The Complete Grand National Championship
Volume II, 1970-1975

Three-wide at Ascot Park with Eddie Wirth, (77), Danny Hockie (45E) and Terry Dorsch (22). Mahony Photo Archives

Gregory R. Pearson

DTG Publications
PO Box 193
Culloden, WV 25510

The Complete Grand National Championship
Volume II 1970-1975

International Standard Book Number (ISBN) 978-0-615-70614-6

Original front cover photo of Jim Rice at San Jose in 1971 by Bill Barrett.

Table of Contents

Acknowledgements/Dedications..………………………………………….. 5

Foreword…………………………………………………………………. 9

Introduction/1970 Season..…………………………………………….…. 11

1971………………………………………………………………………. 95

1972………………………………………………………………………. 163

Grand National Photos, (In Alphabetical Order)………………………….. 235

1973………………………………………………………………………. 321

Cal Rayborn Tribute by Jim McMurren …………………………………. 399

1974………………………………………………………………………. 403

1975………………………………………………………………………. 483

Epilogue………………………………………………………………….. 559

Acknowledgements

Without the help of the following group of people, this book would not have been possible. Thanks to; David Aldana, John Blackstock, Charlie Chapple, Terry Dorsch, Scott Drake, Don Emde, Kathy Estep, Walt Fulton III, Al Gaskill, Dan Gurney, Bob Hansen, Kevin Heath, Darryl Hurst, Noot Irvin, Billy Kennedy Jr., Dennis Mahan, Jimmy Maness, Keith Mashburn, Mark Mederski, Bill Milburn, Steve Morehead, Jimmy Osborne, Chuck Palmgren, Jim Rice, Ronnie Rall, Hank Scott, Jack Warren, Chuck Weber, Hurley Wilvert, Jimmy Zeigler and John Zwerican. All of whom have helped in a notable way in researching this book over the years. Thanks and remembrance to those who have helped and are no longer with us; Bart Markel, Gary Nixon and Wayne Hosaka.

Special thanks to the following;

Bob Herrick, my Michigan based friend and colleague is a lifelong dirt track fan who has accumulated the most comprehensive private collection of racing programs, newspapers, original source documents and periodicals on Class C racing in existence. If you want information on a particular rider or race, Bob is the go-to-guy. He has unselfishly helped me, above and beyond-the-call, with race and rider information, as well as helping to figure out the confusing AMA points system of the early 1970's.

Bert Sumner, from Wisconsin, has been a huge supporter of my first book and in helping to proof-read this work. Bert is from a great racing family; he his father Al, and brother Jim, were all Expert rated riders. Jim tragically lost his life at the Springfield Mile in 2002, in an accident not of his making. Despite this, the Sumner's have never stopped supporting flat track racing. They promote the Dairyland Classic, one of the largest paying non-Nationals in the country, which has been running for nearly 30 years. Bert also established the online Pro Racers Memorial to honor his brother and all Pro racers we have lost. Bert's mother Judy, a skilled English teacher, obviously passed some of her knowledge to Bert. His reading over of my rough draft was a huge help, catching more grammatical errors and goofy mistakes than I care to comment on. Bert, his wife Suzanne and the rest of the Sumner clan are a very bright spot in our sport. Visit Bert's website at www.dairylandclassic.com

Jeff Willis is a longtime local friend, world class motorcycle restorer and racing enthusiast. Jeff graciously loaned me a considerable part of his extensive magazine collection for researching this book. His connections in the motorcycle world have also been a big help. He has always been there to encourage me to continue, even when at times I have been overwhelmed by the project and life in general. Jeff's motorcycle restorations are among the finest in the world. His Harley-Davidson board track racer has been on display at the Smithsonian and the AMA Motorcycle Hall of Fame Museum. His Harley CRS Sprint claimed the Jim Davis award at the AMA's Concourse show in 2003. He specializes in reproducing metal casting of rare items such as engine and frame components, as well as offering complete, exact replica frames for board trackers and other vintage machines.

Dick Mann, two-time Grand National Champion and motorcycle enthusiast of all types, graciously consented to write the foreword for the book. He and wife Kay were very supportive of Volume I, and didn't miss a beat when I asked them for help on this project. Dick is the epitome of the "been there and done it racer"; he could do it all, ride, tune, design and build engines and frames. He also is very insightful and knowledgeable about the history of the sport, gained from years as a racer, businessman and being involved in the politics and bureaucracy of the manufacturers and the AMA. Dick Mann is a true life American hero.

Jim McMurren kindly agreed to right a tribute to his friend Cal Rayborn. McMurren was a great racer in his own right and gave great insight to the period. His thoughts on Cal Rayborn not only help us understand the "racing legend", but also the "regular guy" behind the scenes. Jim was a delight to work with and I deeply appreciate his contribution.

Thanks to the photographers who allowed me to use their fantastic images;

Dan Mahony has always been there whenever I had a question or request. Any history of Grand National racing would be incomplete without the addition of "official" Mahony photos. Their renowned images provide the backbone, photographic record of Grand National racing, both in quality and quantity; a standard, by which all others are measured. Dan and father Walt were part of the racing community and devoted their life's work to racing and captured thousands of classic images. If you are interested in buying some photos, please contact Mahony Photo Archives at; (417) 993-5195 or mahonyphotos@yahoo.com.

Ray Ninness was a Cycle News contributor during the early to mid-1970's. His spectacular images of dirt track and road races were prominently featured in Cycle News and other period publications. Like the Mahony's, Ray was just not a photojournalist. He became part of the racing community and was particularly close to Michigan area racers. Many of Ray's photos have not been widely seen and it is a thrill to have them included in this volume. You can reach Ray through his website, www.f8Photos.com

Californian Bill Barrett was a motorcycle enthusiast who shot some great image of the eras racing. Bill and I became internet buddies and he graciously offered use of his photos. He has been a great west coast supporter of Volume I, and gave me introductions to several California racers.

Other high quality images present in the book were taken by, Bert Shepard, Paul Webb, Craig Stocks, Ben H. Hall and Gerald Baltke.

Thanks to all the great photographers!

Also, thanks to the AMA's Motorcycle Hall of Fame Museum (MHOF), it's Operations Manager Katy Wood and the entire staff. Use of their archival material was essential in researching this project. The museum was founded in 1990, giving the AMA a place to showcase motorcycling history. It is located in Pickerington, Ohio adjacent to the AMA's headquarters. The museum's exhibit halls feature rotating exhibits that highlight different themes of motorcycling history such as "American Dirt Track", "Motocross America", and "Women in Motorcycling". The museum's Motorcycle Hall of Fame honors individuals who have made significant contributions to motorcycling. It is a unique feature of the museum and to be inducted is a prestigious and internationally recognized honor. New members are selected annually. Many riders featured in this book have been inducted into the Hall of Fame. The Motorcycle Hall of Fame Museum is a must see if you are in the Columbus, Ohio area!
Contact them at: (614) 856-2222 or www.motorcyclemuseum.org

Publications Used in Research:

AMA Media Guides, AMA News, American Motorcycling, Classic American Racing Motorcycles by Mick Walker, Cycle, Cycle News, Cycle World, Enthusiast Magazine, Harley Racers by Allan Girdler, Mann of His Time by Ed Youngblood, Modern Cycle, Motorcycle Ace: The Dick Mann Story by Dick Mann and Joe Scalzo, Motorcycle Sport Quarterly, MotorCycle Weekly, Motorcyclist Magazine, Racer: The Story of Gary Nixon by Joe Scalzo, Sturgis: The Story of the Rally by Carl Edeburn, The Bart Markel Story by Joe Scalzo, The Daytona 200: The History of America's Premier Motorcycle Race by Don Emde, Triumph Racing Motorcycles in America by Lindsay Brooke.

Dedications

To my Dad, Robert R. Pearson, for introducing me to the greatest sport on wheels. In good times and bad, our bond through motorcycling has been unshaken.

To my wife Tammy and son Shane; Thanks for your unconditional love, support and patience through the trying times of another project. It almost becomes "normal" to have racing photos, books, magazines, etc., strung through the house, along with endless phone calls and computer time (early and late). I know they will be sorry to see it end for awhile! Thanks guys, without your help, this book would never have happened.

Dick Mann

Ray Ninness Photo

Foreword

Greg Pearson has taken us into the world of GNC racing of the fifties, sixties and mid-seventies. Although forty years have passed, this era is considered by most racing historians the Golden Age of Motorsports. This seems to also apply to Formula One car racing, Champ Car racing, Indianapolis, Moto-cross in England and Europe and Gran Prix Motorcycle racing throughout the world.

When if first got a glimpse of the first edition, I was amazed at what a brilliant job Greg had accomplished. What he had done was make a book basically of results and weave it into a riveting, living story that I could not put down. It brought back memories I had long ago lost and put the ones I remembered into context.

In 1952, I got a job as an apprentice motorcycle mechanic for Hap Alzina, the new West Coast distributor for BSA motorcycles. One of the other employees was a gentleman in his seventies, named Bill Bulger. He had worked for Hap Alzina since the turn of the century and had never owned an automobile, only motorcycles. He had first-hand knowledge of motorcycle racing and the riders in the teens and twenties. He would tell me stories of motorcycle racing in that period. These accounts had a great influence on me. I valued them all of my life. I realized that when Bill passed, that era would be lost.

I have always been aware of the need for preserving the history of our great sport. Thus is the importance of these two editions by Greg. It means this era will live on.

The world was recovering from the WWII and the economy was coming back. Technology was moving forward at an exciting rate, but did not yet dominate any of these sports. The driver or rider was the largest contribution to the results. As Greg relates, since 1954, the AMA Grand National Championship series was unique. Unlike the other specialized forms of racing, a rider would have to compete in various disciplines. This put a premium on consistency and versatility.

The rules for our Class C racing were very restrictive. A few of the riders were always pushing for rule changes that allow for safer conditions, better purses and more sophisticated race bikes. These changes did come about very slowly, but they did occur.

The growing imports of foreign brands, mainly from England, gave the fans a choice other than Indian or Harley Davidson. The sport boomed because of it. These subjects are well brought to light in Greg's first edition 1954-1969. The second edition further documents, in a spellbinding manner, further "changing of the guard", both in riders, brands and technology. The biggest influence in changing the sport near the end of the era was the decline of the British Motorcycle industry, and the rising influence of the Japanese brands. We welcomed the greater sponsorship and larger purses. Unfortunately, this tended to put pressure on the AMA to abandon the concept of the multi-discipline point system. It put an end to the unique era that is documented so well in these two entertaining, informative books.

This does not mean that motorcycling racing in the US has declined, it has only changed. The American sport of Dirt Track racing on long tracks is still, by far, the best motorsport show in the world and will never die. The specialization of U.S. Road racing has resulted in producing many World Champions and our Road racing competitors still set the mark internationally.

Dick Mann
September 8, 2012

Introduction

The Seventies Kick Off!

1970 GNC Season Preview

The premier motorcycle racing series in the United States, the American Motorcyclist Association's Grand National Championship (GNC), had been slowly evolving since the modern points paying series began in 1954. The conservative organization coupled with heavy industry pressure from manufacturers like Harley-Davidson meant things had mostly stayed the same, rules and technical wise, well into the 1960's. Rigid frames, no brakes and the much maligned 500 OHV/750 sidevalve rule had been mainstay items on the tour. If receiving regular updates, your 1954 Harley KR750 dirt tracker could still be competitive in 1969. Great racing throughout, but somewhat stale technically. The growing motorcycle boom in the mid-60's and the subsequent technical advances began to have an effect on the staid series. In 1969 the 500/750 rule was repealed for dirt track and brakes were allowed for the first time. In 1970 the 500/750 rule was gone for pavement competition as well. As the decade closed, rear swing arm suspension, (always legal on production frames, but rarely used on dirt), became the hot set up and rigid frames quickly disappeared. As the 1970's dawned, the AMA GNC truly moved into the modern era.

Huge growth in motorcycle sales had greatly increased GNC interest and support from manufacturers fighting for their share of the lucrative American market. Racing team sizes and budgets billowed. For the first time riders were being offered contracts and sizable salaries. The pressure to win led to the widespread use of specialized lightweight racing components. This was contrary to the original Class "C" rules for the series developed in the 1930's which mandated production only equipment, available to everyone. (A quick review; this was as opposed to Class "A" and "B" rules from the teen's and 1920's that allowed exotic race machines and pieces). Over the years of Class "C" racing, pure racing items slipped in with cursory approval by the AMA. By 1970, purpose built frames, wheels, suspension components and speed equipment were common place. Trackmaster frames built in California by craftsman Ray Hensley were nearly standard for all non-Harley's, (which were the only production racers and had their own frames). The bikes became more, for example, "Triumph engined", than a true Triumph motorcycle. Competition did indeed improve the breed, but the machines were becoming far removed from what the "average Joe" could buy off the dealer's showroom floor. This would lead to long term ramifications for the sport and to at least a partial return to Class "C" rules in the present century.

The series dominant marquee, Harley-Davidson, finally had to develop an OHV 750 to compete under the new rules of 1969/70. The famous KR750 flathead had served well, winning right up to the end with Mert Lawwill taking the 1969 GNC title, straight-up with the ohv machines, at least on dirt. The writing was literally on the wall and the Harley team, led by long time race manager Dick O'Brien, began a crash program to build the required 200 machines required. The new XR750 looked, and in many ways was, a destroked version of the racing 883cc Sportster racing engine, the XLR. The engines shared revamped cases and iron cylinders, with a reworked bottom end due to the shorter stroke. There were also numerous other changes. The new powerplants horsepower, (in the low 60's) was barely what the "scienced out" flathead had produced. Serious teething problems ensued, including the pressed main shafts in the flywheels coming loose, piston rings that self-destructed and even more problematic, chronic overheating due to the iron barrels. While the big Sportster had been raced for years in drag racing and TT, it had not been subject to the WFO nature of oval track and road racing. The problem would plague the "iron XR" throughout its existence. The engines were housed in a tried and true KR style dirt track frame, adorned with beautifully designed fiberglass Wixom tank and seat bases. The road race frames were also virtually unchanged from KR items. The Harley team possessed a formidable squad of riders headed National Champion Mert Lawwill, three-time GNC champ Bart Markel and Mark Brelsford. Other team riders included Walt Fulton III, George Roeder and Larry Darr.

The Triumph and BSA teams were now operating out of the same California headquarters under the direction of veteran Triumph race manager Pete Coleman. Pat Owens was the team crew chief. The teams were well positioned for the season with reliable good handling twins for dirt track; though the machines were still 650's, well under the displacement limit. Both brands would move towards homologating 750 versions, Triumph by mid-season, BSA not till 1971. For pavement, both teams would field the powerful production based 750, 3-cylinder machines. It was essentially the same power plant, thus the bikes were nicknamed "Beezumphs". Dirt track versions would appear with varying success, some with Trackmaster frames, others with the road race chassis. Triumph stars would be Gene

Romero, rookie Don Castro and two-time champ Gary Nixon, still recovering from a devastating leg injury from 1969. BSA's main weapons were Jim Rice and hot rookie Dave Aldana. BSA mainstay, 1963 GNC champ Dick Mann had not been re-signed. Both teams would host road race specialists at the some of the big pavement events.

Yamaha would debut their new 650 OHC twin at Houston. Race team manager Dennis Mahan put together a talented group, including Chuck Palmgren, Neil Keen, Dusty Coppage and rookie Keith Mashburn who rode under the Shell Racing banner. The new engine showed competitive, reliable and was installed in the ubiquitous Trackmaster frame. The teams tried-and-true 350 road racers were capable of running with the larger 750 twins. The Canadian Fred Deeley team with Yvon DuHamel aboard was another threat.

Honda announced it would enter its new CB750 Superbike at Daytona. Dick Mann had not inked a deal with his traditional ride with BSA and through Team Honda's Bob Hansen, signed up to ride one of the bikes at the 200.

Suzuki would return with a strong team on their 500 twins. Riders were Art Baumann, Ron Grant and Jody Nicholas. All were great riders, capable of winning at any event.

Kawasaki did not have an official team, but ran "back door" teams with capable riders like Dave Smith, Mark Williams and racer/journalist Jess Thomas. They offered huge contingency awards for professional racers scoring high finishes on their machines.

Just as the machines were changing dramatically in the 1970's, so were the riders. Most of the top riders of the 1950's and '60's were pretty conservative "blue collar" racers. Many were married and held down regular jobs due to the low purses of the era. The cultural upheavals of the late 1960's touched all parts of society, including motorcycle racing. Many of the younger racers personalities and lifestyles tended to be more freewheeling when compared to their older counterparts. The riders could earn a good living and not have to worry about having to hold down a day job. Veterans like George Roeder, Ralph White and Roger Reiman were cutting back or retiring, while a new generation of charismatic characters like Gene Romero, Dave Aldana, Chuck Palmgren and Mark Brelsford were emerging. They had the talent of the older guys and also liked to have a lot of fun on the road.

The riders and teams faced an arduous 27 race schedule, the biggest in AMA history, that criss-crossed the country from coast-to-coast. Anyone serious about winning the #1 plate would have to attempt as many races as possible. There were 5 TT races, 2 short tracks, 5 road races, 10 half-miles and 5 mile events. New events included the Kent, Wa Road Race, the Palmetto, Ga Half-Mile, a return to the Tulare, Ca Half-Mile and a visit to the new Talladega Superspeedway. Some races gone from the schedule included the Indianapolis and Sears Point Road races.

There was another change in the AMA points system for 1970. The points awarded for each event were in accordance with the purse size rather than just event type. The new system would see confusion and revision during the season. I have chosen to post points and subsequent revisions "as they happened"; that is, you will see the point's standings and revisions as they were listed at the time.

The point system(s) used from 1970-'75 were continually complicated by changes in the way the AMA points were awarded, thus there were several changes and corrections (by the AMA), through the period. In collaboration with Bob Herrick, the points for each race, each season, have been painstakingly reviewed and corrected to the best of my own and Bob's ability. There may be slight variations from the points shown during the period. These variations were necessary when correcting mistakes from the period.

1970 GNC Points System

Position	Over 15,000	12,000 to 14,999	10,000 to 11,999	9,000 to 9,999	8,000 to 8,999	7,000 to 7,999	Up to 6,999
1st	101	86	71	62	53	30	26
2	91	76	61	52	43	16	19
3	82	67	52	42	34	14	13
4	74	59	44	35	26	12	9
5	67	52	37	28	19	10	8
6	61	46	31	22	12	8	7
7	56	41	26	17	8	6	6
8	52	37	22	13	5	5	5
9	49	34	19	10	4	4	4
10	46	31	16	7	3	3	3
11	43	28	13	4	2	2	2
12	40	25	10	1	1	1	1
13	37	22	7				
14	34	19	4				
15	31	16	1				
16	28	13					
17	25	10					
18	22	7					
19	19	4					
20	16	1					
21	13						
22	10						
23	7						
24	4						
25	1						

1970 National Numbers

1. Mert Lawwill, San Francisco, Ca
2. Dick Mann, Richmond, Ca
3. Gene Romero, San Luis Obispo, Ca
4. Bart Markel, Flint, Mi
5. Larry Palmgren, Freehold, NJ
6. Chuck Palmgren, Freehold, NJ
7. Sammy Tanner, Wilmington, Ca
8. Shorty Seabourne, Lawndale, Ca
9. Gary Nixon, Baltimore, Md
10. Neil Keen, Decatur, Ill
11. Jim McMurren, Nestor, Ca
12. Eddie Mulder, Burbank, Ca
13. William Lloyd, Langley Park, Md
14. Gary Davis, Portland, Ore
15. Ralph White, Torrance, Ca
16. Unassigned
17. Unassigned
18. Held open for Mert Lawwill
19. Ray Little, Atlanta, Ga
20. Larry Schafer, Hyattsville, Md
21. Robert Winters, Ft. Smith, Ark
22. Dan Haaby, Orangevale, Ca
23. Dave Bostrom, Service
24. Jim Rice, Palo Alto, Ca
25. Cal Rayborn, Spring Valley, Ca
26. Ed Varnes, Cochranville, Pa
27. Unassigned
28. Al Urich, Omaha, Ne
29. Unassigned
30. Art Baumann, Brisbane, Ca
31. Jimmy Maness, Augusta, Ga
32. Dusty Coppage, Burbank, Ca
33. Bob Bailey, Anaheim, Ca
34. Dallas Baker, Orange, Ca
35. Unassigned
36. Ben Breeding, Decatur, Ill
37. Mel Lacher, San Diego, Ca
38. Tommy Rockwood, Gardena, Ca
39. Duane Buchanan, Pekin, Ill
40. Robert Hinkle, Brookville, Oh
41. Doug Showler, Cleveland, Oh
42. Unassigned
43. Frank Ulicki, Kenosha, Wi
44. Ron Widman, St. Louis, Mo
45. Darrel Dovel, Kansas City, Mo
46. Joe Evans, Bloomington, Ill
47. Pat Gosch, Omaha, Ne
48. Jim Corpe, Temple, Ca
49. Donald Beasley, Evansville, Ind
50. George Longabaugh, Elverson, Pa
51. Dick Woods, Topeka, Ks
52. Ronnie Rall, Mansfield, Oh
53. Larry Roberts, Indianapolis, Ind
54. Allen Smith, Springfield, Ill
55. Roger Reiman, Kewanee, Ill
56. Charles Southgate, Nashville, Tn
57. Carl Williamson, Mill Hall, Pa
58. Jody Nicholas, San Diego, Ca
59. Skip Van Leeuwen, Bellflower, Ca
60. John Tibben, Elmhurst, Ill
61. Ron Grant, Brisbane, Ca
62. Michael Meyer, Reisterstown, Md
63. Walt Fulton, Hacienda Hts., Ca
64. Unassigned
65. Al Gaskill, Utica, Mi
66. Dwayne Walker, Shawnee, Ok
67. Unassigned
68. Unassigned
69. Sonny Burres, Portland, Ore
70. Mark Williams, Cottage Grove, Ore
71. Unassigned
72. Unassigned
73. Sid Carlson, Seattle, Wa
74. Unassigned
75. Harold Lyons, Indianapolis, Ind
76. Jack Forrester, Lafayette, Ind
77. Jimmy Odom, Fremont, Ca
78. Ed Adkins, Seaford, De
79. Unassigned
80. Emil Ahola, Tacoma, Wa
81. Unassigned
82. Jack Warren, Clio, Mi
83. Donald McLeod, Tacoma, Wa
84. Eddie Wirth, Manhattan Beach, Ca
85. Unassigned
86. Unassigned
87. Mark Brelsford, San Bruno, Ca
88. Unassigned
89. Tom Bowersox, South Bend, Ind
90. George Cunha, Johnston, RI
91. Unassigned
92. Jim Jones, Kirkland, Wa
93. William Ruffner, Ft. Worth, Tx
94. Larry Darr, Mansfield, Oh
95. Earl Myers, Kensington, Md
96. Art Barda, Orange, Ca
97. Ron Pierce, Bakersfield, Ca
98. Bob Sholly, Camp Hill, Pa
99. William O'Brien, Waukegan, Ill

1970
Grand National Championship
Schedule

	Race	Location	Date
1	Houston TT	Houston, Tx	February 6, 1970
2	Houston Short Track	Houston, Tx	February 7, 1970
3	Daytona 200 Mile Road Race	Daytona Beach, Fl	March 15, 1970
4	Kent 125 Mile Road Race	Kent, Wa	April 5, 1970
5	Atlanta Half-Mile	Palmetto, Ga	April 19, 1970
6	Cumberland Half-Mile	Cumberland, Md	May 3, 1970
7	Talladega 200 Mile Road Race	Talladega, Al	May 17, 1970
8	Reading Half-Mile	Reading, Pa	May 31, 1970
9	Louisville Half-Mile	Louisville, Ky	June 6, 1970
10	Loudon 100 Mile Road Race	Loudon, NH	June 14, 1970
11	Heidelberg Mini Road Race	Heidelberg, Pa	June 21, 1970
12	Sante Fe TT	Hinsdale, Ill	June 26, 1970
13	Columbus Half-Mile	Columbus, Oh	June 28, 1970
14	San Jose Half-Mile	San Jose, Ca	July 5, 1970
15	Castle Rock TT	Castle Rock, Wa	July 11, 1970
16	Ascot TT	Gardena, Ca	July 18, 1970
17	Santa Rosa Mile	Santa Rosa, Ca	July 26, 1970
18	Tulare Half-Mile	Tulare, Ca	August 1, 1970
19	Terre Haute Half-Mile	Terre Haute, Ind	August 16, 1970
20	Sante Fe Short Track	Hinsdale, Ill	August 21, 1970
21	Peoria TT	Peoria, Ill	August 23, 1970
22	Sedalia Mile	Sedalia, Mo	August 30, 1970
23	Nazareth Mile	Nazareth, Pa	September 6, 1970
24	Indy Mile	Indianapolis, Ind	September 7, 1970
25	Sacramento Mile	Sacramento, Ca	September 13, 1970
26	Ascot Half-Mile	Gardena, Ca	September 19, 1970
27	Oklahoma Half-Mile	Oklahoma City, Ok	October 4, 1970

GNC Round #1 & 2 of 25 **Date:** February 6 & 7, 1970 **Type:** TT and Short Track TT **Venue:** Houston Astrodome **Location:** Houston, Tx	**Purse:** $16,000.00 **Surface:** Dirt **Course Length:** ¼ mile **Laps:** 25 ea

TT National

Factory BSA star Jim Rice rode his backup 650 twin to victory in Friday's TT in front of 16,000 fans at the Houston Astrodome. He passed early leaders Eddie Mulder and Skip Van Leeuwen. The smooth-riding Rice looked as if he was on a Sunday ride; his "sit up straight" riding style belied his blazing speed. As typical at the 'Dome, a lot of new and unusual equipment showed up. Chuck Palmgren, Dan Haaby, Dusty Coppage and Keith Mashburn were debuting Yamaha's new 650 twin, all utilizing Trackmaster frames. Mark Brelsford's success at Houston in 1969 on a Harley Sprint encouraged several to use smaller machines. Brelsford and Mert Lawwill returned on Sprints, Eddie Mulder was on a 360 Montesa, Ronnie Rall on a Bultaco and Dick Mann aboard a 405cc Husky.

Time Trials

In qualifying, 103 entries vied for just 36 spots. Dallas Baker topped the field on a traditional 650 BSA at 29.86. The choice of lightweights appeared to have some merit as Ronnie Rall's Bultaco was 2nd at 30.13 and Mert Lawwill's Sprint a 30.21. Ascot stars Skip Van Leeuwen and Paul Bostrom were next on their Triumph twins. Eddie Mulder (Mon) and Dick Mann (Hus) were close behind. While the smaller bikes were impressive in qualifying, they weren't as strong in competition, lacking the punch to power through traffic.

Heats

Skip Van Leeuwen (Tri) led off the line in what proved to be a wild and wooly heat. Van Leeuwen had a big lead on lap 1 till Dallas Baker, Dan Haaby and several others got tangled up, causing a restart. Van Leeuwen nailed the restart as Baker again had trouble, this time with Norm Robinson. Gene Romero (Tri) came along and with nowhere to go, collected Robinson. On the third try, Van Leeuwen led to the flag followed by Eddie Mulder and Dave Hansen (Tri). Each heat would only transfer the top 3.

The second heat was filled with talent like Ronnie Rall, Paul Bostrom, Jim Rice, Cal Rayborn, Bart Markel and Mark Brelsford. Rayborn jumped the start and was sent to the penalty line. Paul Bostrom quickly took control of the restart and led the whole event. A nice battle developed behind him with Rall, Rick Deane, Rice and Brelsford. Rice moved up smoothly by first Deane and then Rall for 2nd. Brelsford worked his way to 3rd and was the only factory Harley rider to transfer directly to the main. Teammates Markel and Rayborn were done for the night.

Heat 3 followed the restart pattern of the night after a nasty getoff by Larry Wilburn. Eddie Wirth narrowly missed the fallen rider, but John Fishburn didn't and ran over Wilburn, resulting in several broken ribs. Northwest TT star Sonny Burres (Tri) topped the field followed by Ascot veteran Dusty Coppage and Jimmy Odom. GNC champ Mert Lawwill had engine trouble and finished off the pace.

Semi

The semi event would only take the top 3 from the talent-laden field. The field included Dave Aldana, Dan Haaby, Eddie Wirth, and former GNC champs Roger Reiman and Dick Mann. Aldana got a great holeshot, bouncing off of any movable or immovable object on his way to an uncontested win. Mann looked reasonably fast on the Husky motocrosser in 2nd. Reiman held 3rd on his Harley KR till the last lap when Ken Pressgrove (BSA) shot by to set the National starting order.

National

The racers and spectators anticipation grew to a fever pitch as the 12 finalists pulled to the starting grid. "Steady Eddie" Mulder pulled one of his patented holeshots, leading the pack into turn 1 on his two-stroke Montesa. Skip Van Leeuwen was only a bike length behind but overshot Turn 1 allowing Jim Rice and Paul Bostrom by. Rice was on a charge and reeled Mulder in. In the final turn before the front straight, Mulder drifted wide and Rice scooted by. He soon pulled a sizeable lead. Mulder slowly drifted back, eventually finishing in 6th spot. Front runners Dick Mann and Mark Brelsford got together, sending both down. Paul Bostrom moved into 2nd place and ran a solid steady race. Behind him, Van Leeuwen and Dusty Coppage battled it out. Coppage, on the new Yamaha, kept pressing the veteran Triumph rider, but the "Flyin Dutchman" didn't crack under the pressure. Up front, Rice put on a dominant performance, far ahead at the finish, followed by Bostrom, Van Leeuwen, Coppage, highest finishing rookie Dave Aldana, Mulder, Odom, Sonny Burres, Mark Brelsford and Dave Hansen.

Short Track National

A huge Saturday night crowd of 27,880 watched veterans Dick Mann and Mert Lawwill battle for the win at the end of an exciting 25 lap National with GNC champ Lawwill narrowly coming on top. In third was Jimmy Odom. For the second night in a row it was all-California podium. TT winner Jim Rice finished 4th, taking the early season points lead. The evening was spiced up by the appearance of spectacular speedway stars Ivan Mauger and Barry Briggs.

Time Trials

In an unusual occurrence, Keith Mashburn (Yam) and Dave Aldana (BSA) turned in an identical 15.56 to share fast time honors. Mark Brelsford (HD) was 2nd fastest and Gene Romero (Tri) was 3rd. Barry Briggs was 7th fastest on a Yamaha 250 twin screamer that was a hybrid speedway/dirt tracker. The first 20 qualifiers were all in the 15-second bracket.

The short track format was unique in GNC racing. There were four heat races, two semis and the main event. Six riders transferred from the heats to the semis. Then the top six from each semi moved unto the main

Heats

Eddie Mulder and Jim McMurren (HD) jumped the initial start and were sent to the penalty. Dave Hansen (Bul) led early till Chuck Palmgren (Yam) took over and led to the finish. McMurren came from the penalty line in a strong ride for 2nd place.

Dan Haaby (Yam) emerged the leader in Heat 2 after out-dueling a pack that included Don Castro (Tri), Dave Aldana and Roger Reiman. Castro ran in 2nd till the last lap when GNC champ Mert Lawwill snuck by at the line. Ivan Mauger and his Kawasaki speedway/dirt track machine spent the race spinning a Barum knobby looking for traction and finished last in his AMA debut.

The third heat took four tries to successfully get underway. Mark Brelsford (HD), Jimmy Odom (Bul) and Dave Smith all ended up on the penalty stripe. On the restart, three-time National Champion Bart Markel bolted into the lead. The green flag didn't stay out for long as a huge crash occurred in Turn 3, involving several riders including Smith and Sid Carlson. It was a wild wreck with two bikes cart-wheeling into the hay bales. A final restart was successful with Dick Mann on the Jerry Schoffer prepared Ossa taking the win from Harley-Davidson's Mark Brelsford.

Barry Briggs put it all together to win Heat 4 on his screaming twin. He had run at the 'Dome before and he had fitted a Pirelli instead of the speedway tire that Mauger tried. He won the event going away.

Semis

Dan Haaby grabbed the lead of the first semi closely pursued by veterans Mert Lawwill and Dick Mann. Bart Markel went down in front of the pack after hitting a hole. He was unavoidably run over by Ronnie Rall and suffered a broken collarbone. Mann took control on the restart with Lawwill and Mark Brelsford running 2nd and 3rd. Close behind, Jimmy Odom, Dan Haaby and Cal Rayborn all challenged, Brelsford for 3rd. Odom on the A&A, Ray Abrams-prepped Bultaco got the spot from Brelsford.

Semi 2 started off well enough with Barry Briggs impressing with the holeshot. His bike soon faltered and he was shunted to the rear of the pack. Butch Corder led briefly led till Dave Hansen went by with Chuck Palmgren in tow. Gene Romero was moving forward, but on lap 6 he and Corder got together. Jim McMurren with nowhere to go, slammed into Romero's bike at speed. The resultant impact tweaked Romero's arm and ripped McMurren's forks right off his Harley Sprint. Mercifully the race was called complete with Dave Hansen declared the winner.

National

Dick Mann led the pack into Turn 1 with Mert Lawwill and Chuck Palmgren close behind. Jimmy Odom worked his way into the lead pack and passed Palmgren for 3rd. Jim Rice pulled through the pack and was 4th behind Odom. Up front, Mert Lawwill slowly reeled in Mann. Just past midpoint of the 25 lap race he was all over the leader. Mann appeared to lose his edge a little and Lawwill took the lead on lap 19. Mann latched onto Lawwill's rear wheel and would have retaliated, but didn't realize the laps were about to run out. Lawwill motored in for the win closely followed by Mann, Odom hung onto for 3rd despite being hounded by Rice. The rest of the top 10 were Chuck Palmgren, Dave Hansen, 1969 winner Ronnie Rall, Dan Haaby, Jerry Stokes and Mark Brelsford.

Jim Rice's TT win and 4th place in the short track combined to give him the early season points lead. Mert Lawwill was second, Dick Mann third, Paul Bostrom and Jimmy Odom tied for fourth and Skip Van Leeuwen was fifth.

Results

Race: 20 Lap TT National
Race Time: 10:03.03

Rank	Rider	Number	Make
1.	Jim Rice, Palo Alto, Ca	24	BSA
2.	Paul Bostrom, Lake Isabella, Ca	15Y	Tri
3.	Skip Van Leeuwen, Bellflower, Ca	59	Tri
4.	Dusty Coppage, Burbank, Ca	32	Yam
5.	Dave Aldana, Santa Ana, Ca	38X	BSA
6.	Eddie Mulder, Burbank, Ca	12	Tri
7.	Jimmy Odom, Fremont, Ca	77	Tri
8.	Sonny Burres, Portland, Ore	69	Tri
9.	Mark Brelsford, San Bruno, Ca	87	HD
10.	Dave Hansen, Hayward, Ca	22Y	Tri
11.	Dick Mann, Richmond, Ca	2	Hus
12.	Ken Pressgrove, Topeka, Ks	14N	BSA

Race: 10 Lap Amateur Final
Race Time: 5:06.39

Rank	Rider	Number	Make
1.	Terry Dorsch, Sunland, Ca	65R	Tri
2.	John Hateley, Van Nuys, Ca	43R	Tri
3.	Gregory Hodges, Los Gatos, Ca	56Y	Tri

Race: 25 Lap Short Track National
Race Time: 6:41.91

Rank	Rider	Number	Make
1.	Mert Lawwill, San Francisco, Ca	1	HD
2.	Dick Mann, Richmond, Ca	2	Oss
3.	Jimmy Odom, Fremont, Ca	77	Bul
4.	Jim Rice, Palo Alto, Ca	24	BSA
5.	Chuck Palmgren, Freehold, NJ	6	Yam
6.	Dave Hansen, Hayward, Ca	22Y	Bul
7.	Ronnie Rall, Mansfield, Oh	52	Bul
8.	Dan Haaby, Orangevale, Ca	22	Yam
9.	Jerry Stokes, Charleston Heights, SC	67D	Bul
10.	Mark Brelsford, San Bruno, Ca	87	HD
11.	Sonny Burres, Portland, Ore	69	Suz
12.	Steve Scott, Santa Monica, Ca	15X	Bul

Race: Amateur Final
Race Time: 2:43.12

Rank	Rider	Number	Make
1.	Tod Sloan, Fresno, Ca	18Z	Bul
2.	Chuck Joyner, Oregon City, Ore	87Q	Bul
3.	David Lawson, Yukon, Ok	89M	Kaw

Grand National Points Standings after Round 2

Rank	Rider	Pts
1.	Jim Rice	35
2.	Mert Lawwill	26
3.	Dick Mann	21
4.	Paul Bostrom	19
5.	Jimmy Odom	19
6.	Skip Van Leeuwen	13
7.	Dave Hansen	10
8.	Dusty Coppage	9
9.	Dave Aldana	8
10.	Chuck Palmgren	8

- Combined attendance for the weekend was 43,981.
- Mert Lawwill won $1200.00 for the short track. Jim Rice took home a combined $1750.00. Pretty small sums when you consider the attendance!
- Jim Rice emerged as the point's leader after winning the TT and placing 4th in the short track. Underappreciated as a tuner, Rice prepared and tuned all of his own dirt track machinery. The BSA factory only provided the equipment.
- A $500.00 "winner take all" short track Match Race was held after Friday's TT event. Californian Jim McMurren topped World Speedway champ Barry Briggs to claim the prize.
- Yamaha's new 650 twin was approved by the AMA just before the National. Yamaha Race Team boss Dennis Mahan and crew hustled to have the bikes ready.
- California riders utterly dominated the final finishing order both nights.
- The first major indoor motorcycle race was promoted by Sidney Shelenker and Allen Becker of Pace Management in the "Eighth Wonder" of the world, the Houston Astrodome in 1968. Indoor/stadium races were not new; in Long Beach, Ca and in Dayton and Cincinnati, Oh there were popular races on concrete indoor surfaces   In the early 1960's J.C. Agajanian promoted an indoor short track in Indianapolis, In, complete with dirt covering the concrete floor. Pace Management capitalized on the idea making it the biggest and most publicized event of its type. It was a true "ground breaking" event. Racing at the Astrodome and other indoor facilities began to skyrocket in popularity. GNC racing ran successfully in several indoor venues into the mid-1980's. Supercross overtook the popularity of GNC and became a huge draw across the country. Pace Management eventually evolved into powerhouse Clear Channel Productions.
- The Astrodome was built in 1965 and hosted professional sports and premier events for decades. It was originally called the Harris County Domed Stadium, until the famous Astroturf baseball surface influenced its name change. The dirt floor was concreted in the 1980's. It fell on troubled times in the mid 1990's. There were calls for a new more modern stadium. The Houston Oilers left for Tennessee in 1996. Reliant Stadium opened up close to the Astrodome in 2002. The new facility took over hosting premier events in Houston. The Astrodome was regulated to hosting high school games and smaller events. It helped house thousands of Hurricane Katrina survivors. The future of the world's first domed coliseum is unclear, but clearly left its mark in many areas.

1970 Daytona 200
Mann Finally Wins Daytona!

GNC Round #3 of 25 **Date:** March 15, 1970 **Type:** Road Race **Venue:** Daytona International Speedway **Location:** Daytona, Florida	**Purse:** $24,500.00 **Surface:** Pavement **Course Length:** 3.81 miles **Laps:** 53 **Distance:** 200 Miles

The running of the 1970 Daytona 200 saw the AMA move into the modern era of road racing. The antiquated 500/750 rule was finally abandoned. For the first time a 750cc limit was in place for all machines regardless of design. The rule had been changed for dirt track racing in 1969, but for undetermined reasons was not applied to pavement events until the following year. It was definitely a game-changer with the timing coinciding with the emerging Superbike movement. It would be a faceoff between the multi-cylinder "Beezumph's" from BSA/Triumph and new player Honda. The British team(s) spared no expense with the factory bikes featuring special Rob North frames, wind tunnel-tested fairings and 5-speed gearboxes. Equally impressive was the lineup of riders. Triumph had 1967 winner Gary Nixon, Gene Romero, rookie Don Castro and English rider Percy Tait. Heading the BSA list was World Champion Mike Hailwood, lured out of motorcycle retirement, bolstered by Americans Dave Aldana and Jim Rice. What of BSA stalwart Dick Mann? Though ostensibly still on the team, BSA had not assigned Mann one of the new triples. Faced with running an uncompetitive 650 twin, the 1963 GNC champ began exploring his options. He was contacted by American Honda's Bob Hansen about riding the company's new CB750-based machine. Hansen was a long time tuner and team manager; the perfect choice to head up Honda's first major foray into AMA racing. Honda's new machine had set the world on it's ear. It bristled with exotic features descended from Hondas GP experience like a 4-cylinder engine, overhead camshafts, disc brakes and featured electric start. It was a legitimate, affordable superbike that forever changed the American big bike market. Hansen realized Mann's experience and still formidable skills would be a great resource for the new team. Mann joined Ireland's Tommy Robb and Scottish rider Ralph Bryans, both experienced Grand Prix riders on the team.

The other Japanese teams were out in force as well. Factory supported and private Yamahas were a plenty. Many riders capable of winning included Yvon DuHamel, 1969 250 World Champion Kel Carruthers, Ron Pierce and a host of other privateers. Suzuki's 500 twins were to be ridden by Ron Grant, Art Baumann, Geoff Perry Jimmy Odom and Jody Nicholas. Baumann was the first to capture a first two-stroke road race win in 1969 and the other teammates had plenty of speed to win. Among those aboard Kawasaki's potent 500 3-cylinders were New Zealander Ginger Molloy, Mark Williams and Royal Sherbert.

The race marked the debut of Harley-Davidson's new overhead valve XR750. The bikes handling was still superb owing to proven KR gear, but the new engine proved troublesome. It's iron cylinders proved prone to overheating and the bikes couldn't match the speed of it's flathead predecessor. Two-time 200 winner Cal Rayborn, new Grand National champion Mert Lawwill and the rest of the team would have a long week at Daytona.

Time Trials

Gene Romero and tuner Pat Owens chased after speed in the days leading up to qualifying. Pulling out the stops they mounted skinny front tires on both wheels to cut down on rolling and wind resistance. Their savvy gamble payed off with Romero running a blistering 157.342 mph average with trap speeds of 165 around the oval. This destroyed Yvon DuHamel's 1969 speed of 150.511. Mike "The Bike" Hailwood was next at 152.90. Gary Nixon made it an all British top three with a 152.82 lap. Dick Mann was close behind at 152.67. Kel Carruthers was the first two-stroke, his Yamaha turning a 151.719. Jody Nicholas had the fastest Suzuki at 151.33. Mark Williams was the first Kawasaki in 11th spot. Bart Markel had the fastest new Harley, in 15th spot at 147.54. Cal Rayborn had a dismal lap and was 21st fastest. The qualifying after 1970 was switched from the oval to the road course so Gene Romero will forever hold the fastest motorcycle lap at Daytona.

National

Dick Mann pulled a world class holeshot on the hard-accelerating Honda. He had a clear lead but coming hard were the Beezumph-mounted trio of Gene Romero, Gary Nixon and Mike Hailwood. Romero caught Mann going into the infield but ran in too deep, losing at least ten places. A first lap shunt collected Art Baumann and 1963 200 winner Ralph White. Baumann suffered a dislocated elbow; White a seriously tweaked ankle. Mann was being overhauled by the hard running Nixon and Hailwood with Kel Carruthers and Cal Rayborn close behind. Nixon and Hailwood began dicing fiercely. Hailwood was quicker through the infield with Nixon blasting by on the banking. The scrappy American showed no signs of his terrible 1969 accident and cut his famed competitor no quarter. Mann hung close in 3rd. Nixon pulled out a small advantage and Hailwood fell into Mann's clutches. Hailwood's engine had began to overheat and blew out right in front of Mann. The British triples had shown signs of hot running and point bounce was causing detonation in some of the team mounts. The Hondas had troubles of their own. Examination of oil after practice showed rubber particles in the oil from the cam chain tensioners. The standard items were wearing rapidly from the racing camshafts action. Mann knew to only push the big Honda as hard as needed. He soon lost 2nd place to a hard charging Ron Grant. He caught leader Nixon and the two swapped positions all around the course. Grant ruled the infield, Nixon the banking. As race worked into the 20th circuit, Grant had pulled some distance on Nixon and the field. Rayborn had managed to work past Mann but was out with engine trouble on lap 25. A lap, later Grant was preparing to come into the pits when his Suzuki ran low on fuel and seized. He coasted to the pits but was done for the day. After the series of pit stops, Nixon was back firmly in the lead. On lap 31 his Triumph overheated and burnt a piston, like Hailwood. Mann reassumed the lead on Nixon's departure. His Honda was slightly off-song, but still strong. Behind him, Gene Romero was coming. He had worked his way back through the pack and was closing. Through his pit signs, Mann was well aware of Romero's progress. He knew that as long as he kept a reasonable pace that Romero would run out of laps. With his engine running rougher, Mann took the flag with Romero 10 seconds back. Behind the front two, rookie Triumph rider Don Castro was an impressive 3rd in his road race debut, finishing on the lead lap. Yvon DuHamel was 5th, the first two-stroke. Geoff Perry was 6th in his first Daytona race. Soldiering home in 7th was Walt Fulton III, on the first Harley, a faithful flathead KR. Rounding out the top 10 were Ginger Molloy, 1966 Daytona winner Buddy Elmore, Royal Sherbert and TT specialist Dusty Coppage. The race speed of 102.691 was almost exactly one mph faster than Cal Rayborn's 1969 run.

Daytona frontrunners dominated the GNC points; the big points awarded smothered those awarded at Houston. The first six at Daytona were the first six in points. Point's leader Dick Mann, Mert Lawwill and Dusty Coppage were the only riders in the top 10 to have scored at Daytona and Houston Nationals.

Results

Race: 200 Mile Road Race National
Race Time: 1:57:13, (102.691 MPH), New Record

Rank	Rider	Number	Make
1.	Dick Mann, Richmond, Ca	2	Hon
2.	Gene Romero, San Luis Obispo, Ca	3	Tri
3.	Don Castro, Hollister, Ca	81	Tri
4.	Yvon DuHamel, LaSalle, Quebec, Can	5	Yam
5.	Geoff Perry, New Zealand	51	Suz
6.	Walt Fulton, Hacienda Heights, Ca	63	HD
7.	Ginger Molloy, Huntley, New Zealand	78	Kaw
8.	Buddy Elmore, El Paso Tx	79	Tri
9.	Royal Sherbert, Largo, Fl	88	Kaw
10.	Dusty Coppage, Chatsworth, Ca	32	Yam
11.	Al Gaskill, Detroit, Mi	65	Yam
12.	David Aldana, Santa Ana, Ca	13	BSA
13.	Larry Stone, Clarkson, Ga	82	Kaw
14.	Rick Deane, Aspen, Co	74	Yam
15.	Mert Lawwill, San Francisco, Ca	1	HD
16.	Robert Bulmer, Morrice, Mi	53	Yam
17.	Leonard Fortune, Webster City, Ia	42	Tri
18.	Larry Darr, Mansfield, Oh	94	HD
19.	Keith Mashburn, Santa Susana, Ca	33	Yam
20.	Ken Molyneux, Vancouver, Can	89	Yam

Race: 100 Mile Amateur Final
Race Time: 1:29:91, (100.723 MH), New Record

Rank	Rider	Number	Make
1.	Joe "Rusty" Bradley, Dallas, Tx	64	Kaw
2.	Gary Fisher, Parkesburg, Pa	10	Tri
3.	Ray Hempstead, St. Petersburg, Fl	99	Yam

Grand National Points Standings after Round 3

Rank	Rider	Pts
1.	Dick Mann	122
2.	Gene Romero	91
3.	Don Castro	82
4.	Yvon DuHamel	74
5.	Geoff Perry	67
6.	Walt Fulton III	61
7.	Mert Lawwill	57
8.	Ginger Molloy	56
9.	Dusty Coppage	55
10.	Buddy Elmore	52

- Dick Mann finally succeeded at Daytona; he had been competing in the 200 since 1955! Mann won around $4000.00 in purse money, plus a $10,000.00 bonus from Honda.
- Gene Romero received $1000.00 for his daring 157 mph qualifying lap. Cycle magazine gave Pat Owen's $500.00 for tuning the triple to it's record breaking lap.
- Rusty Bradley picked up a whopping $5000.00 contingency award from Kawasaki for winning the 100-Mile Amateur race on a Boston Cycles ride. His winnings totaled $6200.00, topped only by Dick Mann.
- 30,000 fans turned out for the 200.
- 81 riders from 8 countries started the race.
- Last year's top qualifier Yvon DuHamel had trouble in time trials and had to start at the rear of the grid, putting in an amazing ride to 4th.
- The attrition rate for the day was high; only around 26 riders finished the race.
- There was great brand parity with 7 different brands in the top 10!
- Mert Lawwill brought the first new Harley-Davidson XRTT home in 15th place.
- Despite a threat of rain, the race went off without a hitch.
- In rookie Dave Aldana's first road race as an Expert, he was running up in the top 10 till late in the event. When Dick Mann lapped him, Aldana was determined to go to school on the veteran. He hung close, but overcooked it in a corner and fell. Leaving the bike near the track, he walked back to the pits and was advised to get back out there and finish; after all this Aldana still finished 12th!
- Mann lapped everyone but Gene Romero and Don Castro at least once.
- Mann and Bob Hansen were seen by most of Honda's GP team as the "B" team. Advice from the American's about the cam chain tensioner issue was ignored. Mann's machine was the only team bike to finish.
- Ironically after Daytona, both Mann and Bob Hansen had to look for new jobs. The race was a one-off for Honda so Mann went looking for a ride, eventually returning to BSA. Bob Hansen was unceremoniously let go after the race after telling the Honda Racing chief to clam up while he was trying to guide Mann to the win. Hansen would land on his feet with Kawasaki.
- It was not Mann's first "ride" for Honda. At a road race event in the 1960's Honda offered Mann a free minibike if he would give a demonstration ride on one of their 4-cylinder machines. Mann put in a lap on a rough running machine. When he reached for the front brake after finally gaining some speed, the brake promptly locked, throwing Mann off, tweaking his collarbone.
- The Daytona Beach Race course was the scene of motorsport speed measurement and competition starting at the turn of the 20th century. It's wide and smooth beach was perfectly suited to racing. Early contests actually took place at nearby Ormond Beach. The oval course was first used around 1936. It used a section of the A1A highway and beachfront for straightaway's and was hooked together with sandy turns. It evolved into a 4.1 mile layout. The first 200 Mile motorcycle race was held in 1938. Stock cars ran on the same track till 1958, after which they moved to the new Daytona International Speedway. The bikes continued to use the beach course till 1960. In 1961 the race moved to the Speedway, utilizing a 2.00 mile infield road course. The bikes did not yet use any of the famous banking. Speeds and the popularity of the event suffered. In 1964 the bikes moved to the "proper" 3.81 mile road course which used the majority of the stock car banking. Higher speeds and slick fairing-equipped bikes brought excitement back to the 200 event. A chicane was added to the back straight in 1973, but the bikes still run the same basic course today. The Daytona Speedway remains one of the most famous race tracks in the world, the site of many world class events and remains the crown jewel of the NASCAR series.

1.	Gene Romero	Tri	157.342 MPH
2.	Mike Hailwood	BSA	152.905
3.	Gary Nixon	Tri	152.827
4.	Dick Mann	Hon	152.671
5.	Kel Carruthers	Yam	151.719
6.	Jody Nicholas	Suz	151.133
7.	Percy Tait	Tri	150.577
8.	Jim Rice	BSA	149.377
9.	Rod Gould	Yam	149.130
10.	Don Castro	Tri	148.834
11.	Mark Williams	Kaw	148.490
12.	Ron Pierce	Yam	148.343
13.	Robert Winters	Yam	148.099
14.	Ron Grant	Suz	147.783
15.	Bart Markel	HD	147.540
16.	Ginger Molloy	Kaw	146.938
17.	Mark Brelsford	HD	146.914
18.	Ralph White	Yam	146.056
19.	Andres Lascoutz	Kaw	145.678
20.	Larry Schafer	HD	145.583

GNC Round #4 of 25	**Purse:** $8000.00
Date: April 5, 1970	**Surface:** Pavement
Type: Road Race	**Course Length:** 2.25 Miles
Venue: Pacific Raceways	**Laps:** 56
Location: Kent, Wa	**Distance:** 125 Miles

It was a bit of an unusual day at the first Kent National Road Race, held outside Seattle, Washington. Suzuki's Ron Grant, originally from England, but a regular fixture on the AMA circuit, won his one and only GNC event. Grant dueled for much of the race with teammate Art Baumann, who slowed after a couple of falls. Race-long dicing behind finally resulted in Yvon DuHamel and Gary Nixon rounding out the podium. Dave Aldana was impressive in fourth. The talented rookie had few pavement starts, but ran up front all day. The Kent track had one long straight, (dragstrip), connected by a series of tight corners. The technical track, along with the wet conditions, favored the smaller, lighter two-stroke machines. It would have seemed a perfect track for the 350 Yamahas, but save DuHamel's runner-up, there were no other Yamahas in the top 10. Many of their factory and privateer riders had trouble on the day. The BSA/Triumph riders were very impressive wrestling their bulky triples around the tight course with Nixon, Aldana, Romero and Don Castro all in the top 10. Daytona winner Dick Mann was notably absent. The National points leader was still without a ride and missed the event. Harley-Davidson still struggled with overheating problems on the new XR model. Despite early Cal Rayborn heroics, in a repeat of Daytona, Walt Fulton was the first Harley home in 11th on a KR flathead with Mert Lawwill just behind on the first XRTT.

Despite sitting out the event, Dick Mann remained in control of the points race. There were few changes in the order. Yvon DuHamel moved into third, but he like most of the other Daytona scorers in the top 10 would not figure significantly in the points battle. Dave Aldana moved into eight in the standings via his 4th place run at Kent.

Heats

In the first 5-lap heat, Dan Haaby (Yam) pulled the early lead, but was quickly overtaken by Art Baumann and Cal Rayborn. Baumann led the opening circuit with Rayborn taking over on lap 2. Rayborn continued to pull away, but on the last lap an overheated cylinder put out the fire in his Harley. Baumann took the win with Rayborn coasting in for 2nd. A rapidly replaced piston would have Rayborn ready for the National.

Heat 2 saw Tom Rockwood (Yam) pull the holeshot, chased by Yvon DuHamel, Gene Romero and Suzuki riders Jody Nicholas and Ron Grant. Romero took the lead on the next lap. Nicholas was really moving and took over on lap 3, stretching to a big lead at the finish. Teammate Grant took over the runner up spot from Romero.

National

Rain fell right up to race time, with several riders breaking out rain gear. Cal Rayborn shot his repaired Harley out in front, trailed by Ron Grant, Gene Romero, Art Baumann and Jody Nicholas. By lap 3 Rayborn was stretching his lead when his XR slowed and he ducked into the pits. His crew hoped a simple plug change will help, but the bike had suffered terminal overheating again. Grant took over the lead with Romero feeling pressure from Baumann as the track was drying out. Behind the leaders in pursuit are Team Britain's Gary Nixon, Don Castro and Dave Aldana. Coming up behind from a bad start was Yamaha's Yvon DuHamel. On lap 7, Baumann moved by Romero and soon latched onto Grant. The two Suzuki pilots began a heated battle with Grant showing a little power edge on the main straight. Romero was losing time to the leaders and was passed by Nicholas on the 11th lap, making it three Suzuki's up front. Behind Romero, Aldana had moved into 5th ahead of Nixon. The duel up front saw Baumann take over the top spot. Just past lap 25, Nicholas dropped his 3rd place Suzuki in one of the course fast sweepers. He was not seriously injured, but was done for the day. Nixon and DuHamel had moved forward pushing Aldana and Romero back. Dicing continued all over, further mixed up by the leaders gas stops which started around lap 40. Grant's stop was uneventful and comes back out running 4th. Leader Baumann overcooked it in hairpin, damaging his fairing and stopped in the pits. Grant became the leader after pit shuffling with DuHamel, Nixon and Aldana behind. Baumann was back out, flying through the pack. He had closed on Nixon when he crashed again. He got going again, his

Suzuki looking very battered. Grant had a 10-second, but was soon racing heavily with Dave Smith (Kaw). Smith was actually in 6th, but Grant wasn't sure. Grant crossed the line with shadow Smith, rounding out the top ten were DuHamel, Nixon, an impressive Aldana, a beat up but still fast Baumann, Smith, Romero, Castro, Don Emde and Jimmy Odom.

Results

Race: 125 Mile Road Race National
Race Time: 1:31:03.55, (83.022 MPH)

Rank	Rider	Number	Make
1.	Ron Grant, Brisbane, Ca	61	Suz
2.	Yvon DuHamel, LaSalle, Quebec, Can	5	Yam
3.	Gary Nixon, Phoenix, Md	9	Tri
4.	Dave Aldana, Santa Ana, Ca	13	BSA
5.	Art Baumann, Brisbane, Ca	30	Suz
6.	Dave Smith, Lakewood, Ca	11	Kaw
7.	Gene Romero, San Luis Obispo, Ca	3	Tri
8.	Don Castro, Hollister, Ca	81	Tri
9.	Don Emde, Bonita, Ca	35	Yam
10.	Jimmy Odom, Fremont, Ca	77	Suz
11.	Tom Rockwood, Gardena, Ca	38	Yam
12.	Walt Fulton, Hacienda Heights, Ca	63	HD
13.	Mert Lawwill, San Francisco, Ca	1	HD
14.	Ken Molyneux, Vancouver, BC, Can	89	Yam
15.	Mark Williams, Springfield, Ore	70	Kaw
16.	John Black, Portland, Ore	80	Yam
17.	Jim Rice, Palo Alto, Ca	24	BSA
18.	Sonny Burres, Portland, Ore	69	Nor
19.	Dusty Coppage, Burbank, Ca	32	Yam
20.	Leonard Fortune, Webster, Ia	42	Mat

Grand National Points Standings after Round 4

Rank	Rider	Pts
1.	Dick Mann	122
2.	Gene Romero	97
3.	Yvon DuHamel	93
4.	Don Castro	87
5.	Geoff Perry	67
6.	Walt Fulton	62
7.	Mert Lawwill	57
8.	Dave Aldana	57
9.	Ginger Molloy	56
10.	Dusty Coppage	55

- An 18,000 strong turned out. While the AMA and racing faithful hoped they were there for the competition, more than few came to see Evel Knievel jump 18 cars with his American Eagle (Laverda).
- It was nearly a perfect Suzuki weekend. The three team bikes of Ron Grant, Art Baumann and Jody Nicholas occupied the first three starting spots and threatened to sweep the National till the crashes of Nicholas and Baumann.
- Cal Rayborn delivered a neat swan song for the aging Harley-Davidson Sprint road racer, winning the Lightweight Combined event over the two-stroke twins of Gary Nixon, Don Emde and Yvon DuHamel. The AMA had allowed single cylinder machines to run a displacement of 360cc to compete with the 250 twins. While this wouldn't allow the Sprint to win on the horsepower tracks, for the shorter courses it was competitive, at least with Rayborn aboard. For the longer courses, Harley allowed Rayborn to choose other brands to ride.
- Pacific Raceways located near Kent, Wa was built by the Fiorito family in 1959. The facility opened in 1960, featuring a 2.25 mile road course and a ¼ mile drag strip that doubled as the road course main straight. The track was leased out in 1976 and became known as Seattle International Raceway. In 2002 the original owners took back control of the facility and reverted to the original name. The GNC visited the scenic facility only twice. Other series that have used the facility include the NHRA, USAC and the SCCA. Vintage auto racing groups, karts and motorcycles also use the facility. The course is alive and well, hosting frequent track days in addition to major race dates.

1970 Atlanta Half-Mile
Rice Takes First Big Dirt Track of '70

GNC Round #5 of 25 **Date:** April 19, 1970 **Type:** Half-Mile **Venue:** Holiday Downs **Location:** Palmetto, Ga	**Surface:** Dirt **Course Length:** ½ Mile **Laps:** 20 **Distance:** 10 Miles

Jim Rice claimed his 2nd National win of the early season at the return of National racing to Georgia for the first time since 1948. The track outside of Atlanta, Ga proved to be rough and bumpy, giving most riders fits. Second in the National was a back-in-action Dick Mann who made a race out of it late in the goings, but came up short. In third spot, Michigan rider Jack Warren put in his best GNC finish yet. He was aboard an unusual Rickman Norton that seemed to work as well as anything else on the tricky course. The track became very rough in practice resulting in numerous spills. Frank Gillespie went down hard early, setting a trend for the day.

The Harley-Davidson debut of it's XR750 was pretty rocky. National #1 Mert Lawwill and Mark Brelsford showed up, but their air-freighted bikes did not, (see *"Extras"* for more). Georgia's own Jimmy Maness was 4th with Bart Markel and Roger Reiman in at 5th and 9th spots.

There was little change at the top of the points. Only three of the top ten scored points at Atlanta. Dick Mann added to his Daytona points with his runner-up position. Second in points Gene Romero was 10th in the race. Don Castro moved to third in points via his 6th place finish. Jim Rice moved from way back to seventh in points.

Time Trials

Home state favorite Jimmy Maness gave the crowd and Harley-Davidson something to cheer about by notching the fast time of 31.60 aboard his new XR750. Rookie sensation Dave Aldana was right behind on his factory BSA at 31.63.

Heats

Jim Rice (BSA) shot to an early lead on his self-tuned, factory BSA in Heat 1, pursued by South Carolina rider Jerry Stokes. Stokes got seriously out of shape up high in turn 3, launching over the fence, and sustained two broken ribs after impacting a fence post. Roger Reiman moved to 2nd, closely followed by Jimmy Maness. Rice won with the fastest time of the day.

Dick Mann (BSA) got out front quick in Heat 2 which quickly became a follow-the-leader affair with Larry Palmgren (Tri) and Bart Markel (HD) strung out behind him in the other transfer spots.

Jack Warren on that neat Norton put in a convincing run in Heat 3 with points contender Don Castro (Tri) in 2nd and Charlie Seale (HD) 3rd.

Semi

Proving there was still life in the Harley flathead KR, Ray Little took an early lead which he stretched to the finish, putting himself in the main. Joe Barringer (Tri) took 2nd spot with Gene Romero (Tri) just zapping rookie Dave Sehl (HD) for the last transfer spot.

National

Winner of two GNC races in 1969, Larry Palmgren, pulled the holeshot at the start of the National. Dick Mann shot through the pack for second followed by Don Castro, Jim Rice and Jack Warren. Mann took over the lead on lap 2 with Rice moving to 3rd. Rice reeled Mann in and took over on lap 8. Rice then stretched out to a decent lead. Things stayed fairly stable but on lap 18, Mann closed the gap and caught Rice in the last corner. Mann's charge ended when the rough track almost knocked him out of the saddle. Rice crossed the line uncontested.

Results

Race: 20 Lap Half-Mile National
Race Time: 10:55.24

Rank	Rider	Number	Make
1.	Jim Rice, Palo Alto, Ca	24	BSA
2.	Dick Mann, Richmond, Ca	2	BSA
3.	Jack Warren, Clio, Mi	82	Nor
4.	Jimmy Maness, Augusta, Ga	31	HD
5.	Bart Markel, Flint, Mi	4	HD
6.	Don Castro, Hollister, Ca	11Y	Tri
7.	Charlie Seale, St. Louis, Mo	7D	HD
8.	Larry Palmgren, Freehold, NJ	5	Tri
9.	Roger Reiman, Kewanee, Il	55	HD
10.	Gene Romero, San Luis Obispo, Ca	3	Tri
11.	Ray Little, Atlanta, Ga	19	HD
12.	Joe Barringer, Whitnel, NC	55C	Tri

Race: 14 Lap Amateur Half-Mile Final
Race Time: 7:43.46

Rank	Rider	Number	Make
1.	Doug Sehl, Waterdown, Ont., Can	75T	Tri
2.	Gary Fisher, Parkesburg, Pa	99A	Tri
3.	Maurice Fraser, Hamilton, Can	80T	Tri

Grand National Points Standings after Round 5

Rank	Rider	Pts
1.	Dick Mann	148
2.	Gene Romero	100
3.	Don Castro	94
4.	Yvon DuHamel	93
5.	Geoff Perry	67
6.	Walt Fulton III	62
7.	Jim Rice	61
8.	Mert Lawwill	57
9.	Dave Aldana	57
10.	Ginger Molloy	56

- A nice crowd was estimated at 7200.
- Track conditions were very difficult. Riders faced holes and bumps, and a 20-30 mph wind spreading curtains of red dust.
- Jimmy Maness put in his best National finish, finishing 4th aboard his factory/Augusta Harley-Davidson sponsored XR750.
- Daytona winner Dick Mann had finally ironed out a deal with BSA and was back on the circuit.
- Some trick early season machinery turned out. Cal Rayborn's trick Andres-built short rod XR with "El Reverso" cylinders, long intake tubes with Mikuni carburetors had trouble. Veteran Darrel Dovel showed up with a recently assembled BSA Rocket 3. Neither machine made the main.
- Georgia rider/tuner Ray Little had some really cool exhaust systems for the new Harleys. Several bikes sported the pipes including Dave Sehl's. Little was 11th in the National.
- Two-time GNC champ Gary Nixon turned some laps in practice, but his still weak leg from the previous year's Santa Rosa crash was not up to the crater-like track surface.
- Mert Lawwill had won the Ascot Park Expert Main, Friday night before the National. After the race, he and Mark Brelsford, (who finished 3rd at Ascot), dutifully crated up their bikes for the Atlanta flight. Running late, the pair had to change airlines. It worked okay for them, but their crated bikes would not fit the cargo hold of their new flight.
- Future stunt man Bobby Gill placed 5th in the Amateur Final.
- The Holiday Downs facility was primarily a horse racing track, but hosted motorcycle racing numerous times over the years. The GNC would only visit the facility once. Vintage motorcycle racing returned in the 1990's. Today the track is closed.

1970 Cumberland Half-Mile
Lawwill Scores First Win for H-D's XR750

GNC Round #6 of 25 **Date:** May 3, 1970 **Type:** Half-Mile **Venue:** Alleghany County Speedway **Location:** Cumberland, Md	**Purse:** $6000.00 **Surface:** Dirt **Course Length:** ½ Mile **Laps:** 20 **Distance:** 10 Miles

GNC Champ Mert Lawwill avenged missing the first big dirt track of the year by just nipping rookie Expert Dave Aldana on the last lap of the 10-Mile Cumberland Half-Mile. Lawwill, the defending race champion, now had two wins on the year, giving him a milestone 10 GNC wins. It was also historic first win for Harley-Davidson's new XR750. Tuner Jim Belland and Lawwill himself prepared the bike. Aldana appeared to have the event sewn up aboard the Irv Seaver-sponsored, factory BSA at mid-race, but Lawwill ran him down. Larry Palmgren also closed up on Aldana on the last lap to round out the podium.

Dick Mann failed to score any points at Cumberland but still maintained the lead in points with 148. Wholesale changes in the order behind were going on as the season was picking up steam. Mert Lawwill's win catapulted him from eighth to runner-up in the standings with 110 points. Gene Romero added a few points but slipped back a spot at 103. Similar to Lawwill, Dave Aldana's 2nd place in the National gave him a big boost, moving from ninth to fourth in points with 100. Don Castro slipped back to fifth raising his total a little to 98.

Time Trials

The Cumberland track was very fast on this day, with Dave Aldana's self-tuned BSA turning in the fastest Expert lap, at 25.90, breaking the old track record of 26.63. Mert Lawwill (HD) was 2nd fastest at 25.96. Amateur sensation Canadian Doug Sehl, brother of Expert Dave, turned in the fastest time of the day with an amazing 25.40. No other riders broke into the 25 second bracket.

Heats

Mert Lawwill was quickly out front in Heat 1, topping factory BSA-supported Ken Pressgrove. They were headed directly to National. Jack Forrester (HD), Jack Warren (Nor) and Cal Rayborn (HD) were going to the semi.

1969 Cumberland winner Larry Palmgren (Tri) and Mark Brelsford (HD) headed the order in Heat 2, followed by heavy hitters Jim Rice (BSA) and Gene Romero (Tri).

The final heat of the day produced some surprises. Rookies Dave Aldana and Keith Mashburn (Yam) finished 1-2. Relatively unknown Louis Moniz Jr. (HD) was 3rd over fast guys Dick Mann (BSA) and Don Castro (Tri).

Semi

A determined Jim Rice led Triumph riders Don Castro and Gene Romero to the last National tickets.

Main

Mark Brelsford blasted his new XR750 into the lead at the start of the National. He led the first two laps before Larry Palmgren moved by. Dave Aldana was right behind and took the lead on lap 4. Mert Lawwill was running mid-pack, but he methodically worked his way to the front. By lap 13 he moved around Larry Palmgren for 2nd. Lawwill next set his sights on the leader. Aldana had a big lead going into the last lap, but Lawwill was gaining rapidly. Aldana protected the inside line, but Lawwill turned on afterburners, passing a surprised Aldana in turn 3 on the outside. Lawwill only led one lap, but it was the one that counted!

Results

Race: 20 Lap Half-Mile National
Race Time: 9:06.53

Rank	Rider	Number	Make
1.	Mert Lawwill, San Francisco, Ca	1	HD
2.	Dave Aldana, Santa Ana, Ca	38X	BSA
3.	Larry Palmgren, Freehold, NJ	5	Tri
4.	Keith Mashburn, Santa Susana, Ca	30X	Yam
5.	Mark Brelsford, San Bruno, Ca	87	HD
6.	Jimmy Maness, Augusta, Ga	31	HD
7.	Ken Pressgrove, Topeka, Ks	14N	BSA
8.	Dave Smith, Lakewood, Ca	11X	Tri
9.	Don Castro, Hollister, Ca	11Y	Tri
10.	Gene Romero, San Luis Obispo, Ca	3	Tri
11.	Dave Sehl, Waterdown, Ont., Can	21T	HD
12.	Jim Rice, Palo Alto, Ca	24	BSA

Race: 14 Lap Half-Mile Amateur Final
Race Time: 6:19.72

Rank	Rider	Number	Make
1.	Doug Sehl, Waterdown, Ont., Can	75T	Tri
2.	Ron Butler, Union Lake, Mi	11E	Tri
3.	Tod Sloan, Fresno, Ca	18Z	Tri

Grand National Points Standings after Round 6

Rank	Rider	Pts
1.	Dick Mann	148
2.	Mert Lawwill	110
3.	Gene Romero	103
4.	Dave Aldana	100
5.	Don Castro	98
6.	Yvon DuHamel	93
7.	Geoff Perry	67
8.	Walt Fulton III	62
9.	Jim Rice	62
10.	Ginger Molloy	56

- The racetrack at Cumberland opened in 1924 as the Fairgo Race Track. It was a popular horse racing facility for decades till it closed in 1961. It soon reopened for use as an auto racing track, and was known as the Alleghany County Speedway. It has hosted several well known sanctioning bodies including ARCA, USAC, URC as well as the AMA. It continues to be a healthy speed plant today, with late model stock cars being it's main attraction. It is also known as "The Rock". It's setting in the mountainous area of Maryland make it one of the most picturesque racetracks in the country.
- A great crowd of 6000 had to please promoter John Barton.
- Dave Aldana was first alternate for the program when his BSA went on one cylinder. He made the program when Royal Sherbert scratched from the program.
- A broken primary chain put Jim Rice out on lap 1.
- Doug Sehl won his second Amateur race in a row.
- Bart Markel was present, but only as a spectator. He was still recovering from an early season collarbone fracture at the Billy Huber Memorial.

1970 Talladega Road Race
A First for Aldana and BSA at Talladega!

GNC Round #7 of 25 **Date:** May 17, 1970 **Type:** Road Race **Venue:** Alabama International Motor Speedway **Location:** Talladega, Al	**Purse:** $10,000.00 **Surface:** Pavement **Course Length**: 4.0 Miles **Laps**: 50 **Distance:** 200 Miles

Rookie Dave Aldana shocked all involved by winning his first race at the inaugural Talladega 200 on a BSA Rocket III. His race speed of 104.589 set the mark for the fastest event in the U.S. The race was also a first National road race win for one of the British triples. Aldana took a comfortable victory after early leader Gary Nixon had trouble and crashed. The win was a surprise; no one doubted the talented Aldana would notch a win soon, it was just expected to be on dirt, not pavement. This was just his third Expert pavement start! Veteran pavement scratcher Jody Nicholas was the runner-up. BSA team rider Jim Rice put in a great ride in 3rd. Like his winning teammate, Rice was primarily thought of as a dirt tracker. The first-time event at Talladega was generally well received by the riders. It was a high speed track, similar to Daytona in speeds. It favored horsepower and throttle-twisting over technical skills, not hurting Aldana's chances. A decent first race crowd of 13,000 showed for the Bill France-promoted event.

In an unfortunate accident, Kent winner Ron Grant received serious injuries in a starting incident during the Lightweight race. Grant's bike stalled on the first line of the grid and was rear-ended by Amateur Dave Bloom whose vision was obscured by starting line smoke. Grant's left leg was terribly mangled and Bloom received serious arm, shoulder and leg fractures. Both were expected to be out of action for six to twelve months.

Dick Mann put in a good finish when he needed, his 5th place run keeping him in the GNC point's lead with 232. Dave Aldana's big win hoisted him close to Mann, up into second with 205. Jim Rice's surprising pavement run shot him from ninth in points to third. Gene Romero slipped back just a little, his 6th place in the National keeping him in the hunt with 166 points. Don Castro maintained fifth with 141 points, the same for Yvon DuHamel in sixth at 93. Mert Lawwill was the big loser for the week. He finished an out-of-the points 26th and fell from runner-up to seventh in points. By virtue of their strong Talladega runs, Art Baumann, Jody Nicholas and Royal Sherbert all moved into the top 10. High finishing Daytona finishers Geoff Perry, Walt Fulton and Ginger Malloy finally drifted out of top of the points standings.

Time Trials

Like Daytona, Gene Romero and tuner Pat Owens mounted highly inflated front tires on both ends of the factory Triumph Trident. Romero blazed through the flying lap around the Talladega oval at 156.521 mph, just off his Daytona speed. Teammate Gary Nixon was next at 154.901. A little off the two Triumphs speed in 3rd was Dick Mann's BSA turning a 151.711 lap. His young teammate Dave Aldana was next at 151.255. Next were the two-strokes of Ron Grant (Suz) and Jess Thomas (Kaw). Showing an increase in power, the new Harley-Davidsons took the next three spots; Mark Brelsford, (149.695), Mert Lawwill, (148.741) and Cal Rayborn , (148.465). Time would tell if they had reliability to go with their speed. Rounding out the top 10 was Expert/Amateur Don Emde on the Mel Dineson-prepped Yamaha.

National

Gene Romero was first away from the line with Gary Nixon on his rear tire; right behind was a pack containing Don Castro, Mert Lawwill, Dave Aldana, Cal Rayborn and Jody Nicholas. Nixon took over on lap 2 and tried to ditch his pursuers. Aldana was getting in a groove and by lap 5 moved by Romero for 2nd. Early retirees included Ralph White (Kaw), Don Emde, Jess Thomas and the first of many Harley riders, Mark Brelsford. While Aldana chased Nixon, Gene Romero slipped back into a pack including Lawwill, Rayborn, Jody Nicholas, Don Castro (Tri), Jim Rice, Art Baumann (Suz), Tom Rockwood (Yam), Ron Pierce (Yam) and Chuck Palmgren (Yam). By lap 20 Aldana had latched onto Nixon who was fighting a sticky throttle. The two ran hard, swapping positions and paint around the circuit. Nixon pushed a little too hard, running off the track and low-siding. Nixon got help from bystanders to push his Trident out of the dirt to get started. Unfortunately this violated AMA rules and Nixon was black flagged. Aldana had a big lead which he was able to maintain even during pit stops. Behind him Nicholas moved into a solid runner-up position, followed by Rice in 3rd despite making two pit stops. The rest of the order behind stabilized to Baumann, Mann and Romero. The only changes in the late laps was Rockwood dropping Pierce back a spot on the final circuit. Rayborn and Lawwill both fell out with the usual iron XR heat issues and Castro was slowed by clutch trouble. Aldana crossed the stripe for a huge first win for himself and BSA.

Results

Race: 200 Mile Road Race National
Race Time: 1:53:57.93

Rank	Rider	Number	Make
1.	Dave Aldana, Santa Ana, Ca	83	BSA
2.	Jody Nicholas, La Mesa, Ca	58	Suz
3.	Jim Rice, Palo Alto, Ca	24	BSA
4.	Art Baumann, Brisbane, Ca	30	Suz
5.	Dick Mann, Richmond, Ca	2	BSA
6.	Gene Romero, San Luis Obispo, Ca	3	Tri
7.	Tom Rockwood, Gardena, Ca	38	Yam
8.	Ron Pierce, Bakersfield, Ca	97	Yam
9.	Chuck Palmgren, Freehold, NJ	6	Yam
10.	Ken Molyneux, Vancouver, Can	89	Yam
11.	Don Castro, Hollister, Ca	81	Tri
12.	Dave Smith, Lakewood, Ca	11	Kaw
13.	Mark Williams, Springfield, Ore	70	Kaw
14.	Nat Williams, Washington, DC	34	Kaw
15.	Rick Deane, Aspen, Co	74	Yam
16.	Philip Cullum, No. Little Rock, Ark	29	Kaw
17.	Royal Sherbert, Largo, Fl	88	BSA
18.	John Klaus, Houston, Tx	43	Hon
19.	Yvon DuHamel, Lasalle, Can	5	Yam
20.	Keith Mashburn, Santa Susana, Ca	33	Yam

Race: 76 Mile Amateur Road Race Final
Race Time: 42:53.29

Rank	Rider	Number	Make
1.	Rusty Bradley, Dallas, Tx	67	Kaw
2.	Gary Fisher, Parkesburg, Pa	10	Tri
3.	Fred Guttner, E. Detroit, Mi	39	Yam

Grand National Points Standings after Round 7

Rank	Rider	Pts
1.	Dick Mann	232
2.	Dave Aldana	205
3.	Jim Rice	188
4.	Gene Romero	166
5.	Don Castro	141
6.	Yvon DuHamel	136
7.	Mert Lawwill	110
8.	Art Baumann	93
9.	Jody Nicholas	91
10.	Royal Sherbert	74

Extra Extra

- Dave Aldana got his biggest payday yet, $7860.00 in purse and contingency money including a nice $5000.00 bonus from BSA.
- Aldana, Bob Tryon and Dallas Baker had wrenched on the BSA before Daytona. Before the race it was one of the slowest team bikes. Aldana remembers that they installed go-fast factory stuff like different pistons and cylinder heads. The bike was pretty fast at Daytona and by the time they got to Talladega, it was real fast.
- It was another awful day for Harley-Davidson. The bright spot was qualifying with three bikes in the top 10. In the National all the team bikes were out of the race by midway. Even Walt Fulton's trusty KR gave up. Mert Lawwill was listed as the top finisher in 26th place. This was the low point for their 1970 road race season.
- It was a tough day for many teams with less than half the starters going the distance.
- Kawasaki was working the bugs out of their race car style, dry break refueling system, hoping to shave 7-8 seconds off a fuel stop. The system seemed to work well with the factory supported bikes including Dave Smith, Jess Thomas and Rusty Bradley.
- Don Emde put in an amazing ride in the Combined Lightweight race, topping Gary Nixon and Cal Rayborn. Rayborn had forsaken his Kent race winning Harley Sprint for a longer legged Don Vesco Yamaha.
- Rusty Bradley topped Gary Fisher again in the Amateur race, getting another $2500.00 contingency award from Kawasaki. Bradley's speed average in the 76-mile race was 104.448, close to Aldana's GNC speed. The previously scuffed rear tire on Bradley's bike was worn to the cords at the end of the race.
- The birth of "Team Mexican" officially? occurred around the Talladega event. Alluding to their Mexican-American heritage, Southern Californians Gene Romero and Dave Aldana adopted the moniker, seen on the "teammates" helmets.
- The Alabama International Motor Speedway opened September 12, 1969. The huge Talladega speedway cost $4 million dollars to build and featured the longest and fastest oval track in NASCAR at 2.66 miles, featuring 33 degree banking. It was mainly built and funded by NASCAR founder Bill France Sr. Many closed course speed records for cars and motorcycles were set there. The track also featured a 4.0 mile road course that was the fastest on the AMA Grand National circuit. The road course also hosted auto road racing with series such as IMSA. The AMA raced there from 1970-'74 with the events a moderate success. Use of the road course ceased in 1983. The tracks name was changed to the Talladega Superspeedway in 1989. It is one of the most famous racetracks in the world and remains a popular fixture for NASCAR stock car racing.
- There was a major correction/revision in the AMA GNC points system made at the time of the Talladega National. The 1970 points system was to be based on the total purse of the entire event, including preliminary events. An error had been made from the beginning of the season, starting with Houston, that based points paid only on the championship final. This revision was retroactive to the start of the year.

Bonus!
Top 20 Talladega 200 Qualifying Speeds

1.		Gene Romero	Tri	156.521 MPH
2.		Gary Nixon	Tri	154.901
3.		Dick Mann	BSA	151.711
4.		Dave Aldana	BSA	151.255
5.		Ron Grant	Suz	150.258
6.		Jess Thomas	Kaw	150.211
7.		Mark Brelsford	HD	149.695
8.		Mert Lawwill	HD	148.741
9.		Cal Rayborn	HD	148.465
10.		Don Emde	Yam	148.396
11.		Don Castro	Tri	147.595
12.		Ed Moran	Kaw	146.983
13.		Sam Ingram	Hon	146.803
14.		Neville Landrobe	Yam	146.803
15.		Ralph White	Yam	146.668
16.		Art Baumann	Suz	144.718
17.		Walt Fulton	HD	143.675
18.		Mark Williams	Kaw	143.460
19.		Larry Darr	HD	142.415
20.		Ken Molyneux	Yam	142.330

1970 Reading Half-Mile
Rice in the Groove Again

GNC Round #8 of 25	**Location:** Reading, Pa
Date: May 31, 1970	**Surface:** Dirt
Type: Half-Mile	**Course Length**: ½ Mile
Venue: Reading County Fairgrounds	**Laps:** 20
	Distance: 10 Miles

BSA factory star Jim Rice notched his 3rd win of the year at the last Reading National Half-Mile. Further adding to his reputation as the groove master of the circuit, Rice came from way back in the field on a track that was very tough to pass on. It was Rice's 6th overall GNC win. Last year's winner Larry Palmgren was 2nd with Dick Mann 3rd.

It was a really weird day with some relative unknowns like Billy Lloyd, George Lougabaugh and Billy Eves having strong runs while many stars struggled. Harley teamsters Mert Lawwill, Mark Brelsford and Bart Markel failed to make the show. Of the Harley regulars, only Cal Rayborn made it to the main where he had problems. Talladega winner Dave Aldana provided fireworks in the semi, spectacular until he fell off. Gary Nixon proved he could still dirt track despite his weakened leg. He ran very strong early in the event before fading.

Dick Mann's 3rd place finish kept him atop of the standings, but faced a new rival. Jim Rice's win moved him into second in points, 31 points back from Mann. Dave Aldana did not make the main and it cost him, slipping back to third in points. He was still within shouting distance, 40 points behind. There were no other changes in position in the top 10.

Heats

Rookie Don Castro (Tri) shot into the lead of Heat 1 and ran off and hid. Gene Romero (Tri) was a solid 2nd till the halfway mark when he slipped off the groove and fell. A young Billy Eves (BSA) raised a few eyeballs with his capture of the runner-up spot. Californian Frank Gillespie (Tri) grabbed the 3rd position. GNC Champ Mert Lawwill was doing business till his kill switch shorted out.

Ken Pressgrove (BSA) pulled the holeshot in Heat 2 and like Castro did a disappearing act. Gary Nixon (Tri) was having a great dirt track day, running 2nd the whole race. The first good racing of the day was between Dave Aldana (BSA), Mark Brelsford (HD) and Dick Mann (BSA), with veteran Mann taking the transfer.

Larry Palmgren (Tri) repeated the previous heat winners routine in Heat 3 and took a comfortable win. Billy Lloyd (Tri) was 2nd and Jim Rice was 3rd.

Semi

Cal Rayborn was determined to put a factory Harley in the main and was up front the whole distance. Putting the only other Harley in the National was George Longabaugh. Royal Sherbert (BSA) held Mark Brelsford off for 3rd. Dave Aldana put on a great show. He had a bump and grind with somebody as he came off the line, knocking his bike out of gear. He ran up high, reeling in the pack, as he worked forward switching to the groove and shortly thereafter he fell off.

National

Billy Lloyd got the holeshot of his life, leading the pack into turn 1. Lloyd looked strong, but Gary Nixon had momentum and took over on lap 2. In a pack behind Nixon and Lloyd were Don Castro, Larry Palmgren, Ken Pressgrove, George Longabaugh and Billy Eves. Jim Rice was way back in the field. Up front, Nixon pulled a small lead and Lloyd slipped back a couple spots. Rice began slicing his way through the lead pack. By lap 6, he was closing. Around lap 8 he took the lead from Nixon. The former champ quickly dropped back to the 5th position. George Longabaugh who had been running with the lead pack all day, fell on lap 9. On lap 12 Billy Lloyd's day went bad when he hit the wall in turn 2. The red flag came out and he took a ride to the hospital, reportedly suffering serious back injuries. A "flying", (rolling), restart saw Rice maintain his lead with Palmgren and Mann following him home.

Race: 20 Lap Half-Mile National

Rank	Rider	Number	Make
1.	Jim Rice, Palo Alto, Ca,	24	BSA
2.	Larry Palmgren, Freehold, NJ	5	Tri
3.	Dick Mann, Richmond, Ca	2	BSA
4.	Ken Pressgrove, Topeka, Ks	14N	BSA
5.	Gary Nixon, Phoenix, Md	9	Tri
6.	Don Castro, Hollister, Ca	11Y	Tri
7.	Billy Eves, Phoenixville, Pa	11A	BSA
8.	Royal Sherbert, Largo, Fla	30D	BSA
9.	Frank Gillespie, Berkeley, Ca	23Y	Tri
10.	Billy Lloyd, Langley Park, Md	13	Tri
11.	Cal Rayborn, San Diego, Ca	25	HD
12.	George Longabaugh, Elverson, Pa	50	HD

Race: 7 Lap Half-Mile Amateur Final

Rank	Rider	Number	Make
1.	Tod Sloan, Fresno, Ca	18Z	Tri
2.	Dennis Palmgren, Freehold, NJ	42M	Tri
3.	Harry Wynns, Ravenna, Oh	15F	HD

Grand National Points Standings after Round 8

Rank	Rider	Pts
1.	Dick Mann	245
2.	Jim Rice	214
3.	Dave Aldana	205
4.	Gene Romero	166
5.	Don Castro	148
6.	Yvon DuHamel	126
7.	Mert Lawwill	110
8.	Art Baumann	93
9.	Jody Nicholas	91
10.	Royal Sherbert	79

Extra Extra

- British bikes dominated the National. There were five each Triumph's and BSA's. There were only two Harley's in the show, neither running at the finish. Rayborn's blew up and Longabaugh fell off his.
- Bart Markel had recovered from his Billy Huber Memorial injuries. He could not get his XR750 into the program.
- Jim Rice took home at least $1150.00 for the win. A heat race win was worth $60.00.
- The Reading, Pa fairgrounds half-mile track had a long motorsports history. It opened in 1924 and saw prewar action from the AAA and other open wheel cars as well as motorcycles. The track closed because of WWII in 1942 and reopened in 1946. The track was again a hotbed for open wheel midgets, sprints, champ cars and USAC events frequently ran there. Reading is probably most famous for modified stock car racing. Names like Tobias, Brightbill and Weld were legendary in the area. 1970 was the last year GNC motorcycles competed there. The track last ran in 1979, the victim of real estate development. The fairgrounds became the site for the Fairgrounds Square Mall, (sic). The old track, coupes and drivers are celebrated each year by the Reading Fair Racing Historical Society (RFRHS), at the "new" Reading fair.

1970 Louisville Half-Mile
Sehl Wins First National

GNC Round #9 of 25	**Purse:** $7000.00
Date: June 6, 1970	**Surface:** Limestone
Type: Half-Mile	**Course Length:** ½ Mile
Venue: Louisville Downs	**Laps:** 20
Location: Louisville, Ky	**Distance:** 10 Miles

Canadian rookie Expert Dave Sehl claimed his first GNC race at the always spectacular Louisville National. The track had been soaked with rain for days leading up to the event and was in great shape. The smooth-riding Sehl just barely dodged mechanical problems in his heat and the final, but tuner Babe DeMay kept things on track. Cal Rayborn was itching for a dirt GNC win, looked great but just came up short settling for second. Larry Palmgren posted another fantastic finish in 3rd place. Bart Markel, who had won all three previous Nationals at Louisville, had engine problems in his heat and did not make the main. Harley-Davidson's domination at Louisville had continued; a relief to the team after debacle at the previous Reading National.

There were not any changes in the top of the points order. The top three all had various problems during the event. Dick Mann and Jim Rice both made the main but both fell out of the race with trouble. Dave Aldana failed to transfer from the semi. Gene Romero, Don Castro and Mert Lawwill all added to their totals, but not enough to advance positions.

Time Trials

Dick Mann turned the fastest lap of the night on his self-tuned factory BSA. Harley-Davidson's Mark Brelsford was second on the Jim Belland-tuned Harley, followed by Jim Rice on his self-tuned Team BSA machine.

Heats

Gene Romero (Tri) took the lead in Heat 1 with Jim Rice (BSA) hot on his heels. Romero eventually pulled a comfortable lead. Rice kept 2nd with Keith Mashburn (Yam) in 3rd, making it Californians 1- 2- 3. Former GNC champs Bart Markel (HD) and Dick Mann (BSA) both had motor woes. Markel was done for the night; Mann would advance to the Semi.

Cal Rayborn (HD) looked great in Heat 2, stretching to a convincing win over Larry Palmgren (Tri) and Mark Brelsford (HD). Rayborn's heat was the fastest of the night, giving him the pole for the National.

Harley teammates Dave Sehl and Mert Lawwill fought for the lead in Heat 3 with Sehl taking the advantage. His engine slowed on the last lap allowing Lawwill by for the win. Ronnie Rall put his self-sponsored BSA into the National by taking 3rd.

Semi

The crushed limestone track was still in great shape and the Semi was packed with talent itching to make the big show. Rookie Don Castro (Tri) gassed it up and was gone; Dick Mann pressured Castro early in the go, but settled for 2nd. Third place was a battle between Larry Darr (HD), Chuck Palmgren (Yam), Dave Aldana (BSA) and a returning-to-action George Roeder. Aldana had been spectacular all night and was barnstorming up by the hay bails. While battling with Darr, he tried to clean his visor and the two tangled. Dave slowed, Darr continued, following Castro and Mann into the National.

National

Cal Rayborn was doing his best Bart Markel imitation and led the charge into Turn 1. The track offered many racing lines and the pack spread clear across the wide surface. As the field sorted itself out, Dick Mann, Dave Sehl and Larry Palmgren chased the leader. Sehl edged ahead of Rayborn on lap 8, stretching out to a good lead. Behind, Rayborn was a safe 2nd. Bad luck hit Team BSA late in the race. Jim Rice's machine had ignition failure and podium bound Dick Mann's primary chain broke. Larry Palmgren moved into 3rd. Ronnie Rall put in the ride of the night in 4th spot. The plucky Ohioan got a bad start and was running at the rear of the field till late in the race when the

41

cushion specialist rolled it on and passed nearly the entire field in just a few laps. Sehl's XR acted up again late in the race, beginning to smoke when an oil return line came loose. The bike stayed together and Dave "Sehled" to the win.

Results

Race: 20 Lap Half-Mile National
Race Time: 9:09.98

Rank	Rider	Number	Make
1.	Dave Sehl, Waterdown, Ont., Can	21T	HD
2.	Cal Rayborn, Spring Valley, Ca	25	HD
3.	Larry Palmgren, Freehold, NJ	5	Tri
4.	Ronnie Rall, Mansfield, Oh	52	BSA
5.	Don Castro, Hollister, Ca	11Y	Tri
6.	Larry Darr, Mansfield, Oh	94	HD
7.	Gene Romero, San Luis Obispo, Ca	3	Tri
8.	Keith Mashburn, Santa Susana, Ca	30X	Yam
9.	Dick Mann, Richmond, Ca	2	BSA
10.	Jim Rice, Palo Alto, Ca	24	BSA
11.	Mert Lawwill, San Francisco, Ca	1	HD
12.	Mark Brelsford, San Bruno, Ca	87	HD

Race: 7 Lap Half-Mile Amateur Final
Race Time: 6:33.14

Rank	Rider	Number	Make
1.	Maurice Fraser, Hamilton, Can	80T	Tri
2.	Richard Holley, San Diego, Ca	13R	Tri
3.	Ron Butler, Union Lake, Mi	11E	Tri

Grand National Points Standings after Round 9

Rank	Rider	Pts
1.	Dick Mann	249
2.	Jim Rice	217
3.	Dave Aldana	205
4.	Gene Romero	174
5.	Don Castro	160
6.	Yvon DuHamel	136
7.	Mert Lawwill	112
8.	Art Baumann	93
9.	Jody Nicholas	91
10.	Royal Sherbert	79

Extra Extra

- A big field of 62 Experts and 64 Amateurs turned out.
- The night turned out to be a Canadian "Double-Header" and nearly a Sehl "Double-Header". Doug Sehl's Triumph broke while he was leading the Amateur final. Fellow countryman Maurice Frazier took over to capture the win.
- George Roeder returned to action at Louisville. Though he didn't figure in the National results, he topped 54 other Experts at the following day's Regional. Roeder looked stylish as ever on a rigid framed Harley XR.

He sported a different look, wearing a full face Bell Star and using number 3F instead of the traditional #94 which Larry Darr now wore.

- Ronnie Rall put in a long night. The morning of the race he had stuffed his BSA into his private plane back in Mansfield, Oh and flew to the event. Upon arrival, he rented the biggest car he could find and wrestled the bike into the trunk. After a great 4th place finish in the National, he picked up his money, stuffed the bike back in the rental and headed out. By now it was very late and Ronnie could not remember how to get back to the airport. After a couple of hours he finally found it and parked in the airports lot. After a bit of snoozing, Ronnie was awakened by a security guard banging on the window. He was told that, " You can't sleep here, come back at 6:00 am". After more driving around, Ronnie came back at the aforementioned time, loaded up and flew home. He raced at an Ohio half-mile the same day, but not surprisingly, can't remember much about it!
- The Louisville Downs harness track opened in the summer of 1966. It was a well lit, modern facility, featuring a large grandstand. AMA Grand National motorcycle racing started in 1967. The wide, deep cushion surface offered multiple racing lines, providing spectacular side-by-side racing. The track drew big crowds and became a GNC series mainstay. Racing continued until 1991 when the facility was purchased by the Churchill Downs Racetrack and it was turned into a thoroughbred training facility.

1970 Loudon Road Race
Nixon Returns at Loudon!

GNC Round #10 of 25 **Date:** June 14, 1970 **Type:** Road Race **Venue:** Bryar Motorsports Complex	**Location:** Loudon, NH **Surface:** Pavement **Course Length**: 1.6 Miles **Laps:** 63 **Distance:** 100 Miles

Gary Nixon returned to victory lane for the first time since his devastating leg injury of 1969. He bid his time and took advantage of others problems to win the 1970 Loudon Grand National. Nixon rode near the front all day, taking over after front runners Mark Brelsford and Yvon DuHamel had trouble. It was the two-time champs 15th National win and second at Loudon, (the first in 1967). It was the first and only win for the mighty Triumph Trident. Cliff Guild was Nixon's tuner this day. California rider Dave Smith put in his best National finish, quietly putting his Kawasaki into the runner-up spot. Rookie Don Emde continued to show skills beyond his years, scoring his best finish GNC yet on the Mel Dineson Yamaha. Yvon DuHamel recovered from a late race fall while in 2nd place to finish 4th. Walt Fulton once again was the top Harley-Davidson, 5th on the trusty KR, (surely a continuing source of Harley team embarrassment). It was not a good weekend for the factory team. Cal Rayborn fell hard while leading his heat race, apparently breaking his wrist. Things looked up during the National; Mark Brelsford appeared the sure winner till late in the race when "ignition" problems took him out.

The track had been recently resurfaced with some corners widened. Track owner Keith Bryar was an enthusiast and tried to do the job right. Everything seemed rosy, but there were an inordinate number of crashes for the weekend, beginning with Talladega winner Dave Aldana's destruction of his BSA in practice, (David, uninjured of course) and Rayborn's heat race crash. Others coming off during the race included, Jody Nicholas, Jimmy Odom, Don Castro, Chuck Palmgren Tom Rockwood and Ron Pierce. Most, besides Rayborn, walked away uninjured. While the reasons for the spills weren't pinpointed, the fresh track surface seemed to get slippery when the temperature got above the 80 degree mark.

While Dick Mann held onto the GNC points lead, his 13th point finish allowed his pursuers to close ground. Jim Rice had a decent pavement day and closed to within 23 points of Mann. Dave Aldana and Gene Romero both finished in the top 10 at Loudon, adding to their totals. Yvon DuHamel moved Don Castro back a spot for fifth. Gary Nixon's win propelled him up into the top of the standings for the first time in 1970. Mert Lawwill slipped back a spot to eighth. Dave Smith and Walt Fulton's Loudon runs moved them into the top 10.

National

Mark Brelsford looked to turn Harley's terrible pavement luck around and charged out front early. Gary Nixon was right with him, joined by Yvon DuHamel (Yam) and Jody Nicholas (Yam). Brelsford began to stretch out his lead as Nixon and DuHamel diced around the twisty course. Nicholas turned up the wick, passing DuHamel and began to challenge Nixon. He went past the Triumph pilot on lap 14, but dropped his Suzuki the next lap. DuHamel had closed up on Nixon and the two continued to go at it. DuHamel eventually moved by and set out after leader Brelsford. By the midway point DuHamel had reeled in Brelsford and passed him on lap 38. DuHamel stepped off his Yamaha the next lap. He hopped back on quick enough to grab 3rd, ahead of Don Emde (Yam) and Dave Smith (Kaw). Brelsford maintained the top spot till his XR750 let him down on lap 52. Barring any trouble Nixon now had a clear path for the win. Second running DuHamel found himself pressured by youngsters Emde and Smith. Both went by, knocking him to 4th. As the laps ran out, Smith grabbed 2nd from Emde. At the flag it was Nixon, Smith, Emde, DuHamel, Walt Fulton on the tractor KR, fast Northeast privateer Frank Camillieri, Yamaha's Dusty Coppage, Team Mexican's Dave Aldana and Gene Romero, with Jim Rice putting in another solid pavement ride to round out the top 10.

Results

Race: 100 Mile Road Race National
Race Time: 1:22:45.00, 73.08 MPH

Rank	Rider	Number	Make
1.	Gary Nixon, Phoenix, Md	9	Tri
2.	Dave Smith, Lakewood, Ca	11	Kaw
3.	Don Emde, San Diego, Ca	35	Yam
4.	Yvon DuHamel, LaSalle, Can	5	Yam
5.	Walt Fulton, Hacienda Heights, Ca	63	HD
6.	Frank Camillieri, Chelsea, Mass	91	Yam
7.	Dusty Coppage, Chatsworth, Ca	32	Yam
8.	Dave Aldana, Santa Ana, Ca	83	BSA
9.	Gene Romero, San Luis Obispo, Ca	3	Tri
10.	Jim Rice, Palo Alto, Ca	24	BSA
11.	Dan Haaby, Orangevale, Ca	22	Yam
12.	Mert Lawwill, San Francisco, Ca	1	HD
13.	Dick Mann, Richmond, Ca	2	BSA
14.	Hurley Wilvert, Long Beach, Ca	79	Kaw
15.	Larry Schafer, Hyattsville, Md	20	HD
16.	Jess Thomas, Sea Cliff, NY	98	Kaw
17.	Bob Bulmer, Monice, Mi	53	Yam
18.	Ed Varnes, Cochranville, Pa	26	Tri
19.	Frank Gillespie, Berkeley, Ca	23	Tri
20.	Rod Pink, White Plains, NY	72	HD

Race: 60 Mile Amateur National
Race Time: 50:20.00. 72.476

Rank	Rider	Number	Make
1.	Rusty Bradley, Dallas, Tx	67	Kaw
2.	Gary Fisher, Parkesburg, Pa	10	Tri
3.	Fred Guttner, E. Detroit, Mi	39	Yam

Grand National Points Standings after Round 10

Rank	Rider	Pts
1.	Dick Mann	286
2.	Jim Rice	263
3.	Dave Aldana	257
4.	Gene Romero	223
5.	Yvon DuHamel	210
6.	Don Castro	160
7.	Gary Nixon	153
8.	Mert Lawwill	152
9.	Dave Smith	149
10.	Walt Fulton III	131

- A typically large Loudon/Laconia crowd approaching 30,000 turned up for the National.
- Gary Nixon won $2700.00 for his win. He also got $250.00 for winning the fastest heat. Yvon DuHamel claimed the other heat win.
- The win was the third for Triumph at the event, Ed Fisher, (Gary's father), in 1953, with Nixon winning the other two events.
- Mert Lawwill was once again the top Harley-Davidson factory rider at a road race, finishing 12th. His was the only team bike still running.
- Rusty Bradley once again topped rival Gary Fisher in the 100-Mile Amateur race. Kawasaki awarded Bradley another $2500.00, giving him a whopping $10,000.00 in contingency money so far this in 1970!
- Yvon DuHamel topped the Lightweight event over Cal Rayborn who chose to ride his factory Sprint on the tight course.
- This turned out to be the final road race event of the year when the June 21st Heidelberg "Mini" Road Race National was rained out and cancelled, much to the joy of most riders.
- The original Laconia/Loudon event was a motorcycle "happening". Kind of a "Northeast Daytona". Thousands came to the Belknap Recreation Area, to ride, camp and tour the beautiful New Hampshire lakes and mountains. The race was first held in 1940. The track was mostly pavement with a dirt/gravel section thrown in. The year 1963 would be the last year for Laconia at the Belknap Recreation Area. The event had outgrown the area and the crowds were becoming more unruly. The costs for security had risen dramatically. The event would move to the Bryar Motorsport Park in nearby Loudon in 1965. The Bryar Motorsport Complex was built by Keith Bryar, a former World Champion Dog Sledder, starting in 1960 with a kart track. The 1.6 mile road race course was built in 1964 and operated till 1989. The AMA ran GNC's there well into the 1980's. There were also two oval tracks and a drag strip which operated at the complex. In 1990 Bobby Bahre plowed the old courses under and built a 1-mile paved oval which incorporated a road course somewhat reminiscent of the old track. The facility began hosting NASCAR events. Bruton Smith and Speedway Motorsports bought the facility in 2007 and renamed it the New Hampshire Motor Speedway. Over the years the SCCA, WKA and CART have also raced at the facility.

GNC Round #11 of 25 **Date:** June 26, 1970 **Type:** TT **Venue:** Sante Fe Speedway	**Location:** Hinsdale, Il **Surface:** Dirt **Course Length:** **Laps:** 25

Eddie Mulder turned in a great performance at the Sante Fe TT to earn his 5th and final GNC win; (see *Extras*). Mulder had to work for the win against Mark Brelsford who was dominant early in the event and later Skip Van Leeuwen, who dogged Mulder till the end. In third, Chuck Palmgren put in his best performance yet on his Yamaha twin. Mark Brelsford appeared to have the race wrapped until knocked out with mechanical trouble. Unusually cool weather kept the normally healthy Sante Fe crowd count down.

The race had little effect on the points order. Dick Mann, Jim Rice, Gene Romero and Don Castro all added some points to their totals. The only change in position was Dusty Coppage whose 5th place in the National put him in tenth place.

Heats

Fast qualifier Eddie Mulder (Tri) jumped out to lead Heat 1, but Mark Brelsford (HD) proved his equal and shadowed Mulder for the entire race. On the last lap, Brelsford turned up the pace and smoothly pulled by Mulder. Skip Van Leeuwen took the 3rd and last transfer spot. The top three would face off again in the National.

Jim Rice (BSA) jetted into the lead and win of Heat 2. Gene Romero (Tri) had a comfortable 2nd for most of the race till Bart Markel (HD) closed up late. Markel had gotten a poor start, but shot through the field and hounded Romero at the flag, settling for 3rd place. Mert Lawwill was aboard a faithful KR, but a camshaft failed, putting him out for the night.

Heat 3 saw both Dusty Coppage (Yam) and Dick Mann (BSA) lead the event. Coppage fell early, with Mann taking the win. Dave Sehl (HD) took 2nd with Coppage managing to remount for an impressive 3rd place.

Semi

The first start of the Semi ended up in a big pileup in the first turn. On the restart, Dave Aldana (BSA) pulled a nifty holeshot and led to the flag. Don Castro (Tri) was fighting transmission problems, but some hard riding allowed him to nail down the runner-up spot. Chuck Palmgren was 3rd on the Dan Gurney-sponsored Yamaha.

National

Mark Brelsford shot into the lead at the beginning of the National. He immediately stretched into a big lead with Eddie Mulder and Dave Aldana giving distant chase. Skip Van Leeuwen soon moved up and passed Aldana for 3rd. Bart Markel was running 5th when he fell hard, losing several laps before remounting. Not far behind, Gene Romero also fell, but was quickly back up. Brelsford's Harley began missing and soon lost all fire. The likeable Californian was out on lap 8, a probable victory gone. Mulder assumed the lead with Van Leeuwen right on his rear wheel. Chuck Palmgren moved up a spot as Dave Aldana dropped out with engine trouble. Jim Rice worked up from a poor start to take 4th from Don Castro. Late in the race Castro was dropped another spot by Dusty Coppage. As the race closed, Van Leeuwen was applying heavy pressure to Mulder on the last lap, just coming up short.

Results

Race: 25 Lap TT National
Race Time: 15:03.59

Rank	Rider	Number	Make
1.	Eddie Mulder, Burbank, Ca	12	Tri
2.	Skip Van Leeuwen, Hollywood, Ca	59	Tri
3.	Chuck Palmgren, Freehold, NJ	6	Yam
4.	Jim Rice, Palo Alto, Ca	24	BSA
5.	Dusty Coppage, Chatsworth, Ca	32	Yam
6.	Don Castro, Hollister, Ca	11Y	Tri
7.	Dave Sehl, Waterdown, Ont., Can	21T	HD
8.	Dick Mann, Richmond, Ca	2	BSA
9.	Gene Romero, San Luis Obispo, Ca	3	Tri
10.	Bart Markel, Flint, Mi	4	HD
11.	Mark Brelsford, San Bruno, Ca	87	HD
12.	Dave Aldana, Santa Ana, Ca	38X	BSA

Race: 14 Lap Amateur TT Final
Race Time: 8:43.15

Rank	Rider	Number	Make
1.	Ed Hermann, Milwaukie, Ore	27Q	Tri
2.	Robert Robinson, Spencerport, NY	71U	Bul
3.	Jack Hendler, Grand Rapids, Mi	62E	BSA

Grand National Points Standings after Round 11

Rank	Rider	Pts
1.	Dick Mann	291
2.	Jim Rice	272
3.	Dave Aldana	259
4.	Gene Romero	227
5.	Yvon DuHamel	210
6.	Don Castro	167
7.	Gary Nixon	153
8.	Mert Lawwill	152
9.	Dave Smith	149
10.	Dusty Coppage	136

Extra Extra

- Eddie Mulder scored all five of his wins on the most famous TT tracks in the U.S.; Peoria, Ascot, Castle Rock and Sante Fe. He won all three TT's on the schedule in 1966 and was fourth in the National standings that year. Although Mulder also had great runs on ovals and road courses, he was a natural talent on the TT courses. He would have probably won even more races, but his spectacular style often used up his tires and machine. "Fast" Eddie Mulder always added excitement and color to every event at which he appeared.

48

1970 Columbus Half-Mile
Sehl Wins 2nd of the Year at "On Any Sunday" Race
Rice Takes Over Points Lead

GNC Round #12 of 25 **Date:** June 28, 1970 **Type:** Half-Mile **Venue:** Ohio State Fairgrounds **Location:** Columbus, Oh	**Purse:** $9000.00 **Surface:** Dirt-Limestone **Course Length**: ½ Mile **Laps:** 20 **Distance:** 10 Miles

Dave Sehl won his second cushion half-mile of the year in convincing fashion at the famed Charity Newsies benefit National. Sehl quickly dispatched 3-time winner Bart Markel and sailed to a comfortable win on the Babe DeMay-tuned factory Harley. Local favorite Ronnie Rall, winner of this event in 1963, took the runner-up spot late in the race. He narrowly topped Larry Palmgren who turned in yet another impressive podium run. This was the event filmed for Bruce Brown's famous motorcycle movie, "On Any Sunday".

With only three riders in the top 10 in points making the National, there wasn't a lot of change in the top of the GNC order, but there was one big move. Dick Mann didn't make the main and lost his near season-long spot as the GNC points leader. Jim Rice took a narrow 3 point lead via his 6th place finish in the National. The only other change was Mert Lawwill squeaking past Gary Nixon for seventh in points.

Heats

The 1969 Columbus winner and this day's fast qualifier, Mert Lawwill, took control of Heat 1, pursued by Ohio cushion aces Ronnie Rall (BSA) and Larry Darr (HD). Bart Markel, on the move aboard his rigid framed XR, blew by both Darr and Rall just after halfway. Markel was "diamonding" the track, (see *Extras*), which still had some cushion up top. Lawwill had the race in the bag, only to have his motor quit on the last lap. Markel, Rall and Darr all blew by. Lawwill and bike had enough momentum to coast to a semi transfer. This was the fast heat of the day.

Larry Palmgren (Tri) was quickly out in front to lead Heat 3, chased by Louisville winner Dave Sehl (HD). Sehl kept close, passing for the lead at midpoint. Palmgren didn't give up and when Sehl's handling started to go away, he repassed for the lead and win with two laps remaining. Yamaha mounted Keith Mashburn was 3rd.

Gene Romero (Tri) managed the only unchallenged heat win of the day in the last elimination. A talented group behind, Jim Rice (BSA), Frank Gillespie (Tri) and Mark Brelsford (HD) battled for the other two spots to the National. Brelsford took the runner-up slot with Rice getting the last direct transfer.

Semi

Mert Lawwill quickly took the point and despite a badly smoking motor, won the event going away. The 1965 Columbus winner and a crowd favorite, George Roeder (HD), was 2nd with Frank Gillespie getting the last National ticket.

National

Bart Markel was determined to make it four unprecedented wins at Columbus and charged out front at the drop of the flag. Markel was still running the "diamond pattern" which had worked so well in his heat. The track had now grooved up and this was no longer the hot setup. Dave Sehl ran the groove and passed Markel before the first lap was complete. A charging Larry Palmgren also moved by Markel. Behind Markel were Ronnie Rall and Mark Brelsford. Mert Lawwill was flying through the pack, blowing into the lead pack, as high as 3rd behind Palmgren. On lap 12, his throttle cable broke and he was out. Markel continued to slide rapidly backwards in the field. With five to go, Sehl had a big lead. Rall had reeled in Palmgren and the two had a fantastic battle over 2nd spot. The crowd was thrilled and cheered for their home state favorite. With one to go, Rall took the position with Palmgren's last shot coming up just short at the line.

Results

Race: 20 Lap Half-Mile National
Race Time: 9:34.79

Rank	Rider	Number	Make
1.	Dave Sehl, Waterdown, Ont., Can	21T	HD
2.	Ronnie Rall, Mansfield, Oh	52	BSA
3.	Larry Palmgren, Freehold, NJ	5	Tri
4.	Mark Brelsford, San Bruno, Ca	87	HD
5.	Gene Romero, San Luis Obispo, Ca	3	Tri
6.	Jim Rice, Palo Alto, Ca	24	BSA
7.	Frank Gillespie, Berkeley, Ca	23Y	Tri
8.	Larry Darr, Mansfield, Oh	94	HD
9.	Bart Markel, Flint, Mi	4	HD
10.	Keith Mashburn, Santa Susana, Ca	30X	Yam
11.	Mert Lawwill, San Francisco, Ca	1	HD
12.	George Roeder, Monroeville, Oh	3F	HD

Race: 7 Lap Half-Mile Amateur Final
Race Time: No Time Due to Red Flag

Rank	Rider	Number	Make
1.	Rex Beauchamp, Drayton Plains, Mi	34E	HD
2.	Paul Pressgrove, Tecumseh, Ks	28N	BSA
3.	Don Emde, San Diego, Ca	35R	BSA

Grand National Points Standings after Round 12

Rank	Rider	Pts
1.	Jim Rice	294
2.	Dick Mann	291
3.	Dave Aldana	259
4.	Gene Romero	255
5.	Yvon DuHamel	210
6.	Don Castro	167
7.	Mert Lawwill	156
8.	Gary Nixon	153
9.	Dave Smith	149
10.	Dusty Coppage	136

Extra Extra

- A usual overflow 'Newsies crowd of 16,000 plus turned out.
- The "diamond pattern" was a classic brakeless technique whereby the rider would run into the corner very deep, clear up to the guardrail in the middle of the track, scrubbing off speed. He would then turn the bike and have a big run off the top, in effect, lengthening the straightaway.
- It was a rough day for GNC points leaders and other stars. Dick Mann's transmission locked up before his heat race. Dave Aldana was not able to transfer to the main. George Roeder's return was short lived when his bike broke on lap 4. For Mert Lawwill it was two DNF's in one weekend.
- The Amateur Final saw a very scary accident on lap 9 when Gary Fisher, Teddy Newton, Doug Sehl and Ron Butler went down in a chain reaction crash. Gary Fisher sustained back injuries; the others were just beaten up and sore.

- The Ohio State Fairgrounds moved to its present location in 1886 and hosted the Ohio State Fair ever since. Horse racing was one of the most popular events for much of the fairs history. Motorcycle racing grew in prominence with its association with Charity Newsies. The event evolved into a major event on the GNC circuit and ran until 1980. The fairgrounds track also hosted regional events like the Buckeye Classic and many Ohio State Championships. The fairgrounds track and huge grandstands were demolished in 1990. Most of the track is now a parking lot.
- The Charity Newsies promoted the long-running event. They provide clothing to underprivileged children in Columbus, Oh. All profits from the races went directly to the charity. The group was founded in 1907 and is still going strong.
- The first Charity Newsies race was held in 1939. It became an AMA National event in 1953.

GNC Round #13 of 25 **Date:** July 5, 1970 **Type:** Half-Mile **Venue:** Santa Clara Fairgrounds **Location:** San Jose, Ca	**Purse:** $6500.00 **Surface:** Dirt **Course Length:** ½ Mile **Laps:** 20 **Distance:** 10 Miles

Jim Rice took his 4th win of the year at the slick San Jose Half-Mile. Rice was the winningest rider on the circuit; he also boosted his GNC points lead. It was Rice's 7th GNC win. He had San Jose wired; he won the Amateur portion of the National in 1968 and his first GNC in '69. Rice had truly become the master groove track rider on the circuit. He used his brains and rear brake better than anyone else, (for more, see *Extras*). Jimmy Odom almost had a great day-he set fast time, won his heat and led the main till Rice drove by; he had to settle for runner-up. Chuck Palmgren had the AAR Yamaha working and took third.

As usual the tricky San Jose surface sent many top runners packing, including Mert Lawwill and the entire Harley-Davidson team! In fact for the first time in recent memory there was not a single Harley in a GNC dirt track main event.

There were no changes anywhere in the top ten riders. Jim Rice solidified his points lead some over Dick Mann, now leading by 28 points. Mann had a pretty miserable day. He crashed in practice, fought engine problems, winding up last in the National. Third and fourth in points, Dave Aldana and Gene Romero finished 5th and 6th in the race, keeping the points in sight.

Time Trials

Jimmy Odom (Tri) was quickest in qualifying with a 27.25 lap. Don Dudek (Tri) raised some eyebrows with a 27.48. Jim Rice (BSA) was 3rd quickest at 27.60.

Heats

Jimmy Odom scorched to an uncontested win in Heat 1. Chuck Palmgren and the Yamaha twin looked very strong in second. Tom Rockwood (Tri) took the last transfer. Frank Gillespie fell hard at the start, possibly cracking a shoulder blade.

Lloyd Houchins (Tri) pulled the holeshot in Heat 2, pacing the field till Dave Aldana scooted by. Dick Mann was in 3rd, but slipped the groove, losing ground. Dave Smith (Tri) and Dallas Baker (BSA) dueled over the final transfer spot with Smith getting the nod. Dave Sehl (HD), winner at Columbus and Dick Mann (BSA) both failed to transfer to the main and were semi-bound.

Jim Rice had no trouble in Heat 3, quickly motoring into the distance. Eddie Mulder (Tri) was impressive in 2nd spot. Dave Hansen (Tri) was 3rd. Harley teammates Mert Lawwill and Mark Brelsford were 4th and 5th and were headed to the semi.

All the riders that transferred directly out of the heats were California riders. Local slippery groove knowledge was proving valuable this day.

Semi

The Semi lineup at San Jose would have made a great GNC race; Mert Lawwill (HD), Gary Nixon (Tri), Mark Brelsford (HD), Dick Mann, Gene Romero (Tri), Don Castro (Tri) and Dewayne Keeter (Nor) were all in the field. Castro took the win after dueling early with Keeter. Romero and Mann put on a crowd pleasing battle to round out the top 3. Everyone else, including the two most recent GNC Champs, Lawwill and Nixon had to load up.

National

Jimmy Odom tried his best to runaway with the race, but Jim Rice got his BSA locked unto the groove and passed for the lead on lap 3. The rest of the race was pretty much a follow-the-leader affair with little passing. On the way to the win, Rice made nary a bobble and had a straightaway lead on Odom at the finish. Chuck Palmgren put in a solid ride in 3rd, harassing Odom along the way. Eddie Mulder (Tri) held 4th for most of the race till engine woes hit him. Don Castro took over the spot and battling with Dave Aldana along the way. Gene Romero was 6th. GNC points leader Dick Mann had trouble, winding up 12th.

Results

Race: 20 Lap Half-Mile National
Race Time: 9:10.70

Rank	Rider	Number	Make
1.	Jim Rice, Palo Alto, Ca	24	BSA
2.	Jimmy Odom, Fremont, Ca	77	Tri
3.	Chuck Palmgren, Freehold, NJ	6	Yam
4.	Don Castro, Hollister, Ca	11Y	Tri
5.	Dave Aldana, Santa Ana, Ca	38X	BSA
6.	Gene Romero, San Luis Obispo, Ca	3	Tri
7.	Tom Rockwood, Gardena, Ca	38	Tri
8.	Dave Hansen, Haywood, Ca	22Y	Tri
9.	Lloyd Houchins, La Crescenta, Ca	20X	Tri
10.	Eddie Mulder, Burbank, Ca	12	Tri
11.	Dave Smith, Lakewood, Ca	11X	Tri
12.	Dick Mann, Richmond, Ca	2	BSA

Race: 14 Lap Half-Mile Amateur Final
Race Time: 6:34.25

Rank	Rider	Number	Make
1.	Terry Dorsch, Sunland, Ca	65R	Tri
2.	Rex Beauchamp, Drayton Plains, Mi	34E	Tri
3.	Bill Morgan, San Leandro, Ca	25Z	HD

Grand National Points Standings after Round 13

Rank	Rider	Pts
1.	Jim Rice	320
2.	Dick Mann	292
3.	Dave Aldana	267
4.	Gene Romero	262
5.	Yvon DuHamel	210
6.	Don Castro	176
7.	Mert Lawwill	156
8.	Gary Nixon	153
9.	Dave Smith	151
10.	Dusty Coppage	136

Extra Extra

- Jim Rice took home $2000.00 for the win.
- 60-plus Experts signed up.
- A crowd of 5400 watched the race.
- Several Triumph riders were using the recently AMA-approved 750 Triumph kits, including runner-up Jimmy Odom and Gene Romero.
- Starting at San Jose, Gene Romero began receiving help from master tuner C.R. Axtell.

- "Groove Master" Jim Rice was a thinking-man's racer and probably the first of the young "On Any Sunday" generation to understand the use of brakes, especially on slick, grooved tracks. The old guard like Bart Markel, Mert Lawwill and even young chargers like Dave Aldana didn't grow up using brakes and didn't really utilize them. Most still pitched their bikes sideways to slow down, regardless of the surface. Rice was the first to fully exploit the usefulness of the brakes on groove tracks and was now reaping the benefits. Others would figure them out as well, but 1970 was Rice's year.
- The Santa Clara Fairgrounds facility has been the site of a huge variety of tracks and motorsports events. Car racing began in 1948 on the half-mile track. The fairgrounds over the years has seen a dizzying amount of track layouts; 1/8 mile, 1/3 mile, ¼ mile, ½ mile and mile; even a dirt "road course" in the 1950's. The GNC bikes competed on the half-mile from 1967-1973 and 1978, and the mile from 1972-1993. Oval racing ended in 1999 and in 2001 the grandstands was demolished. Today there is a motocross track in use at the fairgrounds. The oval tracks are unused and/or built over. Satellite photos clearly show the outlines of the tracks which produced a rich motorsports history.

1970 Castle Rock TT
It's Mann at the Rock/Takes Back Points Lead

GNC Round #14 of 25 **Date:** July 11, 1970 **Type:** TT **Venue:** Mt. St. Helens Motorcycle Club Grounds **Location:** Castle Rock, Wa	**Purse:** $8000.00 **Surface:** Dirt **Course Length:** ½ Mile **Laps:** 30

GNC veteran Dick Mann posted his second win of the season at Castle Rock after a late struggle with Dave Aldana. The win put him back atop the National points standings. It was Mann's 18th National victory. Mann had come from back in the pack on his self-tuned BSA to catch Aldana late in the race, and when the two got together, Aldana went down. Don Castro assumed 2nd and Mark Brelsford put in a good ride in 3rd. Gene Romero continued his string of great finishes in 4th. Mann's main GNC rival, Jim Rice, had trouble, finishing well back in the order.

Dick Mann's win put him back in the points lead with 345 points. Jim Rice made the main, but scored no points; his tally stayed at 320. Gene Romero's high finish moved him to third in the standings with 288 points. It was his highest ranking yet. Dave Aldana had a rough night; he nearly won the event, but ended up on the ground, scoring no points. He slipped back to fourth in the rankings at 267 points. Don Castro's podium run pushed the rookie to fifth in points at 219. Yvon DuHamel moved back a spot to 6th still at 210 points. Mert Lawwill added some points after a 5th place run in the National. The rest of the top ten stayed the same.

Time Trials

Gene Romero (Tri) topped the order with a quick time of 25.19. The 1968 Castle Rock winner, Skip Van Leeuwen (Tri) was just a tick back at 25.20. Team Harleys Mert Lawwill and Mark Brelsford tied for 3rd spot with an identical 25.23 clocking.

Heats

Mark Brelsford took an easy win in Heat 1, making it look easy over Don Castro (Tri), fast-timer Gene Romero and rookie Dave Hansen (Tri).

Heat 2 saw a good race between Skip Van Leeuwen, Mark Williams (Kaw) and Dave Aldana (BSA). Aldana followed a Van Leeuwen/Williams battle for several laps and then passed them both in the same corner. Aldana went on to the win followed by Van Leeuwen, Williams and Tom Rockwood (Tri).

Mert Lawwill passed early leader Eddie Mulder (Tri) in Heat 3 and stretched out to the win. Mulder dropped back through the order as Dick Mann (BSA) moved into 2nd, with Triumph riders Jimmy Odom and Jimmy Smith taking 3rd and 4th spots.

Semi

Jim Rice (BSA) battled with early with Bill Elder (HD) and Ike Reed (Tri) before taking over the "last chance" win. After much position-swapping behind Rice, Ken Pressgrove (BSA) was 2nd, Glen Adams 3rd with Elder in the 4th and final transfer spot.

National

Harley-Davidson star Mark Brelsford led the field away, chased by teammate Mert Lawwill and rookies Don Castro and Dave Aldana. Castro was on the move, passing Lawwill and then Brelsford on lap 3 to take the lead. Aldana followed suit, moving by the Harley riders and blowing by Castro a lap later. Dick Mann was also charging and moved by Castro and was pressuring Aldana for the lead by lap 8. Castro, Brelsford and Lawwill were followed by Gene Romero and Mark Williams. Mann continued to hound Aldana, looking for a bobble or opening. On lap 19 he made his move in Turn 1; the two touched and Aldana went flipping out of the ball park. "Rubberball" Aldana walked away. Mann continued home with a comfortable win followed by Castro, Brelsford, Romero, Lawwill, Williams, Tom Rockwood, Skip Van Leeuwen, Glen Adams and Bill Elder.

Results

Race: Mile 30 Lap TT National
Race Time: 13:02.64

Rank	Rider	Number	Make
1.	Dick Mann, Richmond, Ca	2	BSA
2.	Don Castro, Hollister, Ca	11Y	Tri
3.	Mark Brelsford, San Bruno, Ca	87	HD
4.	Gene Romero, San Luis Obispo, Ca	3	Tri
5.	Mert Lawwill, San Francisco, Ca	1	HD
6.	Mark Williams, Springfield, Ore	70	Kaw
7.	Tom Rockwood, Gardena, Ca	38	Tri
8.	Skip Van Leeuwen, Hollywood, Ca	59	Tri
9.	Glen Adams, Seattle, Wa	77V	Nor
10.	Bill Elder, Vancouver, Wa	42V	HD
11.	Jimmy Odom, Fremont, Ca	77	Tri
12.	Ken Pressgrove, Topeka, Ks	14N	BSA
13.	Jim Smith, Salem, Ore	19Q	Tri
14.	Dave Hansen, Hayward, Ca	22Y	Tri
15.	Jim Rice, Palo Alto, Ca	24	BSA
16.	Dave Aldana, Santa Ana, Ca	38X	BSA

Race: Amateur TT Final
Race Time: 4:21.20

Rank	Rider	Number	Make
1.	Chuck Joyner, Oregon City, Ore	57Q	Tri
2.	Darrel Cotton, Milwaukie, Ore	10Q	Tri
3.	Ed Hermann, Milwaukie, Ore	27Q	Tri

Grand National Points Standings after Round 14

Rank	Rider	Pts
1.	Dick Mann	345
2.	Jim Rice	320
3.	Gene Romero	288
4.	Dave Aldana	267
5.	Don Castro	219
6.	Yvon DuHamel	210
7.	Mert Lawwill	175
8.	Gary Nixon	153
9.	Dave Smith	151
10.	Dusty Coppage	136

- Dick Mann pocketed $1620.00 for his win.
- Gene Romero received an extra $173.00 for fast time.
- Many stars failed to make the main, (for various reasons), including; Gary Nixon, Cal Rayborn, Dusty Coppage, Yvon DuHamel, Eddie Mulder and Chuck Palmgren.
- The Mount St. Helen's Motorcycle Club first held TT events in 1958. The course is roughly half-mile in length, had 6 turns and no jump. It is shaped kinda like a pinched paperclip. After this first 1965 National, the tour would return many times. The track was rebuilt after the 1980 Mt. St. Helen's eruption. The track has been in operation for over 50 years. Currently the club has been promoting very successful, high paying non-nationals.

GNC Round #15 of 25 **Date:** July 18, 1969 **Type:** TT **Venue:** Ascot Park **Location:** Gardena, Ca	**Purse:** $7500.00 **Surface:** Dirt **Course Length:** ½ Mile, (approx.) **Laps:** 50

GNC Champ Mert Lawwill finally had Lady Luck smile upon him as he won the grueling 50 lap National. It was Lawwill's 3rd win of the season and his 11th overall. By most standards, Lawwill had been having a pretty good season with wins at Houston and Cumberland, but he was down in the points standings, suffering teething problems with the new XR750 as well as plain old bad luck. Besides Lawwill's rough year, he had terrible luck the last few years at the Ascot TT. On this night, he and tuner Jim Belland saw their luck turn around in a big way, with their monster 900cc XLR never missing a beat. He was serious contention several times only to fall out with mechanical trouble. It was a well deserved win for the embattled defending champ. Second place finisher Gene Romero led the majority of the event till Lawwill powered around. Dallas Baker had the best run of his GNC career, finishing 3rd after leading the race early. Points leader Dick Mann soldiered to a solid 4th place finish. GNC contender Jim Rice struggled for the second race in a row, making the main via the semi. He dropped out when his BSA developed oiling problems.

Dick Mann's 4th place run coupled with rival Jim Rice's 20th place finish allowed Mann's lead to stretch by 37, (357 to 320). Gene Romero's runner-up finish kept him close-in-third with 302 points. Romero had yet to win in 1970, but had been consistent all year. He stretched ahead of fourth in points Dave Aldana who finished 11th at Ascot and had 260 points. Don Castro maintained fifth with 217 points. Mert Lawwill's win allowed him to pull within 5 points of sixth in points Yvon DuHamel, 205 points to 210.

Time Trials

1966 Ascot TT winner Eddie Mulder (Tri) turned in a 45.16 lap for fast time. Mulder was the only rider in the 45 second bracket. His time was a remarkably over a half-second quicker than Mark Brelsford's (HD) second place time of 46.06. There was also a big gap back to 3rd fastest Dallas Baker (BSA) at 47.13.

Heats

Fast timer Eddie Mulder set a blistering pace in Heat 1 and disappeared from the pack. Dave Aldana (BSA) was 2nd and Tom Rockwood (Tri) in 3rd. Dick Mann (BSA) worked up from the pack to 4th.

Two-time Ascot winner, (1967 and '68), Skip Van Leeuwen (Tri) took a big win in Heat 2. He was helped when a challenging Mark Brelsford (HD) had his throttle stick and bailed off. Eddie Wirth (Tri) briefly held the runner-up spot before fading. Bob Bailey ended up 2nd with Lloyd Houchins 3rd, both aboard Triumphs.

Heat 3 saw a future main event matchup with Gene Romero (Tri) battling with Dallas Baker (BSA) and Mert Lawwill before taking the win. Don Castro (Tri) had a stuck throttle end his night early.

Semi

Like Sante Fe, Jim Rice (BSA) had to race hard through the semi to make the National. Veteran Ralph White (Tri) made a rare appearance, looking good as he challenged Rice early in the race. Also making the transfer were White, Paul Bostrom (Tri) and Mark Williams (Kaw).

National

Skip Van Leeuwen got the jump in front of the big field, but the advantage was negated by an accident between Paul Bostrom and Tom Rockwood. Rockwood had a boot end up between the shock and wheel of Bostrom's bike. Officials had to cut off the heel of Rockwood's boot to free him. On the restart, Dallas Baker took the point, but Eddie Mulder quickly went by on Lap 2. Mulder and Baker were followed by Dave Aldana who in turn was chased by Gene Romero. Aldana fell beside Ascot's duck pond and Romero went to 3rd. Mert Lawwill was moving through the pack and worked his way to 4th with Skip Van Leeuwen 5th.

Romero moved by Baker and set out for Mulder. Romero chipped away at Mulder's big lead and moved by on around lap 12. Mulder's bike was slowing with ignition trouble and he was forced out shortly before the 20th circuit. Lawwill had been reeling in Baker and passed him about the time of Mulder's retirement. Lawwill next pointed the potent XLR at Romero whose tires had lost their edge. Lawwill soon caught up and after trying to pass Romero on the outside of the half-mile turn several times, he snuck by on the inside on lap 28. Time and luck were with Lawwill this year at Ascot and was stretching his lead clear to the end. Romero and Baker maintained their podium positions to the flag. Dick Mann in 4th, had been patient all night, passing several riders and also moving up as Aldana, Mulder and Van Leeuwen dropped out. Eddie Wirth was 5th. Tom Rockwood and Paul Bostrom recovered nicely from their starting line accident and ended up in 6th and 7th spots. Mark Williams again put his Kawasaki in the main in 8th. Chuck Palmgren was 9th. It was neat to see 1963 Daytona winner Ralph White rounding out the top 10.

Results

Race: 50 Lap TT National
Race Time: 40:34.53

Rank	Rider	Number	Make
1.	Mert Lawwill, San Francisco, Ca	1	HD
2.	Gene Romero, San Luis Obispo, Ca	3	Tri
3.	Dallas Baker, Orange, Ca	34	BSA
4.	Dick Mann, Richmond, Ca	2	BSA
5.	Eddie Wirth, Manhattan Beach, Ca	84	Tri
6.	Tom Rockwood, Gardena, Ca	38	Tri
7.	Paul Bostrom, Lake Isabella, Ca	15Y	Tri
8.	Mark Williams, Springfield, Ore	70	Kaw
9.	Chuck Palmgren, Freehold, NJ	6	Yam
10.	Ralph White, Torrance, Ca	15	Tri
11.	Dave Hansen, Hayward, Ca	22Y	Tri
12.	Gary Nixon, Phoenix, Md	9	Tri
13.	Mike Haney, Inglewood, Ca	48R	Tri
14.	Don Dudek, Redondo Beach, Ca	42X	Tri
15.	Lloyd Houchins, LaCrescenta, Ca	20X	Tri
16.	Jim Berry, Santa Ana, Ca	39X	Tri
17.	Dusty Coppage, Chatsworth, Ca	32	Yam
18.	Keith Mashburn, Santa Susana, Ca	30X	Yam
19.	Sonny Burres, Portland, Ore	69	Tri
20.	Jim Rice, Palo Alto, Ca	24	BSA

Race: Amateur TT Final
Race Time: 12:09.09

Rank	Rider	Number	Make
1.	John Hateley, Van Nuys, Ca	43R	Tri
2.	Al Kenyon, Cupertino, Ca	88Y	Tri
3.	Terry Dorsch, Sunland, Ca	65R	Tri

Grand National Points Standings after Round 15

Rank	Rider	Pts
1.	Dick Mann	360
2.	Jim Rice	320
3.	Gene Romero	317
4.	Dave Aldana	267
5.	Don Castro	219
6.	Mert Lawwill	214
7.	Yvon DuHamel	210
8.	Gary Nixon	154
9.	Dave Smith	151
10.	Dusty Coppage	136

Extra Extra

- Mert Lawwill saved Team Harley from potential embarrassment by placing the XLR in the main. His was the only Milwaukee brand in the National, narrowly avoiding a San Jose Half-Mile National repeat. The rest of the field were TT favorite Triumphs and BSA's along with Mark William's Kawasaki twin.
- 4000 fans turned out.
- Gary Nixon made his first TT in recent memory, finishing a credible 13th. No small feat considering his still weak leg.

1970 Santa Rosa Mile
Rice Takes 5th National at Santa Rosa
Tightens up Points Race

GNC Round #16 of 25	**Purse:** $7500.00
Date: July 26, 1970	**Surface:** Dirt
Type: Mile	**Course Length:** 1 Mile
Venue: Sonoma County Fairgrounds	**Laps:** 20
Location: Santa Rosa, Ca	**Distance:** 20 Miles

Jim Rice's convincing at Santa Rosa gave him 5 wins for the year, putting him back on Dick Mann's heels in the National points battle. The track at Santa Rosa was very similar to the surface of the earlier San Jose Half-Mile. Conditions were so similar that the top finishing positions were exactly the same; Rice, Jimmy Odom and Chuck Palmgren repeated their finish of a month ago at San Jose!

Dick Mann finished 5th in the main and maintained a narrow points lead over Jim Rice, 372 to 359. Rice closed the gap to just 13 with his big points paying win. Gene Romero scored another consistent finish in 7th and his total was a very close 332. Dave Aldana remained in striking distance with 264. GNC Champ Mert Lawwill still had a slim chance at retaining his title with 220. Don Castro was right behind at 219. Yvon DuHamel was the last rider above the 200 mark with 210.

Time Trials

Team Harley's Mark Brelsford rocked the house by posting the quickest lap of the day at 41.79. Not only was he the only rider in the 41 second bracket, he did it on a flathead KR! This was a telling move; it showed the lack of faith the Harley-Davidson team had in the new ohv XR750. Chuck Palmgren had the AAR Yamaha flying and was 2nd at 42.21. Brother Larry Palmgren was right behind on his Triumph at 42.28. Championship hopefuls took the next three spots; Dick Mann (BSA) at 42.65, Jim Rice (BSA) a 42.81 and Mert Lawwill (HD) a 42.82.

Heats

Mark Brelsford's choice appeared to be the right one as he led Heat 1 from wire-to-wire. Dick Mann (BSA) controlled 2nd place till a back from the pack Gene Romero (Tri) scooted by. Mann also had trouble from young Don Castro (Tri) who also snuck by. Mann had enough of this foolishness and managed to get back around Castro for the last transfer spot.

Jim Rice (BSA) dominated Heat 2 in a similar fashion as Brelsford and was not challenged. Chuck Palmgren (Yam) and Cal Rayborn (HD) put some excitement in the program by swapping 2nd spot all through the race. Rayborn got the nod at the end. Rice's heat was a telling three seconds faster than Brelsford's.

Heat 3 showed what racing on the mile was supposed to be about. Triumph-mounted aces Larry Palmgren, Jimmy Odom and Eddie Mulder duked it out the whole race. Mulder pulled the early advantage, leading the first three circuits. Palmgren then took over. Odom took the lead going into the last lap but Palmgren was just able to draft past coming off turn 4 for the win.

Semi

As usual for the 1970 season, the lineup in the "Last Chance Race" would have made a great National. Canadian Dave Sehl whose west coast swing had been dismal, took the win followed by GNC Champ Mert Lawwill and a through the pack Dave Aldana.

National

Surprising no one, Jim Rice pulled the holeshot and quickly pulled out front. Larry Palmgren, Tom Rockwood, Mark Brelsford and Dick Mann trailed early. Palmgren managed to run Rice down, leading laps 2 and 3. Rice moved back to the point on lap 4 and proceeded to motor away from the field. Third place runner Tom Rockwood dropped out with ignition failure. With Rice's disappearing act, it was up to the rest of the field to provide some racing

61

excitement. Dick Mann was a strong third early on, but a misstep off the groove allowed both Eddie Mulder and Jimmy Odom to scoot by. Gene Romero and Chuck Palmgren had both gotten terrible starts but by lap 10 they were challenging the front pack. They soon bumped Mann back two spots. More swapping ensued and at mid-race the order read; Rice, Larry Palmgren, Odom, Romero, Chuck Palmgren, Mulder and Mann. Things heated up as the end of the race neared. Larry Palmgren was knocked from his 2nd spot with Romero taking the spot and Chuck Palmgren following. Romero held the place with two laps to go only to have both Odom and Chuck Palmgren draft past. Mann managed to sneak past Larry Palmgren for 5th. The top ten at the finish were Rice, Odom, Chuck Palmgren, Romero, Mann, Larry Palmgren, Lawwill, Mulder, Lloyd Houchins and Mark Brelsford on the KR.

Results

Race: 20 Lap Mile National

Rank	Rider	Number	Make
1.	Jim Rice, Palo Alto, Ca	24	BSA
2.	Jimmy Odom, Fremont, Ca	77	Tri
3.	Chuck Palmgren, Freehold, NJ	6	Yam
4.	Gene Romero, San Luis Obispo, Ca	3	Tri
5.	Dick Mann, Richmond, Ca	2	BSA
6.	Larry Palmgren, Freehold, NJ	5	Tri
7.	Eddie Mulder, Burbank, Ca	12	Tri
8.	Mert Lawwill, San Francisco, Ca	1	HD
9.	Lloyd Houchins, La Cresenta, Ca	20X	Tri
10.	Mark Brelsford, San Bruno, Ca	87	HD
11.	Dave Aldana, Santa Ana, Ca	38X	BSA
12.	Dave Hansen, Hayward, Ca	22Y	Tri
13.	Don Castro, Hollister, Ca	11Y	Tri
14.	Eddie Wirth, Manhattan Beach, Ca	84	Tri
15.	Frank Gillespie, Berkeley, Ca	23Y	Tri
16.	Carl Patrick, Culver City, Ca	29X	Tri
17.	Cal Rayborn, Spring Valley, Ca	25	HD
18.	Sonny Burres, Portland, Ore	69	Tri
19.	Dave Sehl, Waterdown, Ont., Can	21T	HD
20.	Tom Rockwood, Gardena, Ca	38	Tri

Race: Amateur Final

Rank	Rider	Number	Make
1.	John Hateley, Van Nuys, Ca	43R	Tri
2.	Chuck Joyner, Oregon, City, Ore	87Q	Tri
3.	Dennis Palmgren, Freehold, NJ	42M	Tri

Grand National Points Standings after Round 16

Rank	Rider	Pts
1.	Dick Mann	372
2.	Jim Rice	359
3.	Gene Romero	332
4.	Dave Aldana	269
5.	Mert Lawwill	220
6.	Don Castro	219
7.	Yvon DuHamel	210
8.	Gary Nixon	154
9.	Dave Smith	151
10.	Dusty Coppage	136

Extra Extra

- The Triumph and BSA teams brought out converted road race triples for the first time at Santa Rosa. In practice they proved to be unwieldy and all involved switched to their twins. Dave Aldana suffered a terrible high-side during practice. His throttle hung open going into a turn and as he tried to low-side the bike, the cases caught and send him for a punishing ride. He still managed to make the program, coming home 11th in the National (on a twin), despite a concussion, breaking two fingers, blurred vision and generally having the hell beat out of him. Aldana was one tough dude.
- There were only 4 Harleys out of 20 machines in the main. It was a tough time for the team. Brelsford's use of a KR showed a real lack of confidence in the new XR. Mert Lawwill came home 8th, Brelsford 10th, Cal Rayborn 17th and Dave Sehl 19th.
- The race was sold-out and run under great conditions.
- Though former two-time GNC Champ Gary Nixon didn't transfer at Santa Rosa, it was good to see him in action at the track that had bitten him so badly in 1969.
- John Hateley won another Amateur National.
- The groomed turf track at the Somona County Fairgrounds is still in use today as a betting horse race facility. The track hosted several GNC races in the late 1960's through the early '70's and on the schedule again in 2012.

GNC Round #17 of 25 **Date:** August 16, 1970 **Type:** Half-Mile **Venue:** Terre Haute Speedway **Location:** Terre Haute, In	**Purse:** $6000.00 **Surface:** Dirt **Course Length:** ½ Mile **Laps:** 20 **Distance:** 10 Miles

Dave Aldana put in a very solid and conservative, (for David) ride to win his 2nd National of the year, aboard the self-tuned, BSA factory/Irv Seaver-sponsored ride. He had to pass teammates Ken Pressgrove and Jim Rice to take the win. Pressgrove led early, but motor problems put him out. Rice appeared to be on his way to notching his record 6th win until Aldana worked by. Rice maintained second with Keith Mashburn scored his best National finish yet aboard the Shell Yamaha.

Although Rice didn't win, his runner-up finish allowed him to close within 2 points of points leader Dick Mann; 378 to 380. Mann had a solid run at Terre Haute, placing 5th. Third in points Gene Romero had a disappointing day when his Triumph refused to start for his heat race. He maintained third in points with 332 points. Dave Aldana's win moved him much closer to Romero with 295 points. Don Castro was fifth with 220 points, tying with GNC Champ Mert Lawwill. Lawwill had yet another day of bad luck when his XR quit with a sure heat race transfer in hand.

Time Trials

The fastest Expert time of the day was turned in by groove expert Jim Rice (BSA) at 26.63 with Don Castro (Tri) literally a tick off at 26.64. The fastest overall time of the day was turned in by Amateur John Hateley (Tri) at 26.61. Everybody was way off Bart Markel's 1969 record of 26.03.

Heats

Ken Pressgrove led Heat 1 early till BSA teammate Jim Rice ripped by for the lead and the win. Mark Brelsford was back aboard a KR, running plenty strong in 3rd.

In Heat 2, Keith Mashburn led fellow California rookie Don Castro (Tri) into the National, followed by Jack Warren (Nor).

Championship contender Gene Romero could not get his normally reliable Triumph to fire for Heat 3. Romero's place was taken by an alternate. Dick Mann was out front early with a hungry pack containing Harley riders Mert Lawwill, Bart Markel, (on a KR), Dave Sehl and Jimmy Maness along with BSA's Dave Aldana. Lawwill squeezed ahead to duel with Mann. The two diced heavily till the final circuit when Lawwill's engine quit. Markel took 2nd and Dave Aldana 3rd. Aldana had got together hard with Dave Sehl during the event. It wasn't till the race was over that Aldana noticed that Sehl's carburetor had snapped off and was wedged in his machine.

Semi

Dave Smith (Tri) took a narrow semi win over Georgia rider Jimmy Maness (HD) with Cal Rayborn (HD) returning from his Loudon injury for 3rd.

National

Kansas rider Ken Pressgrove got a great start and led Dick Mann, Jimmy Maness, and Dave Aldana early in the event. Maness's Harley broke up a BSA monopoly. Rice and Aldana moved by Mann and latched onto leader Pressgrove. Mann began to fade a little, Maness a lot. Keith Mashburn moved forward along with Bart Markel. Rice slipped by teammate Pressgrove on lap 9 and one lap later Pressgrove was out with mechanical trouble. Aldana stayed right with Rice as the laps ticked away. The two dueled with Rice on the groove, (where else!), and Aldana up top with David pulling a small advantage. Behind them there was a nifty race for third between Mann, Mashburn and Markel. Mashburn took the last podium spot with Markel edging Mann on the last lap for 4th place. Behind Mann was Dave Smith with a great 6th, Cal Rayborn was 7th with Jimmy Maness ending up 8th. Mark Brelsford was 9th and Norton mounted Jack Warren rounded out the top ten.

Results

Race: 20 Lap Half-Mile National
Race Time: 9:02.74

Rank	Rider	Number	Make
1.	Dave Aldana, Santa Ana, Ca	38X	BSA
2.	Jim Rice, Palo Alto, Ca	24	BSA
3.	Keith Mashburn, Santa Susana, Ca	30X	Yam
4.	Bart Markel, Flint, Mi	4	HD
5.	Dick Man Richmond, Ca	2	BSA
6.	Dave Smith, Lakewood, Ca	11X	Tri
7.	Cal Rayborn, Spring Valley, Ca	25	HD
8.	Jimmy Maness, Augusta, Ga	31	HD
9.	Mark Brelsford, San Bruno, Ca	87	HD
10.	Jack Warren, Clio, Mi	82	Nor
11.	Ken Pressgrove, Topeka, Ks	14N	BSA
12.	Don Castro, Hollister, Ca	11Y	Tri

Race: 14 Lap Half-Mile Amateur Final
Race Time: 6:23.88

Rank	Rider	Number	Make
1.	Rex Beauchamp, Drayton Plains, Mi	34E	HD
2.	John Hateley, Van Nuys, Ca	43R	Tri
3.	Ed Hermann, Milwaukie, Ore	27Q	Tri

Grand National Points Standings after Round 17

Rank	Rider	Pts
1.	Dick Mann	380
2.	Jim Rice	378
3.	Gene Romero	332
4.	Dave Aldana	295
5.	Don Castro	220
6.	Mert Lawwill	220
7.	Yvon DuHamel	210
8.	Dave Smith	158
9.	Gary Nixon	154
10.	Dusty Coppage	136

- Dave Aldana took home $1000.00 for his win.
- This was the last half-mile win for a BSA motorcycle.
- Jim Rice picked up a $50.00 bonus for setting fast time.
- 60 Experts signed in.
- A good crowd of 5000 watched the race.
- There were 4 Harley riders in the 12 rider National. Markel was the most successful, riding his KR to 4th spot.
- Several top road racers opted to compete in an AMA race in Pocono, Pa, instead of Terre Haute. GNC regulars Gary Nixon and Yvon DuHamel topped the $3000.00 event.
- Amateur Rex Beauchamp was now appearing aboard a factory supported Harley-Davidson.
- The Terre Haute Speedway, also known as "The Action Track", was built in 1952 on the grounds of the Wabash Valley Fairgrounds. The track is most famous for it's USAC open wheel heritage, with the greatest drivers of the 1950's-80's competing in Silver Crown, sprint and midget events. It's most famous event is probably the Hut Hundred. The track closed in 1987, but reopened in the 1990's. Today it is struggling with curfew and noise issues. The GNC would run at the track several times. Many of the Midwest open wheel drivers would often turn out to watch their two-wheeled brethren compete.

1970 Sante Fe Short Track
Markel Ties Leonard with 27 Wins!
Rice Takes Points Lead

GNC Round #18 of 25 **Date:** August 21, 1970 **Type:** Short Track **Venue:** Sante Fe Speedway	**Location:** Hinsdale, Ill **Surface:** Dirt **Course Length**: ¼ Mile **Laps:** 25

Bart Markel's amazing come-from-behind win at Sante Fe impressed all present, but it really didn't surprise anyone. The 3-time GNC champ's performances were often dramatically hot or cold. With the win, Markel tied the great Joe Leonard's 27 National victories. The two had very different personalities and styles but both were amazing, dominant talents in their prime. In the race, Jim Rice finished 2nd after passing leader Neil Keen late in the race. Keen, a Sante Fe regular, led for most of the National. Rice and Keen put on a great race, probably slowing both down enough to allow Markel to catch up.

The other big story of the night involved World Speedway Champion Barry Briggs. He was winning his heat race going away when he slowed to miss an accident. AMA officials deemed the race complete as they crossed the line, which dropped Briggs out of contention. Briggs, other riders, and the fans were all very unhappy as chaos ruled for awhile.

Only three of the top ten in GNC points made the main. There was only one change in position, but it was a notable one. Via his runner-up finish, Jim Rice took a very narrow 8 point lead over Dick Mann who was close behind in 4th place.

Time Trials
Bart Markel set fast time on his trick, rigid frame, Lake Injector-equipped Harley Sprint at 15.91. Next was Dallas Baker (Oss) with 16.05.

Heats
The first heat was taken by Charlie Chapple aboard a Neil Keen-sponsored Yamaha. Transferring to the semi behind him were Bart Markel (HD), Bill O'Brien (Bul), Gordon Dusenberry, Don Castro (Tri) and Gary Cape.

Dallas Baker and Mark Brelsford (HD) had a furious race long battle in Heat 2, exchanging the front position several times. Baker held on for the win with transfers going to Brelsford, Ken Pressgrove (BSA), Eddie Mulder and Jack Forrester (HD).

The third heat saw an early battle for the lead between Jim Rice (BSA) and Dave Sehl (HD). Neil Keen moved up from the back to join in. Keen forged ahead and at the flag followed by Rice, Sehl, Chuck Palmgren (Yam), Frank Ulicki (HD) and former GNC Champ and Sante Fe winner Roger Reiman (HD).

The fourth heat was talent-laden with Dick Mann (Oss), Barry Briggs (Yam) and Harley teammates Mert Lawwill and Cal Rayborn. Ohio rider Larry Darr (HD) led early, chased by Briggs on his screaming Yamaha twin dirt track/speedway hybrid. The two swapped the lead several times. With one lap to go, Jimmy Odom came off hard, with two other riders becoming involved, nearly blocking the track. Briggs backed off the gas, allowing nearly the entire field to shoot by. The officials decided to call the race complete as they had crossed the line. Briggs was furious; he thought the scoring should have reverted to the previous lap. He was backed up by Gary Nixon and Neil Keen as well as the vocal Sante Fe crowd. Despite the protests the officials stood by their decision and Briggs was out.

Semis
Charlie Chapple maintained momentum from his heat win in the first semi. He never missed a beat and led the whole way. Those transferring to the main behind were Bill O'Brien, Larry Darr, Dick Mann, Bart Markel and Don Castro.

In Semi 2, Neil Keen and Jim Rice fought over the top spot with Rice thumping to victory on his BSA. Those following into the National included Dave Sehl, Ken Pressgrove, Roger Reiman and Mark Brelsford.

National

Neil Keen shot out to an early lead followed by Charlie Chapple, Jim Rice, Ken Pressgrove, Bill O'Brien and Don Castro. Bart Markel pulled a big wheelie and was at the tail of the field trying to pick his way through. Keen jetted out to a small lead, closely pursued by Rice. Bart Markel began to slice his way into the pack. By lap 4 he was into the top 10. In the next 5 lap stretch, Markel passed the best in the business including Ronnie Rall, Mark Brelsford, Dick Mann, Don Castro, Bill O'Brien, Ken Pressgrove and Charlie Chapple, clear up to 4th place. By lap 10 Markel had caught 3rd place Dave Sehl, moving by on the 15th circuit. Just ahead Rice made a move and passed Keen on lap 16. Keen passed him back two laps later. As the two engaged in their battle, they failed to notice the rapidly approaching #4. Markel blasted by both with 5 laps to go. While they tried hard to retaliate, Markel would not be denied. On the last lap Rice made the last pass of the race, knocking Keen back to 3rd.

Results

Race: 25 Lap Short Track National

Rank	Rider	Number	Make
1.	Bart Markel, Flint, Mi	4	HD
2.	Jim Rice, Palo Alto, Ca	24	BSA
3.	Neil Keen, Decatur, Ill	10	Yam
4.	Dick Mann, Richmond, Ca	2	Oss
5.	Mark Brelsford, San Bruno, Ca	87	HD
6.	Bill O'Brien, Waukegan, Ill	99	Bul
7.	Ken Pressgrove, Topeka, Ks	14N	BSA
8.	Don Castro, Hollister, Ca	11Y	Tri
9.	Charlie Chapple, Flint, Mi	91E	Yam
10.	Larry Darr, Mansfield, Oh	94	HD
11.	Roger Reiman, Kewanee, Ill	55	HD
12.	Dave Sehl, Waterdown, Ont., Can	21T	HD

Race: Amateur Final

Rank	Rider	Number	Make
1.	Rex Beauchamp, Drayton Plains, Mi	34E	HD
2.	Al Kenyon, Cupertino, Ca	88Y	Bul
3.	Chuck Joyner, Oregon City, Ore	87Q	Bul

Grand National Points Standings after Round 18

Rank	Rider	Pts
1.	Jim Rice	397
2.	Dick Mann	389
3.	Gene Romero	332
4.	Dave Aldana	295
5.	Don Castro	225
6.	Mert Lawwill	220
7.	Yvon DuHamel	210
8.	Dave Smith	158
9.	Gary Nixon	154
10.	Dusty Coppage	136

- Sante Fe Speedway was "The" motorcycle short track in the U.S. Located in the Chicago area, its central location in the country led racers from across the land to journey to its regular Wednesday night program. It was the first track to host a Grand National short track in 1961. The track's origins go way back. The first track on the facility was built in 1896 by Frederick Tiedt. It was called Sante Fe Park due to the close proximity to the Sante Fe Railroad tracks. A varied program of horse, auto, motorcycle and bicycle racing took place there. A tornado destroyed the grandstands in late 1920's and racing ceased. After WWII, Tiedt's son Howard began to rebuild the facility. The track reopened in 1953 with a ¼ mile and short ½ mile oval. The track featured stock car, sprint cars, midgets and motorcycle racing. The facility had been visited by many major sanctioning bodies including the AMA, NASCAR, USAC and the World of Outlaws. The track also built a TT course for motorcycle racing and began hosting TT Nationals in 1969. The AMA promoted GNC's on the short track and TT's well into the 1980's. The track was very successful well into the 1990's until suburban encroachment made the land increasingly more valuable. The track closed in 1996 and was bulldozed in 1999 for a housing development.

The Tulare Debacle

The race scheduled for August 1 was headed for trouble early. A series of judgment calls resulted in changes to the original plans, caused a bad track surface and a cancellation of the race, resulting in a near riot. Originally scheduled to be a 20-lap TT, the Tulare Fair Board refused permission to use the infield portion of the facility. Promoter J.C. Agajanian was forced to change the date to a Half-Mile National. Tulare had run a National before, but had a bad reputation for poor lighting and a substandard, sandy surface. Pre-race scouting by track whiz and co-promoter Harold Murrell, showed the track to be hard and raceable. Murrell felt he could improve the track and ripped it down deep, packed and watered it. When practice began race night, the track quickly fell apart. Rider representative Mert Lawwill voiced most riders opinion that the track was dangerous and not capable of holding a National level show. While several racers, including Gary Nixon, Dick Mann and Jim Rice were ready to race, most riders were against the idea. The decision was made to rework the track and try again. Another practice session was held, with the riders having the same decision. After conferring with the AMA officials the race was to be called off. Future dates conflicted with other scheduled races and the event was cancelled. While all this was going on, the crowd was growing restless and agitated. They had not been advised by announcer Roxy Rockwood about what was going on. Rockwood was apparently not in the loop and was hesitant to comment. When the decision was announced at 9:30, the crowd was not happy. When told refunds would be honored by mail only, not on the spot, things got ugly. A small, vocal, probably intoxicated group of "fans" assaulted J.C.Agajanian with beer cans, rocks and sprayed him with a fire extinguisher. His trademark Stetson hat was knocked off his head and he was kicked when he tried to pick it up. He was rescued by ambulance drivers and led to safety. Agajanian did not duck out; he had the driver go to the ticket booth and had his workers refund money to the remaining fans till the money ran out.

This ugly incident should stand as a learning experience. All involved were the best in the business. Agajanian and Murrell were professionals and supporters of the sport. Lawwill and the AMA made the right decision. Rockwood was the premier announcer of the era. Sometimes things just go wrong. A lack of communication between the officials, promoters, and the announcer meant the fans weren't properly informed about what was going on, triggering the explosion of anger. It is important to mention this story; maybe lessons learned about communication can help prevent a similar incident.

1970 Peoria TT
Rice Makes it 6 with Win at Peoria!

GNC Round #19 of 25 **Date:** August 23, 1970 **Type:** TT **Venue:** Peoria Motorcycle Club Grounds	**Location:** Peoria, Ill **Surface:** Dirt **Course Length:** ½ Mile **Laps:** 20

Smooth Jim Rice became the winningest rider by far in 1970 taking his 6th National win at the famed Peoria facility. It was his 9th career National victory. Rice was on a hot streak and looked like a safe bet for taking the GNC title as the season was in its final stretch. He was completely dominant this day at Peoria, setting fast time, winning his heat race and leading the National wire-to-wire. Rice normally prepared his own equipment, but Mike Akatiff tuned his BSA this day. Dave Aldana finished a distant 2nd which added to the rookie's late season championship bid. Rounding out the podium was Gene Romero who continued to rack up great finishes in his own title run. Dick Mann, Rice's other main championship rival, scored few points when his BSA expired on the starting line of the National.

Jim Rice's win allowed him to stretch to a 60 point advantage over Dick Mann, who finished last in the National due to engine trouble. Gene Romero's 3rd place finish allowed him to close up a little. Only the top 3 in the standings scored points at Peoria. There were no changes in positions, except for Chuck Palmgren who moved to tenth in points after a 4th place run in the National.

Time Trials
Jim Rice served notice he was on his game by setting fast time of 29.86, which held till late in the session when Triumph Don Castro turned an identical time. Mark Brelsford (HD) was next at 29.83 and Sonny Burres (Tri) with a 29.92.

Heats
The only real scare Jim Rice had was in Heat 1 when TT ace Sonny Burres shot out to an early lead. Rice applied heavy pressure to the Oregon TT ace. He got a break on lap 4 when Burres Triumph quit. Rice scooted ahead for the win followed by Dave Aldana (BSA) and Dusty Coppage (Yam).

Blast from the past, 1959! Peoria Heavyweight winner Duane Buchannan surprised all the youngsters in Heat 2 by pulling the holeshot. Eddie Mulder (Tri) worked by veteran Buchanan on lap 4. Cal Rayborn (HD) held 3rd. Dick Mann (BSA) was on the move from the back, passing both Rayborn and Buchannan. Mulder took the win followed by Mann, Rayborn and Dave Hansen (Tri) who also passed a fading Buchannan.

In Heat 3 Gene Romero (Tri) took control early, chased by 6-time Peoria winner Bart Markel with Jim Corpe (Kaw) and Mark Brelsford (HD) battling for 3rd. Gary Nixon (Tri) soon crashed hard coming onto the front straight. The gritty two-time champ was knocked out and made a trip to the hospital. Later reports showed he was beat up bad, but no serious injuries. Markel took control on the rolling restart only to face the 1970 "Harley Curse" and the all-time Peoria win leader was out. The always tough at Peoria, Jim Corpe (Kaw), took the point only to have Brelsford go by on lap 8. Skip Van Leeuwen (Tri) passed Romero for 3rd late in the race.

Semi
Title-hopeful Gene Romero knew he couldn't afford to miss out on any National points and quickly took control of the 5-lap semi. Steve Lathrop (BSA), winner of a Peoria spring non-National and Chuck Palmgren (Yam), followed Romero to the main.

National
Jim Rice pulled a big holeshot and the other riders knew it was going to be a long day. Dick Mann's BSA self-destructed on the line and he was out. Eddie Mulder followed with Jim Corpe next who was chased hard by Dave Aldana. Aldana passed Corpe on lap 4. Mulder appeared to fade a little and Aldana and Corpe shot by. Mark Brelsford and Gene Romero were both on the move from the back of the pack. Brelsford passed Corpe for 3rd on lap

71

8. Romero moved Corpe back another spot on lap 10. Rice was long gone, but the top 5 spots were still being settled. Brelsford dropped out late with mechanical trouble with a sure 3rd place in hand. Corpe also suffered a mechanical and was out. Chuck Palmgren had a late charge from the back and moved up behind Romero in 4th. The top 5 at the finish was Rice, Aldana, Romero, Palmgren and Mulder.

Results

Race: 20 Lap TT National

Rank	Rider	Number	Make
1.	Jim Rice, Palo Alto, Ca	24	BSA
2.	Dave Aldana, Santa Ana, Ca	38X	BSA
3.	Gene Romero, San Luis Obispo, Ca	3	Tri
4.	Chuck Palmgren, Freehold, NJ	6	Yam
5.	Eddie Mulder, Burbank, Ca	12	Tri
6.	Skip Van Leeuwen, Bellflower, Ca	59	Tri
7.	Dave Hansen, Hayward, Ca	22Y	Tri
8.	Dusty Coppage, Burbank, Ca	32	Yam
9.	Mark Brelsford, San Bruno, Ca	87	HD
10.	Jim Corpe, Temple, Ca	48	Tri
11.	Steve Lathrop, Grand Rapids, Mi	66E	BSA
12.	Dick Mann, Richmond, Ca	2	BSA

Race: Amateur TT Final

Rank	Rider	Number	Make
1.	Jerry Powell, Cicero, Ind	23H	Tri
2.	Terry Dorsch, Sunland, Ca	65R	Tri
3.	Chuck Joyner, Oregon City, Ore	87Q	Tri

Grand National Points Standings after Round 19

Rank	Rider	Pts
1.	Jim Rice	450
2.	Dick Mann	390
3.	Gene Romero	366
4.	Dave Aldana	338
5.	Don Castro	225
6.	Mert Lawwill	220
7.	Yvon DuHamel	210
8.	Dave Smith	158
9.	Gary Nixon	154
10.	Chuck Palmgren	144

Extra Extra

- The Peoria TT was/is one of the most exciting, longest-running races, (since 1947, less 1971), on the National circuit. It is a cross of a traditional half-mile and smooth scrambles, complete with a jump and right hand corner. The race was unique to the tour; it was the only TT until the Ascot TT was granted a National in 1962. It is a track where area and California TT specialists and a few great all-arounder's did well at.

1970 Sedalia Mile
Romero Puts it All Together at Sedalia
Mann Injured

GNC Round #20 of 25 **Date:** August 30, 1970 **Type:** Mile **Venue:** Missouri State Fairgrounds	**Location:** Sedalia, Mo **Surface:** Dirt **Course Length**: 1 Mile **Laps:** 20 **Distance:** 20 Miles

Gene Romero took a well-deserved win at the Sedalia Mile GNC. Romero had been a serious title threat for all of 1970, but had been winless since his very first win that was way back at the 1968 Lincoln, Ne TT. He and the C.R. Axtell prepped factory Triumph had jelled and had been very strong since the 750 kits came out. The win allowed Romero to gain a little ground on title rival Jim Rice who came in 3rd at Sedalia. Dick Mann was running up front when he had his foot run over, resulting in a broken leg for Mann that could end his championship hope. Rookie Don Castro turned in yet another impressive finish. He ran in the top 5 all day before securing the runner-up spot. Dave Aldana's "go or blow" season continued when mechanical problems knocked him out of his heat race.

Jim Rice maintained the top spot in points with a good run at Sedalia, his total at 502 points. Gene Romero's win allowed him to move into second ahead of injured Dick Mann with 437 points to Mann's 390. Dave Aldana scored no points, but maintained fourth in points with 338. Don Castro added to his total at 286 points. Mert Lawwill was hanging just behind at 264 points.

Time Trials

1964 GNC Champ Roger Reiman (HD) set fast time at 39.96. Although semi-retired, Reiman was a rocket on the Harley tuned by his father Hank. The only other rider to break the 40-second mark was Jim Rice on his factory BSA.

Heats

Fast-timer Roger Reiman tried his best to run off with Heat 1, but Larry Palmgren (Tri) soon ran him down. Dave Aldana gave chase behind till his BSA dropped out with a large hole in its cases. Mert Lawwill (HD) took over 3rd. At the finish it was Palmgren, Reiman, Lawwill with Eddie Mulder (Tri) and Dan Haaby (Yam) also going to the National.

Cal Rayborn (HD) got away first to lead Heat 2. He led the first several laps till Jim Rice scooted by. Hot rookie Don Castro (Tri) also passed Rayborn, but ran out of time to catch Rice. Bart Markel was 4th aboard a faithful Harley KR with Jimmy Odom (Tri) 5th.

Heat 3 was heavily contested the whole distance. Gene Romero controlled most of the race under heavy pressure from Chuck Palmgren and Dick Mann. Romero came out on top followed by Palmgren, Mann, Tom Rockwood (Tri) and Keith Mashburn (Yam).

Semi

Ken Pressgrove on a BSA "3" won the "Last Chance" event over a talented group. Mark Brelsford (HD), Gary Nixon (Tri) and Dallas Baker (BSA) took the remaining National tickets.

National

Roger Reiman showed he still had some fire by taking the point at the wave of the green. Gene Romero surged past into the lead on lap 2 with Don Castro in tow. Jim Rice was also headed forward and moved into 3rd on lap 4. A disappointed Reiman suffered mechanical trouble and dropped from the field. Romero began stretching to a comfortable lead. Behind him Castro was caught by Rice and was also joined by Larry Palmgren. The three had a great race playing the mile shuffle all over the track for several laps. Castro was able to exert some muscle and pull away to a secure 2nd spot. Replacing Castro in the battle was Dick Mann. He drafted up to Palmgren and Rice late in the race. The three were going at it hard when Mann's foot was accidently run over by Rice. Both stayed upright, but Mann suffered a broken leg.

At the finish it was Romero way out front. Castro had a similar lead over Rice. Palmgren's bike quit on the last lap and had Mert Lawwill (HD) sneak by. Palmgren had enough steam and coasted across in 5th. Tom Rockwood (Tri) was 6th, Ken Pressgrove on the "3" was 7th with Chuck Palmgren (Yam), and Team Harley's Mark Brelsford and Bart Markel rounding out the top 10.

Results

Race: 20 Lap Mile National
Race Time: 13:19.30

Rank	Rider	Number	Make
1.	Gene Romero, San Luis Obispo, Ca	3	Tri
2.	Don Castro, Hollister, Ca	11Y	Tri
3.	Jim Rice, Palo Alto, Ca	24	BSA
4.	Mert Lawwill, San Francisco, Ca	1	HD
5.	Larry Palmgren, Freehold, NJ	5	Tri
6.	Tom Rockwood, Gardena, Ca	38	Tri
7.	Ken Pressgrove, Topeka, Ks	14N	BSA
8.	Chuck Palmgren, Freehold, NJ	6	Yam
9.	Mark Brelsford, San Bruno, Ca	87	HD
10.	Bart Markel, Flint, Mi	4	HD
11.	Eddie Mulder, Burbank, Ca	12	Tri
12.	Keith Mashburn, Santa Susana, Ca	30X	Yam
13.	Dan Haaby, Orangevale, Ca	22	Yam
14.	Gary Nixon, Phoenix. Md	9	Tri
15.	Dallas Baker, Orange, Ca	34	BSA
16.	Jimmy Odom, Fremont, Ca	77	Tri
17.	Frank Gillespie, Berkeley, Ca	23Y	Tri
18.	Dick Mann, Richmond, Ca	2	BSA
19.	Cal Rayborn, Spring Valley, Ca	25	HD
20.	Roger Reiman, Kewanee, Ill	55	HD

Race: 10 Lap Amateur Mile National
Race Time: 6:49.45

Rank	Rider	Number	Make
1.	Gary Fisher, Parkesburg, Pa	99A	Tri
2.	Dennis Palmgren, Freehold, NJ	42M	Tri
3.	Richard Holly, San Diego, Ca	13R	Tri

Grand National Points Standings after Round 20

Rank	Rider	Pts
1.	Jim Rice	502
2.	Gene Romero	437
3.	Dick Mann	390
4.	Dave Aldana	338
5.	Don Castro	286
6.	Mert Lawwill	264
7.	Yvon DuHamel	210
8.	Chuck Palmgren	166
9.	Dave Smith	158
10.	Gary Nixon	158

- Things were looking better for Team Harley; 5 bikes made the National and 3 were still running at the finish, Mert Lawwill and Mark Brelsford on XR's, Bart Markel on a KR. George Roeder and Walt Fulton III were also on KR's but didn't make the main.
- Gene Romero's tuning team included C.R. Axtell, Mike Libby and Nick Deligianis. Axtell and Libby normally stayed in California while Deligianis was Romero's main wrench on the road.
- Roger Reiman got around $200.00 for fast time.
- Gary Fisher was back from his Columbus injuries to win the Amateur Final. Rex Beauchamp had clutch trouble just before the race.
- Dave Aldana made an unsuccessful attempt to claim BSA teammate Jim Rice's motorcycle.
- The Sedalia Fairgrounds facility has a rich motorsports history which continues to this day. The mile dirt track oval was built in 1901 with auto racing starting in 1914. Racing on the big track continued on and off till 1998. USAC made the mile a big part of it's champ car and sprint car series. The AMA ran GNC's on the mile from 1968-'70. Racing emphasis was shifted to the fairgrounds half-mile track, (built in 1936), which is still the frequent host of sprint car racing. The AMA also returned to the smaller track in the 1990's.

1970 Nazareth Mile
Chuck Palmgren Scores First Yamaha Win at Nazareth Endurance

GNC Round #21of 25	**Purse:** $12,000.00
Date: September 6, 1970	**Surface:** Dirt
Type: Mile	**Course Length**: 1 1/8 Mile
Venue: Nazareth Speedway	**Laps:** 50
Location: Lehigh Valley, Pa	**Distance:** 50 Miles, (approx.)

Chuck Palmgren and his Yamaha twin scored the first-ever big bore National dirt track win for a Japanese manufacturer. Palmgren on the Dan Gurney-sponsored ride, outlasted, (barely!) a field decimated by mechanical failures. Only 8 of the 20 starters finished the 50 mile grind on the unique Nazareth 1/1/8 mile oval. Palmgren's own machine barely made it to the finish. Gary Nixon put in his best dirt track finish since his 1969 Santa Rosa injury in second place. Consistent rookie Don Castro again impressed with another podium finish in 3rd.

It was a rough day for the GNC points leaders. Jim Rice and Gene Romero both had mechanical trouble and finished way down in the order. Dave Aldana fell in the main and failed to score any points. Only rookie Don Castro had a great day with his runner-up finish.

It was an interesting day for machinery at the mile. The British 3's were out in force for a change. The extra long straights at Nazareth tempted several riders to give them a try. Jim Rice, Gary Nixon, Ken Pressgrove and Don Castro were among the front runners to give the triples a shot. The converted road racers had been abandoned. Remaining attempts with the triples used Trackmaster frames. The Harley team was still having big trouble with the new XR's. They were fast but had sprouted numerous oil coolers to try and cope with their overheating problems. Most other riders went with their traditional Triumph and BSA twins.

Time Trials
Jim Rice was back aboard the Western BSA triple. He topped the field with a rapid 41.13 lap. This broke 1969 Nazareth winner Fred Nix's record time of 42.06. Rice appeared to have made the right choice in machinery. He was the only rider to have won a GNC on the big 3's, at Sedalia, Mo in 1969.

Heats
Jim Rice and his powerful "3" howled to a comfortable win over Cal Rayborn (HD) and Don Castro (Tri) and a spectacular-riding Yvon DuHamel (Yam) in Heat 1.

Dave Aldana aboard his BSA twin and XR750 mounted Mert Lawwill dueled over the Heat 2 victory right up to the end of the race. Aldana took the narrow win. Gene Romero (Tri) took third position.

George Roeder suffered a broken leg on the first lap of Heat 3. On the restart, Gary Nixon took the lead on his triple. Chuck Palmgren (Yam) latched onto Nixon and the two battled to the finish. Nixon pulled out a close win.

Semi
Ken Pressgrove (BSA 3) took his second Semi win in a row with Dave Smith (Tri), Eddie Mulder (Tri), Norm Robinson (BSA) and Keith Mashburn (Yam) joining him in the National.

National
The Harley-Davidson team's hard work on the XR's seemed to be paying off as Mert Lawwill pulled an early lead, followed by teammates Cal Rayborn and Mark Brelsford. The trio jetted off to a sizeable lead over the field. Time would tell if the bikes would make the distance. Dave Aldana, Jim Rice and Chuck Palmgren hooked up in a draft and tried to run the front runners down. By lap 10 they had caught up to Rayborn. Aldana fell as he attempted to pass Rayborn. Chuck Palmgren managed to pass both Rice and Rayborn shortly after. Brelsford was fading back in the field. Palmgren reeled leader Lawwill in and moved by lap 14. On the next lap, Lawwill pulled off with a worn-out rear tire. Rice was all over Palmgren for the next handful of laps, but couldn't quite get by. On lap 29 Rice's triple shed it's primary chain. Palmgren now had a sizeable lead over Rayborn.

Mechanical attrition was hitting the field hard; GNC title-contender Gene Romero, Tom Rockwood, Yvon Duhamel, Keith Mashburn and many others suffered minor to major mechanical trouble. Many tried to fix their maladies and returned laps down to the field. Late in the race Rayborn and his machine joined the mechanical wounded. He was soon joined by teammate Mark Brelsford.

Making their way through the field were Gary Nixon and Don Castro who assumed second and third place on their triples. Dave Sehl had the only XR still running in 5th. Chuck Palmgren probably thought he was next as his Yamaha started missing and slowed. Running way off pace, Palmgren had a big enough lead over Nixon for his Yamaha to stumble across the stripe first.

Results

Race: 50 Lap Mile National
Race Time: 35:02:00

Rank	Rider	Number	Make
1.	Chuck Palmgren, Freehold, NJ	6	Yam
2.	Gary Nixon, Baltimore, Md	9	Tri
3.	Don Castro, Hollister, Ca	11Y	Tri
4.	Dave Sehl, Waterdown, Ont., Can	21T	HD
5.	Dave Smith, Lakewood, Ca	11X	Tri
6.	Frank Gillespie, Berkeley, Ca	23Y	Tri
7.	Eddie Mulder, Burbank, Ca	12	Tri
8.	Cal Rayborn, Spring Valley, Ca	25	HD
9.	Mark Brelsford, San Bruno, Ca	87	HD
10.	Keith Mashburn, Santa Susana, Ca	30X	Yam
11.	Jim Rice, Palo Alto, Ca	24	BSA
12.	Gene Romero, San Luis Obispo, Ca	3	Tri
13.	Yvon Duhamel, LaSalle, Que; Can	5T	Yam
14.	Dave Aldana, Santa Ana, Ca	38X	BSA
15.	Tom Rockwood, Gardena, Ca	38	Tri
16.	Billy Eves, Phoenixville, Pa	11A	BSA
17.	Norm Robinson, Spencerport, NY	82B	BSA
18.	Mert Lawwill, San Francisco, Ca	1	HD
19.	Ken Pressgrove, Topeka, Ks	14N	BSA
20.	Larry Palmgren, Freehold, NJ	5	Tri

Race: Amateur Final
Race Time: 6:59.62

Rank	Rider	Number	Make
1.	Rex Beauchamp, Drayton Plains, Mi	34E	HD
2.	Al Kenyon, Cupertino, Ca	88Y	BSA
3.	Richard Holly, San Diego, Ca	13R	Tri

Grand National Points Standings after Round 21

Rank	Rider	Pts
1.	Jim Rice	530
2.	Gene Romero	462
3.	Dick Mann	390
4.	Dave Aldana	357
5.	Don Castro	353
6.	Mert Lawwill	271
7.	Chuck Palmgren	252
8.	Gary Nixon	234
9.	Yvon DuHamel	232
10.	Dave Sehl	210

Extra Extra

- The Indy Mile was scheduled for the next night, forcing riders and crews on a 600 mile scramble west. Most teams were worn out, except for the BSA/Triumph teams, which flew the riders to Indy.

- George Roeder's broken leg effectively ended his Grand National comeback and his racing career. Roeder had struggled since the return, making just a few races. The popular Ohioan just didn't seem comfortable in this era. One of the most naturally gifted and stylish riders ever, Roeder won 8 Nationals in his career and came agonizingly close to winning the Grand National Crown twice, losing out Dick Mann in 1963 by 1 point and in another narrow tight battle in 1967 with Gary Nixon. He also set a World Speed record in 1965 in a Harley Sprint-powered streamliner. George built a very successful Harley-Davidson shop in Monroeville, Oh. He tutored three of his sons as racers. George Roeder II also had a successful National career. George Roeder Sr. passed away in 2003.

- The track site in Lehigh Valley, Pa was the site of very early motorsports activity, with racing starting in the early 1900's. The track took its modern "D" shaped configuration in 1966. Modified stock car racing was the track's staple through the 1960's. USAC champ and sprint cars also made stops at the speedway. Home state driver Mario Andretti made frequent appearances at the facility. The AMA ran three GNC's at the speedway. The track closed after the 1971 season. The track reopened in 1982 and was altered to a 1 mile distance. It closed again in 1984. Roger Penske purchased the track in 1986. It was paved and the whole facility renovated. It was renamed Pennsylvania International Speedway. Sanctioning bodies that visited the track in it's third generation included, CART, the NASCAR Busch series and the IRL. The track was continually upgraded and in 1993 took back it's original Nazareth Speedway name. Despite most events being successful, the track closed in 2004. In 2007 all building structures were removed, with the grandstands moved to the Watkins Glen road course. The tracks future is unclear, but commercial or residential development seems imminent.

1970 Indianapolis Mile
Aldana Takes Win #3 on Mann's BSA!

GNC Round #22 of 25	**Location:** Indianapolis, In
Date: September 7, 1970	**Surface:** Dirt
Type: Mile	**Course Length**: 1 Mile
Venue: Indianapolis State Fairgrounds	**Laps:** 30
	Distance: 30 miles

Dave Aldana's amazing rookie season continued with his third GNC win coming at the Indy Mile. Aldana rode injured Dick Mann's BSA to a convincing win, bolstering his championship hopes. Tom Rockwood was impressive in second. Larry Palmgren, who won here in 1969, was third. Aldana's title rivals had a mixed day; Gene Romero had a good run in 4th; Jim Rice was running up front before he suffered mechanical failure for the second race in a row. Mann was technically still in the race although his chance of returning to action was in doubt. Always a smart business man, he knew putting Aldana on his bike might make them both some money while he healed.

Jim Rice maintained a slim points lead over Gene Romero, 534 to 521 points. Rice was in contention but engine problems cost him again. The ever-consistent Romero closed the gap to a very small margin. Dave Aldana's win got him on serious contention for the title with 443 points. Dick Mann (390) and Don Castro (360) still had a long shot. With the huge 101 points available to the winner at the upcoming Sacramento Mile, enabling Rice or Romero and could clinch the title. Aldana stood a chance if he did very well and the leaders struggled over the remaining three events. Mann and Castro odds were slimmer than Aldana's.

Time Trials
Mert Lawwill's feast or famine season continued with a fast time on his iron XR at 38.68. It was fast, but would it last?

Heats
Heat wins went to Gene Romero (Tri), Dave Aldana (BSA) and Larry Palmgren (Tri). Mert Lawwill's engine blew in his heat, knocking him out of any chance of repeating as GNC champ.

Semi
Veteran Shorty Seabourne on a Harold Allison-Norton won the semi event.

National
Cal Rayborn on the factory iron XR, showed strength as he thundered out to an early lead. Question was, would the Harley make it to the end before it self-destructed? A hot-running pack containing teammate Mark Brelsford as well as Dave Aldana, Gene Romero (Tri), Jim Rice (BSA), Larry Palmgren (Tri) and Tom Rockwood (Tri) were close behind. Dave Aldana drafted into the lead on lap 4. The pack behind battled heavily with Rayborn and Brelsford's high strung XR's slowing a little. Rockwood and his Triumph powered into 2nd. Aldana began stretching his lead each lap in record breaking fashion. Rice's flywheel came apart and he was out on lap 16. The battle for the podium positions raged with Rockwood fending off Larry Palmgren and Romero. Aldana finished with a half-track lead. Aldana's first task after the race was thanking Mann for loaning him the rapid ride. Rayborn and Brelsford's Harleys did hold together, but faded back to 5th and 6th at the finish.

Results

Race: 30 Lap Mile National
Race Time: 19:57.82

Rank	Rider	Number	Make
1.	Dave Aldana, Santa Ana, Ca	38X	BSA
2.	Tom Rockwood, Gardena, Ca	38	Tri
3.	Larry Palmgren, Freehold, NJ	5	Tri
4.	Gene Romero, San Luis Obispo, Ca	3	Tri
5.	Cal Rayborn, Spring Valley, Ca	25	HD
6.	Mark Brelsford, San Bruno, Ca	87	HD
7.	Dave Sehl, Waterdown, Ont., Can	21T	HD
8.	Walt Fulton, Hacienda Heights, Ca	63	HD
9.	John Weaver, Fort Wayne, Ind	78H	BSA
10.	Shorty Seabourne, Lawndale, Ca	8	Yam
11.	Larry Darr, Mansfield, Oh	94	HD
12.	Ken Pressgrove, Topeka, Ks	14N	BSA
13.	Keith Mashburn, Santa Susana, Ca	30X	Yam
14.	Mark Mayer, Plainfield, Ind	17H	BSA
15.	Neil Keen, Decatur, Ill	10	Yam
16.	Earl Lout, Rock Island, Ill	61P	BSA
17.	Al Gaskill, Utica, Mi	65	HD
18.	Don Castro, Hollister, Ca	11Y	Tri
19.	Jim Rice, Palo Alto, Ca	24	BSA
20.	Gary Nixon, Baltimore, Md	9	Tri

Race: 10 Lap Mile Amateur Final

Rank	Rider	Number	Make
1.	Richard Holly, San Diego, Ca	13R	Tri
2.	Rex Beauchamp, Drayton Plains, Mi	34E	HD
3.	Don Emde, San Diego, Ca	35R	BSA

Grand National Points Standings after Round 22

Rank	Rider	Pts
1.	Jim Rice	534
2.	Gene Romero	521
3.	Dave Aldana	443
4.	Dick Mann	390
5.	Don Castro	360
6.	Mert Lawwill	271
7.	Chuck Palmgren	252
8.	Gary Nixon	235
9.	Yvon DuHamel	232
10.	Larry Palmgren	214

Extra Extra

- Dave Aldana had one major scare towards the end of the race. The bike began to stumble and quit; Aldana frantically looked the bike over and discovered the gas petcocks were nearly shut. He alertly turned them back on and got going without losing the lead. Turns out that before the race, Aldana had fitted his own, larger gas tank to Mann's BSA. It didn't fit just right and during the race, the petcocks got pushed closed.
- Chuck Palmgren had to scratch from the main allowing alternate Walt Fulton into the race. Fulton put in a great 8th on a Harley KR.
- Though another very disappointing day for Mert Lawwill, overall it was a decent day for Harley-Davidson. The Milwaukee brand made up 6 of the 20 starters with all running at the finish.
- The expensive jet ride for the Team BSA/Triumph riders must have paid dividends as the first four riders in the National were all aboard the flight!
- The Indianapolis Fairgrounds are among the oldest and largest in the United States. The mile oval is also known as the "Track of Champions". It has hosted horse racing, and motorsports events including the AMA, USAC and ARCA events for decades. The facility also has a half-mile cushion track inside the mile oval.

1970 Sacramento Mile
Romero Wins Race and Title at Sacto!!!

GNC Round #23 of 25	**Purse:** $16,000.00
Date: September 13, 1970	**Surface:** Dirt
Type: Mile	**Course Length:** 1 Mile
Venue: California State Fairgrounds	**Laps:** 50
Location: Sacramento, Ca	**Distance:** 50 Miles

Gene Romero took the win and wrapped up the Grand National crown at the Sacramento Mile. The 1970 title fight had been one of the tightest in GNC history. Going into the Sacto event, four riders had a shot at Number One; Jim Rice, Gene Romero, Dave Aldana and Dick Mann. Rice had won 6 Nationals on the year and led by 13 points going into the race. He was the best at the slick California grooved tracks and looked like a safe bet. Romero had been consistent all year and very strong of late. Although he had only one win, (Sedalia), the C.R. Axtell-prepped Triumph was as fast as anything on the circuit and received massive preparation before the National. Dick Mann had led the points battle most of the year, but a broken leg at Sedalia just a few weeks prior appeared to have ruined his chances. Amazingly he showed up at Sacto ready to go despite a very swollen and fragile left leg. Rookie Dave Aldana had an outside shot if the others had a bad day.

In the end Romero did not miss a beat, sweeping to the day's fast time, a heat race win and dominating the main event. The win locked up the crown with two races left to run. Tom Rockwood came from the back for a strong 2nd place. Cal Rayborn and his XR survived the 50 lap grind for 3rd. Jim Rice had an terrible day, suffering an awful crash in his heat race, riding hurt in the main for a 15th place finish. Mann was fast but his leg was tender and his bike gave up in the main. Aldana trashed his Beezumph on the first lap of the race.

The Sacto event was the first time Gene Romero time topped the GNC points order all year. His timing couldn't have been better. His total was 622 points. Jim Rice was second with 565. The two remaining Nationals at Ascot and Oklahoma would only pay a maximum of 50 points, locking the title up for Romero.

Time Trials

Gene Romero showed he meant business by clicking off the only sub-41 second lap at 40.60. The factory-backed Triumph had received expert tuning help from the team of C.R. Axtell, Nick Deligianis and Mike Libby. It was a bullet, with Romero's time a half-second quicker than anyone else. Dick Mann surprised everyone with his self-tuned BSA turning the second quickest time at 41.10. Tied for third were Jody Nicholas on the Harold Allison-Norton and Jimmy Odom on the Cycle Import Triumph at 41.16. Harley-Davidson teamsters Mark Brelsford and Larry Darr turned in laps of 41.24 and 41.25 respectively.

Heats

Gene Romero led the first heat from flag-to-flag, but teammate Don Castro was right with him through the race. Title contender Dave Aldana was 3rd on his 3-cylinder BSA, Eddie Wirth (Tri) was 4th.

Heat 2 was taken by iron man Dick Mann, his leg issue appearing not to slow him at all. TT ace Eddie Mulder (Tri) was impressive in 2nd with Keith Mashburn (Yam) and Lloyd Houchins (Tri) in 3rd and 4th.

Dusty Coppage (Yam) pulled the holeshot in Heat 3 which soon turned into a good mile battle. Coppage was joined in a swap fest for first with Cal Rayborn, Frank Gillespie (Tri), Mert Lawwill (HD) and Jody Nicholas. Rayborn took the top spot on lap 4 with Lawwill taking over for good on lap 6. The order behind at the finish was Nicholas, Rayborn and Gillespie.

Heat 4 was a barnburner with a terrifying conclusion. The race had a fantastic five-way battle for the top spots with Gary Nixon on a (Tri "3"), Jimmy Odom, Chuck Palmgren (Yam), Jim Rice (BSA "3"), and Tom Rockwood (Tri) battling heat long for the National transfers. Palmgren led lap 1 with Nixon taking over for lap 2. Odom showed some power by taking the front spot on lap 5. Odom led to the finish with Nixon and Palmgren right behind. The battle for the last transfer went to Rice over Rockwood by a whisker. Going into turn 1, Rice apparently hit a false neutral as he reached for the brake when Palmgren checked up in front of him. He layed his triple down at full bore.

As documented in On Any Sunday, Rice took a very scary ride with both he and the bike going through the fence. A photographer was struck by Rice's machine and was badly injured. Rice received a broken nose and was very shaken up. He did board an ambulance, but did not leave the fairgrounds. After getting patched up and regaining his bearings, Rice decided to ride the main. Tom Cates and crew began straightening out the battered BSA.

Semi

The semi was only 4 laps but created some great dicing. Area racer Ralph Waldman (Tri) led early with Tom Rockwood going by on lap 3. Mark Brelsford also worked by to take 2nd. Waldman held 3rd with veteran Ralph White (Tri) filling out the main event roster.

National

The tension-filled National blasted off the line with Romero pulling ahead. Mann shot by on the backstretch. Dave Aldana bailed off his BSA in Turn 3, necessitating a restart. First alternate Dallas Baker (BSA) filled Aldana's spot. The restart was an exact copy, with Romero leading lap 1. Close behind were Mann, Mert Lawwill and Don Castro. Tom Rockwood was playing catch-up after missing shifts on the start. Lawwill went by Mann for 2nd on lap 4. Don Castro bumped Mann back another spot on lap 8, but soon dropped out with engine trouble. Jody Nicholas was on the move from the pack and took over 3rd place. Rockwood was blitzing through the pack and was in the top 10 by the 10th lap. When Nicholas fell out with oil cooler problems on lap 13, Chuck Palmgren took over 3rd place. Mann left the race on lap 15 after twisting his already hurting leg and a missing engine. Gary Nixon had his "3" howling and passed Palmgren on lap 17. Rockwood was having an amazing ride on the Danny Macias-tuned Triumph and moved into 7th on lap 18.

By the halfway point, Romero had a big lead and was running away with the event. Nixon had reeled Lawwill in and went by on lap 29. Tom Rockwood was up to 6th and pressing Cal Rayborn and Eddie Wirth. Unbelievably Rockwood jetted by both for 4th. Lawwill's machine began misfiring and he fell back through the pack. The order now read Romero, Nixon, Rockwood, Wirth and Rayborn.

With less than 10 to go Rockwood caught Nixon and began applying pressure. A little ways back Mark Brelsford and Jimmy Odom joined up with Wirth and Rayborn and the group began swapping for 4th spot. Romero had cooled his pace a little as the Nixon and Rockwood battle cut his lead to 4 second. With just two laps to go, Nixon got into turn 3 a little hot, and grounded the cases on his triple. Gary went down, unhurt, but out of the race. At the flag Romero still had a decent lead and was followed across the line by Rockwood, Rayborn Wirth, Odom and Brelsford.

Results

Race: 50 Lap Mile National
Race Time: 33:58.67

Rank	Rider	Number	Make
1.	Gene Romero, San Luis Obispo, Ca	3	Tri
2.	Tom Rockwood, Gardena, Ca	38	Tri
3.	Cal Rayborn, Spring Valley, Ca	25	HD
4.	Eddie Wirth, Manhattan Beach, Ca	84	Tri
5.	Jimmy Odom, Fremont, Ca	77	Tri
6.	Mark Brelsford, San Bruno, Ca	87	HD
7.	Lloyd Houchins, La Crescenta, Ca	20X	Tri
8.	Chuck Palmgren, Freehold, NJ	6	Yam
9.	Frank Gillespie, Berkeley, Ca	23Y	Tri
10.	Mert Lawwill, San Francisco, Ca	1	HD
11.	Ralph White, Torrance, Ca	15	Tri
12.	Eddie Mulder, Burbank, Ca	12	Tri
13.	Dallas Baker, Orange, Ca	34	BSA
14.	Gary Nixon, Phoenix, Md	9	Tri
15.	Jim Rice Palo Alto, Ca	24	BSA

Rank	Rider	Number	Make
16.	Keith Mashburm, Santa Susana, Ca	30X	Yam
17.	Jody Nicholas, Newport Beach, Ca	58	Nor
18.	Dick Mann, Richmond, Ca	2	BSA
19.	Don Castro, Hollister, Ca	11Y	Tri
20.	Ralph Waldman, Fairfield, Ca	88Z	Tri

Race: 10 Lap Amateur National
Race Time: 6:52.50

Rank	Rider	Number	Make
1.	John Hateley, Van Nuys, Ca	43R	Tri
2.	Gary Fisher, Parkesburg, Pa	99A	Tri
3.	Terry Dorsch, Sunland, Ca	65R	Tri

Grand National Points Standings after Round 23

Rank	Rider	Pts
1.	Gene Romero	622
2.	Jim Rice	565
3.	Dave Aldana	443
4.	Dick Mann	412
5.	Don Castro	379
6.	Mert Lawwill	317
7.	Chuck Palmgren	304
8.	Tom Rockwood	294
9.	Mark Brelsford	272
10.	Gary Nixon	269

Extra Extra

- The J.C. Agajanian-promoted event offered one of the largest purses in dirt track history of $16,000.00. Contingency awards numbered around $10,000.00.
- Gene Romero's share of the purse was $5000.00.
- A great crowd of 15,000 turned out.
- After his second major spill on one of the converted road race triples, Aldana had enough. It was the last time he would ride a multi on dirt.
- Jim Rice's BSA triple never seemed as quick as previous events. A post-mortem revealed a blown head gasket.
- With everything riding on the line at Sacto, why were two of BSA's best hopes for the championship on the questionable "Beezumphs"? It seems the British brass were very high on their superbike getting as much press as possible and urged all team riders, BSA and Triumph alike, to ride the machines. Romero and Mann refused, going with their twins. The call may have cost BSA the title.
- Rookie expert Ken Pressgrove was killed at the Race of Champions held September 12 at Louisville Downs. The 20-year Kansas racer had earned a place on the BSA team and was a rising star. He had injured his ankle at the Houston Short Track, but was turning in solid performances in the late season.
- The "Old" California State Fairgrounds location in Sacramento hosted the State Fair from 1909 to 1968. The AMA hosted Nationals at the facility starting in 1959. The 1970 Sacto Mile was one of the last major events at the facility. Continued urban growth forced a move further from town to the present Cal Expo location. The races would not return to Sacramento till 1978.

1970 Ascot Half-Mile
Romero Again at Ascot

GNC Round #24 of 25	**Purse:** $6000.00
Date: September 19, 1970	**Surface:** Dirt
Type: Half-Mile	**Course Length:** ½ Mile
Venue: Ascot Park	**Laps:** 20
Location: Gardena, Ca	**Distance:** 10 Miles

Gene Romero, the new 1970 GNC Champ, added icing on the cake by winning the tough Ascot Half-Mile. It was win number three for the season, four for Romero's career. Like the Sacto Mile, Romero topped the field at every opportunity; he set fast time, won his heat and the main. While Romero had nothing to prove to anybody, the victory really confirmed that he was deserving of the GNC title. Harley-Davidson's Mark Brelsford ended the night in 2nd after leading the early laps of the main. Lloyd Houchins netted his best ever GNC finish in 3rd. It was a typical Ascot event with the field made up of Ascot stars and those GNC riders who cut their teeth there. No "outsiders" made the main.

Heats

Keith Mashburn pulled the holeshot on the Shell Yamaha, leading lap 1. Gene Romero had the Axtell Triumph wound up and took the point position on lap 2. Dave Aldana moved up from the pack and knocked Mashburn back a spot on lap 7. At the end of the race, Romero had a comfortable lead with Aldana and Mashburn also transferring directly to the main.

In Heat 2 Norton riders Jody Nicholas and Mel Lacher stormed out front, followed by Jimmy Odom (Tri). Nicholas looked to have the win wrapped up till his Harold Allison-owned machine lost fire in one cylinder. Odom went on to win with Nicholas managing to hold onto the runner-up spot. Lacher was 3rd with Shorty Seabourne on another Norton was semi-bound.

"Fast Eddie" Mulder (Tri) pulled one of his patented holeshots in Heat 3 to establish the early lead. Tom Rockwood (Tri) and Lloyd Houchins (Tri) got together and were running at the back of the field. Defending race winner Mert Lawwill (HD) soon caught and passed Mulder. Unfortunately the "Iron XR Curse" again ruined Lawwill's chances and he was out. Harley teammate Mark Brelsford scooted by Mulder for the lead. Houchins and Rockwood had amazingly ripped through the field and took the other two transfer spots.

Semi

Cal Rayborn (HD) appeared to have the semi wired till Shorty Seabourne went by with two to go. Don Castro (Tri) just edged out Jim Rice (BSA) for the final transfer.

National

Mark Brelsford shot out front at the drop of the flag. Gene Romero and Jody Nicholas gave chase behind. Nicholas briefly moved by, but he was hit by mechanical trouble again and was out. Romero moved forward, catching Brelsford on lap 5. Romero applied heavy pressure and took the lead on lap 7. Romero would pull away for the rest of the event. Brelsford was solid in the runner-up spot with a good lead over 3rd place Houchins. Behind, Dave Aldana and Jimmy Odom battled heavily over 4th place. Aldana eventually took the spot with Odom fading. Shorty Seabourne worked up from the back row to 5th spot. At the flag it was all Romero with the rest of the top 5; Brelsford, Houchins, Aldana and Seabourne.

Results

Race: 20 Lap Half-Mile National
Race Time: 7:54.82

Rank	Rider	Number	Make
1.	Gene Romero, San Luis Obispo, Ca	3	Tri
2.	Mark Brelsford, San Bruno, Ca	87	HD
3.	Lloyd Houchins, La Cresenta, Ca	20X	Tri
4.	Dave Aldana, Santa Ana, Ca	38X	BSA
5.	Shorty Seabourne, Lawndale, Ca	8	Nor
6.	Jimmy Odom, Fremont, Ca	77	Tri
7.	Tom Rockwood, Gardena, Ca	38	Tri
8.	Don Castro, Hollister, Ca	11Y	Tri
9.	Keith Mashburn, Santa Susana, Ca	30X	Yam
10.	Cal Rayborn, Spring Valley, Ca	25	HD
11.	Mel Lacher, San Diego, Ca	37	Nor
12.	Jody Nicholas, San Diego, Ca	58	Nor

Race: 14 Lap Amateur Half-Mile National
Race Time: 5:39.81

Rank	Rider	Number	Make
1.	John Hateley, Van Nuys, Ca	43R	Tri
2.	Gary Fisher, Parkesburg, Pa	99A	Tri
3.	Al Kenyon, Cupertino, Ca	88Y	Tri

Grand National Points Standings after Round 24

Rank	Rider	Pts
1.	Gene Romero	648
2.	Jim Rice	565
3.	Dave Aldana	452
4.	Dick Mann	412
5.	Don Castro	384
6.	Mert Lawwill	317
7.	Chuck Palmgren	304
8.	Tom Rockwood	300
9.	Mark Brelsford	291
10.	Gary Nixon	269

- A bunch of talented racers didn't transfer to the National, including, Jim Rice, Chuck Palmgren, Sammy Tanner, Eddie Wirth, Larry Darr, Gary Nixon and Dewayne Keeter. Ascot was a tough place!
- Triumph representatives presented new Grand National Champion Gene Romero a check for $10,000.00 during intermission festivities.
- Ascot Park was a spectacular stop on the GNC circuit. It was the hub of motorcycle racing in Southern California for decades. It was built over a former city dump and operated as Gardena Speedway. Charismatic J.C. Agajanian renamed it Ascot Park in the late 1950's. Its unique tacky surface hosted sprint cars, stock cars and motorcycles. The short half-mile produced very quick lap times. The place was always packed with fans and racers. Some of the best riders in the country honed their skills at the often dangerous facility. The place was the measuring stick to see how gutsy and skilled you really were as a racer. Ascot regulars often embarrassed top- ranked GNC riders. It would be nearly 20 years before a non-Californian won a National at Ascot. If you could run fast at Ascot, you could go fast anywhere.

GNC Final Round #25	Surface: Dirt
Date: October 4, 1970	Course Length: ½ Mile
Type: Half-Mile	Laps: 20
Venue: State Fair Speedway	Distance: 10 Miles
Location: Oklahoma City, Ok	

Mark Brelsford salvaged some glory from what had been a pretty dismal season for him, (and most of Team Harley), at the final GNC of the year at the Oklahoma City Fairgrounds, aboard a Jim Belland-tuned iron XR750. It was the likeable Brelsford's second National win, the first since his first-ever at the Ascot TT in 1969. New GNC champ Gene Romero put in another great ride, taking 2nd on the narrow groove race track. He pressured Brelsford for the early part of the event. Veteran Larry Palmgren had another solid finish in 3rd. Although Palmgren had gone winless for the season, he had several top ten finishes.

While the top 6 in points for the year remained unchanged, there was still some dicing behind. Brelsford's win shot him up two places from ninth to seventh in points. Correspondingly, Chuck Palmgren and Tom Rockwood who both failed to make the National, fell back to eighth and ninth respectively.

Time Trials

Three-time GNC champ Bart Markel set the fastest time of the day aboard on his self-tuned Harley iron XR at 24.84.

Heats

Larry Palmgren (Tri) topped Heat 1 over heavy hitters Gene Romero (Tri), Mark Brelsford (HD) and a semi-bound Jim Rice (BSA). Palmgren had won the Expert portion of a regional race held at the fairgrounds the day before the Nationals.

Gary Nixon (Tri), whose dirt track performances were getting stronger by the event, led Heat 2 wire-to-wire. Behind, a slugfest on the narrow groove was going on between Mert Lawwill (HD), Keith Mashburn (Yam), Eddie Mulder (Tri) and Chuck Palmgren (Yam). Taking the transfers behind Nixon were Lawwill and Mashburn.

Team BSA's Dave Aldana captured the final heat, followed by Don Castro (Tri), Larry Darr (HD) with Tom Rockwood (Tri) headed to the semi.

Semi

Jim Rice did it the hard way again, winning another semi to get to the National. Fast Triumph guys Eddie Mulder and Frank Gillespie took the final two National tickets.

National

A determined Mark Brelsford (HD) jumped out front at the start of the National and was never headed. Gene Romero (Tri) tried to make a race of it but Brelsford pulled away to a comfortable lead. Brelsford's mentor Mert Lawwll was running in 3rd but was unmercifully hit with bad luck once again and dropped back with mechanical trouble. The narrow groove track kept passing to a minimum till late in the race when Dave Aldana (BSA) caught fire. He moved from deep in the pack and was just behind Romero on lap 17. He pressed Romero hard, but got into a tank slapper and dropped back to 6th at the finish. The order at the final National of 1970 was Brelsford, Romero, Larry Palmgren, Jim Rice, (from the semi), Don Castro, Dave Aldana, Mert Lawwill, Eddie Mulder, Larry Darr and Gary Nixon.

Results

Race: 20 Lap Half-Mile National
Race Time: 8:21.21

Rank	Rider	Number	Make
1.	Mark Brelsford, San Bruno, Ca	87	HD
2.	Gene Romero, San Luis Obispo, Ca	3	Tri
3.	Larry Palmgren, Freehold, NJ	6	Yam
4.	Jim Rice, Palo Alto, Ca	24	BSA
5.	Don Castro, Hollister, Ca	11Y	Tri
6.	Dave Aldana, Santa Ana, Ca	38X	BSA
7.	Mert Lawwill, San Francisco, Ca	1	HD
8.	Eddie Mulder, Burbank, Ca	12	Tri
9.	Larry Darr, Mansfield, Oh	94	HD
10.	Gary Nixon, Baltimore, Md	9	Tri
11.	Frank Gillespie, Berkeley, Ca	23Y	Tri
12.	Keith Mashburn, Santa Susana	30X	Yam

Race: 14 Lap Amateur Half-Mile Final
Race Time: 6:00.15

Rank	Rider	Number	Make
1.	Don Emde, San Diego, Ca	35R	BSA
2.	Dennis Palmgren, Freehold, NJ	42M	Tri
3.	Terry Dorsch, Sunland, Ca	65R	Tri

Grand National Final Points Standings

Rank	Rider	Pts
1.	Gene Romero	667
2.	Jim Rice	574
3.	Dave Aldana	459
4.	Dick Mann	412
5.	Don Castro	392
6.	Mert Lawwill	323
7.	Mark Brelsford	317
8.	Chuck Palmgren	304
9.	Tom Rockwood	300
10.	Gary Nixon	272

Extra Extra

- Great crowd of around 6000.
- The race was billed as the Fred Nix Memorial. Nix was an Oklahoma native and won the National here in 1968. He died in a traffic accident in 1969. Nix's father presented Mark Brelsford the winner's trophy.
- Racing artist Melva Murphy presented Nix's widow, Carol, with a check with proceeds from the Nix print she (Murphy), had painted.
- The State Fair Speedway hosted motorsports for over 50 years. In addition to AMA motorcycles, NASCAR and other touring series, local supermodifieds and late model stock cars have enjoyed a healthy run at the facility. Presently the track is facing the possibility of being paved over and used as a parking lot. Alternative locations and solutions are being explored.

1970 GNC Review

1. Gene Romero
667 Points

Gene Romero and crew persevered, never giving up through the killer 25-race schedule. Romero started the year rough at Houston, failing to make either race while his main rivals for the title, Jim Rice and Dick Mann had great opening rounds. Rice notched a win at the TT and Mann was 2nd at the short track. Things looked up with a 2nd place at Daytona. For the next 8 Nationals, Romero made every race except for the Reading Half-Mile, mostly finishing just inside the top ten. Things began turning around at mid-season due to two things, the use of the new 750cc kits and the tuning skills of C.R. Axtell, Mike Libby and Nick Deligianis. Romero kept up his earlier consistency, but his finishers were more towards the front. Romero and Rice both scored points in 20 of the 25 Nationals run. Romero only scored two wins before the title was decided, coming late in the season at the Sedalia Mile and the Sacramento Mile which paid Romero a fat 101 points, clinching the championship. Rice scored an amazing 6 wins during the year. What really won the title for Romero was his consistent high finishes due to the reliability of his Triumph compared to Rice and his BSA. In the Nationals that Romero made, he only finished outside of the top 10 once, a 12th at Nazareth. Romero added his third win of the year at Ascot after clinching the title. Besides his wins, Romero was 2nd at Daytona, the Ascot TT and the season ending Oklahoma Half-Mile. He was 3rd at the Peoria TT. He was in the top 5 at Columbus, Castle Rock TT, Santa Rosa and the Indy Mile. He had an amazing eight top 10 finishes at Kent, Palmetto, Cumberland, Talladega, Louisville, Loudon, Sante Fe TT and the San Jose Half-Mile. Prior to his win at Sedalia, Romero had only notched one win, in 1968 at the Lincoln TT. His 1970 title fight showed his versatility and skill in all GNC disciplines, remarkable tenacity and belief in himself and crew, after pretty much everyone else had conceded the title to favorites Dick Mann and Jim Rice. The new points system ultimately rewarded consistency over wins.

2. Jim Rice
574 Points

Jim Rice appeared the favorite after taking the points lead from Dick Mann late in the season. He consistently reeled off victories at about every third or fourth start, taking an amazing 6 wins on the year at the Houston TT, Palmetto, Reading, San Jose Half-Mile, Santa Rosa, and Peoria. He was runner-up at Terre Haute and the Sante Fe Short Track. He was an amazing 3rd at Talladega and again at the Sedalia Mile. Rice was in the top 5 three times; at the Houston Short Track, Sante Fe TT and Oklahoma. There were three other finishes in the top 10, at the Louisville Half-Mile, Loudon and Columbus. He ran well in all 5 types of GNC competition. He scored points in the same amount of races as Romero, (20). It is hard to believe on the surface that Rice didn't take the title. The difference was the eight finishes outside the top 10, mostly due to mechanical trouble. In addition Rice's strong suit was on dirt, which except for Sacramento didn't pay nearly as many points as the road races. Rice's terrible day at Sacto ensured Romero's title. A heartbreaker for Rice, who appeared to have the title in-hand, late in the year.

3. Dave Aldana
459 Points

Dave Aldana lived up to all advanced billing, challenging for the title and becoming the highest finishing rookie in the points chase. Aldana scored more points than his two closest challengers, Dick Mann and Don Castro, despite scoring points in fewer races, 15 of 25. He scored a stunning win at the Talladega Road Race which boosted him to 2nd in the championship. He dropped back to 4th as Gene Romero mounted his mid-season charge. Aldana scored two more wins, at Terre Haute and another win aboard Dick Mann's BSA at the Indy Mile, boosted him back to 3rd in points. Going into the title-decider at Sacramento, Aldana had a shot at the title if the other contenders ran into trouble and he did well. It was not to be, but it was still a fantastic season. In addition to his three wins, Aldana nearly won the Cumberland Half-Mile and finished 2nd at the Peoria TT. He had four top 5's at the Houston TT, Kent, and the San Jose and Ascot Half-Miles. Aldana also scored top 10 finishes at Loudon and Oklahoma City. When his bike was running he never finished lower than 12th, and that was Daytona!

4. Dick Mann
412 Points

1963 GNC champion Dick Mann's chances appeared bleak at the start of the 1970 season. Written off by BSA for being too old, Mann picked up the one-off Honda ride, winning at Daytona after years of trying. Mann missed the Kent Road Race, but he and BSA made a deal and it was soon business as usual. Mann held the points lead for most of the year, looking a like he had a great chance to win his second title. Unfortunately an incident late in the season at Sedalia left him with a leg injury and apparently out for the year. Mann sat out a couple of rounds, but showed up at Sacramento, knowing he still had a shot at the title. The odds were against him but it was a valiant try. Despite missing Kent and four of the last five Nationals, Mann finish fourth in the title bid, scoring points in 17 of 25 races. Besides Daytona, he also picked up a win at the Castle Rock TT, was 2nd at the Houston Short Track and Palmetto and 3rd at the Reading Half-Mile. He was a top 5 finisher at Talladega, the Ascot TT, Santa Rosa, Terre Haute and the Sante Fe Short Track. Top 10 finishes were recorded at Louisville, and the Sante Fe TT.

5. Don Castro
392 Points

Don Castro had a fantastic rookie year. Most seasons his record would have easily made him the top first year rider, but this year, there was fellow California rookie Dave Aldana. Nevertheless Castro's performance more than justified his Triumph factory ride. He was 3rd at Daytona on his first try! He also posted a runner-up at the Castle Rock TT and at Sedalia as well as a 3rd at Nazareth Mile. He posted top 5's on the half-miles at Louisville, San Jose and Oklahoma City. His seven top 10 finishes were impressive, coming at Kent, Sante Fe Short Track and TT and the half-miles at Palmetto, Cumberland, Reading and Ascot. Castro was a great all-arounder and his first GNC win was just a matter of time.

6. Mert Lawwill
313 Points

The first Harley-Davidson rider home was Mert Lawwill. It was a trying season for defending champion Lawwill, as well as the entire Harley team. This season marked the lowest finish ever for the Milwaukee brand in the year-end GNC standings. The new XR750 was trouble all year; the team balanced power and reliability all season to no avail. Oil coolers and reduced compression helped some. The iron cylinders posed an insurmountable obstacle that only a new design would help. Despite the gloom and doom, Lawwill posted an impressive three wins for the year. The wins were on three different models; Houston, on a Sprint, Cumberland a promising first win for the XR and the Ascot TT on the 900 XLR. Lawwill turned to his backup KR on several occasions. Besides his wins, Lawwill was never on the podium all year. He did post top 5's at the Castle Rock TT and the Sedalia Mile. He was in the top 10 at just three races, the Santa Rosa and Sacramento Miles and the Oklahoma City Half-Mile. Lawwill scored in just 13 of the 25 rounds.

7. Mark Brelsford
312 Points

Mark Brelsford came in just one point behind his teammate and mentor Mert Lawwill. Though Brelsford's year had problems similar to Lawwill, he did post 18 points scoring finishes. He ended the year the strongest of any of the Harley team. Starting at the Santa Rosa Mile, Brelsford had an amazing 10 in the row run of finishes, right up to the season ender at Oklahoma City, where Brelsford scored his only win of the season. While the team had to feel good about Brelsford's reliability run, one of the finishes was on a Sprint and he resorted to a KR at more than one race. Brelsford also set on the podium at the Castle Rock TT and Ascot Half-Mile and was in the top 5 at Cumberland and Columbus Half-Miles. Impressively, Brelsford was in the top 10 a total of nine times through the year; at both Houston races, the Peoria TT, the Terre Haute Half-Mile and the miles at Santa Rosa, Sedalia, Nazareth, Indy and Sacramento. Brelsford was fast and consistent on all distances and surfaces and showed promise as a future champion once the machinery was "ironed" out.

8. Chuck Palmgren
303 Points

Chuck Palmgren posted many strong finishes during the year, and at the Nazareth Mile gave Yamaha it's first dirt track GNC win, a first for any Japanese manufacturer. In addition to his win, Palmgren was on the podium at the Sante Fe Short Track and the San Jose Half-Mile. He also posted top 5's at the Houston Short Track and the Peoria

TT. Top 10 finishes included the Talladega Road Race, Ascot TT and the Sedalia and Sacramento Miles. He scored points in 10 of 25 events. A veteran campaigner, strong on at all events, especially on dirt, Palmgren's future with the Yamaha twin looked bright.

9. Tom Rockwood
301 Points

Tom Rockwood finished out the year strong with runner-up finishes at the Indy and Sacramento Miles. He was also in the top 10 at Talladega, the Castle Rock TT, Sedalia Mile and San Jose and Ascot half-miles. The young Californian was gaining experience and was putting himself in position to win his first National.

10. Gary Nixon
271 Points

Two-time champion Gary Nixon may not have had the year he wanted, but his comeback after suffering a compound leg fracture in 1969 was impressive. Nixon pulled off another win at his best pavement track, Loudon. He was also 3rd at the Kent Road Race. Nixon showed he could still dirt track despite his weakened leg. He was 2nd at the Nazareth Mile, and 5th at the Reading Half-Mile after leading early. He was running 2nd at Sacramento till late in the race till he drug the cases on his 3-cylinder Beezumph and went down. Nixon was one tough cat and would be back for more.

The big story of the year was obviously the great title chase between BSA teammates Dick Mann, Jim Rice, Dave Aldana and Triumph's Gene Romero. Despite their very different backgrounds and styles, all were pretty evenly matched. A deciding difference may have been in the depth of machinery. Often forgotten, Mann, Rice and Aldana did the majority of bike preparation and tuning themselves. Their machinery was equal to anyone's. Pulling double duty though; riding and tuning at the top level of the sport, was surely a major stressor, physically and mentally. Romero had it a little easier with help from C.R. Axtell and crew.

It was "triumphant" year for the British teams; they took 7 of the top 10 spots, Triumph with 4, BSA had 3. Harley had 2 spots and Yamaha 1. Ten different riders claimed the 25 Nationals. A total of 97 riders scored points in the National Championship races.

The huge 25-race schedule offered Amateur racers plenty of opportunity to gain experience on National level tracks in front of big crowds. Rusty Bradley from Texas made the most press by winning three road races, including Daytona and was awarded huge Kawasaki contingency money; He out earned all Expert riders except for the winner at each event. Tying for the most wins were Michigan rider Rex Beauchamp and California's John Hateley with four wins. Terry Dorsch, Tod Sloan and Canadian Doug Sehl each won two races. Taking one win each were Canadian Maurice Fraser, Ed Hermann, Chuck Joyner, Jerry Powell, Gary Fisher, Rick Holly and Don Emde. Emde's situation was unique. He was an Expert ranked road racer who had several high GNC finishes including a 3rd place finish at Loudon. He earned his Amateur win on the dirt at the Oklahoma City Half-Mile. Other front runners included Ron Butler, Al Kenyon and Dennis Palmgren.

1970 GNC Season Winners

Event	Location	Winner	Machine
TT	Houston, Tx	Jim Rice, Palo Alto, Ca	BSA
Short Track	Houston, Tx	Mert Lawwill, San Francisco, Ca	HD
Road Race	Daytona Beach, Fl	Dick Mann, Richmond, Ca	Hon
Road Race	Kent, Wa	Ron Grant, Brisbane, Ca	Suz
Half-Mile	Palmetto, Ga	Jim Rice, Palo Alto, Ca	BSA
Half-Mile	Cumberland, Md	Mert Lawwill, San Francisco, Ca	HD
Road Race	Talladega, Al	Dave Aldana, Santa Ana, Ca	BSA
Half-Mile	Reading, Pa	Jim Rice, Palo Alto, Ca	BSA
Half-Mile	Louisville, Ky	Dave Sehl, Waterdown, Ont., Can	HD
Road Race	Loudon, NH	Gary Nixon, Cockeysville, Md	Tri
TT	Hinsdale, Ill	Eddie Mulder, Burbank, Ca	Tri
Half-Mile	Columbus, Oh	Dave Sehl, Waterdown, Ont., Can	HD
Half-Mile	San Jose, Ca	Jim Rice, Palo Alto, Ca	BSA
TT	Castle Rock, Wa	Dick Mann, Richmond, Ca	BSA
TT	Gardena, Ca	Mert Lawwill, San Francisco, Ca	HD
Mile	Santa Rosa, Ca	Jim Rice, Palo Alto, Ca	BSA
Half-Mile	Terre Haute, Ind	Dave Aldana, Santa Ana, Ca	BSA
Short Track	Hinsdale, Ill	Bart Markel, Flint, Mi	HD
TT	Peoria, Ill	Jim Rice, Palo Alto, Ca	BSA
Mile	Sedalia, Mo	Gene Romero, San Luis Obispo, Ca	Tri
Mile (1 1/8)	Nazareth, Pa	Chuck Palmgren, Freehold, NJ	Yam
Mile	Indianapolis, Ind	Dave Aldana, Santa Ana, Ca	BSA
Mile	Sacramento, Ca	Gene Romero, San Luis Obispo, Ca	Tri
Half-Mile	Gardena, Ca	Gene Romero, San Luis Obispo, Ca	Tri
Half-Mile	Oklahoma City, Ok	Mark Brelsford, San Bruno, Ca	HD

1971 GNC Season Preview

There were no dramatic changes in riders or teams for the 1971 season. This would tend favor the British teams chances for again taking the top spots in the Grand National series. The Triumph/BSA teams were again given huge budgets and encouraged to take the title no matter the cost. Triumph returned with new GNC champ Gene Romero, two-time champion Gary Nixon, Don Castro and new team member, Tom Rockwood. BSA would return with Jim Rice, Jim Rice, Dave Aldana and their new addition, road race whiz Don Emde. New for the year were exclusive contracts. Team riders could not compete on any other brand of motorcycles. This had a big effect on road racers like Gary Nixon and Don Emde who had both been successful on Yamaha lightweights. It was a frustrating situation given that the team had no competitive small displacement machines. Danny Macias replaced Pat Owens as the team's new crew chief. The triples received new "low boy" frames and some aerodynamic tuning of the bodywork. Engines were given new ignitions and received additional head work and carburetion changes that boosted horsepower over 1970 levels. Dirt track machines were largely unchanged. It was twins only and the unwieldy triples were abandoned. BSA came out with their 750cc, A70 engine during the season.

Harley-Davidson would return with the infamous "iron XR" for 1971. The engines continued to be tweaked in hope of gaining some reliability while still delivering competitive power. Some bikes sported up to four oil coolers to combat overheating. Compression was dialed back. New heads were developed to use twin carburetors. Many designs were tried before settling on one that had both exhaust pipes exit to the left, with the carbs exiting together back to the right, which became the basic setup for all later versions of the XR. Cylinder studs replaced bolts. The problem with the mainshafts coming loose in the flywheels was taken care by making the units together. Despite all the work, the writing was on the wall and while trying to refine the iron engine, back at the factory, work had commenced on a new aluminum engine for 1972. The team was largely the same as 1970; former GNC champs Mert Lawwill and Bart Markel along with Mark Brelsford were joined by Dave Sehl and rookie Rex Beauchamp. Despite the talented riders and crew involved, it was going to be a long year for the team.

Yamaha would carry on much the same with a similar effort as 1970. Chuck Palmgren was the best hope for Grand National success, along with new National Number 19, Keith Mashburn, still operating as a Shell Motors rider. Neil Keen would represent the team at Midwest events. Dusty Coppage continued as their TT specialist. Australian GP star Kel Carruthers would hit the pavement Nationals on Don Vesco machines.

Ron Pierce joined the Suzuki team of Ron Grant, Art Baumann and Jody Nicholas. The group were again aboard the air-cooled 500 twins.

Kawasaki again had no official team, but helped operated several top back door teams. Their stock went up considerably with the signing of long time Yamaha pilot, Yvon DuHamel. Amateur sensation Rusty Bradley was set to make his Expert debut at Daytona. Privateers Cliff Carr and Hurley Wilvert could also be expected to turn in strong runs. Kawasaki now had the riders to be a legitimate contender in the National arena.

There were big changes for the 1971 AMA GNC schedule. The big announcement was the addition of a 250 Mile race at the Ontario Motor Speedway in California, offering a huge $50,000.00 purse, the richest purse ever offered. It was hoped to attract many international stars and a huge crowd. Other new events were road races at Road Atlanta, (Ga) and Pocono Raceway, (Pa). There were two new dirt tracks; the Corona, Ca Half-Mile, and the Livonia, Mi Mile. Gone for the 1971 season were a slew of tracks; the half-mile races at Palmetto, Cumberland and Reading, the Sante Fe TT and Heidelberg Road Race, and the miles at Santa Rosa, Indy and Sacramento. Most famously the famed Peoria TT was off the schedule for the first time since the ever since 1947. Details were not worked out for a National, though a non-National did run there in 1971. The total of races scheduled races dropped from 27 to 21, surely eliciting a sigh of relief from the teams. The new scheduled offered 3 TT's, 2 short tracks, 7 big points road races, 7 half-miles and 2 miles. This was a loss of 2 TT events, 1 road race, 3 half-miles and a whopping reduction of 3 miles. This meant that Nazareth and Livonia were the only mile tracks for the season, with none being held in California.

A dramatic rule change that would affect riders and fans alike was the adopting of a new National numbering system. The new system was based on the finishing order in GNC points from the 1970 season. The AMA was trying to grow the image of professional motorcycle racing. The idea was also backed by new champ Gene Romero. It was felt fans could tell right away who the best riders were, making it easier to understand GNC racing. Many riders had to give up numbers they had held for years. For example, Bart Markel gave up #4 for #32. Ronnie Rall, was now #30 instead of #52. Time would tell if the move would be accepted.

There was another change in the Championship points system. It was an attempt to even out the disparity between road racing and dirt track. It raised the points paid at events with a lower purse. Many had felt it was unfair to load the road races with so many points, not giving the dirt track riders, who were the mainstay of the series, a fair shake. Jim Rice had dominated much of the 1970 season, but because his wins were all on dirt, he did not fare as well as Dick Mann and Gene Romero who scored well at the pavement events. Gene Romero was one of the proponents of the new system.

Although not directly affecting the National series, Amateurs, the second year riders would now be called Juniors. The Amateur name was not an accurate term as they were considered "Professional" racers and were awarded prize money. Rusty Bradley's big earnings in 1970 painfully pointed this out.

1971 GNC Points System

Position	Minimum to $14,999	15,000 to 24,999	25,000 to 49,999	50,000 to 47,999	75,000 to 99,999
1st	82	91	101	112	124
2	74	82	91	101	112
3	67	74	82	91	101
4	61	67	74	82	91
5	56	61	67	74	82
6	52	56	61	67	74
7	49	52	56	61	67
8	46	49	52	56	61
9	43	46	49	52	56
10	40	43	46	49	52
11	37	40	43	46	49
12	34	37	40	43	46
13	31	34	37	40	43
14	28	31	34	37	40
15	25	28	31	34	37
16	22	25	28	31	34
17	19	22	25	28	31
18	16	19	22	25	28
19	13	16	19	22	25
20	10	13	16	19	22

1971 National Numbers

1. Gene Romero, San Luis Obispo, Ca
2. Jim Rice, Palo Alto, Ca
3. Dave Aldana, Santa Ana, Ca
4. Dick Mann, Richmond, Ca
5. Don Castro, Hollister, Ca
6. Mert Lawwill, San Francisco, Ca
7. Mark Brelsford, San Bruno, Ca
8. Chuck Palmgren, Freehold, NJ
9. Tom Rockwood, Gardena, Ca
10. Gary Nixon, Phoenix, Md
11. Yvon DuHamel, LaSalle, Quebec, Can
12. Larry Palmgren, Freehold, NJ
13. Unassigned
14. Cal Rayborn, Spring Valley, Ca
15. Dave Smith, Lakewood, Ca
16. Dave Sehl, Ontario, Ca
17. Walt Fulton, Hacienda Hts., Ca
18. Jimmy Odom, Fremont, Ca
19. Keith Mashburn, Santa Susana, Ca
20. Eddie Mulder, Burbank, Ca
21. Dusty Coppage, Chatsworth, Ca
22. Frank Gillespie, Orinda, Ca
23. Jody Nicholas, La Mesa, Ca
24. Art Baumann, Brisbane, Ca
25. Don Emde, San Diego, Ca
26. Eddie Wirth, Manhattan Beach, Ca
27. Larry Darr, Mansfield, Oh
28. Royal Sherbert, Largo, Fl
29. Lloyd Houchins, La Crescenta, Ca
30. Ronnie Rall, Mansfield, Oh
31. Skip Van Leeuwen, Hollywood, Ca
32. Bart Markel, Flint, Mi
33. Frank Camillieri, Boston, Mass
34. Geoff Perry, Auckland, New Zealand
35. Rick Deane, Aspen, Co
36. Ken Molyneux, Vancouver, B.C.
37. Ron Pierce, Bakersfield, Ca
38. Dallas Baker, Orange, Ca
39. Ginger Molloy, Huntly, New Zealand
40. Dan Haaby, Orangevale, Ca
41. Mark Williams, Springfield, Ore
42. Ron Grant, Brisbane, Ca
43. Robert, Bulmer, Morrice, Mi
44. Al Gaskill, E. Detroit, Mi
45. Buddy Elmore, El Paso, Tx
46. Paul Bostrom, Lake Isabella, Ca
47. Ralph White, Torrance, Ca
48. Shorty Seabourne, Lawndale, Ca
49. Larry Stone, Clarkston, Ga
50. Nat Williams, Washington, D.C.
51. Unassigned
52. John Weaver, Fort Wayne, Ind
53. Larry Schafer, Hyattsville, Mo
54. Dave Hansen, Hayward, Ca
55. Neil Keen, Decatur, Ill
56. Phil Cullum, N. Little Rock, Ark
57. Jess Thomas, Sea Cliff, NY
58. Leonard Fortune, Webster City, Ia
59. John Klaus, Houston, Tx
60. Ed Varnes, Cochranville, Pa
61. Jimmy Maness, Augusta, Ga
62. Billy Eves, Phoenixville, Pa
63. Mark Mayer, Plainfield, Ind
64. Rod Pink, White Plains, NY
65. Jack Warren, Clio, Mi
66. Ralph Waldman, Fairfield, Ca
67. Mike Meyer, Reisterstown, Pa
68. Jack Forrester, Lafayette, Ind
69. Carl Williamson, Mill Hall, Pa
70. Earl Lout, Rock Island, Ill
71. Earl Myers, Bladensburg, Md
72. Norm Robinson, Spencerport, NY
73. Sonny Burres, Portland, Ore
74. W.T. Ruffner, Fort Worth, Tx
75. Bill O'Brien, Waukegan, Ill
76. Charlie Seale, Lantana, Fl
77. Bob Bailey, Compton, Ca
78. Roger Reiman, Kewanee, Ill
79. Jerry Stokes, Charleston Hts., SC
80. John Black, Portland, Ore
81. Gary Boyce, Aspen, Co
82. Phil Hawk, Atlanta, Ga
83. Glen Adams, Seattle, Wa
84. Charlie Chapple, Flint, Mi
85. Bill Lloyd, Langley Park, Md
86. Bill Elder, Vancouver, Wa
87. Jim Corpe, Tustin, Ca
88. Ray Little, Atlanta, Ga
89. Steve Lathrop, Grand Rapids, Mi
90. Mel Lacher, San Diego, Ca
91. Richard Scott, Santa Monica, Ca
92. Joe Barringer, Whitnel, NC
93. Mike Dottley, Birmingham, Al
94. George Longabaugh, Elverson, Pa
95. Ed Moran, Neptune, NJ
96. George Roeder, Monroeville, Oh

1971
Grand National Championship
Schedule

	Race	Location	Date
1	Houston TT	Houston, Tx	January 29, 1971
2	Houston Short Track	Houston, Tx	January 30, 1971
3	Daytona 200 Mile Road Race	Daytona Beach, Fl	March 14, 1971
4	Road Atlanta 125 Mile Road race	Braselton, Ga	April 25, 1971
5	Louisville Half-Mile	Louisville, Ky	June 5, 1971
6	Loudon 100 Mile Road race	Loudon, NH	June 13, 1971
7	Terre Haute Half-Mile	Terre Haute, Ind	June 20, 1971
8	Columbus Half-Mile	Columbus, Oh	June 27, 1971
9	San Jose Half-Mile	San Jose, Ca	July 5, 1971
10	Kent 100 Mile Road Race	Kent, Wa	July 11, 1971
11	Castle Rock TT	Castle Rock, Wa	July 17, 1971
12	Ascot TT	Gardena, Ca	July 24, 1971
13	Corona Half-Mile	Corona, Ca	July 31, 1971
14	Livonia Mile	Livonia, Mi	August 8, 1971
15	Sante Fe Short Track	Hinsdale, Ill	August 13, 1971
16	Pocono 100 Mile Road Race	Mt. Pocono, Pa	August 22, 1971
17	Talladega 200 Mile Road Race	Talladega, Al	September 5, 1971
18	Ascot Half-Mile	Gardena, Ca	September 25, 1971
19	Oklahoma Half-Mile	Oklahoma City, OK	October 3, 1971
20	Nazareth Mile	Nazareth, Pa	October 9, 1971
21	Ontario 250 Mile Road Race	Ontario, Ca	October 17, 1971

1971 Houston Astrodome Short Track and TT
Mann Wins TT as Odom Almost Doubles

GNC Round #1 & 2 of 21	**Purse:** $20,000.00
Date: January 29 & 30, 1971	**Surface:** Dirt
Type: TT and Short Track	**Course Length:** ¼ mile
Venue: Houston Astrodome	**Laps:** 25 TT, 20 Short Track
Location: Houston, Tx	

One of the largest crowds ever assembled for motorcycle racing in America, estimated at over 60,000 for the weekend, watched two exciting nights of racing at the Houston Astrodome. Ageless veteran Dick Mann was in the right place at the right time for the TT win when leader Jimmy Odom had his Triumph's rear wheel collapse on the last lap. Odom came back in an exciting short track race Saturday night. He and Mark Brelsford raced hard, but Odom wasn't going to let another victory get away. If not for the broken wheel during the TT race, Odom may have been the 'Domes first double winner.

TT National

Time Trials
Jimmy Odom started out the weekend right by putting the Les Edwards built, Cycle Imports-sponsored Triumph on the pole with a 28.60. Mark Brelsford finally abandoned the Harley 350 Sprint of the previous two years, going the opposite extreme and was aboard the Jim Belland prepared 900cc XLR. He was 2nd fastest at 28.66. Unfortunately a cracked engine case put him out for the rest of the night. Rounding out the top 5 were Eddie Mulder, Skip Van Leeuwen and rookie John Hateley, all Triumph mounted. The entire top 5 were Ascot TT regulars. GNC champ Gene Romero was very lucky; he qualified 37th and only made the program as an alternate.

Heats
Jimmy Odom led Heat 1 out of the gate, but the race was stopped when Jerry Powell fell on lap 4. Powell didn't make the restart allowing first alternate Gene Romero (Tri) in the program. Odom again led after the restart, chased to the flag by 1969 Houston TT winner Skip Van Leeuwen (Tri) and defending race champion Jim Rice (BSA). New BSA team member Don Emde followed.

Rookie John Hateley led Heat 2 wire-to-wire on the Jack Hateley-tuned Red Line Triumph. BSA factory star Dave Aldana finished 2nd and Dave Hansen (Tri) was 3rd.

Dick Mann was fast and smooth on yet another factory BSA, stretching his lead to a nice advantage at the finish. Ascot regulars Paul Bostrom (Tri), Dan Haaby and Dusty Coppage, (both Yamaha mounted), battled hard for the runner-up position with the JK Cycles sponsored-Bostrom taking a slim advantage at the flag.

Semi
Dallas Baker (BSA) pulled the holeshot at the beginning of the "last chance race". Dusty Coppage ran a close 2nd. Gene Romero had fortune riding with him this night, barely making the program and just nipping Chuck Palmgren (Yam) for the last ticket to the National.

National
John Hateley continued to impress, grabbing the holeshot for the National and leading the first lap. Jimmy Odom was right on Hateley's rear wheel and was quickly by with Dick Mann right with him. Hateley missed a gear and was quickly passed by Skip Van Leeuwen and Dave Aldana. Defending champ Rice fell on lap 5. He quickly remounted, but had lost a lot of ground. Odom and Mann pulled away from the pack containing Van Leeuwen, Aldana and Hateley. At the halfway point Mann began heavily pressuring Odom. The two banged and bumped with Mann briefly surging ahead only to have Odom regain the lead. Jim Rice was ripping through the pack and made it up to 6th place as the laps began to run out. Odom looked to have the win iced, although Mann was right behind. Going into the last lap, Odom's rear wheel failed and Mann scooted by to an easy win. The huge crowd went nuts. Van Leeuwen came

in 2nd, Aldana 3rd, Dave Hansen 4th, Gene Romero the luckiest rider of the night was 5th, Jim Rice with a nice charge to 6th, Dan Haaby 7th, John Hateley 8th in his National debut, Dusty Coppage 9th with Odom scored in 10th spot.

Short Track

A huge, history making crowd numbering over 35,000, watched a determined Jimmy Odom avenge his previous nights disappointment. Odom battled to an extremely tight victory over Mark Brelsford and Charlie Chapple.

Time Trials

Factory Harley Sprints tuned by Jim Belland topped qualifying: Mark Brelsford was the fastest at 15.10 and defending race champion Mert Lawwill turned a 15.33. Speedway star Barry Briggs was 3rd on his 250 Yamaha twin powered machine.

Heats

Mark Brelsford won Heat 1 over new teammate Rex Beauchamp and Tom Rockwood (Tri).

In Heat 2, Mert Lawwill battled with Frank Gillespie (Oss) on his way to the fastest heat of the night. Jimmy Odom (Bul) was 3rd.

Yamaha teammates Dan Haaby and Keith Mashburn had a race long battle in Heat 3. Both were on Yamaha DT-1 based machines. Keeping hopes alive for a second 'Dome win was Dick Mann (BSA) in 3rd.

In the last heat, Rookie John Hateley (Tri) scored his second heat race win of the weekend. Veteran Neil Keen (Yam) was 2nd and rookie Wayne Hosaka (Bul) 3rd.

Semis

The first 6 finishers from each 8-lap semi moved on to the National. In Semi 1, Mert Lawwill battled early with Dan Haaby and Keith Mashburn. Haaby had ignition troubles and dropped out. Dick Mann was done for the night after falling early in the race. Mashburn ran strong, nosing by Lawwill for the lead. This was short-lived as Lawwill regained the top spot with Jimmy Odom also going by Mashburn. Frank Gillespie put on a late charge and also knocked Mashburn back a spot. At the finish it was Lawwill, Odom, Gillespie, Mashburn and Chuck Palmgren (Yam).

Semi 2 saw a spectacular run by Dave Aldana. Getting little straight away speed out of the BSA Starfire based machine, Aldana ran his machine wide open through the corners. He blasted by early leader Mark Brelsford and John Hateley (Tri). Aldana electrified the crowd by riding the high line. Hateley and Brelsford maintained 2nd and 3rd.

National

An altercation between Mark Brelsford and John Hateley caused a complete restart. Brelsford got a nasty hand injury, but made the restart. Mert Lawwill took control on the restart and appeared to be on his way to a repeat victory. Dave Aldana's night ended on lap 2 when his overcooked engine gave out. Lawwill ran strong, but was shadowed by Brelsford and Jimmy Odom. Unbelievably, Lawwill lost the front end of his Sprint on lap 12 and fell. Odom took advantage of the ensuing confusion and captured the lead. Brelsford managed to power by Odom for a couple laps. On lap 16 Odom moved back into the lead. Odom led to the flag still closely chased by Brelsford. Chuck Palmgren had been closing on the front duo and appeared to have a shot at 2nd till Charlie Chapple arrived. He put a bump and grind on Palmgren to take 2nd spot. Chapple scored his best ever Grand National placing with Palmgren falling clear back to 9th place.

Results

Race: 20 Lap TT National
Race Time: 9:49.62

Rank	Rider	Number	Make
1.	Dick Mann, Richmond, Ca	4	BSA
2.	Skip Van Leeuwen, Hollywood, Ca	31	Tri
3.	Dave Aldana, Santa Ana, Ca	3	BSA
4.	Dave Hansen, Hayward, Ca	54	Tri
5.	Gene Romero, San Luis Obispo, Ca	1	Tri
6.	Jim Rice, Palo Alto, Ca	2	BSA
7.	Dan Haaby, Orangevale, Ca	40	Yam
8.	John Hateley, Van Nuys, Ca	43R	Tri
9.	Dusty Coppage, Chatsworth, Ca	21	Yam
10.	Jimmy Odom, Fremont, Ca	18	Tri
11.	Dallas Baker, Orange, Ca	38	BSA
12.	Paul Bostrom, Lake Isabella, Ca	46	Tri

Race: Junior Final

Rank	Rider	Number	Make
1.	Gary Scott, Baldwin Park, Ca	64R	Bul
2.	Loyal Penn, Palos Verdes Estates, Ca	58X	Tri
3.	Roger Ring, National City, Ca	25R	Tri

Race: Mile 25 Lap Short Track National
Race Time: 6:46.84

Rank	Rider	Number	Make
1.	Jimmy Odom, Fremont, Ca	18	Bul
2.	Mark Brelsford, San Bruno, Ca	7	HD
3.	Charlie Chapple, Flint, Mi	84	Yam
4.	Keith Mashburn, Santa Susana, Ca	19	Yam
5.	Rex Beauchamp, Drayton Plains, Mi	34E	HD
6.	Dallas Baker, Orange, Ca	38	Oss
7.	Mert Lawwill, San Francisco, Ca	6	HD
8.	Wayne Hosaka, San Diego, Ca	55X	Bul
9.	Chuck Palmgren, Freehold, NJ	8	Yam
10.	John Hateley, Van Nuys, Ca	43R	Tri
11.	Frank Gillespie, Orinda, Ca	22	Oss
12.	Dave Aldana, Santa Ana, Ca	3	BSA

Race: Junior Final

Rank	Rider	Number	Make
1.	Kenny Roberts, Menlo Park, Ca	80Y	Yam
2.	Gary Scott, Baldwin Park, Ca	64R	Bul
3.	Mike Kidd, Hurst, Tx	72N	Bul

Grand National Points Standings after Round 2

Rank	Rider	Pts
1.	Jim Odom	122
2.	Dave Aldana	101
3.	Dallas Baker	89
4.	John Hateley	86
5.	Dick Mann	82
6.	Skip Van Leeuwen	74
7.	Mark Brelsford	74
8.	Charlie Chapple	67
9.	Dave Hansen	61
10.	Keith Mashburn	61

Extra Extra

- Saturday's short track crowd was the largest to ever watch a GNC dirt track event.
- A total of 212 Expert and Junior riders turned out for Friday's TT. The following nights short track had 225 combined entries.
- Cal Rayborn was disqualified from the short track race after officials claimed he had taken three qualification attempts. Rayborn vehemently denied the charge and although he had had turned a plenty quick time to make the program, he was out.
- A TT exhibition featuring Jim Rice, Skip Van Leeuwen, Jimmy Odom, Dusty Coppage and Mark Brelsford was run after Saturday's short track. Van Leeuwen took the win with Brelsford and Odom tangling on the last lap.
- Juniors Gary Scott and Kenny Roberts put on a great short track battle. Scott led most of the way with Roberts squeaking by with two laps to go. Scott won Friday's TT event. Roberts was put out of action by a spill.
- Rookie Wayne Hosaka was a talented San Diego, California racer whose 8th place finish in the short track gave an indication of his racing potential. Soon after Houston, Hosaka received a broken neck at a regular event at Ascot Park. He was paralyzed and lost most of his feeling from the neck down. Confined to a wheelchair, he successfully overcame the huge new challenges presented to him. He found work in the emerging world of computers. Hosaka became a renowned artist, mainly using a mouth brush to complete his paintings. In 1995, Hosaka started a website called flattrack.com on the burgeoning Worldwide Web. It gave a new center to the world of flat track racing, where ideas could be exchanged and information posted. Complications from his accident troubled him over the years and he passed away on January 16, 2011. While maybe not fulfilling his desire to become a famous racer, Wayne ending up touching far more people as result of his outgoing, positive personality, which was expressed through flattrack.com.

1971 Daytona 200
Mann Repeats at Daytona!

GNC Round #3 of 21 **Date:** March 14, 1971 **Type:** Road Race **Venue:** Daytona International Speedway **Location:** Daytona, Florida	**Purse:** $32,500.00 **Surface:** Pavement **Course Length:** 3.81 miles **Laps:** 53 **Distance:** 200 Miles

The 1971 running of the Daytona 200 had a lot in common with the 1970 event, everything was just bigger! Dick Mann repeated his win, this year on a BSA, with the Honda factory a no-show. National Champion Gene Romero was runner-up again on a Triumph. New BSA team member Don Emde was impressive riding Dick Mann's 1970 regular season bike. The BSA/Triumph team spent lavish amounts on travel, riders and machines. The top four riders, Americans Dick Mann, Gene Romero and English imports Mike Hailwood and Paul Smart were given the latest machines. The new 'low-boys", featured redesigned frames and fairings. The rest of the team rode 1970 machines that had been tweaked by the American teams for more reliability. Besides the aforementioned riders, others were; Dave Aldana, Jim Rice and Don Emde, (BSA) and Gary Nixon, Don Castro and Tom Rockwood (Triumph).

Kawasaki had a formidable crew of riders including 1963 Daytona winner Ralph White, Yamaha convert Yvon DuHamel on factory machines as well as Mike Duff, Cliff Carr, Ginger Molloy, Walt Fulton, Rusty Bradley and Dave Smith. The Suzuki team was largely the same as last year; Ron Grant, Art Baumann and Geoff Perry returned, joined by Ron Pierce. Yamaha's effort was headed by Kel Carruthers on a semi-factory, Don Vesco aided ride, along with Chuck Palmgren, Dusty Coppage, Royal Sherbert, Frank Camillieri, and Jimmy Odom. Honda had bowed out this year, but Gary Fisher was aboard a very fast Krause CB750-based machine.

The Harley-Davidson team hoped to have the worst of their problems ironed out. Reliability was still an issue, but a ton of work over the last year had raised horsepower and speed. 1964 GNC champ and 200 Mile winner Roger Reiman joined stars such as 1968 and '69 winner Cal Rayborn, Mark Brelsford, Mert Lawwill, Dave Sehl and rookie Rex Beauchamp. Other Harley faithfuls included Larry Darr, Ron Widman, DeWayne Keeter and Larry Schaefer.

Tragedy struck on lap 2 of the National. Rookie Expert Rusty Bradley got caught up in front pack traffic and was thrown from his motorcycle. He suffered severe head injuries and never regained consciousness. The well liked Bradley had won the 1970 Amateur event aboard a Kawasaki. His performances had earned him a spot on the Kawasaki team and had a big future in racing. It was the first fatality at the Daytona event since 1953.

Time Trials

The qualifying procedure for 1971 season was changed from a flying lap around the big oval to a lap around the 2.5 mile road course. Not surprising anyone a Beezumph took the top spot. Daytona first timer Paul Smart replete in European type-goggles, styled his way to the top speed of 105.800 mph. A pleasant surprise was that Harley-Davidson riders took the next two positions; Cal Rayborn at 105.678 and Mark Brelsford a 105.613. Don Emde was next on Mann's "old" hi boy with a 105.087. Mike Hailwood rounded out the top 5 with a 105.063 lap. Gary Fisher's big Honda turned a 105.039, Kel Carruthers had the first Yamaha at 104.678, Walt Fulton on his Erv Kanemoto-tuned three cylinder Kawasaki which ran a 104.634, Jody Nicholas had the fastest Suzuki with a 104.534 and Jim Rice rounded out the top ten on his BSA hi boy with a 104.129. Last year's winner Dick Mann ran a 104.019 lap for 11th.

National

Yvon DuHamel pulled the holeshot but was soon swallowed up by a fast pack containing Gary Fisher, Paul Smart, Mike Hailwood and Dick Mann. Lap 2 saw the Rusty Bradley accident occur which also collected Steve McLaughlin and Duane McDaniels. McLaughlin walked away; McDaniels suffered a fractured finger and shoulder injuries. Mert Lawwill had a tire let go on lap 12, suffering a broken elbow and wrist. Fisher led the talented front pack till his Honda slowed and then dropped out with a broken cam chain. Smart, Hailwood and Mann diced heavily for a number of laps. Both Smart and Hailwood swapped the lead with Mann often in 2nd place. Rayborn had been running with leaders till transmission troubles hit. He would continue after repairs, but well down in the order. Running just behind the lead pack, Kel Carruthers, Don Emde, Gene Romero, Roger Reiman, and others who traded positions all over. Smart assumed the lead on lap 13 with Hailwood retiring two laps later with a burnt valve. Smart and Mann continued to run together with Mann testing the waters by taking the lead for a couple laps before Smart reassumed command. Behind the lead duo were Gene Romero and Roger Reiman with Don Emde on the move. As the race neared the 40 lap mark, Smart's BSA began to falter. First Mann and then Romero, Emde and Reiman went by. On lap 42, Smart was too out with valve trouble. Mann now had a clear shot at a second Daytona win and didn't put a wheel wrong to the flag. Romero survived a challenge from young Emde to repeat his runner-up finish of the previous year. Roger Reiman helped regain some Harley pride in 4th for his best 200 finish since 1965. Dirt trackers Jimmy Odom and Chuck Palmgren rode their Yamahas to 5th and 6th. Journalist/racer Jess Thomas had his best finish at the speedway in 7th. Tom Rockwood was 8th, Dave Smith the first Kawasaki in 9th with Kel Carruthers rounding out the top 10. Mann set a new record speed for the event, almost 2 mph faster than his previous year's win.

Results

Race: 200 Mile Road Race National
Race Time: 1:54:55.62 (104.737 MPH) New Record

Rank	Rider	Number	Make
1.	Dick Mann, Richmond, Ca	4	BSA
2.	Gene Romero, San Luis Obispo, Ca	1	Tri
3.	Don Emde, San Diego, Ca	25	BSA
4.	Roger Reiman, Kewanee, Ill	55	HD
5.	Jimmy Odom, Fremont, Ca	18	Yam
6.	Chuck Palmgren, Freehold, NJ	181	Yam
7.	Jess Thomas, Sea Cliff, NY	157	Tri
8.	Tom Rockwood, Gardena, Ca	9	Tri
9.	Dave Smith, Lakewood, Ca	15	Kaw
10.	Kel Carruthers, Sidney, Aus	73	Yam
11.	Frank Camillieri, Chelsea, Mass	33	Yam
12.	Martin Carney, London, Eng	147	Yam
13.	James Dunn, Everett, Mi	171	Yam
14.	Fred Guttner, Detroit, Mi	69	Yam
15.	Cliff Carr, Waterdown, Mass	89	Kaw
16.	Don Castro, Hollister, Ca	5	Tri
17.	Bill Manley, Long Beach, Ca	29	BSA
18.	Dave Aldana, Santa Ana, Ca	3	BSA
19.	Rick Deane, Aspen, Co	35	Yam
20.	Ron Widman, St. Louis, Mo	98	HD

Race: 100 Mile Junior National
Race Time: 1:58.27 (99.925 MPH)

Rank	Rider	Number	Make
1.	Dennis Ponseleit, Sarasota, Fla	28	Hon
2.	Jim Allen, Islington, Ont., Can	65	Yam
3.	John Lysight, Tracy, Que., Can	9	Kaw

Grand National Points Standings after Round 3

Rank	Rider	Pts
1.	Jim Odom	189
2.	Dick Mann	183
3.	Gene Romero	147
4.	Dave Aldana	123
5.	Chuck Palmgren	104
6.	Dallas Baker	89
7.	John Hateley	86
8.	Don Emde	82
9.	Skip Van Leeuwen	74
10.	Mark Brelsford	74
11.	Roger Reiman	74

Extra Extra

- It was the 30th running of the Daytona Classic.
- A crowd of 38,000 turned out.
- There were 89 riders from 6 countries in the starting field.
- There were only 40 bikes running at the finish.
- It was BSA's first Daytona win since Bobby Hill led a team sweep in 1954.
- The win for Dick Mann was his second in a row in two ways. He was also coming off a win at the Houston TT.
- Mann took home around $6600.00 for winning the race, his milestone 20th GNC victory.
- Gene Romero got $3300.00 for second, Don Emde $2300.00 in third.
- While Paul Smart fell out of the running, he was only second to Mann at the pay window. Daytona paid $125.00 a lap to the leader with Smart racking up nearly $4000.00!
- There was a huge difference in speed between the new Beezumph lo-boys and the 1970 versions. Most of the hi-boys were down about 2 seconds per lap compared to the new bikes.
- Most of the heavy hitters for Kawasaki and Suzuki had trouble. Dave Smith was the first Kawasaki rider in 9th place with Cliff Carr 15th. The team bikes of Yvon DuHamel and Ralph White were 53rd and 64th. Not what was hoped for, but better than Suzuki's day. None of their bikes finished the race. Ron Pierce was the first rider home in 51st place.
- Jimmy Odom's 5th place finish kept him narrowly in the GNC points lead over Dick Mann, 189 to 183 points. The rest of the top 5 was; Gene Romero, Dave Aldana and Chuck Palmgren.
- Kel Carruthers repeated his Lightweight win of 1970.
- Dennis Ponseleit on a Honda 750 was the surprise winner in the Junior event after leader Mike Lane dropped out.
- In 1972, Rusty Bradley's parents and the AMA started a scholarship for racers who were college students. Rusty was an engineering student at the University of Texas at Arlington. His parents stayed active in the racing community for years. The scholarship is still active today.

1.	Paul Smart	Tri	105.800 MPH
2.	Cal Rayborn	HD	105.678
3.	Mark Brelsford	HD	105.613
4.	Don Emde	BSA	105.087
5.	Mike Hailwood	BSA	105.063
6.	Gary Fisher	Hon	105.039
7.	Kel Carruthers	Yam	104.678
8.	Walt Fulton	Kaw	104.674
9.	Jody Nicholas	Suz	104.534
10.	Jim Rice	BSA	104.129
11.	Dick Mann	BSA	104.019
12.	Ginger Molloy	Kaw	104.011
13.	Gene Romero	Tri	103.924
14.	Art Baumann	Suz	103.516
15.	Ron Pierce	Suz	103.399
16.	Hurley Wilvert	Kaw	103.213
17.	Rusty Bradley	Kaw	103.127
18.	Ralph White	Kaw	102.810
19.	Don Castro	Tri	102.620
20.	Cliff Carr	Kaw	102.251

1971 Road Atlanta
Carruther's Conquers Road Atlanta!

GNC Round #4 of 21 **Date:** April 25, 1971 **Type:** Road Race **Venue:** Road Atlanta **Location:** Flowery Branch, Ga	**Purse:** $15,000.00 **Surface:** Pavement **Course Length:** 2.52 Miles **Laps:** 49 **Distance:** 125 Miles

Kel Carruthers took a historic first win at the character filled Road Atlanta Raceway. He presented Yamaha with it's first pavement "big bike" GNC win ever, (though Dick Mann won a rare 250 National at Nelson Ledges in 1965). The Australian who had won the 1969 250 World Championship had relocated to the United States to pursue the lucrative AMA road race Nationals. The talented rider/tuner was aboard a Don Vesco owned, factory supported Yamaha. Carruthers had made forays into U.S. racing before, but was pursuing the pavement Nationals full-time.

Carruthers took the lead midway from Cal Rayborn who dropped out with mechanical trouble. Daytona winner Dick Mann finished 2nd after a lengthy scrap with Suzuki's Jody Nicholas, (later disqualified for rules infractions, see Extras). Third went to veteran campaigner Ralph White aboard a factory Kawasaki.

The first-time National at the twisty 2.5 mile facility was a challenge for most riders. The many turns made it difficult to easily set up other riders for a pass. Experienced pavement scratchers took easily to the track. It caused full time dirt trackers to often create their own "lines".

Dick Mann's 2nd place allowed him take the GNC points lead away from Jimmy Odom who finished 11th on the day. Their totals were 265 to 226 points respectively. GNC Champ Gene Romero (6th in the National), maintained third with 203 points. Don Emdes's fine 5th place propelled him from eighth in points to fourth with 143. Carruthers win shot him from way back to a solid fifth in points with 137. Dave Aldana dropped back to sixth with 123.

Heats

The first of two short 5-lap heats was led away by Kawasaki teammates Yvon DuHamel and Ralph White. Don Emde showed he was also a quick study of the new course, moving by for the win on the factory BSA triple. Jody Nicholas had tucked in right behind Emde and took 2nd.

Heat 2 saw Cal Rayborn (HD) and Kel Carruthers battled heavily through the race with Carruthers coming out on top. While everyone knew his reputation, this was the first time he showed his abilities as he defeated the best U.S. road racer. Dick Mann motored behind in 3rd on his Daytona winning BSA.

National

Cal Rayborn's thundering factory XRTT750 led the pack into Turn 1 with Yvon DuHamel and Dick Mann close behind. The end of lap 1 saw Rayborn still up front with resurgent veteran Ralph White moving to 2nd, DuHamel 3rd, Mann 4th and Kel Carruthers 5th. On lap 2 DuHamel had a minor off-course excursion letting Mann by. Mann next managed to get by White. DuHamel kept pace behind, but on lap 3, threw it away at the "bridge turn". Carruthers began a charge, moving by Mann and latching onto leader Rayborn's rear wheel. Dave Aldana moved up behind BSA teammate Mann in 4th only to have his transmission go out on lap 8. As the first 10 laps ticked by, Carruthers was sizing up Rayborn all over the course, biding his time. Further back Jody Nicholas had made his way through the field and was harassing Mann for third with White close behind. Lap 16 saw Nicholas pass Mann only to have the favor quickly returned. On lap 18, Carruthers moved by Rayborn for the lead and steadily pulled away. At midway he had nearly 10 second lead over the field. The battle for 3rd continued to rage between Mann and Nicholas with White hanging on to 4th with Emde 5th. Rayborn dropped out on lap 27 after losing 3rd gear, moving everybody behind up a spot.

Pit stops started after the 30 lap mark; Carruthers was in and out quickly, never losing his lead. Mann lost 2nd, momentarily to Nicholas, whose stop or lack thereof, turned into a fiasco; it led to Nicholas and team being disqualified, (see *Extras*). Nicholas never received a signal to stop and ran out of fuel on lap 42.

Returning to the racing, Carruthers had a huge lead and was lapping the field. Mann was a solid 2nd followed by White and Gary Nixon (Tri) who had methodically worked through the pack, knocking Emde back to 5th. GNC Champ Gene Romero was 6th, Walt Fulton 7th, Jim Rice 8th, Robert Winters 9th and Cliff Carr 10th.

Results

Race: 125 Mile Road Race National
Race Time: 1:26.03 (89.946 MPH)

Rank	Rider	Number	Make
1.	Kel Carruthers, El Cajon, Ca	73	Yam
2.	Dick Mann, Richmond, Ca	4	BSA
3.	Ralph White, Torrance, Ca	47	Kaw
4.	Gary Nixon, Phoenix, Md	10	Tri
5.	Don Emde, San Diego, Ca	25	BSA
6.	Gene Romero, San Luis Obispo, Ca	1	Tri
7.	Walt Fulton, Hacienda Heights, Ca	17	Kaw
8.	Jim Rice, Palo Alto, Ca	2	BSA
9.	Robert Winters, Ft. Smith, Ark	46	Kaw
10.	Cliff Carr, Watertown, Mass	87	Kaw
11.	Ron Grant, Brisbane, Ca	42	Suz
12.	Jimmy Odom, Fremont, Ca	18	Yam
13.	Duane McDaniels, Milford, Mi	58	Yam
14.	Jess Thomas, Sea Cliff, NY	57	Tri
15.	Royal Sherbert, Largo, Fl	28	Yam
16.	Al Gaskill, E. Detroit, Mi	44	Yam
17.	Jeff Sperry, Bakersfield, Ca	41	Yam
18.	Dewayne Keeter, Ojai, Ca	85	Yam
19.	Eddie Mulder, Burbank, Ca	20	Tri
20.	Johnny Isaacs, Riverside, Ca	13	Yam

Race: Junior/Novice 50 Mile Final
Race Time: 35:06.00 (86.153 MPH)

Rank	Rider	Number	Make
1.	Kenny Roberts, Redwood City, Ca	80	Yam
2.	Jerry Christopher, W. Covina, Ca	83	Yam
3.	Jerry Greene, San Mateo, Ca	41	Yam

Grand National Points Standings after Round 4

Rank	Rider	Pts
1.	Dick Mann	265
2.	Jimmy Odom	226
3.	Gene Romero	203
4.	Don Emde	143
5.	Kel Carruthers	137
6.	Dave Aldana	123
7.	Chuck Palmgren	104
8.	Jim Rice	98
9.	Dallas Baker	89
10.	Jess Thomas	87

Extra Extra

- A great crowd of 20,000 turned out for the event.
- It was a double win weekend for Kel Carruthers; he also captured the Lightweight event.
- Besides a bonus from Yamaha for it's first big bike win, Carruthers took home around $5000.00 from the purse and contingencies.
- Carruthers self-tuned, Don Vesco supported, semi-factory Yamaha churned turned out an impressive 62 rear wheel horsepower.
- Kenny Roberts received $480.00 for winning the Junior/Novice Final.
- Ralph White turned in a great podium ride. One of the very few riders to win both the Daytona 200 and Springfield Mile, White had not finished a National road race since 1966.
- It was definitely an experienced trio up front at Road Atlanta. Kel Carruthers was 33 years old, Dick Mann 37 and Ralph White 36!

The Suzuki Refueling Incident

In an interesting bit of strategy, Team Suzuki interpreted AMA pit rules to mean they could pit anywhere on the course that was "safe". Thinking this might give them a quicker stop, they set up their refueling equipment in a Turn 7, away from the pits. First into the impromptu pit area was Ron Pierce. Unfortunately for the team, an official witnessed the incident and sent them packing. During the confusion, front runner Jody Nicholas ran out of fuel.

GNC Round #5 of 21	**Purse:** $10,000.00
Date: June 5, 1971	**Surface:** Limestone
Type: Half-Mile	**Course Length:** ½ Mile
Venue: Louisville Downs	**Laps:** 20
Location: Louisville, Ky	**Distance:** 10 Miles

Canadian cushion master Dave Sehl won his second consecutive Louisville race in a row and the third of his career at the famed Louisville Downs facility, the first half-mile of the year. Sehl had to work hard, coming from the semi to get into the main, but he and super tuner Babe DeMay had it all put together for the National. Dick Mann led till late in the race till a swing arm bolt broke. Limestone specialists Larry Darr and Jack Warren, (also from the semi), rounded out the podium. While British machinery did well in qualifying and the heats and threatened in the National, it was the fifth win in a row for Harley-Davidson at Louisville; they had won every event since the races inception in 1968.

Predictably, cushion specialists dominated the field at Louisville with just four of the top ten in GNC points making the main. Dick Mann ended up 11th at the race, maintained the top GNC points spot with 302 points. GNC Champ Gene Romero managed a 9th on the night, moving up a notch to second with 246 points. Jimmy Odom did not make the race and dropped back to third with 226 points. Dave Aldana who finished a strong 5th jumped a couple of spots from sixth to fourth with 179 points. Jim Rice was right behind Aldana in the race and also moved up behind him in points with 150. Don Emde competed at Louisville, but failed to make the main and dropped from 4th to 6th. Dave Sehl's win gave him his first points of the season and didn't break into the top 10.

Time Trials

Early day moisture in the cushion gave speed to the British teams; in fact there was only one Harley-Davidson in the top 5 during qualifying. Dave Aldana put the fastest lap of the day in aboard his BSA at 25.49. Back from Daytona injuries was Mert Lawwill who was 2nd on his factory Harley with a 25.64 lap. Don Castro (Tri) was 3rd fastest at 25.76. Jim Rice (BSA) was 4th at 25.90 and Ronnie Rall was 5th, turning a 26.20 on the Bill Kennedy Triumph. Dave Sehl was just a tick off at 26.21.

Heats

It was an all British show in Heat 1 as Dave Aldana stormed to victory in leading Jim Rice and Jody Nicholas, (in a rare east coast appearance aboard the Harold Allison Norton). Jack Warren on another Norton was 4th. Aldana's heat time was the fastest of the night by a whopping 2 seconds.

Heat 2 had the best race of the night with cushion stars Bart Markel (HD), Larry Darr (HD), Al Gaskill (BSA), Ronnie Rall and all around fast Mert Lawwill fighting for the transfer spots. Larry Darr controlled most of the race and took the win despite early pressure from 3-time Louisville winner Markel riding up high. Markel's high line did not pay off as Gaskill and Rall snuck by down low. Markel and Lawwill were semi bound.

There were two Sehl's in Heat 3, but the winner was rookie Doug aboard a Triumph. Dick Mann (BSA) made it close, catching Sehl on the last lap. Californian Dave Smith (Tri) took the last direct transfer. Last year's winner Dave Sehl was headed to the semi.

Semi

The "Last Chance" race saw a talented field fight for the three remaining National tickets. Favorites for the win included Dave Sehl, Bart Markel and GNC Champ Gene Romero. Nobody told Jack Warren though and the diminutive Michigan racer blasted to the win with Sehl and Romero in tow. Legend Bart Markel just couldn't go forward and was done for the night.

National

Larry Darr and Dick Mann battled early on lap 1 with Mann soon taking the advantage. Larry Darr maintained 2nd and Dave Sehl with a great back row start was right behind. Mann pulled a good gap on lap 2 as Sehl moved into 2nd, Darr now 3rd and Jim Rice in 4th. Just behind, Gene Romero had a good run going till he slipped down on lap 5. Romero got back in the running, but well back in the order. Jody Nicholas was on the move and slipped by Rice for 4th late in the race

Mann looked to have the race in the bag as he pulled away till a swing arm bolt gave way, dropping the former GNC champ from the race. Sehl assumed the top spot with a big lead over Darr. Jack Warren caught fire late in the race, passing Rice and battling by fellow Norton rider Nicholas for 3rd. He reeled in Darr on the final lap, but had run out of time to complete the pass. Both were closing the distance on Sehl, but it was too little too late as the smooth Canadian took the win.

Results

Race: 20 Lap Half-Mile National
Race Time: 9:09.24

Rank	Rider	Number	Make
1.	Dave Sehl, Atlanta, Ga	16	HD
2.	Larry Darr, Mansfield, Oh	27	HD
3.	Jack Warren, Millington, Mi	65	Nor
4.	Jody Nicholas, Newport Beach, Ca	23	Nor
5.	Dave Aldana, Santa Ana, Ca	3	BSA
6.	Jim Rice, Palo Alto, Ca	2	BSA
7.	Doug Sehl, Waterdown, Ont., Can	6T	Tri
8.	Ronnie Rall, Mansfield, Oh	30	BSA
9.	Gene Romero, San Luis Obispo, Ca	1	Tri
10.	Al Gaskill, E. Detroit, Mi	44	BSA
11.	Dick Mann, Richmond, Ca	4	BSA
12.	Dave Smith, Lakewood, Ca	15	Tri

Race: Junior Final

Rank	Rider	Number	Make
1.	Randy Scott, Carnilla, Ore	57Q	Tri
2.	Carl LeBlanc, Decatur, Al	77L	Tri
3.	Keith Ulicki, Kenosha, Wi	87G	HD

Grand National Points Standings after Round 5

Rank	Rider	Pts
1.	Dick Mann	302
2.	Gene Romero	246
3.	Jimmy Odom	226
4.	Dave Aldana	179
5.	Jim Rice	150
6.	Don Emde	143
7.	Kel Carruthers	137
8.	Chuck Palmgren	104
9.	Dallas Baker	89
10.	Jess Thomas	87

- A huge SRO crowd of 12,200 fans watched the race.
- Though there were only two Harleys in the field, they took the top spots. The rest of the field was a nice mix of four BSA's, two Triumph's and two Norton's.
- The two Norton's in the top 5 of a dirt track National was a rare occurrence indeed!
- Mann's unusual DNF spoiled what probably would have been the first non-Harley victory at Louisville. That occurrence was still a long way off.
- Doug Sehl was the only rookie to make the National, finishing 7th.
- Expert Pat Gosch, 27 years, from Omaha, Ne, passed away May 11, 1971 from injuries he received from a crash at Ascot Park on April 30th. He had been in a coma from the time of the accident. Pat was a great racer and had held National Number 47 from 1967-'70 and was a front-runner on the Midwest fair circuit.

1971 Loudon Road Race
Brelsford Shocks at Loudon!
Only Iron XR Road Race Win

GNC Round #6 of 21	**Purse:** $20,000.00
Date: June 13, 1971	**Surface:** Pavement
Type: Road Race	**Course Length**: 1.6 Miles
Venue: Bryar Motorsports Complex	**Laps**: 63
Location: Loudon, NH	**Distance:** 100 Miles

In a thrilling last lap, last corner shootout, Mark Brelsford took a very narrow win at the Loudon GNC over Kel Carruthers. Brelsford had come from deep in the pack to interrupt a duel between Carruthers and Dick Mann. It was Brelsford's first pavement win, made even more impressive by defeating such talented foes. He also delivered the only road race victory for the troubled Harley iron XR. The short nature of the course helped the hot running machines make it home. Teammate Cal Rayborn came home in 7th spot. It was Brelsford's 3rd GNC win; showing his versatility all had come in three different disciplines, half-mile, TT and road race. Such versatility was the hallmark of past champions and Brelsford was just getting warmed up.

Dick Mann's strong Loudon finish allowed him to maintain the top spot in the GNC chase with 376 points. GNC Champ Gene Romero, much like 1970 was running strong and consistent and his 4th place finish kept Mann close with 307 points. Jimmy Odom failed to score any points at Loudon but was still third with 226 points. Kel Carruthers 2nd place finish in the National moved him from seventh to a tie for fourth with Dave Aldana, (11th at Loudon), with 216.

Jim Rice was 6th at 196. Don Emde, 7th at 192. Mark Brelsford's win moved him into the top ten for the first time since Houston, eighth in points with 165. Chuck Palmgren and Dave Smith rounded out the top ten.

National

Veteran Ralph White (Kaw) showed he still had the necessary fire and led the talented pack off the line. Teammate Yvon DuHamel soon took over with Kel Carruthers (Yam) and Dick Mann (BSA) also giving chase. Carruthers passed DuHamel for the lead on lap 12 with Mann still in 3rd. Mann took the point on the 17th circuit only to have Carruthers go back in front a few laps later. DuHamel stayed with the lead pack through the race, but was hampered by repeated due to his Kawasaki's penchant for fuel. Early front runner White retired with mechanical problems. Where was Mark Brelsford? His crew had fitted a new front tire on the Ron Alexander tuned- XRTT and he was cautiously scuffing it in and was slowly moving through the pack. He did not break into the top ten till the race neared the 20 lap mark.

As the race progressed, veterans Carruthers and Mann played an enjoyable game of cat and mouse, biding their time. Mann patiently studied the former World Champions lines. Although taking the lead briefly on lap 30, Mann was mostly content to motor along. Carruthers likewise wasn't pushing unnecessarily hard. That is until Mark Brelsford showed up around lap 50. The two leaders began to pick up the pace because of Brelsford's pressure. Mann was fighting a chattering rear brake and ran wide in a slow corner, allowing Brelsford by. Brelsford latched onto Carruthers and went by for the lead on lap 54. Carruthers turned up the wick and repassed the upstart dirt tracker two laps later. Brelsford tucked in behind the Yamaha and stayed close over the closing laps. As they entered into the last lap they encountered a bunch of lapped traffic in the final corners. Entering the last turn, Brelsford on the low-side stuffed his Harley under lapper Larry Koup, forcing him wide into Carruthers path. In the drag race to the line, Brelsford won by about a bike length. Mann followed closely in 3rd. DuHamel was 4th and Gene Romero with another great run was 5th. Robert Winters on a private Kawasaki was 6th, Cal Rayborn with engine trouble was 7th, BSA teammates Don Emde and Jim Rice were 8th and 9th with Walt Fulton (Kaw) rounding out the top 10.

Race: 100 Mile Road Race National

Rank	Rider	Number	Make
1.	Mark Brelsford, San Bruno, Ca	7	HD
2.	Kel Carruthers, Sydney, Aus	73	Yam
3.	Dick Mann, Richmond, Ca	4	BSA
4.	Yvon DuHamel, LaSalle, Quebec, Can	11	Kaw
5.	Gene Romero, San Luis Obispo, Ca	1	Tri
6.	Robert Winters, Ft. Smith, Ark	46	Kaw
7.	Cal Rayborn, Spring Valley, Ca	14	HD
8.	Don Emde, San Diego, Ca	25	BSA
9.	Jim Rice, Palo Alto, Ca	2	BSA
10.	Walt Fulton, Hacienda Heights, Ca	17	Kaw
11.	Dave Aldana, Santa Ana, Ca	3	BSA
12.	Don Castro, Hollister, Ca	5	Tri
13.	Frank Camillieri, Boston, Mass	33	Yam
14.	Duane McDaniels, Milford, Mi	8	Yam
15.	Dave Smith, Lakewood, Ca	15	Yam
16.	Dave Damron, Riverside, Ca	89	Kaw
17.	Mert Lawwill, San Francisco, Ca	6	HD
18.	Larry Schafer, Washington, DC	53	HD
19.	Chuck Palmgren, Freehold, NJ	8	Yam
20.	John Hateley, Van Nuys, Ca	48	Tri

Race: Junior Final

Rank	Rider	Number	Make
1.	Loyal Penn, Palo Alto, Ca	68	Yam
2.	Mike Lane, Bakersfield, Ca	4	Kaw
3.	Jim Allen, Ashburn, Ont., Can	65	Yam

Grand National Points Standings after Round 6

Rank	Rider	Pts
1.	Dick Mann	376
2.	Gene Romero	307
3.	Jimmy Odom	226
4.	Kel Carruthers	219
5.	Dave Aldana	219
6.	Jim Rice	196
7.	Don Emde	192
8.	Mark Brelsford	165
9.	Chuck Palmgren	120
10.	Dave Smith	108

Extra Extra

- The traditional Loudon/Laconia race drew a strong 28,000 crowd.
- Mark Brelsford won $3500.00 for his last lap heroics.
- Brelsford was credited with a new race record, bettering Cal Rayborn's 1968 mark by 18 seconds.
- Loudon was a bit of retribution for Harley-Davidson after the debacle at Road Atlanta.
- Several previous Loudon/Laconia winners started the National. On the old course, Dick Mann won in 1960 and '62, Jody Nicholas in 1963. Ralph White was the first winner on the new course in 1965.
- Kel Carruthers won another Lightweight event.
- Great brand diversity in the National; 5 different brands in the first 5 places.
- The podium finishers were aboard three very different motorcycles. The "new" 750 Harley-Davidson was traditional "Class "C" V-twin. The Yamaha a "small" powerful 350 two-stroke twin combining GP and street technology. The BSA was 3-cylinder 750 Superbike based model.

1971 Terre Haute Half-Mile
It's Sehl at Terre Haute

GNC Round #7 of 21 **Date:** June 20, 1971 **Type:** Half-Mile **Venue:** Terre Haute Speedway **Location:** Terre Haute, In	**Purse:** $7,500.00 **Surface:** Dirt **Course Length:** ½ Mile **Laps:** 20 **Distance:** 10 Miles

Dave Sehl won his second dirt track National in a row at the blue-groove Terre Haute "Action Track". Sehl utilized a very different set of skills to win on the slick groove compared to his win at the deep cushion Louisville National. It was Sehl's 4th GNC win. He had to battle with the best in the business in a heavily contested race including Don Castro, Gene Romero and a resurgent Bart Markel. Castro posted his best finish of the year in second. In third was 3-time GNC Champ Bart Markel showing he still had the speed to possibly win that elusive 28th National win to break Joe Leonard's record.

Dick Mann maintained his points lead, riding Dave Aldana's spare BSA to 8th in the final, (this was payback for Mann loaning Aldana a bike at the 1970 Indy Mile, which David won). Mann's total stood at 422 points. Gene Romero's 5th place at Terre Haute raised his total to 363, closing the gap on Mann a little. Jim Rice's 4th place finish moved him into title contention for the first time, moving to third in points with 257. Jimmy Odom failed to make another National and slipped back to fourth with 226. Kel Carruthers and Dave Aldana were next, tied at 219. Mark Brelsford stayed at 165. Dave Sehl's win moved him to 9th with 164. Rookie John Hateley moved back into the top ten at 151.

Time Trials

The hot dusty Indiana somehow offered up a fast surface with 9 riders breaking Bart Markel's 26.03 mark from 1969. Dave Aldana (BSA) was the fastest with a scorching 25.63. John Hateley (Tri) turned a 25.66, Jim Rice (BSA) a 25.71, first Harley rider was Dave Sehl at 25.81 and Gene Romero (Tri) rounding out the first five with a 25.83.

Heats

Fast timer Dave Aldana had to scratch from the first heat when his BSA wouldn't make it to the grid. In the race, Dave Sehl on the factory, Babe DeMay tuned-Harley scooted to a comfortable win. Keith Mashburn (Yam) appeared to have 2nd sewed up with one lap to go when "Black Bart" Markel (HD) went by on the high line. Dave Hansen (Tri) fell unhurt after an early battle with Markel.

Rookie "Lil" John Hateley (Tri) pulled the holeshot in Heat 2, leading the first few laps till GNC Champion Gene Romero zipped past. Hateley turned up the wick and went back by on lap 5. Ronnie Rall on the Bill Kennedy Triumph, dropped Romero back to 3rd on lap 7. At the flag it was Hateley with a fighting Romero back in front of Rall.

Groove maestro Jim Rice hooked up his factory BSA and led all of Heat 3. Don Castro (Tri) ran through the pack for 2nd. Frank Gillespie (Tri) ran 3rd till Tom Rockwood (Tri) went by with three to go.

Semi

Rookie Expert Rex Beauchamp on a Edgar Fuhr-tuned factory Harley was headed to the National, topping Eddie Mulder (Tri) with Dick Mann squeaking through on Aldana's BSA.

National

A very rubbered up groove awaited the 12 finalists. Gene Romero jetted into the lead at the start of the National chased by Bart Markel, Dave Sehl and Don Castro. The fifth go-around saw Markel take the lead much to the delight of the partisan Harley crowd. Markel's stay was short-lived as the next lap Sehl steamed by, pulling Castro along with him. Jim Rice had moved up and began a battle with Romero. Up front Sehl stretched his lead masterfully scrubbing off speed in the groove by pronating the front wheel. Castro was running a higher line, finally getting some breathing room from Markel, who was running an even higher line. Positions remained static as the laps ran out with exception of Rice sneaking by Romero on the last lap for 4th place.

Results

Race: 20 Lap Half-Mile National
Race Time: 8:57.35

Rank	Rider	Number	Make
1.	Dave Sehl, Atlanta, Ga	16	HD
2.	Don Castro, Hollister, Ca	5	Tri
3.	Bart Markel, Flint, Mi	32	HD
4.	Jim Rice, Palo Alto, Ca	2	BSA
5.	Gene Romero, San Luis Obispo, Ca	1	Tri
6.	John Hatelely, Van Nuys, Ca	43R	Tri
7.	Rex Beauchamp, Drayton Plains, Mi	34E	HD
8.	Dick Mann, Richmond, Ca	4	BSA
9.	Tom Rockwood, Gardena, Ca	9	Tri
10.	Eddie Mulder, Burbank, Ca	20	Tri
11.	Ronnie Rall, Mansfield, Oh	30	Tri
12.	Keith Mashburn, Santa Susana, Ca	19	Yam

Results

Race: Junior Final

Rank	Rider	Number	Make
1.	Kenny Roberts, Redwood City, Ca	80Y	Yam
2.	Billy Schaffer, Pine Grove, Pa	52A	BSA
3.	Keith Ulicki, Kenosha, Wi	87G	HD

Grand National Points Standings after Round 7

Rank	Rider	Pts
1.	Dick Mann	422
2.	Gene Romero	363
3.	Jim Rice	257
4.	Jimmy Odom	226
5.	Dave Aldana	219
6.	Kel Carruthers	219
7.	Don Emde	192
8.	Mark Brelsford	165
9.	Dave Sehl	164
10.	John Hateley	151

Extra Extra

- Post-mortem on Dave Aldana's BSA showed an errant paper towel had gotten sucked into the fast qualifier's engine.
- Dick Mann's finish may not have appeared that impressive, but he sure had to work for it. He had trouble getting Aldana's bike up to speed in qualifying and appeared to have missed the program. As luck would have it, a rider scratched and Mann started last in Heat 3. He just made the transfers in both his heat and semi to make the National. Mann steadily worked the pack to his eventual 8th place finish. Whew!
- The Terre Haute crowd had improved over 1970, but at an estimated 3,400, had the lowest attendance of the 1971 series.
- At $7500.00, the Terre Haute and Oklahoma Half-Miles purses were the smallest of the year.

1971 Columbus Half-Mile
Markel Wins 28th!!!

GNC Round #8 of 21 **Date:** June 27, 1971 **Type:** Half-Mile **Venue:** Ohio State Fairgrounds **Location:** Columbus, Oh	**Purse:** $12,000.00 **Surface:** Dirt-Limestone **Course Length:** ½ Mile **Laps:** 20 **Distance:** 10 Miles

Bart Markel wowed the 12,000 plus present at the Charity Newsies-sponsored GNC, winning his 28th AMA National, finally breaking Joe Leonard's long standing record. It was also Markel's fourth win at the famed Columbus event. Markel's luck had been pretty sour the previous couple of years. He did have a bright spot in 1970 when he scored win number 2th on his Sprint at Sante Fe. His experience on the new Harley-Davidson XR750 had been awful. Things had improved of late as Markel's 3rd place at the previous Terre Haute National showed. He looked like the champion of old at Columbus in a dominant performance. Track conditions played to Markel's strengths. The surface retained some cushion and did not groove up badly. Markel' "diamond pattern" of cornering failed him at last year's event, but worked perfectly this day. The 36-year old Markel was unstoppable aboard his self-tuned Harley. Early leader Don Castro hung on for his second runner-up position in a row. Rookie John Hateley scored his best National finish yet in 3rd. Dave Sehl, winner of the two previous half-miles had his Harley-Davidson lunch its transmission on the Nationals first lap. Points leaders Dick Mann and Gene Romero both had trouble and failed to make the main.

Half-mile specialists dominated the Columbus race and most riders at the top of the points chart had a lousy day. Only 3 of the top 10, Jim Rice, Dave Aldana and Dave Sehl, made the National. Not a bunch changed in the standings. Mann stayed atop the standings. Jim Rice pulled within 50 points of second in points Gene Romero. With his 3rd place in the race, John Hateley moved from tenth in points to seventh. Don Castro moved to eighth in the standings.

Time Trials

The circuit's hottest half-miler, Dave Sehl (HD), continued his hot streak, topping the field with a 26.11, setting a NTR. The rest of the top 5 qualifiers were; Don Castro (Tri) at 26.33, three Team Harleys of Mert Lawwill (26.41), Cal Rayborn, (26.43), Bart Markel, (26.47) and BSA's Jim Rice at 26.55.

Heats

Cal Rayborn still trying to notch a national dirt track win, blasted out to lead Heat 1. He led the first seven laps till Dave Sehl hooked up and took the win. Rayborn hung onto 2nd with Keith Mashburn (Yam) in 3rd.

TT ace Eddie Mulder looked very strong in Heat 2, controlling most of the race. Bart Markel broke free of a battle with Don Castro, John Hateley (Tri) and Teddy Newton (BSA) and slowly reeled in Mulder, passing him with two laps to go and holding on for the win. Mulder faded back and was passed by rookies Hateley and Newton.

Crowd favorite, Ohio's own Ronnie Rall (Tri) the 1963 Charity Newsies winner took the Heat 3 win. He had to come from back in the pack, running down early leaders Jim Rice and Larry Palmgren (Tri), taking the lead with two to go.

Semi

Points leader Dick Mann (BSA), Eddie Mulder (Tri) and Rex Beauchamp (HD) got a little anxious to make the main, jumping the start and ending up on the penalty line. Floridian Royal Sherbert and Dave Aldana , both aboard BSA's blasted to the front, capturing the crowd's attention. Don Castro was playing catch up on a factory Triumph, raced by both on the last lap, taking the win. Mann failed to transfer.

National

Jim Rice pulled the holeshot to lead lap 1. Markel was not to be denied though and blasted past Rice into turn 1. Ronnie Rall soon bumped Rice out of 2nd spot with John Hateley running close behind. Don Castro was on the move, riding spectacularly on the outside. He blew by both Rice and Hateley on the same lap. Next he applied pressure to Rall, going by for the runner-up spot just before halfway. Hateley also began moving forward. It took him several laps to get by Rice, then set his sights on Rall. The two diced heavily with Hateley taking the last podium position with 3 laps to go. Up front Markel motored to his 28th historic win with a huge lead.

Results

Race: 20 Lap Half-Mile National

Rank	Rider	Number	Make
1.	Bart Markel, Flint, Mi	32	HD
2.	Don Castro, Hollister, Ca	5	Tri
3.	John Hateley, Van Nuys, Ca	43R	Tri
4.	Ronnie Rall, Mansfield, Oh	30	Tri
5.	Jim Rice, Palo Alto, Ca	2	BSA
6.	Teddy Newton, Pontiac Mi	2E	Tri
7.	Royal Sherbert, Largo, Fla	28	BSA
8.	Larry Palmgren, Freehold, NJ	12	Tri
9.	Dave Aldana, Santa Ana, Ca	3	BSA
10.	Keith Mashburn, Santa Susana, Ca	19	Yam
11.	Cal Rayborn, Spring Valley, Ca	14	HD
12.	Dave Sehl, Atlanta, Ga	16	HD

Race: Junior Final

Rank	Rider	Number	Make
1.	Gary Scott, Baldwin Park, Ca	64R	Nor
2.	Kenny Roberts, Redwood City, Ca	80Y	Yam
3.	Carl LeBlanc, Decatur, Al	77L	Tri

Grand National Points Standings after Round 8

Rank	Rider	Pts
1.	Dick Mann	422
2.	Gene Romero	363
3.	Jim Rice	313
4.	Dave Aldana	262
5.	Jimmy Odom	226
6.	Kel Carruthers	219
7.	John Hateley	218
8.	Don Castro	213
9.	Dave Sehl	198
10.	Don Emde	192

Extra Extra

- Mert Lawwill's bad XR luck struck again when he had to pull off the line in Heat 3 with mag problems.
- In addition to Lawwill, there were a bunch of talented racers who were forced to watch the show. Some others were; Gene Romero, Jim Rice, Mark Brelsford, Chuck Palmgren, Jody Nicholas, Frank Gillespie, Gary Nixon, and Eddie Mulder.
- With the cancellation of the Sacramento Mile, the Columbus Half-Mile and Nazareth Mile tied for the biggest dirt track purse at $12,000.00.
- Junior winner Gary Scott borrowed one of Jody Nicholas's spare Nortons from owner Harold Allison.
- Illustrating the depth of racing at the time, just prior to the 'Newsies, Dick Mann won a half-mile in Urbana, Il on June 25th over John Hateley and Al Kenyon. On June 26th at the Troy Oh Half-Mile, Ronnie Rall topped Bart Markel and Jody Nicholas.

GNC Round #9 of 21 **Date:** July 5, 1971 **Type:** Half-Mile **Venue:** Santa Clara Fairgrounds **Location:** San Jose, Ca	**Purse:** $8000.00 **Surface:** Dirt **Course Length:** ½ Mile **Laps:** 20 **Distance:** 10 Miles

GNC Champ Gene Romero finally put together a win in 1971 at the San Jose Half-Mile. Romero had a great year going, very consistent as in 1970, but with no victories. He became the first rider in two years to knock groove-master Jim Rice out of victory at San Jose. It was Romero's 5th National win. It allowed him to close up to long time points leader Dick Mann in the GNC title chase. Mann made the main event, but again had trouble. Finishing 2nd in the main was Eddie Mulder, posting his one of his best ever oval track finishes. Defending race champion Rice still managed to have a good race, rounding out the podium. Local Expert Nick Theroux had the ride(s) of his career; winning his heat and ending up 5th after running up front all day.

Dick Mann maintained a narrow 11 point lead over Gene Romero 456 to 445. Mann had trouble in the main and ended 12th. Jim Rice remained a close third in points with 380. Jimmy Odom made the main and moved back into fourth in points with 275. Dave Aldana slipped back a spot to fifth with 262 points. Dave Sehl moved up three spots to sixth with 250 points. Mark Brelsford's yo-yoing in and out of the top ten continued, moving back to seventh in with 226 points. Kel Carruthers and John Hateley were nearly tied with 219 and 218 points. Don Castro rounded out the top 10 with 213 points.

Time Trials

Californians set atop the order in qualifying with Frank Gillespie (Tri) at 27.11. Eddie Mulder aboard the Love Brothers Triumph was next at 27.19.

Heats

Heat 1 was stopped by a spectacular accident caused when Terry Dorsch slid down and Dave Aldana clipped his Triumph, sending Aldana and his cart wheeling BSA through the fence. Despite ripping out 30 feet of fence and ended up outside the track, Aldana emerged unhurt. Terry Dorsch made the restart, but then crashed into the fence on the other end of the track. Dorsch was knocked unconscious, but apparently not seriously injured. The race finally turned into a good one with Jimmy Odom (Yam) leading early, chased by Dick Mann (BSA). The two put on a good race, with Mann taking the point at midway. Loudon winner Mark Brelsford (HD) was on the move too and passed both for the win.

Heat 2 was a shocker, early leader Chuck Palmgren (Yam) had to give way to Bay area racer Nick Theroux aboard a Jim Deehan-tuned Triumph, took the lead on lap 3 and held it to the end. Behind, first Gene Romero and then Eddie Mulder bumped Palmgren back, getting the remaining transfer spots. An incident in the early laps of the heat between Cal Rayborn and Theroux ended with Rayborn on the ground, but escaping injury. Evidently Theroux was not slowed.

In Heat 3, Jim Rice (BSA) and a couple of other riders were sent to the penalty line by starter Bob Malley, ("Bouncing Bob"), causing a restart. Veteran Dusty Coppage (Yam) shot out to another lead followed by Dave Sehl (HD). Rice was on a charge and had moved halfway through the pack on the opening lap. Sehl took the lead on lap 3 and was in control till Rice arrived late and went by for the win. Sehl maintained 2nd with Dave Hansen (Tri) getting by Coppage for the last direct transfer to the main.

Semi

Rookie Expert Al Kenyon (BSA), took the win over Dusty Coppage and Dave Smith (Tri).

National

Gene Romero and Jim Rice turned the first lap into a drag race and ran wheel-to-wheel across the stripe of the first go around. Romero pulled a small lead on lap 2. Behind, Rice had to be a little surprised as Nick Theoroux motored by on lap 4. Romero extended his lead and Theroux had his hands full with Rice. Behind the front three were Eddie Wirth (Tri) and Mark Brelsford. Dick Mann was out early with engine trouble. After the halfway point, Theourx began to lose speed from an apparently overcooked tire. Theroux had some big "moments" and Rice slipped off the groove to avoid him. Taking advantage, both Mulder and Brelsford slipped by. Rice managed to repass Brelsford. Theroux had somehow managed to keep his ride in 2nd, but rapidly slipped backward and ended up in 5th spot. The top ten at the flag; Romero with a big lead, Mulder, Rice, Brelsford, Theroux, Dave Sehl, Jimmy Odom, Dave Hansen, Dave Smith and Al Kenyon.

Results

Race: 20 Lap Half-Mile National
Race Time: 8:56.08

Rank	Rider	Number	Make
1.	Gene Romero, San Luis Obispo, Ca	1	Tri
2.	Eddie Mulder, Burbank, Ca	20	Tri
3.	Jim Rice, Palo Alto, Ca	2	BSA
4.	Mark Brelsford, San Bruno, Ca	7	HD
5.	Nick Theroux, San Francisco, Ca	64Y	Tri
6.	Dave Sehl, Atlanta, Ga	16	HD
7.	Jimmy Odom, Fremont, Ca	18	Yam
8.	Dave Hansen, Hayward, Ca	54	Tri
9.	Dave Smith, Lakewood, Ca	15	Tri
10.	Al Kenyon, Cupertino, Ca	88Y	BSA
11.	Dusty Coppage, Chatsworth, Ca	21	Yam
12.	Dick Mann, Richmond, Ca	4	BSA

Race: 12 Lap Junior Final

Rank	Rider	Number	Make
1.	Gary Kapus, Vancouver, Wa	7W	Yam
2.	Bill Morgan, San Leandro, Ca	25Z	Tri
3.	Harry Dring, Oakland, Ca	66Y	BSA

Grand National Points Standings after Round 9

Rank	Rider	Pts
1.	Dick Mann	456
2.	Gene Romero	445
3.	Jim Rice	380
4.	Jimmy Odom	275
5.	Dave Aldana	262
6.	Dave Sehl	250
7.	Mark Brelsford	226
8.	Kel Carruthers	219
9.	John Hateley	218
10.	Don Castro	213

- Gene Romero aboard his factory Nick Deligianis-tuned Triumph broke Harley-Davidson's four-in-a-row win streak.
- A SRO only crowd of 6,600 was present.
- Gary Kapus was the Junior Final winner; favorites Kenny Roberts and Gary Scott had off days, finishing 5th and 9th.

1971 Kent Road Race
Mann Wins Again-Extends Points Lead
Romero Suspended Post-Race

GNC Round #10 of 21	**Purse:** $15,000.00
Date: July 11, 1971	**Surface:**
Type: Road Race	**Course Length:** 2.25 Miles
Venue: Pacific Raceways	**Laps:** 44
Location: Kent, Wa	**Distance:** 100 Miles

Dick Mann captured his third win at the tight, technical Kent, Wa Road Race National. Mann had a humdinger of a battle the whole distance with Kel Carruthers, Don Emde and Cal Rayborn. Unofficially the lead was swapped 39 times over the 100 mile distance. Mann finally pulled a little distance on 2nd place finisher Carruthers who was slowed by a bulky transmission at the worst time, on the last lap. Don Emde was in the lead pack all day and finished a solid 3rd. Cal Rayborn's day ended early as his Harley-Davidson self-destructed again. GNC Champ Gene Romero ended up a credible 4th at the finish.

The top seven in the standings scored points at Kent. The top four did not change position. Dick Mann gained some breathing space over Gene Romero. Romero's win at San Jose had pulled him to within 10 points of the lead. Mann's win at Kent put him 35 points over Romero, 547 to 512. Romero's top 5 kept the Mann in sight. Jim Rice finished 10th, keeping him in the championship with 423. Jimmy Odom, who finished a couple of spots behind Rice, maintained fourth with 312 points. Kel Carruthers was the big mover for the week; his 2nd place finish in the National shot him from eighth to fifth with 301 points. Mark Brelsford, 6th on the day, moved up a spot to sixth in points. Don Emde's 3rd place run moved him into the top 10, right behind with 266 points. Dave Aldana scored no points and slipped from fifth in points to eighth with 262 points.

In a dramatic post-race development, Gene Romero and several other riders were suspended by the AMA for allegedly falsifying some medical documentation. The move could cost Romero valuable championship points necessary to defend his title. For more info, see Extras.

Heats

Cal Rayborn (HD) hungry for some pavement redemption in '71, shot into the lead of Heat 1, never to be seen by the pack again. Kawasaki riders Ralph White and Walt Fulton had a great fight over 2nd place till Dick Mann (BSA) arrived on the last lap, passing both. Fulton took 3rd with White in 4th.

Kel Carruthers (Yam) would have seemed the favorite in Heat 2, but nobody told National champ Gene Romero (Tri). The two had a great scrap with Carruthers taking the spot but really had to work for it. Former champ Mert Lawwill's rotten luck continued as his XRTT blew up during the heat.

National

Yvon DuHamel (Kaw), still chomping at the bit for his first GNC win, led the pack off the line. He controlled the first two laps until Cal Rayborn thundered by. Dick Mann and Kel Carruthers rolled by the early leaders and would set the pace for the rest of the day. Mann's BSA was handling great around the tight course. Carruthers smaller Yamaha was actually faster on the straight portions, but the nature of the course negated the advantage; while Carruthers could pass Mann at various points around the course, he couldn't lead at the line. Behind the two leaders, Rayborn's day ended around the lap 20 mark with piston/overheating problems. Don Emde took over 3rd spot. Further back were Kawasaki teammates DuHamel and White. Gas stops knocked them back to finish 13th and 11th With the leading Kawasaki's slowed, Gene Romero, Walt Fulton and Mark Brelsford (HD) moved up.

Up front, Mann and Carruthers were flying and lapped clear up to 4th place. As the laps wound down, Carruthers still had a shot and was right on Mann. Unfortunately at the worst possible moment, transmission problems caused him to slow slightly, allowing Mann to cross the line uncontested. The order at the finish was: Mann, Carruthers, Emde, Romero, Fulton, Brelsford, Suzuki riders Jody Nicholas, Art Baumann, Dave Smith and Jim Rice.

Race: 100 Mile Road Race National

Rank	Rider	Number	Make
1.	Dick Mann, Richmond, Ca	4	BSA
2.	Kel Carruthers, El Cajon, Ca	73	Yam
3.	Don Emde, San Diego, Ca	25	BSA
4.	Gene Romero, San Luis Obispo, Ca	1	Tri
5.	Walt Fulton, Hacienda, Heights, Ca	17	Kaw
6.	Mark Brelsford, San Bruno, Ca	7	HD
7.	Jody Nicholas, Newport Beach, Ca	23	Suz
8.	Art Baumann, Brisbane, Ca	24	Suz
9.	Dave Smith, Lakewood, Ca	15	Yam
10.	Jim Rice, Palo Alto, Ca	2	BSA
11.	Ralph White, Torrance, Ca	47	Kaw
12.	Jimmy Odom, Fremont, Ca	18	Yam
13.	Yvon DuHamel, LaSalle, Que	11	Kaw
14.	Ron Pierce, Bakersfield, Ca	37	Suz
15.	Cliff Carr, Watertown, Mass	87	Kaw
16.	Don Castro, Hollister, Ca	5	Tri
17.	Tom Rockwood, Gardena, Ca	9	Tri
18.	Mark Williams, Springfield, Ore	41	Kaw
19.	Dave Damron, Riverside, Ca	89	Yam
20.	Hurley Wilvert, Westminster, Ca	51	Kaw

Race: Junior/Novice Final

Rank	Rider	Number	Make
1.	John Green, Carmichael, Ca	52	Yam
2.	Rudy Galindo, Sante Fe, Ca	26	Yam
3.	Jim Chen, Carson, Ca	10	Yam

Grand National Points Standings after Round 10

Rank	Rider	Pts
1.	Dick Mann	547
2.	Gene Romero	512
3.	Jim Rice	423
4.	Jimmy Odom	312
5.	Kel Carruthers	301
6.	Mark Brelsford	282
7.	Don Emde	266
8.	Dave Aldana	262
9.	Dave Sehl	250
10.	Don Castro	238

Extra Extra

- Dick Mann was having a heck of a season, particularly on road courses. He won at Daytona, was 2nd at Road Atlanta, 3rd at Loudon and now a win at Kent. Not to mention his Houston TT win. His run was strongly reminiscent of his 1963 championship run.
- A big crowd of 52 Experts charged off the line in front of 3,500 spectators.
- Though up front all day dicing with Dick Mann, Kel Carruthers never officially led a lap.
- Carruthers captured the Lightweight event.
- Novice John Greene topped the combined Novice/Junior event.
- Team Suzuki had a lackluster day. Last year's winner Ron Grant fell out with mechanical problems. Jody Nicholas and Art Baumann finished 7th and 8th in the National.
- Veteran Dick Hammer made his racing return at Kent. He finished 3rd in the Lightweight race on a Yoshimura Honda. He also ran in the big bike event, but a fall and a derailed chain kept him from finishing.
- Mark Brelsford was hurting during the National after really banging up his hand in the Lightweight race.
- Jack Hateley let the AMA officials have it after they mistakenly black flagged son John Hateley for dropping oil.
- Though a modest success, this was the final GNC to be run at Kent.

The Romero Suspension

Just after the Kent National, the AMA announced that Gene Romero, Skip Van Leeuwen, Dick Hammer and Chuck Palmgren all faced a 15 day suspension for allegedly using a forged doctors signature on some medical forms. The doctor in question was actually a gynecologist! Romero would soon file an appeal. Neil Keen and Dave Aldana were later charged with the same offense.

GNC Round #11 of 21 **Date:** July 17, 1971 **Type:** TT **Venue:** Mt. St. Helens Motorcycle Club Grounds	**Purse:** $11,000.00 **Location:** Castle Rock, Wa **Surface:** Dirt **Course Length**: ½ Mile **Laps:** 30

The race fans in the Northwestern U.S. are among the most devoted anywhere. The 8,200 present got a real thrill on this date, witnessing two historical firsts. It was the first National win for Oregon rider Sonny Burres, it also meant it was the first time the Castle Rock had been won by a Northwestern rider. The crowd always loved to see "their" area stars beat up on the GN regulars when they came to town. Burres had to work hard for his first ever win. He went past early leader Eddie Mulder; struggled with Dave Aldana mid-race and barely fought off determined rookie John Hateley at the flag. The race ended in controversy as the "intial" finish was recalled. Through a scoring error, the race went two laps past the scheduled 30 laps. John Hateley had actually pulled up alongside Burres on "lap 32" making it a very close finish. At the "real" 30 lap distance, Burres had a discernable lead. All involved were eventually satisfied with the validity of the decision. For Hateley it turned out to be his second podium of the year. Crowd favorite Mark Williams, from Oregon hung in there for a solid 3rd place. Jimmy Odom came home in 4th with points leader Dick Mann in 5th.

The track was very slick and rutted by main event time. As per previous years, Castle Rock held National time trials and a full Novice and Junior program Friday before the GNC. The surface became treacherous and numerous riders including former winner and GNC Champ Mert Lawwill going down with injuries.

Like Kent, 7 of the top ten in points made the National at Castle Rock; an impressive performance against the TT specialists. No positions changed in the top 5. Leader Dick Mann added a few more points over Gene Romero. Romero had filed an appeal on his suspension and was allowed to ride, finishing 8th in the National. John Hateley's runner-up finish again moved him into the top 10; this time clear to sixth place.

Time Trials
Mark Williams was back aboard a familiar Triumph after a fairly successful year, frequently on a Kawasaki. The move was a good one as he topped a tough field with a 25.28 time. Sonny Burres also on a Triumph, was next at 25.37. Literally a tick back was Mert Lawwill (HD) at 25.38.

Heats
Heat 1 was all Triumph mounted TT specialists. A war between Chuck Joyner, Eddie Mulder, and Mark Williams was interrupted by a nasty Al Kenyon crash which brought out the red flag. Kenyon suffered a shoulder injury. Mulder went on to take the win, with Williams and Joyner also transferring to the National.

The second heat was a warmup for the main with Sonny Burres eeking out a tough win over John Hateley and last years winner Dick Mann (BSA) passing GNC champ Gene Romero to take 3rd.

Two-time Castle Rock winner Mert Lawwill, (1967 & '69), led Heat 2 early, pressured heavily by BSA riders Dave Aldana and Jim Rice. Lawwill got out of shape and slipped back to 3rd. Aldana continued on to the win, followed by Rice, Lawwill and Jimmy Odom (Yam).

Semi
A talented bunch of riders went at it hard in the "last chance" race. Terry Dorsch and Emil Ahola led the race early. The proceedings were halted by a violent crash involving Don Emde and Eddie Wirth. Wirth was apparently okay, with a shaken up Emde taking a ride to the hospital. Upon the restart Don Castro took control and led Dave Hansen, Terry Dorsch and Emil Ahola to the last four National tickets. All were, you guessed it, Triumph mounted.

National

"Fast Eddie" Mulder pulled the holeshot, but the race was stopped when Chuck Joyner and Pat Marinacci went down in Turn of lap 2. Joyner suffered a broken arm. Mulder led the single file restart only to have Jim Rice fall coming out of turn 4. Luckless for 1971 Mert Lawwill hit Rice's machine and was catapulted into the wall. He suffered hand and wrist injuries. After a long wait for the return of an ambulance, the third restart was on. Mulder again led and held the point till lap 6 when a pressuring Burres went by accompanied by Dave Aldana (BSA). On lap 8, Aldana passed Burres for the lead. Aldana looked to have things wrapped up till lap 14 when he had a big crash in turn 1. His BSA flipped several times, but Aldana once again walked away. Burres reassumed the lead and he and a now close John Hateley put distance on the field. Way back, Dick Mann tried to keep Mark Williams behind him for 3rd place. With a couple laps to go, Williams moved by. Jimmy Odom (Tri) also caught and passed the points leader, knocking him back to 5th. Hateley had been reeling in Burres and on the last lap, he got hooked up coming out of turn 4 on the bottom, but Burres was running the topside and had just a little more traction. Burres took the win by less than a foot.

Results

Race: 30 Lap TT National

Rank	Rider	Number	Make
1.	Sonny Burres, Portland, Ore	73	Tri
2.	John Hateley, Van Nuys, Ca	43R	Tri
3.	Mark Williams, Springfield, Ore	41	Tri
4.	Jimmy Odom, Fremont, Ca	18	Yam
5.	Dick Mann. Richmond, Ca	4	BSA
6.	Eddie Mulder, Burbank, Ca	20	Tri
7.	Terry Dorsch, Granada Hills, Ca	65R	Tri
8.	Gene Romero, San Luis Obispo, Ca	1	Tri
9.	Emil Ahola, Tacoma, Wa	80W	Tri
10.	Pat Marinacci, Seattle, Wa	14W	Tri
11.	Dave Hansen, Hayward, Ca	54	Tri
12.	Don Castro, Hollister, Ca	5	Tri
13.	Jim Rice, Palo Alto, Ca	2	BSA
14.	Dave Aldana, Santa Ana, Ca	3	BSA
15.	Mert Lawwill, San Francisco, Ca	1	HD
16.	Chuck Joyner, Oregon, Ore	87Q	Tri

Race: 10 Lap Junior Final

Rank	Rider	Number	Make
1.	Randy Scott, Corvallis, Ore	57Q	Tri
2.	Don Lipp, Tacoma, Wa	11V	Yam
3.	Gary Scott, Baldwin Park, Ca	64R	Kaw

Grand National Points Standings after Round 11

Rank	Rider	Pts
1.	Dick Mann	603
2.	Gene Romero	558
3.	Jim Rice	451
4.	Jimmy Odom	373
5.	Kel Carruthers	301
6.	John Hateley	292
7.	Dave Aldana	290
8.	Mark Brelsford	282
9.	Don Castro	272
10.	Don Emde	266

Extra Extra

- Mark Williams got $270.00 for setting fast time.
- A big crowd on Friday night watched Expert qualifying and full Junior and Novice programs that were won by Randy Scott (Tri) and Steve Baker (Yam) respectively.

GNC Round #12 of 21 **Date:** July 24, 1971 **Type:** TT **Venue:** Ascot Park **Location:** Gardena, Ca	**Purse:** $10,300.00 **Surface:** Dirt **Course Length:** ½ Mile, (approx.) **Laps:** 50

Mark Brelsford dominated the 50 Lap Ascot TT GNC race to capture his second win of the year. It was Mark's 4th National win, the first coming here at the Ascot TT in 1969. Brelsford led nearly every lap aboard the monster 900cc Harley XLRTT, nearly lapping the whole field. He showed little evidence of a still banged up hand from the Kent Road Race. Dave Aldana challenged late in the race, but a fall ended his charge although he still got up to finish 2nd. Eddie Mulder ran up front the whole night to finish a strong 3rd.

Dick Mann was hoping to extend his points lead over rival Gene Romero who was forced to miss the race when his appeal of his bizarre 15-day suspension was disallowed. Mann was in contention in the TT, but was forced out with a broken crankshaft. The race had no effect on the first four in points although fourth place Jim Odom closed up the gap on Jim Rice. Dave Aldana moved up a couple of spots to 5th. National winner Mark Brelsford went up from eighth to sixth in points. Road race specialist Kel Carruthers slid back in standings from fifth to seventh.

Time Trials

Mark Brelsford muscled the big Jim Belland-tuned Harley to the fastest time of the event with a rapid 45.30. Much further back on the clock was 1966 Ascot TT winner Eddie Mulder (Tri) with a 45.98. Dave Aldana (BSA) just missed the 45 second bracket with a 46.10.

National

Oregon TT ace Mark Williams (Tri) pulled a nice holeshot over the 24 rider field. Unfortunately he overcooked in front the whole pack going into the infield section. Veteran Lloyd Houchins fell trying to avoid Williams and was consequently hit by Dusty Coppage and Tom Rockwood. Houchins suffered a broken wrist. Everybody else involved was okay and made the restart. In contrast with the previous week's melee at Castle Rock, this was fortunately the only serious incident of the night. Williams pulled a second holeshot on the restart, but Mark Brelsford was soon by on lap 2. Williams held onto 2nd place until lap 4, giving into pressure from Eddie Mulder. Dave Aldana also bumped Williams back a spot. Dick Mann was out on lap 10 with bottom end woes. As the race wore on, Brelsford stretched out to a big lead. Second place Mulder was being stalked by Aldana. Aldana reeled Mulder in and passed him at the mid-point of the race. TT specialist Mike Haney was running in the lead pack till an engine failure knocked him out of 4th place on lap 30. He dropped some oil on the track which 5th place Jim Rice promptly found, knocking the championship contender out of the race. Early leader Williams was in and out of the pits with mechanical trouble. In the waning laps of the National Dave Aldana had actually begun to catch leader Brelsford. He pushed a little too hard, sliding down. He kept the engine running and was quickly back up, maintaining 2nd. Top 5 at the finish were Brelsford, Aldana, Mulder, Cal Rayborn, (happy to finish a National!), and Eddie Wirth.

Results

Race: 50 Lap TT National
Race Time: 39:24.15

Rank	Rider	Number	Make
1.	Mark Brelsford, San Bruno, Ca	7	HD
2.	Dave Aldana, Santa Ana, Ca	3	BSA
3.	Eddie Mulder, Burbank, Ca	20	Tri
4.	Cal Rayborn, Spring Valley, Ca	14	HD
5.	Eddie Wirth, Manhattan Beach, Ca	26	Tri
6.	Terry Dorsch, Granada Hills, Ca	65R	Tri
7.	Jimmy Odom, Fremont, Ca	18	Yam
8.	Tom Rockwood, Gardena, Ca	9	Tri
9.	Don Dudek, Redondo Beach, Ca	42X	Tri
10.	Sonny Burres, Portland, Ore	73	Tri
11.	Mark Williams, Springfield, Ore	41	Tri
12.	Dusty Coppage, Chatsworth, Ca	21	Yam
13.	Dave Hansen, Hayward, Ca	54	Tri
14.	Ralph White, Torrance, Ca	47	Tri
15.	Mike Haney, Inglewood, Ca	48R	Tri
16.	Jim Rice, Palo Alto, Ca	2	BSA
17.	Paul Bostrom, Lake Isabella, Ca	46	Tri
18.	Dave Sehl, Atlanta, Ga	16	HD
19.	Don Emde, San Diego, Ca	25	BSA
20.	Bob Bailey, Compton, Ca	77	Tri

Race: 14 Lap Junior Final

Rank	Rider	Number	Make
1.	Kenny Roberts, Redwood City, Ca	80Y	Yam
2.	Gary Scott, Baldwin Park, Ca	64R	Tri
3.	Randy Scott, Corvallis, Ore	57Q	Tri

Grand National Points Standings after Round 12

Rank	Rider	Pts
1.	Dick Mann	603
2.	Gene Romero	558
3.	Jim Rice	473
4.	Jimmy Odom	422
5.	Dave Aldana	367
6.	Mark Brelsford	364
7.	Kel Carruthers	301
8.	John Hateley	292
9.	Don Emde	279
10.	Don Castro	266

- Nice crowd of 9000 was present to witness the 20th Annual Ascot TT.
- Last week's Castle Rock TT runner-up John Hateley could not get on track and missed the National.
- Nice to see Don Emde in the race after being pretty shook up from his spill at Castle Rock.
- Kenny Roberts (Yam) topped rival Gary Scott (Tri) in the Junior Final.
- The night before the National, Ascot hosted the Yamaha Cup on the half-mile The race had a $6000.00 purse and saw Jody Nicholas (Nor) top the Experts, Gary Scott (Tri) the Juniors and Scott Brelsford (Yam), (Mark's younger brother), the Novice division.

Romero's Suspension Continued

The AMA had let Gene Romero race at Castle Rock after he appealed his 15 day suspension. After reviewing the appeal, the AMA rejected it. Romero had served 4 days before the appeal, the 11 remaining knocked him out of the Ascot TT. He would be eligible to ride the upcoming Corona National.

1971 Corona Half-Mile
Odom Wins Chaotic Corona
Romero Takes Points Lead

GNC Round #13 of 21 **Date:** July 31, 1971 **Type:** Half-Mile **Venue:** Corona Raceway **Location:** Corona, Ca	**Purse:** $8000.00 **Surface:** Dirt **Course Length:** ½ Mile **Laps:** 20 **Distance:** 10 Miles

Jimmy Odom took a close win at a mess of a race at the first/last GNC race to be held at Corona. Odom was able to master a very slippery, follow-the-leader surface to claim his second National win of the year. Ascot TT winner Mark Brelsford challenged Odom through the event, but had to settle for the runner-up spot. Groove-master Jim Rice was up front all night and finished 3rd. Gene Romero celebrated his suspension being over by placing 4th and taking over the points lead.

Points leader Dick Mann and a bunch of others were apparently victims of a bad start in the semi event and were left sitting on the starting line. Despite protests led by Mann to bump up the number of riders in the National, no action was taken by the officials. Mann lodged an official protest after the race.

Gene Romero's 4th place finish in the National, along with Mann missing the show put him atop the point's battle, 619 to 603 points. Mann's past history in dealing with the AMA in protests had not gone well in the past, but he knew how to play the game and would hope for the best. Jim Rice's strong finish kept him in third with 540 points. Winner Jimmy Odom closed up the gap some 504 points. Mark Brelsford's 2nd place finish moved him into fifth with 438 points, knocking Dave Aldana back a spot at 387. Kel Carruthers was still seventh with 364 and Eddie Mulder moved into the top 10 with 298 points.

Time Trials

Rising star Don Castro set fast time of 22.44 breaking Terry Dorsch's regional track record. TT ace Eddie Mulder was 2nd with a 22.67. Tom Rockwood was close with a 22.73 lap. All were Triumph mounted.

Heats

Fast-timer Don Castro night was over quickly, sliding down in the first corner. Mark Brelsford (HD) was soon in control of Heat 1, followed by young Californian Dave Hansen (Tri). In 3rd was two-time GNC champ Gary Nixon (Tri), making his first dirt National of the year.

Fast starter Mark Williams (Tri) led Heat 2 for one lap before Jimmy Odom on the A&A Yamaha scooted by. Eddie Mulder applied heavy pressure to Williams and passed him at the stripe on the last lap.

GNC champ Gene Romero (Tri) celebrated his return to action by winning Heat 3. Jim Rice (BSA) and Tom Rockwood followed him into the National. Dick Mann failed to make the transfer and was headed to the semi.

Semi

Controversy reigned in the semi. Dick Mann, Jody Nicholas, Nick Theroux and others had crept over the line with the riders expecting a reset before the start. Instead, Bob Malley waved the flag, with Mann and others sitting on the line as the rest of the field zoomed off. Terry Dorsch (Tri) won the race followed by Keith Mashburn and Chuck Palmgren, both Yamaha mounted. After the race Mann and the other affected riders lobbied vehemently for the officials to allow all the riders to start the National because of the botched start. The protest was to no avail. Dick Mann would file a formal protest before leaving Corona.

National

Starter drama continued in the main, when Eddie Mulder, notorious for messing with officials, was sent to the penalty line along with Tom Rockwood and Mark Williams. It was a rough night for starter Malley. On the restart Jimmy Odom pulled a narrow lead over Jim Rice and Mark Brelsford. Brelsford soon surged by Rice and began breathing down Odom's neck. Brelsford managed to get by on lap 4 with Odom quickly retaking the lead. Gary

Nixon slid down early in the race but managed to keep going. Gene Romero ran 4th and Terry Dorsch 5th. Slippery track conditions mandated follow-the-leader racing, with everyone carefully "two-wheeling" through the corner. They crossed the line in close order, Odom, Brelsford, Rice, Romero and Dorsch. Everyone was ready to move on and forget the event, well except for maybe Jimmy Odom!

Results

Race: Mile 20 Lap Half-Mile National
Race Time: 7:33.54

Rank	Rider	Number	Make
1.	Jimmy Odom, Fremont, Ca	18	Yam
2.	Mark Brelsford, San Bruno, Ca	7	HD
3.	Jim Rice, Palo Alto, Ca	2	BSA
4.	Gene Romero, San Luis Obispo, Ca	1	Tri
5.	Terry Dorsch, Granada Hills, Ca	65R	Tri
6.	Keith Mashburn, Santa Susana, Ca	19	Yam
7.	Eddie Mulder, Burbank, Ca	20	Tri
8.	Dave Hansen, Hayward, Ca	54	Tri
9.	Tom Rockwood, Gardena, Ca	9	Tri
10.	Mark Williams, Springfield, Ore	41	Tri
11.	Chuck Palmgren, Freehold, NJ	8	Yam
12.	Gary Nixon, Phoenix, Md	10	Tri

Race: 14 Lap Junior Final
Race Time: 5:10.90

Rank	Rider	Number	Make
1.	Gary Scott, Baldwin Park, Ca	64R	Tri
2.	Kenny Roberts, Redwood City, Ca	80Y	Yam
3.	Ron Moore, San Bernardino, Ca	37R	Tri

Grand National Points Standings after Round 13

Rank	Rider	Pts
1.	Gene Romero	619
2.	Dick Mann	603
3.	Jim Rice	540
4.	Jimmy Odom	504
5.	Mark Brelsford	438
6.	Dave Aldana	367
7.	Kel Carruthers	301
8.	Eddie Mulder	298
9.	John Hateley	292
10.	Don Emde	279

Extra Extra

- 5000 fans watched the National.
- Jimmy Odom made history by winning the first National Half-Mile on a Yamaha.
- Mark Brelsford put the only Harley-Davidson in the National.
- Many stars missed the show including Don Castro, Dave Aldana, Cal Rayborn and John Hateley.
- Gary Scott topped Kenny Roberts in the Junior main.
- Corona Raceway opened around 1970 and became a very popular dirt "speedplant". The track had ¼ mile and ½ mile dirt tracks, MX course and a 7-mile off-road course. Weekly racing included flat track, TT and MX racing as well as stock car racing on the ¼ mile oval and Figure 8 course. Despite the poor lighting and rough shod appearance of the facility it attracted racers and fans in droves through the 1970's. The ½ mile track was regular stop for SoCal flattrack racers in the early 1970's. The GNC series only made the one troubled stop in 1971. The track ran into the 1980's before closing. It is now covered with apartments, houses and industrial buildings.
- Tragedy struck the Junior event when Loyal Penn received fatal injuries during a multi-bike accident. Penn succumbed to his injuries a couple of days later. Penn was a rising star; his talent was considered nearly equal to Kenny Roberts and Gary Scott. Earlier in the year he won the Novice/Junior Loudon Road Race and had been a front runner at several races including the Houston TT.

1971 Livonia Mile
Rayborn Finally Scores on Dirt!

GNC Round # 14 of 21	**Purse:** $9000.00
Date: August 8, 1971	**Surface:** Cushion
Type: Mile	**Course Length:** 1 Mile
Venue: The Detroit Race Course	**Laps:** 20
Location: Livonia, Mi	**Distance:** 20 Miles

Cal Rayborn scored his first and only dirt track at the dust-shortened Livonia, Mi Mile. Rayborn had been close for years and after years of trying finally won a dirt track National. He was long overdue for a win, dirt or pavement. Cal had been winless since the 1969 season, a victim of the new Harley-Davidson XR's poor reliability as well as plain old bad luck. Besides his success in the overseas Match Races, there had been little for him to be happy about. Brilliant on pavement, he always struggled to score a dirt win. He had led numerous dirt Nationals but just couldn't seem to put it all together till this day at Livonia. It seemed that as hard as Rayborn worked to be a great pavement rider, he worked just as hard on dirt, happy to be one of the guys on the circuit.

The Livonia race was his day, setting fast time, winning his heat and leading the shortened 14-lap National distance. Dust had been an issue all day and despite repeated efforts, it was decided to cut the laps in the final. Chuck Palmgren had his best finish of the year in 2nd. Dave Sehl notched another strong finish in 3rd. Gene Romero was 4th and lengthened his GNC points lead on Dick Mann who suffered mechanical trouble again.

The Livonia facility was a beauty and the Regional event there in 1970, (won by Larry Palmgren), went off without a hitch. The cushion track on this day got rough quickly, followed by nonstop problems with dust. The cushion turned hard down low with more traction available up high which compounded the dust problem.

Gene Romero now topped Dick Mann 680 points to 619. As in 1970, Romero's consistent finishes kept him in the hunt and were paying off. Mann's Corona protest was still being considered and could tip the scales if decided in his favor. Jim Rice finished 5th at Livonia, pulling close to Mann with 596 points. He again had a legitimate shot at the title. Jimmy Odom added some points at Livonia and maintained fourth with 538 points. Dave Aldana maintained sixth in points with 367 points.

Time Trials
Cal Rayborn set fast at time on his factory Harley at 41.02. Dick Mann on his self-tuned factory BSA was 2nd fastest.

Heats
In a preview of the main, Cal Rayborn jumped front of Heat 1 and led every lap. The pack strung out behind with Chuck Palmgren (Yam) and Harley riders Dave Sehl and Larry Darr chasing the pavement ace home. This was the fastest heat of the day.

In Heat 2, Bart Markel showed some horsepower and jetted to a big lead. He dominated the event, but with two laps to go was hit with the XR750 overheating/piston failure curse. Dick Mann took over for the win, followed by title rival Gene Romero and fellow Triumph riders Larry Palmgren and Teddy Newton.

On a slowing, dusty track, Ronnie Rall (Tri) ran off with the last heat win over, Jim Rice (BSA), Keith Mashburn (Yam) and Eddie Mulder (Tri).

Semi
Michigan's own Ron Butler (Tri) looked set to win the "last chance" race till a determined Don Castro (Tri) went by with one to go. A&A Racing sponsored Jimmy Odom (Yam) was 3rd.

National
Cal Rayborn kept his luck going, leading the National in the early laps, trailed by Chuck Palmgren (Yam), Dick Mann and Dave Sehl (HD). Mann dropped out on lap 6. The dust was so bad that the red flag came out shortly. As the riders conferred with the AMA officials waited, the water truck hit the track. It was agreed to shorten the overall

distance to 14 laps from the original 20 lap distance. During the delay Mann made repairs to his machine and was able to resume his earlier spot. On the restart Rayborn kept his earlier pace, still chased by Palmgren. Mann's BSA gave up for good on lap 12, moving Sehl and Gene Romero (Tri) up a spot and that sealed up the top places. Behind was Jim Rice (BSA) in 5th, Larry Darr (HD) 6th, John Weaver (BSA) 7th, Teddy Newton (Tri) 8th, Ronnie Rall 9th and Larry Palmgren. Although there is no doubt Rayborn would have wanted to win the race "straight up", he was happy just to win any race at this point and was especially happy to have the dirt track monkey off his back.

Results

Race: 20 Lap Mile National
Race Time: 9:52.58

Rank	Rider	Number	Make
1.	Cal Rayborn, Spring Valley, Ca	25	HD
2.	Chuck Palmgren, Freehold, NJ	8	Yam
3.	Dave Sehl, Atlanta, Ga	16	HD
4.	Gene Romero, San Luis Obispo, Ca	1	Tri
5.	Jim Rice, Palo Alto, Ca	2	BSA
6.	Larry Darr, Mansfield, Oh	94	HD
7.	John Weaver, Fort Wayne, Ind	52	BSA
8.	Teddy Newton, Pontiac, Mi	2E	Tri
9.	Ronnie Rall, Mansfield, Oh	30	Tri
10.	Larry Palmgren, Freehold, NJ	12	Tri
11.	Keith Mashburn, Santa Susana, Ca	19	Yam
12.	Jimmy Odom, Fremont, Ca	18	Yam
13.	Dennis Palmgren, Freehold, NJ	16A	Tri
14.	Eddie Mulder, Burbank, Ca	20	Tri
15.	Tommy Rockwood, Gardena, Ca	9	Tri
16.	Rex Beauchamp, Milford, Mi	34E	HD
17.	Charles Seale, Lantana, Fl	76	BSA
18.	Dick Mann, Richmond, Ca	4	BSA
19.	Ron Butler, Union Lake, Mi	11E	Tri
20.	Don Castro, Hollister, Ca	5	Tri

Race: Junior Final

Rank	Rider	Number	Make
1.	Kenny Roberts, Redwood City, Ca	80Y	Yam
2.	Carl LeBlanc, Decatur, Al	77L	Tri
3.	Neal Blochinger, Pittsburgh, Pa	28E	BSA

Grand National Points Standings after Round 14

Rank	Rider	Pts
1.	Gene Romero	680
2.	Dick Mann	619
3.	Jim Rice	596
4.	Jimmy Odom	538
5.	Mark Brelsford	438
6.	Dave Aldana	367
7.	Dave Sehl	333
8.	Eddie Mulder	326
9.	Kel Carruthers	301
10.	John Hateley	292

- Chuck, Larry and Denny Palmgren had to be the first brother trio to make a GNC main event. They finished in 2nd, 10th and 13th positions.
- The ride making the biggest buzz of the day was Junior rider Carl "Frenchie" LeBlanc's performance in his heat race. His rear tire went completely flat late in the race, but the fearless Alabama rider never backed off, despite the mile speeds. LeBlanc led most of the Junior main with a shadowing Kenny Roberts sneaking by for the win.
- The Livonia event turned out to be a one-time shot. This is unfortunate as the race drew a huge crowd, numbering around 14,000.
- The Detroit Race Course, (DRC), was situated in Livonia, a suburb of Detroit. It opened in 1950 and enjoyed a long successful run as a betting horse track facility. It hosted motorcycle racing several times over the years. In the late 1990's, the track began to experience hard times and in 1998, offered only video racing. After almost 50 years, the facility was destroyed in 1999 to make way for an industrial complex.

GNC Round #15 of 21 **Date:** August 13, 1971 **Type:** Short Track **Venue:** Sante Fe Speedway	**Location:** Hinsdale, Ill **Surface:** Dirt **Course Length:** ¼ Mile **Laps:** 25

Short track specialist Robert E. Lee scored big in his one and only GNC win at the Sante Fe event. The "Little General", a relatively unknown racer from Texas, shocked the crowd and surely a lot of other riders with the win. Lee had to deal with the spectacular riding of speedway star Barry Briggs early and later to rookie Rex Beauchamp who finished 2nd. Sante Fe regular Neil Keen came from the pack for 3rd. GNC contender Jim Rice, always strong at Sante Fe was 4th.

With the National being the typical short track crap shoot, many of the top riders in the points did not make the main, including Gene Romero and Dick Mann. Only 3 of the top 10 managed to score points. There was only one change for position, but it was a big one. Jim Rice's finish enabled him to take second in points from Dick Mann. Mann was still awaiting the AMA's decision on Corona.

Heats

Fast qualifier Neil Keen (Yam) won Heat 1 over Harley teammates Dave Sehl and rookie Rex Beauchamp. Rounding out the top 5 were Keith Mashburn on the Shell Motors Yamaha and two-time GNC champ Gary Nixon on a factory Triumph.

In Heat 2, Dan Gurney-sponsored Chuck Palmgren (Yam) rolled to the win over Frank Ulicki (HD) and BSA's Dick Mann.

Former GNC champ Roger Reiman (HD), (1964 Sante Fe winner), showed the youngsters how to do it in Heat 3. He scooted to the win aboard his Harley Sprint over Robert E. Lee (Oss) and Royal Sherbert (Bul).

Jim Rice had never won at Sante Fe, but sure looked good on his way to win Heat 4 aboard his underpowered 250 BSA. He topped Barry Brigg's screaming, overpowered Yamaha twin. Eddie Mulder (Tri) was 3rd.

Semis

Semi 1 was a near repeat of Heat 3 with Jim Rice again taking a narrow win over Barry Briggs. Others transferring behind were; Chuck Palmgren, Frank Ulicki, Dave Aldana (BSA), and Charlie Chapple (Yam).

In Semi 2, crowd favorite Neil Keen streaked to a comfortable win followed by Robert E. Lee, Rex Beauchamp and Royal Sherbert.

National

Robert E. Lee, aboard his self-tuned Dick Mann Replica, (DMR) Ossa, shot out to an early lead, pursued by Chuck Palmgren, Barry Briggs and Jim Rice. Briggs quickly took over 2nd, wowing the crowd by forsaking the bottom groove everyone else was on and was rim-riding the screaming 250 twin on the outside. The line worked early on, but he was caught by Rex Beauchamp (HD) who had worked his way through the pack. Beauchamp moved by on lap 8. Brigg's line stopped working and he would eventually fade to 10th spot. Veteran Neil Keen was also on the move and began to battle with 3rd place runner Jim Rice. Rice was tough on the small groove, but Keen moved by after the midpoint of the race. Up front, Lee was on a string and finished the National with a big lead. Rounding out the top 5 were Beauchamp, Keen, Rice and Chuck Palmgren.

Results

Race: 25 Lap Short Track National
Race Time: 6:52.25

Rank	Rider	Number	Make
1.	Robert E. Lee, Ft. Worth, Tx	54N	Oss
2.	Rex Beauchamp, Milford, Mi	34E	HD
3.	Neil Keen, St. Louis, Mo	55	Yam
4.	Jim Rice, Palo Alto, Ca	2	BSA
5.	Charles Chapple, Flint, Mi	84	Yam
6.	Dave Aldana, Santa Ana, Ca	3	BSA
7.	Chuck Palmgren, Freehold, NJ	8	Yam
8.	Roger Reiman, Kewanee, Ill	78	HD
9.	Dave Sehl, Atlanta, Ga	16	HD
10.	Barry Briggs, Southhampton, Eng	7T	Yam
11.	Frank Ulicki, Kenosha, Wi	23G	HD
12.	Royal Sherbert, Largo, Fl	28	Bul

Race: Junior Short Track Final

Rank	Rider	Number	Make
1.	Kenny Roberts, Redwood City, Ca	80Y	Yam
2.	Darryl Hurst, Houston, Tx	34N	Oss
3.	Keith Ulicki, Kenosha, Wi	87G	HD

Grand National Points Standings after Round 15

Rank	Rider	Pts
1.	Gene Romero	680
2.	Jim Rice	657
3.	Dick Mann	619
4.	Jimmy Odom	538
5.	Mark Brelsford	438
6.	Dave Aldana	419
7.	Dave Sehl	333
8.	Eddie Mulder	326
9.	Kel Carruthers	301
10.	John Hateley	292

Extra Extra

- A rocking crowd of 9,200 turned out for the National.
- Lots of hotshoes did not make the main. Some of which were; Last year's winner Bart Markel, Gene Romero, Dick Mann, Jimmy Odom, Mark Brelsford, Eddie Mulder and John Hateley. Roger Reiman was the only heat winner who didn't transfer to the National.
- There was no mention of Barry Briggs never returning to AMA competition after his run in with officials at Sante Fe last year.
- The Briggs Yamaha screamer was built by Kel Carruthers and Don Vesco.
- There were more brothers advancing to the finals this week. Not the Palmgren's though; Frank Ulicki made it to the GNC, with brother Keith competing in the Junior main.

1971 Pocono Road Race
Mann Wins Race-Protest-Points!

GNC Round #16 of 21 **Date:** August 22, 1971 **Type:** Road Race **Venue:** Pocono International Raceway	**Purse:** $15,000.00 **Location:** Pocono, Pa **Surface:** Pavement **Course Length:** 1.8 Miles **Laps:** 55 (approx.) **Distance:** 100 Miles

Dick Mann had things swing back his way at the first ever Pocono National. He topped the race after a great scuffle with Kel Carruthers, giving him the points to top rival Gene Romero. In addition, Mann and seven other riders were given additional points when the AMA unexpectedly decided in the riders favor over the Corona starting line debacle. Those 28 points awarded to Mann helped him back atop the standings. It was win number 4 for the season, equaling his career high mark for one season, in 1964. Mann's GNC win total was now 22, with only Joe Leonard and Bart Markel having more with 27 and 28 wins respectively.

Kel Carruthers was in contention for the win up to the last corner of the race but was forced to settle for the runner-up slot again, similar to the Kent Road Race. Dave Aldana turned in a great pavement ride to round out the podium. Yvon DuHamel suffered the greatest disappointment of the day, though finishing 3rd. As in so many previous road races, DuHamel dominated early, but his two-stroke machines thirst and mechanical problems robbed him of a win, (again). Kawasaki was even offering a $10,000 bonus to the Kawasaki rider that scored its first big-bore National, surely adding to Duhamel's frustration. His day was coming though.

Dick Mann's combination of winning the road race National and points from the Corona race allowed him to take a narrow lead over Gene Romero, 738 to 732. Romero had a good run in the National, finishing 7th. Jim Rice was 8th in the race, and slipped back to third, still close with 706 points. The top 5 had now pulled a huge advantage over the rest of the pack. Jimmy Odom was the closest with 557 points, but was injured at a non-national after Corona and was probably out for the year. Dave Aldana's podium finish moved him up to fifth with 486 points. Mark Brelsford scored a few points and was 6th with 454 points. Dave Sehl remained in seventh, Kel Carruthers was eighth and Don Emde moved back into the top ten with his 6th place finish.

Heats

Yvon DuHamel (Kaw) ripped out front at the start of Heat 1 and was never sighted by the pack again. Jim Rice (BSA) showed his growing pavement prowess by battling with Jody Nicholas (Suz) through much of the race. Two-time champ Gary Nixon (Tri) showed he still had the skills, burning by both Rice and Nicholas for 2nd position. DuHamel's speed would be the faster of the two heats.

GNC champ Gene Romero (Tri) led early in Heat 2, chased by Don Emde (BSA) and by now racing buddies Dick Mann (BSA) and Kel Carruthers (Yam). Emde took the point on lap 2 only to have the two veterans blow by with Mann taking the point. Carruthers managed to get by Mann on the last lap to take the win.

National

The master of "cold tires and a full fuel tank", Yvon DuHamel, pulled the holeshot and immediately raced to a big lead. Kel Carruthers and Dick Mann were 2nd and 3rd, chased by Don Emde, Jody Nicholas and Gene Romero. DuHamel seemed to have everybody covered, but the upcoming pit stops had him worried. Several times he had races nearly won, only to have some kind of Snafu derail his hopes. The stop on lap 34 seemed to go okay, but sure enough his bike had slowed. Kel Carruthers and Mann now controlled the top two spots. DuHamel was now in 3rd, with Jody Nicholas moving past Don Emde and Dave Aldana with Romero behind. Back up front, Mann passed Carruthers for the lead on the 40th circuit. A few laps later Aldana caught fire, passing both Emde and Nicholas to take the 4th spot.

As the laps closed Mann and Carruthers got into some serious dicing. Carruthers was a bit faster on the straights with Mann holding an advantage through the last corners. The two swapped the lead at least five times. With two laps to go, the swapping continued. On the last circuit, Mann had a little more speed through the last corner and narrowly led Carruthers across the stripe. The positions behind were DuHamel, Aldana, Nicholas, Emde, Romero and Rice.

Results

Race: 100 Road Race National
Race Time: 1:07.54

Rank	Rider	Number	Make
1.	Dick Mann, Richmond, Ca	4	BSA
2.	Kel Carruthers, El Cajon, Ca	73	Yam
3.	Yvon DuHamel, LaSalle, Que., Can	11	Yam
4.	Dave Aldana, Santa Ana, Ca	3	BSA
5.	Jody Nicholas, Newport Beach, Ca	23	Suz
6.	Don Emde, San Diego, Ca	25	BSA
7.	Gene Romero, San Luis Obispo, Ca	1	Tri
8.	Jim Rice, Palo Alto, Ca	2	BSA
9.	Ron Pierce, Bakersfield, Ca	37	Suz
10.	Ron Grant, Brisbane, Ca	42	Suz
11.	Don Castro, Hollister, Ca	5	Tri
12.	Duane McDaniels, Milford, Mi	58	Yam
13.	Cliff Carr, Watertown, Mass	87	Kaw
14.	Ginger Molloy, Huntley, NZ	39	Kaw
15.	Hurley Wilvert, Westminster, Ca	51	Kaw
16.	Walt Fulton, Hacienda Heights, Ca	17	Kaw
17.	Marty Lunde, Redondo Beach, Ca	66	Yam
18.	Jimmy Odom, Fremont, Ca	18	Yam
19.	Mark Brelsford, San Bruno, Ca	7	HD
20.	Eddie Mulder, Burbank, Ca	20	Tri

Race: Junior/Novice Final

Rank	Rider	Number	Make
1.	Doug Libby, Dearborn, Mi	88	Yam
2.	Jerry Christopher, W. Covina, Ca	83	Yam
3.	John Greene, San Mateo, Ca	414	Yam

Grand National Points Standings after Round 16

Rank	Rider	Pts
1.	Dick Mann	738
2.	Gene Romero	732
3.	Jim Rice	706
4.	Jimmy Odom	557
5.	Dave Aldana	486
6.	Mark Brelsford	454
7.	Dave Sehl	389
8.	Kel Carruthers	383
9.	Eddie Mulder	335
10.	Don Emde	322

Extra Extra

- Gary Fisher survived a nasty crash in the Lightweight race. He got tangled up with another rider and launched into a 100 mph endo. He walked away, bruised and shaken with road rash on his gloveless hands.
- Kel Carruthers captured yet another Lightweight win.
- Tire problems were a concern at the first time National. The only apparent victim was Gary Nixon who had a blow out early in the main. The two-time GNC champ went down hard, suffering a banged up arm.
- The Pocono International Raceway is a truly unique facility in design, location and ownership. It's trademark "tri-oval" features three distinctly different corners, each designed after three different tracks: Trenton Speedway, Indianapolis Motor Speedway and the Milwaukee Mile. There are three separate infield sections that can be used independently, (allowing simultaneous use of the tracks), or linked together to come up with many different combinations. The tracks location is in the scenic Pennsylvania mountains and is close to major population centers such as Philadelphia and New York City. The track has been run by the Mattioli family since it's opening in 1968. Most major sanctioning bodies have held races at the track including the AMA, NASCAR, USAC, CART, IRL, SCCA. It is frequently used by driving schools and racing clubs. The track underwent a multi-million dollar renovation starting in 1990.

GNC Round #17 of 21 **Date:** September 5, 1971 **Type:** Road Race **Venue:** Alabama International Motor Speedway	**Purse:** $18,000.00 **Location:** Talladega, Al **Surface:** Pavement **Course Length**: 1.8 Miles **Laps:** 55 (approx.) **Distance:** 100 Miles

On a very hot Labor Day race at Talladega, Alabama, Yvon DuHamel finally captured a long overdue AMA National road race. DuHamel had been in serious contention to win a GNC since 1968. Time after time a combination of bad luck and two-stroke maladies, (first with Yamahas, now Kawasakis), had struck him down; seizures, broken pipes, ignition failures, excess fuel consumption. You name it, it happened to Yvon DuHamel. He was an extraordinarily talented and bold racer; he always rode as hard as he could, early or late in a race. His determination never wavered, never giving up on his quest to score a National win. He and Team Hansen finally figured out a pit strategy that worked with the thirsty Kawasaki's. Dick Mann scored another top placing, his second place adding to his points lead over Gene Romero who dropped out while in the top 5. Don Emde showed he was going to win soon with yet another podium finish. Premier road race talents Kel Carruthers and Cal Rayborn both had bad luck. Carruthers had a nasty crash, (not of his making), and Rayborn was again the victim of the Harley-Davidson iron XR curse. Veteran campaigner Ralph White put in an impressive 4th place run.

There was no change in the top 6 in points. Mann stretched his lead over Gene Romero and Dave Aldana added a handful of points. In the rest of the top 10, Kel Carruthers moved up a spot and Don Emde moved up two. Dave Sehl slipped back two spots and Eddie Mulder dropped out of the top 10. With the end of the season approaching, only Mann, Romero, Jim Rice and Dave Aldana had a mathematical shot at the title.

National

New Zealand racer Ginger Molloy (Kaw) shot out in front of the snarling 42 rider pack. Yvon DuHamel went by Molloy as they entered the twisties on lap 1 and stretched a big lead. Molloy had mechanical troubles, retiring on lap 3. DuHamel was setting a blinding pace up front, turning the fastest lap of the day on lap 5 at over 112 mph. Kel Carruthers had broken from the pack into 2nd and was attempting to keep DuHamel in sight. Fighting for 3rd were Dick Mann (BSA) and Cal Rayborn who was praying the blankity-blank XRTT would hold together. He ran a short distance behind Carruthers and witnessed a lapped rider veer right in front of the Australian. Carruthers was promptly sent flying over the bars with he and the bike going end-over-end. Undaunted Carruthers knocked the bike back into rideable shape and took off to the pits. He lost a bunch of positions, but made it back in the race to finish a credible 12th. With Carruthers departure from the front, Mann and Rayborn moved to 2nd and 3rd, carrying on a fantastic side-by-side duel all over the track.

Pit stops, the Achilles heel of the Kawasaki team were coming up as DuHamel neared the 20 lap mark. He decided to pit on lap 17 with a near 30 second lead. The stop was an amazing quick 4 seconds. DuHamel screamed back on the track with Mann and Rayborn still not in sight. Pit stops shuffled the order a bit with Don Emde taking over the runner-up slot from Mann. Mann, 1971's hottest road racer, bore down and despite an oily visor, worked back around Emde. Rayborn had to stop twice in the pits, but still managed to catch and pass Emde as well. Unfortunately, his problems would continue and a frustrated Rayborn faded to 11th spot.

DuHamel never backed off his pace and his lead grew to over a minute late in the race. This allowed him to maintain his lead even after a second fuel stop. GNC champ Gene Romero (Tri) was out with mechanical trouble on lap 38 after running as high as 5th spot. Ralph White worked his way through the field to 4th and may have been a threat to Emde and Mann, but ran out of time. At the finish, DuHamel had a huge lead over BSA teammates Mann and Emde, White and Dave Aldana.

Race: 200 Mile Road Race National
Race Time: 1:49:53

Rank	Rider	Number	Make
1.	Yvon DuHamel, LaSalle, Que., Can	11	Yam
2.	Dick Mann, Richmond, Ca	4	BSA
3.	Don Emde, San Diego, Ca	25	BSA
4.	Ralph White, Torrance, Ca	47	Kaw
5.	Dave Aldana, Santa Ana, Ca	3	BSA
6.	Ron Grant, Brisbane, Ca	42	Suz
7.	Duane McDaniels, Milford, Mi	8	Yam
8.	Dave Smith, Lakewood, Ca	15	Yam
9.	Tom Rockwood, Gardena, Ca	9	Tri
10.	Ken Molyneux, Weston, Ont., Can	36	Yam
11.	Cal Rayborn, Spring Valley, Ca	25	HD
12.	Kel Carruthers, El Cajon, Ca	73	Yam
13.	Don Castro, Hollister, Ca	5	Tri
14.	Dusty Coppage, Chatsworth, Ca	21	Yam
15.	Gene Romero, San Luis Obispo, Ca	1	Tri
16.	John Skinner, Auburn, Ala	35	Yam
17.	Jess Thomas, Sea Cliff, NY	57	Tri
18.	Art Baumann, Brisbane, Ca	24	Suz
19.	Dave Sehl, Atlanta, Ga	16	HD
20.	Gary Fisher, Parkesburg, Pa	30	Hon

Race: 76 Mile Junior Final

Rank	Rider	Number	Make
1.	Mike Lane, Bakersfield, Ca	4	Kaw
2.	R.G. Wakefield, Indianapolis, Ind	76	Kaw
3.	Kenny Roberts, Redwood City, Ca	80	Yam

Grand National Points Standings after Round 17

Rank	Rider	Pts
1.	Dick Mann	820
2.	Gene Romero	760
3.	Jim Rice	706
4.	Jimmy Odom	557
5.	Dave Aldana	547
6.	Mark Brelsford	454
7.	Kel Carruthers	420
8.	Don Emde	409
9.	Dave Sehl	405
10.	Don Castro	356

- A good crowd of around 15,000 turned out despite the oppressive Alabama heat and humidity.
- Yvon Duhamel's record race speed, averaging over 108 MPH, made Talladega the fastest road race course on the circuit.
- It was a big payday for DuHamel. Besides his share of the purse, he received a $10,000.00 bonus for winning Kawasaki's first big bike National.
- Kawasaki's "dry break" refueling system worked very well. Team riders were in and out very quickly. Bob Hansen and crew had the stops down to perfection. As the old saying goes, "necessity is the mother of invention".
- Of the 42 riders starting the National, only 12 finished.
- Gritty Kel Carruthers soldiered to a 12th place finish despite his accident and having to borrow gas from a spectator after running out of gas!
- New Zealand racer Ginger Molloy finally stopped Carruthers winning streak in the Lightweight event. Carruthers was runner-up.
- Sante Fe winner Robert E. Lee had a bad day in the Lightweight race. He injured both ankles in a nasty getoff.

1971 Ascot Half-Mile
First Timer Rockwood Scores in a Thriller!

GNC Round #18 of 21 **Date:** September 25, 1971 **Type:** Half-Mile **Venue:** Ascot Park **Location:** Gardena, Ca	**Purse:** $10,000.00 **Surface:** Dirt **Course Length:** ½ Mile **Laps:** 20 **Distance:** 10 Miles

Factory Triumph star Tom Rockwood claimed a very exciting first win over challengers Jody Nicholas and John Hateley. The crowd of around 10,000 witnessed at least 14 unofficial lead changes in the National. Rockwood aboard the Danny Macias-tuned Triumph fended off Jody Nicholas riding the Harold Allison Norton and John Hateley on the rapid Jack Hateley-tuned Triumph. The win was in doubt right to the end when Rockwood took over, barely topping Hateley and Nicholas. Son of famed announcer Roxy Rockwood, Tom was fast on both dirt and pavement. He cut his teeth at Ascot and it would be the scene of his only National win.

The Ascot surface was very fast with eight riders recording 22 second bracket times, as well producing record breaking heat and main event times.

Dick Mann had one of his best runs ever at Ascot, notching a 6th place finish. Title rival Gene Romero failed to make the main. Mann's finish allowed him to stretch his lead, 872 points to 760, a 112 point gap. Jim Rice managed an 8th place in the final and was a mere 8 points behind Romero. The top three were now well ahead of the rest of the riders. Going into the last three Nationals, only Mann, Romero and Rice still had a mathematical shot at the title. Jimmy Odom who had missed the last several Nationals was finally crow barred out 4th place by Dave Aldana. Mark Brelsford maintained sixth, Dave Sehl moved up to 7th, Kel Carruthers was now eighth, Don Emde was 9th and John Hateley again moved back into the top ten with his 2nd place finish.

Time Trials

No stranger to Ascot, Mark Brelsford was the fastest Expert aboard his factory Harley at 22.66. Jody Nicholas (Nor) was a very close 22.68 which was tied by John Hateley (Tri). Canadian Dave Sehl (HD) showed he could ride the clay as well as the cush' with a 22.79. Tom Rockwood (Tri) clocked in at 22.80. Junior Kenny Roberts (Yam) set the fastest overall time of the night with a blistering 22.54.

Heats

Fast-timer Mark Brelsford immediately shot out front and was never challenged. Dave Sehl grabbed 2nd. Lloyd Houchins, was apparently recovered from his early season injuries and scored the last transfer spot. Brelsford's winning time set a new 10-lap record.

Heat 2 saw a preview of the National with Jody Nicholas and Tom Rockwood battling for the lead. The two had a great duel with Nicholas holding the point and Rockwood applying heavy pressure. GNC champ Gene Romero (Tri) was stuck in the pack and fell while trying to break through. The defending champ was out for the night, missing out on desperately needed points. As the laps waned, Rockwood managed to finally work past Nicholas for the win. Amazingly, Rockwood's heat time was 3 seconds faster than Brelsford's briefly held record. The final transfer was taken a strange way. Frank Gillespie (Tri) held the spot at the finish, but a flagging mistake sent him around an additional lap. He went down hard as he dropped the bike to avoid riders on the "real" cool down lap. Gillespie suffered a fractured clavicle. He was advanced to the National and given last place points and money.

Heat 3 witnessed an early battle between BSA star Dave Aldana and fast as ever Ascot regular Mel Lacher (Nor). It took John Hateley a few laps to get going as he tracked the lead duo down. He soon went by both and headed to the win. Points leader Dick Mann (BSA) just managed to get the last transfer to the semi.

Semi

The talent laden semi would have made a great National. Among those fighting for the last spots in the National were Dick Mann, Jim Rice (BSA), Mark Williams (Tri), Keith Mashburn (Yam), Paul Bostrom (Tri), Don Castro (Tri) and 4-time Ascot winner Sammy Tanner (Nor). Local star Dewayne Keeter on a Harley KR, launched into the lead over the aforementioned stars and ran away for the win. Rice and Mann struggled from the back, both passing Mashburn for the final transfer spots in the National.

National

Tom Rockwood shot ahead of the pack, opening up a small gap. He was joined on lap 2 by Jody Nicholas and John Hateley. Nicholas returned the pressure Rockwood gave him in their heat and made the pass for the lead on lap 9. Nicholas looked strong, but began feeling the effects of a rapidly wearing rear tire. The lead changed numerous times with Rockwood back on top by the 12th circuit. Hateley was still a close 3rd. Rockwood could not shake Nicholas, who often stuck a wheel out front, but couldn't close the deal. When Nicholas made a few bobbles, Hateley was right there and scorched by on lap 18. He was soon all over Rockwood who managed to find just enough speed to keep the closing Hateley at bay. It was one of the most exciting finishes in Ascot history. Dave Sehl put in an impressive ride in 4th, Mert Lawwill was 5th, Dick Mann had one of his best Ascot rides in 6th, and Lloyd Houchins was 7th, Jim Rice in 8th, Keeter an impressive 9th on his KR and Dave Aldana in 10th.

Results

Race: 20 Lap Half-Mile National
Race Time: 7:47.94

Rank	Rider	Number	Make
1.	Tom Rockwood, Gardena, Ca	9	Tri
2.	John Hateley, Van Nuys, Ca	43R	Tri
3.	Jody Nicholas, Newport Beach, Ca	23	Nor
4.	Dave Sehl, Atlanta, Ga	16	HD
5.	Mel Lacher, San Diego, Ca	90	Nor
6.	Dick Mann, Richmond, Ca	4	BSA
7.	Lloyd Houchins, La Crescenta, Ca	29	BSA
8.	Jim Rice, Palo Alto, Ca	2	BSA
9.	Dewayne Keeter, Ojai, Ca	44X	HD
10.	Dave Aldana, Santa Ana, Ca	3	BSA
11.	Mark Brelsford, San Bruno, Ca	7	HD
12.	Frank Gillespie, Orinda, Ca	22	Tri

Race: 14 Lap Junior Final

Rank	Rider	Number	Make
1.	Kenny Roberts, Redwood City, Ca	80Y	Yam
2.	Ron Moore, San Bernardino, Ca	37R	Tri
3.	Dennis Kanegae, Garden Grove, Ca	51X	Tri

Grand National Points Standings after Round 18

Rank	Rider	Pts
1.	Dick Mann	872
2.	Gene Romero	760
3.	Jim Rice	752
4.	Dave Aldana	587
5.	Jimmy Odom	557
6.	Mark Brelsford	491
7.	Dave Sehl	466
8.	Kel Carruthers	420
9.	Don Emde	409
10.	John Hateley	366

- Kenny Roberts captured yet another Junior event. Scott's main rival Gary Scott sat out the event due to a broken wrist suffered at the Corona half-mile the previous week. Eastern invader Frenchie LeBlanc fell while leading his heat race.
- DeWayne Keeter became the last rider to put a Harley-Davidson KR into a GNC event. He was very much with the program in 9th place.

1971 Oklahoma City Half-Mile
Romero Wins OK Shootout-Tightens Up Points Battle

GNC Round #19 of 21	**Purse:** $7,500.00
Date: October 3, 1971	**Surface:** Dirt
Type: Half-Mile	**Course Length:** ½ Mile
Venue: State Fair Speedway	**Laps:** 20
Location: Oklahoma City, Ok	**Distance:** 10 Miles

GNC champ Gene Romero's back was against the wall as the 1971 season was drawing to a close. His fall at Ascot cost him and he responded well to the pressure, winning at the rough, rutted Oklahoma track aboard the C.R. Axtell/Mike Libby prepped, Nick Deligianis-tuned factory Triumph. The National was lucky to run at all after heavy rains rolled through the area. Racers were forced to bring out there vans and after much packing, the track was finally runnable. The program was further delayed till the track doctor arrived.

In the "Fred Nix Memorial" main event Eddie Mulder led much of the race and finished a very strong 2nd. This season had produced some of "Fast Eddie's" best ever oval track runs. Dave Aldana came from back in the pack to finish 3rd. Jim Rice was 4th. Points leader Mann was in the hunt and finished 5th, negating some of Romero's advantage. If Romero was to retain his title he would have to run very well at the remaining Nationals at Nazareth and Ontario.

Dick Mann kept a decent advantage of 86 points over race winner Gene Romero. While Jim Rice still had a slight chance in third, the title chase was coming down to the top two with just two races left. Both were very consistent riders with Romero maybe having a slight horsepower advantage at Nazareth. Mann was clearly the stronger road racer headed into Ontario. This had to make him the favorite when taking into consideration the huge road race points that were at stake at the season finale.

Time Trials

Jim Rice set the fastest time on the rough track at 25.06. Charlie Seale was back a bit with a 25.34. Both were BSA mounted.

Heats

Heat 1 offered the riders about any line they were brave enough to try as there was traction across the surface. Traditional groove rider Jim Rice (BSA) showed he was smart and opportunistic, immediately going to the high line and running away with the race. Triumph riders Terry Dorsch and Mark Williams took the other transfer spots.

John Weaver (BSA) a strong Indiana competitor, had the crowd checking their programs as he led three-time GNC champ Bart Markel (HD), Charlie Seale (BSA) and 1963 GNC champ Dick Mann, also on a BSA. Markel was experimenting with lines all over the track and closed up on Weaver, but couldn't make a pass stick. Seale eventually dropped Markel back to 3rd. Mann also challenged Markel for the last transfer spot, but had to settle for 4th and a semi ticket.

The third heat featured a nifty battle between "Team Mexican" Dave Aldana (BSA) and Gene Romero (Tri). Aldana rode the bottom rail for a narrow win. Hot rookie John Hateley (Tri) was 3rd.

Semi

Dave Sehl (HD) topped a field of heavy hitters in the last chance event. Grabbing the last two National tickets were Dick Mann (BSA) and Eddie Mulder (Tri).

National

Dave Aldana guessed just right at the flag, immediately pulling out a gap on the field. Charlie Seale was next, followed by Gene Romero, Eddie Mulder and Jim Rice. Mulder was on a charge and passed Aldana on lap 5. Mulder began stretching to a big lead. Romero bumped Seale back to 3rd. Seale would continue to slip back and finished in 8th. With 10 laps to go, Romero had begun to close on Mulder with Aldana 3rd and Rice running the high line in 4th.

On lap 15, Romero caught and passed Mulder and pulled away to a small gap at the finish. Behind the front two were Aldana, Rice, Dick Mann, Bart Markel, John Weaver, Charlie Seale, John Hateley, Terry Dorsch and Mark Williams.

Results

Race: 20 Lap Half-Mile National

Rank	Rider	Number	Make
1.	Gene Romero, San Luis Obispo, Ca	1	Tri
2.	Eddie Mulder, Northridge, Ca	20	Tri
3.	Dave Aldana, Santa Ana, Ca	3	BSA
4.	Jim Rice, Palo Alto, Ca	2	BSA
5.	Dick Mann, Richmond, Ca	4	BSA
6.	Bart Markel, Flint, Mi	32	HD
7.	Dave Sehl, Atlanta, Ga	16	HD
8.	John Weaver, Fort Wayne, Ind	52	BSA
9.	Charlie Seale, Lantana, Fl	76	BSA
10.	Terry Dorsch, Granada Hills, Ca	65R	Tri
11.	John Hateley, Van Nuys, Ca	43R	Tri
12.	Mark Williams, Springfield, Ore	41	Tri

Race: Junior Final

Rank	Rider	Number	Make
1.	Kenny Roberts, Redwood City, Ca	80Y	Yam
2.	Dave Rupe, Oklahoma City, Ok	38M	Tri
3.	Robert Ely, Kansas City, Ks	24K	BSA

Grand National Points Standings after Round 19

Rank	Rider	Pts
1.	Dick Mann	928
2.	Gene Romero	842
3.	Jim Rice	813
4.	Dave Aldana	654
5.	Jimmy Odom	557
6.	Dave Sehl	515
7.	Mark Brelsford	491
8.	Kel Carruthers	420
9.	Eddie Mulder	413
10.	Don Emde	409

1971 Nazareth Mile
Romero Wins 2nd In a Row!

GNC Round #20 of 21	**Purse:** $12,000.00
Date: October 9, 1971	**Surface:** Dirt
Type: Mile	**Course Length**: 1 1/8 Mile
Venue: Nazareth Speedway	**Laps:** 30
Location: Lehigh Valley, Pa	**Distance:** 30 Miles, (approx.)

Gene Romero narrowed Dick Mann's point lead at the rescheduled, rain shortened Nazareth 1 1/8 Mile National. Romero took control of the race after early leader Cal Rayborn had trouble and dropped back. Rival Dick Mann chased Romero to the end of the race. Rain showers during the event made the surface slippery and when a rider fell on lap 31, the AMA officials called the race complete. Not a big deal on the surface, but Dick Mann was the rider who fell. Romero protested on the spot because the decision would give Mann 2nd place back. He did not file an official protest though. This was somewhat surprising as a decision in Romero's favor might have been a title decider. A classy move on Romero's part and a lucky break for Mann. Don Castro put in a late race charge to grab the last podium spot. Cal Rayborn hurt his foot while up front and managed to hang onto 4th place, his best finish since Livonia.

Gene Romero's win narrowed the point gap to 78 points; the championship would be decided by the final National at Ontario. It was really Mann's championship to lose. If he did well he would take the title. Romero had to hope for a top finish with Mann having some bad luck. Jim Rice suffered a DNF at Nazareth, effectively putting him out of the title chase. Dave Aldana maintained 4th in points. Dave Sehl's 8th place finish in the National moved him to fifth place in the standings, his highest ranking of the year.

Heats

Dick Mann (BSA) led the first heat away with Mark Brelsford (HD) and fast qualifier Keith Mashburm (Yam) breathing down his exhaust pipes. After three circuits, Mashburn moved by Brelsford for 2nd and tried to reel Mann in. Brelsford soon mounted a charge of his own, getting back by Mashburn and taking the lead from Mann with one lap to go. Mann managed to make a final pass for the lead in the last turn.

Dave Sehl (HD) pulled the holeshot in Heat 2, but teammate Cal Rayborn had control as they headed down the backstretch. Rayborn pulled out a fairly comfortable lead to the finish followed by Sehl and Eddie Mulder (Tri).

BSA star Jim Rice led Heat 3, wire-to-wire, with Gene Romero (Tri) close at the finish. Dave Aldana (BSA) was 3rd.

National

Threatening weather further added to drama as the race began. Dick Mann (BSA) pulled the holeshot but Cal Rayborn (HD) had a healthy horse this day and drafted by on lap 2. Keith Mashburn's Yamaha was also running strong and was close behind the lead duo, followed by Gene Romero (Tri). Romero soon moved by Mashburn for 3rd. He and title rival Mann engaged in a great battle, exchanging spots several times. Behind them Jim Rice (BSA) was on the move and passed Mashburn for 4th. Leader Rayborn began to slow, a victim of hitting a rock with his sliding foot. He faded a little, but hung on to 4th. Around the 10th circuit, it was the GNC points leaders out front; Romero held the point, followed by Mann and Rice. A few laps later, Rice's engine gave up and he slid into the fence, unhurt. Romero and Mann continued to pull away from the pack, now chased by Don Castro (Tri) who appeared late in the race, knocking Rayborn back another spot. Just as Romero looked to be home free, rain had begun to fall. Mann slid his BSA down in turn 4 and the red flag came out. They decided to shorten the distance to 30 laps. Mann and Rayborn both got their positions back. Romero did not lodge an official protest and Mann left Nazareth with a solid points lead heading to the final race at Ontario. He appeared to be holding the cards for his second championship. Still, less than 80 points separated the two; going into the race anything was possible.

Results

Race: Mile 50 Lap Mile National
Race Time:

Rank	Rider	Number	Make
1.	Gene Romero, San Luis Obispo, Ca	1	Tri
2.	Dick Mann, Richmond, Ca	4	BSA
3.	Don Castro, Hollister, Ca	5	Tri
4.	Cal Rayborn, Spring Valley, Ca	25	HD
5.	Keith Mashburn, Santa Susana	19	Yam
6.	Dave Aldana, Santa Ana, Ca	3	BSA
7.	John Hateley, Van Nuys, Ca	43R	Tri
8.	Dave Sehl, Atlanta, Ga	16	HD
9.	Mark Brelsford, San Bruno, Ca	7	HD
10.	Jimmy Maness, Augusta, Ga	61	HD
11.	Don Twigg, Hagerstown, Md	15D	Tri
12.	Terry Dorsch, Granada Hills, Ca	65R	Tri
13.	Roger Reiman, Kewanee, Ill	78	HD
14.	Larry Darr, Mansfield, Oh	27	HD
15.	Norm Robinson, Spencerport, NY	72	BSA
16.	Doug Sehl, Waterdown, Que., Can	6T	Tri
17.	John Weaver, Fort Wayne, Ind	52	BSA
18.	Gary Nixon, Phoenix, Md	10	Tri
19.	Jim Rice, Palo Alto, Ca	2	BSA
20.	Eddie Mulder, Northridge, Ca	20	Tri

Race: Junior Final

Rank	Rider	Number	Make
1.	Kenny Roberts, Redwood City, Ca	80Y	Yam
2.	Keith Ulicki, Kenosha, Wi	87G	HD
3.	Herb Potts, Richmond, Va	25C	Yam

Grand National Points Standings after Round 20

Rank	Rider	Pts
1.	Dick Mann	1002
2.	Gene Romero	924
3.	Jim Rice	826
4.	Dave Aldana	706
5.	Dave Sehl	561
6.	Jimmy Odom	557
7.	Mark Brelsford	534
8.	John Hateley	452
9.	Don Castro	423
10.	Eddie Mulder	423

- A solid crowd of 5000 was present.
- Keith Mashburn on the Shell Yamaha set a new record during qualifying, 40.78 at 99.58 mph.
- Junior Kenny Roberts scored another win. His big east coast rival Frenchie LeBlanc was inconsolable after his bike broke an ignition wire while running a close second in the main.

GNC Final Round #21	Purse: $53,100.00
Date: October 17, 1971	Surface: Pavement
Type: Road Race	Course Length: 1.8 Miles
Venue: Ontario Motor	Laps: 69 Per Segment
Speedway	Distance: 250 Miles, 2 X 125
Location: Ontario, Ca	Mile Segments

The modern, cavernous Ontario Speedway hosted one of the biggest paying road races ever, billed as the Champion Spark Plug Classic, running a lengthy 250 miles, split into two segments. A big crowd of 33,000 turned out to watch the road race stars at the modern Ontario facility. Though state of the art, most riders found the layout to be bland and featureless. The big purse overcame any serious course objections. International star John Cooper on a factory BSA topped all the regular AMA competitors in his U.S. debut. He narrowly topped fellow international star Kel Carruthers in a true photo finish. Ron Grant finally was able to put the Suzuki teams woes behind him to finish 3rd. The race was run with Olympic style scoring with two 125-lap segments.

Dick Mann was able to do well enough, (6th, & 19th), to finish 9th overall. It turned out to be enough. Gene Romero gave it all he had, up front before crashing in Heat 1, but managing to lead Heat 2 till knocked out with mechanical trouble. Luck just went Mann's way. It was a great championship between the two California riders. They were from different generations and had very different personalities. What they had in common was great skill and determination.

Cooper's winning BSA was claimed after the race by another competitor. See "*Extras*" for more details.

Heats

Ralph White (Kaw) led Heat 1 for the first couple laps till Dick Mann (BSA) and Cal Rayborn (HD) ripped by. On lap 3, Rayborn took over and led to the finish.

Yvon DuHamel (Kaw) led Heat 2 flag-to-flag. Gary Nixon was strong on Paul Smart's specially prepared factory Triumph but couldn't close on the fleet Canadian. Despite a practice crash, Kel Carruthers (Yam) was with the program in 3rd. GNC champ Gene Romero (Tri) was impressive in 4th.

National
Segment 1

Fast qualifier Yvon DuHamel (Kaw) shot out to an early lead, but two-time GNC champ Gary Nixon quickly caught the French-Canadian. Nixon's luck had been awful in 1971 and he was out to show he was still one of the best. He and DuHamel staged a titanic battle. DuHamel's Kawasaki triple had power to spare on the long straightaways, but Nixon's better handling Triumph could easily move by on the twisties. The two traded the lead all over the big course. Behind early were Cal Rayborn (HD), John Cooper (BSA), Kel Carruthers (Yam) and Dick Mann (BSA). Gene Romero (Tri) ran close behind, but hit an infield slick spot and went down, seriously jeopardizing his title chances. He was scored in 41st place. Rayborn fell out of serious contention with recurring engine troubles. Cooper took over 2nd, Carruthers was 3rd with Mann slipping back to 6th. The win was decided by pit strategy. As usual DuHamel's thirsty Kawasaki necessitated a fuel stop. Nixon was supposed to stop as well, but gambled he could go the whole distance. His gutsy move paid off. He gained a big lead when DuHamel pitted.

Segment 2

Gary Nixon sensed victory was at hand and led the field away for Heat 2. DuHamel stalled his Kawasaki on the line and once underway was tearing through the pack. By lap 6 DuHamel was already up to 3rd. Soon after, Jess Thomas's Triumph sprayed oil all over Turn 8. Nixon rode right into it, crashing hard. John Cooper managed to avoid the oil and continued on with the lead in hand. Behind a huge melee ensued with numerous riders involved including DuHamel, Dick Mann, Dave Aldana, and Reg Pridmore. Fortunately no one was seriously injured and all got moving again, at least to the pits.

Cooper continued to lead with Kel Carruthers and Gene Romero right behind. Romero's luck seemed to be turning; if he stayed up front he could take over the points lead. Romero turned up the wick and impressively passed both international stars. Unbelievably Romero's Triumph broke a throttle cable on lap 27, and the fairy tale comeback was over. Even worse for Romero, Mann had returned to the track after the accident and was moving at good speed. The rest of the race saw a fantastic battle between Cooper and Carruthers. The two cleanly swapped the lead countless times over the last 12 laps. Carruthers had the point over the last couple of laps. He had a small lead coming out of the last corner but Cooper was able to draft the Yamaha pilot and nipped Carruthers at the line by inches. Jim Rice was 3rd, Dave Smith 4th, and Ginger Malloy 5th. A beat and battered Dick Mann and machine soldiered in 19th place, good enough to make him the 1971 AMA Grand National Champion. It was his second title, the first in 1963, giving him the longest span between GNC titles in history.

Results

Race: 250 Mile Road Race National

Rank	Rider	Number	Make
1.	John Cooper, London England	28	BSA
2.	Kel Carruthers, El Cajon, Ca	73	Yam
3.	Ron Grant, Brisbane, Ca	42	Suz
4.	Dave Smith, Lakewood, Ca	15	Yam
5.	Art Baumann, Central Valley, Ca	24	Suz
6.	Jim Rice, Palo Alto, Ca	2	BSA
7.	Ginger Molloy, Huntley, New Zealand	39	Suz
8.	Don Castro, Hollister, Ca	5	Tri
9.	Dick Mann, Richmond, Ca	4	BSA
10.	Fred Guttner, E. Detroit, Mi	69	Yam
11.	Tom Rockwood, Gardena, Ca	9	Tri
12.	Ralph White, Torrance, Ca	47	Kaw
13.	Gary Nixon, Phoenix, Md	10	Tri
14.	Hurley Wilvert, Westminster, Ca	51	Yam
15.	Larry Schafer, Washington, D.C.	53	HD
16.	Don Emde, San Diego, Ca	25	BSA
17.	Cliff Carr, Arlington, Mass	87	Kaw
18.	Bert Clark, Vancouver, B.C.	43	Yam
19.	David Damron, Riverside, Ca	89	Yam
20.	John McGillivray, Los Angeles, Ca	94	BSA

Race: Junior Final

Rank	Rider	Number	Make
1.	Mike Lane, Bakersfield, Ca	4	Kaw
2.	Mike Kidd, Hurst, Tx	72	Yam
3.	Jerry Greene, San Mateo, Ca	41	Yam

Grand National Points Final Standings

Rank	Rider	Pts
1.	Dick Mann	1057
2.	Gene Romero	924
3.	Jim Rice	893
4.	Dave Aldana	706
5.	Dave Sehl	561
6.	Jimmy Odom	557
7.	Mark Brelsford	534
8.	Kel Carruthers	521
9.	Don Castro	479
10.	John Hateley	452

Extra Extra

- John Cooper took home a whopping $14,500.00 of Ontario's purse.
- Other British stars didn't fare as well;
    - Phil Read was slated to ride a trick Kawasaki for Team Monotrac and Wes Cooley. When the bike wasn't ready for what Read considered adequate practice time, he vacated the premises. California racer George Kerker took over the ride.
    - Rod Gould shipped his own exotic Yamaha over for the race, but didn't get it to the AMA in time for approval. Mel Dineson offered up one of his racers, but Gould, decided to bow out.
    - Barry Sheene rode a Deeley Yamaha. He ran well, but engine trouble knocked him to 24th overall.
- John Cooper's winning, exotic BSA was briefly claimed by California racer Bob Bailey. Bailey was a veteran Triumph campaigner and like many others was upset that the latest trick factory parts weren't available to privateers, violating the letter and spirit of Class "C" racing. He followed the AMA's due process and put up the required $2500.00 and was preliminarily awarded Cooper's BSA. Triumph/BSA's Doug Hele was mortified. The bike had won some prestigious oversea races including the Race of Champions. It was fitted with a special lightweight primary drive and Rob North frame and other neat goodies. Hele offered Bailey a low boy frame and race shop engine. Being a Triumph faithful and just trying to keep the factory honest, Bailey accepted, much to Hele's relief!
- The Ontario Motor Speedway was an extravagant attempt at a modern motorsports complex. The track opened in 1970 featuring a modified 2.5 mile copy of the Indianapolis Motor Speedway, a full infield road course and drag strip. There were 155,000 permanent seats. The complex covered 800 acres and cost $25.5 million to build. It boasted features now seen at NASCAR superspeedways; air conditioned corporate suites, full time restaurant, escalator, advanced scoring and timing, an early version of "safe" walls and modern individual garages for race teams. The track was located about 40 miles east of Los Angeles. Major sanctioning groups like USAC, NASCAR, NHRA and the AMA all hosted events there. The track had great potential, but was never a financial success. It was too much, too soon, too ahead of its time. Early events were successful, but the track soon slid into major financial trouble. Besides racing some huge concerts like California Jam I and II were held there. The AMA Nationals held there never drew the hoped for attendance. Crowds of less than 20,000 looked meager in a facility that held over 150,000. The last GNC ran in 1975. Despite best efforts the track closed in 1980 and was subsequently demolished for commercial development. The owners had given it a valiant try; there was not an understanding at the time on how to fund a major speedway and how track could benefit the community and state. There were not enough incentives and tax breaks offered which today can benefit modern facilities. Private money was not enough to keep the huge facility afloat. Newer facilities such as the California Speedway, (now Auto Club Speedway), just 15 miles from the Ontario site, benefited from the lessons learned by this pioneer effort.

1971 Season Review

1. Dick Mann
1057 Points

After being nearly written off for being over the hill at the beginning of the 1970 season, Dick Mann had been on an absolute tear. He had led the points most of year before being put out by injury. He started out the 1971 season even stronger, winning the Houston TT and Daytona. He was under heavy pressure from defending GNC champ Gene Romero every race, all year. Romero briefly took over the points just after mid-season, but Mann's consistency paid off. He won four Nationals during the year; besides the Houston TT and Daytona wins, he also scored at the Kent and Pocono Road Races. He was the dominant road racer for the year, topping all comers, including the pavement specialists. Besides his three pavement wins, he placed 2nd at Road Atlanta and Talladega, 3rd at Loudon, and his 9th place at Ontario which was enough to clinch the title in the last round from Romero. Mann scored big in the seven pavement races on the schedule, giving him over half of his seasons points total. His year on dirt was much rougher, mainly due to mechanical trouble. He still managed a 2nd at Nazareth, 5th places at the Castle Rock TT and Oklahoma City Half-Mile and a 6th at the Ascot Half-Mile. He scored points in 17 of the 21 races. Mann was 38 years old and it had been eight years since his first Grand National Championship in 1963.

2. Gene Romero
924 Points

Gene Romero had a very strong year, nipping at Dick Mann's heels up until the last race of the year at Ontario. If not for his strange suspension involving forged medical papers and failing to score at some critical late season Nationals, he may have repeated as Grand National Champion. He ran consistently through mid-season, notching a win at the San Jose Half-Mile. Despite missing the Ascot TT due to his suspension, he still managed to take the points lead after Livonia. Mann soon surged back, retaking the points lead after winning the Pocono Road Race. The two stayed close right to the end of the year. Romero had a bad night at Ascot, but reeled off back-to-back wins at Oklahoma City and Nazareth. Going into the final race, the title rivals were less than 80 points apart. Luck just didn't go Gene's way, with a crash and mechanical ills putting him out of contention. Besides his three wins, Romero was 2nd again at Daytona, was top 5 at the Houston TT, Loudon Road Race, Terre Haute, Kent, Corona and Livonia. Top 10's were scored at Road Atlanta, Louisville, Castle Rock and Pocono. Romero scored point in 15 of 21 events.

3. Jim Rice
893 Points

Jim Rice had a great year by most standards; he held 3rd in points nearly all year, had numerous top placings and earned points in 18 races, more than any other racer. He had to be somewhat disappointed though that after scoring 6 GNC victories in 1970, he went winless in 1971. He was only on the podium twice, at San Jose and Corona. There were top 5's at Terre Haute, Columbus, Sante Fe and Oklahoma City. Rice had top 10's at the Houston TT, half-miles at Ascot and Louisville and impressively on the pavement at Road Atlanta, Loudon, Kent, Pocono and Ontario. Late in the season he was the only other rider with a real shot at the #1 plate besides Mann and Romero.

4. Dave Aldana
706 Points

Dave Aldana's season was similar to teammate Jim Rice; successful, but off of last year's form. After exploding onto the scene in rookie year, reeling off three wins, Aldana went winless in 1971. He was 2nd at the Ascot TT, 3rd at the Houston TT and Oklahoma City Half-Mile. There were two top 5's at Louisville and Pocono. His four top 10's were at Columbus, Sante Fe, the Ascot Half-Mile and Nazareth. Aldana was in and out of the top 5 in points most of the year. While not in contention for the title, he worked into 4th in points by a string of top 10 finishes at the end of the year, only failing to score points at Ontario. He scored points in 14 of the 21 races.

5. Dave Sehl
561 Points

Canadian Dave Sehl had great year, notching back-to-back half-mile wins at Louisville and Terre Haute. He was also 3rd at Livonia and a surprising 4th at Ascot, where outsiders usually suffer. Sehl had top 10 runs at Sante Fe, Nazareth and the San Jose and Oklahoma City Half-Miles. While considered a dirt track specialist, Sehl did score some road race points through the year. He scored points in 12 of 21 races.

6. Jimmy Odom
557 Points

Talented, fun loving Jim Odom, had a real shot at the #1 plate till derailed by injury at a non-National event late in the year. Odom started out the year by winning the Houston Short Track and nearly winning the TT. He also scored a win at the ill-fated Corona Half-Mile. He was a career best 5th at Daytona, 4th at the Castle Rock TT and 7th at both San Jose and the Ascot TT. He remained high up in the points standing despite running only one of the last seven races. Odom scored points in 11 of the 21 events. The A&A sponsored rider was the top privateer of the year.

7. Mark Brelsford
534 Points

Things looked to be better for Team Harley for 1971. They hoped to have the iron XR running more reliably but were only partly successful. Despite scoring a large number of wins, they actually fared worse in the overall standings than 1970, with Mark Brelsford finishing a spot below Mert Lawwill's previous year mark. This set a new low mark for the marquee in GNC history. There were some bright spots for Brelsford however; he scored a stunning win at Loudon and also a win at the Ascot TT. He was also runner-up at the Houston TT and Corona Half-Mile and 6th at the Kent Road Race. He scored points in just 8 events. Things would look up for Team Harley and Brelsford in 1972.

8. Kel Carruthers
521 Points

Australian GP star Kel Carruthers rode just the pavement Nationals in a semi-factory Yamaha effort out of Don Vesco's shop. Carruthers was Dick Mann's main rival through the year. He won the Road Atlanta National and was runner-up an amazing four times at Kent, Pocono and losing by inches at Loudon and Ontario. Carruthers scored points in 7 Nationals.

9. Don Castro
479 Points

Though Don Castro slipped back a little from 1970, he was still solidly in the top 10. He had a bit of an up and down year, but was 2nd at both Terre Haute and Columbus, 3rd at Nazareth and 8th at Ontario. He earned points in 8 events.

10. John Hateley
452 Points

"Lil' John Hateley was the most successful rookie of the season. He rode out of his father Jack's Triumph dealership. Hateley nearly won the Castle Rock TT and was also 2nd at the Ascot Half-Mile. Other great finishes were a 3rd at Columbus, a 6th at Terre Haute, 7th at Nazareth and top 10 finishes at both Houston Nationals.

Despite a seemingly miserable year, Harley-Davidson won more races than any other brand; 6 for the year! There was a dramatic four-in-a row blitz that included Mark Brelsford's spectacular Loudon win and Bart Markel's 28th National win at Columbus. Later in the year Brelsford won the Ascot TT on the monster XLR and Cal Rayborn claimed his long awaited dirt track win at Livonia. 1969 GNC champion Mert Lawwill suffered through injuries and went winless for the first time since 1966. The iron XR ran it's last factory race at Ontario. Lessons hard learned on the troublesome engine would be applied to the new alloy XR750 that would appear in 1972. The 1971 had the most wins ever by different manufacturers; 7 different brands scored victories. BSA and Triumph tied with 5 wins each. Yamaha had two wins, one on pavement, and one on dirt. Kawasaki finally claimed its first big pavement win. Bultaco and Ossa split the two short track races. Twelve different riders claimed victories during the 21 race season. A total of 96 racers scored AMA Grand National points.

Kenny Roberts absolutely dominated the year's Junior events, winning 9 of the 21 events; 8 on dirt, 1 on pavement. Gary Scott won 3 dirt track races. Randy Scott and Mike Lane each won 2 events, the former on dirt, and the latter on pavement. Winning 1 event each were; Dennis Ponseleit (Daytona), Gary Kapus, John Green, Doug Libby and Loyal Penn. Penn lost his life at an accident at Corona. A very talented group of other front runners included Carl "Frenchie" LeBlanc, Mike Kidd, Jerry Greene, Jim Allen, Keith Ulicki, Billy Schaffer, Jerry Christopher, Jimmy Zeigler, Bill Morgan. Many we will hear from again.

1971 GNC Winners

Event	Location	Winner	Machine
TT	Houston, Tx	Dick Mann, Richmond, Ca	BSA
Short Track	Houston, Tx	Jim Odom, Fremont, Ca	Bul
Road Race	Daytona Beach, Fl	Dick Mann, Richmond, Ca	BSA
Road Race	Braselton, Ga	Kel Carruthers, El Cajon, Ca	Yam
Half-Mile	Louisville, Ky	Dave Sehl, Waterdown, Ont., Can	HD
Road Race	Loudon, NH	Mark Brelsford, San Bruno, Ca	HD
Half-Mile	Terre Haute, Ind	Dave Sehl, Waterdown, Ont., Can	HD
Half-Mile	Columbus, Oh	Bart Markel, Flint, Mi	HD
Half-Mile	San Jose, Ca	Gene Romero, San Luis Obispo, Ca	Tri
Road Race	Kent, Wa	Dick Mann, Richmond, Ca	BSA
TT	Castle Rock, Wa	Sonny Burres, Portland, Ore	Tri
TT	Gardena, Ca	Mark Brelsford, San Bruno, Ca	HD
Half-Mile	Corona, Ca	Jim Odom, Fremont, Ca	Yam
Mile	Livonia, Mi	Cal Rayborn, Spring Valley, Ca	HD
Short Track	Hinsdale, Ill	Robert E. Lee, Ft. Worth, Tx	Oss
Road Race	Mt. Pocono, Pa	Dick Mann, Richmond, Ca	BSA
Road Race	Talladega, Al	Yvon DuHamel, LaSalle, Que., Can	Kaw
Half-Mile	Gardena, Ca	Tom Rockwood, Gardena, Ca	Tri
Half-Mile	Oklahoma City, OK	Gene Romero, San Luis Obispo, Ca	Tri
Mile (1 1/8)	Nazareth, Pa	Gene Romero, San Luis Obispo, Ca	Tri
Road Race	Ontario, Ca	John Cooper, England	BSA

The 1972 GNC Season Preview

The status quo of the two years of Team Britain domination was about to change. Economic realities and new machines/technology were about to shake things up dramatically. The huge BSA/Triumph teams of the previous years were gone. Unbelievably, the BSA factory that had just won the AMA Grand National Championship, was soon to be out of business. The beleaguered company had suffered mismanagement and poor sales as the Japanese companies grew. Defending champion Dick Mann was the only team rider; Jim Rice, Dave Aldana and Don Emde were now privateers. Things weren't much better at Triumph; most of the team was cut, including Gary Nixon, Don Castro and Tom Rockwood. Only 1970 GNC champ Gene Romero was in place at the start of the season. Rookie Gary Scott would receive support as the season progressed. The team's motorcycles reflecting the current realities were in a holding pattern. There was no money for new racing models. The existing machinery would only see minor refinements as other companies were introducing new, technically advanced racers.

Harley-Davidson, who had suffered through two years with the iron XR, had high hopes for their new alloy version. The new project took cues from the KR and iron XR engine development. The successful ideas and lessons learned from the iron engine were integrated. The redesigned engine received new cases, one-piece forged flywheels and mainshafts, an oversquare bore/stroke, huge alloy cylinder heads with new valve angles and valve gear. The new engine was good, but there were problems with the main bearings, piston rings and valve train. These issues would slowly be solved. The out- of-the-box alloy engine was not as strong as the raced iron version, but the platform the team needed to reliably add horsepower over the years was finally in place. Delays in getting the required 200 examples produced for AMA inspection meant the team would miss Daytona. The bikes would debut on the dirt at the Colorado Mile in late April. Team riders were largely the same as 1971; 1969 GNC champ Mert Lawwill, Mark Brelsford, three-time champ Bart Markel, Dave Sehl and Rex Beauchamp. 1964 National champ Roger Reiman, a Harley rider his whole career, got a ride with Krause Honda to ride a CB750 based machine.

Yamaha put together their biggest racing effort yet. Riders and machines were resplendent in matching yellow and black, "bumble bee" livery. Team riders included veterans Jimmy Odom, Keith Mashburn, spectacular rookie Kenny Roberts and GP star Kel Carruthers who would contest road races only. The 650 twin based dirt track machines were competitive and still being developed. The team had new model 350 road racers that despite giving away power to some of the new 750 two-strokes, were very capable of winning.

Kawasaki had a formidable line up of machines and riders for 1972. Their new 750 triple two stroke made lots of power and was housed in frame designs, proven with the smaller 500. Two-time National champion Gary Nixon and English star Paul Smart joined Yvon DuHamel as riders.

Suzuki made big news with their new production based, water-cooled 750 triple. The engines pumped out gobs of horsepower and despite being a new design and rather heavy, the bikes appeared to handle well. A talented squad of riders including Ron Grant, Art Baumman, Jody Nicholas would comprise the domestic team. New Zealand rider Geoff Perry would hit some of the big road races.

In an important development for dirt track racing, Goodyear made their DT1 racing tire available to all racers. Testing began in 1971. This was the first tire made specifically for flat track racing. Department of Transportation (DOT) street legal tires like Pirelli's Universal and Dunlop's K70 had been the norm for years.

The number of Grand Nationals for 1972 increased to 24, an increase of 3 events. New races included half-miles at Long Island, NY and Salem, Ore, a mile at Chicago, Ill and the exciting Laguna Seca road race course. Returning events included the Peoria TT, the Indianapolis Road Race and mile racing at Indianapolis In, San Jose, Ca and Atlanta, Ga. Events off the scheduled were the Kent and Pocono road races, half-miles at Terre Haute, Oklahoma City and Corona, and miles at Livonia and Nazareth. Significant were the increases of mile races on the schedule to five and road races to seven. With the return of Peoria, there were now 4 TT races, and the loss of one half-mile, down to six. For the first time, the AMA established a Manufacturer Championship. Similar to the rider's championship, points would be awarded throughout the year.

The National numbers assigned by points standing from 1971 was abolished by the AMA. The rule was unpopular with the riders and especially by the fans whom had trouble identifying their traditional favorites. Several riders kept their 1971 numbers, but they tended to be those who earned their first National number that year like Dave Sehl and Keith Mashburn. Most veterans opted for their old numbers. Former National champions were now the only ones who could use a single digit, i.e., Bart Markel was number 4, Roger Reiman number 5, Mert Lawwill number 7 and Gary Nixon number 9.

1972 National Numbers

1. Dick Mann, Richmond, Ca
2. Unassigned
3. Gene Romero, San Luis Obispo, Ca
4. Bart Markel, Flint, Mi
5. Roger Reiman, Kewanee, Ill
6. Unassigned
7. Mert Lawwill, San Francisco, Ca
8. Unassigned
9. Gary Nixon, Phoenix, Md
10. Neil Keen, St. Louis, Mo
11. Don Castro, Hollister, Ca
12. Eddie Mulder, Burbank, Ca
13. Dave Aldana, Santa Ana, Ca
14. Cal Rayborn, Spring Valley, Ca
15. Ralph White, Carson, Ca
16. Dave Sehl, Waterdown, Ont., Can
17. Yvon DuHamel, LaSalle, Quebec, Can
18. Jimmy Odom, Fremont, Ca
19. Keith Mashburn, Santa Susana, Ca
20. Dave Smith, Lakewood, Ca
21. Robert Winters, Ft. Smith, Ark
22. Terry Dorsch, Granada Hills, Ca
23. Dave Hansen, Hayward, Ca
24. Jim Rice, Palo Alto, Ca
25. Don Emde, San Diego, Ca
26. Cliff Carr, Watertown, Ca
27. Duane McDaniels, Milford, Mi
28. Royal Sherbert, Largo, Fl
29. Larry Palmgren, Freehold, NJ
30. Art Baumann, Brisbane, Ca
31. Rex Beauchamp, Drayton Plains, Mi
32. Dusty Coppage, Chatsworth, Ca
33. John Weaver, Ft. Wayne, Ind
34. Dallas Baker, Orange, Ca
35. John Cooper, Derby England
36. Charles Chapple, Flint, Mi
37. Mel Lacher, San Diego, Ca
38. Chuck Palmgren, Freehold, NJ
39. Jess Thomas, Sea Cliff, NY
40. Ted Newton, Pontiac, Mi
41. Ginger Molloy, Brisbane, Ca
42. Fred Guttner, Detroit, Mi
43. Richard Wallar, Bothell, Wa
44. Dewayne Keeter, Oaji, Ca
45. Doug Sehl, Waterdown, Ont., Can
46. Paul Bostrom, San Pablo, Ca
47. Charlie Seale, Lantana, Fl
48. Allen Kenyon, Cupertino, Ca
49. Dave Damron, Riverside, Ca
50. Frank Camillieri, Chelsea Ma
51. Hurley Wilvert, Long Beach, Ca
52. Ronnie Rall, Mansfield, Oh
53. Larry Schafer, Hyattsville, Md
54. Robert E. Lee, Ft. Worth, Tx
55. Jim Jones, Kirkland, Wa
56. Charles Thiekle, Seattle, Wa
57. Edward Hermann, Milwaukie, Ore
58. Jody Nicholas, Newport, Ca
59. Skip Van Leeuwen, Hollywood, Ca
60. Chuck Joyner, Oregon City, Ore
61. Ron Grant, Brisbane, Ca
62. John Goad, Richmond, Va
63. Walt Fulton, Santa Ana, Ca
64. Nick Theroux, San Francisco, Ca
65. Al Gaskill, East Detroit, Mi
66. John Skinner, Auburn, Ala
67. Pat Marinacci, Seattle, Wa
68. Michael VanBibber, Albuquerque, NM
69. Sonny Burres, Portland, Ore
70. Mark Williams, Springfield, Ore
71. Jimmy Maness, Augusta, Ga
72. Michael Anderson, Van Nuys, Ca
73. Kel Carruthers, El Cajon, Ca
74. Paul Pressgrove, Tecumseh, Ks
75. Donald Twigg, Hagerstown, Md
76. Frank Gillespie, Berkeley, Ca
77. Robert Davis, Battle Creek, Mi
78. David Lawson, Yukon, Ok
79. Lloyd Houchins, La Crescenta, Ca
80. Emil Ahola, Tacoma, Wa
81. Gordon Duesenberry, Wichita, Ks
82. Jack Warren, Millington, Mi
83. Glen Adams, Seattle, Wa
84. Eddie Wirth, Manhattan Beach, Ca
85. William O'Brien, Waukegan, Ill
86. William Elder, Vancouver, Wa
87. Mark Brelsford, San Bruno, Ca
88. Tom Rockwood, Gardena, Ca
89. Jimmie Smith, Salem, Ore
90. Ike Reed, Salem, Ore
91. Mike Haney, Inglewood, Ca
92. Gregory Edmunds, Oxon Hill, Md
93. Gary Bailey, Torrance, Ca
94. Larry Darr, Mansfield, Oh
95. George Russell, Owings Md
96. Ed Varnes, Cochranville, Pa
97. Ron Pierce, Bakersfield, Ca
98. John Hateley, Van Nuys, Ca
99. Michael Sponseller, Phoenix, Md

1972
Grand National Championship
Schedule

	Race	Location	Date
1	Houston TT	Houston, Tx	January 28, 1972
2	Houston Short Track	Houston, Tx	January 29, 1972
3	Daytona 200 Mile Road Race	Daytona Beach, Fl	March 12, 1972
4	Road Atlanta 125 Mile Road Race	Braselton, Ga	April 16, 1972
5	Colorado Mile	Colorado Springs, Co	April 30, 1972
6	Ascot TT	Gardena, Ca	May 6, 1972
7	San Jose Mile	San Jose, Ca	May 21, 1972
8	Louisville Half-Mile	Louisville, Ky	June 4, 1972
9	Loudon 100 Mile Road Race	Loudon, NH	June 11, 1972
10	Indianapolis 125 Mile Road Race	Indianapolis, Ind	June 18, 1972
11	Columbus Half-Mile	Columbus, Oh	June 25, 1972
12	San Jose Half-Mile	San Jose, Ca	July 2, 1972
13	Salem Half-Mile	Salem, Ore	July 9, 1972
14	Castle Rock TT	Castle Rock, Wa	July 16, 1972
15	Laguna Seca 125 Mile Road race	Monterey, Ca	July 23, 1972
16	Roosevelt Half-Mile	Long Island, NY	July 29, 1972
17	Homewood Mile	Chicago, Ill	August 5, 1972
18	Peoria TT	Peoria, Ill	August 13, 1972
19	Sante Fe Short Track	Hinsdale, Ill	August 18, 1972
20	Indy Mile	Indianapolis, Ind	August 26, 1972
21	Talladega 200 Mile Road Race	Talladega, Al	September 3, 1972
22	Atlanta Mile	Atlanta, Ga	September 10, 1972
23	Ascot Half-Mile	Gardena, Ca	September 24, 1972
24	Ontario 250 Mile Road race	Ontario, Ca	October 1, 1972

GNC Round #1 & 2 of 24 **Date:** January 28 & 29, 1972 **Type:** TT and Short Track **Venue:** Houston Astrodome **Location:** Houston, Tx	**Purse:** $20,000.00 **Surface:** Dirt **Course Length:** ¼ mile **Laps:** 25 TT, 20 Short Track

By 1972, AMA Grand National racing was growing by leaps and bounds. Spectator appeal was up and multi-factory efforts were at their height. The Astrodome races were growing along with National racing. The 1972 season opener drew record crowds which witnessed the debut of one of the most stellar groups of youngsters to ever hit the GNC scene. Future superstar Kenny Roberts' incredible natural talent set the motorcycle racing world on its ear. Nobody ever rode Houston, especially the TT course, like Roberts. His debut at the 'Dome was the most remarkable since Brad Andres at Daytona in 1955. Roberts' perennial rival in California events, Gary Scott, also made a big splash at Houston. Scott was nearly equal to Roberts speed, but with a much different style. Roberts was spectacular like Bart Markel, while Scott was more comparable to Gary Nixon. Along with the two Californians, another future star, Texan Mike Kidd, made his inaugural Grand National appearance. While not a rookie, youngster John Hateley also reflected the changing of the guard in GNC racing. Hateley was the highest finishing rookie at Houston in 1971 and was unbeatable this year on the TT. Roberts may have had something for Hateley, but a fall early in the event prevented him from catching Hateley. His charge to the front though was spectacular and let all present know that he was something special. Roberts would not be denied at the next night's short track race.

TT National

Things started off normally enough in TT qualifying. GNC champ Dick Mann set the early fast time on his factory BSA, till bested by Posa Enterprises sponsored Mark Williams (Tri).

Fast-timer Williams bested Eddie Mulder (Tri) in Heat 1. After that, the youngsters dominated the heats. Kenny Roberts (Yam) ran away with Heat 2 over Dave Hansen (Tri) and Dick Mann. John Hateley (Tri) was unbeatable in the last heat over Frank Gillespie (Tri). The traditional favorites hadn't won a single heat.

Semi action saw Al Kenyon (BSA) topping Gary Scott (Tri) and Paul Bostrom (Tri) for the last three National spots.

National

The 22,000 strong crowd watched a determined, if slightly shaky, John Hateley quickly jump out front. After a few laps, 'Lil John grew more comfortable and stretched his lead. Behind him, both Mark Williams and Kenny Roberts fell off. Williams was out while Roberts push started his Yamaha twin and continued. The order settled down with Hateley followed by, Mulder, Brelsford, Dave Hansen and Dick Mann. Nobody knew that a force of nature named Kenny Roberts was coming. He began charging through the field, quickly moving into the lead pack. He got the crowd's attention when he passed Mann for 5th. They began cheering him on and Roberts was using up every inch of the tight Astrodome track. He was next harassing Hansen and the crowd had forgotten about leader Hateley. Roberts was quickly by Hansen and soon did the same to Brelsford for 3rd and the crowd went nuts. Up front, Hateley had a big lead and Mulder began to notice the closing Roberts. With only a couple of laps to go, Roberts gobbled up the territory and closed on Mulder. In the last turn, Roberts has a shot and goes high coming out of the last turn, coming up just short with Mulder hanging on to second. Hateley crossed the stripe with a comfortable lead.

Short Track National

The rookies continued to look strong in Saturday's Short Track National. Fast qualifier Gary Scott (Kaw) looked dominant, winning his heat and semi. Kenny Roberts (Yam) did likewise in his events. More rookies, home state favorite Mike Kidd (Bul) and wild man Carl "Frenchie" LeBlanc (Yam) easily made the main. A handful of veterans also made the show, including three-time GNC champ Bart Markel (HD), 1969 winner Ronnie Rall (Bul), Eddie Mulder (Yam), and Chuck Palmgren (Yam). Others in the main were Robert E. Lee (Oss), Dave Hansen (Suz), Gary Landry (Oss) and Todd Sloan (Bul). More amazing than those who made the main, were those who didn't; Gary Nixon, Mark Brelsford, Dick Mann, Gene Romero, Cal Rayborn, Don Castro, and Roger Reiman. Romero and Mann were riding slow, ill-handling factory supplied Rickman's. Mann qualified 47th of 48 qualifiers and was last in his heat. Romero made it into the semis only to run in last as well. There was a real turn-around in the machines in the race: all were two-strokes except Bart Markel's lone Harley Sprint. A real switch compared to the first few years of the event when the Sprints were near dominant.

National

Many of the 37,000 strong crowd were rooting for spectacular Kenny Roberts or Texas favorite Mike Kidd or maybe Bart Markel, who represented the old guard. Roberts left little doubt of his intentions by bolting into the lead aboard his Ray Abrams-tuned Trackmaster Yamaha single. Kidd tried to keep close in 2nd, trailed by Dave Hansen, Bart Markel, Frenchie LeBlanc and 1971 Sante Fe winner Robert E. Lee, another Texan. Lee put in just a few laps till his Ossa had an engine seizure. Markel was strong on his thumper in 4th, hounded by LeBlanc who was riding a high line. LeBlanc did everything but fall off trying to get around the old champ. Gary Scott had picked the wrong front tire on his Kawasaki and struggled all night. Up front, Roberts stretched his lead while Kidd was trying to fend off a pressuring Hansen. Markel's Sprint broke allowing LeBlanc into 4th. He began seriously harassing Hansen for the last podium spot, hanging off his bike, bouncing through ruts and not surprisingly, finally falling off. An ecstatic Kenny Roberts pulled away to a big victory. The future "King" of GNC racing was just getting started at Houston in 1972.

Results

Race: 25 Lap TT National
Race Time: 10:14.10

Rank	Rider	Number	Make
1.	John Hateley, Van Nuys, Ca	98	Tri
2.	Eddie Mulder, Burbank, Ca	12	Tri
3.	Kenny Roberts, Modseto, Ca	80Y	Yam
4.	Mark Brelsford, Los Altos, Ca	87	HD
5.	Gary Scott, W. Covina, Ca	64R	Kaw
6.	Dave Hansen, Hayward, Ca	23	Tri
7.	Dick Mann, Richmond, Ca	1	BSA
8.	Mark Williams, Springfield, Ore	70	Tri
9.	Frank Gillespie, Reseda, Ca	76	Tri
10.	Skip Van Leeuwen, Sherman Oaks, Ca	59	Tri
11.	Al Kenyon, Cupertino, Ca	48	Bul
12.	Paul Bostrom, San Pablo, Ca	46	Tri

Race: Junior TT Final

Rank	Rider	Number	Make
1.	Joe Brown, Paso Robles, Ca	19Z	Yam
2.	Steve Snider, Tulare, Ca	12Z	Bul
3.	Rex Barrett, Pomona, Ca	21X	Yam

Race: 25 Lap Short Track National
Race Time: 7:02.40

Rank	Rider	Number	Make
1.	Kenny Roberts, Modesto, Ca	80Y	Yam
2.	Mike Kidd, Hurst, Tx	72N	Yam
3.	Dave Hansen, Hayward, Ca	23	Suz
4.	Gary Scott, W. Covina, Ca	64R	Kaw
5.	Eddie Mulder, Burbank, Ca	12	Yam
6.	Gary Landry, Lake Charles, La	34L	Oss
7.	Chuck Palmgren, Freehold, NJ	38	Yam
8.	Tod Sloan, Fresno, Ca	18Z	Bul
9.	Ronnie Rall, Mansfield, Oh	52	Bul
10.	Carl LeBlanc, Medina, Oh	77F	Yam
11.	Bart Markel, Flint, Mi	4	HD
12.	Robert E. Lee, Ft. Worth, Tx	54	Oss

Race: Junior Short Track Final

Rank	Rider	Number	Make
1.	Mike O'Brien, Danville, Ca	75Z	Bul
2.	Gary Lozano, Stockton, Ca	70Y	Bul
3.	Jimmy Lee, Bedford, Tx	49N	Bul

Grand National Points Standings after Round 2

Rank	Rider	Pts
1.	Kenny Roberts	250
2.	Eddie Mulder	180
3.	John Hateley	150
4.	Dave Hansen	150
5.	Gary Scott	140
6.	Mike Kidd	120
7.	Mark Brelsford	80
8.	Gary Landry	50
9.	Dick Mann	40
10.	Chuck Palmgren	40

Extra Extra

- The riders share of Houston's big purse was increasing with John Hateley taking home around $3300.00 for his TT win.
- Hateley missed a shot at a weekend double when he couldn't get his unusual CZ engined machine into the short track race.
- Some notables not qualifying for the TT National included 1970 winner Jim Rice, Cal Rayborn, Ronnie Rall and Bart Markel.
- Gary Scott rode his Kawasaki Big Horn based racer to top 5's in both events. His tuners switched the top end components from 350 to 250 for the short track race.
- Bultaco's new Astro debuted at Houston. The new model was named for the venue and was designed after National victories by Ronnie Rall and Jim Odom. Many were aboard the new machine including Jim Rice, Gary Nixon, Don Emde, Al Kenyon and Gary Fisher.
- During the short track National, Frenchie LeBlanc noticed his bike slowing. He managed to jam an adrift carburetor back onto his Yamaha's engine and kept going.

- Exhibition races followed each nights programs. Texan Robert E. Lee thrilled Friday's TT crowd by topping a star studded short track event. The TT exhibit after the short track, turned into as much show as race. Kenny Roberts, John Hateley, Mark Brelsford and Eddie Mulder popped wheelies, jumped in tandem and rubbed elbows all around the course.

GNC Round #3 of 24
Date: March 12, 1972
Type: Road Race
Venue: Daytona International Speedway
Location: Daytona, Florida

Purse: $43,000.00
Surface: Pavement
Course Length: 3.81 miles
Laps: 53
Distance: 200 Miles

The 1972 Daytona event marked big changes in racing and the motorcycle world in general. The huge British teams with unlimited budgets were gone. BSA was in dire financial straits with Triumph also in trouble. The Japanese teams, particularly Kawasaki and Suzuki, showed up in strength. This reversal of fortune reflected the motorcycle economy at the time. The Japanese factories were leading in the sales world and the European companies were on the decline. The BSA and Triumph teams were cut to just Dick Mann and Gene Romero; everyone else was scratching for rides. There were no specially-imported stars. Gary Nixon and Paul Smart moved to the Kawasaki team, (aka Team Hansen), with Yvon DuHamel. With no other factory rides available, the other cut riders did the best they could. Don Emde was luckier than most and received sponsorship from Motorcycle Weekly aboard a Mel Dineson Yamaha. The only other former team rider to figure in the results was Tom Rockwood. Another company with trouble of a different sort was Harley-Davidson. They ran out of time in preparation of the new aluminum-cylinder XR750. Active team members were not allowed to ride on a competitor's machine. Two-time 200 winner Cal Rayborn along with the other factory riders, were forced to sit out the big race. Roger Reiman, who placed a fine 4th place in the 1971 event, secured a ride on a fast Krause Honda along with Gary Fisher.

The Norton factory backed by the John Player cigarette company, made a Daytona appearance for the first time since 1964. Phil Read and Peter Williams were aboard trick, great handling twins. While way down on power, the talented scratchers were with the program, especially through the infield.

For the first time ever, Yamaha showed up with a recognizable team effort. The factory bikes were a new short stroke, production-based 350 with a 6-speed transmission. The bikes and leathers featured a striking yellow, black and white scheme. Riders included veteran Kel Carruthers, Jimmy Odom, Keith Mashburn and Houston short track winner, rookie Kenny Roberts.

The big news speed-wise at Daytona was the debut of the Suzuki and Kawasaki 750's. The water-cooled Suzuki and the enlarged Kawasaki triples put up very fast lap times with trap speeds in the 170 mph range. On the surface, they seemed unbeatable, but their high horsepower and Daytona's track produced unforeseen troubles. The bikes were shredding their rear tires in a handful of laps. There was no way the bikes could go the distance on the present tires. Despite the best efforts of Dunlop, they could not recommend the use of their tires. Goodyear came up with a last-minute effort but it would not last either. It was a case of one technology outpacing another. Tires had not ever been a problem to this magnitude at Daytona. The weight of the new machines, the Suzukis in particular, combined with high horsepower and the track's banking caused the situation. If the tire problem wasn't bad enough, the new 750's were also breaking drive chains, further adding to Kawasaki and Suzuki's worries.

Time Trials

Living up to expectations, Suzukis dominated qualifying, taking the top three spots. Art Baumann ran a record-breaking 110.363 mph lap, nearly 5 mph faster than Paul Smart's 1971 time. His trap speed was a scorching 171.75. Teammate Jody Nicholas was next with a 108.658 lap, trap speed 166.05. Geoff Perry turned a 107.517; not surprising, but Perry was actually on an older 500 twin. His trap speed of 152.54 was nearly 20 mph off Baumann's! Rounding out the top 5 was Gary Fisher's Honda; 106.989 with trap speed of 159.57 and Kenny Roberts 106.103 whose fastest speed was 152.54.

National

In a repeat of the 1971 race, Yvon DuHamel led the pack away early with Art Baumann taking over as they entered the infield. DuHamel settled into 2nd with Jody Nicholas, and a pack with Gary Nixon, Roger Reiman, and

Cliff Carr being the early front runners. Baumann was suddenly out of the race on lap 9 with ignition troubles. DuHamel took the point and led for six more laps till his first fuel stop, (of three), for his thirsty Kawasaki. Jody Nicholas became the new leader. DuHamel would soon retire with mechanical trouble. Suzuki's Ron Grant was riding a smart race on his new triple, trying to make the tires and chain last. No matter, he was put out before halfway with clutch troubles. He joined other fast guys on the sidelines including Nixon (seizure) and Kel Carruthers, Ralph White (crash victims). Nicholas set a fast pace and led the next portion of the race till his rear tire let go on lap 27. Gary Fisher took over briefly, but was soon out with a broken oil tank on his Honda.

By the second half of the race most all the expected favorites were out or experiencing trouble, allowing a crop of dark horses to emerge. Challengers for the top spot included Phil Read, Dave Smith, Don Emde, Ray Hempstead, Roger Reiman and Geoff Perry. The last round of pit stops continually shook up the lead order. Dave Smith and Phil Read both had troubles on their stops, knocking them out of contention for the win. Hempstead and Emde emerged as frontrunners, but were soon joined by Suzuki's last hope, Perry. Not known during the race, but Perry was actually a lap down after fouling a plug at the start. Perry took the apparent lead on lap 45 with Emde and Hempstead doing some heavy dicing. With two laps to go, Perry's bike broke it's chain. Emde pulled away from Hempstead with some drafting help from laps down Dick Mann and led to the finish. The rest of the top 5 behind Emde and Hempstead were Smith, Read and Fred Guttner. It was a remarkable, historic win for Emde in a number of ways. Daytona had always been the stomping grounds for the factories, particularly so in the years immediately preceding this event. Former BSA factory rider Emde became the first full fledged privateer to win the event in the modern GNC era. It was Yamaha's first Daytona win, marking the first two-stroke win as well as the smallest engine used. Emde joined father Floyd Emde, the 1948 winner, as the only father-son duo to win the event. A day to remember for Don Emde, Mel Dineson, and Yamaha. A day that the vaunted Suzuki and Kawasaki teams would probably rather forget as they had no riders on their new machines in the top 20.

Results

Race: 200 Mile Road Race National
Race Time: 1:56:27.63 (103.358 MPH)

Rank	Rider	Number	Make
1.	Don Emde, San Diego, Ca	25	Yam
2.	Ray Hempstead, St. Petersburg, Fla	99	Yam
3.	Dave Smith, Lakewood, Ca	20	Yam
4.	Phil Read, Surrey, Eng	22	Nor
5.	Fred Guttner, E. Detroit, Mi	42	Yam
6.	Eddie Mulder, Northridge, Ca	12	Tri
7.	Jimmy Odom, Union City, Ca	18	Yam
8.	Michael Ninci, Kansas City, Mo	95	BSA
9.	Duane McDaniels, Milford, Mi	27	Yam
10.	James Dunn, Everett, Wa	50	Yam
11.	Mark Williams, Springfield, Ore	70	Yam
12.	George Kerker, Glendale, Ca	90	Hon
13.	Jim Allen, Vancouver, B.C., Can	85	Yam
14.	Geoff Perry, Aukland, NZ	96	Suz
15.	Johnny Lane, Bakersfield, Ca	44	Yam
16.	Keith Masburn, Santa Susana, Ca	19	Yam
17.	Larry Darr, Mansfield, Oh	94	HD
18.	Conrad Urbanowski, Miramar, Fla	80	Yam
19.	Don Twigg, Hagerstown, Md	75	BMW
20.	Doug Libby, Dearborn, Mi	87	Yam

Race: 100 Mile Junior Road Race Final
Race Time: 58:58.79 (103.316 MPH) New Record

Rank	Rider	Number	Make
1.	Ronnie Dottley, Birmingham, Al	64	Yam
2.	Jean Lysight, Tracy, Quebec, Can	39	Yam
3.	James Chen, Carson, Ca	21	Hon

Grand National Points Standings after Round 3

Rank	Rider	Pts
1.	Kenny Roberts	250
2.	Eddie Mulder	240
3.	Don Emde	180
4.	Dave Hansen	150
5.	John Hateley	150
6.	Ray Hempstead	144
7.	Gary Scott	140
8.	Mike Kidd	120
9.	Dave Smith	120
10.	Phil Read	96

Extra Extra

- 63 riders made up the starting grid.
- Two-strokes dominated the race, taking 14 of the first 20 places.
- Don Emde took home around $14,000.00 for his win.
- Emde was lucky to make it to the 200, let alone win. A serious crash in the Lightweight race left Emde with a very tweaked shoulder. He managed to convince the track doctor he was OK and started the race. On the third lap his Yamaha began to seize. He pulled in the clutch lever, almost turned into the pits, but instead popped the clutch and rode on with no trouble.
- Bob Hansen left Honda after Dick Mann's 1970 win and went to work for Kawasaki. The very experienced race team manager was tapped to lead the unofficial Kawasaki team.
- The 1972 race was run under joint AMA and FIM sanctions. The FIM allowed 6-speed transmissions and Yamaha had their new machine duly approved in time for the race.
- By most accounts, the AMA would have flexed the rules to allow Harley-Davidson to compete at Daytona even if they were short the required 200 machines. Harley probably made the right move to stay home rather than debuting the new XR750 at engine-punishing Daytona.
- The BSA/Triumph teams ran U.S. produced Wenco chassis, essentially a lightweight copy of the Rob North low boy item.
- Dick Mann and Gene Romero had nothing but trouble through Speedweek. Despite Danny Macias and crews best efforts, the bikes were down on power and having problems with a new ignition system. Things did not improve and the winner and runner-up from the last two Daytona races finished outside the top 20.
- A bright spot for Dick Mann was being awarded a new Datsun 240Z for being Cycle magazines Rider of the Year.
- The highest finishing British bike was TT star Eddie Mulder, placing 6th on an ex-factory Triumph high-boy. It was Mulder's best and last Daytona run.
- Emerging super-tuner Kevin Cameron had mostly hand-crafted a new 750 race engine after Kawasaki couldn't or wouldn't supply him with the necessary pieces. Cameron and rider Cliff Carr had to have some satisfaction when their bike had legs on the factory machines. Carr was knocked out of contention after crashing in some oil.

- Another trick private Kawasaki was the aluminum monocoque-framed machine of Frenchman Eric Offenstadt. The bike was fast, but an early race crash involving Kel Carruthers put him out of the running.
- Art Baumann's factory Suzuki mechanics, Tanaka and Kita, were awarded $500.00 for wrenching Baumann's bike to fast time.
- Cycle mag's Jess Thomas was part of Don Vesco's team along with Dave Smith and Mike Lane. Thomas finished 21st, Lane 15th and Smith on the podium in third.
- Dave Smith also won the Lightweight event over Kenny Roberts, riding Kel Carruthers' winning machine from 1971.
- Kenny Roberts was knocked out of his first 200 with a flat tire on lap 20.
- Roberts still emerged with the GNC points lead with Eddie Mulder close behind with the addition of Daytona points. Don Emde's 200 win moved him way up to 3rd in points.
- The heavyweight Suzukis could shred any tire present if pressed hard. Despite testing fine in Japan, the loads imposed by the stresses of Daytona's banking were not anticipated.
- While their Yoshimura-prepped engines ran, well the Krause team Hondas still ran into problems. Both Gary Fisher and Roger Reiman were forced out with cracked oil tanks.
- Larry Darr brought his Iron XR in 17th for the top Harley finish. It was the brand's lowest finish in modern GNC history.
- Don Twigg's BMW was close behind in 19th.

GNC Round #4 of 24	**Purse:** $20,000.00
Date: April 16,1972	**Surface:** Pavement
Type: Road Race	**Course Length:** 2.52 Miles
Venue: Road Atlanta	**Laps:** 49
Location: Flowery Branch, Ga	**Distance:** 125 Miles

Jody Nicholas and his factory Suzuki appeared dominant at the Road Atlanta National. It seemed Nicholas had won his third GNC and it would have also been the first win for Suzuki's 750 triple. Unfortunately for the Suzuki team, the water-cooled machines were under scrutiny starting at technical inspection. Indeed there was an official protest after the race. It seemed the bikes cylinder heads were special and the rules dictated production items to be used. The AMA later ruled the heads were illegal and second place runner Yvon DuHamel was declared the winner. DuHamel teammate Paul Smart was 2nd and Gene Romero moved to 3rd after Ron Grant's Suzuki was also disqualified.

The disqualification was a shame for Jody Nicholas who, despite running up front recently at both road race and dirt Nationals, had not won a race since 1963. In addition, Suzuki just seemed to be the unlucky manufacturer who got caught. Most teams had been running questionable and downright illegal pieces and most of the time got away with it.

Kenny Roberts padded his points lead over Eddie Mulder by 40 points, 290 to 240 points. Mulder scored no points at Road Atlanta. Neither did Don Emde who hung onto third. John Hateley placed 12th and moved up a spot in the standings, as did 11th place finisher Ray Hempstead. Yvon DuHamel's win moved him to 6th. Dave Hansen did not compete and dropped from fourth to seventh in the standings. Gary Scott dropped a spot to eighth, Dave Smith was ninth. Mike Kidd fell back into a tie with Dick Mann who was back in the top 10.

Heats

Gary Nixon, getting well acquainted with his new Kawasaki, shot out to lead Heat 1 early. He was chased by a gang headed by Art Baumann (Suz) and Roger Reiman on the Honda four-stroke. Baumann soon worked forward, taking over the lead. Paul Smart was on the move from the field and bumped Reiman out of 3rd spot. Behind at the finish were Kel Carruthers (Yam), Ron Grant (Suz), Gene Romero (Tri) and Cliff Carr (Kaw).

Yvon DuHamel led the charge off the line in Heat 2 pursued early by Don Emde (Yam) and Dick Mann (BSA). Jody Nicholas was making his way forward and on lap 4 passed DuHamel for the lead. Soon after, rain hit the track, prompting a red flag. The race was called complete with the top order; Nicholas, DuHamel, Ron Pierce (Yam), Gary Fisher (Yam) and Dick Mann.

National

At the start of the 125-Mile National, Team Green showed the strength of their Kawasakis with Yvon DuHamel, Paul Smart and Gary Nixon up front early. The Suzukis of Art Baumann and Jody Nicholas had a more sedate start, but were on the move. By lap 4 the blue & white Suzukis split up the "Green Meanies" with first Baumann and then Nicholas dropping Nixon back to 5th. On lap 6 Baumann passed Paul Smart and began gaining on leader DuHamel. Two laps later he made the pass; his lead was quickly cut short as the Suzuki began missing. DuHamel retook the lead, but a spark plug wire came loose, sending him to the pits. Nicholas took over the lead till lap 25 when he stopped for fuel. Smart assumed the point till lap 28 when Nicholas charged by as Smart pulled in for his stop. Further back, 1970 GNC champ Gene Romero was tearing past some notable pavement scratchers like Nixon, Kel Carruthers (Yam) and rookie Kenny Roberts (Yam). He moved into 5th position behind Ron Grant.

At the front on lap 35 was Nicholas, DuHamel, Smart, Grant and Romero. Cliff Carr was putting in a great ride on the Kevin Cameron Kawasaki. He was running in the top 5 till he ran out of gas. He got running again, but dropped out with bottom end trouble. Leader Nicholas continued to stretch his lead and at the finish was followed by DuHamel, Smart, Romero, Dick Mann, Nixon, Carruthers, Roberts and Gary Fisher.

Jody Nicholas and Team Suzuki weren't surprised when they were protested after the race. Although the final decision would not come for a couple weeks, all the factory Suzukis were disqualified from the final order and barred from competing in future events for the foreseeable future.

Results

Race: 125 Mile Road Race National

Rank	Rider	Number	Make
1.	Yvon DuHamel, La Salle, Quebec, Can	17	Kaw
2.	Paul Smart, Kent, Eng	8	Kaw
3.	Gene Romero, San Luis Obispo, Ca	3	Tri
4.	Dick Mann, Richmond, Ca	1	BSA
5.	Gary Nixon, Phoenix, Md	9	Kaw
6.	Kel Carruthers, El Cajon, Ca	73	Yam
7.	Kenny Roberts, Modesto, Ca	60	Yam
8.	Gary Fisher, Parkesburg, Pa	10	Hon
9.	Roger Reiman, Kewanee, Ill	5	Hon
10.	Dave Smith, Lakewood, Ca	20	Yam
11.	Ray Hempstead, St. Petersburg, Fla	99	Yam
12.	John Hateley, Van Nuys, Ca	98	BSA
13.	Conrad Urbanowski, Miramar, Fla	80	Yam
14.	Keith Mashburn, Santa Susana, Ca	19	Yam
15.	Robert Winter, Ft. Smith, Ark	11	Yam
16.	Jim Allen, Islington, Ont., Can	85	Suz
17.	Gary Scott, West Covina, Ca	64	Yam
18.	John Samways, Louisville, Ky	35	Kaw
19.	Duane McDaniels, Milford, Mi	27	Yam
20.	Bob Bailey, Carson, Ca	77	Tri

Race: Junior 50 Mile Road Race Final

Rank	Rider	Number	Make
1.	Jerry Greene, San Mateo, Ca	57	Kaw
2.	Jim Evans, San Bernardino, Ca	47	Yam
3.	James Chen, Carson, Ca	21	Hon

Grand National Points Standings after Round 4

Rank	Rider	Pts
1.	Kenny Roberts	290
2.	Eddie Mulder	240
3.	Don Emde	180
4.	John Hateley	159
5.	Ray Hempstead	154
6.	Yvon DuHamel	150
7.	Dave Hansen	150
8.	Gary Scott	144
9.	Dave Smith	135
10.	Mike Kidd	120
11.	Dick Mann	120

- Till the protest was settled in late April, everything was held up; official finishing positions, payout and points.
- A similar inspection of Yamaha's new engine passed without incident.
- Several competitors from the recent Anglo-American Match Races were still waiting for their bikes to arrive from overseas. The Team Suzuki bikes made it in fairly comfortable time. Cal Rayborn ended up on a ride brought in from Milwaukee. Dick Mann and Gene Romero's machines didn't make it till Saturday morning. Romero had earlier borrowed one of the Krause Honda's to get some track time.
- The new aluminum Harley XR750 still wasn't ready. Rayborn's race machine continued the iron XR's tradition and fried itself early in the National.
- Kenny Roberts junked his bike in practice and rode Kel Carruthers spare in the race.
- Kel Carruthers won the Combined Lightweight race.
- Junior winner Jerry Greene pocketed $3000.00 from Kawasaki's still-formidable contingency program.
- Tire development continued with new wide-pattern Dunlop's making an appearance on the Team Suzuki's.
- Putting the cap on a weird weekend, after the races Dave Smith managed to fall out of Gary Fisher's vehicle, sustaining a concussion and other injuries.

1972 Colorado Mile
Rice Burns at Pike Peak

GNC Round #5 of 24 **Date:** April 30, 1972 **Type:** Mile **Venue:** Pikes Peak Turf Club **Location:** Colorado Springs, Co	**Purse:** $12,000.00 **Surface:** Dirt **Course Length**: 1 Mile **Laps:** 25 **Distance:** 25 Miles

Jim Rice was simply unstoppable at the inaugural Colorado Mile National. He won both his heat and the main on his self-tuned BSA in convincing fashion. Rice was now a privateer and perhaps had something to prove, piloting his self-tuned BSA to victory in the first "real" dirt National of the year. It was milestone GNC win number 10 for Rice, his first since the 1970 season. Mark Brelsford rode the new alloy Harley-Davidson XR750 to an impressive 2nd place. Points leader Kenny Roberts was 3rd. The day at the Pikes Peak Turf Club featured very gusty winds blowing across a sandy, slick and bumpy mile track. There were numerous accidents on the tricky course. Former GNC champion Bart Markel suffered a broken pelvis in a nasty heat race fall.

Kenny Roberts' podium finish lengthened his points lead to a 390 point total. Eddie Mulder was hanging right in there with his 9th place in the main keeping him in second with 260. Mark Brelsford and Mike Kidd both had a good race and were now tied at 200 points. Daytona winner Don Emde was a no-show in the main and slipped back to 5th with 180. John Hateley scored a few points in 17th and had 163 points. Pavement racer Ray Hempstead was hanging in there with 154. Tied at 150 points were winner Jim Rice, Yvon DuHamel, Dave Hansen and Gary Scott.

Time Trials

Mark Brelsford had to bring a smile to Dick O'Brien's face by topping qualifying on his new Jim Belland-tuned XR750 at 42.78. Rounding out the top 5 were City Cycle Centers Gary Scott (Tri) 42.82, Jim Rice (BSA) 42.83, Cal Rayborn aboard his new factory XR750 at 42.88 and Team Yamahas Kenny Roberts, a 43.00. Four different brands in the top 5; nice brand parity!

Heats

Five of the six official Harley team wound up in Heat 1. Mark Brelsford took the holeshot and was soon accompanied by teammate Cal Rayborn who passed nearly half the field with a daring high line move through turns 1 and 2. Charlie Seale (BSA) took 3rd over Rex Beauchamp (HD) and Yamaha mounted Mike Kidd. Harley factory pilots Mert Lawwill and Dave Sehl missed the cut and were semi-bound.

GNC champ Dick Mann (BSA) and Kenny Roberts had a great battle throughout Heat 2 with Roberts squeaking out the win. Bart Markel was beating and banging with Gary Scott over 3rd spot. The battle ended with the two-time National champ hitting the ground very hard, breaking his pelvis. Scott continued and finished ahead of 4th place runner Gene Romero (Tri).

In Heat 3 Jim Rice pulled the holeshot and rapidly put the field behind him. On lap 4, Jody Nicholas, aboard Dave Sehl's spare Harley, hooked his steel shoe in the fence and went down hard. He took Dave Hansen down with him. Nicholas was banged up, Hansen was okay. Rice won the race going away followed by Chuck Palmgren (Yam), John Hateley (Tri), Frank Gillespie (Nor) and Jimmy Odom (Yam).

Semi

Keith Mashburn (Yam) led the first few laps of the laps of the semi, with Dave Sehl, Mert Lawwill and Eddie Mulder in hot pursuit. Lawwill took over the top spot with Sehl dropping back with engine troubles. The top 3 were set as Lawwill, Mashburn and Mulder. The event sent five riders to the National and Ron Moore and Randy Scott battled their way to the last National tickets.

National

    Mark Brelsford pulled the holeshot and led the first lap closely followed by Jim Rice, Kenny Roberts and Mike Kidd. Rice found a small opening and snuck by Brelsford on the inside. Brelsford tucked in close behind. Both ran very close to the tall inside rail, almost underneath it. Kenny Roberts, on a slightly higher line, closed up on Brelsford. Close behind the leaders were Kidd, Cal Rayborn, John Hateley, Charlie Seale and GNC champ Dick Mann. Up front, Rice was flying, soon lapping the back markers. Rayborn's XR's handling went away and he faded through the field. Mann was working his way forward when his BSA's engine gave out. Keith Mashburn flew through the pack from a back row start to nail down 5th spot by the finish. Just behind, Charlie Seale topped a struggle with Gene Romero and Don Castro (Tri). Rice was untouchable and lapped clear up to 5th place. At the finish he had a half track lead on Brelsford, with the order behind, Roberts, Kidd, Mashburn, Seale, Romero, Castro, Eddie Mulder and Jimmy Odom.

Results

Race: 25 Lap Mile National
Race Time: 17:54.16

Rank	Rider	Number	Make
1.	Jim Rice, Palo Alto, Ca	24	BSA
2.	Mark Brelsford, Los Altos, Ca	87	HD
3.	Kenny Roberts, Modesto, Ca	80Y	Yam
4.	Mike Kidd, Hurst, Tx	72N	Yam
5.	Keith Mashburn, Santa Susana, Ca	19	Yam
6.	Charlie Seale, Lantana, Fla	47	BSA
7.	Gene Romero, San Luis Obispo, Ca	3	Tri
8.	Don Castro, Hollister, Ca	11	Tri
9.	Eddie Mulder, Burbank, Ca	12	Nor
10.	Jimmy Odom, Fremont, Ca	18	Yam
11.	Ron Moore, Bernardino, Ca	37R	Tri
12.	Randy Scott, Philomath, Ore	57Q	Tri
13.	Mert Lawwill, San Francisco, Ca	7	HD
14.	Frank Gillespie, Berkeley, Ca	76	Tri
15.	Gary Scott, W. Covina, Ca	64R	Tri
16.	Cal Rayborn, Spring Valley, Ca	14	HD
17.	John Hateley, Van Nuys, Ca	98	Tri
18.	Rex Beauchamp, Milford, Mi	31	HD
19.	Dick Mann, Richmond, Ca	1	BSA
20.	Chuck Palmgren, Freehold, NJ	38	Yam

Race: Junior Final

Rank	Rider	Number	Make
1.	Steve Droste, Waterloo, Ia	26K	Yam
2.	Scott Brelsford, San Bruno, Ca	84Y	HD
3.	John Caldwell, Chula Vista, Ca	31R	Tri

Grand National Points Standings after Round 5

Rank	Rider	Pts
1.	Kenny Roberts	390
2.	Eddie Mulder	260
3.	Mark Brelsford	200
4.	Mike Kidd	200
5.	Don Emde	180
6.	John Hateley	163
7.	Ray Hempstead	154
8.	Jim Rice	150
9.	Yvon DuHamel	150
10.	Dave Hansen	150
11.	Gary Scott	150

Extra Extra

- An impressive crowd of around 12,000 turned out for the first time, Don Brymer-promoted event.
- In an unusual move, the program also featured a full Novice and Junior program. The AMA had stopped running "regular" Junior support races in 1971. Motorcycle-jumper-turned racer, Steve Droste, won the Junior event with Randy Brackett topping the Novice division.
- It was two Brelsfords in the top two. Mark's younger brother Scott was 2nd in the Junior race on a new factory-supported XR750.
- Though the new Harley-Davidson was hardly a world beater in it's debut, the results were encouraging and improvements were forthcoming.
- Dave Aldana was a surprising no-show. He had made a deal with Kawasaki to ride the Elsinore Grand Prix!
- Former Ascot star Elliot Shultz turned up and qualified a Shell Yamaha in 9th place. Shultz hadn't ridden since injury in 1969. In the 1960's Shultz rode Shell Thuett's Royal Enfield to numerous Ascot wins. Despite the promising qualifying run, Shultz didn't make the National.
- The Pikes Peak Turf Club (and subsequent incarnations) has had an interesting history with many ups and downs. The track, located south of Fountain, Co, opened for horse racing in 1965. From the beginning the facility struggled to find a steady audience. Like other such venues, other ways to generate revenue were tried, including concerts and motorcycle racing. Some regional races ran as early as 1969. The AMA paid a visit to the "Colorado Mile" in 1972 and 1973. The facility was first-rate, but as with so many other mile cushion tracks, it did not hold up well to motorcycle racing. Questionable track conditions led to numerous spills and accidents. Despite impressive crowd turnouts, the series did not return. More up-and-down years led to the closure of the track in 1984. The track was sold in 1990 and reopened as Pikes Peak Meadows, again hosting horse racing. The results were disastrous and the track closed in less than three months. Owners said the facility would host concerts and auto racing. In 1996 C.C. Myers Raceway Associates, Inc., took over the facility and begin building Pikes Peak International Raceway, with intentions on hosting NASCAR and IRL events. A new state-of-the-art facility featuring a 1-mile banked oval and 1.3 mile road course was built at a cost of $35 million dollars. For almost a decade, the track hosted the IRL, NASCAR Busch and Craftsman Truck Series, USAC open wheel races and AMA Superbikes. Despite this, the track was losing money and had not signed up NASCAR's premier Cup division, which many thought would save the track. The facility was taken over by Lehman Brothers in 2001, when the owners couldn't cover their debt. The last premier races were run in 2005. International Speedway Corporation, under the name of the Rocky Mountain Speedway Corporation, bought the facility soon after. The track reopened in 2008 and is currently operating as a "participant and corporate focused" motorsports complex. Numerous car, kart and motorcycle clubs such as the SCCA hold autocross and "Test and Tune" days there. Bob Bondurant has a driving school there. NASCAR teams test there because of the first rate facility and the fact they can't test at an active NASCAR sanctioned track. It is unclear if there will be attempts to once again host large scale events at the facility.

Bonus!
Top 10 Colorado Mile Qualifying Times

1.	Mark Brelsford	HD	42.78 seconds
2.	Gary Scott	Tri	42.82
3.	Jim Rice	BSA	42.83
4.	Cal Rayborn	HD	42.88
5.	Kenny Roberts	Yam	43.00
6.	Chuck Palmgren	Yam	43.19
7.	Tom Rockwood	Tri	43.25
8.	Dick Mann	BSA	43.31
9.	Elliot Shultz	Yam	43.42
10.	Dave Sehl	HD	43.43

1972 Ascot TT
Brelsford Wins 3rd Ascot TT!
6 Nationals, 6 Different Winners!

GNC Round #6 of 24 **Date:** May 6, 1972 **Type:** TT **Venue:** Ascot Park **Location:** Gardena, Ca	**Purse:** $10,000.00 **Surface:** Dirt **Course Length**: ½ Mile, (approx.) **Laps:** 25

Mark Brelsford once again dominated at the Ascot TT, one of his favorite venues. He was untouchable all night, setting fast time, winning his heat and completely controlling the main event. It was his third victory at the event, with his first win GNC win ever in 1969 and winning again in 1971. It was his fifth National win. Rookie Gary Scott was 2nd with John Hateley 3rd, both Triumph mounted. GNC points leader Kenny Roberts had engine trouble early and had to borrow Junior Gary Lozno's ride. He was out of the event early with a crash.

Kenny Roberts' 19th place-finish only added a couple of points to his total, now at 392. Mark Brelsford's win shot him into second in points and within shouting distance of Roberts with 350 points. "Steady" Eddie Mulder finished 7th in the race, but slipped back to third with 300 points. Gary Scott was the big mover of the week: His runner-up finish catapulted him clear up to fourth with 270. John Hateley finished 3rd behind Scott in the race and was also just behind him in points with 263. Likewise, Jim Rice's 4th in the main placed him just back from Hateley at 230. Mike Kidd failed to make the main and dropped from a tie for third to way back to seventh. Don Emde continued a backslide; now eighth, still at 180. Ray Hempstead was 9th with 154. Dave Hansen and Yvon Duhamel remained tied at 150.

Time Trials

Mark Brelsford's decision to once again ride the monster Belland/Lawwill 900cc Harley XLR seemed to be the right one, managing to break his own track record with a 44.87. In a preview of the National, Gary Scott was 2nd quickest followed by John Hateley.

Heats

Giving a preview of the coming National, Mark Brelsford was up and gone on his way to Heat 1 domination. Jim Rice (BSA) was a distant 2nd with Keith Mashburn (Yam) 3rd. Team Mexican's Dave Aldana (BSA) and Gene Romero (Tri) rounded out the top 5.

GNC champ Dick Mann (BSA) pulled the holeshot in Heat 2 with Triumph guys Gary Scott and Eddie Mulder giving chase. Mann led till late in the race when Scott muscled by. Mulder held onto 3rd, Kenny Roberts on his borrowed Yamaha was 4th and Ed Hermann (Tri) 5th. National points contender Mike Kidd fell off during the race and was done for the night.

Cal Rayborn, on a new XR750, put in a convincing ride top capture Heat 3. He topped a stellar field of Triumph mounted TT racers: Terry Dorsch, John Hateley, two-time Ascot TT winner Skip Van Leeuwen and Mike Haney.

Semi

Mert Lawwill took the semi event aboard a new XR750.

National

Mark Brelsford immediately grabbed the lead on the very strong Sportster-based machine. First lap carnage saw Kenny Roberts collect Mert Lawwill, both going down and failing to make the restart. On the second start, Brelsford was closely pursued by Colorado winner Jim Rice (BSA), Dick Mann and Gary Scott. Scott soon muscled his way by for 2nd place, but had nothing for Brelsford. Rice and Mann continued to hang onto 3rd and 4th. As the laps wound down, Brelsford continued to stretch his lead. Mann's machine began missing and he dropped from contention. The same fate befell Gene Romero. John Hateley had worked his way forward and closed on the leaders. He applied heavy pressure to 3rd place Rice all over the track before working by late in the race. Behind Hateley were; Dave Aldana, Cal Rayborn, Eddie Mulder, Frank Gillespie, Skip Van Leeuwen and Todd Sloan.

Results

Race: Mile 25 Lap TT National
Race Time: 19:09.17

Rank	Rider	Number	Make
1.	Mark Brelsford, Los Altos, Ca	87	HD
2.	Gary Scott, W. Covina, Ca	64R	Tri
3.	John Hateley, Van Nuys, Ca	98	Tri
4.	Jim Rice, Palo Alto, Ca	24	BSA
5.	Dave Aldana, Santa Ana, Ca	13	BSA
6.	Cal Rayborn, Spring Valley, Ca	14	HD
7.	Eddie Mulder, Northridge, Ca	12	Tri
8.	Frank Gillespie, Berkeley, Ca	76	Tri
9.	Skip Van Leeuwen, Hollywood, Ca	59	Tri
10.	Tod Sloan, Fresno, Ca	18Z	Tri
11.	Ed Hermann, Milwaukie, Ore	57	Tri
12.	Mike Haney, Inglewood, Ca	91	Tri
13.	Dusty Coppage, Chatsworth, Ca	32	Tri
14.	Gene Romero, San Luis Obispo, Ca	3	Tri
15.	Dick Mann, Richmond, Ca	1	BSA
16.	Terry Dorsch, Granada Hills, Ca	22	Tri
17.	Keith Mashburn, Santa Susana, Ca	19	Yam
18.	Roger Ring, Imperial Beach, Ca	25R	Tri
19.	Kenny Roberts, Modesto, Ca	80Y	Yam
20.	Mert Lawwill, San Francisco, Ca	7	HD

Race: Junior Final
Race Time: 11:04.03

Rank	Rider	Number	Make
1.	Joe Brown, Pasto Robles, Ca	19Z	Yam
2.	Larry Gino, San Bernardino, Ca	96R	Tri
3.	Rick Newby, Bakersfield, Ca	23Z	Tri

Grand National Points Standings after Round 6

Rank	Rider	Pts
1.	Kenny Roberts	392
2.	Mark Brelsford	350
3.	Eddie Mulder	300
4.	Gary Scott	270
5.	John Hateley	263
6.	Jim Rice	230
7.	Mike Kidd	200
8.	Don Emde	180
9.	Ray Hempstead	154
10.	Dave Hansen	150
11.	Yvon DuHamel	150

Extra Extra

- Mark Brelsford took home around $2000.00 from the purse.
- This was the first year that the traditional 50-lap distance was reduced to 25-laps.
- Cal Rayborn had flown up from Laguna Seca after qualifying for a sports car race earlier in the day.
- Junior Astrodome TT winner Joe Brown claimed his second big TT win aboard his Yamaha.
- California riders dominated the 20 rider field. Only Oregon rookie Expert Ed Hermann prevented a complete sweep.
- Bob Bailey and Skip Van Leeuwen got together hard in practice. Van Leeuwen was OK, but Bailey was transported to the hospital for work on a separated shoulder.
- Keith Mashburn fell in the National, taking a trip to the hospital with possible leg injuries.
- Many star riders failed to make the National for a variety of reasons: Mark Williams, Don Castro, Tom Rockwood, Chuck Joyner, Jimmy Odom, Chuck Palmgren, Sonny Burres, Al Kenyon, Randy Scott were just some of those who missed the show.

GNC Round #7 of 24	**Purse:** $12,000.00
Date: May 21, 1972	**Surface:** Dirt
Type: Mile	**Course Length**: 1 Mile
Venue: Santa Clara Fairgrounds	**Laps:** 25
Location: San Jose, Ca	**Distance:** 25 Miles

Jim Rice scored a dramatic win at the return of GNC mile racing at the Santa Clara Fairgrounds in front of nearly 30,000 fans, winning his second consecutive mile race. The race was the first on the big San Jose track since 1958. Rice brushed the inside railing around the halfway mark in the race, separating his shoulder. He was running in 4th spot at the time and amazingly clawed his way to the front, staging a terrific battle with Kenny Roberts, barely edging the super rookie at the flag. Third place went to early leader Rex Beauchamp. Gary Scott dominated the National before a blown engine knocked him out late in event. Rice's second win of the year made him the first repeat winner of 1972, breaking a streak of 6 different winners. GNC point's contender Mark Brelsford pulled off the track by mistake with a semi win in hand, costing him valuable points.

Kenny Roberts 2nd place run combined with Brelsford's mistake, gave him some breathing room in the points contest. His 511 points was way ahead of San Jose winner and new second place Jim Rice's 380 total. Brelsford slipped back to 3rd, still with 350 points. Eddie Mulder was 14th on the day, slipping back to fourth with 307. John Hateley maintained fifth at 303. Gary Scott's blown engine forced him back a couple of spots to sixth with 274. Dick Mann was back in the top 10 at 228 points. Mike Kidd again missed a National, dropping back a spot, still with 200. Like Mann, Gene Romero reappeared in the top of the table, seventh with 197. Don Emde continued to barely hang on; tenth with 180.

Time Trials

Mert Lawwill posted fast time of 39.90 on the new XR750, closely followed by teammate Cal Rayborn at 39.95. Gary Scott (Tri) was 3rd quick at 40.17, followed another Harley, ridden by Dave Sehl who turned a 40.20. Surprisingly, San Jose master Jim Rice didn't qualify in the top 10.

Heats

Mark Brelsford (HD) led the field away in Heat 1 closely chased by teammate Dave Sehl as well as Yamaha riders Chuck Palmgren, Kenny Roberts and Frank Gillespie (Nor). Sehl took the lead on lap 3 and Brelsford began to fade. Gillespie showed speed on the Nick Deligianis-built Norton and moved to 2nd. At the flag it was Sehl, Gillespie and Roberts. Behind, Palmgren, John Hateley (Tri) and Brelsford were headed to the semi.

Always a quick starter, Cal Rayborn pulled the holeshot in Heat 2. He looked like a safe bet for the win, but Rayborn's poor luck continued as his XR dropped a valve on the third lap. Don Castro (Tri) took over the lead with BSA riders Jim Rice and Dave Aldana in 2nd and 3rd respectively. Castro also experienced engine trouble and began dropping back on lap 5. Rice took over the lead with 2nd place Aldana sub coming first to Dick Mann (BSA) and then Tom Rockwood. Aldana was semi bound.

Gary Scott (Tri) blew off the line in Heat 3, never to be seen by the pack again. Rex Beauchamp (HD) and Mark Williams (Tri) put on a nifty duel for 2nd with Beauchamp getting the spot. Close behind them Eddie Mulder and Gene Romero, both Triumph mounted, were headed to the semi. Scott's time was the fastest heat of the day.

Semi

Jimmy Odom led a talent-laden semi away on his factory Yamaha to lead lap 1. Don Castro drafted by for the lead with Mark Brelsford taking over 2nd. Triumph riders Ron Moore and Lloyd Houchins punted Jimmy Odom back to 5th. Odom, riding hard to get back up front, got into the rough stuff coming out of the 4th turn on lap 4 and was thrown off his bike in a nasty looking wreck. Odom was okay, but the bike was trashed. Brelsford had a safe looking lead with one lap to go, but slowed, thinking the white flag was the checkers, allowing teammate/buddy Mert

Lawwill to zip past. He pulled Moore, Castro and Todd Sloan into the main with him. Brelsford thought the race was over and pulled off the track. By the time he realized what had happened, it was too late and would score no points on the day.

National

Gary Scott quickly took control of the 25-mile National, wresting the top spot from Rex Beauchamp on lap 2. He immediately began stretching his lead. Close behind, Beauchamp fell into battle with Frank Gillespie and Jim Rice. Coming through the pack Kenny Roberts and Dick Mann were reeling in the lead group. Rice hit the inside rail on lap 9, allowing Roberts and Mann to close up. Rice quickly recovered, never backing off the gas, but was now riding with one hand. Rice, Roberts and Mann caught Gillespie, who was slowing. The Roberts/Mann show was picking up steam and they teamed up to pass Rice. They also moved by Rex Beauchamp. On lap 17, Scott's dominant Triumph came apart and Mann took over the lead with Roberts on his rear wheel. Lap 18 saw Rice turn up the wick, (one-handed!), and moved past Beauchamp for 3rd. Roberts moved by Mann for the lead on lap 19. Rice was now gaining and soon passed Mann for 2nd. By lap 23 Rice had reeled in Roberts and began applying pressure. Mann's BSA was missing and faded slightly. Rice drafted by Roberts at the stripe with one to go. Roberts repassed in turns 1-2. On the backstretch Rice drafted back by. Roberts drove it hard into turn 3 and they are wheel-to-wheel. Rice stayed on the groove coming out of turn 4 with Roberts sliding a little wide, allowing Rice to cross the line first. A thrilling finish, with the top 5; Rice, Roberts, Mann, Beauchamp and Chuck Palmgren.

Rice took an extra lap to figure out how to stop the bike. He made a quick stop in Victory Circle and then headed to get checked out by the medical crew. Rice had now won the first two big oval track races of the year, shutting out all other brands including the new alloy Harley-Davidson. Very impressive runs by the independent Rice, aboard a brand that was nearly out of business.

Results

Race: 25 Lap Mile National
Race Time: 17:03.74

Rank	Rider	Number	Make
1.	Jim Rice, Portola Valley, Ca	24	BSA
2.	Kenny Roberts, Modesto, Ca	80Y	Yam
3.	Dick Mann, Richmond, Ca	1	BSA
4.	Rex Beauchamp, Milford, Mi	31	HD
5.	Chuck Palmgren, Freehold, NJ	38	Yam
6.	Gene Romero, San Luis Obispo, Ca	3	Tri
7.	John Hateley, Van Nuys, Ca	98	Tri
8.	Mark Williams, Springfield, Ore	70	Tri
9.	Mert Lawwill, San Francisco, Ca	7	HD
10.	Dave Aldana, Santa Ana, Ca	13	BSA
11.	Tom Rockwood, Gardena, Ca	88	Tri
12.	Tod Sloan, Fresno, Ca	18Z	Tri
13.	Dave Sehl, Waterdown, Ont., Can	16	HD
14.	Eddie Mulder, Northridge, Ca	12	Nor
15.	Dave Hansen, Hayward, Ca	23	Tri
16.	Eddie Wirth, Manhattan Beach, Ca	84	Yam
17.	Gary Scott, W. Covina, Ca	64R	Tri
18.	Frank Gillespie, Berkeley, Ca	76	Tri
19.	Ron Moore, San Bernardino, Ca	37R	Tri
20.	Don Castro, Hollister, Ca	11	Tri

Race: Junior Final

Rank	Rider	Number	Make
1.	Scott Brelsford, San Bruno, Ca	84Y	HD
2.	Rex Barrett, Pomona, Ca	21X	Tri
3.	Jim Rawls, Arlington, Tx	41N	Yam

Grand National Points Standings after Round 7

Rank	Rider	Pts
1.	Kenny Roberts	511
2.	Jim Rice	380
3.	Mark Brelsford	350
4.	Eddie Mulder	307
5.	John Hateley	303
6.	Gary Scott	274
7.	Dick Mann	228
8.	Mike Kidd	200
9.	Gene Romero	197
10.	Don Emde	180

Bonus!
Top 10 San Jose Mile Qualifying Times

1.	Mert Lawwill	HD	39.90 seconds
2.	Cal Rayborn	HD	39.95
3.	Gary Scott	Tri	40.17
4.	Dave Sehl	HD	40.20
5.	Tom Rockwood	Tri	40.27
6.	Eddie Mulder	Nor	40.32
7.	John Hateley	Tri	40.38
8.	Dick Mann	BSA	40.43
9.	Rex Beauchamp	HD	40.58
10.	Mark Brelsford	HD	40.62

1972 Louisville Half-Mile
It's Brelsford and Harley at Louisville

GNC Round #8 of 24 **Date:** June 4, 1972 **Type:** Half-Mile **Venue:** Louisville Downs **Location:** Louisville, Ky	**Purse:** $10,000.00 **Surface:** Limestone **Course Length:** ½ Mile **Laps:** 20 **Distance:** 10 Miles

Mark Brelsford scored the alloy XR's first ever GNC win with the new bike taking five of the first six places at the Louisville National. It was a sigh of relief for Team Harley to return to the cushion track at which had won every race held. It was Brelsford's 2nd win of the year and the 6th of his career. He closed up the points battle to within 11 points of Kenny Roberts who did not make race. Two-time Louisville winner, (1970 and '71), Dave Sehl, tried to make it three in a row, coming up a little short in 2nd place. Third place Gary Scott's Triumph was the only non-Harley in the top 6. The entire program was run during the day on Sunday after rain washed out the almost-completed heats on Saturday night.

Kenny Roberts maintained a very narrow points lead over Mark Brelsford; 511 to 500 points. This was the closest anyone had been to Roberts all season. Roberts had a miserable weekend, scoring no points. Jim Rice sat out the race, waiting for his shoulder to heal, but still hung onto third with 380 points. Gary Scott's strong 3rd place moved him from sixth in points to fourth with 374 points. John Hateley was 7th in the National and hung onto fifth in points at 343 points. Eddie Mulder scored no points and dropped from fourth to sixth, "steady" 307. GNC champ Dick Mann had an off weekend, staying at 228 points. Rookie Mike Kidd was impressive at 200 points. Gene Romero had 197. Rounding out the top 10 was Don Emde at 180.

Time Trials
Despite the coming Harley juggernaught, Triumph of Burbank sponsored John Hateley set fast time of 25.84, within shouting distance of Dick Mann's 1969 record of 25.32.

Heats
Cal Rayborn's (HD) dirt track confidence was up and blasted into the lead of Heat 1. Chuck Palmgren (Yam) was a solid 2nd, with fast-timer John Hateley in 3rd. Hateley passed Palmgren on lap 7 for the runner-up spot. He set sail for Rayborn, catching and passing the pavement star on the last lap.

Mark Brelsford took control of Heat 2 on the Jim Belland-tuned XR750 and rode unchallenged to the win. Points leader Kenny Roberts made one circuit before his Yamaha broke. Mert Lawwill (HD) ran 2nd with Michigan cushion specialist Teddy Newton (BSA) in 3rd. Fellow Michigan rider Rex Beauchamp ran Newton down on the last lap to make it Team Harley, 1-2-3. Brelsford's heat time was the fastest of the night.

Heat 3 went to Ohio cushion rider Larry Darr on the Edgar Fuhr tuned-Harley, still after his first GNC win. He led the Canadian's Dave and Doug Sehl into the National. All were Harley mounted.

Semi
Teddy Newton, always strong at Louisville, put in a great ride to win the "last chance event". Triumph riders Gary Scott and Larry Palmgren picked up the other two tickets to the National. Gene Romero (Tri) and Keith Ulicki (HD) had a great battle over 4th with Ulicki coming out on top, but still a spot short of the big show.

National
Holeshot artist Cal Rayborn nailed the start again, leading pole-sitter Mark Brelsford and crew into turn 1. Larry Darr's night ended quickly when he slid his XR down in turn 3 of the opening lap. Rayborn and Brelsford ran together, chased by a pack containing Dave Sehl, Rex Beauchamp, Gary Scott and Doug Sehl. Rayborn was running a line very tight to the inside rail while Brelsford was sliding spectacularly around up higher. Brelsford was all over Cal and on lap 7 took over the lead for good. Soon after Dave Sehl also worked by Rayborn and took off after the

new leader. Gary Scott, clear from the semi, also hassled Rayborn and went by on lap 10. Rayborn had lost the handle and slid back to an eventual 6th place finish.

In the closing laps, Sehl narrowed the gap, but at the flag it was Brelsford by 30 feet or so. Scott was 3rd, Beauchamp in 4th and Doug Sehl 5th.

Results

Race: 20 Lap Half-Mile National
Race Time: 8:56.26

Rank	Rider	Number	Make
1.	Mark Brelsford, Los Altos, Ca	87	HD
2.	Dave Sehl, Waterdown, Ont., Can	16	HD
3.	Gary Scott, W. Covina, Ca	64R	Tri
4.	Rex Beauchamp, Milford, Mi	31	HD
5.	Doug Sehl, Waterdown, Ont., Can	45	HD
6.	Cal Rayborn, Spring Valley, Ca	14	HD
7.	John Hateley, Van Nuys, Ca	98	Tri
8.	Teddy Newton, Pontiac, Mi	40	BSA
9.	Mert Lawwill, San Francisco, Ca	7	HD
10.	Larry Palmgren, Freehold, Ca	29	Tri
11.	Chuck Palmgren, Freehold, NJ	38	Yam
12.	Larry Darr, Mansfield, Oh	94	HD

Race: Junior Final 6:24.11

Rank	Rider	Number	Make
1.	Scott Brelsford, San Bruno, Ca	84Y	HD
2.	Jim Rawls, Arlington, Tx	41N	Yam
3.	Del Armour, Denver, Co	9M	HD

Grand National Points Standings after Round 8

Rank	Rider	Pts
1.	Kenny Roberts	511
2.	Mark Brelsford	500
3.	Jim Rice	380
4.	Gary Scott	374
5.	John Hateley	343
6.	Eddie Mulder	307
7.	Dick Mann	228
8.	Mike Kidd	200
9.	Gene Romero	197
10.	Don Emde	180

- Making it an all-Brelsford weekend, Scott Brelsford won the Junior event.
- Kenny Roberts toasted both his factory Yamahas on Saturday. He borrowed Keith Mashburn's spare Shell Yamaha which suffered the same fate in Roberts' heat race on Sunday.
- Dick Mann had a similar weekend. He suffered two blown engines and a fall before the weekend was done.
- John Hateley's fast Triumph was the subject of a claim by Joe Barringer after Sunday's National. Despite Barringer posting the required $2500.00, luck was with Hateley who got to take the bike back home.
- Goodyear's new DT1 was prevalent, used by many including winner Brelsford.
- Saturday's fast guys included fast timer Corky Keener on Bart Markel's Harley and heat winners Larry Darr and Jimmy Maness. On Sunday, Keener's bike broke, Maness didn't transfer out of his heat. Darr won his heat, but fell in the opening laps of the main.
- Ronnie Rall was aboard the F&S Suzuki 750 triple. He timed in an amazing 5th on Saturday night. On Sunday, Rall ran a strong 5th in his heat, but didn't transfer out of the semi.

1972 Loudon Road Race
Go-Fast Fisher Wins
Brelsford Takes Points Lead

GNC Round #9 of 24 **Date:** June 11, 1972 **Type:** Road Race **Venue:** Bryar Motorsports Complex **Location:** Loudon, NH	**Purse:** $25,000.00 **Surface:** Pavement **Course Length**: 1.6 Miles **Laps:**63 **Distance:** 100 Miles

Second-generation racer Gary Fisher had everything click for him in a near perfect weekend at Loudon. He turned in a pavement double, winning the Lightweight and GNC race. Fisher had been riding the Krause-prepared 750 Honda, but after trying it out, he decided he would be better off on his own, more nimble 350 Yamaha. Though this would be his one and only GNC win, Fisher remained a strong road race competitor through the 1970's.

The race marked the debut for the Harley-Davidson XRTT. Last year's winner, Mark Brelsford put one in 2nd after a race long battle with some of the best pavement racers in the country. His high placing allowed him to take over the GNC lead from Kenny Roberts for the first time this season. Roberts finished way back with transmission problems after running strong for most of the race. In 3rd was Gene Romero. Never yet given his due as a road racer, Romero put in a remarkable ride on the twisty circuit with the bulky Triumph Trident.

Mark Brelsford had been knocking on the door and took over the points lead in a big way, his total at 632. Kenny Roberts mechanical problems dropped him way back, scoring no points: his total remained at 511. John Hateley was showing great all-around skills and his surprising 7th place run in the National moved him from sixth in points to third. Young Hateley had to be considered a legitimate title contender. Gary Scott held onto fourth in with 382 points via his 14th place finish. Jim Rice scored no points at Loudon and slipped way back from third to sixth in points. Eddie Mulder slipped back a spot with 307 points, entering into a tie with Gene Romero (who finished on the podium). Dick Mann, finished 6th, and fell back to eighth, now at 283 points. Mike Kidd held ninth with 200 points and Loudon winner Gary Fisher rounded out the order with 195 points.

National

A determined Cal Rayborn, (he had not recorded a GNC road race win in nearly two years), blasted into the lead on lap 1. He had a 20 yard lead on Gary Fisher and Yvon DuHamel. Rayborn's glory only lasted for a couple laps, the victim of a broken valve spring. Fisher surged by for the lead with DuHamel in tow. DuHamel soon began slipping back with transmission problems as well as new Goodyears that were not hooking up. Paul Smart moved into 2nd followed by points contenders Kenny Roberts and Mark Brelsford, accompanied by Gene Romero. This group swapped 2nd place furiously with each rider taking the place at least once. Roberts took the spot around the 20 lap mark and was gaining on Fisher when his transmission packed up. Romero was putting in an amazing ride, taking over 2nd place until his Triumph began misfiring. Brelsford took over 2nd place for good. DuHamel's transmission finally ground itself to bits and he was out with 6 laps to go. As the laps wound down, Fisher had a 10+ second lead over Brelsford, Romero held on to 3rd, Paul Smart (Kaw) was 4th, Kel Carruthers (Yam) came from way back for 5th, GNC champ Dick Mann (BSA) was 6th, John Hateley (Tri) was 7th, Rayborn suffered into 8th, Marty Lunde (Yam) 9th and Ron Pierce (Yam)10th.

Results

Race: 100 Mile Road Race National

Rank	Rider	Number	Make
1.	Gary Fisher, Parkesburg, Pa	10	Yam
2.	Mark Brelsford, Los Altos, Ca	87	HD
3.	Gene Romero, San Luis Obispo, Ca	3	Tri
4.	Paul Smart, Kent, Eng	8	Kaw
5.	Kel Carruthers, El Cajon, Ca	73	Yam
6.	Dick Mann, Richmond, Ca	1	BSA
7.	John Hateley, Van Nuys, Ca	98	Tri
8.	Cal Rayborn, Spring Valley, Ca	14	HD
9.	Marty Lunde, Hermosa Beach, Ca	66	Yam
10.	Ron Pierce, Bakersfield, Ca	97	Yam
11.	Mashiro Wada, Japan	20	Kaw
12.	Jim Allen, Islington, Ont., Can	85	Suz
13.	Keith Mashburn, Santa Susana, Ca	19	Yam
14.	Gary Scott, W. Covina, Ca	64	Yam
15.	Fred Guttner, E. Detroit, Mi	42	Yam
16.	Gary Nixon, Phoenix, MD	9	Kaw
17.	Dave Sehl, Waterdown, Ont., Can	16	HD
18.	R.G. Wakefield, Indianapolis, Ind	74	Kaw
19.	Andy Lascoutx, Ashland, Mass	92	Yam
20.	Dave Damron, Riverside, Ca	49	Suz

Race: 50 Mile Junior Final

Rank	Rider	Number	Make
1.	Jim Evans, San Bernardino, Ca	47	Yam
2.	James Chen, Carson, Ca	21	Hon
3.	Jeff March, Acme, Pa	33	Yam

Grand National Points Standings after Round 9

Rank	Rider	Pts
1.	Mark Brelsford	632
2.	Kenny Roberts	511
3.	John Hateley	387
4.	Gary Scott	382
5.	Jim Rice	380
6.	Eddie Mulder	307
7.	Gene Romero	307
8.	Dick Mann	283
9.	Mike Kidd	200
10.	Gary Fisher	195

- A huge 30,000 strong crowd turned out for Sunday's race.
- Gary Fisher took home around $7000.00 from the purse and contingency awards.
- Fisher's father Ed won the 1953 Laconia event on a Triumph.
- The Fisher's picked up the winning bike from Fred Deeley, the Canadian Yamaha distributer the Wednesday before the race. It received a quick motel blueprint the weekend of the race, but was otherwise a painfully stock TR-3.
- The Suzuki team was still on hiatus from the Road Atlanta disqualification. They were slated to return at Talladega.
- Kawasaki paid for track use on Wednesday and got a free day thrown in by the track on Thursday. When Kawasaki failed to show, racer friendly Bryar let anyone use the facility.
- Don Vesco's military-like organization had a rough weekend. Most team-members including experts Gary Scott, Steve McLaughlin and Jess Thomas all had some kind of trouble.
- Two-time Loudon winner Gary Nixon, (1967 & '70), also had a rough weekend. He was tossed off hard during the Lightweight race and didn't figure in the National.

1972 Indianapolis Road Race
Rayborn Wins 4th at Indy

GNC Round #10 of 24	**Purse:** $20,000.00
Date: June 18, 1972	**Surface:** Pavement
Type: Road Race	**Course Length:** 2.5 Miles
Venue: Indianapolis Raceway Park, (IRP)	**Laps:** 50
Location: Indianapolis, In	**Distance:** 125 Miles

The Grand National Championship returned to Indianapolis Raceway Park (IRP) for the first time since 1969. Cal Rayborn obviously had an affinity for the course, scoring his fourth win in a row at the facility. It was milestone win number 10 for Calvin. His last pavement win was here, way back in 1969. Hard to believe the nations most talented road racer had been winless so long. He had suffered through seemingly endless mechanical trouble with the new Harley XR's. His perseverance seemed to finally be paying off and his XRTT never missed a beat.

Rayborn battled with Yvon DuHamel early before DuHamel had to pit for ignition problems. DuHamel charged back late in the race to claim a distant 2nd. Gene Romero impressed once again in a fine pavement finish in 3rd. Point's leader Mark Brelsford saw his hopes for a top finish disappear late in the race when throttle problems forced him out.

Mark Brelsford held onto the GNC points lead despite his DNF. Kenny Roberts finished 6th and narrowed the points margin to 71, 632 to 561. Gary Scott moved into third in with 442 points via his 5th place finish in the National. Gene Romero's podium really shot him up in the standings, moving from seventh to fourth with 407 points. John Hateley slid back to fifth with 387 points.

Heats

Cal Rayborn (HD) and Yvon DuHamel (Kaw) were the heat victors. DuHamel's time was a new 5-lap record. It was also around 9 seconds quicker than Rayborn's time.

National

The fastest Gary's on pavement, Nixon (Tri) and Fisher (Yam), led the field into Turn 1. Fisher took the lead before the lap was out. Yvon DuHamel had an uncharacteristically bad start, but was leading by lap 2. Cal Rayborn was also on the move, battling with Kawasaki test rider Masahiro Wada. They both knocked Fisher and Nixon back.

Up front, DuHamel's Kawasaki started slowing and around lap 10, headed to the pits with a possible fouled plug. Rayborn took over the lead and Fisher moved back to 2nd, followed by Ron Pierce. After a few laps, Fisher seemed to fade and Ron Pierce took the runner-up spot chased by Gene Romero (Tri) and Paul Smart (Kaw), with Fisher back to 5th. Wada crashed on lap 15 with a thrown chain. Positions 3-5 stayed in constant flux at mid race. Kel Carruthers (Yam) joined the battle for a time but was sidelined with a fractured intake manifold. GNC points leader Mark Brelsford (HD) also joined in the fun. Pit stops really mixed up the order with Fisher taking over 2nd when Pierce stopped, then Brelsford as Fisher came in. DuHamel's Kawasaki was now running cleanly, breaking into the top 5 and passing Romero on the 42nd lap for 3rd. DuHamel was then closing on Brelsford who helped the French-Canadian's charge when he dropped out with throttle problems. Pierce began dropping back late in the race with a slipping clutch. Gary Scott, on a Don Vesco Yamaha, and Kenny Roberts on a factory one, both had moved up through the ranks. Scott battled with Fisher over 4th while Roberts watched. At the finish it was Rayborn, DuHamel, Romero, Fisher, Scott and Roberts.

Race: 125 Mile Road Race National

Rank	Rider	Number	Make
1.	Cal Rayborn, Spring Valley, Ca	14	HD
2.	Yvon DuHamel, LaSalle Quebec, Can	17	Kaw
3.	Gene Romero, San Luis Obispo, Ca	3	Tri
4.	Gary Fisher, Parkesburg, Pa	10	Yam
5.	Gary Scott, W. Covina, Ca	64	Yam
6.	Kenny Roberts, Modesto, Ca	60	Yam
7.	Ron Pierce, Bakersfield, Ca	97	Yam
8.	Paul Smart, Santa Ana, Ca	8	Kaw
9.	Cliff Carr, Arlington, Mass	26	Kaw
10.	Dick Mann, Richmond, Ca.	1	BSA
11.	Keith Mashburn, Santa Susana, Ca	19	Yam
12.	Steve McLaughlin, Duarte, Ca	55	Yam
13.	Fred Guttner, E. Detroit, Mi	42	Yam
14.	Dave Sehl, Waterdown, Ont., Can	16	HD
15.	R.G. Wakefield, Indianapolis, Ind	74	Kaw
16.	Larry Schafer, Washington, DC	53	HD
17.	V.E. Brown, Portland, Ore	65	Yam
18.	Mike Kidd, Hurst, Tx	72	Yam
19.	Mike Lane, Bakersfield, Ca	44	Yam
20.	Robert Ely, Kansas City, Ks	54	Hon

Race: 50 Mile Junior Final

Rank	Rider	Number	Make
1.	Jim Deehan, Pacifica, Ca	73	Kaw
2.	Jerry Greene, San Mateo, Ca	57	Kaw
3.	Jim Evans, San Bernardino, Ca	47	Yam

Grand National Points Standings after Round 10

Rank	Rider	Pts
1.	Mark Brelsford	632
2.	Kenny Roberts	561
3.	Gary Scott	442
4.	Gene Romero	407
5.	John Hateley	387
6.	Jim Rice	380
7.	Eddie Mulder	307
8.	Dick Mann	298
9.	Cal Rayborn	288
10.	Gary Fisher	275

1972 Columbus Half-Mile
Lawwill Returns to Victory at Columbus!

GNC Round #11 of 24 **Date:** June 25, 1972 **Type:** Half-Mile **Venue:** Ohio State Fairgrounds **Location:** Columbus, Oh	**Purse:** $12,000.00 **Surface:** Dirt-Limestone **Course Length**: ½ Mile **Laps:** 20 **Distance:** 10 Miles

Mert Lawwill's win at the Charity Newsies-promoted National ended an extended dry spell caused by the mechanical ills of the Harley iron XR and just plain old bad luck. Lawwill had been winless since the 1970 Ascot Half-Mile. It was GNC win number 12 for Lawwill and his 2nd at Columbus, the other coming in 1969. Lawwill had a tough struggle with rookie Gary Scott, who came close to scoring his first win. Scott led late in the event till Lawwill trucked by on his Jim Belland/self-tuned factory Harley-Davidson.

Points leaders Mark Brelsford and Kenny Roberts both had lousy days; making it to the semi, but running well out of the transfer spots. Brelsford hung onto the top spot. Gary Scott's runner-up finish allowed him to narrowly pass Roberts for second by one point. Gene Romero 7th place finish solidified his fourth place standing. John Hateley added some points and maintained fifth. Jim Rice stayed in sixth, Dick Mann moved to seventh. Cal Rayborn's Indy Road Race win and top 10 at Columbus moved him to eighth in points. Eddie Mulder and Gary Fisher rounded out the order.

Time Trials

1970 Columbus winner Dave Sehl set fast time at a blazing 26.15 on his Babe DeMay-tuned factory Harley, breaking his own year-old track record. Gary Scott (Tri) was close with a 26.22. Rex Beauchamp (HD) was 3rd at 26.25. GNC champ Dick Mann (BSA) was 4th at 26.29 and closing out the top 5 was Eddie Mulder (Tri), turning a 26.59.

Heats

Dave Sehl led the field away in Heat 1 after a couple of false starts. John Hateley, always fast at Columbus, kept it close in 2nd. The track had begun to groove up while Sehl and Hateley rode the bottom, Dick Mann wowed the crowd, flying by both on the high side, taking over by lap 4. Mann stretched out to a big lead. Hateley worked by Sehl for 2nd and that's how they finished.

California rivals Gary Scott and Kenny Roberts (Yam) blasted out front in Heat 2, chased by Cal Rayborn (HD), Terry Dorsch (Tri) and Mert Lawwill. Lawwill moved into 3rd and latched onto Roberts. With three to go, Roberts bobbled and Lawwill took 2nd. Rayborn also managed to get by Roberts for the last direct transfer.

Heat 3 was a barn burner with Ohio favorite Larry Darr (HD) taking the early lead, chased by a talented bunch including Dave Aldana (BSA), Frank Gillespie (Nor), Tom Rockwood (Tri) and Gene Romero (Tri). Beauchamp took over on lap 2 with Darr slipping back. Romero was flying from mid-pack and on the last lap, both he and Gillespie passed Beauchamp in the fastest heat of the day.

Semi

Larry Darr was determined to put a Buckeye into the National and ran off with the race. Kenny Roberts was close behind in the opening moments. Chuck Palmgren (Yam) quickly displaced Roberts for 2nd. Roberts was finding no traction and was slipping backward. Tom Rockwood and Don Castro (Tri) had a great side-by-side duel till Rockwood slid down unhurt in turn 1. Darr, Palmgren and Castro were headed to the National.

National

Mert Lawwill pulled a huge holeshot from the outside of Row 1 and stretched his lead down the back straight. Pole- sitter Gene Romero managed to head the rest of the pack for 2nd. Mann tried a huge slide job on Romero going into turn 3, sliding wide allowing not only Romero, but also Gary Scott and Chuck Palmgren, to go by. Scott soon

195

caught and scooted by Romero for second. On lap 4 John Hateley dropped out with clutch trouble. Scott began reeling in Lawwill and passed him around midway for the lead. Behind the leaders, Romero and Palmgren had a crowd pleasing duel for 3rd. Dick Mann couldn't get hooked up on the groove and slid back a little in the order. Up front, Lawwill stayed right on Scott waiting for the rookie to make a mistake. It finally happened on the 17th lap, with Lawwill running it in deep on Scott and taking the lead back. Palmgren had a comfortable advantage in 3rd. Don Castro made a late race charge on Romero for 4th with Mann right behind. On lap 19 Romero slipped off the groove, losing several spots.

At the finish it was Lawwill with a good advantage over Scott. Palmgren was 3rd, Castro 4th, Mann 5th, Frank Gillespie 6th, Romero salvaging 7th in a photo finish with Larry Darr, with Cal Rayborn and Rex Beauchamp rounding out the top 10.

Results

Race: 20 Lap Half-Mile National
Race Time: 8:53.06 (New Record)

Rank	Rider	Number	Make
1.	Mert Lawwill, San Francisco, Ca	7	HD
2.	Gary Scott, W. Covina, Ca	64R	Tri
3.	Chuck Palmgren, Freehold, NJ	38	Yam
4.	Don Castro, Hollister, Ca	11	Tri
5.	Dick Mann, Richmond, Ca	1	BSA
6.	Frank Gillespie, Berkeley, Ca	76	Nor
7.	Gene Romero, San Luis Obispo, Ca	3	Tri
8.	Larry Darr, Mansfield, Oh	94	HD
9.	Cal Rayborn, Spring Valley, Ca	14	HD
10.	Rex Beauchamp, Milford, Mi	31	HD
11.	Dave Sehl, Waterdown, Ont., Can	16	HD
12.	John Hateley, Van Nuys, Ca	98	Tri

Race: Junior Final

Rank	Rider	Number	Make
1.	Jim Rawls, Arlington, Tx	41N	BSA
2.	Steve Droste, Waterloo, Ia	26K	Yam
3.	Jim Crenshaw, Davis, Ca	21Y	Nor

Grand National Points Standings after Round 11

Rank	Rider	Pts
1.	Mark Brelsford	632
2.	Gary Scott	562
3.	Kenny Roberts	561
4.	Gene Romero	447
5.	John Hateley	396
6.	Jim Rice	380
7.	Dick Mann	358
8.	Cal Rayborn	308
9.	Eddie Mulder	307
10.	Gary Fisher	275

Extra Extra

- It was the 20th Annual Charity Newsies Grand National race.
- Columbus was traditionally a Harley-Davidson track, taking 15 of the 18 modern era Nationals. The exceptions were Dick Klamfoth winning on a BSA in 1958 and '59, Gary Nixon on a Triumph in 1968.
- The new alloy XR had now claimed 4 victories in 6 starts. There were 5 in the Columbus National, starting to stem the tide of the imports from the previous couple of years.
- Exemplifying the extraordinary brand parity of the era, all five of the "big" brands were represented in the top 6 spots.
- Junior Scott Brelsford's heat race time was faster than any of the Expert heats. Brelsford fell in the main, which was claimed by JR Rawls.

1972 San Jose Half-Mile
Romero Repeats at San Jose

GNC Round #12 of 24 **Date:** July 2, 1972 **Type:** Half-Mile **Venue:** Santa Clara Fairgrounds **Location:** San Jose, Ca	**Purse:** $12,000.00 **Surface:** Dirt **Course Length:** ½ Mile **Laps:** 20 **Distance:** 10 Miles

Gene Romero took his first win of 1972 at the San Jose Half-Mile, repeating last year's win. It was Romero's 8th National win. He took the lead early in the event and ran unchallenged to the finish. Runner-up Chuck Palmgren was on the podium for the second week in the row. GNC points leader Mark Brelsford added more points towards the championship by finishing in 3rd. Romero's win put him firmly in the points race. Other title contenders Gary Scott and Kenny Roberts didn't fare as well, with Roberts dropping back in the championship.

Mark Brelsford remained strong and consistent, still firmly in charge at the top of the points order with a 732 total. Top Gary Scott's 6th at San Jose kept him close at 612. 1970 GNC champion Gene Romero moved solidly into the chase, just knocking Kenny Roberts out of third, 597 to 581. Jim Rice had a good National and his 4th place run moved him back into the top 5 with 460. John Hateley slipped back to sixth, with Dick Mann stationary in seventh. Chuck Palmgren's runner-up in the National moved him to eighth. Cal Rayborn and Eddie Mulder were ninth and tenth.

Time Trials

A very fast San Jose track saw a score of riders break Frank Gillespie's 1971 track record of 27.10, led by Mert Lawwill (HD) at 26.61. Keith Mashburn was close behind at 26.67. Dave Sehl (HD) was 3rd at 26.70. Gary Scott (Tri) and Cal Rayborn (HD) tied for 4th quickest with a 26.79. In all, 13 riders bested the existing record time, including Norton- mounted Gillespie, just squeaking past at 27.09. Junior Scott Brelsford continued to impress; he set the absolute fastest time of the day at 26.58!

Heats

Mert Lawwill, hot off his Columbus win and fast qualifying time, stormed out front to lead Heat 1. The race was red flagged on lap 2 after Frank Gillespie and Gary Scott got together. Lawwill took up where he left off, winning the heat handily. Jim Rice (BSA) was 2nd with Harley teamster Rex Beauchamp in 3rd. Championship contender Scott managed to work his way into a semi berth in 5th.

Gene Romero was on the gas in Heat 2, outdistancing Keith Mashburn (Yam) who was close in the opening laps. Cal Rayborn (HD) was showing good dirt track form in 3rd spot.

Canadian Harley star Dave Sehl, led Heat 3 wire to wire over California riders, Kenny Roberts (Yam) and Terry Dorsch (Tri). National champ Dick Mann (BSA) was behind and semi-bound.

Semi

Al Kenyon (BSA) shot out to an early lead in the semi event with Gary Scott quickly taking the point away. Mark Brelsford was on the move and bumped Kenyon back another spot. Kenyon would continue to slip back as a battle between Ron Moore (Tri) and Chuck Palmgren (Yam) raged past. Moore and Palmgren swapped places several times with Palmgren finally taking the advantage. Scott set a blistering 10-lap pace and was followed to the main by Brelsford and Palmgren. Dick Mann did not make the transfer.

National

Keith Mashburn led the way at the start of the 20-lap race. He only led briefly as a determined Gene Romero steamed by. Romero proceeded to check out to a comfortable lead. Mashburn had swingarm trouble and dropped to an 11th place finish. Semi-winner Chuck Palmgren moved into 2nd with two-time San Jose Half-Mile winner Jim Rice in 3rd. The order at halfway was Romero, Palmgren, Rice, Dave Sehl and Mert Lawwill. Mark Brelsford and Gary

Scott had hooked up and were working their way through the pack. They altered the running order towards the end of the race. Brelsford bumped Rice back to 4th, with Scott taking 6th from Lawwill. Up front, Brelsford had latched onto Chuck Palmgren and was applying heavy pressure. Veteran Palmgren didn't slip though, just holding off Brelsford. Leader Romero was not to be caught and cruised to a comfortable victory.

Results

Race: 20 Lap Half-Mile National

Rank	Rider	Number	Make
1.	Gene Romero, San Luis Obispo, Ca	3	Tri
2.	Chuck Palmgren, Freehold, NJ	38	Yam
3.	Mark Brelsford, Los Altos, Ca	87	HD
4.	Jim Rice, Portola Valley, Ca	24	BSA
5.	Dave Sehl, Waterdown, Ont., Can	16	HD
6.	Gary Scott, W. Covina, Ca	64R	Tri
7.	Mert Lawwill, San Francisco, Ca	7	HD
8.	Terry Dorsch, Granada Hills, Ca	22	Tri
9.	Kenny Roberts, Modesto, Ca	80Y	Yam
10.	Cal Rayborn, Spring Valley, Ca	14	HD
11.	Keith Mashburn, Santa Susana, Ca	19	Yam
12.	Rex Beauchamp, Milford, Mi	31	HD

Race: Junior Final

Rank	Rider	Number	Make
1.	Scott Brelsford, San Bruno, Ca	84Y	HD
2.	Jim Rawls, Arlington, Tx	41N	BSA
3.	Tom White, Huntington Beach	42R	Tri

Grand National Points Standings after Round 12

Rank	Rider	Pts
1.	Mark Brelsford	732
2.	Gary Scott	612
3.	Gene Romero	597
4.	Kenny Roberts	581
5.	Jim Rice	460
6.	John Hateley	396
7.	Dick Mann	358
8.	Chuck Palmgren	331
9.	Cal Rayborn	323
10.	Eddie Mulder	307

1972 Salem Half-Mile
Brelsford Takes 3rd of 1972!

GNC Round #13 of 24 **Date:** July 9, 1972 **Type:** Half-Mile **Venue:** Oregon State Fairgrounds **Location:** Salem, Ore	**Purse:** $12,000.00 **Surface:** Dirt **Course Length:** ½ Mile **Laps:** 20 **Distance:** 10 Miles

Mark Brelsford took his third win of the year at the first-time National at Salem, Oregon. He battled past early front runners Rex Beauchamp and Jim Rice on his Jim Belland-tuned Harley. It was Brelsford's 7th career win. Rice ran up front through the National, ending up 2nd. Gary Scott once again put in a strong run, finishing 3rd to round out the podium. Rain washed out qualifying that was scheduled on Saturday. The whole program moved to Sunday. The sky again threatened, but cleared up right before race time.

Mark Brelsford was making a strong run at the Championship as the schedule moved past the halfway point. He added to his points lead over Gary Scott, their totals now 882 and 712 points respectively. Kenny Roberts raised his total to 641 points, topping Gene Romero's 617 points for fourth. They finished 5th and 9th respectively at Salem. Jim Rice continued to impress; he was fifth in points after running only five Nationals. His total was 580 points. Chuck Palmgren jumped to sixth with 411.

Time Trials

Team Harley had their XR750's running fast and reliable at Salem. They dominated time trials, taking the top 4 spots, led by Cal Rayborn, Rex Beauchamp, Dave Sehl and Mert Lawwill.

Heats

Chuck Palmgren hoped to shake up the Harley contingent in Heat 1, running out front on the Dan Gurney Yamaha. Early leader Gene Romero (Tri) had to work hard to hold off fast timer Cal Rayborn on the Andres-tuned Harley in 3rd.

In Heat 2, Jim Rice (BSA) pulled the holeshot, but Michigan half-mile ace Rex Beauchamp was by before two laps were out. Don Castro (Tri) stayed close, taking the last transfer in 3rd.

Dave Sehl shot out in front of Heat 3, but slipped off the groove. Gary Scott (Tri) assumed the lead, but repeated Sehl's mistake in turn 3 and Kenny Roberts (Yam) went by for the lead. Mark Brelsford was on the move, passing Scott and Roberts, taking the win. Scott and Roberts followed, with Sehl semi-bound. Brelsford had the fastest heat and thus the pole for the National.

Semi

Dave Sehl was determined to make the main and took the lead at the green flag and led to the finish. Frank Gillespie (Nor) finished 2nd and Keith Mashburn (Yam) 3rd, taking the last ticket to the National. Dick Mann missed transferring to his second National in a row.

National

Jim Rice showed his pipes of his self-tuned BSA to the field at the start of the National. Chuck Palmgren stayed close in 2nd. Rex Beauchamp blasted by Palmgren on the backstretch. Just back were Mark Brelsford, Kenny Roberts, Gene Romero and Dave Sehl. On lap 2, Beauchamp shot past Rice on the back straight. Brelsford was also on the move and knocked Palmgren out of 3rd spot. By lap 8, Kenny Roberts passed Palmgren for 3rd. Up front, Rex Beauchamp could taste his first win and was pulling away from his challengers. On lap 9 his XR began running rough and he was soon out and Brelsford took over.

By lap 14, Brelsford was extending his lead with Palmgren taking 3rd back from Roberts. Cal Rayborn was hanging right in there and moved into the 5th spot, passing Romero. Gary Scott had been working his way forward through the pack, and with 3 laps to go went around Roberts and then quickly by Palmgren for 3rd. He was gaining ground on front runners Rice and Brelsford, but just ran out of time. Brelsford still had a straight away lead at the finish.

Results

Race: 20 Lap Half-Mile National

Rank	Rider	Number	Make
1.	Mark Brelsford, Los Altos, Ca	87	HD
2.	Jim Rice, Portola Valley, Ca	24	BSA
3.	Gary Scott, W. Covina, Ca	64R	Tri
4.	Chuck Palmgren, Freehold, NJ	38	Yam
5.	Kenny Roberts, Modesto, Ca	80Y	Yam
6.	Frank Gillespie, Berkeley, Ca	76	Nor
7.	Cal Rayborn, Spring Valley, Ca	14	HD
8.	Dave Sehl, Waterdown, Ont., Can	16	HD
9.	Gene Romero, San Luis Obispo, Ca	3	Tri
10.	Keith Mashburn, Santa Susana, Ca	19	Yam
11.	Don Castro, Hollister, Ca	11	Tri
12.	Rex Beauchamp, Milford, Mi	31	HD

Race: Junior Final

Rank	Rider	Number	Make
1.	Jim Crenshaw, Davis, Ca	21Y	Nor
2.	Tom White, Huntington Beach, Ca	42R	Tri
3.	Scott Brelsford, San Bruno, Ca	84Y	HD

Grand National Points Standings after Round 13

Rank	Rider	Pts
1.	Mark Brelsford	882
2.	Gary Scott	712
3.	Kenny Roberts	641
4.	Gene Romero	617
5.	Jim Rice	580
6.	Chuck Palmgren	411
7.	John Hateley	396
8.	Cal Rayborn	363
9.	Dick Mann	358
10.	Eddie Mulder	307

Extra Extra

- The state capitol of Salem has been home of the Oregon State Fair since 1862. The fair celebrated the rural culture of farming, livestock and crafts. A one mile horse track was built in 1893 and became one of the main attractions of the fair. An impressive 6,500 seat grandstand was built in 1929. Motorcycle racing made some appearances over the years, with the GNC series paying just the one visit in 1972. The fair grew steadily over the years and in recent times has hosted over 400,000 people over its 12-day schedule. Like many fairs, the attractions have moved away from their agricultural roots and cater to more urban tastes. The grandstands were torn down in 2002 and in 2004 a new pavilion/exhibition area, along with more parking, were built over the racetrack area. Some good news for motorsports fans occurred in 2009 when flattrack bikes and quads started racing indoors at the fairgrounds.

1972 Castle Rock TT
Scott Wins First at the 'Rock

GNC Round #14 of 21 **Date:** July 16, 1972 **Type:** TT **Venue:** Mt. St. Helens Motorcycle Club Grounds	**Purse:** $12,000.00 **Location:** Castle Rock, Wa **Surface:** Dirt **Course Length**: ½ Mile **Laps:** 25

Rookie Gary Scott, who had been knocking on victories door all season, notched his first ever GNC win at the Castle Rock National. Throughout his career, Scott would continue to have an affinity for Triumphs and TT racing. Scott dominated the night's event, setting a new track record in time trials, winning his heat and running away with the main. Jim Rice, always strong at TT events, was 2nd over TT specialist and crowd favorite Mark Williams.

GNC points leader Mark Brelsford struggled in the main, finishing 8th, allowing Gary Scott to close up in the standings. The gap was now only 50 points, 912 to 862. Kenny Roberts had an off night in 9th. Gene Romero did not make the main. This combined with Jim Rice's 2nd place propelled him to third points with 700. Roberts was now fourth with 661 points and Gene Romero fifth with 617 points. There was a big gap back to sixth place Chuck Palmgren at 411. Seventh was Dick Mann at 408, John Hateley eighth with 396, Cal Rayborn 9th at 317. Eddie Mulder rounded out the top 10 with 307.

Heats

The first heat of the night got off to a rocky start with area rider Ross Roberts, falling in front of the pack. Despite the melee, the race continued. Gary Scott on the Eddie Hammond tuned, City Cycle Center Triumph, shot out to the win over Kenny Roberts (Yam), Terry Dorsch (Tri) and one of the crowd favorites, Chuck Joyner (Tri).

Cal Rayborn (HD) looked very strong in Heat 2, controlling most of the race. With two laps to go, Jim Rice (BSA) scooted by for the win. Points leader Mark Brelsford (HD) worked his way from the pack for 3rd. Last year's Junior winner Randy Scott on a Fred's Distributing sponsored Triumph was 4th.

Ike Reed, on the Kawasaki Town Triumph, tried his best to run off with Heat 3, but was run down by Posa Enterprises rider Mark Williams (Tri) on lap 2. Williams then proceeded to motor away to the win. Reed hung onto 2nd with California TT specialist Mike Haney taking 3rd. The top 3 were all Triumph mounted. Dave Aldana (BSA) was 4th.

Semi

The semi event turned into a barnburner as Al Kenyon (BSA) and John Hateley (Tri) went at it hammer and tong. The two diced fiercely, swapping the top spot all over. The battle ended when Hateley's Triumph locked up, sending him off the track. Kenyon continued for the win. Dick Mann (BSA) was 2nd, making his first National in the last three starts. Dave Aldana (BSA) and Frank Gillespie (Tri) filled out the final National spots.

National

The first start of the National turned into a big mess. Mike Haney (Tri) came off directly in the paths of Randy Scott and Terry Dorsch, sending all involved to the surface. All were apparently okay, making it back for the restart. Mark Williams jumped out front on the restart and opened up a small lead over Cal Rayborn. Lap 2 saw Jim Rice and Gary Scott both pass Rayborn. Two laps later, Scott passed Rice for 2nd and set out after Williams. He quickly reeled in the locals favorite, passing him on lap 7. Scott then proceeded to check out on the field. Rice also closed on Williams, applying pressure for several laps, finally getting by late in the race. Behind was TT ace Chuck Joyner, Dave Aldana (BSA) and Dick Mann (BSA). At the finish it was Scott with a huge lead followed by Rice, Williams, Joyner, Aldana, Mann, Terry Dorsch, Mark Brelsford, Kenny Roberts and local racer Jim Jones.

Results

Race: 25 Lap TT National

Rank	Rider	Number	Make
1.	Gary Scott, W. Covina, Ca	64R	Tri
2.	Jim Rice, Portola Valley, Ca	24	BSA
3.	Mark Williams, Springfield, Ore	70	Tri
4.	Chuck Joyner, Oregon City, Ore	60	Tri
5.	Dave Aldana, Santa Ana, Ca	3	BSA
6.	Dick Mann, Richmond, Ca	1	BSA
7.	Terry Dorsch, Granada Hills, Ca	22	Tri
8.	Mark Brelsford, Los Altos, Ca	87	HD
9.	Kenny Roberts, Modesto, Ca	80Y	Yam
10.	Jim Jones, Kirkland, Wa	55	Tri
11.	Al Kenyon, Cupertino, Ca	48	BSA
12.	Randy Scott, Philomath, Ore	57Q	Tri
13.	Cal Rayborn, Spring Valley, Ca	14	HD
14.	Ike Reed, Salem, Ore	90	Tri
15.	Frank Gillespie, Berkeley, Ca	76	Tri
16.	Mike Haney, Inglewood, Ca	91	Tri

Race: Junior Final

Rank	Rider	Number	Make
1.	Tom White, Huntington Beach, Ca	42R	Tri
2.	Jim Crenshaw, Davis, Ca	21Y	Nor
3.	Jim Rawls, Arlington, Tx	41N	BSA

Grand National Points Standings after Round 14

Rank	Rider	Pts
1.	Mark Brelsford	912
2.	Gary Scott	862
3.	Jim Rice	700
4.	Kenny Roberts	661
5.	Gene Romero	617
6.	Chuck Palmgren	411
7.	Dick Mann	408
8.	John Hateley	396
9.	Cal Rayborn	371
10.	Eddie Mulder	307

1972 Laguna Seca Road Race
It's Rayborn at First Laguna Race

GNC Round #15 of 24 **Date:** July 23, 1972 **Type:** Road Race **Venue:** Laguna Seca Raceway **Location:** Monterey, Ca	**Purse:** $20,000.00 **Surface:** Pavement **Course Length:** 1.8 Miles **Laps:** 69 **Distance:** 125 Miles

Cal Rayborn won the first-ever Grand National event at Laguna Seca which was billed as the Kawasaki Superbike International. It was his 2nd win of the year and his 11th and final GNC win. After an early race melee, originated by Yvon DuHamel, Rayborn worked himself into the lead and was never headed. Gene "quit calling me dirt tracker" Romero once again podiumed on his Triumph Trident. Rookie Expert Kenny Roberts was beginning to show his pavement chops and came home 3rd despite losing his front brake lever along the way. Mark Brelsford had tire trouble and scored no points. Gary Scott finished, really tightening up the points race.

Mark Brelsford saw his points advantage over Gary Scott cut to just 10 points, 912 to 902. Kenny Roberts podium moved him back to third in points with 761 points. Gene Romero's runner-up showing shot him back to fourth with 737. Jim Rice's limited schedule still had him in contention with 700. Cal Rayborn's win moved him up to seventh.

Heats

The two hottest road racers of 1972, Cal Rayborn and Yvon DuHamel, captured the two preliminary heats. In Heat 1, Rayborn on the Harley-Davidson alloy XRTT reeled off an easy win, running lap times around 1:15.

Heat 2 with DuHamel aboard the Kawasaki triple, passed early leader Gary Fisher (Yam) and was running times nearly two seconds faster than Rayborn. Overall, heat times were nearly identical though. Finishing behind were teammates Gary Nixon and Paul Smart, giving hope to Team Hansen for a win at the Kawasaki-sponsored event.

National

As expected, Yvon DuHamel rocketed his Steve Whitelock tuned-Kawasaki off the line, with the field in formation behind him. His hopes ended quicker than anyone expected. Going into turn 4 at around 100 mph, his bike began running off–song. He quickly looked down to check out the problem; when he looked back up he was off the course. The bike tossed DuHamel off and began flipping wildly. Unfortunately it shot right back across the track. Kenny Roberts and Gary Fisher just squeezed past, but some riders behind were not so lucky. Cliff Carr got a faceful of the DuHamel Kawasaki, followed by Dick Mann and Jerry Christopher. Fortunately, no one was seriously injured. The accident enabled Roberts and Fisher to speed way out front. Kawasaki teammates Paul Smart and Gary Nixon were behind trying to close up. Rayborn was pacing the leaders back in 6th. On lap 2, road race ace Jim Dunn fell very hard, suffering serious injury.

Back up front, Fisher moved by Roberts in the corkscrew. Rayborn was on the march forward, getting by Nixon and Smart, and heading out after Roberts. Nixon fell just before the corkscrew; he was able to continue, but was well back in the running. Around lap 10, Rayborn moved by Roberts for 2nd, with a following Paul Smart doing the same. At this point, Fisher had a 5-second plus lead. Rayborn was slowly reeling him in when Fisher's Yamaha began slowing with clutch trouble. Rayborn went by for the lead on lap 18. Soon after, Smart also moved past Fisher. Rayborn really got into a groove and at the halfway point had around a 20-second lead. Behind, the thirsty two-strokes of Roberts and Smart had to pit, giving up 2nd and 3rd spots. Mark Brelsford made a brief appearance up front till slowed by a leaking front tire. Gene Romero had moved way up when Roberts and Smart pitted and managed to pass both when they rejoined the race. Roberts then passed Smart whose bike slowed with cracked exhaust. The front order was now set. Rayborn got a scare when he thought his XRTT was running out of gas. The bike was expected to go the full distance and the crew scrambled to ready for a fuel stop. On the last lap, Rayborn limped to the finish. Turns out the bike had plenty of fuel; a faulty carburetor was to blame. Behind Rayborn, Romero, Roberts and Smart were Kel Carruthers, Mike Lane, Gary Scott, Fisher, Jim Allen and Conrad Urbanowski.

Results

Race: 125 Mile Road Race National

Rank	Rider	Number	Make
1.	Cal Rayborn, Spring Valley, Ca	14	HD
2.	Gene Romero, San Luis Obispo, Ca	3	Tri
3.	Kenny Roberts, Modesto, Ca	60	Yam
4.	Paul Smart, Santa Ana, Ca	8	Kaw
5.	Kel Carruthers, El Cajon, Ca	73	Yam
6.	Mike Lane, Bakersfield, Ca	44	Yam
7.	Gary Scott, W. Covina, Ca	64	Tri
8.	Gary Fisher, Parkesburg, Pa	10	Yam
9.	Jim Allen, Islington, Ont., Can	85	Suz
10.	Conrad Urbanowski, Miramar, Fla	80	Yam
11.	John Hateley, Van Nuys, Ca	98	Tri
12.	Bob Bailey, Gardena, Ca	77	Tri
13.	Don Emde, San Diego, Ca	25	Yam
14.	Fred Guttner, Detroit, Mi	42	Yam
15.	Jess Thomas, Sea Cliff, NY	39	Yam
16.	Mike Ninci, Kansas City, Mo	95	BSA
17.	Eddie Mulder, Northridge, Ca	12	Tri
18.	Dave Smith, Lakewood, Ca	20	Yam
19.	Reg Pridmore, Santa Barbara, Ca	82	BMW
20.	George Kerker, Glendale, Ca	90	Hon

Race: Junior Final

Rank	Rider	Number	Make
1.	Jerry Greene, San Mateo, Ca	57	Kaw
2.	Steve Baker, Bellingham, Wa	41	Yam
3.	Howard Lynggard, Glendora, Ca	7	Yam

Grand National Points Standings after Round 15

Rank	Rider	Pts
1.	Mark Brelsford	912
2.	Gary Scott	902
3.	Kenny Roberts	761
4.	Gene Romero	737
5.	Jim Rice	700
6.	Cal Rayborn	521
7.	Chuck Palmgren	411
8.	Dick Mann	408
9.	John Hateley	406
10.	Eddie Mulder	311

Extra Extra

- A great crowd of around 30,000 helped assure that the Laguna Race would return on the GNC schedule.
- Brand diversity still reigned with 4 different brands in the top 4. There were also 5 brands in the top 10.
- There was still no Team Suzuki, but Jim Allen brought home a private entry in 9th place.
- Gary Scott was 7th in his first ride on a Triumph Trident.
- Goodyear showed up with some new design slicks.

- Walt Fulton fell hard in the practice at the same corner as Deeley teammate Jim Dunn.
- Gary Fisher captured the Lightweight event, wowing the photog's with big wheelies along the way.

GNC Round #16 of 24	**Purse:** $15,000.00
Date: July 29, 1972	**Surface:** Cushion-covered matting
Type: Half-Mile	**Course Length:** ½ Mile
Venue: Roosevelt Raceway	**Laps:** 20
Location: Long Island, NY	**Distance:** 10 Miles

Chuck Palmgren won his first National since Nazareth in 1970 at the one-off National at the Roosevelt Half-Mile in Long Island, NY. Making it even sweeter, the race was known as the Yamaha Gold Cup and it marked Yamaha's first big-bore dirt track win of the year. It was Palmgren's 4th GNC win. Team Harley-Davidson's Mert Lawwill and points leader Mark Brelsford finished out the podium. A disappointed Larry Darr ended up 4th after battling with Palmgren for the lead late in the race. He slipped backwards in the waning laps of the event. Brelsford's points rival Gary Scott hurt his shoulder in a heat race crash, earning no points and possibly knocking him out of upcoming events.

The surface at Roosevelt Raceway was unique; it consisted of rubber mats covered with a synthetic cushion surface. The motorcycles blew the cushion surface off the mats in the corners, offering great traction. The surface on the straights stayed intact. While possibly a great surface for horse, spinning dirt track motorcycle tires quickly found their way through to the matting.

For the first time in a long while there were no major changes in the top 5 of the GNC points order. Mark Brelsford was able to pad his lead over Gary Scott, who didn't make the main event. Gene Romero added a few points in 8th place. Kenny Roberts had a rotten weekend; mechanical problems kept him out of the main. Jim Rice was a no-show in the National. Chuck Palmgren's win pushed him into sixth, switching places with Cal Rayborn. Dick Mann and John Hateley stayed locked in at eighth and ninth. Mert Lawwill moved into tenth, knocking Eddie Mulder out of the top 10 for the first time this season.

Time Trials

Gary Scott (Tri) and Chuck Palmgren tied for the fastest time of the day, turning in identical 26.77's.

Heats

GNC hopeful Gary Scott had his night end early, falling off on lap 1 of the first heat. Teddy Newton and Billy Eves were also caught up in the accident. Scott tweaked his shoulder pretty badly and Newton suffered hand injuries. Of the three, only Eves made the restart. Dick Mann (BSA) shot out front on the restart. He looked unstoppable till his chain or a shock came loose, locking his rear wheel on lap 7. He was fortunate to get the bike stopped without incident.

Chuck Palmgren took control of Heat 2 with Don Castro, aboard a Yamaha instead of his normal Triumph and Dave Sehl (HD) following. Gene Romero (Tri) knocked Sehl out of the last transfer spot late in the race.

Ohio hotshoe Larry Darr (HD) put in a strong ride in Heat 3. He led the whole race, with teammate Mert Lawwill catching him with one to go, but Lawwill could not get around the fast Buckeye.

Semi

GNC points leader Mark Brelsford was forced to run the last chance event. Terry Dorsch (Tri) led most of the race with Brelsford nipping him in a crowd-pleasing pass at the stripe. Texas rookie Mike Kidd was 3rd aboard a Triumph.

National

Little-known cushion specialist Billy Eves was the early leader till Chuck Palmgren rolled by followed by Don Castro. Close behind were Larry Darr, Mert Lawwill and Mark Williams (Tri). Mark Brelsford was deep in the pack, but moving up. Castro couldn't maintain the pace and began fading back. Eves also began to fade, eventually winding up in 10th spot. Darr moved into 2nd and was soon all over Palmgren. Lawwill ran 3rd with Brelsford applying heavy pressure to Williams for 4th. Darr finally found an opening and passed Palmgren entering Turn 3 on lap 9. Palmgren stayed right with Darr, never more than a few bike lengths back. Lawwill and Brelsford were keeping it close, just behind. The group freight-trained around for a number of laps, with Palmgren often side-by-side with Darr. With 4 laps to go, Palmgren slipped underneath Darr for the lead. Darr went a little wide and both Lawwill and Brelsford slipped past, setting the top spots. Mike Kidd was very impressive, working up to 5th place. At the flag, Palmgren had the biggest lead of the night with the rest of the top ten, Lawwill, Brelsford, Darr, Kidd, Castro, Williams, Romero, Terry Dorsch and Billy Eves.

Results

Race: 20 Lap Half-Mile National

Rank	Rider	Number	Make
1.	Chuck Palmgren, Freehold, NJ	38	Yam
2.	Mert Lawwill, San Francisco, Ca	7	HD
3.	Mark Brelsford, Los Altos, Ca	87	HD
4.	Larry Darr, Mansfield, Oh	94	HD
5.	Mike Kidd, Hurst, Tx	72N	Tri
6.	Don Castro, Hollister, Ca	11	Yam
7.	Mark Williams, Springfield, Ore	70	Tri
8.	Gene Romero, San Luis Obispo, Ca	3	Tri
9.	Terry Dorsch, Granada Hills, Ca	22	Tri
10.	Billy Eves, Phoenixville, Pa	41A	BSA
11.	Larry Palmgren, Freehold, NJ	29	Tri
12.	Dave Aldana, Santa Ana, Ca	13	BSA

Race: Junior Final

Rank	Rider	Number	Make
1.	Jim Rawls, Arlington, Tx	41N	Yam
2.	James Houston, Richmond, Va	58C	Tri
3.	Scott Brelsford, San Bruno, Ca	84Y	HD

Grand National Points Standings after Round 16

Rank	Rider	Pts
1.	Mark Brelsford	1012
2.	Gary Scott	902
3.	Gene Romero	767
4.	Kenny Roberts	761
5.	Jim Rice	700
6.	Chuck Palmgren	561
7.	Cal Rayborn	521
8.	Dick Mann	408
9.	John Hateley	406
10.	Mert Lawwill	360

- This was the 2nd Annual Yamaha Gold Cup at Roosevelt Raceway. The first was a non-National, won by Dave Sehl.
- Overwatering of the tricky surface before the heats may have contributed to Gary Scott's mishap. Heat 1 started right after a bout of watering and the riders were not given a "sighting" lap to check conditions.
- In a switching of rides, Mike Kidd was riding a Triumph with Don Castro aboard Kidd's former K&N Yamaha. Both had good nights, finishing 4th and 5th.
- Bart Markel was back in action for the first time since his pelvic fracture at the Colorado Mile. He turned competitive laps, but didn't make the National.
- The Junior main ended in controversy. JR Rawls had the chain on his Yamaha break on what appeared to be the last lap. Scott Brelsford scooted by to take the checkers. While Brelsford was celebrating in Victory Circle, it was announced that the race had run a lap too many and Rawls was the winner! Jubilation for Rawls; disappointment for Brelsford.
- Roosevelt Raceway lived a turbulent 48-year history; battling bankruptcy, setting new standards for any racing facility, hitting huge success, and finally facing a sad decline. The track was located near the site of the first horse track in the United States, which was built in 1664! This was the first organized sport of any kind in America. The site was later part of the Roosevelt Airfield. In 1936 a car racetrack was built on the grounds which hosted the Vanderbilt Cup for two years. Investors converted it to a horse track, which opened in 1940. Pre-war success was modest. George Levy, the moving force behind the track, faced bankruptcy and government investigations between 1942 and 1944. He managed to make it through to see the track boom in the post-war years. The huge population in the Long Island area turned out in droves and the track became hugely successful. It became the first racetrack to be listed on the American Stock Exchange. The track had a huge $20 million dollar upgrade in 1956, including a 5-story grandstand with a hospital and two restaurants. The track surface received a state-of-the-art system, utilizing perforated rubber mats, covered with a synthetic cushion surface. This allowed quick drainage in the event of rain. A 105,000 watt lighting system was installed. Closed-circuit television enabled the races to be seen all through the new grandstand. Don Brymer successfully promoted a Yamaha Gold Cup motorcycle race at the facility in 1971. It became a National in 1972. Despite the success of the events, motorcycles never returned. Roosevelt Raceway also hosted successful concerts in the 1970's. Off-track betting and other attractions in the area led to a serious decline at the track through the seventies. The track changed hands in 1984 and closed in 1988. The land had become hugely valuable and the track grounds were developed into shopping centers. The huge grandstands stood still until 2002. The stands and track area were covered by condominiums in 2006.

GNC Round #17 of 24	**Purse:** $12,000.00
Date: August 5, 1972	**Surface:** Cushion
Type: Mile	**Course Length:** 1 Mile
Venue: Washington Park	**Laps:** 25
Location: Homewood, Ill	**Distance:** 25 Miles

GNC Champion Dick Mann had it all come together at the rough surface, one-time-only Homewood Mile, outside of Chicago, Il. It was a perfect match of Mann, machine and track. The 39 year-old veteran put on an amazing display, lapping clear up to 4th place finisher Chuck Palmgren! Mann, like fellow veteran Bart Markel, excelled on rough tracks. Despite his age, Mann was in excellent shape and his love of motocross and off-road riding gave him an edge on moonscape-like surfaces.

It was remarkable win, in-and-of itself, but it also established a racing precedent. Mann became the first rider to ever complete a modern day, Grand National Championship "Grand Slam". He had previously won every type of National event, short track, half-mile, TT and road race; leaving only a mile event. The win at Homewood gave him the final piece of the puzzle. Remarkably, Mann had been on the circuit 13 years before a mile win.

Current GNC points leader Mark Brelsford trucked in way behind Mann at the end of the race followed by teammate Rex Beauchamp.

There was little change through the top 10. Brelsford's runner-up spot boosted his lead over 11th place finisher Gary Scott by 225 points. Gene Romero's 10th place added a few points in third. Kenny Roberts machines again let him down, failing to make the main. The only change in positions were Dick Mann and Cal Rayborn swapping seventh and eighth.

Time Trials

Mert Lawwill stopped the clocks the quickest on his Jim Belland/self-tuned, Team Harley XR at 41.13. Teammate and protégé Mark Brelsford was close behind on the second Belland wrenched machine at 41.17. Third quickest and last rider below the 42 second mark was GNC champ Dick Mann on his self-tuned factory BSA, running a 41.23.

Heats

Harley-Davidson riders dominated Heat 1 with Dave Sehl taking the win over Larry Darr and Doug Sehl. Fast timer Mert Lawwill dropped out with mechanical trouble.

In Heat 2 teammates Mark Brelsford and Rex Beauchamp topped Gary Scott (Tri). Scott was still recovering from shoulder injuries suffered at the Roosevelt National.

Dick Mann (BSA) gave a preview of the upcoming main by running away with Heat 3. Chuck Palmgren put the AAR Yamaha in the show by taking 2nd spot. Cal Rayborn was 3rd aboard his factory Harley.

Semi

Bart Markel (HD) showed he was coming back to form after his Colorado Mile injuries by taking the semi win. Kenny Roberts had a sure 2nd spot till his Yamaha lunched it's engine late in the race. The title contender was done for the night.

National

Dick Mann picked the outside pole of the National at the start and immediately set sail. By lap 2, he already had at least a 10 bike length lead. Larry Darr, who had been very strong of late, was running 2nd, followed by Mark Brelsford, Gary Scott, Rex Beauchamp and Dave Sehl. Scott's bike suffered a mechanical problem and quickly dropped out. Darr appeared to slow a little, with Brelsford moving by into 2nd on lap 4. Beauchamp also passed Darr a lap later. Darr next fell back into Dave Sehl's clutches and Sehl moved by on lap 11.

Up front, Mann was way out front, lapping the field. He had an insurmountable lead, barring trouble. The podium positions were set around halfway, but there was much position-swapping behind. Chuck Palmgren powered his way into the top 5, getting into a good scrap with Darr and Dave Sehl. Palmgren showed his Yamaha's power by moving past Sehl into 4th. Bart Markel had been running way back in the field, but worked into the top 10 just after half distance. He managed to move by a fading Darr into 6th spot. Doug Sehl passed Gary Fisher (Nor) late in the race for 8th, with Gene Romero (Tri) rounding out the top 10.

Mann had passed/lapped 16 top riders on his historic ride and was actually catching 4th place Chuck Palmgren at the end. Truly, one for this, and all record books.

Results

Race: 25 Lap Mile National

Rank	Rider	Number	Make
1.	Dick Mann, Richmond, Ca	1	BSA
2.	Mark Brelsford, Los Altos, Ca	87	HD
3.	Rex Beauchamp, Milford, Mi	31	HD
4.	Chuck Palmgren, Freehold, NJ	38	Yam
5.	Dave Sehl, Waterdown, Ont., Can	16	HD
6.	Bart Markel, Flint, Mi	4	HD
7.	Larry Darr, Mansfield, Oh	94	HD
8.	Doug Sehl, Waterdown, Ont., Can	45	HD
9.	Gary Fisher, Parkesburg, Pa	9A	Nor
10.	Gene Romero, San Luis Obispo, Ca	3	Tri
11.	Jack Warren, Millington, Mi	82	HD
12.	Cal Rayborn, Spring Valley, Ca	14	HD
13.	Jim Rice, Palo Alto, Ca	24	BSA
14.	Frank Gillespie, Berkeley, Ca	76	Nor
15.	Jody Nicholas, Newport, Ca	58	HD
16.	Gary Scott, W. Covina, Ca	64R	Tri
17.	Ed Hermann, Milwaukie, Ore	57	Tri
18.	Frank Ulicki, Kenosha, Wi	23G	HD
19.	Corky Keener, Goodrich, Mi	31E	Yam
20.	Carl LeBlanc, Elyria, Oh	77F	Tri

Race: Junior Final

Rank	Rider	Number	Make
1.	Scott Brelsford, San Bruno, Ca	84Y	HD
2.	Billy Field, Brunswick, Oh	48L	Nor
3.	Steve Droste, Waterloo, Ia	26K	Yam

Grand National Points Standings after Round 17

Rank	Rider	Pts
1.	Mark Brelsford	1132
2.	Gary Scott	907
3.	Gene Romero	782
4.	Kenny Roberts	761
5.	Jim Rice	708
6.	Chuck Palmgren	641
7.	Dick Mann	558
8.	Cal Rayborn	530
9.	John Hateley	406
10.	Mert Lawwill	360

Extra Extra

- Dick Mann's performance had to be partially credited to his trick Jim Dour-built BSA engine. Most of the credit for the win though, must assuredly go to Dick Mann being in the saddle.
- This was the BSA brands 58th and last Grand National Championship win.
- Bart Markel's return to the top level of GNC racing was remarkable. The run at Homewood would be one of the strongest in the late stages of his career.
- Kenny Roberts again suffered through engine troubles. He had used up all of his engines and the one that let go in his semi was a borrowed piece from Team K&N.
- "Road racer" Gary Fisher put in a 9th place aboard Ron Wood's neat Norton.
- Scott Brelsford won his 4th Junior National.
- Washington Park Race Track was one of the many horse racing tracks to be built around the Chicagoland area. It actually existed in two different locations. The first was located in the Woodlawn community area and opened in 1883. The track was initially successful, but political and social pressures against gambling eventually caused the track to close in 1905. The track had some interesting history. Early auto racing include match races between gasoline and electric powered cars. At the time the two types had nearly equal numbers and a race at the track in 1900 saw a gasoline powered machine beat an electric car for the first time. Over time, the track itself disappeared but the stables survived and are now part of the DuSable Museum of African-American History. The second track opened in 1926, in the midst of a horse track boom during the period of the "Roaring '20's". It was built outside the Homewood village area. A new railway line connected the track directly with Chicago-proper. The track remained healthy and popular for decades, if not as prestigious as some other area tracks like Arlington Park. The AMA Grand National series visited the facility for the successful Don Brymer-promoted 1972 race. The track was to be on the schedule for 1973, but was cancelled when the permits for the event were revoked over concerns about dust and noise. The tracks main grandstand burned in the winter of 1977. It was not rebuilt and the track went out of business. The area was used for commercial and residential development in the early 1990's.

GNC Round #18 of 24 **Date:** August 13, 1972 **Type:** TT **Venue:** Peoria Motorcycle Club Grounds **Location:** Peoria, Ill	**Purse:** $12,000.00 **Surface:** Dirt **Course Length:** ½ Mile **Laps:** 25

Dick Mann put on a TT riding clinic at the famous Peoria Motorcycle Club grounds. Mann had now posted back-to-back GNC wins, giving him 2 victories for the year. This victory, the 24th of Mann's career, would be the great champion's last National win. His first win had come at Peoria and he won the famed race 5 times: 1959, 1964, 1967, 1969 and now 1972. The reigning GNC champ was still too far back to challenge for the 1972 title, but he was making a late season charge. TT ace Sonny Burres led early, later battling with Mann and veteran Mert Lawwill, ending the day in 2nd spot. In 3rd position was Mert Lawwill. His TT form was back but had throttle problems which slowed him late in the event.

Mark Brelsford finished 5th on the day, further stretching his lead over Gary Scott, 1192 to 927 points. The rest of the top 5 added some points to their totals. Dick Mann was again on the move, his win boosting him into sixth. The only other change in position was Mert Lawwill and John Hateley swapping the last spots in the top 10.

Time Trials

Privateer Jim Rice (BSA) the 1970 Peoria winner, and Mert Lawwill on his factory Harley-Davidson, tied for the top spot at 29.61. They were just a tenth of a second off Bart Markel's track record. Dick Mann (BSA) clocked into fifth spot.

Heats

Jim Rice had the track wired in Heat 1, leading the whole distance. Eddie Wirth (Tri) ran 2nd place early in the event only to have Dave Aldana go by on the jump. Wirth fell out of transfer range as Frank Gillespie and 1964 Peoria Lightweight winner Ronnie Rall moved by. Both were Triumph mounted. Kenny Roberts (Yam) had a huge moment at the beginning of the race and scratched his way through the field to grab 5th and a semi-berth.

Mert Lawwill and Dick Mann gave a preview of the National in Heat 2. The two veterans kept it close with Mann threatening in the turns only to have Lawwill power away on the front straight. They would finish 1-2. Behind, GNC point's leader Mark Brelsford (HD) led Mike Haney (Tri) into the Main. Frenchie Leblanc (Tri) was close behind, but semi-bound.

Bob Bailey (Tri) pulled the holeshot in Heat 3, but Sonny Burres (Tri) and Ed Hermann (Tri) were quickly by. Burres and Hermann had a nifty duel going. The two traded the lead back and forth, but Hermann's engine quit with four laps to go, giving Burres an uncontested lead. Behind them, Bailey had disappeared from the scene, replaced by Randy Scott (Tri) and Buddy Powell. They gave way to charging 5-time Peoria winner Bart Markel (HD), Gene Romero (Tri) and Jim Jones (Tri). At the flag it was Burres with a big lead, Markel, Romero and Jones.

Semi

Bob Bailey wired his second start of the night, but quickly fell to a charging Don Castro on the K&N Yamaha. Gary Scott (Tri) ran second early followed by Frenchie Leblanc and Kenny Roberts. Roberts was on the move and soon into the runner-up spot. LeBlanc fell out on lap 3 with mechanical trouble. With two laps to go, Roberts worked by Castro for the win. Behind were Scott and Al Kenyon. All four headed to the final.

National

At the start of the National, Sportytops sponsored-Sonny Burres and Mert Lawwill led a very even start off the line. Jim Rice was just behind, but a shorted kill button put him out just after the jump on lap 1. Burres took command followed by Lawwill, Dick Mann, Mark Brelsford and Don Castro from the back row. Lawwill began breathing down Burres' tailpipes and went by on lap 4 in the second turn. Dick Mann, in turn, began to pressure Burres, making the pass over the jump on lap 7 for second. The three front runners had a big lead over the following pack. Mark Brelsford had taken 4th spot after a duel with Castro. Dave Aldana had moved up and dropped Castro back another spot. Kenny Roberts was also in the mix. All were soon challenged by a charging Mike Haney (Tri).

Back up front, Mann's pressure on Lawwill paid off and he moved by near the halfway mark. Lawwill was being hampered by sticking throttles and Burres moved back into second. The top three were now set. For Mann, it seemed like a repeat of Homewood. He was lapping through the field, past talent like Gene Romero and Bart Markel, clear up to 9th position. Further back Haney, moved through the pack, taking 4th spot from Brelsford. Aldana and Roberts both dropped out and Don Castro moved into 6th spot.

At the checkered, the top 5 was Mann, Burres, Lawwill, Haney and Brelsford.

Results

Race: 25 Lap TT National

Rank	Rider	Number	Make
1.	Dick Mann, Richmond, Ca	1	BSA
2.	Sonny Burres, Portland, Ore	69	Tri
3.	Mert Lawwill, San Francisco, Ca	7	HD
4.	Mike Haney, Inglewood, Ca	91	Tri
5.	Mark Brelsford, Los Altos, Ca	87	HD
6.	Don Castro, Hollister, Ca	11	Yam
7.	Ronnie Rall, Mansfield, Oh	52	Tri
8.	James Jones, Kirkland, Wa	55	Tri
9.	Gary Scott, W. Covina, Ca	64R	Tri
10.	Bart Markel, Flint, Mi	4	HD
11.	Gene Romero, San Luis Obispo, Ca	3	Tri
12.	Frank Gillespie, Berkeley, Ca	76	Tri
13.	Dave Aldana, Santa Ana, Ca	13	BSA
14.	Kenny Roberts, Modesto, Ca	80Y	Yam
15.	Al Kenyon, Cupertino, Ca	48	BSA
16.	Jim Rice, Portola Valley, Ca	24	BSA

Race: Junior Final

Rank	Rider	Number	Make
1.	John Einarsson, Shelton, Wa	12W	HD
2.	Mike Caves, Galesburg, Ill	2P	Tri
3.	Scott Brelsford, San Bruno, Ca	84Y	HD

Grand National Points Standings after Round 18

Rank	Rider	Pts
1.	Mark Brelsford	1192
2.	Gary Scott	927
3.	Gene Romero	792
4.	Kenny Roberts	769
5.	Jim Rice	714
6.	Dick Mann	708
7.	Chuck Palmgren	641
8.	Cal Rayborn	530
9.	Mert Lawwill	460
10.	John Hateley	406

1972 Sante Fe Short Track
Gerald Shakes 'em up at Sante Fe

GNC Round #19 of 24 **Date:** August 18, 1972 **Type:** Short Track **Venue:** Sante Fe Speedway	**Location:** Hinsdale, Ill **Surface:** Dirt **Course Length:** ¼ Mile **Laps:** 25

Short track specialist Mike Gerald took his first GNC win at the Sante Fe speed plant. Gerald took the lead late in the race when Mike Kidd, dominant to that point, had his bike break. Don Castro took 2nd spot with Darryl Hurst in 3rd spot. Both Gerald and Hurst were on Ossa DMR's (Dick Mann Replicas). It was a banner race for Ossa, with Mike Johnson's Junior victory giving the brand two big wins. Gerald's win was the third and final GNC win for Ossa. The track was in great shape with any number of lines working on the ¼ mile clay oval.

The race was notable for Gerald's first win as well as the huge number of GNC regulars who didn't make the event. A short list would include: Dick Mann, Mark Brelsford, Mert Lawwill, Cal Rayborn, Gary Scott, Dave Aldana, Neil Keen, Chuck Palmgren and three-time winner Gary Nixon.

The event was not kind to riders in the top 10 in GNC points with just three of them- Kenny Roberts, Jim Rice and Gene Romero making the main. Because so few made the race, there was not a lot of change in position in the points battle. The big change was Kenny Roberts moving back into third position in points. He now trailed Gary Scott by just 89 points; 937 points to 848. Point's leader Mark Brelsford was still in reach at 1192.

Semis

It took a couple of tries to get the first Semi off, with Mike Gerald leading the restart, closely pursued by rookie Mike Kidd (Bul), and Rex Beauchamp aboard his Harley Sprint, the only competitive four- stroke of the night. Beauchamp made the wrong line choice early in the race and dropped way back in the order. The 1970 Sante Fe winner, Bart Markel (HD), wasn't as lucky, falling off on lap 3. Gerald would lead the whole race, but young Kidd was right on his tail. Beauchamp managed to work his way into a transfer spot as the laps ran out. He was the only member of Team Harley to make the National.

Texas short tracker Darryl Hurst (Oss) jumped out in front of Semi 2 and led wire-to-wire. Behind was a great race between last year's Sante Fe winner Robert E. Lee (Oss) and Team K&N's Don Castro (Yam). Lee controlled the first half the race with Castro taking over to the finish. John Skinner (Bul) took 4th with Bultaco mounted Jim Rice 5th and Gene Romero putting the only factory Rickman in the National. Teammates Dick Mann and Gary Scott failed to make the race.

National

Don Castro launched his Yamaha out front at the start of National. He got into turn 1 too hot, sliding to the top of the track. Taking advantage were Mike Kidd, Mike Gerald, Darryl Hurst and Robert E. Lee. Castro tucked in behind. Battling for the lead, Kidd and Gerald fought hard, running side by side for several laps. Kidd finally pulled a small lead. Behind, Castro had worked his way back up to 3rd through a snarling pack containing Kenny Roberts (Yam), Darryl Hurst and Charlie Chapple (Kaw). Following were Rex Beauchamp on the lone Harley, Jim Rice, Frenchie Leblanc (Yam) and Gene Romero. Robert E. Lee went to the pits with compression release trouble on lap 10, reentering the race far behind.

Up front, Mike Kidd appeared to be headed for his first GNC victory, when suddenly he slowed and pulled off, victim of a broken coil bracket. Realizing the implication, Gerald gassed it up rode the remainder of the race on a string. In second Castro actually closed it up at the end but ran out of time. Hurst made a late race move around Roberts for 3rd with Kenny making it close till the end. Rex Beauchamp put in an impressive race in 5th spot against a field of two-strokes.

215

Race: 25 Lap Short Track National

Rank	Rider	Number	Make
1.	Mike Gerald, Baton Rouge, La	29L	Oss
2.	Don Castro, Hollister, Ca	11	Yam
3.	Darryl Hurst, Houston, Tx	34N	Oss
4.	Kenny Roberts, Modesto, Ca	80Y	Yam
5.	Rex Beauchamp, Milford, Mi	31	HD
6.	Jim Rice, Portola Valley, Ca	24	Bul
7.	Carl LeBlanc, Elyria, Oh	77F	Yam
8.	Gene Romero, San Luis Obispo, Ca	3	Ric
9.	Charlie Chapple, Flint, Mi	36	Kaw
10.	Robert E. Lee, Ft. Worth, Tx	54	Oss
11.	Mike Kidd, Hurst, Tx	72N	Bul
12.	John Skinner, Auburn, Ala	66	Bul

Race: Junior Final

Rank	Rider	Number	Make
1.	Mike Johnson, Flint, Mi	94E	Oss
2.	Teddy Poovey, Garland, Tx	42N	Bul
3.	Fred Smith, Memphis, Tn	18L	Yam

Grand National Points Standings after Round 19

Rank	Rider	Pts
1.	Mark Brelsford	1192
2.	Gary Scott	927
3.	Kenny Roberts	848
4.	Gene Romero	822
5.	Jim Rice	763
6.	Dick Mann	708
7.	Chuck Palmgren	641
8.	Cal Rayborn	530
9.	Mert Lawwill	460
10.	John Hateley	406

GNC Round #20 of 24 **Date:** August 26, 1972 **Type:** Mile **Venue:** Indianapolis State Fairgrounds **Location:** Indianapolis, In	**Purse:** $12,000.00 **Surface:** Dirt **Course Length**: 1 Mile **Laps:** 25 **Distance:** 25 miles

Chuck Palmgren showed that his Dan Gurney Yamaha still had had the ponies to top the best Harley-Davidsons at the Indy Mile, winning his second race of the year. Engine builder Johnny Miller and tuners Dick Bender and Palmgren himself had built a rocket. The Milwaukee brand dominated the top 10, taking 8 spots. It was Chuck Palmgren's 5th and final GNC victory. In the event he had to outrun Harley teammates Dave Sehl and Cal Rayborn. Early leader Rayborn looked dominant until slowed with minor mechanical trouble. The other big story was Bart Markel's performance through the day. Markel was spectacular during his heat, Semi win and then coming from the back row to place 6th in the National. He showed there was still fire in the former 3-time GNC champs belly.

Mark Brelsford's 5th place finish helped boost him to a whopping 315 point advantage over Gary Scott. Scott had trouble and could only manage an 11th place finish. Gene Romero had a solid 7th place run which boosted him back into third over Kenny Roberts who again had engine trouble, finishing way back. Chuck Palmgren's win moved him to fifth, his highest placing of the year. His advancement pushed Jim Rice, Dick Mann, Cal Rayborn and Mert Lawwill all back a spot. Dave Sehl's runner-up brought him into the top 10.

Brelsford was very close to clinching the title. Gary Scott still had a legitimate shot at the title if Brelsford had trouble over the last few races. Gene Romero and Kenny Roberts could still play a factor, but only with bad luck from Brelsford and Scott combined with wins or very high placings on their parts.

Heats

Fast qualifier Cal Rayborn, (37.74) led Heat 1 from wire to wire. Dave Aldana (BSA) ran a distant 2nd. Gary Scott took 3rd after a nearly race long-battle with Jim Rice (BSA) and Dave Sehl (HD).

Heat 2 saw Harley-Davidson teammate Mert Lawwill do likewise. He led a Harley sweep with Doug Sehl and Rex Beauchamp in the next two spots. Bart Markel stole the show in this heat. He apparently fouled a plug on the line and the field was already out of turn 2 when he got rolling. A switched on Markel caught the field and nabbed 7th spot and a semi transfer at the flag.

Completing a Team Harley-Davidson heat sweep, GNC point's leader Mark Brelsford took the Heat 3 win. He didn't have as easy time as his teammates. He had to first fend off persistent GNC champ Dick Mann (BSA); then he was pressured heavily by Chuck Palmgren. Palmgren actually snatched the lead with two laps to go, but Brelsford managed to get back by on the next go around.

Semi

Bart Markel, still pumped from his heat race, blitzed to the front of the Semi and checked out. He was chased early on by 2-time GNC champ Gary Nixon (Tri) who soon had mechanical trouble and dropped back. Following Markel into the main were Dennis Palmgren (HD), Georgian Jimmy Maness and Kenny Roberts (Yam).

National

Cal Rayborn, always a great starter, shot out in front of the 20 rider field. Tucked in behind were Mert Lawwill and Chuck Palmgren. Lap 3 saw Palmgren draft by for 2nd spot. As Rayborn and Palmgren checked out, Lawwill maintained 3rd, followed by, Mark Brelsford, Rex Beauchamp and Doug Sehl. Mark Williams and Kenny Roberts both dropped out early with mechanical problems. Shortly before the 10-lap mark, Rayborn's XR began losing a little speed, due to a possible valve train problem. Palmgren began closing the distance and pressuring the great road race star. Palmgren moved by on lap 12 and soon began opening up a gap. Doug Sehl dropped out shortly after while in 4th spot.

Coming through the pack were Bart Markel and Dave Sehl. As they neared the 20-lap mark, Sehl passed Brelsford for 4th with Markel close behind. Sehl had speed on the field, (except for Palmgren!), and slowly reeled in Rayborn and Lawwill. He passed both on lap 23. There was no catching Palmgren out front, who took the win by a wide margin over Sehl, Rayborn, Lawwill, Brelsford, Markel, Gene Romero, Rex Beauchamp, Denny Palmgren and Keith Ulicki. GNC points contender Gary Scott fell back to 11th position at the flag.

Results

Race: 25 Lap Mile National
Race Time:

Rank	Rider	Number	Make
1.	Chuck Palmgren, Freehold, NJ	38	Yam
2.	Dave Sehl, Waterdown, Ont., Can	16	HD
3.	Cal Rayborn, Spring Valley, Ca	14	HD
4.	Mert Lawwill, San Francisco, Ca	7	HD
5.	Mark Brelsford, Los Altos, Ca	87	HD
6.	Bart Markel, Flint, Mi	4	HD
7.	Gene Romero, San Luis Obispo, Ca	3	Tri
8.	Rex Beauchamp, Milford, Mi	31	HD
9.	Denny Palmgren, Freehold, NJ	16A	HD
10.	Keith Ulicki, Kenosha, Wi	87G	HD
11.	Gary Scott, W. Covina, Ca	64R	Tri
12.	Dave Aldana, Santa Ana, Ca	13	BSA
13.	Dick Mann, Richmond, Ca	1	BSA
14.	Teddy Newton, Pontiac, Mi	40	BSA
15.	Terry Dorsch, Granada Hills, Ca	22	Tri
16.	Doug Sehl, Waterdown, Ont., Can	45	HD
17.	Jim Rice, Portola Valley, Ca	24	BSA
18.	Jimmy Maness, Augusta, Ga	71	HD
19.	Kenny Roberts, Modesto, Ca	80Y	Yam
20.	Mark Williams, Springfield, Ore	70	Tri

Race: Junior Final

Rank	Rider	Number	Make
1.	Scott Brelsford, San Bruno, Ca	84Y	HD
2.	Steve Gardner, Peoria, Ill	36S	HD
3.	Del Armour, Denver, Co	9M	HD

Grand National Points Standings after Round 20

Rank	Rider	Pts
1.	Mark Brelsford	1252
2.	Gary Scott	937
3.	Gene Romero	862
4.	Kenny Roberts	851
5.	Chuck Palmgren	791
6.	Jim Rice	767
7.	Dick Mann	716
8.	Cal Rayborn	630
9.	Mert Lawwill	540
10.	Dave Sehl	419

Extra Extra

- The Harley train was clearly picking up steam. Chuck Palmgren was followed across the line by XR750's in positions 2-6. Harley's made up 7 of the top 10.
- Junior Scott Brelsford captured win number 5. The top 4 in the Junior main were Harleys.
- Bart Markel's heat ride was the talk of the pits and stands. Markel was indeed fired up; he had now made 3 of 4 Nationals since his return.
- Kenny Robert's engine woes continued. Another three engines bit the dust. Two of the factories and a spare Shell engine in the National.
- 1968 winner Larry Palmgren broke his foot in early action.
- Don Castro appeared in a spare set of Gary Scott's Triumph leathers aboard the K&N Yamaha.
- Speaking of leathers, Jimmy Manness's white and pink Harley-Davidson-style leathers were really cool.
- While it was Chuck Palmgren's final National win, the fun-loving talented rider/tuner remained a fixture on the GNC circuit into the late 1970's. His involvement with legend Dan Gurney would eventually lead to a permanent spot with Gurney's All American Racers shop.

GNC Round #21 of 24 **Date:** September 3, 1972 **Type:** Road Race **Venue:** Alabama International Motor Speedway **Location:** Talladega, Al	**Purse:** $21,500.00 **Surface:** Pavement **Course Length:** 1.8 Miles **Laps:** 50 **Distance:** 200 Miles

Yvon Duhamel scored his second GNC of the year at the very hot Labor Day race in Talladega, Al. It was Duhamel's day and after a brief skirmish with Team Suzuki's Jody Nicholas, Duhamel was unchallenged. He was the defending Talladega race champion. It was GNC win number three for the French Canadian. The day was blistering hot and the 90+ temperatures took out Nicholas and several other riders. Duhamel's Kawasaki teammate, Gary Nixon, put in a great 2nd place. He was the only rider that Duhamel didn't lap. Art Baumann's 3rd place finish was remarkable. He rode the event with a broken collarbone and cracked ribs. The event saw the return of the factory Suzukis to National competition, with all engine components now AMA approved.

GNC points leader Mark Brelsford suffered engine trouble on the last lap but still came home 7th, helping to cement his championship. His luck was much better than his points rivals; they all had major trouble. Gary Scott only made 5 laps before mechanical troubles hit his Triumph. Gene Romero ran in the top ten for much of the day before his Triumph suffered an ignition failure. Kenny Roberts ran upfront till near midway when he was once again cursed with engine trouble. For all intents and purposes, the GNC crown was Brelsford's. A decent showing at the upcoming Atlanta Mile would put the championship away.

Time Trials

Yvon DuHamel shattered Kel Carruthers track record of 109.190 with a scorching 113.207 mph lap aboard the Steve Whitelock prepared Kawasaki. Jody Nicholas on one of the returning Suzukis was next, nearly 3 mph off DuHamel's speed at 110.361. Paul Smart (Kaw) turned a 110.243 lap. Kel Carruthers (Yam) was right on his former record speed with a 109.789 lap. Rounding out the top 5 was Kenny Roberts turning a speed of 109.489.

National

The start of the National was somewhat surprising when Jody Nicholas led lap one, ahead of traditional fast starter Duhamel, by 30-40 feet. Duhamel got by in the infield turns with Nicholas taking the lead again in the banking. Duhamel soon took over for good, although Nicholas stayed close for the next 10 laps. Cal Rayborn, winner of the last two pavement Nationals, had been down on power the whole week. He was out on lap 3 with piston failure. Behind the lead duo was the riding-injured Art Baumann in third, who was being challenged by Team Yamaha's Kel Carruthers and Kenny Roberts. Kawasaki riders Gary Nixon and Paul Smart were close behind.

Early fuel stops mixed up the order a little with Roberts and Carruthers moving up during Nicholas's stop. Jody began to feel the effects of the heat, pitting again soon after and stopping completely by lap 29. Some of Team Yamaha soon ran into trouble as well. Roberts retired on lap 20 with engine trouble. Soon after, Kel Carruthers went out with mechanical trouble as well. When he stopped in the pits, the heat overcame him and he collapsed. He took a trip to the hospital to recover. All the attrition considerably changed the running order. Paul Smart moved into 3rd position. Gene Romero and Dick Mann had been glued together through much of the race and they moved into the top 5. Romero's strong day ended on lap 42 with engine woes. Ron Pierce moved into 4th spot ahead of Mann with Mark Brelsford in tow. Brelsford looked to have a great day when his engine let go with one to go. This set the top order as Duhamel, (who had now lapped up to second spot!), Nixon, Baumann, Smart, Mann, and Pierce. Brelsford's lap total salvaged 7th place. DuHamel set a new race record speed of 110.441 mph.

Results

Race: 200 Mile Road Race National
Race Time: 1:47:55.633 (110.441) New Record

Rank	Rider	Number	Make
1.	Yvon DuHamel, LaSalle, Quebec, Can	17	Kaw
2.	Gary Nixon, Phoenix, Md	9	Kaw
3.	Art Baumann, Brisbane, Ca	30	Suz
4.	Paul Smart, Santa Ana, Ca	8	Kaw
5.	Dick Mann, Richmond, Ca	1	BSA
6.	Ron Pierce, Bakersfield, Ca	97	Yam
7.	Mark Brelsford, Los Altos, Ca	87	HD
8.	Conrad Urbanowski, Miramar, Fl	80	Yam
9.	R.G. Wakefield, Indianapolis, Ind	74	Kaw
10.	Ray Hempstead, St. Petersburg, Fl	99	Yam
11.	Cliff Carr, Watertown, Mass	26	Yam
12.	George Kerker, Glendale, Ca	90	Hon
13.	Bob Bailey, Carson, Ca	77	Tri
14.	Gary Fisher, Parkesburg, Pa	10	Yam
15.	Reg Pridmore, Santa Barbara, Ca	82	BMW
16.	Stan Friduss, Gainesville, Fl	78	Yam
17.	Ron Grant, Brisbane, Ca	61	Suz
18.	Roger Reiman, Kewanee, Ill	5	Hon
19.	Keith Mashburn, Santa Susana, Ca	19	Yam
20.	Don Emde, San Diego, Ca	25	Yam

Race: 76 Mile Junior Final

Rank	Rider	Number	Make
1.	Jerry Greene, San Mateo, Ca	57	Kaw
2.	Jim Evans, San Bernardino, Ca	47	Yam
3.	Scott Brelsford, San Bruno, Ca	84	HD

Grand National Points Standings after Round 21

Rank	Rider	Pts
1.	Mark Brelsford	1292
2.	Gary Scott	937
3.	Gene Romero	862
4.	Kenny Roberts	851
5.	Chuck Palmgren	791
6.	Dick Mann	776
7.	Jim Rice	767
8.	Cal Rayborn	630
9.	Mert Lawwill	540
10.	Dave Sehl	420

- Despite the heat a big crowd of over 18,000 turned out.
- The new record speed made it the fastest 200 Mile National yet run.
- It was a big day for frontrunners Yvon DuHamel and Gary Nixon. With purse and contingencies, DuHamel took home around $18,300.00, Nixon about $9350.00.
- Jerry Greene also took home more Kawasaki money for winning the Junior race on the Erv Kanemoto tuned ride. His total winnings exceeded $4000.00.
- The heat took a toll on other riders including Dave Sehl and Eddie Mulder.
- The high temperatures also contributed to the high mechanical attrition with just 21 of 40 bikes running at the end of the race.
- It was a rough day for Harley-Davidson: between the heat and other mechanical issues, no factory bikes finished. Scott Brelsford's 3rd in the Junior race was the high point of the weekend.
- Even the usually stone-reliable Yamahas had trouble. Both Kel Carruthers and Kenny Roberts were done early. Keith Mashburn had the only factory supported bike that made the distance.
- The returning Suzuki's all featured new beefed-up frames, (and stock appearing cylinder heads).
- The individualistic Kawasaki teams had different frames for different riders. Yvon DuHamel a modified production item, Gary Nixon a one-off team designed item and Paul Smart a Seeley item.
- Horsepower for all the Kawasakis was reportedly near 110 hp.
- Cliff Carr was aboard a Don Vesco Yamaha instead of his usual Kevin Cameron Kawasaki; he finished 11th

Bonus!
Top 20 Talladega 200 Qualifying Speeds

1.	Yvon DuHamel	Kaw	113.207 MPH
2.	Jody Nicholas	Suz	110.361
3.	Paul Smart	Kaw	110.243
4.	Kel Carruthers	Yam	109.789
5.	Kenny Roberts	Yam	109.489
6.	Art Baumann	Suz	109.380
7.	Cal Rayborn	HD	108.967
8.	Gary Nixon	Kaw	108.556
9.	Gary Fisher	Yam	108.425
10.	Mark Brelsford	HD	108.409
11.	Mert Lawwill	HD	107.727
12.	Don Emde	Yam	107.270
13.	Ron Pierce	Yam	107.166
14.	Dave Sehl	HD	106.672
15.	Gene Romero	Tri	106.864
16.	Ron Grant	Suz	106.658
17.	Mike Lane	Yam	106.179
18.	John Hateley	Tri	105.809
19.	Jim Allen	Suz	105.688
20.	Dave Smith	Yam	105.084

1972 Atlanta Mile
Sehl Wins First of the Year
Brelsford Clinches GNC Title!

GNC Round #22 of 24 **Date:** September 10, 1972 **Type:** Mile **Venue:** Lakewood Raceway **Location:** Atlanta, Ga	**Purse:** $15,000.00 **Surface:** Dirt **Course Length**: 1 Mile **Laps:** 25 **Distance:** 25 miles

Dave Sehl took his first win of the 1972 season in dominating fashion at the Atlanta Mile. He took command early and stretched to a big lead at the flag aboard a Babe DeMay tuned-factory Harley-Davidson. It was the Canadian's 5th GNC victory. Teammate Rex Beauchamp was 2nd and Don Castro posted a podium finish on the K&N Yamaha. Eddie Mulder turned a great oval track run in 4th.

Mark Brelsford had an off day, but so did title rival Gary Scott. Brelsford clinched the Grand National crown with two races- Ascot and Ontario-to go.

This was the AMA series first return to the Lakewood Raceway since 1948. The once famous track was on its last legs; both the track and facilities were in poor shape. Due to the narrow nature of the track, main event finalists were reduced from the normal 20 riders to 16.

Time Trials

Rex Beauchamp turned the clocks quickest on his factory Harley-Davidson at 38.59. Teammate Dave Sehl was 2nd fastest with a 38.84, Triumph mounted Gary Scott was 3rd at 39.07. Rounding out the top 5 were Dave Aldana on a Nick Deligianis-tuned Norton at 39.41 and Gene Romero's factory Triumph at 39.45.

Heats

Chuck Palmgren (Yam) gave Rex Beauchamp some grief early on in Heat 1, before mechanical trouble took him out. Beauchamp sped home for the uncontested win, followed by teammates Mert Lawwill and Cal Rayborn in the fastest heat of the day.

Dave Sehl led wire-to-wire in Heat 2. Behind him, Triumph mounted Gene Romero and Eddie Mulder had a ding-dong battle over second. They traded the spot repeatedly doing the "Mile Shuffle" the whole race. A charged-up Mulder came out on top. Frank Gillespie was next, riding Chuck Palmgren's backup Yamaha.

Heat 3 was a pressure-cooker with title rivals Mark Brelsford and Gary Scott going head to head. Brelsford's title was on the line while Scott had nothing to lose. Brelsford took the early lead while Scott applied heavy pressure. They went at it for several laps till Mark missed the groove on lap 6. Scott and Don Castro (Yam) both went by. Brelsford struggled a bit with Keith Ulicki (HD) but managed to snag 4th spot and a National ticket.

Semi

With less spots open in the National than usual, the "last chance race" turned out to be the race of the day. The field was talent laden with stars like; Kenny Roberts (Yam), John Hateley (Tri), Jimmy Maness (HD) and three, count 'em three former Grand National Champions in the form of Bart Markel (HD), Dick Mann (BSA), and Gary Nixon (Tri). Hometown favorite Maness was the early leader followed by the GNC champs. Dick Mann surged into the lead on the 2nd lap but dropped out with electrical gremlins. Markel repeatedly drafted to the head of the pack, only to run into the corners too deep and slide off the groove, usually taking somebody else with him. The rest of the race was a hammer and tong affair as everyone mentioned, sans Mann, fought for the transfer spots. At the flag it was Roberts, Maness, Hateley and Markel managing to get tickets to the big show. Gary Nixon put on a great race, coming up just short.

National

A hungry Dave Sehl powered the Babe DeMay-tuned Harley into the lead and immediately set "Sehl". Mark Brelsford and Rex Beauchamp were right behind. Brelsford quickly fell off the pace; Sehl's bike had a small oil leak, coating Mark's face shield. He pulled off to clean his visor, returning at least a lap down. Somehow Beauchamp had clear enough vision to continue a distance behind. Gary Scott, who was running third, had a real chance to score points, given Brelsford's trouble. Just behind, Don Castro was fighting it out with Eddie Mulder. Castro pulled free of Mulder and began to fight with Scott over third. The two seemed very even till 6 laps to go, when Scott's Triumph began to misfire. Scott rapidly dropped through the ranks, his title hopes disappearing. At the flag, it was Sehl with a huge lead over Beauchamp, Castro, Mulder and Mert Lawwill. Gary Scott finished in 13th spot, only one ahead of Mark Brelsford. Although he wasn't sure at the time, Brelsford had just become the 1972 AMA Grand National Champion!

Results

Race: 25 Lap Mile National

Rank	Rider	Number	Make
1.	Dave Sehl, Waterdown, Ont., Can	16	HD
2.	Rex Beauchamp, Milford, Mi	31	HD
3.	Don Castro, Hollister, Ca	11	Yam
4.	Eddie Mulder, Northridge, Ca	12	Tri
5.	Mert Lawwill, San Francisco, Ca	7	HD
6.	Keith Ulicki, Kenosha, Wi	87G	HD
7.	Doug Sehl, Waterdown, Ont., Can	45	HD
8.	Cal Rayborn, Spring Valley, Ca	14	HD
9.	Kenny Roberts, Modesto, Ca	80Y	Yam
10.	Gene Romero, San Luis Obispo, Ca	3	Tri
11.	John Hateley, Van Nuys, Ca	98	Tri
12.	Bart Markel, Flint, Mi	4	HD
13.	Gary Scott, W. Covina, Ca	64R	Tri
14.	Mark Brelsford, Los Altos, Ca	87	HD
15.	Frank Gillespie, Berkeley, Ca	76	Yam
16.	Jimmy Maness, Augusta, Ga	71	HD

Race: Junior Final

Rank	Rider	Number	Make
1.	Scott Brelsford, San Bruno, Ca	84Y	HD
2.	Billy Field, Brunswick, Oh	48L	Nor
3.	Steve Gardner, Peoria, Ill	36S	HD

Grand National Points Standings after Round 22

Rank	Rider	Pts
1.	Mark Brelsford	1299
2.	Gary Scott	945
3.	Gene Romero	877
4.	Kenny Roberts	870
5.	Chuck Palmgren	791
6.	Dick Mann	776
7.	Jim Rice	767
8.	Cal Rayborn	660
9.	Mert Lawwill	600
10.	Dave Sehl	569

- The original race location for this date was at Arlington Park, the "Chicago Mile". When that facility revoked the race permit, due to "noise, air and dust possibilities", promoter Don Brymer moved the event to the old Atlanta racetrack.
- The Lakewood Speedway had a long and storied career. The track was known as the "Indianapolis of the South". It's racing history from 1917-1981, included motorcycle, horse, open wheel and stock car racing. All the major motorsports sanctioning bodies staged races there, including the AAA/USAC, AMA, IMCA and NASCAR. Built in 1916 as part of the Great Southeastern Fairgrounds, the track circled a water reservoir/lake. The first and second turns were very squared off due to proximity of a local road, Lakewood Avenue. Turns three and four were more rounded and traditional. The inaugural race in 1917, featured horse and motorcycle racing. Auto racing would soon follow. The track drew big crowds and was considered a first class facility. It was a regular stop for the Indy Cars. NASCAR first sanctioned races there in 1948 and became an important part of the series early history. Things began to go downhill in the 1950's. The track and grounds were getting tired and received no updating. The last Indy Car race was held in 1958. With the opening of the nearby Atlanta International Raceway, NASCAR switched venues, making its last appearance at Lakewood in 1959. Racing continued with mostly local and regional events. The big one-mile oval was a very dangerous place. The squared off first turns were the scene of many grinding crashes. Competitors paid a heavy price at Lakewood, with 14 known fatalities, of which at least two were motorcycle racers. The AMA National circuit visited the track several times over the years. It was the scene of the only "dead heat" finish ever at a National. Bobby Hill and Billy Huber were both credited with a win at the 1948 event. The series return in the Seventies was troubled by poor track conditions and facilities, mirroring the problems with the now rundown speedway itself. The AMA's last try in 1973 met with disastrous results. The track itself continued to host stock car and open wheel racing up to 1979. Returning to the tracks original roots, the last event ever held was a horse race in 1981. It was not successful. The track afterwards saw only local flea markets and concerts. Over the years, the lake was partially filled, and items such as an amphitheater, parking lots and access roads were built over the grounds. Today, the only recognizable link to Lakewood's racing past is its grandstand. Racing historian Brandon Reed has done a great job of keeping the racing memories of Lakewood alive. Much more information is available at georgiaracinghistory.com.

GNC Round #23 of 24	Purse: $10,000.00
Date: September 24, 1972	Surface: Dirt
Type: Half-Mile	Course Length: ½ Mile
Venue: Ascot Park	Laps: 20
Location: Gardena, Ca	Distance: 10 Miles

Rookie Gary Scott may have run out of time for the Grand National title, but his victory at Ascot showed he never gave up. Scott dominated the day setting fast time, winning the fastest heat and controlling most of the National. The race was held in the daytime for the first time in the 14-year history of the event. The reason was for filming for ABC's "Wide World of Sports". Instead of the usual lightning fast, tacky surface, riders were faced with a narrow, slick groove. Scott's main rival for the day was Tom Rockwood, who led the National early, before giving way to Scott. Amazingly, Rockwood had almost drowned just days before the race, (see *"Extras"*). Mert Lawwill rounded out the podium and was the first Harley home. 1972 GNC champ Mark Brelsford finished out the dirt track year in 4th.

Time Trials

Tom Rockwood's year old daytime record (non-national) was broken by several riders. Gary Scott on the Eddie Hammond tuned, City Cycle Center Triumph, was the fastest with a 23.50, Mert Lawwill (HD) was second at 23.75, Rockwood's Danny Macias's Triumph was third at 23.78 and Don Castro on a Triumph instead of the K&N Yamaha, was fourth at 23.86. Dick Mann qualified for the program on Gene Romero's spare Triumph after his own BSA gave up in practice.

Heats

Gary Scott quickly jumped out front of Heat 1 and led wire-to-wire. Terry Dorsch (Tri) ran up front early before Chuck Palmgren (Yam) and Don Castro worked by.

In Heat 2, Tom Rockwood was involved in a first lap shunt with three other riders. Rockwood did not let it deter him as he quickly moved to the front on the restart. He led Dave Aldana (BSA) home by a small margin. Aldana was also involved in the first lap crash.

Much of Team Harley-Davidson competed in Heat 3. Mark Brelsford took a narrow win over Mert Lawwill and Dave Sehl. It would be the highlight of the day for the Milwaukee brand.

Semi

The last chance for 3 riders, turned into a California shoot-out. Dave Hansen (Tri) jumped out front early, chased by Terry Dorsch (Tri) and Jim Rice (BSA). Rex Beauchamp (HD) fell while running in the front pack. Dorsch got by Hansen after a few laps. Rice came from back in the pack, zapping both Hansen and Dorsch for the win.

National

Tom Rockwood really wanted to win his second Ascot National in a row and pulled a nice holeshot off the line. As expected, Gary Scott was right behind, followed by Mert Lawwill, Chuck Palmgren and Dave Sehl. Both Jim Rice and Dave Aldana fell down on lap 1 in unrelated slick-groove incidents. Scott reeled Rockwood in and went by on the seventh circuit. Rockwood maintained a sold 2ⁿᵈ position. Mark Brelsford got a lousy start and had been carefully moving his way forward into the lead pack. Chuck Palmgren had moved past the Harley team members into 3rd place. Just past halfway, Palmgren overcooked the groove, allowing Sehl and Brelsford by. With three laps to go, Brelsford moved into the 4th spot. This set the top order as Scott, Rockwood, Lawwill, Brelsford and Sehl.

Results

Race: 20 Lap Half-Mile National

Rank	Rider	Number	Make
1.	Gary Scott, W. Covina, Ca	64R	Tri
2.	Tom Rockwood, Gardena, Ca	88	Tri
3.	Mert Lawwill, San Francisco, Ca	7	HD
4.	Mark Brelsford, Los Altos, Ca	87	HD
5.	Dave Sehl, Waterdown, Ont., Can	16	HD
6.	Chuck Palmgren, Freehold, NJ	38	Yam
7.	Terry Dorsch, Granada Hills, Ca	22	Tri
8.	Dave Hansen, Hayward, Ca	23	Tri
9.	Don Castro, Hollister, Ca	11	Tri
10.	Randy Scott, Philomath, Ore	57Q	Tri
11.	Dave Aldana, Santa Ana, Ca	13	BSA
12.	Jim Rice, Portola Valley, Ca	24	BSA

Race: Junior Final

Rank	Rider	Number	Make
1.	Tom Horton, Lancaster, Ca	75X	Tri
2.	Barry Patrick, Garland, Tx	82N	Nor
3.	Mike Caves, Galesburg, Ill	2P	Yam

Grand National Points Standings after Round 23

Rank	Rider	Pts
1.	Mark Brelsford	1379
2.	Gary Scott	1095
3.	Gene Romero	877
4.	Kenny Roberts	870
5.	Chuck Palmgren	841
6.	Dick Mann	776
7.	Jim Rice	776
8.	Mert Lawwill	700
9.	Cal Rayborn	660
10.	Dave Sehl	629

Extra Extra

- Just four days before the Ascot National, Tom Rockwood had been pulled unconscious out of the Pacific. He was rushed to intensive care with almost no breathing or pulse. Rockwood recovered and was released the day before the race.
- The very slick conditions contributed to lots of favorites failing to make the National including; Kenny Roberts, Dick Mann, John Hateley, Gene Romero, Keith Mashburn, Cal Rayborn and Eddie Mulder.
- Sonny Burres got launched over the fence in practice when his Triumph's engine seized. He walked away with a tweaked ankle.
- Tom Horton became the 14th different Junior winner of the year. Dominant Scott Brelsford slipped off the groove and fell early in the main.

GNC Final Round #24 Date: October 1, 1972 Type: Road Race Venue: Ontario Motor Speedway Location: Ontario, Ca	Purse: $68,675.00 Surface: Pavement Course Length: 1.8 Miles Laps: 69 Per Segment Distance: 250 Miles, 2 X 125 Miles

England's Paul Smart had proven himself one of the best road racers in the world when he topped all comers, including Giacomo Agostini at the 1972 Imola, Italy event. Despite this, he had yet to win an AMA Grand National race aboard his factory Kawasaki. His win at the 2nd Annual Champion Spark Plug Motorcycle Classic gave him his first major U.S. win. Not only did he beat the best GNC regulars, including Cal Rayborn, Yvon Duhamel, Kel Carruthers, Gary Nixon and others. He also defeated international stars like fellow Englishman and last year's winner John Cooper, Phil Read, Peter Williams as well as Italian star Renzo Pasolini. Finishing second to Smart was New Zealand's Geoff Perry. First American home was great all-arounder and new Grand National Champion, Mark Brelsford. The event used Olympic style scoring which combined the scores from each of two 125-mile events. The lowest score would take the win. In the event of a tie, the finish in the second round was given preference. Although the event wasn't drawing the crowds the promoters expected to the sprawling Ontario complex, the huge purse of over $68,000.00 sure brought out road racings biggest stars.

Heats

Yvon Duhamel (Kaw) quickly took control of the first heat only to fall early in the race. Cal Rayborn (HD) went on for an impressive four-stroke win over Gary Fisher (Yam). Duhamel's spill would force him to start at the rear for the National.

Striking a blow for privateers everywhere in Heat 2 was Cliff Carr aboard the Kevin Cameron tuned Arlington Motors Kawasaki. Englishman Carr and Cameron had been struggling with their 750 triple for two seasons and were starting to find the reliability to go along with the speed of their Kawasaki. When things went right they were a match for the factory teams. Things went right in this race. Carr led wire-to-wire with Paul Smart breathing down his neck.

National
Segment 1

Gary Nixon (Kaw) shot into the lead of the first 125-miler with Cliff Carr, Paul Smart and Yamaha's Kenny Roberts giving chase. Cal Rayborn (HD) was on the move and sliced by Roberts for 4th spot. Unbelievably, Yvon Duhamel broke into the top 10 by the third lap. Coming from the last row, he had passed over 40 riders! Several riders experienced trouble in the early laps and had to pit, including Gene Romero, Don Emde and Eddie Mulder. Up front, Carr was pressuring Nixon and passed for the lead on lap 7. Nixon followed Carr for a couple of laps, then wicked it back up front. Cal Rayborn and Art Baumann both got tangled up with a lapped rider and were done for the day. The order by lap 10 was Nixon, Carr, Smart, Carruthers and Duhamel clear up to 5th. British stars John Cooper (BSA), and Norton -mounted teammates Phil Read and Peter Williams were riding formation behind the lead pack. Mark Brelsford (HD) was moving quickly through the pack after having to fix a fouled plug at the start. Jody Nicholas (Suz) crashed hard in the infield, breaking his right shoulder and collarbone. Up front Duhamel kept up his amazing charge, passing Carr for second on lap 14. As he closed on Nixon, the leaders transmission packed up and Gary was out of the running. As the 20-lap mark neared, the Kawasakis gas stops began. The stops shook the order up with Kel Carruthers leading teammate Kenny Roberts. Roberts took the point on lap 24. Close behind were the Kawasakis of Duhamel, Carr and Smart. Duhamel's charge ended on lap 31 when he got together with a lapped rider. Duhamel fell hard, breaking his elbow. The very tough Canadian got back on and rode to the pits.

Leader Roberts stopped for gas on the 32nd circuit. Carruthers' assumed the lead and despite signals to stop for gas, kept pushing clear to the checkers. The top 5 at the flag were, Carruthers, Kenny Roberts, Cliff Carr, Geoff Perry and Paul Smart.

Segment 2

The start of the final 125 miles saw Cliff Carr and Paul Smart battle through the first lap, with Carr pulling a narrow lead. Team Yamaha's race went bad quickly with Kenny Roberts out with crank problems on lap 3, and Carruthers experiencing engine trouble soon afterward. Carr continued to maintain a small lead over Smart, with Geoff Perry in third. Mark Brelsford was also running with the lead pack. Mechanical trouble knocked more front runners out including Dick Mann, Ron Pierce and Dave Aldana. By lap 15, Team Hansen's Nixon and Duhamel had knifed their way through the pack to 4th and 10th spots respectively. A few laps later, pit stops started with Nixon, Smart and Perry pulled in. Carr stayed out looking very strong when suddenly he was out with crankshaft failure. Paul Smart took over the lead and he continued on to the finish, stretching his lead as he went. Mark Brelsford was very impressive on the underpowered but good-handling XRTT. Geoff Perry moved Brelsford back a spot. Renzo Pasolini was on the move despite a rough running engine in his Harley-Davidson. He and Brelsford began a nifty duel for third. Behind this duel ran Don Vesco sponsored Dave Smith (Yam) who was first dropped a spot by Cal Rayborn and then faced a last lap challenge by John Cooper. Late in the race, Pasolini passed Brelsford for 2nd spot. On the last lap Cooper passed Smith for 6th position. This set the top finishing order as Paul Smart, Geoff Perry, Renzo Pasolini, Mark Brelsford, Cal Rayborn, John Cooper and Dave Smith.

Results

Race: 250 Mile Road Race National
Race Time: Heat 1, 1:25.13 (87.926 MPH)
             Heat 2, 1:25.16 (87.926 MPH)

Rank	Rider	Number	Make
1.	Paul Smart, London, Eng	8	Kaw
2.	Geoff Perry, Auckland, NZ	96	Suz
3.	Renzo Pasolini, Varese, Italy	2	HD
4.	Mark Brelsford, Los Altos, Ca	87	HD
5.	John Cooper, Derby, Eng	28	BSA
6.	Mert Lawwill, San Francisco	7	HD
7.	Gary Fisher, Parkesburg, Pa	10	Yam
8.	Dave Smith, Lakewood, Ca	20	Yam
9.	Conrad Urbanowski, Miramar, Fl	80	Yam
10.	John Hateley, Van Nuys, Ca	98	Tri
11.	Art Baumann, Brisbane, Ca	30	Suz
12.	Steve McLaughlin, Duarte, Ca	55	Hon
13.	Gary Scott, W. Covina, Ca	64	Tri
14.	Kel Carruthers, El Cajon, Ca	73	Yam
15.	Ron Grant, Brisbane, Ca	61	Suz
16.	Cliff Carr, Watertown, Mass	26	Kaw
17.	Jim Dunn, Everett, Wa	71	Yam
18.	George Kerker, Glendale, Ca	90	Hon
19.	Paul Higgins, Islington, Ont., Can	6	Yam
20.	Keith Mashburn, Santa Susana, Ca	19	Yam

Race: Junior Final
Time: 87:42.0 (85.901 MPH) New Record

Rank	Rider	Number	Make
1.	Jerry Greene, San Mateo, Ca	57	Kaw
2.	Steve Baker, Bellingham, Wa	40	Yam
3.	Jeff March, Elm, NJ	33	Yam

Grand National Points Final Standings

Rank	Rider	Pts
1.	Mark Brelsford	1483
2.	Gary Scott	1105
3.	Gene Romero	877
4.	Kenny Roberts	871
5.	Chuck Palmgren	841
6.	Dick Mann	776
7.	Jim Rice	776
8.	Mert Lawwill	765
9.	Cal Rayborn	660
10.	Dave Sehl	629

Extra Extra

- A solid crowd of over 23,000 turned out for the National.
- Paul Smart's winnings were a whopping $30,400.00. Geoff Perry received $7150.00 for second, Renzo Pasolini $4525.00 for third and first American Mark Brelsford $3200.00 for fourth.
- Smart's winning ride was tuned by talented rider/wrench Hurley Wilvert.
- The Harley-Davidson team had three bikes in the top 10; impressive for machines that had been largely written off.
- Finnish 250 World Champion Jarno Saarinen was slated to ride the event, but seriously tweaked his leg in practice and sat out the event.
- Cliff Carr and tuner Kevin Cameron had a real chance of capturing the whole event on their private Kawasaki, till their street bike crank gave out.
- 55 riders started the first segment, 44 the second.
- Kel Carruther's won the Combined Lightweight race.
- Jerry Greene captured his 4th Junior event. His winnings totaled $3925.00.

1972 Season Review

1. Mark Brelsford
1483 Points

Mark Brelsford had everything come together in 1972; his great all around riding ability, the faith that Dick O'Brien, Mert Lawwill and Jim Belland had in him combined with the new XR750, to win the 1972 AMA Grand National Championship. Brelsford scored 3 wins on the year, the first ever for the alloy engine at Louisville as well as the Salem Half-Mile and Ascot TT. He nearly repeated his past year's win at Loudon and was also 2nd at the Colorado and Chicago Miles. He was also on the podium at the San Jose and Long Island Half-Miles. Top 5 finishes were scored at the Houston and Peoria TT's, Indy Mile, Ascot Half-Mile and the Ontario Road Race. Brelsford was also in the top 10 at Castle Rock and Talladega. He made 16 of the 24 races, only finishing outside of the top 10 one time. He chased down early season GNC points leader, rookie Kenny Roberts by mid-season. He was pressured through the last half of the year by another rookie, Gary Scott. It was close, but Brelsford's high, consistent finishes over the last 5 rounds locked up the title.

2. Gary Scott
1105 Points

When Mark Brelsford plotted strategy before the 1972 season he figured on guys like Gene Romero, Dick Mann and Mert Lawwill. No one considered rookies like Gary Scott and Kenny Roberts to be legitimate title threats. Gary Scott was in Roberts shadow during their Junior year, but he showed he was also a formidable force in the GNC. Scott won two races; the Castle Rock TT and the season ending Ascot Half-Mile. He was 2nd at the Ascot TT and fought with Mert Lawwill over the win at Columbus before settling for the runner-up slot. He was 3rd at the Louisville and Salem Half-Miles. Scott was in the top 5 at both Houston races and showed his road race abilities with a 5th at the Indy Road Race. He was in the top 10 at the San Jose Half-Mile and Laguna Seca Road Race. He was extremely consistent, scoring points in 20 of the 24 rounds, more than any other rider, including an unmatched 12 race finishing streak through mid-season. He slowly worked his way into the points battle, taking the 2nd spot from Roberts after Columbus. Scott held on ferociously, pressuring Brelsford and had a legitimate shot at the title till the last four rounds when Brelsford pulled out some breathing room. Scott's efforts earned him growing attention from the Triumph factory, which provided him with more support, including Trident road racers during the last half of the season.

3. Gene Romero
877 Points

Despite the ongoing changes at Triumph, Gene Romero was still determined to make a run at the title. As typical, he suffered through the Houston races, and was then sabotaged by electrical trouble at Daytona. He got on track at with a 3rd at Road Atlanta and made a strong drive through the middle of the season. He won the San Jose Mile and moved into 3rd in points. He had a couple of bad races, slipping back in the standings. After a second at Laguna Seca and a solid run at the Long Island Half-Mile, he took back 3rd from Roberts The two traded the spot, with Romero just edging the rookie out by a handful of points. He was close enough that if the title rivals had a problem he could have had a shot at the championship. Besides the finishes noted, he was also on the podium at the Loudon and Indy Road Races. He also had an incredible runs of top 10's at the San Jose, Indy and Atlanta Miles, as well as the Columbus, Salem and Long Island Half-Miles. Out of his 16 finishes he was out of the top 10 just two times.

4. Kenny Roberts
871 Points

Kenny Roberts amazing Junior season was enough to land him a full-fledged Yamaha factory ride. Nevertheless most GNC observers didn't expect the young Californians performance. Roberts came on like a whirlwind at Houston, winning the short track and placing 3rd in the TT, taking the early season points lead. Though he didn't score any points at Daytona, he continued to lead the standings up to the Loudon National. Some DNF's caused him to slide back. He bounced back, battling with Gene Romero, but repeated mechanical trouble with both his dirt trackers and road racers ruined his chances for a top 3 GNC finish. Roberts was on the podium at the San Jose Mile, Columbus and Laguna Seca. He was in the top 5 at the Salem Half-Mile and Sante Fe Short Track. Top 10 finishes included the Road Atlanta and Indy Road Races, San Jose Half-Mile, Castle Rock TT and Atlanta Mile. Roberts ran very competitively at all types of tracks and surfaces. There was no doubt he was a contender for future championships if his machinery would hold up.

5. Chuck Palmgren
841 Points

Chuck Palmgren was no longer on the factory Yamaha team, but there was no shortage of speed in his performances. If anything, his Dan Gurney AAR prepped machine was often faster than the Yamaha factories bikes, and was at times faster than anything on the circuit. He scored a big win at the Indy Mile and the unusual Long Island Half-Mile. Palmgren was also on the podium at the Columbus and San Jose Half-Miles. He was in the top 5 at the Salem Half-Mile and San Jose and Chicago Miles. Top 10 runs were placed at the Houston Short Track and Ascot Half-Mile. Palmgren scored points in 11 of 24 rounds.

6. Dick Mann
776 Points

Defending GNC champ Dick Mann was probably the most disappointed rider of the season. The schedule, heavily laden with big points paying road races and TT's looked tailor made for the veteran. The season started well enough with a 7th at the Houston TT. Electrical problems knocked the back-to-back Daytona champion out of the 200. Mann bounced back with a 4th at Road Atlanta. Then, starting a pattern, he had mechanical trouble and then bounced back. He was turning in solid performances, but engine trouble and bad luck never let him get his season on track. It wasn't all bad though, Mann turned in a show stopping performance at the Homewood Mile, lapping most of the field. It was Mann's first mile win, completing the series first ever Grand Slam; Mann had won every discipline in the GNC, TT, short track, half-mile, mile and road race. Others like Carroll Resweber, Gary Nixon and Bart Markel had been close, but never closed the deal. Mann turned in back-to-back wins by claiming the Peoria TT. It was his last GNC victory, at the site of his first win back in 1959.

7. Jim Rice
776 Points

After losing his BSA factory ride, Jim Rice still hit the circuit, but ran a limited schedule. Winless since 1970, no one was quite sure of his chances. Rice stunned everyone by taking a huge win at the Colorado Mile. He ran 4th at the Ascot TT and soon after won the San Jose Mile, cracking his shoulder blade along the way. Despite only running a few races, Rice was way up in the standings. Rice took a four race hiatus to let his shoulder heal. He came back with three great finishes; he was 4th at the San Jose Half-Mile, and 2nd at both the Salem Half-Mile and Castle Rock TT. Rice's finishes the rest of the year were often sabotaged by mechanical trouble and bad luck. He did manage a 6th at the Sante Fe Short Track. Rice scored points in 11 rounds.

8. Mert Lawwill
765 Points

While surely not the results he hoped for, 1972 was a big improvement over the previous year for Mert Lawwill. He scored a win at the Columbus Half-Mile, was 2nd at the Long Island Half-Mile and 3rd at both the Peoria TT and Ascot Half-Mile. Other highlights were a 5th at Atlanta and top 10's at the San Jose Mile and Half-Mile, Louisville and Ontario. Mechanical issues still dogged Lawwill through the year.

9. Cal Rayborn
660 Points

While the previous year's Livonia win was satisfying, it had been a frustrating two years since the nation's best road racer had claimed a pavement win. Rayborn took two wins on the year, at the Indy and Laguna Seca Road Races. It was his 4th win at IRP. The rest of his season saw mixed results, but he managed a strong 3rd at the Indy Mile and top 10's at the Ascot TT, Atlanta Mile, Loudon and at the Louisville, Columbus and Salem Half-Miles.

10. Dave Sehl
629 Points

The fast dirt track specialist from Canada was in the top 10 for the second year in a row. He won the Atlanta Mile and nearly won his third Louisville race in a row. He was also 2nd at the Indy Mile. Other season highlights were three 5th place finishes at the San Jose and Ascot Half-Miles and the Chicago Mile.

There were 6 brands that scored GNC wins in 1972. Harley-Davidson was once again the win leader, taking 7 wins for the season, taking the first ever Manufacturer Championship. Yamaha had 5 wins, Triumph and BSA had 4 each, Kawasaki 3 and Ossa 1. Illustrating the competitiveness of the period, from Peoria to the Ascot Half-Mile, each of the 6 brands scored a win. There was an amazing 16 different winning riders taking wins on the 24 event schedule.

While there was not one dominant Junior rider like Kenny Roberts of the previous year, Scott Brelsford and Jerry Greene each scored 4 wins; Brelsford on dirt, Greene on pavement. Joe Brown won two TT's, Jim Rawls two dirt tracks. Mike O'Brien, Ronnie Dottley, Steve Droste, Jim Evans, Jim Deehan, Jim Crenshaw, Tom White, John Eienarsson, Mike Johnson and Tom Horton all claimed one victory each. Some other top Juniors for the year were Steve Baker, Billy Field, Mike Caves, Teddy Poovey and Del Armour.

1972 GNC Winners

Event	Location	Winner	Machine
TT	Houston, Tx	John Hateley, Van Nuys, Ca	Tri
Short Track	Houston, Tx	Kenny Roberts, Woodside, Ca	Yam
Road Race	Daytona Beach, Ca	Don Emde, San Diego, Ca	Yam
Road Race	Braselton, Ga	Yvon DuHamel, LaSalle, Que., Can	Kaw
Mile	Colorado Springs, Co	Jim Rice, Palo Alto, Ca	BSA
TT	Gardena, Ca	Mark Brelsford, Woodside, Ca	HD
Mile	San Jose, Ca	Jim Rice, Palo Alto, Ca	BSA
Half-Mile	Louisville, Ky	Mark Brelsford, Woodside, Ca	HD
Road Race	Loudon, NH	Gary Fisher, Parkesburg, Pa	Yam
Road Race	Indianapolis, Ind	Cal Rayborn, Spring Valley, Ca	HD
Half-Mile	Columbus, Oh	Mert Lawwill, San Francisco, Ca	HD
Half-Mile	San Jose, Ca	Gene Romero, San Luis Obispo, Ca	Tri
Half-Mile	Salem, Ore	Mark Brelsford, Woodside, Ca	HD
TT	Castle Rock, Wa	Gary Scott, Baldwin Park, Ca	Tri
Road Race	Monterey, Ca	Cal Rayborn, Spring Valley, Ca	HD
Half-Mile	Long Island, NY	Chuck Palmgren, Freehold, NJ	Yam
Mile	Chicago, Ill	Dick Mann, Richmond, Ca	BSA
TT	Peoria, Ill	Dick Mann, Richmond, Ca	BSA
Short Track	Hinsdale, Ill	Mike Gerald, Baton Rouge, La	Oss
Mile	Indianapolis, Ind	Chuck Palmgren, Freehold, NJ	Yam
Road Race	Talladega, Al	Yvon DuHamel, LaSalle, Que., Can	Kaw
Mile	Atlanta, Ga	Dave Sehl, Waterdown, Ont., Can	HD
Half-Mile	Gardena, Ca	Gary Scott, Baldwin Park, Ca	Tri
Road Race	Ontario, Ca	Paul Smart, England	Kaw

Bonus!
1972 Year End Points Fund Payout
(Grand National Champion awarded extra 10% of Fund Total)

1.	Mark Brelsford	1483 Points	$6,234.11
		10% Bonus	5,718.45*
		Total	11,952.56
2.	Gary Scott	1105	4,645.10
3.	Gene Romero	877	3,686.66
4.	Kenny Roberts	871	3,661.44
5.	Chuck Palmgren	841	3,535.32
6.	Dick Mann	776	3,262.08
7.	Jim Rice	776	3,262.08
8.	Mert Lawwill	765	3,215.84
9.	Cal Rayborn	660	2,774.45
10.	Dave Sehl	629	2644.14
11.	Rex Beauchamp	506	2,127.08
12.	Don Castro	461	1,937.91
13.	John Hateley	436	1,832.82
14.	Yvon DuHamel	420	1,765.56
15.	Eddie Mulder	391	1,643.65
16.	Gary Fisher	384	1,614.23
17.	Mike Kidd	273	1,147.62
18.	Mark Williams	213	895.39
19.	Don Emde	189	794.50
20.	Frank Gillespie	187	786.10
		Total of Point Fund	57,184.53

A selection of
Grand National Championship Riders

The most spectacular rider in 1970's GNC racing, Dave Aldana. One of the best to not win #1, he won 4 Nationals in his career, each in a different discipline, just a short track win of a "Grand Slam". He rode for top teams of the era including BSA, Norton and Suzuki. Aldana was inducted into the Motorcycle Hall of Fame (MHOF) in 1999. Mahony Photo Archives

Aldana was blazingly fast in his rookie year of 1970. He won 3 Nationals and finished 3rd in the GNC standings. Notice the rooster tail coming off that BSA; it is over Aldana's head! Mahony Photo Archives

Aldana and Jay Springsteen at the 1975 Columbus Charity Newsies. "Who is that kid?" Robert Pearson Photo

Aldana might be wearing Norton leathers, but that's a Yamaha TZ700 he is riding. Through the early 1970's, he was not given his due as a pavement racer, despite winning the 1970 Talladega National. His rides on the Yamaha during the 1974 season helped him land a Suzuki factory ride the following year. Ray Ninness Photo

Aldana pushing hard on a Nick Deligianis-prepped Harley TT bike. Always in the hunt on a TT course, Aldana won the 1973 Ascot TT on a factory Norton. Note the cool "Bones" leathers and the Neil Keen tribute #10. Both snubs at the AMA stuffed shirts! Mahony Photo Archives

Michigan's Dave Atherton, one of the best riders of the period to not be awarded a National Number, despite being a GNC contender and strong Regional performer. Atherton's sons, Brian and Kevin became noted AMA flat trackers. Ray Ninness Photo

Dallas Baker leads Dave Hansen (11X), Al Urich (28) and Kenny Pressgrove (14N) at the 1970 Sedalia Mile. A skilled craftsman, Baker turned out his own frames and components. He was a top TT contender on the GNC trail, finishing 3rd at the 1970 Ascot TT. Photo courtesy of Joe Neff

Bellingham, Wa native Steve Baker at speed. Baker grew up on Northwestern dirt tracks, but his association with Canadian Yamaha importer, Trevor Deeley, led to a top-flight pavement career. Mild-mannered in appearance, Baker was a fierce competitor. He would go on to great National and International racing success. Baker was inducted into the MHOF in 1999. Ray Ninness Photo

Pavement specialist Art Baumann at the 1971 Talladega National. He was the first to score a big bore two-stroke National win, at Sears Point in 1969 for Suzuki. A top-flight rider, Baumann rode for both the Suzuki and Kawasaki factory teams. He was a threat at any road race, but frequent crashes and bad luck prevented another National win. Baumann passed away in 2011. Ray Ninness Photo

One of the best dirt trackers of the period, "Michigan Mafia" member, Rex Beauchamp. He was picked up for a rare Harley-Davidson sponsorship during his Amateur year of 1970. He struggled with injuries in his early Expert years, but scored a National win at Terre Haute in 1973. He would add wins at Toledo and the San Jose Mile by the end of 1975. Beauchamp was tragically killed in a street bike accident in 1988. He was inducted into the MHOF in 2007. This spectacular image from Louisville remains one of the greatest in motorsports. Mahony Photo Archives

Beauchamp leads fellow Harley riders (and brothers), Doug Sehl (45) and Dave Sehl (16). Ray Ninness Photo

Gotta love the '70's! Beauchamp gets a send off from a Nasco Oils girl before the 1974 Toledo GNC. Couldn't have hurt; Rex scored his 2nd National win shortly after the photo! Ray Ninness Photo

California privateer Tom Berry fights the roost at Ascot. Berry was a top -10 GNC oval track competitor; very tough in home state events. Mahony Photo Archives

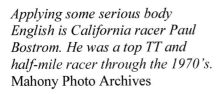

Applying some serious body English is California racer Paul Bostrom. He was a top TT and half-mile racer through the 1970's. Mahony Photo Archives

The 1972 Grand National Champion Mark Breslford on his Harley dirt tracker; unfortunately a rare site. The talented, versatile rider worked hard for the #1 plate and had little chance to enjoy it. A devastating crash at Daytona caused him to miss the majority of 1973. Brelsford healed up and returned in 1974, only to suffer another serious injury. He decided to call it a day and retired. He was inducted into the MHOF in 1998. Mahony Photo Archives

Though thought of as a dirt tracker, Brelsford's pavement skills were impressive, scoring a surprise last turn win at Loudon in 1971 over Kel Carruthers and Dick Mann. It was Brelsford's and the iron XR's only GNC pavement win. He is pictured here at IRP. Ray Ninness Photo

Like the rest of Team Harley, Brelsford struggled through the XR750's development, but was the most successful on the team winning 4 of 6 of his National wins between 1970-'72 on the new machines. Bill Barrett Photo

Lawwill and protégé Brelsford at the Ascot TT. Brelsford was a great student and a perfect match for the Jim Belland/Lawwill 900cc XLR. He won 3 Ascot National TT 's on the monster machine named "Goliath". Mahony Photo Archives

Scott Brelsford aboard Erv Kanemoto's Kawasaki H2R screamer. Besides Kenny Roberts', Brelsford was the most successful multi-cylinder two-stroke rider. He was in the top ten at the summer San Jose Mile and won a Pacific Coast Regional on the machine. Mahony Photo Archives

Brelsford in his rookie year of 1973 at Toledo, leading Dave Aldana (13), unknown and John Skinner (66). He claimed a GNC the same season at the dust shortened Atlanta Mile. Older brother Mark retired in 1974; Scott quietly retired at the end of 1975. Mahony Photo Archives

Sonny Burres (69), being chased by Dick Mann (1) and Ron Moore (37R) at Ascot. The Oregon star won National TT's at Castle Rock in 1971, and Peoria in 1975. While thought of as a TT rider, Burres was versatile in all disciplines and a talented tuner as well.
Mahony Photo Archives

Ohio oval track specialist Ricky Campbell, getting all he can out of his Yamaha on a cushion track. His performances only got stronger when he switched to the dominant Harley-Davidsons. That's Michigan racer (33X) Tom Cummings working the high line.
Ray Ninness Photo

Englishman Cliff Carr and crew in action at Talladega. Kevin Cameron, (manning the fuel hose), tuned Carr's privateer and factory Kawasaki's in the early 1970's. Carr later switched to a Suzuki factory ride. Carr put in great rides, including a 2nd place at Laguna Seca in 1973. Other shots at victory were often derailed by mechanical trouble. Ray Ninness Photo

The multi-talented Australian Kel Carruthers was the 1969 250 World Champion and won the Isle of Man twice. He began racing in the U.S. in the early 1970's for Don Vesco and later the Yamaha factory. He raced and acted as crew chief for the whole team. He won Nationals at Road Atlanta and Talladega before retiring. He continued on, managing Yamahas road race team and acted as mentor to Kenny Roberts. He was inducted into the MHOF in 1999. Mahony Photo Archives

Carruthers on a very clean 350 Yamaha at Road Atlanta in 1972. Ray Ninness Photo

Gifted rider Don Castro raced for both Triumph and Yamaha factory teams. Great on dirt and pavement, Castro came painfully close to victory on numerous occasions, finally notching a win at the 1973 San Jose Half-Mile. He finished in the top ten in GNC points for three years. He was inducted into the MHOF in 2010. Ray Ninness Photo

Castro was one of the best pavement racers of the era, coming up just short of a GNC win several times. He was 3rd at Daytona in 1970 and 4th in 1974. Ray Ninness Photo

Dirt trackers never give up! Castro having a serious moment on the cushion. Mahony Photo Archives

Don Castro wicks up the Erv Kanemoto Kawasaki H2R inside of (34) Darryl Hurst, (93) JR Rawls and (62) Corky Keener. Note the duct tape on Castro's old Yamaha factory leathers. Mahony Photo, courtesy of Darryl Hurst

Illinois Expert Mike Caves at Toledo, Oh in 1974. His career took off when he teamed with former GNC champ Roger Reiman. A good all-around racer, Caves was best on the TT courses. He was always a threat at his home state Peoria TT, finishing 3rd at the 1974 event. Ray Ninness Photo

Michigan rider Charlie Chapple going hard on his Yamaha half-miler. He was best known for his short track skills, finishing 3rd at Houston in 1971. Ray Ninness Photo

Dusty Coppage was the Yamaha's factory TT specialist in the early 1970's. He scored a 4th in the XS650 based machines debut at Houston in 1970. An underrated road racer, he was 10th at Daytona and 7th at Loudon in 1970. He scaled back his racing in 1971, running occasional GNC events through the mid-'70's. Mahony Photo Archives

The first woman to earn an Expert license, Diane Cox. The Oregon state rider was a Castle Rock regular. She qualified for several GNC programs, missing the National transfers by a whisker. Mahony Photo Archives

Georgia rider Roger Crump burst onto the scene in 1974, setting fast time at the Houston Short Track. He was also fast on the big ovals, turning in impressive performances on Bill Kennedy's Triumph. Frequent injury prevented Crump from showing his true potential. Ray Ninness Photo

One of the eras best cushion riders, Ohio's Larry Darr. One of the best racers to not win a GNC, Darr came close on several occasions, including the 1971 Louisville Half-Mile, finishing 2nd. His career was cut short after a 1973 accident at Daytona. Ray Ninness Photo

The always on-the-gas Terry Dorsch. The California rider was a consistent front runner at all GNC dirt tracks, but was best known for his TT skills. His best finish was a 3rd at the 1973 Ascot TT. Mahony Photo Archives

A neat two for one shot, in alphabetical order! Number 7F is Ohio racer Scott Drake, the "Xenia Zephyr". Drake found early success on Delbert Bushes' BSA before moving to a Harley-Davidson. He is dueling with (92) Iowa racer, Steve Droste. Droste had a unique career as a motorcycle jumper/daredevil before switching to pro racing, full time. He teamed up with tuner Tex Peels and began reeling off great runs including a 4th at the 1974 Toledo Half-Mile, the night Ray Ninness took this photo.

"Captain America" Gordon Dusenberry, was a tough Midwest competitor, popular with fans and other racers alike. Ray Ninness Photo

French-Canadian Yvon DuHamel aboard the Deeley Yamaha in 1970. DuHamel and team came painfully close to winning a National for years only to have one trouble or another. Ben H. Hall Photo, courtesy of Betzel Smith

DuHamel made a move to a Kawasaki factory ride in 1971 and finally got a National win at Talladega. You can almost feel the excitement as DuHamel is pushed to Victory Circle by tuner Steve Whitelock. DuHamel went on to win 5 GNC road races, the last at Ontario in 1973. Ray Ninness Photo

Nobody rode harder than DuHamel! Much like a Bart Markel on pavement, he was always on the gas, as this image from IRP in 1972 shows. He was inducted into the MHOF in 1999. Ray Ninness Photo

254

Don Emde on his way to his historic 1972 Daytona 200 win on the Mel Dineson Yamaha. It was the first Daytona win for a two-stroke, first Yamaha Daytona win, smallest engine to win the race and first and only father/son combo to win the 200 (father Floyd won on the beach in 1948!) Don Emde was inducted into the MHOF in 1999, father Floyd in 1998! Photo courtesy of Don Emde

Emde working past #55 Steve McLaughlin and #22 Phil Read on the way to his Daytona victory. It was the start of a 13-year Yamaha win streak at Daytona. Mahony Photo Archives

Don and Floyd at IRP in the early 1970's Ray Ninness Photo

California racer Jim Evans was one of the top privateer road racers of the period. Top finishes included a 3rd places at Daytona in 1973 and Talladega in 1974. This photo shows him at Daytona aboard a Mel Dineson tuned Yamaha. Mahony Photo Archives

Race face on, Pennsylvania rider Billy Eves readies for action. Robert Pearson Photo

Always a crowd favorite, oval specialist Eves ran strong at Regional and National events aboard his fast Larry Mohan-tuned Triumph. His best GNC finish was a 3rd at the 1975 Toledo Half-Mile. Ray Ninness Photo

Second-generation racer Gary Fisher. Like his father Ed, Gary captured his lone National win at Loudon/Laconia; Dad did it in 1953, son in 1972. He scored his win as a privateer, but also rode the Krause Honda CB750 machine and served a stint as a Yamaha factory rider. Mahony Photo Archives

A solid dirt tracker, here is a rare shot of Fisher aboard his factory Yamaha two-stroke TT bike in 1973. Mahony Photo Archives

Walt Fulton and crew practice a pit stop at the 1971 Talladega National. Fulton was a great road racer and while on the Harley-Davidson factory team in 1970, turned in some of the team's best pavement finishes on a faithful flathead KR while the rest of the riders struggled with the new "iron" XRTT. He moved to this Erv Kanemoto tuned Kawasaki in '71. Ray Ninness Photo

Tough Al Gaskill aboard a neat BSA dirt tracker in the early 1970's. Gaskill earned a lot of purse money at Regional and National dirt tracks. He was also a strong pavement runner, finishing 11th at Daytona in 1969 and '70. Ray Ninness Photo

John Gennai was a blindingly fast Junior at Ascot Park, frequently outpacing the Experts on his Triumph. He received Harley-Davidson support in his rookie year of 1974. He had some success, but eventually returned to his familiar Triumph. He was 2nd at the 1975 Ascot TT after leading much of the race. Here he leads teammates Mert Lawwill (7) and Jim Rice(24). Mahony Photo Archives

The "Ragin'Cajun" hisself, Mike Gerald. The Louisiana rider was one of the best short trackers of the 1970's. He won 3 Nationals including 2 in-a- row at Sante Fe. His last and biggest win is pictured here at Houston in 1974. Like Daytona in 1970, Honda mounted a huge effort, won the race and pulled out. Mahony Photo Archives

Fearless Frank Gillespie was a successful GNC campaigner throughout the 1970's. His best finish was a 3rd at the 1973 San Jose Mile. The Californian rode a wide variety of machines, including Triumphs, Nortons, Harleys and the Yamaha pictured here. Mahony Photo Archives

Veteran California racer Mike Haney scored a surprise win at the 1973 Houston TT after Kenny Roberts ran into trouble. Here Haney tries out an old school 21" front wheel at the San Jose Mile. Mahony Photo Archives

Another California TT privateer, Dave Hansen, topped Roberts for the Houston TT crown in 1974. Hansen rode to the win on a Les Edward's prepared, Champion Frame sponsored Triumph. Mahony Photo Archives

Fast Californian "Lil" John Hateley. He was stylish and fun to watch on all surfaces. His first National win was at the 1972 Houston TT. In this classic Mahony photo, a feet-up, sideways Hateley is tucked in and reaching for the triple trees at the 1974 Toledo National. Mahony Photo Archives

Hateley "in the paint" at the San Jose Mile. Mahony Photo Archives

An accomplished motocross rider, Hateley was an especially strong TT rider. Here he launches a Norton at Ascot. Mahony Photo Archives

Like many Northwestern riders, "Oregon Guy" Ed Hermann was categorized as a TT specialist, but was an accomplished half-miler as well. Mahony Photo Archives

Californian Rick Hocking was a real-life cowboy as well as a natural born throttle twister. His speed and toughness always brought him to the front of TT's and rough surfaces. He caught fire late in his rookie year of 1974, winning the Golden Gate Mile and Ascot Half-Mile. He was a top GNC competitor through the 1970's. He is pictured here on the monstrous Champion CB750 miler at San Jose. Hocking passed away in 2011. Mahony Photo Archives

While showing some promise, the neat Doug Schwerma built machine was not a success. Like all four-stroke multis, the excess width of the cases were always a problem. Mahony Photo Archives

Hocking, wearing #13, engaged in a serious battle with champ Kenny Roberts at Ascot in 1975. Mahony Photo Archives

Hocking tries out Schwerma's Yamaha TZ750 at Ascot Park, here paced by Corky Keener. While obviously a handful on a short half-mile, Hocking set fast time the first time out. Mahony Photo Archives

Indiana's Gary Horton styles his Triumph on the cushion. Mahony Photo Archives.

California hotshoe Tom Horton. While normally staying close to home, Horton was 3rd at the 1974 Houston Short Track. Mahony Photo Archives

Wayne Hosaka aboard Pete Pistone's cool Rickman Triumph at Ascot in 1970. His career was cut short by injury and was confined to a wheelchair. Hosaka touched thousands through his website, Flattrack.com. He passed away in 2011. Mahony Photo Archives

Expert Lloyd Houchins riding indoors on a Harley Sprint. Like many fast California riders, Houchins stayed close to home, but could run up front anywhere. He was a career best 3rd at the 1970 Ascot Half-Mile. He finished in the top 10 at 4 of the 5 California GNC's held in 1970. Houchins was tragically killed at the 1973 San Jose Half-Mile. Mahony Photo Archives

Houston's own Hurst scoring his huge win at Houston. Previously Hurst was on the podium at the Sante Fe Short Track in 1972 and '73. Photo courtesy of Darryl Hurst

Darryl Hurst leads Hank Scott at the 1975 Houston Short Track. The white haired kid beside the banner in the stands is Hurst's nephew, future World Champion, Kevin Schwantz. Photo courtesy of Darryl Hurst.

Hurst with the Houston winning Yamaha at Donelson's Cycle in 2012. Robert Pearson Photo

Spectacular Michigan rider Mike Johnson, short tracking on an Ossa. Johnson was also a great cushion half-mile rider. Ray Ninness Photo

Rookie Expert Alex Jorgenson fighting the Ascot dirt clods aboard the Ron Wood Norton. Jorgenson ran very well at Ascot in 1975; dominating the weekly shows late in the year. At the season ending Ascot National, he set fast time and finished 5th in the National. "Jorgy" was just getting started! Mahony Photo Archives

Washington state TT specialist Chuck Joyner won the Castle Rock National in 1973 and 1975. He remained competitive through the decade. Mahony Photo Archives

"Michigan Mafia" member, Corky "Mr. Dirt" Keener. Keener turned Expert in the mid-1960's, but got his second-wind, finding Grand National glory in the seventies. He warmed up by dominating East coast Regionals before teaming up with Bart Markel to win his first National at Louisville in 1974. With full-on Harley-Davidson support, Keener won another 3 Nationals by the end of 1975. Ray Ninness Photo

Keener at the edge, or a little beyond, in this classic Ray Ninness photo.

Popular California rider DeWayne Keeter during a rare East Coast swing, at Toledo, Oh in 1974. He was an Ascot regular, where he scored a runner-up finish in 1968 National Half-Mile. He was tragically killed at Ascot in 1975. Ray Ninness Photo

Second-generation racer Al Kenyon watching track preparation before the 1971 San Jose Half-Mile. Al's father, Harold was also a great California Expert. Bill Barrett Photo

Small, but tough Texan, Mike Kidd. He fought frequent injury early in his career, but still managed to score 2 GNC wins. The first at the 1974 Columbus National (Triumph's last oval win) and then the all-Harley show at Terre Haute in 1975. Greater glory awaited Kidd in future GNC competition. Mahony Photo Archives

Mel Lacher on his Andres-tuned Harley KR, duels with Cal Rayborn (25) who is riding a new "iron" XR. At the time a good running KR was a match for it's replacement. Mahony Photo Archives

Classic Mahony image of Mert Lawwill aboard his KR in 1970. Lawwill, saddled with defending his championship with the troubled "iron" XR, occasionally had to dig out his old sidevalve racer. He still managed 3 wins on the year, coming in 6th in the GNC standings. Mahony Photo Archives

Lawwill styling at Columbus; he won Nationals at the track in 1969 and 1972. Mahony Photo Archives

Lawwill and Jack Dunn prepping an iron XR750 during the 1971 season. Bill Barrett Photo

Mert Lawwill celebrating his 1973 Peoria TT win. Lawwill won 15 Nationals in his career and was the 1969 GNC champ. He was a road race shy of a GNC "Grand Slam". Not for a lack of trying, Lawwill finished in the top 5 three times at Daytona. He could do it all, he was a great rider who also became a world class tuner and chassis builder. With the release of On Any Sunday he became one of the most recognized motorcycle racers in the world. He was inducted into the MHOF in 1998. Craig Stocks Photo

Lawwill aboard one of the legendary 900cc XLR TT bikes he and Jim Belland put together. Mahony Photo Archives

A case of what might have been-Southern wild man Carl"Frenchie" LeBlanc had a short, spectacular career. Riding a Bill Kennedy Triumph during his Junior year, LeBlanc was the only real East Coast competition for dominant Kenny Roberts. He had a succesful rookie Expert year, finishing in the top ten at the Houston and Sante Fe Short Tracks. LeBlanc suffered serious head injuries at Ascot Park, effectively ending a promising career. Ray Ninness Photo

This photo from Columbus in 1971 was a microcosim of LeBlanc's season long battle with Kenny Roberts. He was this close all year. Mahony Photo Archives

Texas short track ace Robert E. Lee #54 ducks for the low line at Houston in 1972. Always a threat on the bull rings, Lee won the Sante Fe National in 1971. Also pictured here are Tod Sloan (18Z), Ronnie Rall (52), Jimmy Maness (71) and Keith Mashburn (19). Mahony Photo Archives

Dick Mann's 1971 GNC title came eight years after his first championship in 1963. He won 8 Nationals between 1970-'72 including two Daytona 200 wins, giving him a total of 24 wins, at the time only behind Bart Markel and Joe Leonard in career wins. His last victory was at Peoria in 1972, the scene of his first National win in 1959! He became the first rider to score a GNC "Grand Slam" when he won the Homewood Mile in 1972. Mahony Photo Archives

Ahh, the glamorous life of a two-time Grand National champion! Mahony Photo Archives

Mann surveys the scene at the Livonia Mile in 1971. What a crowd! Ray Ninness Photo

Mann wrenches on a very sano Triumph dirt tracker in 1974, his last year on the GNC circuit. Mahony Photo Archives

One of the most successful road racers of the early 1970's, Mann won 4 pavement Nationals between 1970-'71. Here he leads Gene Romero, with whom he waged a fierce battle for the 1971 GNC title. Ray Ninness Photo

Colorful Georgia dirt tracker, Jimmy Maness. Maness raced for Augusta Harley-Davidson, with factory support. He dominated southern Regional races through the 1970's. A tough competitor at cushion GNC's, Maness notched best finishes of 4th at the 1970 Atlanta Half-Mile and 5th at Louisville in 1974. Maness brightened up the sport with his pink and white leathers. He retired from two-wheel racing in 1979, beginning a succesful career in dirt track stock cars. A class act! Photo Courtesy of Jimmy Maness

Bart and Jo Ann Markel celebrate after Markel's historic 28th National win at the 1971 Columbus National. He had finally broken Joe Leonard's long standing record. It was his last National victory. Markel was inducted into the MHOF in 1998. Mahony Photo Archives

Markel guns his "iron" XR around the Livonia Mile in 1971. Markel remained competitive on the circuit till retirement in 1974, even bouncing back from a broken pelvis suffered at the Colorado Mile in 1972. Ray Ninness Photo

One of the first Yamaha factory riders, Keith Mashburn rode under the Shell Motors banner from 1970-'71. In 1972 he joined the "official" team. A top GNC talent, Mashburn would retire way too early after a team shakeup in 1973. Mahony Photo Archives

Hard charging Rob Morrison aboard the Ron Wood Norton at Ascot. A top 10 GNC talent, Morrison went on to join the Norton-Villers team in 1975. Mahony Photo Archives

East meets West in a short track territorial dispute between #11 Jim McMurren (California) and #52 Ronnie Rall (Ohio). From the looks of McMurren's front number plate, it wasn't the first of the night! Photo Courtesy of Jim McMurren

Ohio Rookie Expert Steve Morehead started out on a Harley-Davidson, but a switch to Bill Kennedy's Triumph was a great fit; Morehead earned his National Number on the bike for 1975, before going onto future GNC glory . He was inducted into the MHOF in 2004. Ray Ninness Photo

California hotshoe Ron Moore launches off the line. Moore was an Ascot regular and finished 2nd to Kenny Roberts at the 1973 Ascot National. Mahony Photo Archives

Mulder at the San Jose Half-Mile in 1971. Though known as a TT specialist, Mulder had several top oval track finishes including a 2nd at the '71 Oklahoma Half-Mile. Bill Barrett Photo

Eddie Mulder on his way to winning the 1970 Sante Fe TT, the last of his 5 National wins, all on TT courses. Mahony Photo Archives

Michigan cushion ace Teddy Newton #40, aboard his BSA, tries to scoot around #9F Jimmy Zeigler's Yamaha at Louisville in 1972. Mahony Photo Archives

Two-time Grand National Champion Gary Nixon (1967 and '68), suffered a serious leg injury in 1969. The injury thwarted his dirt track skills, but he retained his pavement skills. Tough guy Nixon bounced back in 1970 to win the Loudon National. He switched to Kawasaki in 1972 and had a serious run at the title in 1973, winning 3 Nationals and finishing 3rd in the chase. Ray Ninness Photo

Nixon leads the pack at the start of the 1974 Loudon National. Nixon and Loudon were a perfect match. He won there 4 times on 3 different types of machines, including the Suzuki pictured here. This was Nixon's 19th and final GNC win. He was inducted into the MHOF in 1998. Gary Nixon passed away in 2011. Ray Ninness Photo

Nixon chased by former 250 World Champion Kel Carruthers. Ray Ninness Photo

Nixon tries out Erv Kanemoto's Kawasaki H2R at the 1974 San Jose Mile. Mahony Photo Archives

Bill O'Brien #99, leads a talented group including #73 Sid Carlson and #10 Neil Keen. Photo Courtesy of Jim McMurren

Multi-talented Jimmy Odom claimed his two National victories in 1971, at the Houston Short Track and the Corona Half-Mile. Odom rode for top teams of the era including a Yamaha factory ride and a long time stint with A&A Racing. Ray Ninness Photo

Fun-loving Odom engaging in some serious pit racing at Talladega in 1971, along with, L to R, Don Vesco, Yvon DuHamel and friends. Ray Ninness Photo

Ohio hotshoe Jimmy Osborne. Osborne thrilled himself and the hometown crowd when he placed 4th in the 1975 Toledo National, the highest placing Buckeye in the race. Bert Shepard/Silver Shutter Photo, courtesy of Jimmy Osborne

The youngest of the three racing Palmgren brothers, Denny. Here aboard a Triumph, he would later switch to a Larry Schafer-prepared Harley. Palmgren was very tough at Northeast Regionals and Nationals.
Ray Ninness Photo

The eldest of the Palmgren brothers, Larry won two Nationals in 1969. He ran very strong in 1970, notching an incredible run of 5 podium finishes. Despite this, Palmgren scaled back his racing and retired in the early 1970's. Mahony Photo Archives

GNC veteran Chuck Palmgren at speed at his favorite type of event, the mile. He began the decade on the Yamaha factory team, scoring the first win for the XS650 at the Nazareth Mile. Palmgren left the factory team and began a long-term association with car racing legend Dan Gurney and All-American Racing (AAR). The pairing up led to arguably the fastest Yamahas on the circuit. Great on all dirt tracks, Palmgren also managed a 6th at Daytona in 1971. He scored the last of his GNC wins at the Indy Mile in 1972. Palmgren still works for AAR in Santa Ana, Ca. He was inducted into the MHOF in 2009. Mahony Photo Archives

One of Palmgren's AAR Yamahas, restored by Stan Millard and owned by John Carr, here on display at the Springfield Mile in 1999. Robert Pearson Photo

Palmgren fighting the dust early on at the Roosevelt Raceway. He went on to score his 3rd National win later that night. Dan Mahony Photo, courtesy of Chuck Palmgren

Palmgren working past Cal Rayborn on his way to winning the 1972 Indy Mile. Mahony Photo Archives, Photo courtesy of Chuck Palmgren

Palmgren on a Yamaha XS650-based road racer, leads Gary Scott and friend at Ontario in 1972. Palmgren was no slouch on the pavement, he was 6th at Daytona in 1971. Photo Courtesy of Chuck Palmgren

Geoff Perry was a champion motorcycle racer from New Zealand. The factory Suzuki rider was 5th at his first Daytona 200 in 1970. He began racing the GNC circuit on a regular basis. He won the Road Atlanta National in 1973. He was killed in a commercial plane crash in the South Pacific later in the season. Ray Ninness Photo

California racer Ron Pierce raced at GNC pavement events through the 1970's. He normally rode as a Yamaha privateer. Some his best finishes of the period were in 1975 with an 8th at Daytona and 4th at Laguna Seca. Ray Ninness Photo

Texas racer Teddy Poovey, half-miling on a Harley XR750. He was also a strong short track racer; he was part of the 1975 Powerdyne factory team. Ray Ninness Photo

Ohio's Ronnie Rall rode a variety of machines through the 1970's. His best finish of the period was a 2nd at Columbus in 1970 on his own BSA. He also had top 5's on Bill Kennedy's Triumph in 1971 at Columbus and Louisville. He tried the wild F & S Suzuki Triple with limited success. He is pictured here on Jimmy Clarke's XR750. Rall tended to ride close to home, making good fair money. His last National was at Columbus in 1973. Ray Ninness Photo

Rall wrestling with the Suzuki "Water Buffalo". Notice his riding style in comparison with the accompanying photo on the left; Rall is way up on the edge of the seat to get that thing turned. It was a beast to ride! Mahony Photo Archives

The great Cal Rayborn at Loudon in 1973. The '70's were a trying period for Rayborn. He seemed to suffer more mechanical issues with the new XR's than the other team riders. He scored just 3 of his 11 National wins from 1970-'73. Rayborn knew that Harley-Davidson was done in road racing and had decided to ride for Suzuki at the end of the '73 season. He was tragically killed at an off-season club race in New Zealand. Rayborn was inducted into the MHOF in 1999. Ray Ninness Photo

You can almost feel Cal Rayborn's satisfaction after finally scoring his long awaited dirt track National win at the Livonia Mile in 1971. Look at the huge crowd! Ray Ninness Photo

Jim Rice contributed this fantastic photo and accompanying caption; *"You could trust Cal, and during a San Jose Half Mile National heat race, I tried to pass him on the outside of each turn, while he stayed on the inside of the groove to give me more room. I wasn't able to pass him, and after the race I thanked him for his good racing manners. Cal said, "That was fun...wasn't it?" Sure was Cal!*

Either somebody's late or somebody's early; clowning around with Mert Lawwill before the 1971 San Jose Half-Mile. Bill Barrett Photo

Multi-time World Champion Phil Read (22), leads Chuck Palmgren (38), John Cooper (28) and (21) Peter Williams at Ontario in 1972. Courtesy of Chuck Palmgren

1964 GNC champ Roger Reiman shields his ears against some bike; probably a blankity-blank 2-stroke. The 4-stroke stalwart gave the iron XRTT it's best Daytona finish, a 4th in 1971. He tried this Krause Honda out in 1973. Reiman made his last GNC appearances in 1974. He was tragically killed at Daytona in 1997 in a Legends Race. He was inducted into the MHOF in 1998. Mahony Photo Archives

Big" Mike Renlsow on the Rocky Cycle CB750 at Ascot. Renslow rode some wild machinery; notably this bike and a Suzuki triple he won a non-national with. Renslow passed away in 2010. Mahony Photo Archives

Jim Rice in a beautiful feet-up slide at Roosevelt Raceway in 1971. Rice was one of the greatest riders of the era. He won 6 Nationals in 1970 and just missed winning the GNC title. He is the only rider to win a dirt track National on a four-stroke multi-cylinder machine, winning the Sedalia Mile in his rookie year of 1969 on a BSA Triple. When BSA went out of business, Rice ran 1972 with limited sponsorship, claiming two wins against the factory teams. In 1973 Rice switched to Harley-Davidson, winning his 12th and final National at Columbus. He was inducted into the MHOF in 2001. Mahony Photo courtesy of Jim Rice

The BSA factory team running in formation at Ascot in 1971; Rice, Aldana and Mann. The three also share something else in common; Each did most of their own tuning and bike preparation. They had no full-time mechanics. Mahony Photo courtesy of Jim Rice

Rice had this slide down, while at speed on the half-mile portion of the Castle Rock TT. He never touched the dirt, just stepped off when the bike stopped! Photo courtesy of Jim Rice

The moment Jim Rice's bid for the 1970 GNC title ended at Sacramento. Rice hit a false neutral entering the corner and stepped off at 120 MPH. He was lucky to walk away. Photo courtesy of Jim Rice

Georgia rookie Expert Jay Ridgeway at the Sante Fe short track on a familiar Woody Kyle Kawasaki. Photo Courtesy of Chuck Weber.

"King" Kenny Roberts earned his title by excelling at every GNC discipline. In his rookie year of 1972, he scored one win and finished 3rd in the GNC chase. In 1973, he picked up 3 wins on his way to his first title. He became "King" in 1974, winning 6 Nationals and became the second rider to score a "Grand Slam". In 1975 he again scored 6 wins, but lost the title to Gary Scott. Despite this, it was a year of legend; he scored a single season Grand Slam and won the Indy Mile on the infamous TZ750. Paul Webb Photo

Roberts was one of the few to really make a Yamaha dirt tracker work; more to will and daring than anything else. Here he stays just ahead of the Harleys of Doug Sehl (45) and Scott Brelsford (19) at Toledo in 1974. Mahony Photo Archives

Roberts practicing on the legendary TZ750-miler. At the 1975 Indy Mile, Roberts had never seen the bike till day of the race! By main event time he nearly had the beast figured out. In this Dan Mahony photo, Roberts is being chased by Triumph rider Steve Morehead; definitely different ends of the technology scale!

Roberts grew up dirt tracking and was uncomfortable in his early pavement forays. A quick learner, Roberts was schooled by Yamaha team captain Kel Carruthers. Roberts did not win a road race on the way to his first championship in 1973. Roberts and the new TZ700 clicked in 1974 and he dominated the pavement races, racking up 3 wins. Many believe that Roberts won his 2nd title due to his road race wins. Amazingly, he would have won the championship on dirt track points alone! Roberts road race skills would continue to grow, eventually enabling him to conquer the World Championship. Ray Ninness Photo

Roberts getting it on at the 1974 Syracuse Mile. Paul Webb Photo

Likeable and talented Tom Rockwood, announcer Roxy Rockwood's son. Tom was successful on the dirt and pavement. He earned a spot on the 1971 Triumph team and won the Ascot Half-Mile at the end of that season. Ray Ninness Photo

While primarily thought of as a dirt tracker, Rockwood was 7th at Daytona in 1969 and 8th in 1971, the year this photo was taken. Mahony Photo Archives

California racer Gene Romero turned Expert in the mid-1960's, best known as a TT rider. He learned the ropes through the '60's and became one of the most versatile riders in the series. He earned his first win in 1969 at the Lincoln, Ne TT. He teamed up with C.R.Axtell and company in 1970, helping him to win the #1 plate. He narrowly lost the title to Dick Mann the next year. Romero was a contender through the '70's switching from Triumph to Yamaha in 1974. Besides his dirt track skills, Romero became an accomplished road racer, winning Ontario in 1974 and at Daytona in 1975 for the last and biggest of his 12 National wins. He was inducted into the MHOF in 1998. Mahony Photo Archives

It ain't easy being a National champ! Note the limestone blasted front plate and lack of rear brake in this Mahony photo from the 1971 Louisville National.

Romero stylin' at Louisville in 1973. Mahony Photo Archives

Romero at Loudon in 1973 with new teammate Gary Scott on his rear wheel. Romero earned his road race chops on the Trident, turning in great rides, including consecutive runner-up finishes at Daytona in 1970 and '71. Ray Ninness Photo

Romero at Loudon in 1974. He quickly adjusted to the new bike, scoring two of the biggest wins of his career, at Ontario and Daytona. Ray Ninness Photo

Texan Bubba Rush (41N), dices with (48) Pat McCaul. Rush had a strong rookie season in 1975, making several main events, including a podium finish at the Sante Fe Short Track. Mahony Photo Archives

California Expert Bobby Sanders hustles his Yamaha around Ascot Park. Mahony Photo Archives

Georgia rider Greg Sassaman was picked up by Harley-Davidson in his Junior year of 1974. Unknown outside of the Southeast, rookie Expert Sassaman set the dirt track community on it's ear by winning the 1975 spring San Jose Mile. He was having a great season till injured at Terre Haute. Ray Ninness Photo

Hank Scott, Gary's younger brother, lets it all hang out in this fantastic image from 1974. Riding like this saw him win the Syracuse Mile and become the top rookie of the year. Scott went onto a very successful GNC career and was inducted into the MHOF in 2000. Ray Ninness Photo

In 1975, Scott began riding Shell Thuett's fast Yamahas. Here he battles with Eddie Wirth at Ascot. Mahony Photo Archives

A spectacular Dan Mahony image of Gary Scott in his Harley-Davidson debut at Houston in 1974. Scott battled fiercely to win the coveted #1 plate. He first finished behind Mark Brelsford in 1972 and then arch rival Kenny Roberts in 1973-'74. His perseverance finally paid off by winning the 1975 Grand National Championship Scott was inducted into the MHOF in 1998. Mahony Photo Archives

Scott in a typical Ascot battle with Keith Mashburn (19), Sammy Tanner (7X), Kenny Roberts (80Y) and Gene Romero (3). There was no shortage of talent at the famous Gardena, Ca speed plant! Mahony Photo Archives

Often overlooked for his pavement skills, Scott was one of the last to put 4-strokes up front at 1970's Nationals. He rode the wheels of his Trident in 1973, making the podium at Loudon and Laguna Seca. In 1974-'75, he put the Harley XRTT in the top 10 at several Nationals. Ray Ninness Photo

The Harley Wrecking Crew at the San Jose Mile; Gary Scott just in front of Corky Keener and Rex Beauchamp.
Mahony Photo Archives

A bit of self-indulgence here. I was 11 years-old when my Dad snapped this photo. Gary Scott had just won the 1975 Columbus National and was on his way to the National Championship. A great day for both of us!

Randy Scott was a top flight racer from Oregon. He was a top 10 threat, particularly on the TT tracks. He was on the podium at both the Houston TT and Castle Rock Nationals in 1973. Ray Ninness Photo

Canadian Dave Sehl's relaxed riding style belied his blazing speed. He won 6 dirt track Nationals, including the Atlanta Mile and 3 Louisville Half-Miles. Ray Ninness Photo

Sehl gets ready for another race in half-mile land. Robert Pearson Photo

One of the best riders to not win a GNC, Doug Sehl, Dave's brother. He was a skilled campaigner on dirt and pavement. Doug looked a sure bet to win a National, especially at the 1974 Indy Mile, where he came up just short. Ray Ninness Photo

Washington States Randy Skiver was a big guy for a dirt tracker, but natural talent made up for any extra size. Skiver was always a top TT contender whose period finishes included a 4th at the 1974 Castle Rock GNC. Courtesy of Randy Skiver and Shawn McDonald.

English star Paul Smart was fast and one of the pioneers of the modern "knee scratching" style. He scored GNC wins for both Kawasaki and Suzuki factory teams. He was fast qualifier at Daytona on 3 occasions; not as fortunate in the race, he managed a 9th place in 1974. Mahony Photo Archives

Smart with tuner Hurley Wilvert at Ontario in 1972. Also visible is tuner Steve Whitelock sitting on Yvon DuHamel's #17 and Suzuki's Jody Nicholas conferring with his crew. Photo Courtesy of Hurley Wilvert

Southern gentleman Charlie Southgate. A very good dirt tracker, Southgate carried National Number 56 in the late 1960's and 1970. Hard working and enthusiastic, Southgate epitomizes the spirit of the American motorcycle racer.
Photo courtesy of Charles Southgate

One of the greatest dirt trackers of all time, Michigan's Jay Springsteen. His rookie year of 1975 included two wins and numerous other top placings which landed him 3rd in the GNC standings and into a full-fledged Harley ride. He completed the mid-70's "Michigan Mafia" with Rex Beauchamp and Corky Keener. He was inducted into the MHOF in 2003. Ray Ninness Photo

Fresh faced teenage brothers Jay and Ken Springsteen. The two were top ranked Novices and starting with their Junior year, were sponsored by dirt track enthusiast Rich Gawthrop, owner of the T-shirt company Vista-Sheen. Ray Ninness Photo

Ken Springsteen working hard to stay in front of "Mr. Dirt", Corky Keener. Mahony Photo Archives

Pennsylvania racer Billy Schaeffer gets ready for action. He was a top GNC racer through the 1970's. Pictured here on a Yamaha, he would soon end up on a Harley-Davidson. From the looks of the visor taped to his helmet, this must be a cushion racetrack. Ray Ninness Photo

One of the best half-milers in the business, Charlie Seale. He battled frequent injury, but still managed to be a dominant Regional racer and a top 5 GNC contender. Ray Ninness Photo

Sammy Tanner was back in a major way at Ascot in the early 1970's. He rode a variety of machines including the Harold Allison Norton pictured here. Tanner was inducted into the MHOF in 1999. Mahony Photo Archives

Michigan rider Jack Warren put together an unusual Norton/Rickman combination. It worked well and during 1970, Warren dominated local half-miles and was 3rd at the 1970 Atlanta National. In 1971 he was 3rd at the Louisville National and won the Louisville Race of Champions. Gerald Baltke Photo, courtesy of Jack Warren

Oregon star Mark Williams, one of the best riders to not win a GNC; Williams posted numerous top finishes, but was never quite able to close the deal. Considered a TT specialist, Williams was a very good all around racer. He was recruited by the 1975 Norton-Villers factory team. Williams was the most successful of the team riders and led the early season Camel Pro points standing, in contention till the team disbanded mid-season. He was seriously injured at the San Jose Mile later that year when a practice crash left him paralyzed. Williams passed away in 2012. Ray Ninness Photo

Super rider/tuner Hurley Wilvert on a factory Suzuki at Daytona in 1975. One of the unsung heroes of GNC racing, Wilvert was a very good California club racer and bike wrench, who ran a few Nationals in 1970. He wanted a job in racing and managed to get on the Kawasaki team as Paul Smart's tuner. When Smart left the team, Wilvert managed to talk his way onto Smart's former ride! The decision paid off for all concerned as Wilvert was on the podium at Charlotte in 1973 and was 3rd at the 1974 Daytona 200; the highest finish for any Kawasaki rider yet. Photo courtesy of Hurley Wilvert

Californian Eddie Wirth rode a variety of machines, including Triumphs, Yamahas and Harley-Davidsons, with success on the GNC circuit. While a GNC TT winner (1969 Sante Fe), Wirth was strong on the ovals as well. He later became a successful CRA sprint car driver. Mahony Photo Archives

TT legend of the 1960's Skip Van Leeuwen, still had the goods in the new decade. He was 3rd at the 1970 Houston TT and 2nd at the Sante Fe TT. He was runner-up at Houston in 1971 and began a limited schedule, running his last Ascot TT in 1972. Mahony Photo Archives

Wisconsin racer Keith Ulicki, like his brother Frank, were top 10 GNC contenders. They were perennially Harley mounted, as Frank worked at the factory and Keith ran out of the family dealership, Uke's Harley-Davidson. Ray Ninness Photo

Representing the underappreciated tuners on the circuit is Kawasaki's Chris Young. Young worked on Art Baumann's bikes and like most of the tuners of the era, put in very long hours for limited money and glory. Photo courtesy of Hurley Wilvert

The start of the 1975 Toledo Grand National, which Cycle News termed "Heartbreak City" for #89 Jimmy Zeigler. After Corky Keener (62) and Gary Scott (64) went by, Zeigler was still headed to a podium finish when his XR750 quit just yards from the checkers. Bert Shepard/Silver Shutter Photo, courtesy of Jimmy Zeigler

Okay, a little more reminiscing, Jimmy Zeigler and I in 1975. Nice guy Zeigler was an Ohio area crowd favorite. His son Justin is a fine dirt tracker (and nice guy as well!)

A classic shot of Jimmy Zeigler on Bill Kennedy's clean Trackmaster Triumph from 1973. Note the ex-Larry Darr factory Harley leathers Zeigler is wearing.
Ray Ninness Photo

Big riders meeting at IRP in 1972. Lots of famous faces in there. How many can you pick out? Ray Ninness Photo

The 1973 GNC Season Preview

Harley-Davidson had set the world back on its axis by reclaiming the Grand National title in 1972. Things looked good for them to repeat in 1973. The alloy XR750 had most of its kinks worked out and was becoming the dominant dirt track machine. On pavement, the team's bikes were at least as strong as the other four strokes, but the writing was on the wall as the two-stroke multis got faster. Mark Brelsford led the team, now joined by his brother, Scott, as well as Mert Lawwill, Bart Markel, Rex Beauchamp, Dave Sehl and Cal Rayborn.

After his strong rookie performance, Gary Scott was made a full-fledged member of Team Triumph. Returning was Gene Romero, who was just behind Scott in the 1972 championship. They were joined by two-time champion Dick Mann after the demise of his long time sponsor BSA. His road race machinery was the same, just repainted in Triumph colors. Bob Tryon was the new race manager. The Triumph factory was still in big financial trouble and this would be the last year for a multi-rider team. The machinery, both on dirt and pavement, was getting long in the tooth, but the talented squad could be expected to turn in competitive performances.

Kenny Roberts would return as Yamahas best hope for taking the GNC crown. Roberts looked to be headed to the title in 1972, only to be derailed by mechanical trouble. For 1973 Roberts would receive the talented tuning skills of Shell Theutt, Bud Meyers and Bud Aksland. Kel Carruthers would contest all the pavement races and act as the team road manager/crew chief. Great all-arounder Don Castro and pavement star Gary Fisher were added to the team. Long-time team member Keith Mashburn and Jimmy Odom were looking for rides. Equipment for the season would include the new 750 kit approved for the dirt track twin and the appearance of a new, water-cooled 350 for pavement. If the team could keep machines under Roberts, they had a great shot at the title.

The other Japanese teams came back in full force for 1973 with their biggest teams and budgets yet. Suzuki riders included Paul Smart, from Kawasaki, 1972 Daytona winner Don Emde, Ron Grant and Geoff Perry. Kawasaki returned with Yvon DuHamel, Gary Nixon, long-time Suzuki pilot Art Baumann, with Hurley Wilvert and Cliff Carr also receiving factory support. Honda would return for Daytona only, for the first time since Dick Mann's 1970 win. Most of the teams would appear with Grand Prix stars at Daytona.

Norton mounted a full-time effort for Dave Aldana. They had supported tuner Nick Deligianis's efforts on a Trackmaster framed machine, which both Frank Gillespie and Aldana rode with success. New dirt track machines would feature C&J frames. They would also enter all road races with some imported stars making appearances.

There were a number of AMA rule changes for 1973. Junior races run in conjunction with the Nationals were scrapped. Instead a Trophy Race, (read consolation race), would be held just before the National. It was also now more difficult to make a half-mile main event; In the qualifying heat races, only the top two riders would transfer directly, rather than three. The two Semi events would transfer two riders each. The short track format was now changed to match the half-mile program, no longer having a unique formula. Road races would also see the addition of a semi event. Expert short track machinery was now changed to 360 cc singles or 250 twins machines. Big bore machinery was limited to 750 for all classes, including TT events. This would end appearances of Team Harleys legendary 900 XLR's.

The 1973 AMA Grand National Championship scheduled remained at 24 events. New dates on the schedule saw returns to the Terre Haute Half-Mile and Pocono Road race, with first time road races at Charlotte Motor Speedway and Dallas. Gone from the schedule were the Indianapolis Road Race, Homewood Mile and the half-miles at Long Island and Salem, Ore. The number of road races was up to a series high of nine events. The Japanese manufacturers jumped into the series with both feet, helping to put up money for several events such as the Kawasaki Superbike event at Laguna Seca. They surely hoped that winning on Sunday would help move units on Monday. Half-mile events, long considered the mainstay event type on the schedule shrank to just five events. This was the fewest number of half-miles on the trail since 1966, when there were only 14 events total. There were four mile events, down one, with TT's and short tracks status quo with four and two events respectively.

The 1973 schedule would favor the riders and teams running for the championship that could field the strongest all around effort. Team Yamaha riders, particularly Kenny Roberts had to be favored; they had competitive bikes for all five types of GNC events. Suffering the most would be Harley-Davidson. Clearly lacking on pavement, the team could previously count on dirt track dominance. As always they were the strongest players at the mile events. Their bread and butter events though, the half-miles, had been cut drastically. Much the same could be said for Team Triumph. They were probably a little better off than Harley on pavement. On dirt their aging warhorses were still competitive on ovals, but the lack of half-miles hurt them too. Neither team had truly competitive road racers or short trackers.

The nine road races certainly coincided nicely with the big teams that Suzuki and Kawasaki were fielding. The surplus of rich road races gave them the incentive to go all out. The "pavement only" riders stood to do well financial and with the amount of events, could figure in the championship. Just as the heavy of schedule of dirt tracks in past championships favored certain brands, (okay, Harley-Davidson), the schedule of 1973 would clearly favor those who could score points across the board, which was Kenny Roberts and Yamaha.

1973 National Numbers

1. Mark Brelsford, Woodside, Ca
2. Dick Mann, Richmond, Ca
3. Gene Romero, San Luis Obispo, Ca
4. Bart Markel, Flint, Mi
5. Roger Reiman, Kewanee, Ill
6. Unassigned
7. Mert Lawwill, San Francisco, Ca
8. Unassigned
9. Gary Nixon, Phoenix, Md
10. Neil Keen, St. Louis, Mo
11. Don Castro, Hollister, Ca
12. Eddie Mulder, Burbank, Ca
13. Dave Aldana, Santa Ana, Ca
14. Cal Rayborn, Spring Valley, Ca
15. Mike Gerald, Baton Rouge, La
16. Dave Sehl, Waterdown, Ont., Can
17. Yvon DuHamel, LaSalle, Quebec, Can
18. Jimmy Odom, Fremont, Ca
19. Keith Mashburn, Santa Susana, Ca
20. Dave Smith, Lakewood, Ca
21. Gary Fisher, Parkesburg, Pa
22. Terry Dorsch, Granada Hills, Ca
23. Dave Hansen, Hayward, Ca
24. Jim Rice, Palo Alto, Ca
25. Don Emde, San Diego, Ca
26. Cliff Carr, Arlington, Mass
27. Duane McDaniels, Milford, Mi
28. Conrad Urbanowski, Miramar, Fl
29. Larry Palmgren, Freehold, NJ
30. Art Baumann, Brisbane, Ca
31. Rex Beauchamp, Drayton Plains, Mi
32. Dusty Coppage, Beaverton, Ore
33. Tod Sloan, Fresno, Ca
34. Darryl Hurst, Houston, Tx
35. Randy Skiver, Everett, Wa
36. Charlie Chapple, Flint, Mi
37. Ron Moore, San Bernardino, Ca
38. Chuck Palmgren, Freehold, NJ
39. Brad Lackey, Pinole, Ca
40. Teddy Newton, Pontiac, Mi
41. Billy Eves, Phoenixville, Pa
42. Fred Guttner, Detroit, Mi
43. Johnny Lane, Bakersfield, Ca
44. DeWayne Keeter, Ojai, Ca
45. Doug Sehl, Waterdown, Ontario, Can
46. Paul Bostrom, San Ramon, Ca
47. Charlie Seale, Lantana, Fl
48. Al Kenyon, Cupertino, Ca
49. Dennis Palmgren, Freehold, Ca
50. Randy Scott, Philomath, Ore
51. George Kerker, Glendale, Ca
52. Ronnie Rall, Mansfield, Oh
53. Bob Bailey, Gardena, Ca
54. Robert E. Lee, Ft. Worth, Tx
55. Jim Jones, Kirkland, Wa
56. Marty Lunde, Hermosa Beach, Ca
57. Ed Hermann, Milwaukie, Ore
58. Richard Schroder, Falls Church, Va
59. Skip Van Leeuwen, Hollywood, Ca
60. Chuck Joyner, Oregon City, Ore
61. Ron Grant, Brisbane, Ca
62. Corky Keener, Goodrich, Mi
63. Walt Fulton, Santa Ana, Ca
64. Gary Scott, West Covina, Ca
65. Jimmy Weinert, Middletown, NY
66. John Skinner, Auburn, Al
67. Pat Marinacci, Seattle, Wa
68. Wyman Priddy, Ft. Worth, Tx
69. Sonny Burres, Portland, Ore
70. Mark Williams, Springfield, Ore
71. Jimmy Maness, Augusta, Ga
72. Mike Kidd, Hurst, Tx
73. Kel Carruthers, El Cajon, Ca
74. Paul Pressgrove, Tecumseh, Ks
75. Jim Dunn, Everett, Wa
76. Frank Gillespie, Berkeley, Ca
77. Carl LeBlanc, Elyria, Oh
78. Ron Wakefield, Indianapolis, Ind
79. Lloyd Houchins, La Crescenta, Ca
80. Kenny Roberts, Lower Lake, Ca
81. Gordon Duesenbery, Wichita, Ks
82. Jack Warren, Millington, Mi
83. Steve McLaughlin, Duarte, Ca
84. Gary L. Bailey, Clovis, NM
85. Richard Wascher, Renton, Wa
86. Keith Ulicki, Kenosha, Wi
87. Hold for Mark Brelsford
88. Tom Rockwood, Gardena, Ca
89. Gary Jones, Hacienda Heights, Ca
90. Ike Reed, Salem, Ore
91. Mike Haney, Inglewood, Ca
92. Gunnar Lindstrom, S. Plainfield, NJ
93. Gregory Edmunds, Oxom Hill, Md
94. Larry Darr, Mansfield, Oh
95. Michael Ninci, Kansas City, Mo
96. Ed Varnes, Cochranville, Pa
97. Ron Pierce, Bakersfield, Ca
98. John Hateley, Van Nuys, Ca
99. Ray Hempstead, St. Petersburg, Fl

1973
Grand National Championship
Schedule

	Race	Location	Date
1	Houston TT	Houston, Tx	January 26, 1973
2	Houston Short Track	Houston, Tx	January 27, 1973
3	Daytona 200 Mile Road Race	Daytona Beach, Fl	March 11, 1973
4	Dallas 75 Mile Road race	Dallas, Tx	April 1, 1973
5	San Jose Half-Mile	San Jose, Ca	May 20, 1973
6	Road Atlanta 75 Mile Road Race	Braselton, Ga	June 3, 1973
7	Louisville Half-Mile	Louisville, Ky	June 9, 1973
8	Loudon 75 Mile Road Race	Loudon, NH	June 17, 1973
9	Columbus Half-Mile	Columbus, Oh	June 24, 1973
10	San Jose Mile	San Jose, Ca	July 1, 1973
11	Colorado Mile	Colorado Springs, Co	July 7, 1973
12	Castle Rock TT	Castle Rock, Wa	July 14, 1973
13	Ascot TT	Gardena, Ca	July 21, 1973
14	Laguna Seca 75 Mile Road Race	Monterey, Ca	July 29, 1973
15	Sante Fe Short Track	Hinsdale, Ill	August 3, 1973
16	Peoria TT	Peoria, Ill	August 5, 1973
17	Terre Haute Half-Mile	Terre Haute, Ind	August 12, 1973
18	Pocono 75 Mile Road Race	Mt. Pocono, Pa	August 19, 1973
19	Indy Mile	Indianapolis, Ind	August 25, 1973
20	Talladega 150 Mile Road Race	Talladega, Al	September 2, 1973
21	Atlanta Mile	Atlanta, Ga	September 10, 1973
22	Charlotte 75 Mile Road Race	Charlotte, NC	September 16, 1973
23	Ontario 250 Mile Road Race	Ontario, Ca	September 30, 1973
24	Ascot Half-Mile	Gardena, Ca	October 6, 1973

GNC Round #1 & 2 of 24 **Date:** January 26 & 27, 1973 **Type:** TT and Short Track **Venue:** Houston Astrodome **Location:** Houston, Tx	**Purse:** $24,000.00 **Surface:** Dirt **Course Length:** ¼ mile **Laps:** 25 TT, 20 Short Track

The rookie stars of 1972-Kenny Roberts, Gary Scott and Mike Kidd-were now all legitimate GNC contenders. All of them, particularly Roberts, thirsted for another shot at Houston glory. Roberts was clearly the fastest rider on the TT course, young or old. He tossed the 750 Yamaha around the tight track like a motocrosser. Although he was determined to win the TT, he unfortunately stalled his Yamaha while in complete command of the race, letting veteran Mike Haney by for the win. Again, he assuaged his disappointment by winning the short track event for the second year in a row. Although Jimmy Odom had come close to the Houston double in 1971, it seemed just a matter of time before Roberts would be the first.

The 1973 Astrodome races drew another huge crowd with a combined two-day attendance of 64,183! The races had become a happening, not just a novelty.

TT National

Heats

Fast qualifier Kenny Roberts blitzed to the first heat race win with a time that was 5 seconds quicker than any other heat. Slowed little by a restart caused after a crash involving DeWayne Keeter and Greg Hodges, Roberts finished with a big advantage over Mike Kidd (Tri) and Jimmy Odom. Odom was off the Yamaha team and back aboard the same Triumph he rode in 1971.

Several riders, including defending race champion John Hateley (Tri), jumped the original start of Heat 2 and were placed on the penalty line. New GNC champ Mark Brelsford, one of two riders left on the front row, led the restart with TT aces Sonny Burres (Tri) and Terry Dorsch (Tri) giving chase. Hateley desperate to get up front, got tangled up with Todd Sloan, both going down. Hateley got going again, but ran out of time to secure a semi transfer and was out for the night. Brelsford went on for the win with Burres and Dorsch following.

Redline Frames-sponsored Mike Haney (Tri) bested fellow TT aces Randy Scott and five-time National TT winner Eddie Mulder, all astride Triumphs. Mulder had a poor start and was charging to the front when he ran out of race. Illinois rider Mike Caves (Tri) put in a wild ride trying to get by Yamaha factory rider Don Castro for 4th. Despite all his pyrotechnics, he came up short and headed for the semi.

Triumph factory star Gary Scott headed fellow Meridian riders Paul Bostrom, and Gary Nixon protégé Steve Delagarno in Heat 4.

Semis

1971 Houston TT winner Jimmy Odom led Mike Caves to the win in Semi 1. In Semi 2, Terry Dorsch and Dave Hansen (Tri) took the last two spots in the National with hometown hero Darryl Hurst (Yam), owner of a Houston area Yamaha shop, just missing in 3rd.

Trophy Race

While Eddie Mulder would have preferred to be in the National, he made the best of the situation winning the first Trophy Race of the year. Fellow Californians Don Castro and Tom White rounded out the podium spots.

National

To no one's surprise, the yellow and black flash that was Kenny Roberts blasted out to the early lead. Roberts was spectacular, sliding the Yamaha on its cases and flying higher and further off the jump than anyone else. Mike Haney and Randy Scott gave chase. By lap 10, Roberts had a big lead over Haney. Coming off the jump on lap 11, Roberts lost concentration for a split second and stalled the big Yamaha twin as he slid into the corner. His crew jumped to his aid, but officials stopped them from helping Roberts. Confusion reigned as one of the new rules for the season was allowing outside help to restart a stalled bike. He valiantly tried to bump start the bike himself, but the high compression machine was against him and soon, the whole pack was by. Roberts got some pushing help from Eddie Wirth to get started, and began ripping through the pack. Haney couldn't believe his luck and didn't squander his opportunity. He rode the remaining portion of the race on a string, making no mistakes. Randy Scott gave chase but soon had to deal with pressure from Jimmy Odom, who took 3rd when Mike Kidd crashed with two laps to go. Roberts ended up in 10th spot, two laps down.

Short Track National

Very similar to the previous year, expectations ran high for Kenny Roberts to again sweep the short track to avenge his TT stumble. Somewhat surprising, he was well down on the grid in 21st in qualifying with unknown Mike O'Brien (Bul) on the pole.

There was a lot of new and unusual machinery at the short track. The 250cc machinery had been replaced by 360's for 1973. Triumph Team members Gary Scott and Gene Romero were ostensibly aboard factory Rickman Montesas, although the frames had been changed to Boyd's and Stelling's items! They handled much better than last year's team bikes and were competitive despite still being 250's. Since BSA's racing effort had been dissolved, 1971 GNC champion Dick Mann was also on the Triumph team. He was aboard a BSA B40-based machine that dated from the 1950's. Yamahas were very prevalent in a variety of aftermarket frames. Stock and aftermarket-framed Bultaco's were also common. Team Harley members were aboard their aging but still competitive Sprints. Dave Aldana was riding the same fast rotary-valve Kawasaki that Gary Scott rode in 1972, now up to 350cc.

Heats

Fast qualifier Mike O'Brien led early, but was quickly swallowed up by Kenny Roberts and Dick Mann. Mann held the inside line on his neat thumper as he dueled with Roberts on the opening lap. Roberts turned up the wick on the Shell Theutt-tuned Yamaha and blasted by on the outside, opening up a large advantage. Mann was a solid 2nd and O'Brien 3rd. Roberts' win was nearly 4 seconds faster than the other heats!

After a blown first start in Heat 2, Gary Scott ran handlebar-to-handlebar with Fred Smith (Yam) and Mike Gerald (Oss). Scott and Smith dueled for the lead with Scott pulling the advantage and win despite his Rickman/Montesa tying up at the stripe. Mike Gerald gave early chase, until he got tangled up with Mike Caves, who was pulling off the track with mechanical trouble. Gerald lost a bunch of places but rode like a madman to get a semi transfer.

The crash-filled third heat lived up to the Roman Coliseum atmosphere that could pervade the Astrodome arena. The event began with a jumped start, moving most of the field including Mike Kidd and Dallas Baker to the penalty line, leaving only Harley teammates Rex Beauchamp and Bart Markel in their original front row spots. The mad rush into the first turn led to a huge crash, with bikes and riders flying through the air. Texan Robert E. Lee came out on the short end of the deal and was out for the night. Alternate Gordon Duesenberry replaced him. The riders went to the line for restart number three. Rex Beauchamp and Todd Sloan crashed hard together, again stopping the event. Sloan became a star for the night when he looped his Ossa over backward going back to the line. The crowd laughed and cheered over the get off. Quick-thinking Sloan did a dramatic bow to the crowd and was greeted by thunderous applause.

The riders still had a race to run. Dave Aldana, in as an alternate for Rex Beauchamp, was now set to entertain the crowd. He had entered the race as an alternate after Robert E. Lee was carted off. Aldana wound up his Kawasaki and headed to the top of the track. He and leader Mike Kidd teamed up for a classic "High/Low" battle. They crossed the line repeatedly side-by-side. Unnoticed by the battling duo, Texan Buck Boren (Yam) had been quickly reeling them in. On the last lap Boren slipped past both with Kidd edging Aldana for 2nd.

Heat 4 was amazingly sedate after the previous craziness. Last year's TT winner John Hateley (Bul) scored a fairly easy win over 1971 Short Track winner Jimmy Odom. Odom was aboard a crusty 250 Yamaha, when his new 360 unit broke in practice.

Semis

Mike O'Brien pulled the holeshot in Semi 1 but Dave Lawson (Kaw) soon shot by. TT winner Mike Haney (Hon) and Tom White (Yam) soon engaged O'Brien in a good battle for the last transfer spot. Lawson took the victory with White getting past both Haney and out-of-luck fast timer O'Brien.

Fred Smith led Semi 2 early with Dave Aldana's rim-riding quickly bringing him up to 2nd place. He and Smith went at it hot and heavy, bringing the crowd to it's feet. At the finish, the two crossed the line side-by-side in a photo finish. It was several minutes after the race when Aldana was declared the winner by a tread width.

Trophy Race

Californian Tom Horton (Bul) led the Trophy Race wire-to-wire over road race ace Cal Rayborn (HD). The lead duo topped a field of notables including TT winner Mike Haney, Bart Markel and Mike O'Brien.

National

Favorites of the nearly 37,000 crowd were, in no particular order, Kenny Roberts, spectacular Dave Aldana and of course Texas sons Mike Kidd and Buck Boren. At the start, Gary Scott tore into the lead with Dick Mann and Kenny Roberts right with him. Mann had his vintage BSA's battery wire come off and he was out. Scott maintained a low line with Roberts pressuring hard. When Scott slipped wide coming out of Turn 4 on the third lap, Roberts shot by, never to be headed. Scott maintained 2nd and Jimmy Odom held 3rd. The rest of the pack struggled to keep up. Mike Kidd worked past Buck Boren for 4th and tried to catch Odom to no avail. Boren repassed Kidd, only to have both Kidd and a charging Dave Aldana go by. At the finish, it was Roberts with a half lap lead over Scott, Odom, Kidd, Aldana, Boren, Fred Smith, Dave Lawson, John Hateley and Tom White.

Results

Race: 25 Lap National TT
Race Time: 11:31.50

Rank	Rider	Number	Make
1.	Mike Haney, Torrance, Ca	91	Tri
2.	Randy Scott, Philomath, Ore	50	Tri
3.	Jimmy Odom, Fremont, Ca	18	Tri
4.	Gary Scott, W. Covina, Ca	64	Tri
5.	Dave Hansen, Hayward, Ca	23	Tri
6.	Mark Brelsford, Woodside, Ca	1	HD
7.	Paul Bostrom, San Ramon, Ca	46	Tri
8.	Sonny Burres, Portland, Ore	69	Tri
9.	Terry Dorsch, Granada Hills, Ca	22	Tri
10.	Kenny Roberts, Los Altos, Ca	80	Yam
11.	Mike Kidd, Hurst, Tx	72	Tri
12.	Mike Caves, Peoria, Ill	2P	Tri

Trophy Race

Rank	Rider	Number	Make
1.	Eddie Mulder, Burbank, Ca	12	Tri
2.	Don Castro, Hollister, Ca	11	Yam
3.	Tom White, Huntington Beach, Ca	42R	Nor
4.	Gary Nixon, Phoenix, Md	9	Tri
5.	Scott Brelsford, Daly City, Ca	84Y	HD
6.	Ronnie Rall, Mansfield, Oh	52	Tri
7.	Dave Sehl, Waterdown, Ont., Can	16	HD
8.	Darryl Hurst, Houston, Tx	34	Yam
9.	Eddie Wirth, Dana Point, Ca	84X	Yam
10.	Keith Mashburn, Santa Susana, Ca	19	Tri
11.	Phil Darcy, Beaumont, Tx	11N	Yam
12.	Dave Lawson, Yukon, Ok	89M	Tri

Race: 20 Lap Short Track National
Race Time: 5:20.73

Rank	Rider	Number	Make
1.	Kenny Roberts, Los Altos, Ca	80	Yam
2.	Gary Scott, W. Covina, Ca	64	Ric
3.	Jimmy Odom, Fremont, Ca	18	Yam
4.	Mike Kidd, Hurst, Tx	72	Bul
5.	Dave Aldana, Santa, Ana, Ca	13	Kaw
6.	Buck Boren, Kleburg, Tx	98N	Yam
7.	Fred Smith, Memphis, Tn	18L	Yam
8.	Dave Lawson, Yukon, Ok	89M	Kaw
9.	John Hateley, Van Nuys, Ca	98	Bul
10.	Tom White, Huntington Beach, Ca	42R	Mon
11.	Dick Mann, Richmond, Ca	2	BSA
12.	Joe Brown, Paso Robles, Ca	19Z	Yam

Trophy Race

Rank	Rider	Number	Make
1.	Tom Horton, Lancaster, Ca	75X	Bul
2.	Cal Rayborn, Spring Valley, Ca	14	HD
3.	Mike O'Brien, Danville, Ca	75Z	Bul
4.	Dave Hansen, Hayward, Ca	23	Hus
5.	Gordon Duesenberry, Wichita, Ka	81	Bul
6.	Gene Romero, San Luis Obispo, Ca	3	Ric
7.	Mert Lawwill, San Francisco, Ca	7	HD
8.	Bart Markel, Flint, Mi	4	HD
9.	Tod Sloan, Fresno, Ca	33	Oss
10.	Billy Schaeffer. Pine Grove, Pa	52A	Bul
11.	Bob Scally, Mtn View, Ca	71Z	Bul
12.	Mike Haney, Torrance, Ca	91	Hon

Grand National Points Standings after Round 2

Rank	Rider	Pts
1.	Gary Scott	200
2.	Jimmy Odom	200
3.	Kenny Roberts	165
4.	Mike Haney	150
5.	Randy Scott	120
6.	Mike Kidd	100
7.	Dave Aldana	60
8.	Dave Hansen	60
9.	Mark Brelsford	50
10.	Buck Boren	50

- Mike Haney scored his only GNC win at the TT. It was his 12th year as a Pro rider.
- Haney brought a big bore Maico to the 'Dome along with the traditional Triumph. Looks like he made the right choice.
- Triumph machines dominated the National, taking 10 places. The only dissenters were the factory Yamaha and Harley-Davidson of Kenny Roberts and Mark Brelsford.
- National Champion Brelsford looked a little tentative at Houston, placing a 6th in the TT and failing to make the short track.
- Jim Rice, the 1970 TT winner, did not attend the event.
- Dick Mann was forced out of the TT event early with a broken frame in hot laps.
- Bart Markel only spectated at Friday's TT. He did run the short track program, making it into the Trophy Race.
- For the first time since the inaugural 1968 short track, there were no Harley Sprints in the National.
- Dick Mann's vintage BSA was the only four stroke in the short track.
- Tuning whiz Erv Kanemoto barely got Gary Scott's seized machine back together after the heat race for the National. The 250 Montesa ran strong and lasted.
- Kenny Roberts' new team of tuners; Shell Thuett, Bud Meyers and Bud Askland had a very successful debut.
- Junior invitational events, called the Gulf Coast Gold Cup Races, (whew!), pitted racers from Texas and Louisiana against each other. In the short track race, Rick Simmons, Jimmie Lee and Tim Rubsan made it a Texas 1-2-3 finish. It was Texas again in the TT with Rubsan topping Bob Ewell and Louisiana rider Dan Spencer.

1973 Daytona 200
Saarinen Outlasts the Heavyweights

GNC Round #3 of 24 **Date:** March 11, 1973 **Type:** Road Race **Venue:** Daytona International Speedway **Location:** Daytona, Florida	**Purse:** $35,000.00 **Location:** Daytona, Florida **Surface:** Pavement **Course Length:** 3.84 miles **Laps:** 52 **Distance:** 200 Miles

The factory teams were back as big as ever in 1973. The mammoth budgets and numerous riders and bikes of the British teams had been neatly replaced by the Japanese efforts. Kawasaki launched the biggest attack with six full-on riders: Art Baumann from Suzuki, Yvon DuHamel, Gary Nixon, Masahiro Wada, Hurley Wilvert and Cliff Carr. Suzuki had acquired Kawasaki's Paul Smart, last year's winner Don Emde, in addition to returning riders Ron Grant and Geoff Perry. Yamaha debuted new water-cooled 350's ridden by Kel Carruthers, Kenny Roberts, new team members Don Castro and Gary Fisher. Keeping up the Daytona tradition of importing European stars was Yamaha's bringing in 250 World Champion Jarno Saarinen from Finland. Team Honda made it's first official effort since 1970; The Japanese crew prepped bikes for Steve McLaughlin and Morishito Sumiya.

Harley-Davidson's best hopes were two-time 200 winner Cal Rayborn, new National Champion Mark Brelsford and Harley's own imported star, Italian Renzo Pasolini. Team BSA, who had claimed the 1971 race and AMA Championship were gone. Gene Romero and Gary Scott were now joined by Dick Mann, whose BSA was resprayed in Triumph livery. Norton had a made a big splash in 1972 and returned with a special monocoque frame for Peter Williams, with John Cooper and Dave Aldana aboard more traditional machines. Besides the factory teams, fast semi-factory and private entries were fielded by teams such as Mel Dineson, Don Vesco, Krause Honda and hordes of independent Yamahas.

The tire issues from the previous year had led the Daytona Speedway and AMA to come up with a chicane on the backstretch to slow the bikes down. It added some distance to the track, now listed as 3.84 miles and knocked a lap off of the race. While done with rider safety in mind, the chicane received mixed reviews. Riders and tire engineers felt it could actually add to tire wear due to slowing down and accelerating hard out of the section. Both top and complete lap speeds dropped. Dunlop and Goodyear had both come out with new tire designs over the previous season. While still a concern, the tires available were thought capable of going the distance.

The Suzukis were fast out of the box with Paul Smart leading the team. Team Green was a little down on speed in comparison, with Masahiro Wada by far the fastest. Unlike the Suzuki team-which had very uniform bikes and tuning, Kawasaki riders and tuners acted somewhat independently, with very different setups. By qualifying time though, all bikes showed similar speed. The Yamahas could not match the blinding speed of the multi 750's, but their lap times were competitive, and the smaller engines required fewer gas stops. Team Manager Kel Carruthers faced some unforeseen issues with the new machines. Some gears in the transmission had not been machined properly, causing the bikes to pop out of gear. This necessitated splitting the cases and working down the offending gears by hand. Crankshaft main bearing failures were also an issue. Team Honda's machines had shown impressive, if inconsistent lap times. The Harley-Davidson's of Brelsford and Rayborn showed surprisingly good trap and lap speeds. The Norton's handled well, but the advanced frame designs could not make up for an antiquated, underpowered engine.

Time Trials

Qualifying went mostly as predicted, with the Suzuki and Kawasakis dominating the top 10. Proving that their team "switcharoo" didn't slow them, Paul Smart (Suz) was fastest at 101.871 mph with Art Baumann (Kaw) running a 100.758. Close behind was Geoff Perry this year on a 750 Suzuki at 100.754. Teammate Ron Grant, who intended only to race at Daytona, ran a 100.137. Kawasaki teammates Masahiro Wada and Yvon DuHamel turned speeds of 100.101 and 99.877 respectively. Yamaha team machines of Gary Fisher and Kenny Roberts, (riding with a dirt bike-induced groin injury), were next at 99.560 and 98.848. Ron Pierce was the first privateer on a Vesco Yamaha at 98.707. Cal Rayborn was very impressive on his XRTT, rounding out the top 10 with a 98.503.

National

Daytona's biggest crowd ever, numbering over 61,000 was on hand for the event. In a change to cut down on first lap crashes, the opening lap procedure had the riders heading directly into the infield instead of going around the big oval first. A Kawasaki trio of Gary Nixon, Art Baumann and Yvon DuHamel led the charge into Turn 1. At the conclusion of lap 1, DuHamel had taken over, followed Baumann and Nixon. Fast qualifier Paul Smart was way down in the running after blowing through the chicane and was then held by track officials till the majority of the field passed. Smart would rocket through the field, but an engine seizure would knock him out later in the race. At the front, Nixon watched Baumann and DuHamel dice heavily though the opening laps. On lap 9, Steve Dalgarno fell in the infield turn. Dalgarno either hit or dropped some fluids causing leaders DuHamel and Baumann to crash when they came into the corner side-by-side. Both returned to the race, but dropped out with trouble from the spill. Soon after Mark Brelsford came into an infield turn flat out only to find teammate Larry Darr in the race line. Brelsford rear-ended Darr in a horrifying accident. Darr and machine were sent spinning off the track. Brelsford's gas tank and exhaust system were torn apart at the same time. Raw gasoline hit the open exhaust and rider and machine were engulfed in a fireball. Brelsford suffered serious multiple fractures and amazingly, only minor burn injuries. Darr suffered severe leg injuries. Gary Nixon now became the race leader. Nixon opened up a nice advantage over the next 10 laps till his Kawasaki seized. Geoff Perry had been in 2nd and now led. His time up front was brief; within a lap his Suzuki lost fire. A bad day for Team Harley-Davidson got worse when Cal Rayborn's bike seized at speed at the chicane. Rayborn was tossed off hard, breaking a collarbone and several ribs. Back to the race, Gary Fisher had been battling with Jarno Saarinen and Ron Grant and took over the lead. He led for around 5 circuits before slowing for a pit stop and then out for good with bottom end problems. Grant took over in front of Saarinen, but was soon struck by the day's leaders curse, and was also out with ignition failure. Similar to 1972, attrition had knocked out many favorites, but this year there were still some heavyweights up front. Saarinen didn't put a wheel wrong over the remaining laps to win with a comfortable margin. Kel Carruthers ran a steady race in finishing 2nd in his best Daytona run. Rookie Jim Evans, aboard Don Emde's former Motorcycle Weekly, Mel Dineson sponsored Yamaha, outlasted a battle with Dave Smith, who ran out of fuel for 3rd. Dick Mann rode fast and patient ride taking his "Triumph" to 4th spot. Both Evans and Mann came from way back on the grid, 56th and 62nd respectively, putting in amazing rides. Privateer Conrad Urbaowski (Yam) was a fine 5th. Morio Sumiya put one of the factory Hondas into 6th. Don Emde, the lone survivor of the Suzuki team, soldiered to a 7th place finish. Rounding out the top 10 were Mick Grant, Don Castro and Steve McLaughlin. There were no Kawasaki team bikes left running at the finish.

Results

Race: 200 Mile Road Race National

Rank	Rider	Number	Make
1.	Jarno Saarinen, Turku, Finland	10	Yam
2.	Kel Carruthers, San Diego, Ca	73	Yam
3.	Jim Evans, San Bernardino, Ca	47	Yam
4.	Dick Mann, Richmond, Ca	2	Tri
5.	Conrad Urbanowski, Miramar, Fl	28	Yam
6.	Morio Sumiya, Tokyo, Japan	15	Hon
7.	Don Emde, Chula Vista, Ca	25	Suz
8.	Mick Grant, Wakefield, England	60	Yam
9.	Don Castro, Hollister, Ca	11	Yam
10.	Steve McLaughlin, Duarte, Ca	83	Hon
11.	Harry Cone, Sherman, Tx	77	Yam
12.	Frank Gillespie, Danville, Ca	76	Yam
13.	Dave Smith, Lakewood, Ca	20	Yam
14.	Gary Scott, Baldwin Park, Ca	64	Tri

Rank	Rider	Number	Make
15.	Doug Sehl, Waterdown, Ont., Can	45	HD
16.	Robert Winters, Ft. Smith, Ark	4	Yam
17.	Mert Lawwill, San Francisco, Ca	7	HD
18.	Martin Sharpe, Northhants, England	104	Yam
19.	Andy Lascoutx, Ashland, Mass	92	Yam
20.	George Kerker, Glendale, Ca	51	Hon

Grand National Points Standings after Round 3

Rank	Rider	Pts
1.	Gary Scott	208
2.	Jimmy Odom	200
3.	Kenny Roberts	165
4.	Mike Haney	150
5.	Kel Carruthers	144
6.	Randy Scott	120
7.	Jim Evans	120
8.	Dick Mann	106
9.	Mike Kidd	90
10.	Conrad Urbanowski	72

Extra Extra

- A new record crowd of 62,200 witnessed the race.
- An equally-huge crowd of 94 riders from 12 countries took the green.
- Jarno Saarinen took at least $12,350.00 home to Finland.
- Saarinen may have had a leg up on the other Yamaha riders as he rode a prototype of the new water-cooled bike on the GP circuit.
- Last practice session, showing blistering of the rear Goodyear on Steve McLaughlin's factory Honda, led to wholesale last minute tire changing to Dunlops. The new tires were slightly bigger, leading to clearance problems on several bikes and cutting an oil line on McLaughlin's.
- Besides the DuHamel/Baumann crash/retirement and Nixon's seizure, the rest of team's ailments included engine problems for Masahiro Wada and flat tires for Hurley Wilvert and Cliff Carr. Carr's ailment occurring while in the lead pack.
- Top Harley-Davidson survivors were Doug Sehl and Mert Lawwill who were 16th and 17th. Renzo Pasolini was scored in 52nd place.
- Dave Smith ran out of gas for the second year in a row while battling for a top spot. He still managed to finish 14th.
- Don Castro was in the lead pack till slowed by a fuel tank leak, fading back to 9th.
- The John Player Norton's had a mixed day. Peter Williams fell out of the top 20 after minor mechanical trouble. Dave Aldana was doing business on the oldest bike on the team till his machine gave up. John Cooper's machine also went out with mechanical trouble.
- Gary Fisher topped the Lightweight race on his factory Yamaha.
- 1966 Daytona winner Buddy Elmore returned for his last run at the 200, finishing 20th on a Yamaha.
- Third place finisher Jim Evans' father, Don, took back to back Amateur wins in 1949 and '50.
- In a sad note, both Jarno Saarinen and Renzo Pasolini were both killed later in the season at the Italian Grand Prix.

Top 15 Daytona 200 Qualifying Speeds

1.		Paul Smart	Suz	101.871 MPH
2.		Art Baumann	Kaw	100.758
3.		Geoff Perry	Suz	100.754
4.		Ron Grant	Suz	100.137
5.		Mashiro Wada	Kaw	100.101
6.		Yvon DuHamel	Kaw	99.877
7.		Gary Fisher	Yam	99.560
8.		Kenny Roberts	Yam	98.848
9.		Ron Pierce	Yam	98.707
10.		Cal Rayborn	HD	98.503
11.		Jarno Saarinen	Yam	98.105
12.		Mike Lane	Hon	97.966
13.		Mark Brelsford	HD	97.945
14.		Dave Smith	Yam	97.848
15.		Yutaka Oda	Yam	97.730

GNC Round #4 of 24 **Date:** April 1, 1973 **Type:** Road Race **Venue:** Dallas International Motor Speedway **Location:** Lewisville, Tx	**Purse:** $25,000.00 **Surface:** Pavement **Course Length:** 2.5 **Laps:** 30 **Distance:** 75 Miles

Factory Suzuki rider Paul Smart outpaced a strong field at the one and only Dallas Grand National Championship Road Race. Smart took over the lead when a dominant Yvon Duhamel fell out of the lead just past halfway. A very tough Gary Nixon barely topped a persistent Kenny Roberts to round out the podium. For Englishman Paul Smart, the event was his second and final GNC victory. It was Suzuki's first "official" victory since Ron Grant's 1970 Kent, Wa win. The rough and bumpy Dallas circuit used a drag strip to hook the twisty sections together. A small spectator turnout hurt the chances for a GNC return to the facility.

In an interesting move, the AMA shook up the road race qualifying method by adding a Semi event along with the two regular heats. Each heat would have the first fifteen racers advance to the main with the remainder headed to the semi event. The top ten from the semi would go to the National. The change was to try and get the road racers to mix it more 'ala dirt track. The day's racing did turn out to be hotly-contested with great battles in all events.

Kenny Roberts 3rd place finish moved him ahead of Gary Scott who was 10th on the day. The top two totals were 285 and 226. Jimmy Odom and Mike Haney didn't score any points and slipped back to third and fifth respectively.

Heats

The master of the "full tank and cold tires", Yvon Duhamel (Kaw), blitzed into the early lead of the first 8-lap heat race. Straining to keep up was a tight pack composed of Yamaha teammates Kenny Roberts and Don Castro, Japanese star Masahiro Wada (Suz) and Cliff Carr (Kaw). Roberts surged ahead with two laps to go, but Duhamel was long gone. Wada had moved into third, barely holding off a charging Castro at the finish. Just behind, Carr held off a spirited charge from Canadian Doug Sehl on a Harley-Davidson XRTT.

Heat 2 saw Gary Fisher (Yam) pull the holeshot closely followed by Art Baumann (Kaw) and New Zealand's Geoff Perry (Suz). Englishman Baumann took over on lap 2 and turned on the afterburners. Perry powered by Fisher on the main straight to take over 2nd spot. Gary Nixon (Kaw) was on the move, knocking Fisher back another spot and set his sights on Perry. Nixon quickly moved by Perry by lap 4. Also charging was Paul Smart (Suz) who soon joined the battle for second. He passed Perry and was all over Nixon. With one lap to go, Smart went by Nixon, with Perry hounding the two-time Grand National Champion for third. Nixon was not intimidated by the international stars and repassed Smart to take a second behind the checked out Baumann.

Semi

Veteran Ron Grant (Suz) quickly took command of the Semi event followed by 1969 Grand National Champion Mert Lawwill (HD) and Canadian rookie expert Steve Baker (Yam). Baker showed his already considerable pavement skills by moving by Lawwill on lap 3 and latching on to Grant. Baker's 350 Yamaha was all over Grant through the twisties, but Grant would simply motor away on the straights. Baker twice had runs on the outside of Grant on the front straightaway in the closing laps only to be forced wide and back off the gas. At the flag it was Grant and Baker, followed by Lawwill who just held off a persistent Steve Dalgarno at the stripe.

National

To no one's surprise, Yvon Duhamel blasted off line ahead of the other 39 riders. Behind him, Art Baumann, Hurley Wilvert (Kaw), Masahiro Wada, Kenny Roberts, Gary Nixon and Paul Smart scrapped over the next positions. Baumann tossed his Kawasaki away in turn 2 on the third lap. Wada began fading and Nixon was in 2nd spot by lap 6. Smart moved by Nixon soon after. Kenny Roberts moved out of the pack and was soon hounding

Nixon for third. Further back, there was a great "international" battle between Wada, Don Castro, Gary Fisher, Doug Sehl, Jerry Greene and Geoff Perry.

Up front, Duhamel was flying, pulling distance on the field on every lap. Unfortunately his factory Kawasaki let him down this day on lap 14; out with a broken piston. Smart was the new leader by a large margin, with Nixon trying to close the gap. Nixon's efforts were stymied by the relentless charge of "dirt tracker" Kenny Roberts. The two went at it fairing to fairing all over the course with neither able to break away. Roberts managed to get past, but Nixon got the bit between his teeth and finally put the upstart behind him on lap 22. Behind them, Fisher and Perry had broken free of the multi-rider battle and were going at it for fourth. As the laps wound down, Nixon, finally free of Roberts, actually whittled Smart's lead down, but just ran out of race. Roberts maintained third with Geoff Perry topping Fisher in the closing laps. Castro likewise got by Wilvert. Doug Sehl put in a great race on the Harley-Davidson, with Steve Baker and Gary Scott rounding out the top 10.

Results

Race: 75 Mile Road Race National

Rank	Rider	Number	Make
1.	Paul Smart, Sante Fe Springs, Ca	8	Suz
2.	Gary Nixon, Phoenix, Md	9	Kaw
3.	Kenny Roberts, Los Altos, Ca	80	Yam
4.	Geoff Perry, Auckland, NZ	65	Suz
5.	Gary Fisher, Parkesburg, Pa	21	Yam
6.	Don Castro, Hollister, Ca	11	Yam
7.	Hurley Wilvert, Westminster, Ca	91	Kaw
8.	Doug Sehl, Waterdown, Ont., Can	45	HD
9.	Steve Baker, Bellingham, Wa	41	Yam
10.	Gary Scott, Baldwin Park, Ca	64	Tri
11.	Jim Dunn, Everett, Wa	75	Yam
12.	Robert Winters, Ft. Smith, Ark	4	Yam
13.	Mike Ninci, Kansas, Mo	96	Yam
14.	Steve McLaughlin, Duarte, Ca	83	Hon
15.	Ron Pierce, Bakersfield, Ca	97	Yam
16.	Buddy Elmore, El Paso, Tx	81	Yam
17.	Conrad Urbanowski, Miramar, Fl	28	Yam
18.	Steve Dalgarno, Baltimore, Md	114	Yam
19.	Gene Romero, San Luis Obispo, Ca	3	Tri
20.	Paul Higgens, Islington, Ont., Can	6	Yam

Grand National Points Standings after Round 4

Rank	Rider	Pts
1.	Kenny Roberts	285
2.	Gary Scott	226
3.	Jimmy Odom	200
4.	Paul Smart	180
5.	Mike Haney	150
6.	Kel Carruthers	144
7.	Gary Nixon	144
8.	Jim Evans	120
9.	Randy Scott	120
10.	Dick Mann	106

- The Dallas International Motor Speedway had an unusually short and tragic history. The state-of-the-art track was built in 1969 and featured an NHRA sanctioned ¼ mile dragstrip with a large, distinctive timing tower.. The track ran the high profile NHRA SpringNationals it's opening year. A 2.5 mile road course, ½ mile paved oval and ¼ mile dirt track were later added, part of the owners vision of a complete motorsports complex. The tracks second year was disastrous; repeated rainouts and flooding sent the track deep in debt. Complaints from neighbors about noise and traffic did not help and led to a 10:00 pm curfew. In a money saving move, the tracks sanction was changed to the less expensive IHRA division. In 1971 a news reporter riding in Art Arfon's jet dragster was killed when the vehicle went out of control, also killing two spectators. The track sank under mounting debts and ran it's last season in 1973. It was sold to the Xerox corporation soon after. The company never developed the property. The timing tower stood till the early 1990's. Eventually a Honda dealership and shopping center were built on the site. Today, no traces remain of the hard luck facility.

1973 San Jose Half-Mile
Castro Scores First Win!
Gary Scott Takes Points Lead
Lloyd Houchins Fatally Injured

GNC Round #5 of 24 **Date:** May 20, 1973 **Type:** Half-Mile **Venue:** Santa Clara Fairgrounds **Location:** San Jose, Ca	**Purse:** $12,000.00 **Surface:** Dirt **Course Length**: ½ Mile **Laps:** 20 **Distance:** 10 Miles

Yamaha factory pilot Don Castro scored his first (and only) GNC win at the San Jose GNC Half-Mile event. The talented Castro grew up just down the road in Hollister, Ca, making this a very popular victory. Gary Scott put in an impressive ride from mid-pack for 2ⁿᵈ position. Scott's strong finish, coupled with a DNF for points leader Kenny Roberts, put Scott atop the GNC points race. Rex Beauchamp was the first non-Californian and Harley-Davidson rider home in third. The track was typical daytime San Jose, with a slick, narrow, black groove negating much passing. This coupled with the new AMA format of just two riders from each heat and each semi made it a nerve racking day for the whole field. Those not making the main went to a Trophy Race.

Tempering the excitement of the day was the great loss of California rider Lloyd Houchins during the second heat race. The accident occurred at the flag when Houchins and another rider got together. Houchins was a popular, successful professional racer. He was a top 10 GNC competitor with several top placings including a podium finish at Ascot in 1970. There were also other tragedies the same day on the international scene; see "*Extras*".

Gary Scott climbed back atop the GNC points standings via his runner-up finish in the main. Kenny Roberts only made a couple laps in the National before suffering a mechanical problem. His 12ᵗʰ place dropped him in behind Scott in the rankings. Don Castro's win blasted him up to third in points out of nowhere. Jimmy Odom did not make the National and slipped back to the fourth spot.

Time Trials

Kenny Roberts (Yam) shattered rookie Scott Brelsford's track record of 26.58 (set last year as a Junior) with a new mark of 26.08. Robert's fantastic lap raised some eyebrows, but it was only 'cause he was way quicker than anybody else. The next closest time was Scott Brelsford breaking his own time with a more reasonable 26.43. Three more riders broke the old record including Cal Rayborn (HD) at 26.47, Mert Lawwill (HD) a 26.50 and Gene Romero (Tri) at 26.56.

Heats

Fast-timer Kenny Roberts blasted to the holeshot of Heat 1 and never looked back. Jim Rice, master of "the notch" at San Jose was strong in the second and last direct transfer. Rice was aboard, surprise; a Harley-Davidson XR750, instead of his usual BSA. Rice had spent almost his entire career aboard BSA's; but times were a changing and Rice looked good in his V-twin debut. He had been dominant at San Jose over the years and it was a great place to try his new ride. Close in 3ʳᵈ spot was last year's winner Gene Romero (Tri).

Don Castro repeated teammate Roberts disappearing acting in Heat 2, winning by a comfortable margin in the fastest heat of the afternoon. Runner-up Gary Scott took the other transfer aboard his factory Triumph. In 3ʳᵈ spot was Scott Brelsford, on a factory Harley like brother Mark, the GNC champ. Brelsford tangled handlebars with veteran Chuck Palmgren, who took the 4ᵗʰ spot on his Dan Gurney/Steed Yamaha. Lloyd Houchin's fatal accident occurred when Houchin's and Pat McCaul got tangled up fighting for 5ᵗʰ position. McCaul was not seriously injured.

In Heat 3, Michigan's Rex Beauchamp (HD) scored the only non-Californian heat win of the day. Mike Kidd, on the Big D Triumph, rode hard from way back into the 2ⁿᵈ spot to break up a Harley sweep as Beauchamp's teammates Cal Rayborn and Dave Sehl were third and fourth.

Mert Lawwill (HD) took an easy-looking win in Heat 4 followed by Randy Scott on the Fred's Distributing/Torco Triumph, rookie Larry Gino (Tri) and Frank Gillespie (Yam).

Semis

Only two riders transferred to the National from each semi. Scott Brelsford, headed veteran Eddie Mulder (Tri) by a comfortable margin in Semi 1. Cal Rayborn riding hurt, (see *Extras*) still had desire, if not stamina, led the early laps in Semi 2. Gene Romero was a solid 2nd, but Chuck Palmgren was about to disrupt the order. He slipped by Romero and pressured a tiring Rayborn off the groove soon after. Romero was also coming, knocking Rayborn back to 3rd to take the last transfer to the National.

Trophy Race

Cal Rayborn hadn't given up, shooting out front, but quickly slipped the groove again. Canadian Dave Sehl put his factory Harley-Davidson out front ahead of the Triumphs ridden by Californians Pat Marinacci and Frank Gillespie. Rayborn slipped way back by the end of the race.

National

Kenny Roberts pulled another holeshot at the start of the National with Don Castro, Rex Beauchamp and Mike Kidd on his heels and the rest of the field stringing out behind. Roberts' ride was over after two laps with a reported broken ignition wire. Castro assumed the top spot and began pulling away. Gary Scott, who was as far back as 7th spot, put on the ride of the day. He worked into the top 5, passing Jim Rice for fourth. He began applying heavy pressure to Mike Kidd. At the halfway point, Kidd slid down in turn 3, possibly because of fading brakes. Kidd suffered leg injuries from the fall. Scott, now third, next set his sights on Beauchamp. After several laps of pressure, Scott moved by with 3 laps remaining. Castro, benefitting from all the racing going on behind, stretched to a big lead at the flag. Scott was making up distance, but had to settle for 2nd spot. Beauchamp was a solid third, Rice was 4th in a fine Harley debut and rookie Scott Brelsford was very impressive rounding out the top 5 in his first National.

Results

Race: 20 Lap Half Mile National

Rank	Rider	Number	Make
1.	Don Castro, Hollister, Ca	11	Yam
2.	Gary Scott, Baldwin Park, Ca	64	Tri
3.	Rex Beauchamp, Milford, Mi	31	HD
4.	Jim Rice, Portola Valley, Ca	24	HD
5.	Scott Brelsford, Daly City, Ca	84Y	HD
6.	Mert Lawwill, San Francisco, Ca	7	HD
7.	Randy Scott, Portland, Ore	50	Tri
8.	Chuck Palmgren, Freehold, NJ	38	Yam
9.	Mike Kidd, Hurst, Tx	72	Tri
10.	Gene Romero, San Luis Obispo, Ca	3	Tri
11.	Eddie Mulder, Northridge, Ca	12	Tri
12.	Kenny Roberts, Los Altos, Ca	80	Yam

Trophy Race

Rank	Rider	Number	Make
1.	Dave Sehl, Waterdown, Ont., Can	16	HD
2.	Pat Marinacci, Seattle, Wa	67	Tri
3.	Frank Gillespie, Berkeley, Ca	76	Yam
4.	Terry Dorsch, Granada Hills, Ca	22	Tri
5.	Sonny Burres, Portland, Ore	69	Tri
6.	Chuck Joyner, Oregon City, Ore	60	Tri

Rank	Rider	Number	Make
7.	Dave Hansen, Hayward, Ca	23	Tri
8.	DeWayne Keeter, Oakview, Ca	44	HD
9.	Cal Rayborn, Spring Valley, Ca	14	HD
10.	Eddie Wirth, Dana Point, Ca	84X	Yam
11.	Tom Rockwood, Gardena, Ca	88	Tri
12.	Larry Gino, San Bernardino, Ca	96R	Tri

Grand National Points Standings after Round 5

Rank	Rider	Pts
1.	Gary Scott	346
2.	Kenny Roberts	294
3.	Don Castro	234
4.	Jimmy Odom	200
5.	Paul Smart	180
6.	Randy Scott	160
7.	Mike Haney	150
8.	Kel Carruthers	144
9.	Gary Nixon	144
10.	Jim Evans	120

Extra Extra

- Don Castro's GNC win was a long time coming. He had turned Expert in 1970 and put in stints as a Triumph factory rider and as a privateer before being picked up by Yamaha who recognized his great all-around talent.
- Castro's win was the bright spot in a dark day for motorcycle racing. In addition to the loss of Lloyd Houchins, two other well known racers lost their lives on this day. Recent Daytona winner Jarno Saarinen and Renzo Pasolini were both killed in a multi-rider crash at Monza, Italy during the Italian Grand Prix. Saarinen was a former 250 World Champion. Pasolini was the 250 Italian National Champion and had finished 3rd at the 1972 Ontario National.
- Cal Rayborn was hampered by his collarbone that he broke at Daytona and reinjured at the British Match Races and at Imola.
- Jim Rice had received some tuning help from legend Tom Sifton to get his new Harley-Davidson dialed in.
- Rick Hocking (Yam) topped Triumph riders John Gennai and Dan White in a Junior Invitational race.
- 84 Experts vied for the 36 rider field.
- The Main featured great brand variety; 5 Triumphs, 4 Harley-Davidsons and 3 Yamahas.

1973 Road Atlanta
Geoff Perry Wins Close Road Atlanta
Roberts Back atop GNC Points

GNC Round #6 of 24 **Date:** June 3, 1973 **Type:** Road Race **Venue:** Road Atlanta **Location:** Flowery Branch, Ga	**Purse:** $22,000.00 **Surface:** Pavement **Course Length:** 2.52 Miles **Laps:** 29 **Distance:** 75 Miles

New Zealand star Geoff Perry scored his one and only GNC victory at Road Atlanta by a very narrow margin over Kel Carruthers. The two battled right to the flag with a charge by Carruthers coming up less than a foot short. It was Suzuki's second road race National win in a row. Kenny Roberts had another strong pavement run, and his third place finish put him atop the GNC points once again. Yvon Duhamel put in the ride of the day after an off-course excursion while leading early dropped him way back. Duhamel charged through the field and finished a fast-closing 4th place.

Kenny Roberts' GNC point total was up to 404, topping Gary Scott, who managed an 11th place in the National. Kel Carruthers runner-up finish moved him to third in points, up from eighth. Carruthers, like most of the pavement-only riders, really didn't figure into the race for the GNC crown. Don Castro failed to score any points and slipped back a spot, his total still at 234.

Heats

Gary Nixon shot out front at the start of Heat 1 aboard the Erv Kanemoto-tuned factory Kawasaki. Nixon was followed early on by Kenny Roberts (Yam), Dallas winner Paul Smart and his Suzuki teammate Geoff Perry. By lap 2, Smart had moved by Roberts for second and was closing on Nixon. On lap 6, just as Smart closed up, Nixon had a connecting rod break. Smart cruised to the finish, trailed by Roberts, Perry, Cliff Carr (Kaw) and Gary Fisher (Yam).

Heat 2 saw another Kawasaki bolt out front, but this time Yvon Duhamel's ride was strong till the end. Duhamel stretched out to a huge lead by the finish. Making it a Kawasaki sweep of the top 3 spots were teammates Art Baumann and Hurley Wilvert.

Semi

Trying to salvage the day, Erv Kanemoto and the rest of the Nixon crew performed a rapid engine swap for the Semi/consolation race. In the race, Ron Grant (Suz) led early till Nixon worked by on the third lap. Nixon looked strong, but incredibly, on lap 6 another rod let go, destroying the cases. Grant went on to the win followed by Frank Gillespie and Howard Lynggard.

National

Kel Carruthers got a fantastic holeshot off the line, chased by Yvon Duhamel, Paul Smart, and Kenny Roberts. DuHamel soon worked by Carruthers for the lead. When Duhamel crossed the line at the end of lap 1, he had an amazing 4 second + lead over the field. The French-Canadian hit turn 1 with a little over-exuberance, running off course as a result. He did not fall, but was now way back in the middle of the 40 rider field. Smart took over the lead, but just a couple of laps later crashed out of contention in Turn 7. Kenny Roberts now assumed the lead with Carruthers right with him. They were soon joined by a charging Geoff Perry. The smaller Yamahas could pull some ground in the corners, but that 750 Suzuki had big power on the straights. On the tenth lap, Carruthers moved to the lead with Perry following and Roberts falling to third. Two laps later, Perry took the top spot with Carruthers moving back by on lap 16. Roberts faded a bit with a cooked rear tire.

At the midway point of the race, the lead trio was followed by Gary Fisher (Yam), Art Baumann (Kaw) and a flying Duhamel. Over the closing laps, Perry and Carruthers continued swapping the lead. On the last lap, Carruthers had the advantage through the slow corners, but he bobbled coming into the last turn allowing Perry to grab the preferred inside line. Despite this, Carruthers got a great drive on the outside, but another wobble allowed Perry to hold on for the win by less than a foot. Roberts held third ahead of a rapidly-closing Duhamel. Rounding out the top ten were Gary Fisher, Cliff Carr, Jerry Greene, Hurley Wilvert, Dave Smith and a thoroughly out-powered Cal Rayborn.

Results

Race: 75 Mile Road Race National

Rank	Rider	Number	Make
1.	Geoff Perry, Auckland, NZ	65	Suz
2.	Kel Carruthers, San Diego, Ca	73	Yam
3.	Kenny Roberts, Los Altos, Ca	80	Yam
4.	Yvon DuHamel, LaSalle, Ont., Can	17	Kaw
5.	Gary Fisher, Parkesburg, Pa	21	Yam
6.	Cliff Carr, Arlington, Mass	26	Kaw
7.	Jerry Greene, San Mateo, Ca	57	Yam
8.	Hurley Wilvert, Westminster, Ca	91	Kaw
9.	Dave Smith, Lakewood, Ca	20	Yam
10.	Cal Rayborn, Spring Valley, Ca	14	HD
11.	Gary Scott, Baldwin Park, Ca	64	Tri
12.	Jim Evans, San Bernardino, Ca	47	Yam
13.	Doug Libby, Milford, Mi	89	Yam
14.	Ron Pierce, Bakersfield, Ca	97	Yam
15.	Steve McLaughlin, Duarte, Ca	83	Yam
16.	Mike Ninci, Kansas City, Mo	95	Yam
17.	Robert Winters, Ft. Smith, Ark	4	Yam
18.	Marty Lunde, Hermosa Beach, Ca	56	Yam
19.	Dick Mann, Richmond, Ca	2	Tri
20.	Jeff March, Acme, Pa	32	Yam

Grand National Points Standings after Round 6

Rank	Rider	Pts
1.	Kenny Roberts	404
2.	Gary Scott	357
3.	Kel Carruthers	276
4.	Don Castro	234
5.	Jimmy Odom	200
6.	Paul Smart	180
7.	Geoff Perry	165
8.	Randy Scott	160
9.	Mike Haney	150
10.	Gary Nixon	144

- Yvon DuHamel set a new lap record during the National of 94.7 mph.
- Team Suzuki was forced to hack about half an inch off their seat tops by the AMA. Apparently a switch to a higher profile tire and longer shock absorbers raised the bikes height a hair over the seat height allowed.
- The Yamaha Grand Prix team officially withdrew from the 1973 season due to the death of Jarno Saarinen and injuries to teammate Hideo Kanaya suffered at the Italian GP.
- Cal Rayborn and Gary Scott were the first four strokes home in 10th and 11th places. Dick Mann was back in 19th.
- Yamaha announced they were planning to sell a 700cc version of their present 500 4 cylinder GP racer over the coming months, with a price tag of around $3500.00. Kel Carruthers and Gary Fisher were to jet to Japan to test the bike right after Road Atlanta.
- Ted Henter topped the Junior race over John Long and Billy Labrie; all were Yamaha mounted.

1973 Louisville Half-Mile
Canadian "Sehl's" to Third Louisville GNC
Harley Sweeps First Five

GNC Round #7 of 24	**Purse:** $12,000.00
Date: June 9, 1973	**Surface:** Limestone
Type: Half-Mile	**Course Length:** ½ Mile
Venue: Louisville Downs	**Laps:** 20
Location: Louisville, Ky	**Distance:** 10 Miles

For the third time in four years, Canadian cushion-master Dave Sehl won the Louisville National. Sehl's mastery of the track rivaled Bart Markel's three wins; though Markel's were all back-to-back. Sehl's run was interrupted by Mark Brelsford's 1972 win, when Sehl was the runner-up. It was not an easy night though as Sehl had to come from a Semi event on the Babe DeMay-tuned factory Harley just to make the show. It was half-mile specialist Sehl's sixth and final GNC win. Veteran teammate Mert Lawwill had his best run of the year in second. Jim Rice scored his best finish yet aboard his new Harley-Davidson XR750. Michigan riders Rex Beauchamp and Corky Keener made it a top 5 sweep for the Harley brand. All seven Louisville GNC's had been won by the Milwaukee brand.

There was not much change in the top order of the GNC points. Gary Scott and Kenny Roberts finished 6th and 7th, allowing Scott to close within 37 points of leader Roberts. There were no changes in the top 5 spots. Due to their great runs at Louisville, Rex Beauchamp, Jim Rice and Mert Lawwill all moved into the top 10.

Time Trials

1969 Grand National champ Mert Lawwill reeled of an impressive 25.34 to top the 70+ National entries. Literally one tick off was San Jose winner Don Castro at 25.35. Castro had shod his factory Yamaha with a Dunlop Universal Trials rear tire, wowing the crowd with huge roostertails up near the fence during practice and qualifications.

Heats

Mert Lawwill quickly shot out in front of the pack in Heat 1, pursued by Dave Sehl. As Lawwill stretched his lead, Gary Scott (Tri) began applying pressure to Sehl for the second transfer spot. On lap 5, Scott got by Sehl in the first turn. Two-time winner Sehl was headed to the semi. This set the first three spots in what would be the fastest heat of the night.

Two-time GNC Champion Dick Mann looked strong on his new factory Triumph, leading the first lap of Heat 2 till Don Castro fell in turn 3 after making contact with Gene Romero (Tri). Castro's bike was back on the line for the restart, with Mann repeating his holeshot. Chuck Palmgren (Yam) held second most of the race, but had to fend off persistent Jimmy Zeigler aboard Delbert Bushes's rapid BSA. Palmgren just managed to keep the diminutive Ohioan behind him to grab the spot with Zeigler and the rest of the pack semi-bound. Mann's win was the only non-Harley bright spot of the night.

Veteran Jim Rice scooted out to the early lead of Heat 3 ahead of GNC points leader Kenny Roberts. Roberts pressured hard early, but after getting way out of shape, settled in behind Rice. Behind Roberts', Corky Keener, Gary Nixon (Tri) and Keith Ulicki battled over third spot. Keener secured third with Ulicki zapping Nixon for fourth.

Rex Beauchamp blasted off the line in Heat 4, never to be seen by the pack again. Rookie Expert Scott Brelsford ran second, hotly pursued by Dave Aldana (Nor) and Charlie Seale (HD). Aldana took the spot on lap 3 only to have his kill button short, knocking him out of contention. Brelsford regained the transfer spot and followed Beauchamp into the National with Seale trailing.

Semis

In the first Semi event, Dave Sehl did not squander his last shot at the National, quickly rolling out front to a big lead. Michigan cushion ace Teddy Newton put his BSA into the big show with a solid second. Behind the front runners, Larry Darr, Charlie Seale and Frank Gillespie squabbled over third. Darr, still on the mend from his Daytona injuries, took the position, which was made a little easier when Seale dropped out with engine woes.

343

In Semi 2, Don Castro took control early with Corky Keener giving chase. Keener worked by on lap 4. Castro looked to have the last spot to the National sewed up till forced out with ignition troubles. Rookie Mike Johnson (HD) was the recipient of Castro's spot and would advance to his first GNC ahead of former GNC champs Gary Nixon and Gene Romero and veterans Ronnie Rall and Cal Rayborn.

Trophy Race

The 12-lap Trophy Race turned into an early battle between fellow Buckeyes Larry Darr and Jimmy Zeigler. Veteran Darr topped second year-Expert Zeigler in a good race. Darr appeared back in form from his Daytona injuries. Keith Ulicki took third with former National champs Gary Nixon and Gene Romero, both on Triumphs, rounding out the top 5.

National

Dave Sehl and Mert Lawwill pulled ahead of the field at the start of the 20-lap National and quickly disappeared. Despite the track being grooved up by National time, there was still some good racing behind the first two riders. Corky Keener and Jim Rice ran nose-to-tail for much of the race. Rice managed to slip by for the last podium spot with three laps to go. Gary Scott ran in 5th spot early in the race ahead of Rex Beauchamp. Beauchamp passed Scott and caught the Keener/Rice battle late in the race. On the last lap, he passed Keener for 4th position. Kenny Roberts ran the high line through much of the race and had managed to pass Dick Mann for 8th spot at the halfway point and Chuck Palmgren for 7th with 3 laps to go. At the flag it was Sehl, Lawwill, Rice, Beauchamp, Keener, Scott, Roberts, Palmgren, Mann and Scott Brelsford rounding out the top ten.

Results

Race: 20 Lap Half-Mile National

Rank	Rider	Number	Make
1.	Dave Sehl, Waterdown, Ont., Can	16	HD
2.	Mert Lawwill, San Francisco, Ca	7	HD
3.	Jim Rice, Palo Alto, Ca	24	HD
4.	Rex Beauchamp, Milford, Mi	31	HD
5.	Corky Keener, Goodrich, Mi	62	HD
6.	Gary Scott, W. Covina, Ca	64	Tri
7.	Kenny Roberts, San Carlos, Ca	80	Yam
8.	Chuck Palmgren, Freehold, NJ	38	Yam
9.	Dick Mann, Richmond, Ca	2	Tri
10.	Scott Brelsford, Daly City, Ca	84Y	HD
11.	Mike Johnson, Flint, Mi	14E	HD
12.	Teddy Newton, Pontiac, Mi	40	BSA

Race: Trophy Race

Rank	Rider	Number	Make
1.	Larry Darr, Mansfield, Oh	94	HD
2.	Jimmy Zeigler, Bellville, Oh	9F	BSA
3.	Keith Ulicki, Kenosha, Wi	86	HD
4.	Gary Nixon, Phoenix, MD	9	Tri
5.	Gene Romero, San Luis Obispo, Ca	3	Tri
6.	Terry Dorsch, Granada Hills, Ca	22	Tri
7.	Steve Gardner, Peoria, Ill	38P	HD
8.	Eddie Wirth, Dana Point, Ca	84X	Yam
9.	Frank Gillespie, Berkeley, Ca	76	Yam
10.	Bert Cummings, Flint, Mi	97E	HD
11.	Cal Rayborn, Spring Valley, Ca	14	HD
12.	Randy Scott, Philomath, Ore	50	Tri

Grand National Points Standings after Round 7

Rank	Rider	Pts
1.	Kenny Roberts	444
2.	Gary Scott	407
3.	Kel Carruthers	276
4.	Don Castro	234
5.	Jimmy Odom	200
6.	Paul Smart	180
7.	Rex Beauchamp	180
8.	Jim Rice	180
9.	Mert Lawwill	175
10.	Geoff Perry	165

Extra Extra

- Dave Sehl took home $2300.00 for his efforts.
- Larry Darr's take for the Trophy Race was $350.00.
- While this was Dave Sehl's last National win, he continued to be a top National and Regional contender into the late 1970's. The dirt track specialist scored 6 Grand National wins at some of the most famous venues on the circuit, including 3 victories at Louisville, the Charity Newsies and Terre Haute half-miles and the 1972 Atlanta Mile. He finished 10th in the 1972 GNC points standings. Ronnie Rall said Sehl was so smooth and controlled that he always looked like he was out for a Sunday ride.
- Around Louisville time came the painful news that AMA Grand National Champion Mark Brelsford had to have the bones in his hand reset. The report ended any hopes that Brelsford would return in 1973.

1973 Loudon Road Race
Nixon Returns!!!

GNC Round #8 of 24 **Date:** June 17, 1973 **Type:** Road Race **Venue:** Bryar Motorsports Complex	**Location:** Loudon, NH **Surface:** Pavement **Course Length:** 1.6 Miles **Laps:** 47 **Distance:** 75 Miles

Never-say-die Gary Nixon notched his first GNC win in three years at the Loudon National Road Race. It had been a long, trying period. He had been dropped unceremoniously by Triumph, generally written off by many and suffered repeat injuries. He was right at home on the Erv Kanemoto-tuned factory Kawasaki. It was Nixon's 16th GNC win; his last was at Loudon in 1970. He also won the event in 1967. It was an especially satisfying weekend for Nixon, who swept the weekend by also capturing the Lightweight race. Kenny Roberts was the early leader in the GNC race. Roberts growing road race prowess could not contain the pure Nixon determination on this day. Kenny was about half a minute distant at the flag. Also showing great pavement abilities was Gary Scott, 3rd on the aging Triumph Trident. Scott was doing his best to keep title rival Roberts at bay. He now trailed Roberts by 59 points in the race for the title. Gary Nixon's win shot him from nowhere to third in points.

Heats

The 1972 winner at Loudon, Gary Fisher (Yam) led the pack away in Heat 1. Yvon Duhamel (Kaw) was right on Fisher's heels. Running close behind was Ron Pierce (Yam). Cal Rayborn (HD) ran in 4th spot early on. Loudon was a track where the great Rayborn skills could overcome the Harley's power deficiency, but Cal was still riding hurt. Cliff Carr (Kaw) and Steve McLaughlin (Yam) both passed Rayborn, who began fading from the lead pack. Gary Scott was moving through the field and was soon behind McLaughlin. Up front, Duhamel was applying pressure to Fisher. His efforts finally paid off, barely nipping Fisher at the line. Pierce held 3rd, with Scott managed to work his way to 4th spot.

Heat 2 was a good Gary Nixon (Kaw)-Kenny Roberts (Yam) show, with Nixon controlling the tempo. Roberts made it close till the waning laps when Nixon pulled ahead. A distant Jim Allen was 3rd with Don Castro close behind. Both were Yamaha-mounted. Kawasaki factory rider Art Baumann crashed out of the program in this heat.

Semi

Reg Pridmore put in an impressive win in the Semi event aboard a Butler & Smith BMW. The win showed the value at Loudon of great handling and riding ability vs. pure horsepower.

National

Kenny Roberts scooted out front at the start of the race with Gary Nixon, Yvon DuHamel, and Jim Allen close behind. DuHamel was quickly into the pits with throttle cable problems. Although repaired and back in the fray, the problem probably contributed to a subsequent piston seizure and DNF. On the track, Nixon soon took the top spot with Roberts a secure 2nd. Gary Scott worked the big Triumph forward past Gary Fisher, Ron Pierce and then Evans to capture 3rd spot. Nixon was not to be denied with Roberts and Scott, deeply engaged in the GNC points battle, were happy to be up front and weren't pushing their luck. Though pretty early in the race, the top 3 positions were set. Cal Rayborn had started the race, but was out before lap 10 because of his lingering injuries. Don Castro was out later for similar issues. Up front at midpoint saw the leading trio stretch their respective advantages. Behind, Gary Fisher had hung unto 4th, but was battling a lower end problem as well as a persistent Steve McLaughlin and Cliff Carr. By late in the race, McLaughlin was a solid 4th with both Fisher and Carr out with mechanical trouble. As the laps waned, Geoff Perry (Suz) mounted a late race charge to 5th, passing Jim Evans and Hurley Wilvert (Kaw). This set the top 5 at the finish as Nixon, Roberts, Scott, McLaughlin and Perry. The crowd was thrilled by Nixon's second win and Gary celebrated with them with a stylish wheelie down the front stretch.

Results

Race: 75 Mile Road Race National
Race Time: 58.51, (76.682 MPH)

Rank	Rider	Number	Make
1.	Gary Nixon, Phoenix, Md	9	Kaw
2.	Kenny Roberts, San Carlos, Ca	80	Yam
3.	Gary Scott, W. Covina, Ca	64	Tri
4.	Steve McLaughlin, Duarte, Ca	83	Yam
5.	Geoff Perry, Auckland, NZ	65	Suz
6.	Hurley Wilvert, Westminster, Ca	91	Kaw
7.	Jim Evans, San Bernardino, Ca	47	Yam
8.	Marty Lunde, Hermosa Beach, Ca	56	Yam
9.	Dick Mann, Richmond, Ca	2	Tri
10.	Jerry Greene, San Mateo, Ca	57	Yam
11.	Mert Lawwill, San Francisco, Ca	7	HD
12.	Dave Aldana, Santa Ana, Ca	13	Nor
13.	Kurt Leibmann, Bergenfield, NJ	59	BMW
14.	Mike Ninci, Kansas City, Mo	95	Yam
15.	Ron Grant, Brisbane, Ca	61	Suz
16.	Gene Romero, San Luis Obispo, Ca	3	Tri
17.	Doug Libby, Milford, Mi	89	Yam
18.	Reg Pridmore, Santa Barbara, Ca	84	BMW
19.	George Miller, Oakland, Ca	66	Yam
20.	Bart Myers, New Brunswick, NJ	68	Yam

Grand National Points Standings after Round 8

Rank	Rider	Pts
1.	Kenny Roberts	576
2.	Gary Scott	517
3.	Gary Nixon	309
4.	Kel Carruthers	2716
5.	Don Castro	234
6.	Geoff Perry	231
7.	Jimmy Odom	200
8.	Mert Lawwill	186
9.	Paul Smart	180
10.	Rex Beauchamp	180
11.	Jim Rice	180

Extra Extra

- Gary Nixon won a combined $19,000.00 from his two wins. This included a $10,000.00 bonus from Kawasaki.
- Nixon's win in the Combined Lightweight was a thriller, passing Kenny Roberts in the last corner for the victory.
- Rain washed out Saturday's Lightweight event which was run under sunny skies before the National.
- Last year's winner Gary Fisher was very disappointed over his DNF on lap 34. A win this day would have been on the 20th anniversary of father Ed's 1953 Loudon victory.
- Coming off wins at Dallas and Atlanta, the factory Suzuki's weren't really in the hunt at Loudon. The big bikes suffered handling and gearing problems all weekend. Geoff Perry managed a 5th place finish.

- Steve McLaughlin scored his best National finish yet in 4th.
- The short circuit helped equalize machinery. The four strokes had a good day. Gary Scott was an impressive 3rd place for his best National pavement finish. Teammate Dick Mann was 9th. Mert Lawwill was 11th and first Harley after Cal Rayborn dropped out. Dave Aldana was 12th on a factory Norton followed by Kurt Liebman on a Butler & Smith BMW.
- Both Aldana and Steve McLaughlin ran the short course *sans* fairings.
- Expert Steve Dalgarno's younger brother Brian, received $500.00 towards his college education from the Rusty Bradley Scholarship program.

1973 Columbus Half-Mile
Rice Wins on a Harley!

GNC Round #9 of 24	**Purse:** $13,000.00
Date: June 24, 1973	**Surface:** Dirt-Limestone
Type: Half-Mile	**Course Length:** ½ Mile
Venue: Ohio State	**Laps:** 20
Fairgrounds	**Distance:** 10 Miles
Location: Columbus, Oh	

Groove-master Jim Rice showed he was well acquainted with his new Harley-Davidson by taking a close victory at the 30th[t] Annual Charity Newsies Half-Mile. A successful last minute plug swap before the start saved the day for Rice. He then battled hard, first with Dave Sehl and later Mert Lawwill and Kenny Roberts right to the flag. It was Rice's 12th and final career GNC win. Two-time Newsies winner Lawwill worked hard through the event. He was strong early, dropped back, then finally making a strong run at Rice at the end. GNC points leader Roberts was in the lead pack all afternoon and finished right on Lawwill's rear wheel. Louisville GNC winner Dave Sehl was in contention for the win until he lost an argument with Roberts over a spot on the groove in turn one and went down mad, but unhurt. Track conditions on this day were unusual for Columbus. A very cool and foggy morning led to a fast moisture laden surface that was conducive to fast qualifying times and which had a bit of cushion instead of the typical blue groove.

Kenny Roberts podium run added a big 100 points to his points total, now 676 to rival Gary Scott's 517. Scott fought carburetion problems all day and failed to transfer to the main. Jim Rice's win shot him out of the pack, clear up to third in points. Gary Nixon scored no points and dropped back a spot. Mert Lawwill's 2nd place finish moved him three spots, up to fifth. Despite scoring some points in 6th, Don Castro dropped back a spot to sixth. Road racer Kel Carruthers dropped from fourth to seventh. Rex Beauchamp's 4th place finish allowed him to move up to eighth. Geoff Perry fell from sixth to ninth. Jimmy Odom hung onto tenth despite not making the National.

Time Trials
Mert Lawwill (HD) was top qualifier for the second dirt GNC in a row. Lawwill broke George Roeder's 1967 lap record of 26.63 with a sizzling 25.93. Dave Sehl (HD) was right behind at 25.94. These were the only two riders with time in 25 second range. Kenny Roberts (Yam) was 3rd fastest at 26.22. Eight riders were under the old record.

Heats
1969 GNC Champ Mert Lawwill quickly took control of Heat 1 and led wire to wire. Jim Rice followed at a distance, the two factory Harley riders taking the only direct transfers. Don Castro and Frank Gillespie had a great Yamaha battle throughout the race. Castro on the factory bike held privateer Gillespie at bay until the last lap when Gillespie snuck past at the stripe. Alas, both were semi bound.

In Heat 2 Dave Aldana looked very strong dominating the race on the neat factory Norton, setting fastest heat time. Dave Sehl (HD) trailed in second spot. Point's runner-up Gary Scott (Tri) was struggling a little and was a ways back in third.

Heat 3 looked like Corky Keener runaway aboard a Bart Markel tuned Harley-Davidson. Kenny Roberts (Yam) was apparently mired back in the pack till he came alive, passing four riders including, Rex Beauchamp (HD), Jimmy Zeigler (BSA), Teddy Newton (HD) and Chuck Palmgren (Yam), in one lap. Roberts set sail for Keener, going by with four to go. The large crowd was suitably impressed!

Seemingly ageless two-time GNC Champion Dick Mann on a factory Triumph showed impressive speed in Heat 4, topping Ohio crowd favorite Ronnie Rall (HD). Wisconsin racer Keith Ulicki, (perennially Harley mounted!), was third. Pole sitter Gene Romero had missed a shift at the start of the race, but worked his way back to 4th spot.

Semi's
Veteran Larry Palmgren (Tri) took the lead early in Semi 1. Don Castro and Frank Gillespie began restaging their heat race battle early in the race, which also saw Palmgren drop out with bike problems. Just like the first heat race,

Castro led with Gillespie nipping at his heels. Gillespie again topped his fellow Californian in the closing laps. Both were headed to the National. Harley riders Scott Brelsford and Larry Darr were close behind.

Michigan cushion ace Teddy Newton ran off early in Semi 2 till Rex Beauchamp ran him down just before halfway. 1970 GNC champ Gene Romero took the final ticket to the Main away from Newton on lap 6.

Trophy Race

A crop of great riders who just missed the National had a chance to make a few bucks in the Trophy Race. A restart was necessary after riders including Jimmy Maness, Dave Lawson, Larry Darr and Teddy Newton were accused of jumping the start and were forced to the penalty line. Doug Sehl shot out front and disappeared from the pack. Chuck Palmgren ran second till about halfway when he started fading back in the pack. Scott Brelsford took over second spot. Larry Darr was a strong 3rd till Keith Ulicki went by with one to go. Teddy Newton rounded out the first 5, all Harley mounted.

National

Riders were unsure how track conditions would play out for the 20 lap National. There was still some rideable cushion at the top of the groove; the question was, how long would it last? Jim Rice experienced some last moment drama just before the National. Upon starting his bike, it oil-fouled a spark plug. Jim's helper had spare plugs and they swapped out the plugs before the two-minute clock ran out. Despite this, the bike fouled another plug and Rice was pushed off the line. Fate was smiling on Rice, as two riders fell on the opening lap, causing a restart. An unknown mechanic offered Rice two more plugs. These were installed and Rice made the restart. He had to pin the Harleys throttle wide open to keep the plugs clean.

Mert Lawwill, hoping to make it two 'Newsies in a row, jumped out in front to lead lap one, chased by Rice, Kenny Roberts and Dave Sehl. Rice, up high, led the field out of turn 2. Lawwill seemed to be a little uncomfortable at first, as evidenced by slipping back to 4th on lap 2, just ahead of Rex Beauchamp. Outside pole sitter Dave Aldana quickly fell back early in the race. Up front, Rice was at the top of the groove and beginning to pull away from Roberts, who was riding a similar line. Sehl began riding a lower line and was heavily pressuring Roberts. Lawwill continued to struggle, falling back to 5th spot as Beauchamp moved by. Nearing the halfway point, Sehl moved by Roberts for 2nd spot and closed on Rice. On lap 10, Sehl trucked by Rice on the bottom of turns 1 and 2. The ever-studious Rice dropped in behind him and began to watch the Canadian's line. Roberts also moved down and joined the leading duo. Three laps later, Rice moved by Sehl to regain the lead. The drama wasn't over yet, as the trio drew even going down the front straight into turn 1 on lap 14. Roberts and Sehl tried to occupy the same portion of groove, got together, with Sehl ending up on the surface. Lawwill had gotten things figured out by this point and remounted a charge, passing Beauchamp and heading to the front. He caught and passed Roberts around lap 16. Both had momentum and closed up on leader Rice with two to go. Rice was pressured but managed to dig down and maintain a small lead as he crossed the finish on lap 20 with Lawwill a length or two back, holding off a threatening Roberts.

Results

Race: 20 Lap Half-Mile National

Rank	Rider	Number	Make
1.	Jim Rice, Palo Alto, Ca	24	HD
2.	Mert Lawwill, San Francisco, Ca	7	HD
3.	Kenny Roberts, San Carlos, Ca	80	Yam
4.	Rex Beauchamp, Milford, Mi	31	HD
5.	Corky Keener, Goodrich, Mi	62	HD
6.	Don Castro, Hollister, Ca	11	Yam
7.	Dick Mann, Richmond, Ca	2	Tri
8.	Dave Aldana, Santa Ana, Ca	13	Nor
9.	Frank Gillespie, Berkeley, Ca	76	Yam
10.	Gene Romero, San Luis Obispo, Ca	3	Tri
11.	Ronnie Rall, Mansfield, Oh	52	HD
12.	Dave Sehl, Waterdown, Ont., Can	16	HD

Race: Trophy Race

Rank	Rider	Number	Make
1.	Doug Sehl, Waterdown, Ont., Can	45	HD
2.	Scott Brelsford, Daly City, Ca	84Y	HD
3.	Keith Ulicki, Kenosha, Wi	86	HD
4.	Larry Darr, Mansfield, Oh	94	HD
5.	Teddy Newton, Pontiac, Mi	40	HD
6.	Jimmy Zeigler, Bellville, Oh	9F	BSA
7.	Chuck Palmgren, Freehold, NJ	38	Yam
8.	Mike Johnson, Flint, Mi	14E	HD
9.	Merlyn Plumlee, Colorado Springs, Ca	52M	Tri
10.	Jimmy Maness, Augusta, Ga	71	HD
11.	Dave Lawson, Yukon, Ok	89M	Yam
12.	Eddie Wirth, Dana Point, Ca	84X	Yam

Grand National Points Standings after Round 9

Rank	Rider	Pts
1.	Kenny Roberts	676
2.	Gary Scott	517
3.	Jim Rice	330
4.	Gary Nixon	309
5.	Mert Lawwill	306
6.	Don Castro	284
7.	Kel Carruthers	276
8.	Rex Beauchamp	260
9.	Geoff Perry	231
10.	Jimmy Odom	200

Extra Extra

- The very talented Jim Rice scored all of his 12 wins on the dirt; 6 half-miles, 4 miles and 2 TT's. Six of the wins came in 1970, when Rice came agonizingly close to winning the National title. His dozen wins tied him with legends Brad Andres, Bobby Hill and Dick Klamfoth. He was the only rider to win a dirt track event on a 3-cylinder Beezumph. He was a top contender in the Grand National Championship, finishing runner-up in 1970, third in 1971 and seventh in 1972.

GNC Round #10 of 24 **Date:** July 1, 1973 **Type:** Mile **Venue:** Santa Clara Fairgrounds **Location:** San Jose, Ca	**Purse:** $13,000.00 **Surface:** Dirt **Course Length**: 1 Mile **Laps:** 25 **Distance:** 25 Miles

Gene Romero topped a hotly contested San Jose Mile, winning his first of the year and becoming the 10th different GNC winner of the year. Romero's 9th National victory came in a classic mile battle. There were well over 20 unofficial lead changes. Romero on his Gary Feil-tuned Triumph narrowly topped teammate Gary Scott on the last lap, followed closely by Frank Gillespie who put in his best career ride in 3rd. Though they swept the top two spots, the Triumphs were at the peak of their development and Romero's win would be the brand's last National Mile victory.

Kenny Roberts continued to lead the GNC standings, but suffered a mechanical failure in the main, scoring a single point. Gary Scott's runner-up finish narrowed the championship gap to 40 points, 677 to 637. Don Castro finished 5th in the race and moved into third with 344 points. Jim Rice had bike troubles and dropped to fourth with 334. Gary Nixon was 14th in the main and dropped to fifth with 316. Rex Beauchamp continued to climb in the standings, moving up two spots to sixth with 310. Mert Lawwill did not make the main and dropped a spot, his total was 306. Kel Carruthers was now back to eighth, still at 276. Dick Mann ran a strong 4th in the National and moved into ninth in the standings. Geoff Perry rounded out the top 10 with 231.

Time Trials

The San Jose track was resurfaced before the event and proved to be very fast. Four riders broke Mert Lawwill's track record of 39.90. Fastest was Gary Scott (Tri) aboard the Brent Thompson-tuned factory Triumph at 39.46, followed by Harley's Rex Beauchamp with a 39.51, Eddie Mulder (Tri) impressed with 39.73 and Jim Rice (HD), who turned in a 39.76. Former record holder Lawwill (HD) was fifth at 39.92. While the Harley-Davidson camp was making the alloy XR750 strong, the venerable Triumph Speed Twin would be tough at the first mile of the year.

Heats

Heat one took several attempts to get underway, delayed by several incidents, the most noticeable ending with Mert Lawwill's XR in two pieces after an altercation with Gary Scott. Mert was unhurt, but done for the day. The mounting pile of broken motorcycles and hay bales caused the officials to pull the riders off the track with the race being completed after the other heats. Once underway, Scott led uncontested to the win trailed by Dave Sehl, Terry Dorsch and Mark Williams, all Triumph mounted except for Harley teamster Sehl. Sehl was aboard a backup after his primary bike lost its engine in practice. Scott's time was a new record and the fastest heat of the day.

More racing action was found in Heat 2 with Rex Beauchamp and Chuck Palmgren on the Dan Gurney Yamaha, swapping the lead repeatedly through most of the race. Reeling them in at the end was two-time GNC Champ Dick Mann (Tri), who dropped Palmgren to 2nd with Beauchamp taking the win. Jim Odom (Tri) topped Harley team member Scott Brelsford for the last direct transfer spot to the National.

Ascot scorcher Dewayne Keeter (HD) was out front early in Heat 3 with Yamaha riders Kenny Roberts, Gary Nixon and Dave Lawson close behind. Nixon was riding one of Chuck Palmgren's spare AAR bikes. Roberts moved to the point, with Keeter trying to maintain contact in second. Lawson, Nixon and Tom Rockwood argued over the two remaining transfer spots with Nixon impressing by taking the 3rd spot with Lawson hanging onto 4th at the finish.

Local hero Don Castro (Yam) pulled a neat holeshot in the final heat, only to be passed by road race star Cal Rayborn (HD). Close behind was a snarling pack made up of Gene Romero, Jim Rice (HD) and Frank Gillespie. When Castro slipped off the groove, all three shot by. Rice moved out of the pack to nail down second, with Gillespie and Romero arguing over third. At the finish, Rayborn took a comfortable win, followed by Rice, Gillespie and Romero. Castro was semi-bound. Winner Rayborn finally appeared healed from his early season injuries.

Semi's

Scott Brelsford (HD) and Eddie Wirth (Yam) topped the first semi after an early scuffle with rookie Tom Horton (Tri). Don Castro ran away with Semi 2 with John Hateley (Tri) taking second from Dave Aldana (Nor) late in the race. The track seemed to be getting faster, as Castro's 10-Lap time was a new record and the fastest of the day.

Trophy Race

The Nick Deligianis-tuned factory Norton of Dave Aldana led Triumph riders Randy Scott and Todd Sloan to the flag in the "Consi".

National

The track was watered just before the National. The riders were given a lap for a look-see. When GNC title contender Kenny Roberts pulled up, his Yamaha was making "expensive noises" and he was out. The remaining racers shot off the line with Frank Gillespie getting a great start from row 2 to take the early lead. Chuck Palmgren's Yamaha broke a primary chain on the line and he joined Roberts to spectate. Back to the race, where Rex Beauchamp took over before the first lap was over. Gillespie maintained second, with Dave Sehl, Jim Rice and Gary Scott following. Rice's Harley had bottom end trouble and he was out on lap 8. Beauchamp was still up front at the halfway mark with Gillespie and Sehl on his heels. Close behind were Scott and Romero, joined by Don Castro. This pack was letting it all hang out with first Scott and then Castro slipping the groove and trading spots all over. They reeled in first three and Scott blasted by all for the lead on lap 13. Beauchamp briefly retook the lead only to lose it quickly and slide backwards out of the top 5. Dick Mann had been on the move and now joined the lead battle. With 15 laps down Romero, Scott and Gillespie became the dominant forces. The factory Triumphs were closely matched, giving no quarter as the laps ticked by. Gillespie's fast Yamaha was right on their heels. On the last lap, Scott led into turn 3. Coming out of the last corner, Romero's CR Axtell tuned mount gained a slight advantage and pulled Scott to the flag. Gillespie held 3rd spot, Mann worked his way to an impressive 4th, Castro was 5th and Beauchamp was the first Harley home in 6th.

Results

Race: 25 Lap Mile National

Rank	Rider	Number	Make
1.	Gene Romero, San Luis Obispo, Ca	3	Tri
2.	Gary Scott, Baldwin Park, Ca	64	Tri
3.	Frank Gillespie, Berkeley, Ca	76	Yam
4.	Dick Mann, Richmond, Ca	2	Tri
5.	Don Castro, Hollister, Ca	11	Yam
6.	Rex Beauchamp, Milford, Mi	31	HD
7.	Scott Brelsford, Daly City, Ca	84Y	HD
8.	Dave Sehl, Waterdown, Ont., Can	16	HD
9.	Cal Rayborn, Spring Valley, Ca	14	HD
10.	Dave Lawson, Yukon, Ok	89M	Yam
11.	DeWayne Keeter, Ojai, Ca	44	HD
12.	Jimmy Odom, Fremont, Ca	18	Tri
13.	John Hateley, Van Nuys, Ca	98	Tri
14.	Gary Nixon, Phoenix, Md	9	Yam
15.	Mark Williams, Springfield, Ore	70	Tri
16.	Terry Dorsch, Granada Hills, Ca	22	Tri
17.	Jim Rice, Palo Alto, Ca	24	HD
18.	Eddie Wirth, Dana Point, Ca	84X	Yam
19.	Chuck Palmgren, Freehold, NJ	38	Yam
20.	Kenny Roberts, San Carlos, Ca	80	Yam

Race: Trophy Race

Rank	Rider	Number	Make
1.	Dave Aldana, Santa Ana, Ca	13	Nor
2.	Randy Scott, Philomath, Ore	50	Tri
3.	Tod Sloan, Fresno, Ca	33	Tri
4.	Tom Horton, Lancaster, Ca	75X	Tri
5.	Pat Marinacci, Seattle, Wa	67	Tri
6.	Ike Reed, Salem, Ore	90	Tri
7.	Terry Sage, Stockton, Ca	70Z	Tri
8.	Al Kenyon, Cupertino, Ca	48	BSA

Grand National Points Standings after Round 10

Rank	Rider	Pts
1.	Kenny Roberts	677
2.	Gary Scott	637
3.	Don Castro	344
4.	Jim Rice	334
5.	Gary Nixon	316
6.	Rex Beauchamp	310
7.	Mert Lawwill	306
8.	Kel Carruthers	276
9.	Dick Mann	270
10.	Geoff Perry	231

1973 Colorado Mile
Roberts Takes First Mile

GNC Round #11 of 24 **Date:** July 8, 1973 **Type:** Mile **Venue:** Pikes Peak Turf Club **Location:** Colorado Springs, Co	**Purse:** $12,000.00 **Surface:** Dirt **Course Length:** 1 Mile **Laps:** 25 **Distance:** 25 Miles

Kenny Roberts snatched his first ever mile victory away from Rex Beauchamp in the last seconds of the bomb-crater like Colorado Mile GNC. The cushion mile horse track had been hit hard by heavy rain the day before, shortening the Junior program. The track was rutted and bumpy, resulting in the AMA shortening the heats to 5 laps and the main to 16. Roberts who had early in the year won the Houston Short Track, became the first rider to repeat a win in 1973, breaking a 10 race streak. It was heartbreak for Team Harleys Rex Beauchamp. He had been in contention for the win at the recent San Jose Mile, and at Colorado it looked like he had the victory wrapped up. Rookie Expert Scott Brelsford finished out the podium behind Beauchamp for his best National finish yet. A surprise to all was Gary Nixon's 4th place finish aboard Chuck Palmgren's backup AAR Yamaha. He was second in his heat and despite his weakened leg, was up front the whole National. Despite being written off by many, the former two-time Grand National Champion, (1967 and '68), was again a legitimate title contender.

Kenny Roberts win really boosted his GNC points lead over Gary Scott, 827 points to 697. Rex Beauchamp's runner-up finish moved him from sixth in points clear up to third. Gary Nixon's surprising dirt track performance moved him up a spot to fourth. Don Castro slipped back a couple of spots to fifth, as did Jim Rice going from fourth to sixth.

Time Trials
Despite the awful track conditions, there was an abundance of traction available. Kenny Roberts (Yam) ran a 40.94 lap on the Shell Theutt tuned factory Yamaha, shattering Mark Brelsford's 1972 time of 42.78. Roberts was the only rider in the 40 second range. Triumph mounted Dick Mann was next with a 41.47 lap. Team Norton's Dave Aldana was close with a 41.71. The Harleys of Jim Rice and Rex Beauchamp rounded out the top 5 with laps of 41.80 and 41.81 respectively. In all a total of 18 racers broke Mark Brelsford's record.

Heats
Fast qualifier Kenny Roberts blasted away from the pack in Heat 1, setting the fastest heat time of the night. Rex Beauchamp and Scott Brelsford were next followed by Charlie Seale (HD).

In Heat 2, the ever popular Dick Mann topped teammate and San Jose Mile winner Gene Romero. Keith Ulicki on the Uke's Harley-Davidson and Frank Gillespie on his self-sponsored Harley took the other two transfer spots.

Title contender Gary Scott (Tri) took the Heat 3 win over Dave Aldana, Yamahas Don Castro and privateer Stan Johnson (Yam).

Mike Kidd (Tri) won Heat 4 over resilient Gary Nixon, Eddie Wirth (Yam) and Cal Rayborn (HD).

Semis
Putting the second AAR Yamaha in the National, Chuck Palmgren ran off with a comfortable win in the first semi over Dave Sehl (HD). Both advanced to the big show.

1964 GNC champ Roger Reiman (HD) and Terry Dorsch on the Bel-Ray/Jardine Headers/Skyway Triumph, put on a crowd pleasing race in Semi 2. The two swapped the point several times. Frank Ulicki (HD) further spiced things up by passing both late in the race for the win. Dorsch took the final transfer over Reiman.

Trophy Race

Roger Reiman was again out front, this time leading the 10-lap Trophy Race for the first several circuits. On lap 3, Steve Droste (Yam) powered his Yamaha past the inside of Reiman. Droste moved away for an easy win. Reiman held 2nd with are rider Merlyn Plumlee (Tri) in 3rd.

National

The shortened 16-Lap National was initially led by Dave Aldana, but Dick Mann pounded past for the lead coming out of the second turn. Rex Beauchamp was following and was also soon by Aldana. Mann looked to be running away with the event when suddenly a bottom end failure put him out on lap 5. Beauchamp's way to win looked clear, but by lap 8 he was being shadowed by Kenny Roberts who had emerged from the pack. Roberts continued to gobble up real estate and was on the Harley riders tailpipes as the race closed. Beauchamp was feeling the pressure and on the last lap, Roberts snuck past going into turn 3. Beauchamp was able to edge back ahead through turn 4. Coming out of the corner Beauchamp drifted just a little high, giving Roberts just enough room to drive by off the bottom, taking a narrow advantage as they crossed the stripe. It was elation for Roberts and another frustrating finish for Beauchamp. Scott Brelsford was a big distance back for his best finish yet, followed by tough guy Nixon, Gary Scott, Dave Aldana, Mike Kidd, Charlie Seale, Gene Romero and Stan Johnson. This was the last time the AMA would return to the Colorado Mile.

Results

Race: 16 Lap Mile National
Race Time: 11:31.25

Rank	Rider	Number	Make
1.	Kenny Roberts, San Carlos, Ca	80	Yam
2.	Rex Beauchamp, Milford, Mi	31	HD
3.	Scott Brelsford, Daly City, Ca	84Y	HD
4.	Gary Nixon, Phoenix, Md	9	Yam
5.	Gary Scott, Baldwin Park, Ca	64	Tri
6.	Dave Aldana, Santa Ana, Ca	13	Nor
7.	Mike Kidd, Hurst, Tx	72	Tri
8.	Charlie Seale, Lantana, Fl	47	HD
9.	Gene Romero, San Luis Obispo, Ca	3	Tri
10.	Stan Johnson, Albuquerque, NM	48M	Yam
11.	Chuck Palmgren, Freehold, Ca	38	Yam
12.	Eddie Wirth, Dana Point, Ca	84X	Yam
13.	Cal Rayborn, Spring Valley, Ca	14	HD
14.	Frank Ulicki, Kenosha, Wi	23G	HD
15.	Don Castro, Hollister, Ca	11	Yam
16.	Terry Dorsch, Granada Hills, Ca	22	Tri
17.	Keith Ulicki, Kenosha, Wi	86	HD
18.	Frank Gillespie, Berkeley, Ca	76	Yam
19.	Dick Mann, Richmond, Ca	2	Tri
20.	Dave Sehl, Waterdown, Ont., Can	16	HD

Race: 10 Lap Trophy Race
Race Time: 3:46.10

Rank	Rider	Number	Make
1.	Steve Droste, Waterloo, Ia	26K	Yam
2.	Roger Reiman, Kewanee, Ill	5	HD
3.	Merlyn Plumlee, Colorado Springs, Co	52M	Tri
4.	Delbert Armour, Denver, Co	10M	HD
5.	Phil Darcy, Beaumont, Tx	11N	Yam
6.	Nick Theroux, San Francisco, Ca	64Y	Tri

Grand National Points Standings after Round 11

Rank	Rider	Pts
1.	Kenny Roberts	827
2.	Gary Scott	697
3.	Rex Beauchamp	430
4.	Gary Nixon	396
5.	Don Castro	350
6.	Jim Rice	334
7.	Mert Lawwill	306
8.	Kel Carruthers	276
9.	Dick Mann	272
10.	Geoff Perry	231

1973 Castle Rock TT
Joyner Wins First at Wild Castle Rock!

GNC Round #12 of 24 **Date:** July 14, 1973 **Type:** TT **Venue:** Mt. St. Helens Motorcycle Club Grounds	**Purse:** $13,000.00 **Location:** Castle Rock, Wa **Surface:** Dirt **Course Length:** ½ Mile **Laps:** 25

Local Castle Rock specialist Chuck Joyner was in the right place at the right time to win his first National. He and several other riders took advantage of the chaos that ensued after early leader Gary Scott's nasty high side. Joyner didn't have an easy time of it though, as GNC points leader Kenny Roberts worked on him for most of the event, but in the end, Roberts had to settle for the runner-up spot and the valuable GNC points. Third spot went to another local favorite, Randy Scott. He put in a solid ride and had the best GNC finish of his career

The track at Castle Rock was unique, matched by it's rabid fans who numbered 7,800 plus, to cheer their regional heroes and Joyner, from Oregon City, Ore delivered on this night. Topping the night for Joyner was that it was also his 23rd birthday!

Kenny Roberts 2nd place finish raised his points by 256 points over Gary Scott, who was scored 16th on the National after his crash. Rex Beauchamp scored no points, but held onto third in points. Jim Rice finished 4th in the race and jumped from sixth in points to fourth. Don Castro finished 5th in the race and held onto fifth in points. Gary Nixon slipped back to sixth.

Time Trials

Setting the stage for the night, Chuck Joyner (Tri) was fastest in qualifying at 25.01. Dry track conditions slowed times way off Mark Williams' record of 23.81. Following were Frank Gillespie (Yam) at 25.15, Gary Scott (Tri) a 25.16 and Mert Lawwill with a 25.20.

Heats

Chuck Joyner on the Fred's Distributing sponsored Triumph, looked strong in Heat 1, but Jim Rice (HD), a two-time GNC TT winner, soon moved past for the lead. Rice stretched the lead to the finish in the fastest heat of the night. Joyner hung onto 2nd spot with Sonny Burres (Tri) capturing 3rd.

Factory Yamaha pilot Don Castro ran off and hid from the pack in Heat 2. Two-time winner at Castle Rock (1967 and '69) Mert Lawwill (HD), while giving heavy chase to young Castro, went down hard in the northeast turn. Lawwill was okay, but was done for the night. Gene Romero (Tri) and Frank Gillespie followed Castro to the finish and into the National.

GNC points rivals Kenny Roberts and Gary Scott were both in Heat 3, assuring an interesting race. Roberts pulled the holeshot and led lap one. Scott was all over Roberts and went by on lap 2. Scott ran the remainder of the race with Roberts breathing down his neck, but didn't let the pressure get to him, taking the win. Dave Aldana (Nor), grabbed the last transfer in 3rd spot.

Local TT hotshoe Mark Williams (Tri) was out front honkin' when the race was red flagged on lap 5. Tom White dropped his bike in a corner, and was struck by John Hateley, who was thrown over the handlebars. Al Kenyon rode into the pile of bodies and bikes and went down as well. White had a suspected arm fracture; both Hateley and Kenyon made the restart. After the restart, Williams rode to a comfortable win, trailed by Ike Reed and John Einarsson. The top 3 were all Triumph-mounted.

Semis

The two semis would each send two riders on to the main. Californian's Tom Horton and Terry Dorsch scooted out front and battled for the top spot. After several laps, Dorsch had come out on top and pulled a small lead. While the two had been racing hard, Dick Mann, an 8-time GNC TT winner, including Castle Rock in 1970, snuck up and passed Horton right at stripe on the last lap.

Randy Scott and Pat Marinacci put on a similar race as the previous semi. They kept the swap-fest between the two, with Scott coming out on top. All riders mentioned in the semi events were aboard; you guessed it, Triumph twins.

Trophy Race

John Hateley got the holeshot in the Trophy event, chased by Randy Skiver. The two traded the top spot a couple of times with Skiver taking the advantage and holding to the flag. Hateley was runner-up and Eddie Wirth was third.

National

Mark Williams, still hungry for his first GNC win, blasted off the starting line with Don Castro and Gary Scott right with him. Scott quickly moved by Castro and onto Williams' rear wheel. Putting the factory ponies to good use, Scott got a good drive on Williams out of the last corner, pulling alongside and passing in the first turn. Castro temporarily came through to the front, only to have Scott and Williams drop him back to third. Castro was soon engaged in battle with Kenny Roberts and Chuck Joyner. Further back, Jim Rice, Terry Dorsch and Gene Romero had a similar fight going on. Gary Scott looked strong out front, but pushed a little too hard coming out of the dog leg and high-sided big time. Scott was lucky to escape serious injury as the pack pummeled him from all directions. Gary's night and a chance to gain points on Kenny Roberts was over. In the confusion that followed, Chuck Joyner was now the leader with Roberts all over him. Randy Scott and Jim Rice were behind, fighting over 3rd spot. Terry Dorsch followed with Don Castro and Mark Williams ending up in a tussle with Gene Romero. With a lot of laps left, Chuck Joyner faced a tall order in keeping a charging Kenny Roberts behind him. Joyner was up to the task, as Roberts tried him all over the track for 20 laps, to no avail. Randy Scott came out on top of a tough battle with Jim Rice, with Terry Dorsch rounding out the top 5.

Results

Race: 25 Lap TT National

Rank	Rider	Number	Make
1.	Chuck Joyner, Oregon City, Ore	60	Tri
2.	Kenny Roberts, San Carlos, Ca	80	Yam
3.	Randy Scott, Philomath, Ore	50	Tri
4.	Jim Rice, Palo Alto, Ca	24	HD
5.	Terry Dorsch, Granada Hills, Ca	22	Tri
6.	Don Castro, Hollister, Ca	11	Yam
7.	Gene Romero, San Luis Obispo, Ca	3	Tri
8.	Mark Williams, Springfield, Ore	70	Tri
9.	Sonny Burres, Portland, Ore	69	Tri
10.	Dick Mann, Richmond, Ca	2	Tri
11.	Frank Gillespie, Berkeley, Ca	76	Yam
12.	Ike Reed, Salem, Ore	90	Tri
13.	Pat Marinacci, Seattle, Wa	67	Tri
14.	Dave Aldana, Santa Ana, Ca	13	Nor
15.	Jim Einarsson, Shelton, Wa	12W	Tri
16.	Gary Scott, Baldwin Park, Ca	64	Tri

Race: Trophy Race

Rank	Rider	Number	Make
1.	Randy Skiver, Everett, Wa	35	Tri
2.	John Hateley, Van Nuys, Ca	98	Tri
3.	Eddie Wirth, Dana Point, Ca	84X	Yam
4.	Dick Wascher, Renton, Wa	85	Tri

Grand National Points Standings after Round 12

Rank	Rider	Pts
1.	Kenny Roberts	959
2.	Gary Scott	703
3.	Rex Beauchamp	430
4.	Jim Rice	422
5.	Don Castro	415
6.	Gary Nixon	396
7.	Mert Lawwill	306
8.	Dick Mann	289
9.	Kel Carruthers	276
10.	Randy Scott	270

Extra Extra

- Chuck Joyner was riding friends Ed Hermann's Triumph. Hermann had been injured at San Jose a few weeks earlier.
- Triumphs dominated the results, taking 11 of 16 spots. Jim Rice saved potential Harley-Davidson embarrassment by putting the sole Milwaukee machine in the National. Kenny Roberts, Don Castro and Frank Gillespie were all Yamaha mounted. Dave Aldana put the lone Norton in the final.
- Chuck Joyner was the 11th different winner in 12 events.

1973 Ascot TT
Aldana Makes History at the Ascot TT!

GNC Round #13 of 24	**Purse:** $12,000.00
Date: July 21, 1973	**Surface:** Dirt
Type: TT	**Course Length:** ½ Mile,
Venue: Ascot Park	(approx.)
Location: Gardena, Ca	**Laps:** 25

Dave Aldana broke a long dry spell with his Ascot TT win and scored Norton's first modern era AMA dirt track GNC win. Aldana had not won a National since the Indy Mile in the "On Any Sunday" year of 1970. While the Norton marquee had scored AMA National wins, they were pre-1954, with pure racing singles (see "*Extras*"); no one had won with a twin. Aldana's C&J framed machine was built and tuned by Nick Deligianis. An unusually patient Dave Aldana paced leader Gary Scott for the majority of the race till Scott's bike had an oil leak and fell off the pace. It was another frustrating night for Scott, who has had continuing bad luck of late, whether of his doing or mechanical trouble. GNC points rival and leader Kenny Roberts finished a strong second, further dimming Scott's championship hopes. For Roberts, it was his second runner-up position in a row. Simply put, he was riding well and things were going his way. Terry Dorsch continued to improve and put in a solid ride for third, his best National finish ever.

As the season moved past midpoint, Kenny Roberts' 2nd place, combined with Gary Scott's meager points in 19th, gave Roberts a huge 374 points advantage. Jim Rice's solid 9th place run moved him into third past Rex Beauchamp, who failed to score any points. Don Castro added a few points, hanging onto fifth. Gary Nixon kept sixth, despite failing to make the race. Dick Mann moved to seventh, dropping Mert Lawwill back one spot. Dave Aldana's win and Scott Brelsford's 4th place moved them into ninth and tenth respectively in points.

Time Trials
Putting the three top brands at the top of the qualifying board were Kenny Roberts on the factory Yamaha at 46.24, Mert Lawwill on the Harley-Davidson Motor Co. ride 46.27, 1966 winner Eddie Mulder ran a 46.45 on his privateer Triumph. Gary Scott fought a misfiring engine, but still ran a 46.78. Terry Dorsch (Tri) rounded out the top 5 with a 46.80.

Heats
Castle Rock winner Chuck Joyner (Tri) was out front early in Heat 1 till slowed with engine trouble. John Hateley (Tri) and Kenny Roberts (Yam) battled heavily with Roberts finally taking the spot with 4 laps to go. Terry Dorsch (Tri) was a close 3rd. Tom Horton (Tri) and Eddie Wirth (Yam) squabbled over the final transfer spot with Horton getting the nod at the stripe.

Dave Aldana was headed on his way to the fastest time of the night in Heat 2, with Mert Lawwill taking 2nd position and Tom Rockwood (Tri) in 3rd. The real race was for the final transfer spot with Dewayne Keeter (HD), Cal Rayborn (HD) and Randy Scott (Tri) all involved in a good battle. Life was made easier for Keeter when both of his rivals suffered mechanical trouble.

Don Castro continued to impress aboard his factory Yamaha, leading Heat 3 with Eddie Mulder and Dick Mann (Tri) giving chase. Mulder's Triumph lost a cylinder and Mann was into second. Late in the race, Mann took over the top spot, with Castro hanging close behind. Jimmy Odom (Yam) and Brian LaPlante (Tri) bumped the still-running Mulder just out of a transfer. LaPlante was on his way to his first National.

A crash by rookie Ron Powell (Yam) brought out a red flag on the 2nd lap of Heat 4. Jim Rice (HD) jumped out front with Gary Scott running him down for the lead in two laps. With one lap to go, Gene Romero (Tri) also moved Rice back a spot. Randy Skiver (Tri) took the last spot to the National.

Semis
Al Kenyon (Tri) was the early leader in the first Semi. Cal Rayborn (HD) quickly took over with Pat McCaul (Tri), rookie Jim Crenshaw (Nor) and veteran TT racer Dusty Coppage (Tri) all heading to the front. As the race

progressed, Kenyon fell out of contention, and McCaul crashed out just past halfway. Rayborn took the win and he and Crenshaw were headed to the National.

Eddie Wirth was out front first in Semi 2 followed by Frank Gillespie (Yam) and Eddie Mulder. Mulder passed both before lap 2 started. Scott Brelsford was on the move, passing Gillespie and catching Wirth. Wirth was pressed hard by the rookie Brelsford, who took the position by inches at the flag. Wirth, the 1969 Sante Fe TT winner, was just out of the transfer spot all night.

Trophy Race

Eddie Wirth finally had things go his way in the Trophy Race, a "consolation" for a rough night. He passed early leader Dusty Coppage after a couple of laps and proceeded to run away with the race. Randy Scott worked his way through the field, passing Coppage late in the going for second. Wirth however, was long gone and took a comfortable win.

National

Gary Scott was first off the line with Dave Aldana, Kenny Roberts and Mert Lawwill in tow. As the laps counted off, Scott and Aldana pulled a gap on the field, with Roberts keeping them in sight. Dick Mann was on the move and knocked Lawwill back a spot when he grabbed 4th. Terry Dorsch headed up a second pack of riders including Scott Brelsford, Gene Romero and Don Castro. John Hateley was with the group till he lost the front of his Triumph in the 2nd turn. As the distance neared midway, Scott was still holding off a pressuring Aldana. Roberts and Mann still pursued. Dorsch was on the charge and had moved past Lawwill. He next set his sights on Mann. Dorsch soon worked by for 4th. Mann tried to retaliate, but hit a slick spot and fell down. He got going again, but lost several places. Things began to change up front; Scott had an oil line begin to leak, coating his rear tire. He began to slip and slide and Aldana was soon by. Aldana shot to a big lead as Scott tried to keep going. Roberts and Dorsch moved into 2nd and 3rd. Scott Brelsford had mounted a strong late race charge and was up to 4th. Low sliders Hateley and Mann were 5th and 6th. Scott tried to keep the wounded Triumph going to salvage some points, but the bike cruelly expired with one lap to go. Aldana cruised in for a historical Norton win and the end of a long dry spell for himself. In "Victory Circle", the bike burst into flames when the battery cables were unhooked. A spark from the battery and a leaky float bowl resulted in a spectacular fireball. The fire was quickly extinguished as Aldana and tuner Nick Deligianis roared with laughter about the weird occurrence.

Results

Race: 25 Lap TT National
Race Time: 19:20.93

Rank	Rider	Number	Make
1.	Dave Aldana, Santa Ana, Ca	13	Nor
2.	Kenny Roberts, San Carlos, Ca	80	Yam
3.	Terry Dorsch, Granada Hills, Ca	22	Tri
4.	Scott Brelsford, Daly City, Ca	84Y	HD
5.	John Hateley, Van Nuys, Ca	98	Tri
6.	Dick Mann, Richmond, Ca	2	Tri
7.	Gene Romero, San Luis Obispo, Ca	3	Tri
8.	Mert Lawwill, San Francisco, Ca	7	HD
9.	Jim Rice, Palo Alto, Ca	24	HD
10.	Tom Rockwood, Gardena, Ca	88	Tri

Rank	Rider	Number	Make
11.	Eddie Mulder, Northridge, Ca	12	Tri
12.	Jimmy Odom, Fremont, Ca	18	Tri
13.	Randy Skiver, Everett, Wa	35	Tri
14.	Don Castro, Hollister, Ca	11	Yam
15.	Jim Crenshaw, Davis, Ca	21Y	Nor
16.	Tom Horton, Lancaster, Ca	75X	Tri
17.	DeWayne Keeter, Oakview, Ca	44	HD
18.	Brian LaPlante, Tustin, Ca	40X	Tri
19.	Gary Scott, Baldwin Park, Ca	64	Tri
20.	Cal Rayborn, Spring Valley, Ca	14	HD

Race: Trophy Race

Rank	Rider	Number	Make
1.	Eddie Wirth, Dana Point, Ca	84X	Yam
2.	Randy Scott, Portland, Ore	50	Tri
3.	Dusty Coppage, Beaverton, Ore	32	Tri
4.	Frank Gillespie, Berkeley, Ca	76	Yam
5.	Dave Sehl, Waterdown, Ont., Can	16	HD
6.	Ron Powell, Palmdale, Ca	31X	Tri
7.	Jim Einarrson, Shelton, Ca	12W	Tri
8.	Ike Mizen, Los Angeles, Ca	60R	Tri
9.	Terry Sage, Stockton, Ca	70Z	Tri
10.	Jim Berry, Newport Beach, Ca	19X	Tri
11.	Bob Bailey, Gardena, Ca	53	Tri
12.	Larry Gino, San Bernardino, Ca	96R	Tri

Grand National Points Standings after Round 13

Rank	Rider	Pts
1.	Kenny Roberts	1079
2.	Gary Scott	705
3.	Jim Rice	442
4.	Rex Beauchamp	430
5.	Don Castro	412
6.	Gary Nixon	396
7.	Dick Mann	339
8.	Mert Lawwill	336
9.	Dave Aldana	308
10.	Scott Brelsford	295

Extra Extra

- Dave Aldana picked up a $2000.00 bonus from Norton in addition to his purse winnings.
- It was the Norton marquees first National win since Bill Tuman's 1953 Dodge City 200 Mile win. The brand had much success before 1954. Dick Klamfoth had won 3 Daytona 200's and Chet Dykgraff was the 1946 Grand National Champion after he won that year's Springfield Mile.
- It was a big weekend for Aldana and Norton. Aldana also won Friday's prestigious Yamaha Gold Cup race, staged on Ascot's half-mile track.
- Gary Scott's night started badly when his Triumph showed up late and incomplete. He chased mechanical issues all night and seemed to have things ironed out till the bike began leaking oil.

- California riders completely dominated the National, filling 19 of the 20 starting spots. Washington state resident Randy Skiver was the lone interloper.
- It was the 12th Annual Ascot TT.
- More bad news for the racing world came out of the South Pacific. Geoff Perry was killed in a plane crash off the coast of Tahiti. Perry was a factory Suzuki rider who competed internationally as well as on the Grand National circuit. He had won his first National early in the season at Road Atlanta.

Bonus!
Top 10 Ascot TT Qualifying Times

1.	Kenny Roberts	Yam	46.24 seconds
2.	Mert Lawwill	HD	46.27
3.	Eddie Mulder	Tri	46.45
4.	Gary Scott	Tri	46.78
5.	Terry Dorsch	Tri	46.80
6.	Dave Aldana	Nor	47.02
7.	Dick Mann	Tri	47.07
8.	Gene Romero	Tri	47.07
9.	John Hateley	Tri	47.11
10.	Cal Rayborn	HD	47.17

1973 Laguna Seca
Nixon Zaps 'Em Again!

GNC Round #14 of 24	**Purse:** $22,500.00
Date: July 29, 1973	**Surface:** Pavement
Type: Road Race	**Course Length**: 1.8 Miles
Venue: Laguna Seca Raceway	**Laps:** 40
Location: Monterey, Ca	**Distance:** 75 Miles

Gary Nixon won his second road race in a row at the Kawasaki sponsored, (and dominated), Laguna Seca National. Nixon captured the Loudon Road Race earlier in the year. It was his 17th career win. Nixon had trailed teammate Yvon DuHamel throughout most of the race, till the fiery Canadian dropped his leading machine in the corkscrew section. Nixon motored on for an uncontested win on his Erv Kanemoto-tuned machine. Fellow Kawasaki teammate Cliff Carr survived a leaking rear brake for the runner-up spot. Team Triumphs Gary Scott brought home his aged Trident an impressive third spot. His finish allowed him to gain some ground on GNC title rival Kenny Roberts. Roberts along with most of the Yamaha team had a rough weekend. Roberts was running with the lead pack till sidelined late in the race with a broken chain. Team manager/racer Kel Carruthers also dropped out with mechanical trouble. Gary Fisher broke his collarbone in practice, reportedly when trying to perfect his wheeling technique which had gotten him a lot of press here in 1972. Don Castro was the lone factory Yamaha rider to finish the National. Suzuki had a similarly rotten weekend. Paul Smart struggled with transmission problems all day, causing him to over-rev the engine which finally had enough and came apart. Ron Grant retired with mechanical gremlins. Teammate Geoff Perry had been lost previous to the National in a plane crash over the Pacific. For a change, Team Kawasaki had everything, (well mostly), go their way, just in time to win their self-sponsored event.

Showing his never-die-attitude, Gary Scott's impressive podium run narrowed Kenny Roberts lead by 110 points, though Roberts still had a strong lead in the GNC points battle, 1079 to 815. Gary Nixon's win put him into third, though a long ways back at 561 points. Jim Rice scored some pavement points, but slipped back to fourth in the standings. Don Castro put in a good 9th place finish, maintaining fifth. Rex Beauchamp slipped from fourth to sixth, scoring no points, static at 430. Former champs Dick Mann and Mert Lawwill maintained their positions in seventh and eighth. Dave Aldana added some points with a 10th in the National, but stayed in ninth in points. Scott Brelsford hung onto tenth in points.

Heats

Things started off right for Team Green in Heat 1 with Hurley Wilvert out front early, followed closely by green shadows Cliff Carr and Art Baumann. By lap 2, Wilvert had dropped to 3rd behind Carr and Baumann. Behind, riders on three different brands of bikes scrapped for 4th spot. Steve Baker (Yam) battled with 1970 GNC champ Gene Romero and Norton rider Dave Croxford. At the front, Carr and Baumann fought right to the flag, with Carr taking the narrow win. Wilvert was 3rd with Baker prevailing in 4th.

In a virtual repeat of the first heat, three factory Green Machines jetted out front in Heat 2. Yvon DuHamel led teammates Gary Nixon and imported Japanese star Masahiro Wada through the early stages of the race. DuHamel pulled a gap on Nixon, going on to a convincing win. Wada fell into the clutches of last year's winner Cal Rayborn and Triumphs Gary Scott. Wada was overtaken by the impressive 4-stroke duo. At the flag it was DuHamel, Nixon, Rayborn, Scott, Wada and Kenny Roberts, Suzuki's best hope for the National, Paul Smart, fell out with transmission difficulties and would have to run the Semi event.

Semi

Roger Ring (Yam) led the early goings of the Semi, but gave way to a charging Paul Smart on his hastily repaired Suzuki. Moving through the pack were Marty Lunde (Yam) and Harley mounted Doug Sehl. Neither rider had started their heat, due to a blown engine and a crash respectively. Both moved past Ring who held onto 4th with Paul Smart way out front.

National

In a sight that had to warm Kawasaki Team Manager Bob Hansen's heart, it was six Kawasaki clones out front on Lap 1. Yvon DuHamel led, followed by Cliff Carr, Gary Nixon, Art Baumann, Marashio Wada and Hurley Wilvert. Wilvert soon dropped out when a spark plug self-ejected out of his bikes engine. Wada also had problems and had to pit, but did return to action. DuHamel began to pull away from now 2nd place Nixon, Carr and Baumann. GNC contenders Gary Scott and Kenny Roberts were duking it out over 5th out with Cal Rayborn and Norton's Peter Williams doing the same just behind.

As the race settled in, DuHamel held his lead over Nixon and as many behind began experiencing trouble, including teammate Carr. The rear brake caliper on Carr's machine began leaking fluid, resulting in a loss of braking and tire grip as the fluid coated his tire. Wada's Kawasaki continued to have problems. Yamaha Team Captain Kel Carruthers was sidelined by mechanical ills. Rayborn's Harley began to go off-song and Paul Smart was again struggling with transmission problems.

Back at the front, Nixon was catching DuHamel. The French-Canadian's was possibly slowed due to excess fuel coming out of the float bowels on his Kawasaki, misting his rear tire. As he tried to stay ahead of the closing Nixon, he fell coming out of the corkscrew while trying to put Rayborn a lap down. DuHamel jumped back up quickly, frustrated but uninjured. Nixon was now free and clear to the finish with Carr soldiering along behind. Art Baumann looked to have 3rd place sewed up till ignition trouble dashed hopes for a Kawasaki sweep of the podium. Kenny Roberts chain broke with 5 laps to go. Gary Scott moved up to 3rd spot upon Baumann's departure. Scott's placing was due to hard riding and a steady attrition rate In front of him. Steve Baker topped a late race duel with Peter Williams for 4th. Jim Evans managed to sneak past Rayborn for 6th in the last few corners. Rounding out the top 10 were Steve McLaughlin, lone factory Yamaha rider Don Castro and Dave Aldana on the domestic Team Norton.

Results

Race: Mile 75 Mile Road Race National
Race Time: 49:55.76

Rank	Rider	Number	Make
1.	Gary Nixon, Phoenix, Md	9	Kaw
2.	Cliff Carr, Arlington, Mass	26	Kaw
3.	Gary Scott, Baldwin Park, Ca	64	Tri
4.	Steve Baker, Bellingham, Wa	41	Yam
5.	Peter Williams, Hants, Eng	15	Nor
6.	Jim Evans, San Bernardino, Ca	47	Yam
7.	Cal Rayborn, Spring Valley, Ca	14	HD
8.	Steve McLauglin, Duarte, Ca	83	Yam
9.	Don Castro, Hollister, Ca	11	Yam
10.	Dave Aldana, Santa Ana, Ca	13	Nor
11.	Marty Lunde, Hermosa Beach, Ca	56	Yam
12.	Jim Rice, Palo Alto, Ca	24	HD
13.	Dick Mann, Richmond, Ca	2	Tri
14.	John Hateley, Van Nuys, Ca	98	Yam
15.	Howard Lynggard, Monrovia, Ca	102	Yam
16.	Mert Lawwill, San Francisco, Ca	7	HD
17.	Gene Romero, San Luis Obispo, Ca	3	Tri
18.	Dave Croxford, Ruislip, England	19	Nor
19.	Masahiro Wada, Nishimari, Japan	6	Kaw
20.	Dave Damron, San Bernardino, Ca	99	Suz

Grand National Points Standings after Round 14

Rank	Rider	Pts
1.	Kenny Roberts	1079
2.	Gary Scott	815
3.	Gary Nixon	561
4.	Jim Rice	452
5.	Don Castro	434
6.	Rex Beauchamp	430
7.	Dick Mann	348
8.	Mert Lawwill	342
9.	Dave Aldana	325
10.	Scott Brelsford	295

GNC Round #15 of 24 **Date:** August 3, 1973 **Type:** Short Track **Venue:** Sante Fe Speedway **Location:** Hinsdale, Ill	**Purse:** $12,000.00 **Surface:** Dirt **Course Length:** ¼ Mile **Laps:** 25

The "Ragin' Cajun" from Louisiana, Mike Gerald, repeated his 1972 win at the Sante Fe GNC short track. That, in itself, was not unusual 'cause besides being a high energy, fun character, Gerald was an excellent short track specialist. What was unusual was the fact that the top 4 were exactly the same as 1972! Don Castro, Darryl Hurst and Kenny Roberts also repeated their previous year's finishes. It was a dominant night for Yamaha two strokes; taking the first 8 spots in the National. More like the Lightweight road races of the day! For this race report, machine makes will only be mentioned if they are non-Yamahas!

With only three of the top 10 in points in the National, Kenny Roberts, Don Castro and Rex Beauchamp, there weren't any dramatic changes. Kenny Roberts piled on another 82 points over Gary Scott who failed to make the National. Their totals now stood at 1159 and 817 respectively. Gary Nixon remained in third with 561. Castro's runner-up performance in the National moved him into fourth past Jim Rice, now with 554 points. Beauchamp added some points with his 11th place finish. Dick Mann earned a few points with a 2nd place finish in the Trophy Race.

Heats

Pole sitter for Heat 1 was "Coon Ass" himself, Mike Gerald. His pole time of 15.97 was the only time under 16 seconds. Gerald was in the zone and dominated the heat. Dave Aldana was the early runner-up, but his Kawasaki seized. Mike Kidd (Bul), no slouch himself at Sante Fe, took the spot and last direct transfer. Fred Smith was 3rd, followed by Gordon Duesenberry (Bul), and Bill Fields (Bul).

Texan short track ace Darryl Hurst had things a little easier in Heat 2 when Teddy Newton and Harley teammates Mert Lawwill, Jim Rice were sent to the penalty line after the initial start. Hurst took the win over Corky Keener, Charlie Chapple and Dick Mann,t6 aboard his 350 BSA.

The 1971 Sante Fe winner Robert E Lee topped the final heat of the night. Rex Beauchamp came from a bad start to grab 2nd away from teammate Dave Sehl on his very rapid Harley Sprint; it would be the only 4-stroke to end up in the National. Behind Sehl was Chuck Palmgren, Pat McCaul and Charlie Seale.

Don Castro's chances for transferring out of Heat 4 to the Main looked bad when he jumped the initial start and was placed on the penalty line. Instead it seemed to fire Castro up and he proceeded to march to the front, passing everyone in front of him including leader and teammate Kenny Roberts! Gary Scott had his Montesa seize on the last lap, but still had a semi berth.

Semis

Tennessee rider Fred Smith led Buckeye Billy Field (Bul) into both of their first National appearances in their semi. Gary Scott had his bike seize again and he was done for the night.

Chuck Palmgren on his AAR ride ended up in a nifty battle with Neil Keen-backed Charlie Chapple. It was nip and tuck through their entire semi with Palmgren just edging out Chapple at the finish. Dick Mann was 3rd and headed to the Trophy Race.

Trophy Race

Popular Gordon Duesenberry topped the Trophy Race ahead of Dick Mann, who rode the wheels off his BSA, but just couldn't catch the leading Bultaco. Charlie Seale was 3rd.

National

The man to beat at Sante Fe, Mike Gerald, took control from early leader Robert E. Lee before lap 1 was out and he immediately jumped out in front and opened up a gap on the field. Lee would fade backwards the rest of the night. Don Castro did his best to keep Gerald in sight while trying to fend off pressuring Rex Beauchamp, who had his

Sprint humming. Some real racing was going on back in the field between Corky Keener, Chuck Palmgren, Charlie Chapple and on- the- move rides by Darryl Hurst and Kenny Roberts. Hurst and Roberts both methodically worked through the pack. Hurst was up to 4th spot late in the going and Roberts moving by Keener and Palmgren with around 5 to go. Keener managed to gain another spot late by getting around Palmgren. Up front, Gerald was long gone and Castro was still trying to hold off Beauchamp. Castro got a break when Beauchamp's Sprint gave up on lap 22, moving those behind up a spot. Things stabilized over the remaining laps with the top 5 at the flag reading Gerald, Castro, Hurst, Roberts and Keener.

Results

Race: 25 Lap Short Track National

Rank	Rider	Number	Make
1.	Mike Gerald, Baton Rouge, La	15	Yam
2.	Don Castro, Hollister, Ca	11	Yam
3.	Darryl Hurst, Houston, Tx	34	Yam
4.	Kenny Roberts, San Carlos, Ca	80	Yam
5.	Corky Keener, Goodrich, Mi	62	Yam
6.	Chuck Palmgren, Freehold, NJ	38	Yam
7.	Charlie Chapple, Flint, Mi	36	Yam
8.	Fred Smith, Memphis, Tn	18L	Yam
9.	Mike Kidd, Hurst, Tx	72	Bul
10.	Robert E. Lee, Ft. Worth, Tx	54	Yam
11.	Rex Beauchamp, Milford, Mi	31	HD
12.	Billy Field, Brunswick, Oh	48L	Bul

Race: Trophy Race

Rank	Rider	Number	Make
1.	Gordon Dusenberry, Wichita, Kan	81	Bul
2.	Dick Mann, Richmond, Ca	2	BSA
3.	Charlie Seale, Lantana, Fl	47	Bul
4.	Dale Furst, Sanford, Mi	48E	Oss
5.	Dave Sehl, Waterdown, Ont., Can	16	HD
6.	Tim Buckles, Houston, Tx	43M	Yam
7.	Pat McCaul, San Jose, Ca	48Y	Oss
8.	Mike Johnson, Flint, Mi	14E	Oss
9.	Steve Dalgarno, Baltimore, Md	66C	Bul
10.	Jim Rice, Palo Alto, Ca	24	HD
11.	Frank Ulicki, Kenosha, Wi	23G	HD
12.	Paul Pressgrove, Tecumseh, Ka	74	Bul

Grand National Points Standings after Round 15

Rank	Rider	Pts
1.	Kenny Roberts	1159
2.	Gary Scott	815
3.	Gary Nixon	561
4.	Don Castro	554
5.	Jim Rice	452
6.	Rex Beauchamp	430
7.	Dick Mann	348
8.	Mert Lawwill	342
9.	Dave Aldana	325
10.	Scott Brelsford	295

1973 Peoria TT
Lawwill Hot in Peoria!

GNC Round #16 of 24 **Date:** August 5, 1973 **Type:** TT **Venue:** Peoria Motorcycle Club Grounds **Location:** Peoria, Ill	**Purse:** $14,000.00 **Surface:** Dirt **Course Length:** ½ Mile **Laps:** 25

After years of trying, Mert Lawwill withstood the hot weather and competition to finally capture the Peoria GNC TT. It was National win number 13 for veteran Lawwill, who was a three-time TT winner, (twice at Castle Rock, once at Ascot), but never at Peoria. Lawwill's hottest competition came from high-flying Ascot TT winner Dave Aldana. Ahead of his time "Extreme Rider" Aldana was getting a lot of altitude and sailing much further over the revamped Peoria jump than anyone else in practice, including a crash on landing as well! This concerned (scared?) other riders and officials so much that heavy equipment was brought out to lower the jump! This did not deter Aldana who still took a banzai approach. He led the main till Lawwill went by near halfway and his engine went sour. GNC points leader Kenny Roberts in another solid ride, assumed 2nd place when Aldana began going backwards. Four-time Peoria winner Dick Mann came from far back to run up front, averted near disaster twice and still managed to nail down the final podium spot. Lawwill became the 14th different winner in 16 Nationals.

Kenny Roberts came out of the Sante Fe/Peoria weekend looking like very safe bet to take his first Grand National Championship. His lead over rival Gary Scott was 414 points, 1279 to 865. The two were way ahead of the rest of the pack. Don Castro had moved into third in points with a 584 point total. Gary Nixon managed to hang onto fourth, despite scoring no points. Jim Rice, usually strong at both events, had struggled on his Harley rides and dropped back to sixth. Dick Mann still held seventh, Rex Beauchamp slipped back to eighth. Dave Aldana and Gene Romero stayed in the last two spots.

Time Trials

Though it is unclear what role the twice-revised jump played in his run, Kenny Roberts (Yam) set a NTR with a 29.56 lap. The record was previously held by Mert Lawwill and Jim Rice with an identical 29.61.

Heats

Kenny Roberts led the entire distance in Heat 1, but received pressure the entire way. Though on opposite ends of the experience spectrum, rookie Scott Brelsford (HD) and veteran Dick Mann (Tri) showed near-equal speed and harassed Roberts the whole distance. The three factory riders took the direct tickets to the National. Finishing a short distance back were Californians Al Kenyon and Terry Dorsch, both Triumph mounted.

The 1970 winner of this event, Jim Rice, may have switched from BSA to Harley-Davidson, but there was no change in his speed. In the second heat, Rice stretched to a huge lead at the finish. Louisville winner Dave Sehl (HD) ran in 2nd spot till the last lap when GNC hopeful Gary Scott scooted by for the spot.

A neat holeshot in Heat 3 by Rex Beauchamp (HD) was negated when Dave Aldana (surprise!) got off hard on the factory Norton, bringing out a red flag. Mert Lawwill assumed command on the restart, chased savagely by the "Rubberball" Aldana. In a preview of the final, Lawwill's more conservative approach won out. Randy Scott (Tri) was third.

Chuck Joyner (Tri), victor at Castle Rock, led the whole way in Heat 4, but had to fend off a determined Don Castro (Yam) the whole distance. Yamaha riders Chuck Palmgren and Eddie Wirth had a good fight over the last direct transfer, with the decision decided in Palmgren's favor on the last lap. For Wirth the day was' a la the Ascot TT where he just missed transferring to the National all night.

Semis

Steve Dalgarno fell in the slippery first turn at the start of Semi 1. On the restart, Terry Dorsch and Al Kenyon renewed their heat race duel. This time the positions were reversed at the finish, but the important part was that both were headed to the final.

The second semi looked to be a battle between two former GNC TT winners, Gene Romero, (Lincoln 1968) and Eddie Wirth (Sante Fe 1969) but battling the two was a big surprise, short track specialist Mike Gerald! Gerald battled back and forth with the veterans, managing to come out on top with Romero second and a frustrated Wirth bound for the Trophy Race.

Trophy Race

This turned into more of an endurance event, as jumped starts and two red flags caused delays. On lap 2, Clarence "Punk" Wells and Pat Marinacci came off and out. In went alternates Darryl Hurst (Yam) and Jimmy Zeigler (Tri). Gordon Dusenberry (Tri) led the restart pressured hard by Keith Ulicki (HD). Nearing halfway Ulicki went down, taking Dusenberry with him. When the event finally got going again, Cal Rayborn (HD) tried to run off, but TT ace Sonny Burres (Tri) ran him down for the win.

National

Not surprising any of the 12,000+ present, Dave Aldana "banzied" the start, chased by Mert Lawwill, Scott Brelsford, Kenny Roberts, Dave Sehl and the rest of the hungry pack. Jim Rice fell in Turn 2, and despite tweaking his ankle, managed to get up and take off after the pack. Despite Aldana's pyrotechnics, he was hampered by a misfiring engine and a strong riding Lawwill. Mert took the lead on the 11th circuit. Aldana would continue, but began sliding rearwards. Scott Brelsford, who had a great day going in 3rd spot, crashed soon after in the first turn(s). Roberts now had a pretty comfortable 2nd spot. Aldana, Dave Sehl, Chuck Palmgren, Dick Mann, Gary Scott and Terry Dorsch all squabbled over top 5 positions. Scott and Aldana slipped a little off the pace, while Sehl had trouble, eventually finishing 12th. Mann put on a great charge into 3rd, pulling distance on Scott, Palmgren and Dorsch. Lap 20 saw near-disaster for Roberts who had his bike slide out from under him. With pushing help from Champion chassis man Doug Schwerma, Roberts got moving again. Mann closed up on Roberts, but nearly came off after the jump and then like Roberts, actually slid down in the same treacherous turn. He kept the bike running however, losing no positions. Out front, Lawwill was way ahead of Roberts; Mann maintained 3rd. On lap 23 both Palmgren and Dorsch went by Scott, setting the top 5.

Results

Race: 25 Lap TT National
Race Time: 12:50.12

Rank	Rider	Number	Make
1.	Mert Lawwill, San Francisco, Ca	7	HD
2.	Kenny Roberts, San Carlos, Ca	80	Yam
3.	Dick Mann, Richmond, Ca	2	Tri
4.	Chuck Palmgren, Freehold, NJ	38	Yam
5.	Terry Dorsch, Granada Hills, Ca	22	Tri
6.	Gary Scott, Baldwin Park, Ca	64	Tri
7.	Dave Aldana, Santa Ana, Ca	13	Nor
8.	Don Castro, Hollister, Ca	11	Yam
9.	Gene Romero, San Luis Obispo, Ca	3	Tri
10.	Al Kenyon, Cupertino, Ca	48	BSA
11.	Jim Rice, Palo Alto, Ca	24	HD
12.	Dave Sehl, Waterdown, Ont., Ca	16	HD
13.	Mike Gerald, Baton Rouge, La	15	Tri
14.	Scott Brelsford, Daly City, Ca	84Y	HD
15.	Chuck Joyner, Oregon City, Ore	60	Tri
16.	Randy Scott, Philomath, Ore	50	Tri

Race: Trophy Race

Rank	Rider	Number	Make
1.	Sonny Burres, Portland, Ore	69	Tri
2.	Cal Rayborn, Spring Valley, Ca	14	HD
3.	Buddy Powell, Noblesville, Ind	18H	Tri
4.	Eddie Wirth, Dana Point, Ca	84X	Yam
5.	Rex Beauchamp, Milford, Mi	31	HD
6.	Jim Crenshaw, Davis, Ca	21Y	Tri
7.	Gordon Dusenberry, Wichita, Ka	81	Tri
8.	Jimmy Zeigler, Bellville, Oh	9F	Tri
9.	Mike O'Brien, Danville, Ca	75Z	Tri
10.	Raymond Smith, Chicago, Ill	25P	Tri
11.	Darryl Hurst, Houston, Tx	34	Yam
12.	Keith Ulicki, Kenosha, Wi	86	HD

Grand National Points Standings after Round 16

Rank	Rider	Pts
1.	Kenny Roberts	1279
2.	Gary Scott	865
3.	Don Castro	584
4.	Gary Nixon	561
5.	Mert Lawwill	492
6.	Jim Rice	462
7.	Dick Mann	448
8.	Rex Beauchamp	440
9.	Dave Aldana	365
10.	Gene Romero	312

1973 Pocono Road Race
Nixon Makes it Three RR's in a Row!

GNC Round #17 of 24 **Date:** August 19, 1973 **Type:** Road Race **Venue:** Pocono International Raceway **Location:** Pocono, Pa	**Purse:** $15,000.00 **Surface:** Pavement **Course Length:** 2.8 Miles **Laps:** 27 **Distance:** 75 Miles

Making believers out of remaining naysayers, Gary Nixon dominated for his third National road race in a row. Nixon had the only "Green Meanie" left running at the end of the 75-Mile race. His Erv Kanemoto-tuned ride expired as he crossed the checkers. It was GNC win number 18 for two-time GNC champ Nixon. GNC point leader Kenny Roberts put in yet another solid road race finish in 2nd, way behind Nixon at the end. In 3rd was Roberts' teammate Gary Fisher, who passed more riders than anybody all weekend. Fisher had to start at the back of the grid after not starting his heat race after a total ignition failure.

The Pocono circuit was nearly universally disliked by the racers. Changed from it's 1.8 mile length from the 1971 GNC, it was a mile longer due to inclusion of a high speed straight with a chicane. The track ranged from blindingly fast to first gear twisties in the infield. It's surface was also treacherously slippery and inconsistent. Where there was traction one lap, there was none the next. Threats of rain did not help the rider's moods. A weak field of 32 Experts signed in.

Kenny Roberts continued to add to his points lead, getting very close to clinching the championship. Gary Scott turned in another great performance on his Trident, finishing 5th, trying to keep Roberts in sight. Nixon's third win moved him back into third in points, bumping Don Castro back a spot. Other than this, there were no other changes within in the top 10.

Heats

The first heat race turned into a Kawasaki procession, not that there wasn't some good racing. Yvon Duhamel (Kaw) shot out to the early lead with Gary Nixon (Kaw) right on his rear wheel. The two jetted away from the rest of the field. Trying to maintain contact were Cliff Carr (Kaw) and Kenny Roberts (Yam). Duhamel and Nixon looked as if they were on a mile dirt track, draft-passing through the event. Art Baumann made it four Kawasakis out front, dispatching Roberts back a spot. On the last lap, Nixon mounted a charge, taking the win over DuHamel.

It was Kawasaki Green out front again in Heat 2, but this time just the lone bike of master tuner/rider Hurley Wilvert . Wilvert had to work hard to keep ahead of an unexpected challenger, Cal Rayborn on a strong Harley-Davidson XRTT. After so many disappointments in '73, Calvin and machine were switched on this day, the big V-twin keeping Wilvert's triple in its sights. Ron Grant was in 3rd early, till caught up in a closing pack including Don Castro (Yam) and Gary Scott (Tri). Wilvert held Rayborn at bay for the win, with Castro in 3rd, Scott in 4th with Grant rounding out the top 5. Notable non-finishers included Gary Fisher, who never turned a lap due to ignition woes, and Paul Smart (Suz), who tossed it away in the new chicane, tweaking his ribs.

Due to threatening weather and slim rider count, the Semi race was scrapped.

National

Gary Nixon pulled the holeshot over DuHamel this time as the field shrieked, howled and rumbled away. Duhamel snuck by before the first lap was done. Nixon made what turned out to be the last pass for the lead on lap 3. Behind the leaders were Cal Rayborn, Hurley Wilvert and Art Baumann. Starting a bad Kawasaki day for all but one, Baumann was out early with a broken shifter. He was joined on lap 10 by DuHamel, whose 750 had a terminal failure. Wilvert moved into 2nd spot, chased again by Rayborn. Not far back were Cliff Carr, Kenny Roberts, Gary Fisher, Gary Scott and Jim Evans (Yam). Fisher had knifed through the pack from nearly dead last, passing 20-plus riders in the process. On lap 12, Rayborn's day was done with an unusual clutch basket failure. Just a couple of laps after Rayborn, Wilvert's run in 2nd was terminated with another Kawasaki death rattle. Cliff Carr also went out, not like Wilvert, but with a flat rear tire. Up front, Nixon stretched to a half-a-minute over his shook-up list of pursuers;

Roberts, Fisher, Evans and Scott. This set the top 5 for the duration. It wasn't without drama for Nixon, as he ran out of fuel just in sight of the flag.

Results

Race: 75 Mile Road Race National

Rank	Rider	Number	Make
1.	Gary Nixon, Phoenix, Md	9	Kaw
2.	Kenny Roberts, San Carlos, Ca	80	Yam
3.	Gary Fisher, Parkesburg, Pa	21	Yam
4.	Jim Evans, San Bernardino, Ca	47	Yam
5.	Gary Scott, Baldwin Park, Ca	64	Tri
6.	Ron Grant, Brisbane, Ca	61	Suz
7.	Don Castro, Hollister, Ca	11	Yam
8.	Conrad Urbanowski, Miramar, Fl	288	Yam
9.	Doug Libby, Milford, Mi	89	Yam
10.	Steve McLaughlin, Duarte, Ca	83	Yam
11.	Reg Pridmore, Santa Barbara, Ca	84	BMW
12.	Dave Aldana, Santa Ana, Ca	13	Nor
13.	Bart Myers, New Brunswick, NJ	68	Yam
14.	Dick Mann, Richmond, Ca	2	Tri
15.	Jean Lysight, Tracy, Que., Can	113	Yam
16.	Gene Romero, San Luis Obispo, Ca	3	Tri
17.	Larry Schafer, Hyattsville, Md	23	HD
18.	R.G. Wakefield, Indianapolis, Ind	78	Yam
19.	James Metrando, Poughkeepsie, NY	46	Yam
20.	Torello Tacchi, Chicago, Ill	86	Suz

Grand National Points Standings after Round 17

Rank	Rider	Pts
1.	Kenny Roberts	1411
2.	Gary Scott	931
3.	Gary Nixon	726
4.	Don Castro	628
5.	Mert Lawwill	492
6.	Jim Rice	462
7.	Dick Mann	456
8.	Rex Beauchamp	440
9.	Dave Aldana	375
10.	Gene Romero	315

Extra Extra

- Gary Nixon took home at least $15,842.00 for the weekend.
- Rain showers just before the National caused many to ponder their tire choices. Cal Rayborn made the switch to "rains" only to switch back when the sun came out.
- The 350 factory Yamaha appeared with modified production front disc brakes. They seemed to work okay, but were heavy.
- Kenny Roberts broke a clutch cable with around 5 laps remaining, but still held down the runner-up spot.
- Reg Pridmore was impressive aboard the Butler & Smith BMW, finishing 11th ahead of a lot of machinery that was supposed to be faster. Dave Aldana was just behind on the factory Norton.

- Junior John Long provided a shocker in the Combined Lightweight race, outrunning Kenny Roberts, Yvon DuHamel, Gary Nixon and Gary Fisher!
- The track's slippery nature was not helped by an onsite car racing school that put in lots of laps, as well as a National Motocross race held at the track the same weekend.
- The event was part of the Governor-proclaimed "Pennsylvania Motorcycle Week". The races themselves were billed as the Koni-Pocono Jamboree and Road Race Nationals.
- The Terre Haute National scheduled for August 12, 1973 was rained out and was rescheduled for September.

1973 Indianapolis Mile
Lawwill Again, at Indy!

GNC Round #18 of 24	**Location:** Indianapolis, In
Date: August 25, 1973	**Surface:** Dirt
Type: Mile	**Course Length**: 1 Mile
Venue: Indianapolis State Fairgrounds	**Laps:** 25
	Distance: 25 miles

Former GNC champion Mert Lawwill scored his second win of 1973 at the action-packed Indy Mile National. In a program full of good racing as well as a lot of attrition, Lawwill's Jim Belland/self-tuned XR750 had the horsepower and longevity to top an all-star field. Lawwill's efforts were aided when race leader Dave Sehl blew an engine, allowing the former champ to take the lead, which he stretched to the checkers. On what was the strongest Yamaha in the field, factory or private, last year's winner, Chuck Palmgren, was a front-runner throughout the event and finished in the runner-up position. Kenny Roberts got seriously out of shape early in the event, but proceeded to march through the field, up to 3rd position. Roberts really let it all hang out, as his Yamaha appeared down on ponies compared to the other front runners.

Roberts continued to stretch his points lead, now at 535 points over Gary Scott who finished 6th in the National. Gary Nixon scored no points, but held onto third in points. Mert Lawwill's win moved him up a spot, bumping 14th place finisher Don Castro to fifth. Jim Rice finished 12th and stayed put in sixth. Dave Aldana had a great run on his Norton, finishing 4th and moving up two spots in the standings to seventh. Dick Mann and Rex Beauchamp both finished well back in the National and each fell back a position in the points. Scott Brelsford finished 5th and broke into the top 10.

Time Trials

Mert Lawwill started the day out right, breaking Cal Rayborn's track record of 37.54 with a 37.52. Lawwill's performance once again showed the dedication he had to extract every pony out of his Harley-Davidson. Foretelling the finish later in the day, Chuck Palmgren's Yamaha was the second fastest bike in the field, not far back with a 37.93. These were the only two riders to break into the 37-second bracket. Former record holder Rayborn was 3rd quickest at 38.09. Kenny Roberts was 4th with a 38.44. Piloting his very fast factory Norton into the 5th spot with a 38.49 lap was Dave Aldana. Gary Scott ran a 38.52 on the fastest Triumph present. This made four different brands of machines in the top 6 qualifiers, illustrating the great brand parity present in 1973.

Heats

Mert Lawwill's domination continued as he marched out front quickly and ran away with the first 10-lap heat. Rex Beauchamp held second throughout the event despite constant pressure from Dick Mann (Tri) and Dave Aldana, who traded spots the whole race. Third went to Aldana with Mann right on his heels; the top four headed to the National.

Heat 2 found 1964 GNC champ Roger Reiman, always known for fielding a fast Harley, bolting out front at the wave of the green. He held the point for one lap before Gary Scott, Chuck Palmgren, Gene Romero (Tri) and Don Castro (Yam) drafted by. Palmgren showed the AAR machine's power advantage and immediately opened up a big lead and held on for the win. Castro topped the factory Triumphs, leading Scott and Romero into the big race. Reiman put in a good race, holding onto 5th, but was semi-bound.

Pole sitter Cal Rayborn led teammate Jim Rice away in Heat 3. Rayborn looked strong, quickly putting a near-100-foot lead on Rice. The Harley teamsters were trailed by the private Harley of Charlie Seale and Triumph mounted Mike Kidd. Fifth place runner Tommy Rockwood (Tri) had his engine let go on lap 8. With one lap to go, Rayborn's engine developed a carburetion problem and began running rough as he passed the white flag on one cylinder. Rice sailed by for the win, trailed by Seale and Kidd. Rayborn managed to just squeak across the line in 4th, ahead of Frank Ulicki, to grab the last direct transfer.

Dave Sehl (HD) and Kenny Roberts put on one of the best races of the night in Heat 4. Sehl was usually in command as they crossed the finish line, but a determined Roberts continually ran his machine in very deep, unofficially taking the lead numerous times. Sehl's Harley power paid off in the end and led where it counted. Behind the leaders, Gary Nixon, aboard a spare AAR Yamaha, battled with California riders Frank Gillespie (Yam) and Terry Dorsch (Tri) throughout the event. In the end, two-time GNC champ Nixon had to settle for 5th behind Gillespie and Dorsch.

Semis

Team Harley-Davidson rookie Scott Brelsford showed plenty of speed in Semi 1 and jetted off to the win. He won by a big margin over Del Armour (HD) who was also headed to the National.

Roger Reiman tried to run off again in the last semi, but was quickly gathered up by Gary Nixon, Mike Collins (Tri) and Dave Atherton (BSA). Nixon tried his best to hold the lead, but Mike Collins was a little faster. Nixon and Atherton dueled hard for the remaining National ticket. Atherton narrowly took the position in the closing laps.

Trophy Race

Texas short track ace Darryl Hurst (Yam) tried to run off with the "Consolation Race", but by lap 5 had to give up the lead to Georgia Harley rider Jimmy Maness. The two traded the spot a couple of times before Maness took over for good. Their squabble allowed Steve Droste (Yam) to catch and pass Hurst in the waning laps. Hurst also faced pressure from Ike Mizen, but held the 3rd spot.

National

The expected Lawwill holeshot failed to materialize, but he was a close 4th off the line behind Dave Sehl, Dave Aldana and Charlie Seale. Aldana shot by Sehl to lead lap 1, with Sehl quickly grabbing the spot back. The two riders hooked up in a draft and pulled a big lead on the field. As the early laps ticked by, Lawwill was up to 3rd, trying to gain on the lead duo. On lap 8, Sehl's Harley had it's bottom end let go and he was done. Aldana held the lead, but Lawwill soon motored by. Reeling Aldana in was Jim Rice, accompanied by Chuck Palmgren and Kenny Roberts, who was charging after getting out of shape during the early laps. Charlie Seale soon dropped out with mechanical trouble, which became all too common during the race. Seale joined the aforementioned Sehl, as well as Rex Beauchamp, Terry Dorsch and Dick Mann; there would be others. Just past the halfway mark, Lawwill had a big lead over Rice, who in turn had a similar lead over Aldana, Palmgren and Roberts. Aldana's Norton began to lose its edge, and Palmgren and Roberts moved to 3rd and 4th. It looked like the top 5 were set when on the last lap, Rice's engine let go, moving everybody behind up a spot, including Scott Brelsford, who moved to 5th. The top ten were; Lawwill, Palmgren, Roberts, Aldana, Brelsford, Gary Scott, Gene Romero, Frank Gillespie, Del Armour and Cal Rayborn, whose Harley was off-song again. Around half the field eventually fell out with mechanical problems, with Dave Atherton and Don Castro joining those already mentioned.

Results

Race: 25 Lap Mile National
Race Time: 16:21.88

	Rider	Number	Make
1.	Mert Lawwill, San Francisco, Ca	7	HD
2.	Chuck Palmgren, Freehold, NJ	38	Yam
3.	Kenny Roberts, San Carlos, Ca	80	Yam
4.	Dave Aldana, Santa Ana, Ca	13	Nor
5.	Scott Brelsford, Daly City, Ca	84Y	HD
6.	Gary Scott, Baldwin Park, Ca	64	Tri
7.	Gene Romero, San Luis Obispo, Ca	3	Tri
8.	Frank Gillespie, Berkeley, Ca	76	Yam
9.	Del Armour, Denver, Co	10M	HD
10.	Cal Rayborn, Spring Valley, Ca	14	HD
11.	Mike Collins, Albuquerque, NM	16M	Tri
12.	Jim Rice, Palo Alto, Ca	24	HD
13.	Dave Atherton, White Pigeon, Mi	15E	BSA
14.	Don Castro, Hollister, Ca	11	Yam

	Rider	Number	Make
15.	Mike Kidd, Hurst, Tx	72	Tri
16.	Charlie Seale, Lantana, Fl	47	HD
17.	Dick Mann, Richmond, Ca	2	Tri
18.	Dave Sehl, Waterdown, Ont., Can	16	HD
19.	Terry Dorsch, Granada Hills, Ca	22	Tri
20.	Rex Beauchamp, Milford, Mi	31	HD

Race: 12 Lap Trophy Race

Rank	Rider	Number	Make
1.	Jimmy Maness, Augusta, Ga	71	HD
2.	Steve Droste, Waterloo, Ia	26K	Yam
3.	Darryl Hurst, Houston, Tx	34	Yam
4.	Ike Mizen, Los Angeles, Ca	60R	Tri
5.	Eddie Wirth, Dana Point, Ca	84X	Yam
6.	Mike Johnson, Flint, Mi	14E	HD

Grand National Points Standings after Round 18

Rank	Rider	Pts
1.	Kenny Roberts	1521
2.	Gary Scott	986
3.	Gary Nixon	726
4.	Mert Lawwill	657
5.	Don Castro	636
6.	Jim Rice	472
7.	Dave Aldana	463
8.	Dick Mann	460
9.	Rex Beauchamp	441
10.	Scott Brelsford	368

Extra Extra

- Dave Sehl's early departure in the National was also a big blow to Team Norton's Dave Aldana. According to David, his Norton was fast, but couldn't lead the fastest machines that day. He and Sehl made perfect drafting partners. They were pulling away from the pack when Sehl's Harley blew and Aldana knew it would just be a matter of time before Lawwill and crew would reel him in. His 4th place run was his season's best oval track performance on the Nick Deligianis-tuned Norton.

Bonus!
Top 10 Indy Mile Qualifying Times

1.	Mert Lawwill	HD	37.52 seconds
2.	Chuck Palmgren	Yam	37.93
3.	Cal Rayborn	HD	38.09
4.	Kenny Roberts	Yam	38.44
5.	Dave Aldana	Nor	38.49
6.	Gary Scott	Tri	38.52
7.	Jim Rice	HD	38.53
8.	Dave Sehl	HD	38.57
9.	Rex Beauchamp	HD	38.61
10.	Gene Romero	Tri	38.71

GNC Round #19 of 24 **Date:** September 2, 1973 **Type:** Road Race **Venue:** Alabama International Motor Speedway	**Purse:** $20,000.00 **Location:** Talladega, Al **Surface:** Pavement **Course Length:** 1.8 Miles **Laps:** 38 **Distance:** 150 Miles

Kel Carruthers and the Yamaha crew may not have the most rapid machines during the 1973 season, but they had the steadiest. As the whole Kawasaki team and the fastest Suzuki either exploded or imploded, Carruthers soldiered on to his second and final GNC victory. Carruthers was the Yamaha team's manager, bike builder and tuner as well as a rider. This would be the talented Australian's last year in competition. Behind Carruthers, there were five other Yamahas rounding out the top 5. Rookie Canadian Steve Baker swept past unsuspecting veteran riders on his way to a very impressive 2nd spot aboard a Fred Deeley ride. Factory rider Gary Fisher rounded out the podium, with fellow team member Don Castro 4th and Jim Evans aboard the Mel Dineson entry was 5th. Many were expecting a sweep of the top spots at Talladega, but not by Yamaha!

GNC points leader Kenny Roberts' bike gave up late in the race, scoring just a few points. It would have been a perfect time for Gary Scott to score another top finish on his aging Triumph, but he had trouble as well. It was a missed opportunity for Scott to reel Roberts in with the fat road race points available. Their points gap remained about the same. Don Castro and Dick Mann were the only other in the GNC top ten to finish in the top of the order. Castro was 4th and Mann 12th. Both moved up a spot in the standings.

Time Trials

The grid for the 150 Miler was set with traditional flying laps. 'Ala Daytona, a chicane had been installed to slow the 750's down. The change knocked around 3 mph off the lap speeds. There were no heats and no Semi event due to the very slender 29 rider field. The front row of the grid was dominated by the big 750's. Two-time winner Yvon DuHamel was fastest with a 110.344 lap. He was joined by most of the Kawasaki team including Gary Nixon, Art Baumann and Cliff Carr. Only Paul Smart's Suzuki was the only non-Green bike on the front row. Team Yamaha, would start mostly from row 2, but time was on their side this day.

National

Gary Nixon, who was hoping to make it four road race Nationals in a row, led the grid away at the drop of the green. Yvon Duhamel stayed right with the two-time champ, taking a few shots, but not quite getting by. Right behind were Art Baumann and Hurley Wilvert, making it all Kawasaki up front. Wilvert slid off hard and was out on lap 4: the first Team Green casualty. Behind, Carruthers and crew bided their time. They, along with Paul Smart, knew the thirsty Kawasaki pit stops would begin soon. So it was, on lap 13, when Nixon and Duhamel came in. All went well till the Kawasaki curse knocked Nixon out on the next lap. Paul Smart had worked by the Yamahas into the lead, with DuHamel trying to make up lost ground. Smart pulled in for fuel on lap 18. His stop was a disaster as the fuel nozzle was stuck in the tank for an agonizingly long time. Abusing the Suzuki hard, he set out after DuHamel, who now had a half-a-minute lead. Around lap 23, DuHamel exploded the carefully prepared Steve Whitelock engine. The bike was on fire, forcing DuHamel to bail off with the bike still moving. Paul Smart stepped into the lead with a good gap to back to Carruthers and Cal Rayborn (HD). Rayborn had steadily worked his way forward as the two-strokes pitted. Just before the 30th lap, both leaders were gone when Rayborn's throttle malfunctioned and Smart's Suzuki had its bottom end give up. Carruthers inherited a nice lead over a gaggle of Yamahas, including Don Castro, Gary Fisher, Kenny Roberts and unknown Steve Baker. As Fisher and Castro dueled, they were joined by young Baker. They assumed this guy was a lap down and let him go. Roberts had his bike expire in the closing laps. Fisher got past Castro for third and the order for the finish was Carruthers, Baker, Fisher, Castro, Jim Evans and in 6th was Ron Grant aboard a Suzuki, the first non-Yamaha.

Results

Race: 150 Mile Road Race National

Rank	Rider	Number	Make
1.	Kel Carruthers, El Cajon, Ca	73	Yam
2.	Steve Baker, Bellingham, Wa	41	Yam
3.	Gary Fisher, Parkesburg, Pa	21	Yam
4.	Don Castro, Hollister, Ca	11	Yam
5.	Jim Evans, San Bernardino, Ca	47	Yam
6.	Ron Grant, Brisbane, Ca	61	Suz
7.	Doug Libby, Milford, Mi	89	Yam
8.	Steve McLaughlin, Duarte, Ca	83	Yam
9.	Bart Myers, New Brunswick, NJ	68	Yam
10.	Gene Romero, San Luis Obispo, Ca	3	Tri
11.	Harry Cone, Sherman, Tx	77	Yam
12.	Dick Mann, Richmond, Ca	2	Tri
13.	R.G. Wakefield, Indianapolis, Ind	78	Yam
14.	Robert Winters, Ft. Smith, Ark	4	Yam
15.	Gary Scott, Baldwin, Park, Ca	64	Tri
16.	Marty Lunde, Hermosa Beach, Ca	56	Yam
17.	Torello Tacchi, Chicago, Ill	86	Suz
18.	Doug Sehl, Waterdown, Ont., Can	45	HD
19.	Cal Rayborn, Spring Valley, Ca	14	HD
20.	Stan Friduss, Gainesville, Fl	79	Yam

Grand National Points Standings after Round 19

Rank	Rider	Pts
1.	Kenny Roberts	1521
2.	Gary Scott	943
3.	Gary Nixon	724
4.	Don Castro	716
5.	Mert Lawwill	657
6.	Jim Rice	472
7.	Dick Mann	470
8.	Dave Aldana	463
9.	Rex Beauchamp	441
10.	Kel Carruthers	441

Extra Extra

- Kel Carruthers pocket $6275.00 from the Talladega purse.
- The fastest Kawasaki bikes were running trap speeds in the 175 mph range. The Suzukis were very close to the same speeds. The best Yamahas were just under 160 mph. The four strokes just weren't close.
- Cliff Carr tore up his Kevin Cameron-tuned Kawasaki in late morning practice and was forced to spectate the rest of the day.
- Some of the Triumph Triples were fighting ignition problems right up to race time. Dick Mann managed to catch the departing pack, Gary Scott joined the field a lap down.
- Gene Romero finished 10th on his Triumph for the best four stroke finish. Dick Mann was 12th, Gary Scott 15th. Harley riders Doug Sehl and Cal Rayborn were 18th and 19th.
- It was wall-to-wall Yamahas in the Combined Lightweight as well. Kenny Roberts took the win, followed by Gary Fisher, Kel Carruthers and Don Castro. Pocono winner John Long was 5th.

1973 Terre Haute Half-Mile
Beauchamp Wins First!

GNC Round #20 of 24 **Date:** September 3, 1973 **Type:** Half-Mile **Venue:** Terre Haute Speedway **Location:** Terre Haute, In	**Purse:** $12,000.00 **Location:** Terre Haute, In **Surface:** Dirt **Course Length:** ½ Mile **Laps:** 20 **Distance:** 10 Miles

Fulfilling the confidence that Harley-Davidson and Dick O'Brien placed in him, Rex Beauchamp scored his first ever GNC win at the rescheduled Terre Haute Half-Mile. Beauchamp first got factory support as an Amateur and Harley had maintained their support. His rookie Expert year in 1971 was rough; Rex suffered through several injuries as well as the Iron XR. In 1972, his luck had improved, but 1973 was his breakout year. He seemed destined for a win after several strong runs such as the Colorado Mile and Sante Fe short track. Only bad luck had kept him out of the top spot. The likeable Michigan rider was a natural talent in the Bart Markel tradition. He never stopped trying and believing he could do it. Beauchamp had to fight past a determined Charlie Seale and veteran Dave Sehl for the win. In the closing laps, Mert Lawwill was coming hard in second, but ran out of laps. Sehl led the most laps on the day, but faded to third via Beauchamp, Lawwill and rough track conditions. Charlie Seale had one of his best days ever, leading the race early and hanging on to a finish in 4th spot.

Kenny Roberts and Gary Scott finished 5th and 6th, with the points gap remaining about the same, their totals now 1581 and 1043 respectively. Mert Lawwill's runner-up finish propelled him up two spots to third with 777. Gary Nixon and Don Castro scored points in the Trophy Race, but each slipped back a spot. Rex Beauchamp's win moved him from ninth to sixth in points. Jim Rice and Dick Mann both lost two positions in the standings with Kel Carruthers still rounding out the tenth spot.

Time Trials
The bumpy, fast, clay "car-type" surface seemed to favor the Milwaukee V-twins. Harley teamsters Rex Beauchamp, (25.70), Cal Rayborn, (26.00) and Mert Lawwill, (26.04) posted the fastest times of the day. A skimpy field of 34 riders signed up for qualifications.

Heats
In Heat 1, Jim Rice, on another factory supported Harley, jumped in front of pole sitter Beauchamp and the rest of the field. Dick Mann (Tri) moved into 2nd spot, followed by Beauchamp. As the laps wound down, Beauchamp moved past Mann and pressured Rice till the laps ran out. As these heats only took the top 2, Mann was headed to the semis.

Heat 2 started out as yet another faceoff between rivals Kenny Roberts (Yam) and Gary Scott (Tri). Scott moved into the lead with Roberts in tow. The two began trading the lead all over the track. Mert Lawwill soon joined the fracas. The wide Terre Haute surface meant plenty of racing room for the top 3. As the laps ran down, the situation was in doubt. On the last lap, the three crossed the line side-by-side. Lawwill took a very narrow win with Roberts moving with him to the National. Gary Scott was semi-bound.

It was all Harley-Davidson in Heat 3; Dave Sehl, the 1971 Terre Haute winner, won with comparative ease. Charlie Seale moved from midpack to take 2nd spot. Rookie Scott Brelsford was 3rd. Seale's private XR split the factory bikes of Sehl and Brelsford.

Dave Aldana (Nor) always seemed to run good at Terre Haute, and took the win in Heat 4, followed by Chuck Palmgren (Yam) and Illinois rider Mickey Greene.

Semis
Triumph teammates Dick Mann and Gene Romero were quickly out front in Semi 1, gaining a comfortable lead on the pack. Mann looked to have it in the bag, but with one to go his engine fell on its face, allowing Romero, Scott Brelsford, (HD) and Frank Gillespie (Yam) to blow past. Only Romero and Brelsford would move on.

Cal Rayborn charged to the lead in Semi 2 and never looked back. Gary Scott and Don Castro (Yam) battled hard all over the track for the very last ticket to the National in a tough matchup. Scott managed to top Castro after some great action.

Trophy Race

Don Castro took the Trophy race win handily over Teddy Poovey and Dave Atherton. Castro barely made the program after losing an engine in Heat 1. The low rider count, combined with Doug Sehl scratching from the program, got Don a shot in the semi.

National

The race took two tries to get started after Scott Brelsford went down spectacularly in turn 3. Brelsford made the restart. Accused of jumping the start, Gary Scott and Gene Romero were sent to the penalty line Jim Rice repeated his heat race holeshot, leading the field into turn 1. There almost as many lines as riders, as the field sorted itself out. Charlie Seale raised a few eyebrows as he looked strong in the 2nd spot, followed by Dave Sehl, Kenny Roberts, Rex Beauchamp and Gary Scott. Mert Lawwill was way back in the early going. Sehl soon moved Seale back to 3rd position. Mert Lawwill was now beginning to slice his way through the pack. Rice looked uncatchable out front till lap 7, when ignition problems sidelined him for the day. Since his win at Columbus, Rice's luck had seemed to sour with either mechanical trouble or spills haunting him. Sehl now assumed the lead, with Seale behind. Beauchamp and Lawwill had dropped Roberts back to 5th spot. Just past halfway, Beauchamp passed Seale for the runner-up spot. He now set his sights on leader Sehl. Lap 16 saw Beauchamp take the top spot while Lawwill dropped Seale back to 4th. The still-charging Lawwill passed Sehl on the last lap, but ran out time as Beauchamp took the win.

Results

Race: 20 Lap Half-Mile National

Rank	Rider	Number	Make
1.	Rex Beauchamp, Milford, Mi	31	HD
2.	Mert Lawwill, San Francisco, Ca	7	HD
3.	Dave Sehl, Waterdown, Ont., Can	16	HD
4.	Charlie Seale, Lantana, Fl	47	HD
5.	Kenny Roberts, San Carlos, Ca	80	Yam
6.	Gary Scott, Baldwin Park, Ca	64	Tri
7.	Cal Rayborn, Spring Valley, Ca	14	HD
8.	Dave Aldana, Santa Ana, Ca	13	Nor
9.	Gene Romero, San Luis Obispo, Ca	3	Tri
10.	Chuck Palmgren, Freehold, NJ	38	Yam
11.	Scott Brelsford, Daly City, Ca	84Y	HD
12.	Jim Rice, Palo Alto, Ca	24	HD

Race: Trophy Race

Rank	Rider	Number	Make
1.	Don Castro, Hollister, Ca	11	Yam
2.	Teddy Poovey, Garland, Tx	42N	HD
3.	Dave Atherton, White Pigeon, Mi	15E	BSA
4.	Del Armour, Denver, Co	10M	HD
5.	Gary Nixon, Phoenix, Md	9	Yam
6.	Eddie Wirth, Dana Point, Ca	84X	Yam

Grand National Points Standings after Round 20

Rank	Rider	Pts
1.	Kenny Roberts	1581
2.	Gary Scott	1043
3.	Mert Lawwill	777
4.	Gary Nixon	726
5.	Don Castro	724
6.	Rex Beauchamp	591
7.	Dave Aldana	493
8.	Jim Rice	481
9.	Dick Mann	470
10.	Kel Carruthers	441

1973 Atlanta Mile
Scott Brelsford Wins Debacle
Roberts Clinches GNC Title!

GNC Round #21 of 24	**Purse:** $15,000.00
Date: September 10, 1972	**Surface:** Dirt
Type: Mile	**Course Length**: 1 Mile
Venue: Lakewood Raceway	**Laps:** 25
Location: Atlanta, Ga	**Distance:** 25 miles

Scott Brelsford deserved better than having his first (and only) win come at the mess that was the 1973 Atlanta Mile GNC. The Lakewood facility was usually troublesome, with an inconsistent, rough, dusty surface. They had a perfect storm this day: terrible dust, ineffective track preparation, late program and unhappy fans. Veteran promoter Don Brymer fortunately escaped without bodily harm. The National only made it a few laps, officially 5 before being called. Gary Scott was listed as in 2nd position and Rex Beauchamp was 3rd. The race paid no National points; riders were paid according to their finishing positions. Scott Brelsford would later lodge a protest, arguing if the results were "official" enough for the riders to be paid, the National points should be similarly awarded.

On a brighter note, Kenny Roberts clinched the Grand National Championship with three rounds remaining. He had a 538 point lead and only 480 points were available in the remaining events. Roberts' performances had included two wins so far, and many top 5's. Runner-up Gary Scott had been plagued with mechanical trouble and a bad string of luck, (similar to Roberts' performance the year before). For Scott, it was two years in a row where he just missed the top spot.

Time Trials
Indy winner Mert Lawwill posted the quickest time at 41.67 aboard his factory supported, Jim Belland/self-tuned Harley-Davidson. Rex Beauchamp (HD) and Kenny Roberts (Yam) were next, tied at 41.75. Gary Scott (Tri) ran a 41.75. Reflecting the poor track conditions, times were way off Rex Beauchamp's record of 38.59.

Heats
Scott Brelsford had showed great speed and versatility in his rookie year and it was apparent early in the Atlanta program as he won the first and fastest heat wire-to-wire. He powered his Bill Werner/Fausto Vitello prepped factory Harley ahead of Mile wizard Mert Lawwill, Dave Sehl (HD) and Don Castro (Yam). All transferred directly to the National.

Terre Haute winner Rex Beauchamp had his factory Harley humming and after passing early leader Dick Mann (Tri), disappeared with the win in Heat 2. Mike Kidd (Tri) and two-time GNC champ Mann were making a race of it for 2nd spot. The two traded places all over the dusty battlefield for most of the heat, with Kidd coming out on top. Road race ace Cal Rayborn (HD) held on for the final transfer spot.

Similar to the last event, Heat 3 saw the leader run away, this time GNC points leader Kenny Roberts (Yam), with the real race behind him. Gene Romero (Tri) and Dave Aldana (Nor) went at it with Romero ending up with the runner-up position. Two-time GNC champ and tough guy Gary Nixon (Tri) showed he could still dirt track by finishing in 4th spot on the rough track.

Heat 4 was a battle between Gary Scott and Jim Rice (HD) who was hoping his luck would improve. Scott led early, with Rice taking over on lap 2. Scott applied heavy pressure and just managed to nip Rice in a "photo finish". Chuck Palmgren took 3rd spot on the AAR/Steed Yamaha. Rounding out the transfer spots was Harley-mounted, Florida hotshoe Charlie Seale (HD).

Semis
Frank Gillespie, on the rapid Gillespie Racing Yamaha, dominated the first Semi with Keith Ulicki on the Uke's HD ride in second.

Home state favorite Jimmy Maness (HD) gave the crowd something to cheer about when he won Semi 2. Canadian Doug Sehl, also Harley mounted, took the last spot to the National.

Trophy Race

JR Rawls and Teddy Poovey made it two for Texas in the Trophy Race. Eddie Wirth, on the Shell Racing Yamaha, rounded out the top 3.

National

Scott Brelsford blasted off the line and led the riders into turn 1. Once the field got rolling, only the first handful of riders were visible. The rest were lost in a huge dust cloud. The race had been started in the sunset and the riders were nearly blinded by the sun/dust combination as they came onto the front straight. Riders began pulling off led by Jim Rice, Dick Mann and Mert Lawwill. A few more laps were run before the officials red flagged the event.

Controversy reigned as AMA Pro Racing Ref Bill Boyce and Referee Charlie Watson tried to figure out what to do as well as trying to calm the agitated racers. After meeting with Rider Representatives including Gary Nixon, Dick Mann, Mert Lawwill and Cal Rayborn, (all of whom were in the National), the officials decided to call the race complete. No National points, but money would be paid based on finishing position. The riders were pacified, but the fans were not. They had sat through a hot, dusty, drawn-out program and a near riot began. Bottles were thrown, insults hurled and the police moved in. Peace was restored and the crowd went home. Scott Brelsford definitely was capable of winning and was credited with the weird 5 Mile victory. Kenny Roberts was the new GNC champ, but this too was under strange conditions and little celebration was evident as the day closed at Atlanta.

Results

Race: 25 Lap Mile National

Rank	Rider	Number	Make
1.	Scott Brelsford, Daly City, Ca	84Y	HD
2.	Gary Scott, Baldwin Park, Ca	64	Tri
3.	Rex Beauchamp, Milford, Mi	31	HD
4.	Chuck Palmgren, Freehold, NJ	38	Yam
5.	Gene Romero, San Luis Obispo, Ca	3	Tri
6.	Kenny Roberts, San Carlos, Ca	80	Yam
7.	Dave Aldana, Santa Ana, Ca	13	Nor
8.	Don Castro, Hollister, Ca	11	Yam
9.	Mike Kidd, Hurst, Tx	72	Tri
10.	Gary Nixon, Phoenix, Md	9	Tri
11.	Jimmy Maness, Augusta, Ga	71	HD
12.	Keith Ulicki, Kenosha, Wi	86	HD
13.	Doug Sehl, Waterdown, Ont., Can	45	HD
14.	Frank Gillespie, Berkeley, Ca	76	Yam
15.	Charlie Seale, Lantana, Fl	47	HD
16.	Cal Rayborn, Spring Valley, Ca	14	HD
17.	Dave Sehl, Waterdown, Ont., Can	16	HD
18.	Dick Mann, Richmond, Ca	2	Tri
19.	Mert Lawwill, San Francisco, Ca	7	HD
20.	Jim Rice, Palo Alto, Ca	24	HD

Race: Trophy Race

Rank	Rider	Number	Make
1.	JR Rawls, Grande Prairie, Tx	41N	HD
2.	Teddy Poovey, Garland, Tx	42N	HD
3.	Eddie Wirth, Dana Point, Ca	84X	Yam
4.	Jim Houston, Richmond, Va	18C	HD
5.	Johnny Goad, Richmond, Va	62C	HD

GNC Round #22 of 24 **Date:** September 16, 1973 **Type:** Road Race **Venue:** Charlotte Motor Speedway **Location:** Charlotte, NC	**Purse:** $25,000.00 **Surface:** Pavement **Course Length:** 1.8 Miles **Laps:** 42 **Distance:** 75

Yvon DuHamel finally put it all together to score his first win of 1973. The talented French-Canadian had run up front all year, but one problem or another had kept him out of victory circle. DuHamel thoroughly dominated this day at the tight Charlotte circuit. While no one else could have probably caught him this day, his job was made easier when many contenders had mechanical trouble, including three-time 1973 road race winner Gary Nixon, Paul Smart, Cal Rayborn and Art Baumann. In addition, Dick Mann and Dave Aldana sat out the event after being injured at a local half-mile race before the National. Mann suffered a suspected bruised kidney and Aldana a broken finger. While for all intents and purposes, Kenny Roberts had wrapped up the GNC title at Atlanta; his solid 2nd place finish at Charlotte really sealed the deal. Late in the race, Hurley Wilvert secured the last podium spot from teammate Cliff Carr whose bike was suffering transmission problems.

Even though the championship was decided, Gary Scott didn't let up wheeling his Trident to an impressive 5th spot. Don Castro's 6th place put him back in front of the topsy-turvy points battle behind Scott.

The last Charlotte road race was sparsely attended by both spectators and riders. Only 36 competitors signed in and the standard 75-Mile program was altered accordingly. Instead of two 20-lap heats and a semi, two 5-lap heat races would set the grid, with no semi event.

Heats

Yvon DuHamel was up and gone in Heat 1, the short 5-lap distance a perfect match for his flat-out style. Paul Smart's Suzuki was sluggish off the start, but he got the engine cleaned out and ripped through the pack for 2nd place. Suzuki teammate Ron Grant was 3rd, Kenny Roberts (Yam) 4th and Cal Rayborn (HD) 5th. Gary Nixon, the hottest road racer of the year, was left sitting on the line with ignition woes.

It was all Team Green early in Heat 2, with hard luck Art Baumann out front, pursued by teammates Hurley Wilvert and Cliff Carr, with Steve Baker giving chase on the Deeley Yamaha. About the time Baumann looked to be turning his luck around, his engine locked up on lap 3, right in front of the lead pack. Baker took advantage of the confusion, shooting the 350 Yamaha past the powerhouse Kawasaki's. While Wilvert and Carr tried, there was no catching the fleet Washington youngster.

National

Yvon DuHamel immediately put the hammer down at the start of the 75-Mile National, leading teammate Hurley Wilvert, Yamaha's Don Castro and Steve Baker away on the opening lap. Cliff Carr quickly picked his way through the lead pack and moved into 2nd place behind DuHamel. Art Baumann had started the race at the back of the field, but a brand new engine gave up in just a few laps. Teammate Gary Nixon was having better luck from his last row start; by the end of lap 1, he had passed half the field. DuHamel and Carr pulled a gap over the following pack, now consisting of Grant, Castro, Ron Grant and Kenny Roberts. Nixon continued to slice through the field, knocking on the door of the top 10 by lap 5. On lap 6, Paul Smart blew a tire and was out. Cal Rayborn was trying his best to stay with the lead pack, but his Harley began misfiring and he dropped out on lap 13. He was soon joined by Nixon, whose heroic charge to the front was cut short by another ignition failure.

At the front of the pack DuHamel stretched his lead over Carr whose transmission was beginning to act up. Roberts snatched 3rd place from Wilvert. As the race hit the mid-way point, Roberts caught the slowing Carr and took over 2nd place. Carr was having trouble with the first two gears; a necessity in the Charlotte slow speed twisties. Heat winner Steve Baker dropped out with ignition trouble. As the laps ticked off, DuHamel had a nearly 20-second lead over Roberts, who had a comfortable lead over everybody else. Carr continued to drop back and Wilvert took over

3rd. Carr slipped back to 7th at the finish. Ron Grant moved to 4th and Gary Scott moved his Triumph past Don Castro late in the race. DuHamel gave the peace sign as he passed the stripe on the final lap, soon heading off to collect the big Kawasaki contingency money with tuner Steve Whitelock.

Results

Race: 75 Mile Road Race National

Rank	Rider	Number	Make
1.	Yvon DuHamel, LaSalle, Ont., Can	17	Kaw
2.	Kenny Roberts, San Carlos, Ca	80	Yam
3.	Hurley Wilvert, Westminster, Ca	91	Kaw
4.	Ron Grant, Brisbane, Ca	61	Suz
5.	Gary Scott, Baldwin Park, Ca	64	Tri
6.	Don Castro, Hollister, Ca	11	Yam
7.	Cliff Carr, Arlington, Mass	26	Kaw
8.	Gary Fisher, Parkesburg, Pa	21	Yam
9.	Steve McLaughlin, Duarte, Ca	83	Yam
10.	Jean Lysight, Tracy, Que., Can	113	Yam
11.	Doug Libby, Milford, Mi	89	Yam
12.	Bart Myers, New Brunswick, NJ	68	Yam
13.	Harry Cone, Sherman, Tx	77	Yam
14.	Larry Schafer, Hyatsville, Md	23	HD
15.	R.G. Wakefield, Indianapolis, Ind	78	Yam
16.	Doug Sehl, Waterdown, Ont., Can	45	HD
17.	Stan Friduss, Gainesville, Fl	79	Yam
18.	Gene Romero, San Luis Obispo, Ca	3	Tri
19.	Jeff March, Springfield, Ill	32	Yam
20.	Steve Baker, Bellingham, Wa	41	Yam

Grand National Points Standings after Round 22

Rank	Rider	Pts
1.	Kenny Roberts	1713
2.	Gary Scott	1109
3.	Don Castro	779
4.	Mert Lawwill	777
5.	Gary Nixon	726
6.	Rex Beauchamp	591
7.	Dave Aldana	493
8.	Jim Rice	481
9.	Dick Mann	470
10.	Kel Carruthers	441

1973 Ontario Road Race
DuHamel Wins Twice!

GNC Round #23 of 24 **Date:** September 30, 1973 **Type:** Road Race **Venue:** Ontario Motor Speedway **Location:** Ontario, Ca	**Purse:** $53,100.00 **Surface:** Pavement **Course Length:** 1.8 Miles **Laps:** 69 Per Segment **Distance:** 250 Miles, 2 X 125 Mile Segments

Kawasaki's Yvon DuHamel closed out the year strong, winning both 125-mile legs of the Ontario/Champion Spark Plugs race. Not only did he have identical results in both segments, so did the other first 6 finishers! For DuHamel it was his second GNC Road Race win in a row and the fifth of his career. It was also the last National win for the fiery French-Canadian. Team Kawasaki had seemingly solved their engines' tendency to devour their own reciprocating assemblies. Gary Nixon finished out a great year with two runner-up finishes, harassing DuHamel in both races. Teammate Art Baumann finally had great run after a terrible year.

The Ontario facility was still generally disliked by the riders, (except those getting the big $$), as well as fans. The facility had been troubled since opening, struggling to find fans, particularly the motorcycle type. It was still hanging on, it seemed just a question of how long.

Gary Nixon's runner-up finishes finally settled the dust-up between himself, Don Castro and Mert Lawwill over third in points. The Roberts-Scott duel for the title had been static for a long time, but the rest of the positions had constantly changed through the season.

Heats

The short heat races on Saturday probably had the best bang for the buck, racing-wise, but there were few fans. Heat 1 had to give Art Baumann (Kaw) hope, as he edged out Kenny Roberts and teammate Yvon DuHamel (Kaw). Rounding out the top 5, quite a ways back, was Steve Baker on the Yamaha Motor Canada ride and a hopeful Cal Rayborn (HD).

Heat 2 may have been the race of the weekend. Gary Scott was riding the war horse Triumph Trident for all it was worth, mixing it up with fast machines of Team Kawasaki, Gary Nixon and Cliff Carr. To make up for the raw two-stroke straightaway power of Nixon and Carr, Scott was blazing through the infield on guts and the still great handling of his Triumph. The three repeatedly swapped places on the track, Kawasaki's ruling the WFO sections, Triumph the twisties. Scott led coming out of the last corner, but Carr and Nixon powered by at the stripe. They were trailed by Hurley Wilvert (Kaw) and Paul Smart (Suz).

Segment 1

Team Green headed out front at the start with Yvon DuHamel away first, chased by Art Baumann and Gary Nixon. Trying to keep them honest were Kenny Roberts, Cliff Carr, Don Castro and the rest of the pack. Nixon was working on Baumann and squeezed past on lap 6. Coming from the back, Paul Smart was on a tear and moved past Hurley Wilvert for 6th. The four strokes were having a rough day: Cal Rayborn and Mert Lawwill had their Harleys break at almost the same time, albeit for different reasons. Dave Aldana's Norton was parked by an oil leak. Gary Scott was running near the front pack, pushing hard he fell, but got going again quickly. His seat had also come loose, making a tough task even harder and went down again pretty hard while fighting with Steve Baker. Up front, Nixon pressured DuHamel and worked by for the lead. This of course just fired DuHamel up and the two began swapping places all over. The thirsty Kawasakis were soon due for fuel, around the 17th lap. Nixon's stop was faster and the chase continued. Eight laps later and DuHamel was by for good. The positions remained relatively static till the end with them coming home, DuHamel, Nixon, Baumann, Roberts, Smart, Baker, Kel Carruthers, Ron Pierce, Gene Romero with the first four stroke and Gary Fisher.

Segment 2

Gary Nixon pulled a tremendous holeshot in the last segment, leading by close to a football field length into turn 1. Chasing were Art Baumann, Kenny Roberts, Cliff Carr and Yvon DuHamel, (a poor start for the French-Canadian). Carr went to work, moving past Roberts and Baumann before engine woes hit him again. DuHamel began a steady march forward and soon moved in behind Nixon. The two began to go at it again, neither having a clear advantage. Finally, DuHamel cleared away, turning the fastest laps of the race. Behind, Roberts was all over Baumann, taking the advantage in the corners, with Baumann ripping by on the straights. Baumann exerted control after the first pit stops. The leaders also pitted, with Nixon's stop being a little quicker. Duhamel mounted another charge, but Nixon had cooled it anyway to save rapidly wearing rear tire. So it was, as DuHamel stretched away to another win, with the top 6 settling into the same order as Segment 1.

Results

Race: 250 Mile Road Race National

Rank	Rider	Number	Make
1.	Yvon DuHamel, LaSalle, Ont., Can	17	Kaw
2.	Gary Nixon, Phoenix, Md	9	Kaw
3.	Art Baumann, Brisbane, Ca	30	Kaw
4.	Kenny Roberts, San Carlos, Ca	80	Yam
5.	Paul Smart, Sante Fe Springs, Ca	8	Suz
6.	Steve Baker, Bellingham, Wa	41	Yam
7.	Kel Carruthers, El Cajon, Ca	73	Yam
8.	Gene Romero, San Luis Obispo, Ca	3	Tri
9.	Ron Pierce, Bakersfield, Ca	97	Yam
10.	Ron Grant, Brisbane, Ca	61	Suz
11.	Jim Evans, San Bernardino, Ca	47	Yam
12.	Dick Mann, Richmond, Ca	2	Tri
13.	Reg Pridmore, Santa Barbara, Ca	84	BMW
14.	Dave Damron, San Bernardino, Ca	99	Suz
15.	Larry Schafer, Hyatsville, Md	23	HD
16.	Dave Smith, Lakewood, Ca	20	Yam
17.	R.G. Wakefield, Indianapolis, Ind	78	Yam
18.	Conrad Urbanowski, Miramar, Fl	28	Yam
19.	Roger Ring, Imperial Beach, Ca	55	Yam
20.	Cliff Carr, Arlington, Mass	26	Kaw

Grand National Points Standings after Round 23

Rank	Rider	Pts
1.	Kenny Roberts	1809
2.	Gary Scott	1109
3.	Gary Nixon	820
4.	Don Castro	781
5.	Mert Lawwill	777
6.	Rex Beauchamp	591
7.	Dave Aldana	493
8.	Kel Carruthers	489
9.	Dick Mann	482
10.	Jim Rice	481

Extra Extra

- The crowd of around 15,000 had shrunk from 23,000 the year before.
- Yvon DuHamel won $27,800.00 from the purse for his win. Gary Nixon got $14,900.00 for 2nd.
- Kawasaki contingency money was substantial: DuHamel got $10,000.00, Nixon $6000.00 and Art Baumann $4000.00.
- DuHamel had his clutch lever broken off in the first lap in an altercation with Dave Smith. It didn't seem to slow him down.
- Art Baumann's 3rd place was sorely needed. He had not finished a National all year.
- John Hateley had his Yamaha seize at speed during practice and was tossed off. A close-following Dave Smith collected him and both went down hard. Smith got a dinged shoulder and Hateley a good amount of road rash.
- Yamaha's PR department filmed new GNC champ Kenny Roberts and the rest of the team during practice.
- Gary Scott, never given his due as a road racer, impressed those present in Heat 2 by putting it on road race pros like Gary Nixon, Cliff Carr, Hurley Wilvert and Paul Smart. He was often the fastest through the tight section, only giving up ground on the straights. He was doing business in Segment 1 till his seat came loose and he crashed. He came back more subdued in Segment 2 to finish 15th.
- It was a bad day for Team Norton. Peter William's long trip from England ended quickly, as his trick ride sprung a fuel leak on the line. Teammate Dave Aldana turned in some laps in Segment 1, but eventually pulled in with engine trouble.
- Gary Fisher was disqualified from Segment 2 while running up front due to a refueling technicality. He fell over during his pit stop, taking the gas man with him. The approved can was damaged, and the bike was refueled with a funnel;, a rules infraction.
- Last year's winner Paul Smart had carburetor trouble all day. Although it took him awhile to get rolling, he claimed a 5th in both segments.
- Gene Romero was the first four stroke home: 8th on his Triumph.
- Reg Pridmore finished out a strong 1973 season. He was 12th on the Butler & Smith BMW.
- The track was in terrible financial straits. It was losing millions of dollars each year. The Ontario race was an on-again-off-again proposition till a group led by JC Agajanian stepped forward to promote the event.
- The event continued to be troubled by low attendance, a featureless track, poor spectator visibility, slick track conditions and overzealous security that harassed journalists.
- Yvon DuHamel was a natural talent on pavement, comparable to Bart Markel on dirt. Nobody ever worked a motorcycle harder, from the drop of the green to the finish. The French-Canadian was sponsored early on by Fred Deeley, the Canadian Yamaha distributer. He was in contention to win numerous Nationals, only to be let down by the frailties of the eras two-stroke machinery. DuHamel was blindingly fast, setting the first 150 mph+ lap at Daytona in 1969, also making his Yamaha the first two-stroke to top Daytona's grid. His switch to Kawasaki in 1971 paid off with a victory at Talladega, also Kawasaki's first AMA Grand National win. He won a total of 5 National races. DuHamel was also successful in the emerging production class, forerunner of the Superbike class, winning numerous races. He also competed internationally for Kawasaki. The versatile DuHamel was not known as a dirt tracker, but was a capable rider, again making history by placing a 350 twin screamer in the top ten at the 1968 Sacramento Mile. DuHamel semi-retired in the mid-1970's but continued to compete in selected events with success into the 1990's. He also had a successful pro career in snowmobile racing, competing in the motorcycle off-season.

1973 Ascot Half-Mile
Roberts Finishes '73 With Style!

GNC Final Round #24	**Purse:** $14,000.00
Date: October 6, 1973	**Surface:** Dirt
Type: Half-Mile	**Course Length:** ½ Mile
Venue: Ascot Park	**Laps:** 20
Location: Gardena, Ca	**Distance:** 10 Miles

Kenny Roberts topped off his championship season in fine form by taking the final race of the season at Ascot Park. Roberts was running up front early in the National and then benefitted when leader Dave Aldana slid down. He was joined on the podium by Ascot regular Ron Moore, who came from dead last at the start, clear up to 2nd place. TT specialist Randy Scott showed fine oval track form, settling for 3rd after pressuring Moore late in the race. Championship runner-up Gary Scott failed to make the program; suffering mechanical trouble and still hurting from his crash at Ontario.

Gene Romero had a rough season, but finished strong with an 8th place run at Ontario and 4th this night at Ascot. It propelled him from outside the top ten in points, clear up to seventh. Mert Lawwill wrapped up fourth place in the championship with a 5th in the National. Don Castro did not make the main and had to settle for fifth position after a fine battle with Lawwill and Gary Nixon for much of the year.

Time Trials

The track surface at Ascot this night was fast and tacky, which helped 12 riders to break into the 22 second range. Mert Lawwill set the fastest mark of the night on his Jim Belland/self-tuned factory Harley at 22.33. Ron Moore, on the Love Brothers Triumph ran a 22.34. Kenny Roberts was close with a 22.43 on his factory Yamaha. Team Mexican members Gene Romero (Tri) and Dave Aldana (Nor) tied for 4th with an identical 22.59. Dick Mann rounded out the top 5 with a 22.74. Don Castro (Yam) was in the 22's, but had a nasty get-off after his run.

Heats

Mert Lawwill led Heat 1 off the line and dominated the race from beginning to end. Gene Romero was the only rider to keep Lawwill in sight from his distant 2nd spot. Behind the two front runners, a struggle for 3rd between DeWayne Keeter (HD), Terry Dorsch (Tri) and Pat McCaul (Nor). McCaul just nipped Keeter at the stripe.

Mike Collins (HD) pulled a nifty holeshot in Heat 2, but veterans Cal Rayborn and Dick Mann (Tri) were soon by. Ron Moore was charging and soon moved by the two famous front runners and took off for a big win. Mann took over 2nd with 1971 Ascot winner Tommy Rockwood moving into 3rd, as Rayborn slipped back to 5th behind Collins.

Don Castro showed no ill effects from his qualifying crash, pulling the holeshot in Heat 3. He was soon shuffled back to 3rd as first Randy Scott (Yam) and soon after Kenny Roberts and Tom Horton (Tri) ripped by. Scott and Roberts warred over the position, with Roberts on the low line moving by the rim riding Scott. Roberts moved out to a comfortable lead to take the win. Scott held 2nd despite late pressure from Horton with Castro 4th.

Steve Baker (Yam) led the last heat off the line, but crowd favorite Dave Aldana soon took over. Scott Brelsford (HD) was up front, but was out with mechanical trouble on lap 3. Aldana blitzed away for the win. A battle for 2nd ensued between Mark Williams (Tri), John Hateley (Tri) and road race specialist Baker. Williams took control of the position, with Hateley barely edging out an aggressive Baker. Baker, mild mannered in appearance only, raised more than a few eyeballs with his go-for-broke style this night at Ascot.

Semis

A determined Tom Horton quickly hustled out front of the first semi. Behind, a war had broken out between Pat McCaul, Jim Rice (HD), Steve Baker and Terry Dorsch. Dorsch dropped out with mechanical trouble. Horton led the group for most of the event. Rice put in a strong last lap effort to take the transfer behind winner Horton.

Ascot regular Dewayne Keeter duked it out with John Hateley and Tommy Rockwood early in Semi 2. Keeter soon got rolling though and went on for the win. Hateley and Rockwood went at it hard, with "Lil John" taking the last National ticket in the closing laps.

Trophy Race

Shell Racing's Eddie Wirth (Yam) took control of the Trophy Race and despite early pressure, went on for the win. Pat McCaul moved into 2nd past early runner-up Steve Droste (HD). Tommy Rockwood was on a charge from back in the pack, nailing McCaul in the final turn for 2nd, McCaul hung unto 3rd ahead of Steve Baker and Droste.

National

Dave Aldana jumped out front of the National, just heading off Mert Lawwill as they headed down the backstretch with Kenny Roberts close behind. Aldana soon had clear sailing and opened up a small lead. Roberts went by Lawwill on lap 5. The two closed up tight on Aldana. There may have been contact between Aldana and Roberts, as Aldana slid down in turns 3-4. Roberts was up and gone, with Lawwill and a close following DeWayne Keeter taking evasive action to miss Aldana. They were soon swallowed up by a pack led by Ron Moore, Randy Scott and Gene Romero. Moore and Scott pulled away from Romero and proceeded to battle handlebar to handlebar as the laps waned. Up front, Roberts was gone; Moore just held off Scott. Romero was 4th, Lawwill salvaged 5th, with the rest of the top 10, John Hateley, Mark Williams, Tom Horton, Dick Mann and Dewayne Keeter.

Results

Race: 20 Lap Half-Mile National
Race Time: 7:39.17, (New Record)

Rank	Rider	Number	Make
1.	Kenny Roberts, San Carlos, Ca	80	Yam
2.	Ron Moore, San Bernardino, Ca	37	Tri
3.	Randy Scott, Portland, Ore	50	Tri
4.	Gene Romero, San Luis Obispo, Ca	3	Tri
5.	Mert Lawwill, San Francisco, Ca	7	HD
6.	John Hateley, Van Nuys, Ca	98	Tri
7.	Mark Williams, Springfield, Ore	70	Tri
8.	Tom Horton, Lancaster, Ca	75X	Tri
9.	Dick Mann, Richmond, Ca	2	Tri
10.	DeWayne Keeter, Oakview, Ca	44	HD
11.	Jim Rice, Palo Alto, Ca	24	HD
12.	Dave Aldana, Santa Ana, Ca	13	Nor

Race: Trophy Race

Rank	Rider	Number	Make
1.	Eddie Wirth, Dana Point, Ca	84X	Yam
2.	Tom Rockwood, Gardena, Ca	88	Tri
3.	Pat McCaul, San Jose, Ca	48Y	Nor
4.	Steve Baker, Bellingham, Wa	42W	Yam
5.	Steve Droste, Waterloo, Ia	26K	HD
6.	Charlie Seale, Lantana, Fl	47	HD
7.	Dennis Kanegae, Costa Mesa, Ca	5X	Yam
8.	Mike Collins, Albuquerque, NM	16M	HD
9.	Larry Gino, San Bernardino, Ca	96R	Tri
10.	Charles Thielke, Santa Ana, Ca	56X	Tri
11.	Frank Gillespie, Berkeley, Ca	76	Yam
12.	Cal Rayborn, Spring Valley, Ca	14	HD

Grand National Final Points Standings

Rank	Rider	Pts
1.	Kenny Roberts	1959
2.	Gary Scott	1109
3.	Gary Nixon	870
4.	Mert Lawwill	837
5.	Don Castro	779
6.	Rex Beauchamp	591
7.	Gene Romero	518
8.	Dave Aldana	502
9.	Dick Mann	501
10.	Jim Rice	491

Extra Extra

STOP THE PRESSES!!!

Scott Brelsford Wins Protest-Atlanta Points To Be Paid!

A week after the Ascot National, the AMA surprised one and all, by awarding points to Atlanta Mile winner Scott Brelsford and all main event finishers. The decision substantially changed the points totals of the Top Ten finishers in the Grand National Championship. Three riders had their positions affected; Scott Brelsford moved to 9th, Dick Mann went to 10th, and unfortunate Jim Rice was dropped out of the Top Ten.

Grand National "Official" Final Points Standings

Rank	Rider	Pts
1.	Kenny Roberts	2014
2.	Gary Scott	1241
3.	Gary Nixon	887
4.	Mert Lawwill	839
5.	Don Castro	812
6.	Rex Beauchamp	701
7.	Gene Romero	584
8.	Dave Aldana	546
9.	Scott Brelsford	543
10.	Dick Mann	504

1973 Season Review

1. Kenny Roberts
2014 Points

With brilliant riding, dependable machinery and a schedule that favored his versatility, Kenny Roberts romped to a huge points victory in the Grand National Championship. Roberts and championship rival Gary Scott started out fairly even in the opening rounds of the series. Due to consistent finishes at Houston and Daytona, Scott was actually ahead in the standings, despite Roberts win at the Houston Short track. Roberts took over the points lead for good at Round #6 at Road Atlanta. Scott kept turning in consistent finishes though, keeping the points totals close. The turning point of the season for Roberts was his win at the Colorado Mile. After this race, the points gap widened and Roberts marched to the title. Showing remarkable versatility, his three wins came at different types of events; the Houston Short Track, the Colorado Mile and the Ascot Half-Mile. He came narrowly close to scoring a pavement win with runner-up finishes at Loudon, Pocono and Charlotte. Roberts was also amazingly close to a TT win; he essentially gave the win away at Houston and then proceeded to finish 2nd at each of the remaining TT's on the schedule, Castle Rock, Ascot and Peoria. He was also on the podium at Road Atlanta, Columbus and the Indy Mile. Top 5 finishes included the Sante Fe Short Track, Terre Haute Half-Mile and Ontario Road Race. Finishes in the top 10 were scored at the Houston TT, Louisville and Atlanta. Roberts put up high consistent finishes everywhere the series ran, racking up points in 22 of 24 races.

2. Gary Scott
1241 Points

After Gary Scott's runner-up performance as a rookie to Mark Brelsford in the 1972 GNC race, his chances looked great for 1973. Despite the Triumph teams aging machinery, Scott was in the hunt for much of the season. While he turned impressive rides all season, his failure to score a win and match Kenny Roberts podium finishes kept the #1 plate just out of his reach. Had things gone just a little differently, Scott may have been the first rider to take the championship without scoring a win. He briefly led the GNC points after the fifth round, the San Jose Half-Mile. He stayed very close to Roberts in the chase up to mid-season, often within 40-50 points. His season derailed after Roberts win at the Colorado Mile. Scott looked to turn the tables at the next race, the Castle Rock TT, but fell off while in the lead. More bad luck at the Ascot TT again put him out while out front. After this point, Scott valiantly battled back, but Roberts usually always finished a few spots ahead, finally salting away the championship. Scott had a season most riders would envy. He was runner-up four times; at the Houston Short Track, the San Jose Half-Mile and Mile and at Atlanta. He was impressive on the Triumph Trident, giving the once mighty superbike its best remaining National finishes, on the podium at both Loudon and Laguna Seca and in the top 5 at Pocono and Charlotte. He had a great run going at Ontario before minor troubles led to a crash. Other top 5's were had at the Houston TT and Colorado Mile. Top 10 runs included races at Dallas, Louisville, Peoria, Indy and Terre Haute. Scott competed in 20 of the 24 races on the schedule. While most racers would have been thrilled with the successful season, Scott would not be satisfied till he took the GNC title.

3. Gary Nixon
887 Points

Despite the nine rich points paying road race Nationals, Gary Nixon was the only mostly pavement racer to break into the top 10. He did it in a big way, winning three pavement races at Loudon, Laguna Seca and Pocono. He was 2nd at both Dallas and Ontario. Written off by many, the former two-time GNC champ was the hottest road racer of 1973. Nixon also showed up at many dirt track Nationals, managing to snag a 4th at the Colorado Mile and 10th at the Atlanta Mile. With Nixon's questionable left leg and other injuries it is ironic that his best dirt finishes were at the worst condition race tracks. Typical Nixon, when you counted him out, he would come through. His third place overall in the championship was very impressive. He did not have the tools to compete week in and week out with his younger competitors. He choose his battles wisely and the veteran scored points in just 8 Nationals compared to Roberts and Scott who were in over 20 events…aah, if for but a stronger leg. It was Nixon's last appearance in the GNC top 10.

4. Mert Lawwill
839 Points

With defending GNC champ Mark Brelsford out for the season with injuries, Harley-Davidson's best hope was venerable Mert Lawwill, the 1969 GNC champ. Lawwill gave it a great try, having some good success, but was troubled by crashes and mechanical trouble. He scored two late season wins at the tough Peoria TT and the fast Indy Mile. He reeled off three half-mile runner-ups at Louisville, Columbus and Terre Haute. He was 5th at the Ascot Half-Mile and 6th at the San Jose Half-Mile. Pavement finishes were hampered by slow machinery and breakdowns. Nevertheless the veteran had the best factory showing, scoring his total in just 11 events.

5. Don Castro
812 Points

With the aid of his Yamaha factory ride, Don Castro was back in the top 10 of National points. He will probably remember 1973 though as the year he finally scored a Grand National win. Castro had been frustratingly close numerous times, so his long awaited victory at the San Jose Half-Mile, close to his home in Hollister, Ca, had to be especially satisfying. Castro's other top finishes included a 2nd at Sante Fe, a 4th at the San Jose Mile and 4th on the pavement at Talladega. He scored a slew of top 10's at Daytona, Dallas, Columbus, Castle Rock, Laguna Seca, Peoria, Pocono, Atlanta and Charlotte. Castro competed in 17 events, putting together 11 finishes in a row, between Columbus and Terre Haute, more than anybody else on the circuit.

6. Rex Beauchamp
701 Points

After battling injury and the iron XR for the past couple of years, Rex Beauchamp finally put it all together to score his first National win. He lost a squeaker to Kenny Roberts at the Colorado Mile, but came back late in the year to win the rescheduled Terre Haute Half-Mile. The dirt track specialist made the most of the limited oval track schedule. He was 3rd at the San Jose Half-Mile and Atlanta Mile, 4th at Louisville and Columbus and 6th at the San Jose Mile. He scored at 8 events, all dirt ovals.

7. Gene Romero
584 Points

In many ways 1970 GNC champ had a great year; he won Triumphs last Mile at San Jose and was a consistent top 10 finisher on the trail. Compared to the past three years where he had placed in the top three in points; 1973 was a disappointment. Besides the San Jose win, Romero was in the top 5 only twice, at the Atlanta Mile and Ascot Half-Mile. A talented road racer, Romero struggled all year, managing best finishes of 8th at Ontario and 10th at Talladega. He was also in the top 10 at the San Jose Half-Mile, Columbus, Colorado, Castle Rock Ascot, and Peoria TT's, Indy and Terre Haute. Romero worked hard, scoring in 17 of the 24 events, but just didn't seem to have the speed or luck of past years.

8. Dave Aldana
546 Points

Dave Aldana had a good year for the factory Norton team. He notched the marquees only modern era GNC win at the Ascot TT. The bike showed strong power, finishing 4th at the Indy Mile. Aldana's other top runs included a 5th place at the Houston Short Track and top 10's at Columbus, Colorado and Terre Haute. He was spectacular at the Peoria TT, looking set for a top finish till slowed with mechanical trouble. The teams road racer handled well, but was well down on power. His best pavement finish was a 10th at Laguna Seca.

9. Scott Brelsford
543 Points

Scott Brelsford's decision to protest the Atlanta Mile paid off big, with the bounty of winners points putting him into the Top Ten. The win helped him cement his spot as the top rookie of the year. Brelsford was also on the podium at Colorado and in the top 5 at the San Jose Half-Mile and Indy Mile. He was 7th at the San Jose Mile. Brelsford joined Mert Lawwill as the only Harley-Davidson team member in the top 10 in points. It had to be a bittersweet year for Scott Brelsford; he had a successful year, but was without support and companionship of older brother Mark after the 1972 Grand National Champion's accident at Daytona.

10. Dick Mann
504 Points

Two-time GNC champ Dick Mann rounded out the top 10. He went winless for the first time since his partial retirement in 1966. His season was very similar to teammate Gene Romero's. Both ran hard, making most main events, but just never got up to speed. Neither was able to match the pace of new teammate Gary Scott. Mann was a season best at 3rd place at Peoria, turned in a credible 4th at Daytona and at the San Jose Mile. There were 6 top 10's at Louisville, Loudon, Columbus, Castle Rock and Ascot TT's and Ascot Half-Mile. In the past, the large number of road races would have played in Mann's favor, but other than his Daytona run, he just didn't have the luck or speed needed. Mann scored in 16 of 24 events. The respected veteran been ranked in the top 10 in points every year except one since 1956; This was his last appearance in the top 10 riders.

There were was a record 18 different winners in the 24 event schedule. Riders scoring Grand National points numbered 107.

Yamaha was the dominant brand for the second year running, taking the Manufacturer Championship with 7 total wins and slews of road race entries, Harley-Davidson had 5 victories, Kawasaki had 5 (their most ever), Triumph 3 and Norton 1.

The 1973 season was unique in Grand National history. The series high 9 road races gave a boost Kenny Roberts season, and put primarily road racer Gary Nixon back in the championship hunt. The schedule led to the most competitive season ever with 18 different winners in the 24 event schedule. There was a huge variety of bikes in the top 5 of both dirt track and road race Nationals. This season marked the last season that Team Triumph would be a significant overall force and a coming Yamaha big bore racer, would make 1973 the final year that that the other Japanese teams were competitive, and would render the remaining four stroke bikes obsolete.

1973 GNC Winners

Event	Location	Winner	Machine
TT	Houston, Tx	Mike Haney, Torrance, Ca	Tri
Short Track	Houston, Tx	Kenny Roberts, Woodside, Ca	Yam
Road Race	Daytona Beach, Fl	Jarno Saarinen, Finland	Yam
Road Race	Dallas, Tx	Paul Smart, Sante Fe Springs, Ca	Suz
Half-Mile	San Jose, Ca	Don Castro, Gilroy, Ca	Yam
Road Race	Braselton, Ga	Geoff Perry, New Zealand	Suz
Half-Mile	Louisville, Ky	Dave Sehl, Waterdown, Ont., Can	HD
Road Race	Loudon, NH	Gary Nixon, Cockeysville, Md	Kaw
Half-Mile	Columbus, Oh	Jim Rice, Palo Alto, ca	HD
Mile	San Jose, Ca	Gene Romero, San Luis Obispo, Ca	Tri
Mile	Colorado Springs, Co	Kenny Roberts, Woodside, Ca	Yam
TT	Castle Rock, Wa	Chuck Joyner, Oregon City, Ore	Tri
TT	Gardena, Ca	Dave Aldana, Santa Ana, Ca	Nor
Road Race	Monterey, Ca	Gary Nixon, Cockeysville, Md	Kaw
Short Track	Hinsdale, Ill	Mike Gerald, Baton Rouge, La	Yam
TT	Peoria, Ill	Mert Lawwill, San Francisco, Ca	HD
Road Race	Mt. Pocono, Pa	Gary Nixon, Cockeysville, Md	Kaw
Mile	Indianapolis, Ind	Mert Lawwill, San Francisco, Cat	HD
Road Race	Talladega, Al	Kel Carruthers, San Diego, ca	Yam
Half-Mile	Terre Haute, Ind	Rex Beauchamp, Milford, Mi	HD
Mile	Atlanta, Ga	Scott Brelsford, Daly City, Ca	HD
Road Race	Charlotte, NC	Yvon DuHamel, LaSalle, Que., Can	Kaw
Road Race	Ontario, Ca	Yvon DuHamel, LaSalle, Que., Can	Kaw
Half-Mile	Gardena, Ca	Kenny Roberts, Woodside, Ca	Yam

Calvin Rayborn II, 1940-1973

Cal Rayborn II was America's premier road racer of the late 1960's and early '70's. He claimed back-to-back Daytona 200 wins in 1968 and 1969 and scored 11 Grand National wins in his career. Rayborn was a versatile racer, capable of top finishes on dirt ovals and TT tracks as well as pavement. These skills enabled him to finish third in the GNC standings twice. Rayborn's had an early interest in motorcycles and held a job as a motorcycle courier, delivering blueprints around San Diego. He also began racing local TT's and scrambles. He and Don Vesco became friends and he tried his hand at club road racing. He turned Expert in 1965 and soon began as association with former GNC champ Brad Andres and his father Len, who provided rapid machinery. His first National win was at Carlsbad in 1966. Harley racing chief Dick O'Brien took and instant liking to Rayborn, who raced Milwaukee produced machines through the majority of his career. Rayborn racked up his wins over a short seven year span, using his dirt track skill of pronating his front wheel to scrub off speed to give him an edge. His skill levels neatly matched the final incarnations of the KR road racer. The combination of the two, were dominant at Daytona in the late 1960's.

Rayborn's association with the new iron XR750 was fraught with breakdowns and disappointment for two years. There were a few bright spots; in 1970 Rayborn set a land speed record of 265.492 in a Harley powered streamliner. His lone National win for the period was a long awaited dirt track win, coming at the dust-shortened Livonia Mile. In early 1972, Rayborn ventured to England to compete at the Transatlantic Match races on Walt Faulk's iron XRTT. At the time, most Europeans didn't think much of American racers pavement skills, believing most were foot dragging dirt trackers. Rayborn changed this perception by winning half of the 6 rounds on tracks he had never seen before and tying as the top scorer. His performance made him an instant legend in England. Rayborn's fortunes changed for the better with aluminum XR750, winning his last two Nationals at Indianapolis and Laguna Seca in 1972. Despite the success, the new bike still had teething problems and more importantly was becoming overwhelmed by the new Japanese multi-cylinder superbikes. Rayborn made the difficult decision to leave Harley-Davidson at the end of 1973 to find a competitive pavement ride. He decided on the Suzuki team and during the off season, ventured to New Zealand. At a club race at Pukekohe, he rode a Suzuki formerly ridden be native star Geoff Perry who died in a commercial plane crash during the season. Rayborn was tragically killed when the bike seized, throwing him off at speed. There has been speculation as to why Rayborn was even on the bike, but he was a racer and was surely just trying to become acquainted with the big bore two-strokes he would soon be racing. News of his death was greeted by shock and dismay. Rayborn was very popular with fans and friends. He was a racer's racer who enjoyed being on the road and chasing the #1 plate on dusty dirt tracks around the United States as just one of the guys. The 33 year-old left behind a wife and family. His son Cal Rayborn III, became a noted road racer in the 1980's. Rayborn was inducted into the MHOF in 1999. (Photo at top courtesy of Jim McMurren.)

Jim McMurren Remembers Friend, Cal Rayborn

Jim McMurren grew up San Diego area of California and like many teenage boys in the late 1950's and early '60's, became obsessed with motorcycles. He found a kindred spirit in Calvin Lee Rayborn. The two were good friends who began racing at the many tracks that existed at the time. The two raced and traveled together through their amateur and early pro careers. McMurren was a very good racer; National Number 11 for several years. He was a particularly strong short tracker. He scaled back his racing after 1970 and though not spending as much time with Rayborn, remained close till the end.

I asked Jim to put down some thoughts about his friendship with Cal Rayborn. He helps give insight to the person and the racer most people only know through legend. He talks about Lou Kaiser; a man who acted as a father figure to Cal, keeping him on track as a person and teaching him about motorcycles. I am honored that Jim contributed to this remembrance of a true American hero.

The following is in Jim McMurren's own words;

Calvin and I were only weeks apart in age and started riding in our early teens, about 14 I guess. This was about average for our time. We had a couple of other friends who rode with us and I think we were fortunate that the small bike thing started as we grew. From 1955-1965 the number of brands of small, fast, sophisticated motorcycles (also relatively cheap) was phenomenal. Of course we had the usual scrambles TT and cross country races. We lived in a rural area. But the emerging of Calvin the road racer was due to two factors. We had lots of pavement racing in California. Paradise Mesa, a one mile airstrip course, sort of a paved TT. Another was Hour Glass Field, also an airstrip but a much bigger one. Willow Springs ran once a month and Riverside was built about 1958. Eventually we had Carlsbad Raceway. All these within 15 min to 2-3 hour drive. The other factor was the military and building boom in San Diego. Blueprint companies were working three shifts and guess who got to deliver the goods? Print shaggers! Calvin and I and a dozen other guys rode motorcycles all over San Diego County delivering blueprints. We did this for a couple of years putting on 100-150 miles a day, 5 or 6 days a week. Of course every trip for us was a new road-race. We got really good and felt like we could do anything on a motorcycle. Calvin was fast and he got even faster during this time. It was a struggle and took a few years, but finally after a few sponsors he got hooked up with Leonard Andres about 1966. He then became the Cal Rayborn everyone got to know. I'm sad he never got the #1 plate. He certainly had the talent and equipment. As you pointed out in your first book, he was under-rated as a dirt tracker and should have won more nationals, but it wasn't to be.

Louie Kaiser was in his mid-fifties when he took Calvin into his home. Calvin was in about his sophomore year in high school. Calvin's mom had remarried and moved to Las Vegas and Calvin wanted to stay in San Diego. Louie was the icon of the motorcycle scene in So. California. Everyone knew and loved Lou. He was a machinist, turner, engine builder and just a great guy. He was like the Rob North to all the racers. Calvin asked Louie if he could stay with him and he agreed as long as Calvin went to school and had decent grades. Ruth, Louie's wife, kept a strict hand on Calvin and Calvin just hated her. He hated to be told what to do. But Calvin graduated and probably wouldn't have without their help and guidance. Calvin was like a son to Louie. He definitively helped Calvin to become the prodigy he was. Louie was with Calvin in New Zealand when he was killed. After sending Calvin's body home he had to go to Australia to get Calvin and Mert Lawwill's race car running and ready to race. It had to be a very tough time for Lou. He just lost his son. Years before, 1956 or 57, Lou had another protégé of his killed at Gardena Speedway in LA. Jimmy Phillips. Lou didn't do much after Calvin died. He was getting older. He went to a few races at Brown Field but just faded away. He died when he was 80 years old. He was a wonderful guy and helped Calvin in myriad way in his formative years.

Jim tells us about this picture; *Cal's first win*
Calvin on a 165 Harley road racing Circa 1957 Hour
Glass Field- a Navy WWII training facility. This was
Calvin's first win. He beat a Canadian champion on an
MV (in picture). The 165 was tuned by Lou Kaiser and
had only a 3 speed transmission, worn out street tires, tiny
brakes and was laughed at before the race. But not after!
He beat about a dozen of us and people started to realize
what natural ability he had. Photo Courtesy of Jim
McMurren

Calvin and me at Ascot on 250s 1962. 108 me and
Calvin 286.
If you look at Calvin's eyes and his throttle hand you
can see there is a problem and that was a rider going
down right in the groove. I was able to sneak by him
on the inside, but Calvin, with nowhere to go, rode
right over the downed bike. I could see him flying up in
the air like going over a jump. They stopped the race
at the start line and I'm thinking how bad it looked for
Calvin. Then he comes riding up on his Honda with
the bars turned down like a Bonneville racer. He didn't
even fall. His pit crew turned the bars up, tightened
the bolts and we were ready for a restart. Photo
Courtesy of Jim McMurren

National numbers 11 and 25; Jim McMurren and Cal
Rayborn, run in close quarters at Sante Fe. That's Neil
Keen on the outside. Photo Courtesy of Jim McMurren

Jim and Calvin hanging out away from the races.
Appears Jim is attempting to make an important point!
Photo Courtesy of Jim McMurren

Jim McMurren and Sid Carlson

Like most racers living the "gypsy" life on the road, Jim McMurren formed strong friendships, some of which have lasted a lifetime. Case in point is Jim's friendship with Sid Carlson. Carlson carried National Number 73 for several years and was well known on the fair and GNC circuit. He and McMurren traveled and raced together for years. They have remained friends for decades and still work for the same company in California!

Carlson on his rigid framed Harley Sprint in the late 1960's. Mahony Photo Archives

.

Carlson nearly tries out the "safety barrier" at the Oklahoma City half-mile. Photo Courtesy of Jim McMurren.

Carlson and McMurren getting after it at Sante Fe. Note: no gloves, no brakes and race posters protecting the carbs. Mahony Photo Archives

The 1974 GNC Season Preview

There was big news on several fronts for the 1974 season; a radical new Yamaha road racer, new factory rides for several top stars and a trial three-race sponsorship deal by prospective series sponsor, cigarette company R.J. Reynolds, via their Camel brand.

Yamaha had become dominate in most classes of road racing in the 1970's and didn't want to lose their advantage. They knew that their 350 was soon to be left behind once the other Japanese manufacturers perfected their 750's. Yamaha felt its racing reputation was at stake and stepped up with the radical TZ700; a 700cc, 4-cylinder water-cooled two-stroke. Out of the box, the reed-valve engine made around 90 horsepower and a well thought out chassis was a good handler in most situations. The new bike really raised the ante in big bore road racing. No one was really expecting a company to ante up and build 200 examples of an exotic, complicated production road racer. In true Class "C" fashion, Kawasaki and Suzuki had modified big bore production machines into racers, pretty much as the British had done. Harley-Davidson was the only other company to build the required quantities of a large displacement, pure racer. Their XRTT piggybacked with the 200 examples of their pure dirt XR, (twice; iron and aluminum!). No one else had done it on recent times. The bike was developed through 1973 and Daytona would see it's U.S. debut.

The TZ700 would strengthen the chances for new Grand National Champion Kenny Roberts to repeat his title. Shell Theutt, Bud Meyers and Bud Aksland would return to tune the champs bikes. The company's proven 750 dirt tracker wasn't ideal in slippery track conditions, but the bikes were competitive against the Harley-Davidsons on most oval and TT courses. Yamahas 360 two-stroke single had become the most dominant short track power plant. Joining Roberts was 1970 GNC champ Gene Romero. The long-time Triumph factory rider had a difficult 1973 season aboard equipment that had passed it's developmental peak. Romero still possessed formidable dirt track skills and the new TZ700 would prove to be a good match for his road race talents which had still not been fully realized (a National victory).

Harley-Davidson had a rough 1973 and bolstered it's chances to get the title back by enlisting Gary Scott. The former Triumph rider was great on dirt ovals and TT's and had been impressive on pavement. He would be near the front on dirt and could be counted on to give the XRTT a heck of a ride on shorter courses like Loudon and Laguna Seca. The 1972 GNC champ Mark Brelsford would return to action after missing most of 1973 following his terrifying Daytona crash. He had endured a lengthy recovery and several operations on his hand. Time would tell if the versatile Brelsford could recapture his pre-injury form. His younger brother, Scott, would return wearing National Number 19. Mert Lawwill had been the highest placing Harley rider in 1973. The 1969 Grand National champ still had great speed on the dirt ovals and was a potent TT racer. Rex Beauchamp closed out the previous year strongly and the dirt specialist could be expected to be in the hunt on the miles and half-miles.

The Triumph Corporation was still limping along financially and fielded just one rider, Texan Mike Kidd. The Triumph dirt track machinery could still get it done on the right day. He would be aboard the same Brent Thompson tuned bikes that Gary Scott rode in 1973. Less was expected on pavement due to Kidd's inexperience and the rapidly dating Triumph triples.

Kawasaki fielded a smaller team than 1973, headed by Yvon DuHamel and returning riders Art Baumann and Hurley Wilvert. There were little apparent changes in the machinery from the previous season. The hottest road racer in 1973, Gary Nixon, moved to Suzuki along with former teammate Cliff Carr. Paul Smart signed on again with the Suzuki team. Gone from the team was Ron Grant, who had had retired, and Geoff Perry had been tragically lost in a plane crash.

Missed by all of the racing fraternity was Cal Rayborn. Arguably America's finest road racer of the period, he had suffered through the XR750's teething problems just in time for the road race version to be obsolete. The handwriting was on the wall at the end of 1973 and Rayborn left Harley-Davidson and was working on a deal with Suzuki. He was killed in a crash in New Zealand. Rayborn had scored 11 National wins, including back-to-back Daytona victories in 1968 and '69. Rayborn was well liked by fans and other racers. He seemed to enjoy just being part of the circuit and was thrilled to score his only dirt track win on the mile at Livonia.

The 1974 Grand National schedule was similar to the previous year. Three road races, at Dallas, Charlotte and Pocono were gone from the schedule, the road race totals back to a more normal 6 races. The San Jose Half-Mile and the infamous Atlanta Mile were also scratched. New on the schedule was the Denver and Toledo Half-Miles and the circuit would return to the Syracuse Mile for the first time since 1953. There were 23 races on the schedule, down one from 1973.

There was a change from the 1973 dirt track advancement procedure. For 1974, the first 3 finishers in each heat race would advance to the National instead of 2. Just the winner of each semi would advance, giving a total of 14 at half-miles and short tracks. Mile races would stay the same with the top 4 advancing from the heats and two from each semi. Points would be paid to the first 20 riders at road races and miles. At half-miles and short tracks, the 14 in the National and the first 6 in the Trophy race would get points.

1974 National Numbers

1. Kenny Roberts, Woodside Ca
2. Dick Mann, Richmond, Ca
3. Gene Romero, San Luis Obispo, Ca
4. Bart Markel, Flint, Mi
5. Roger Reiman, Kewanee, Ill
6. Mark Brelsford, Woodside, Ca
7. Mert Lawwill, Tiburon, Ca
8. Unassigned
9. Gary Nixon, Cockeysville, Md
10. Neil Keen, St. Louis, Mo
11. Don Castro, Gilroy, Ca
12. Eddie Mulder, Northtridge, Ca
13. Dave Aldana, Santa Ana, Ca
14. Cal Rayborn, Spring Valley, Ca
15. Mike Gerald, Baton Rouge, La
16. Dave Sehl, Waterdown, Ont., Can
17. Yvon DuHamel, LaSalle, Quebec, Can
18. Jimmy Odom, Fremont, Ca
19. Scott Brelsford, Daly City, Ca
20. Dave Smith, Lakewood, Ca
21. Gary Fisher, Parkesburg, Pa
22. Terry Dorsch, Granada Hills, Ca
23. Dave Hansen, Hayward, Ca
24. Jim Rice, Portola Valley, Ca
25. Don Emde, Chula Vista, Ca
26. Cliff Carr, Arlington, Mass
27. Jim Evans, San Bernardino, Ca
28. Conrad Urbanowski, Mirimar, Fl
29. Larry Palmgren, Freehold, NJ
30. Art Baumann, Brisbane, Ca
31. Rex Beauchamp, Milford, Mi
32. Steve Baker, Bellingham, Wa
33. Paul Smart, Santa Ana, Ca
34. Darryl Hurst, Houston, Tx
35. Randy Skiver, Everett, Wa
36. Charlie Chapple, Flint, Mi
37. Ron Moore, San Bernardino, Ca
38. Chuck Palmgren, Freehold, NJ
39. Hurley Wilvert, Westminster, Ca
40. Doug Libby, Milford, Mi
41. Billy Eves, Phoenixville, Pa
42. Fred Smith, Memphis, Tn
43. Jerry Greene, San Mateo, Ca
44. DeWayne Keeter, Ojai, Ca
45. Doug Sehl, Waterdown, Ontario, Can
46. Paul Bostrom, San Ramon, Ca
47. Charlie Seale, Lantana, Fl
48. Al Kenyon, Cupertino, Ca
49. Buck Boren, Kleberg, Tx
50. Randy Scott, Philomath, Ore
51. Dave Lawson, Yukon, Ok
52. Ronnie Rall, Mansfield, Oh
53. Bart Myers, New Brunswick, NJ
54. Robert E. Lee, Ft. Worth, Tx
55. Tom Horton, Lancaster, Ca
56. Marty Lunde, Hermosa Beach, Ca
57. Ed Hermann, Portland, Ore
58. Robert Winters, Fort Smith, Ark
59. Jean Lysight, Tracy, Que., Can
60. Chuck Joyner, Oregon City, Ore
61. Ron Grant, Brisbane, Ca
62. Corky Keener, Flint, Mi
63. Reg Pridmore, Goleta, Ca
64. Gary Scott, Baldwin Park, Ca
65. Delbert Armour, Denver, Co
66. John Skinner, Auburn, Al
67. Pat Marinacci, Seattle, Wa
68. Larry Schafer, Hyattsville, Md
69. Sonny Burres, Portland, Ore
70. Mark Williams, Springfield, Ore
71. Jimmy Maness, Augusta, Ga
72. Mike Kidd, Euless, Tx
73. Kel Carruthers, San Diego, Ca
74. Paul Pressgrove, Tecumseh, Ks
75. Jim Dunn, Everett, Wa
76. Frank Gillespie, Danville, Ca
77. Eddie Wirth, Dana Point, Ca
78. Ron Wakefield, Indianapolis, Ind
79. Stan Johnson, Albuquerque, NM
80. Tom White, Huntington Beach, Ca
81. Gordon Duesenbery, Witchita, Ks
82. Harry Cone, Sherman, Tx
83. Steve McLaughlin, Duarte, Ca
84. Mike Collins, Albuquerque, NM
85. Mike Johnson, Flint, Mi
86. Keith Ulicki, Kenosha, Wi
87. James Einarsson, Shelton, Wa
88. Tom Rockwood, Gardena, Ca
89. Jimmy Zeigler, Bellville, Oh
90. Ike Reed, Salem, Ore
91. Mike Haney, Torrance, Ca
92. Steve Droste, Waterloo, Ia
93. Jim Rawls, Grand Prairie, Tx
94. Ted Poovey, Garland, Tx
95. Michael Ninci, Kansas City, Mo
96. Bill Schaeffer, Pinegrove, Pa
97. Ron Pierce, Bakersfield, Ca
98. John Hateley, Van Nuys, Ca
99. Steve Dalgarno, Baltimore, Md

1974
Grand National Championship
Schedule

	Race	Location	Date
1	Houston TT	Houston, Tx	February 1, 1974
2	Houston Short Track	Houston, Tx	February 2, 1974
3	Daytona 200 Mile Road Race	Daytona Beach, Fl	March 10, 1974
4	San Jose Mile	San Jose, Ca	May 19, 1974
5	Colorado Half-Mile	Denver, Co	May 26, 1974
6	Road Atlanta 75 Mile Road Race	Braselton, Ga	June 2, 1974
7	Louisville Half-Mile	Louisville, Ky	June 8, 1974
8	Loudon 75 Mile Road Race	Loudon, NH	June 16, 1974
9	Columbus Half-Mile	Columbus, Oh	June 23, 1974
10	San Jose Mile	San Jose, Ca	July 7, 1974
11	Castle Rock TT	Castle Rock, Wa	July 13, 1974
12	Ascot TT	Gardena, Ca	July 20, 1974
13	Laguna Seca 75 Mile Road Race	Monterey, Ca	July 28, 1974
14	Sante Fe Short Track	Hinsdale, Ill	August 9, 1974
15	Peoria TT	Peoria, Ill	August 18, 1974
16	Indy Mile	Indianapolis, Ind	August 24, 1974
17	Talladega 75 Mile Road Race	Talladega, Al	September 1, 1974
18	Syracuse Mile	Syracuse, NY	September 8, 1974
19	Toledo Half-Mile	Toledo, Oh	September 21, 1974
20	Terre Haute Half-Mile	Terre Haute, Ind	September 22, 1974
21	Golden Gate Mile	Albany, Ca	September 29, 1974
22	Ontario 250 Mile Road Race	Ontario, Ca	October 6, 1974
23	Ascot Half-Mile	Gardena, Ca	October 12, 1974

1974 Houston Astrodome TT and Short Track
Honda, Hansen and Gerald Top Houston

GNC Round #1 & 2 of 23 **Date:** February 1 & 2, 1974 **Type:** TT and Short Track **Venue:** Houston Astrodome **Location:** Houston, Tx	**Purse:** $28,000.00 **Surface:** Dirt **Course Length:** ¼ mile **Laps:** 25 TT, 20 Short Track

The Houston races were always the site of new bikes, riders, leathers and sponsorship deals. The 1974 race combined almost all of these elements when Honda decided to launch an all out attack on the Houston Short Track. Much like their assault on Daytona in 1970 with Dick Mann and Bob Hansen, they put all the right components together for victory. They enlisted the help of Doug Schwerma of Champion frames and the tuning talent of legend Al Gunter for the one-off effort. Riders included veterans Mike Gerald, Dave Hansen and rookies John Gennai and Rick Hocking, all from California.

At Friday nights, TT Dave Hansen was the surprise winner on his Champion Frames-sponsored Triumph, smoking his way to a solid win over Kenny Roberts who once again came up short after a poor start. On Saturday Hansen and Mike Gerald replete in Honda leathers, dominated the small oval. Gerald led Hansen in a 1-2 freight train with the four stroke Hondas hooking up perfectly to the slick Astrodome track. Record crowds of over 68,000 attended the weekend's events.

TT National

Houston promoters had brought in California track whiz Harold Murrell in an attempt to smooth out the unpredictable temporary dirt surface. The track was less bumpy, although a little slick and more one grooved than in the past. The layout was altered to take out some of the infield twisties, making for a faster track. A virtual who's who of Grand National stars crashed in practice, including former National TT winners Mert Lawwill, a returning-to-action Mark Brelsford and Gene Romero. Northwest TT star Randy Scott had a terrible looking crash off the jump, severely tweaking his shoulder. Tough guy Scott rode on and eventually made the National. A crowd of around 32,000 watched Friday nights TT.

Time Trials

Dave Hansen (Tri) set the fastest time of the night at 23.78 on his Les Edwards tuned Triumph. The 1972 TT winner John Hateley was aboard a Yamaha instead of his usual Triumph and ran a 23.94. Kenny Roberts (Yam) was next with a 23.95. New Harley Team member Gary Scott, Mark Williams (Tri) and rookie Expert Rick Hocking (Yam) turned identical 24.10's to round out the top 5.

Heats

"Steady Eddie" Mulder (Tri) riding with Jack Hateley Enterprises sponsorship, pulled one of his patented holeshots in Heat 1. Mulder looked good, but KRW Helmets/Fred's Distributing sponsored Mark Williams and fast timer Dave Hansen soon passed the multi-time National TT winner. Williams led early before Hansen went on for the win. Mulder hung onto 3rd for the last direct transfer. Rookie Charlie Brown (Tri) was 4th. The 1972 GNC champ, Mark Brelsford was in his first dirt track event since Houston last year, put in a strong charge from the back of the pack for 5th after being tangled up in a first lap crash with Rob Morrison. Former GNC champs Mert Lawwill and Gene Romero struggled in the rear of the pack.

Act two was dominated by John Hateley aboard his new Jack Hateley tuned 750 Yamaha. He launched the big twin over the jump like a motocrosser, wowing the crowd. Gary Scott was fast in 2nd place on his new Bill Werner-tuned ride. Texas hope Jim Rawls was also strong on his Harley in 3rd. Chuck Palmgren (Yam) was 4th and semi-bound.

New Grand National Champion Kenny Roberts debuted his #1 plate in Heat 3. He and Tom White (Tri), always a strong runner at Houston, argued over the top spot with some serious handlebar rattling. Roberts won the battle and surged ahead to the win. Dave Aldana (Nor) was 3rd. Randy Scott rode with his injured shoulder to an impressive 4th. Don Castro was out for the night after getting tangled up over the jump and crashing heavily.

Unusual for Houston, there had not been a lot of restarts and crashes yet; that all changed in Heat 4. Mike Kidd's neat holeshot on the lone factory Triumph was negated by two grinding crashes involving a gaggle of riders including Rex Beauchamp (HD), Ed Salley (Yam) and Jimmy Lee (Tri). Beauchamp's bike broken gas tank was repaired with duct tape and he made the restart. Rookie Rick Hocking on a Champion-framed Yamaha led the restart, but Texas crowd favorite Kidd took the lead and the win. John Gennai was charging forward and took 2nd as Hocking's ride slowed.

New for 1974 was the 14 rider field, two more than in previous years. Three riders came out of each heat and the two semis were essentially last chance qualifiers with only the winner advancing, making an already tough to make National tougher.

Semis
Mark Brelsford was determined to earn a spot in the National and jumped out to a narrow lead. He stayed just ahead of a battle raging between Chuck Joyner (Tri), Mert Lawwill, Robert E. Lee (Yam) and Gene Romero. Romero ended up going down hard, knocking himself unconscious. He was up again soon, but done for the night. Brelsford took the win after the restart followed by Joyner and Lawwill.

Never-say-die Randy Scott led Semi 2 wire-to-wire in an impressive win. Behind, Sonny Burres (Tri) was in 2nd place early, but Houston native Darryl Hurst (Yam) and Gil Reed (Tri) managed to slip past.

Trophy Race
Chuck Joyner led fellow Northwest TT ace Sonny Burres to win the Trophy Race with Jimmy Lee in 3rd. All were Triumph mounted.

National
Gary Scott pulled a tasty holeshot over the talent laden field, but his out-of-control landing off the jump allowed Dave Hansen and Mike Kidd to get by. John Hateley, who was running with the leaders, lost time in avoiding Scott. The early order was Hansen, Kidd, Scott and Hateley. Kenny Roberts got a horrible start and was trying to move through the field. Mid-pack action saw Jim Rawls crash, nearly taking Dave Aldana with him. Aldana continued only to fall three laps later in the same spot. The same corner also got Hateley, who tucked the front end of his Yamaha. All the while, Roberts was blasting through the pack. The Houston crowd was cheering him on; now accustomed to Roberts "come from behind" runs. Roberts was 4th after Hateley's crash and quickly moved by Scott. The crowd went wild as he closed up on Kidd for 2nd. He moved Kidd over going through Turn 1 and set out after Hansen. Although he was reeling the leader in, Roberts ran out of race. Smooth-riding Hansen took a win for the underdogs, similar to Mike Haney's 1973 win.

Short Track
A huge crowd of 36,888 turned up Saturday to cheer on their favorites. The surprise fast qualifier was Georgia rookie Roger Crump (Bul) at 15.20. John Hateley (Yam) was 2nd fastest for two nights in a row, turning in a 15.24. Mert Lawwill, who won the 1970 event, wowed everyone by putting his Harley Sprint in at 3rd fastest with a 15.27. The Honda team was trying to get their mounts sorted out with Mike Gerald 19th and Dave Hansen 22nd fastest. Kenny Roberts was in the same boat with his Yamaha and was way back in the order. The track was fast and smooth, but a thin blue groove meant little traction anywhere else.

Heats
Roger Crump proved his fast time was no fluke and dominated the first heat. Jimmy Lee was a solid 2nd until his Yamaha quit on the last lap. Pat McCaul (Yam) took over the spot at the finish. Kenny Roberts came from a second row start to finish an uncharacteristic 3rd, but he was in the National. Crump's time set a new record for the heat races.

Heat 2 was an exciting run featuring a duel between Dave Hansen, Rob Morrison (Bul), John Hateley and Phil McDonald (Yam) all of whom took a turn leading. McDonald and Bill Schaeffer had an altercation, bringing out the red flag with 3 laps to go. Morrison took the lead on the restart until Hansen forced his way by. Hateley and Ed Salley (Yam) battled over the last transfer spot with Drew Pate's-sponsored Salley just getting the nod at the line.

The third heat had to be restarted after an incident involving Houston's own Darryl Hurst (Yam) and Ohio rider Scott Drake. Rookie Hank Scott, (yep, Gary's younger brother), on another Pate's Yamaha ride would lead the early laps. "Ragin' Cajun" Mike Gerald, cheered on by a huge contingent of Louisiana fans, put a wheel on Scott, moving by on the last lap for the win. Rookie Tom Horton and Scott followed, both Yamaha mounted. Gerald's time topped Crump's for another 10 lap record.

Heat 4 started with 1971 winner Jimmy Odom (Yam) and Pat Marinacci (Hon) being accused of jumping the start and were moved to the penalty line. Odom crashed with Don Graham (Bul) on the restart. When it finally got going, the race was a crowd pleaser with relatively unknown Houston resident Tim Buckles (Bul) leading the race from start to finish. Mert Lawwill was doing business on his Harley Sprint till midway when valve train problems hit. Behind Buckles, a "battle royale" for the remaining transfer spots between a Yamaha quartet made up of Chuck Palmgren, Robert E. Lee, Corky Keener and Gene Romero. They rode together in a tight pack with Lee passing Palmgren for 2nd. Keener and Romero were semi bound.

Semis

Jim "JR" Rawls made his second National of the weekend by taking a comfortable victory in Semi 1. Gene Romero beat and banged his way to 2nd over a star studded field that included Corky Keener, Gary Nixon and Mike Kidd.

John Hateley won Semi 2 after a race long battle with motorcycle stunt man/jumper-turned-racer, Steve Droste (Yam). Behind them, John Gennai, Fred Smith and Gary Scott were headed to the Trophy Dash. Unbelievably, Dave Aldana, Mark Brelsford and Bart Markel were done for the night.

Trophy Race

Scoring the first major Honda dirt track win so far was John Gennai in the Trophy Race win. Second went to Gene Romero, who continued to ride the wheels off of his new factory Yamaha short tracker, pressing Gennai for much of the event. Corky Keener was 3rd. Gary Scott hadn't had much luck all night on his first ride on a Harley Sprint and was 4th.

National

Mike Gerald started on the pole for the 20-Lap National. He and new teammate Dave Hansen bolted to the front of the pack. The Murrell-prepared track was fairly smooth, but unlike past years, there was only one line. The fast line was on the pole and passing was difficult. Gerald and Hansen stuck to the bottom of the track and rode the Honda freight train away from the pack. It was not an easy "team" ride for Gerald; Hansen was hungry for another victory and the two had several bumps and grinds, but Gerald would not be denied. Tom Horton had the best run of his National career, running 3rd on the Shell Motors Yamaha. Roger Crump had an impressive debut in 4th. Kenny Roberts came from a back row start and could only manage a 5th place finish; A far cry from the past two years when the champ dominated the event. At the finish, Gerald was ecstatic and the large and loyal group of Louisiana fans went nuts.

Results

Race: 25 Lap TT National
Race Time: 10:21.31

Rank	Rider	Number	Make
1.	Dave Hansen, Hayward, Ca	23	Tri
2.	Kenny Roberts, Woodside, Ca	1	Yam
3.	Mike Kidd, Euless, Tx	72	Tri
4.	Gary Scott, Baldwin Park, Ca	64	HD
5.	Rick Hocking, Fremont, Ca	31Z	Yam
6.	Mark Williams, Springfield, Ore	70	Tri
7.	Eddie Mulder, Northridge, Ca	12	Tri
8.	Mark Brelsford, Woodside, Ca	6	HD
9.	Randy Scott, Philomath, Ore	50	Tri
10.	John Hateley, Van Nuys, Ca	98	Tri
11.	John Gennai, Hayward, Ca	16Y	HD
12.	Dave Aldana, Santa Ana, Ca	13	Nor
13.	Tom White, Huntington Beach, Ca	80	Tri
14.	JR Rawls, Grand Prairie, Tx	93	HD

Race: 14 Lap Trophy Race
Race Time: 5:54.02

Rank	Rider	Number	Make
1.	Chuck Joyner, Oregon City, Ore	60	Tri
2.	Sonny Burres, Portland, Ore	69	Tri
3.	Jimmy Lee, Bedford, Tx	19N	Tri
4.	Gilbert Reed, Salem, Ore	90	Tri
5.	Mert Lawwill, San Francisco, Ca	7	HD
6.	Bob Ewell, Dallas, Tx	40N	Yam
7.	Bob Sanders, Whittier, Ca	5R	Yam
8.	Mike Caves, Galesburg, Ill	2P	Tri
9.	Robert E. Lee, Fort Worth, Tx	54	Yam
10.	Darryl Hurst, Houston, Tx	34	Yam

Race: 20 Lap Short Track National
Race Time: 5:20.01

Rank	Rider	Number	Make
1.	Mike Gerald, Baton Rouge, La	15	Hon
2.	Dave Hansen, Hayward, Ca	23	Hon
3.	Tom Horton, Lancaster, Ca	55	Yam
4.	Roger Crump, Resaca, Ga	4C	Bul
5.	Kenny Roberts, Woodside, Ca	1	Yam
6.	Chuck Palmgren, Freehold, NJ	38	Yam
7.	Pat McCaul, San Jose, Ca	48Y	Yam
8.	John Hateley, Van Nuys, Ca	98	Yam
9.	Hank Scott, Hixson, TN	20R	Yam
10.	Tim Buckles, Houston, Tx	23N	Bul
11.	JR Rawls, Grand Prairie, Tx	93	Bul
12.	Rob Morrison, Granada Hills, Ca	10E	Bul
13.	Ed Salley, Roswell, Ga	62C	Yam
14.	Robert E. Lee, Fort Worth, Tx	54	Yam

Race: 14 Lap Trophy Race
Race Time: 3:40.70

Rank	Rider	Number	Make
1.	John Gennai, Hayward, Ca	16Y	Hon
2.	Gene Romero, San Luis Obispo, Ca	3	Yam
3.	Corky Keener, Flint, Mi	62	Yam
4.	Gary Scott, Baldwin Park, Ca	64	HD
5.	Steve Droste, Waterloo, Ia	92	Yam
6.	Mike Kidd, Euless, Tx	72	Ric
7.	Gary Nixon, Cockeysville, Md	9	Kaw
8.	Fred Smith, Memphis, Tn	42	Yam
9.	Charlie Chapple, Flint, Mi	36	Yam
10.	Bill Morgan, San Leandro, Ca	25Z	Yam

Grand National Points Standings after Round 2

Rank	Rider	Pts
1.	Dave Hansen	270
2.	Kenny Roberts	180
3.	Mike Gerald	150
4.	Mike Kidd	101
5.	Tom Horton	100
6.	Gary Scott	80
7.	Roger Crump	80
8.	Rick Hocking	60
9.	Chuck Palmgren	50
10.	Mark Williams	50

Extra Extra

- Dick Mann wasn't able to ride at Houston; He was still recovering from a broken leg suffered while motocrossing. He put his time to good use, helping ABC Television's Jim McKay from Wide World of Sports, and filmmaker Bruce Brown, cover the weekend happenings for future broadcast. Mann would be healed up by Daytona time.
- Dave Hansen's 1-2 finishes made him the closest yet to an Astrodome "Double". He left Houston with the GNC points lead.
- Roger Crump pocketed $100.00 for setting fast short track time.
- Larry Cooper won the Junior Invitational Short Track over Guy McClure, both Bultaco mounted. In qualifying, McClure bettered the Expert's times with a 14.91.

Top 10 Houston TT Qualifying Times

1.	Dave Hansen	Tri	23.78 seconds
2.	John Hateley	Yam	23.94
3.	Kenny Roberts	Yam	23.99
4.	Rick Hocking	Yam	24.10
5.	Mark Williams	Tri	24.10
6.	Gary Scott	HD	24.10
7.	Don Castro	Yam	24.12
8.	Mike Kidd	Tri	24.13
9.	Eddie Mulder	Tri	24.20
10.	JR Rawls	HD	24.29

Bonus!
Top 10 Houston Short Track Qualifying Times

1.	Roger Crump	Bul	15.20
2.	John Hateley	Yam	15.24
3.	Mert Lawwill	HD	15.27
4.	Tim Buckles	Bul	15.30
5.	Jimmy Lee	Yam	15.33
6.	Steve Droste	Yam	15.40
7.	Tom Horton	Yam	15.40
8.	Chuck Palmgren	Yam	15.42
9.	Gary Scott	HD	15.44
10.	Dave Aldana	Ric	15.45

1974 Daytona 200
Agostini First at Daytona!

GNC Round #3 of 23
Date: March 10, 1974
Type: Road Race
Venue: Daytona International Speedway
Location: Daytona, Florida

Purse: $52,000.00
Surface: Pavement
Course Length: 3.84 miles
Laps: 52
Distance: 200 Miles

The 1974 running of the "200" was a game changer for Daytona as well as road racing in general. Despite winning the previous two Daytona events, Yamaha knew that their 350 was soon to be left behind and Daytona saw the debut of the radical TZ700. The bike benefited from Yamahas rich road racing experience. A 500cc version had raced throughout Europe in 1973. The bike was very fast out of the gate and a well thought out chassis was a good handler in most situations. Reliability seemed good except for the four flat-sided expansion chambers that were prone to cracking. On the surface it would seem that the Kawasaki and Suzuki teams would have things well in hand, at least till the TZ's bugs were worked out. They had several years development and had comparable power and speeds to the Yamaha. Unfortunately both brands still suffered nagging reliability problems. This was at least partially due to the fact that they were highly stressed production items. The new Yamaha was essentially two sets of tried and true 350 top ends on a new crankcase. It would not take long to science out the engine. Time was already running out for the other teams. Despite being a pricy new model, multitudes of factory and private TZ700's showed up at Daytona.

In addition to their formidable motorcycle, Yamaha assembled it's the strongest team riders yet. No one could argue with the success of imported Grand Prix stars at Daytona, this year Yamaha had one of the greatest ever; 13-time World Champion Giacomo Agostini. He was joined by fellow GP riders Teuvo Lansivuori and Hideo Kanaya. U.S. team members included GNC champ Kenny Roberts, Gene Romero and Don Castro. Last year's winner Jarno Saarinen was lost in a racing accident shortly after Daytona.

The Suzuki team which had been very stable over the last several years added some new faces. Just for the event they imported their own GP stars Barry Sheene and Ken Araoka. Gary Nixon and Cliff Carr, victims of Kawasaki's racing cutback, joined Paul Smart on the U.S. based squad. Long time Suzuki rider Ron Grant had retired. 1972 Daytona winner Don Emde did not compete. Geoff Perry was lost in an airplane accident over the Pacific in 1973. Another sad loss felt by all was Cal Rayborn's absence. He had signed with Suzuki but was killed in a racing accident in New Zealand. The big Suzuki's still had the speed to run with all comers, they just needed to go the distance.

A much abbreviated Kawasaki team showed up at Daytona. The only returning riders were Yvon DuHamel, Art Baumann and Hurley Wilvert. A much different scene than the attack launched in 1973. While all the team riders were capable of winning, the air-cooled team bikes seemed down on power and needed the reliability to finish; something that none of the factory machines did the previous year.

The four-stroke teams were all woefully down on power, most giving up around 20 mph on the banking. Harley-Davidson's main road race talent was now Mark Brelsford. The 1972 GNC champ bravely returned to the scene of his horrific crash. Mark was capable of winning on pavement, as demonstrated by his 1971 Loudon win, but his ride clearly was not. He was joined by his younger brother Scott, Roger Reiman and new teammate Gary Scott. Norton brought back their very cool monocoque rides with Dave Aldana and Peter Williams riding. Butler & Smith brought a custom framed, hot rod BMW for Reg Pridmore. The once world beating factory British triples were represented by the sole Triumph of Mike Kidd. Even Dick Mann had moved on, now aboard a Don Vesco TZ700. The Honda effort of the previous year was not in evidence. The four strokes all handled great and looked cool, but were out of the hunt. The appearance of the mighty Yamaha TZ700 marked the end of an era and the start of a new one.

The race was shortened to 180 miles under pressure from government decrees to not waste fuel during the period's gasoline crunch.

Due to mixed reaction from all involved, the back straight chicane was tweaked to allow faster entry and exit. The change was well received by the riders.

413

Time Trials

Paul Smart once again topped qualifying on his Suzuki, showing that the Yamahas weren't completely invincible. He ran a lap in 2.08:06 at 107.949. Lap times were quicker due to the changed chicane; 24 riders topped the Paul Smart's previous record of 101.871. Joining him on the front row were Hideo Kanaya (Yam), Kenny Roberts (Yam), Barry Sheene (Suz) and Giacomo Agostini (Yam). Row two was; Gary Nixon (Suz), Teuvo Lansivuori (Yam), Yvon DuHamel (Kaw), Cliff Carr (Suz) and Akiyasu Motohashi (Yam).

National

While Don Castro managed to lead briefly off the line, Giacomo Agostini wanted no part of an early race pileup and really gassed it up, despite dead cold tires and a full fuel load and jetted away from the pack. Following at the end of lap 1 were the more restrained group of Hideo Kanaya, Don Castro, Gary Nixon, Yvon DuHamel, Barry Sheene, Paul Smart and a horde of other fast guys. Kanaya was the only rider making time on the fleeing leader. He began stuffing his Yamaha harder and harder through the infield corners. Finally, on lap 5 he pushed too hard in the infield sweeper, tossing the bike away spectacularly. He was beat up and suffered at least an ankle fracture. With the pack beginning to reel him in, Agostini cooled his blistering pace. Barry Sheene, Kenny Roberts and Gary Nixon were all over the World Champion by lap 8. DuHamel was having shifting problems and was dropping back. Sheene took over the lead in the infield, soon followed by Roberts and Nixon. The trio then diced around the track for several laps, trailed by Agostini. Roberts soon faded back with a suspected overheating engine, but hung unto the group. A second group of riders including Teppi Lansivuori, John Long, Don Castro, Cliff Carr, Paul Smart and Hurley Wilvert were shuffling positions behind. When pit stops began, the Suzuki team ran into a debacle; all the riders were using the same quick fill station which malfunctioned. Several team riders were held up before the backup system used. Worse for the team, frontrunner Sheene dropped out on lap 25. The stops of Nixon, Roberts and Nixon went smoothly and they continued to dispute the lead. Roberts began to slow with cracked pipes and a still hotter engine. Nixon came in for his last stop and was now in the drivers seat. The 1967 Daytona winner had the race in hand; he was only a short distance behind Agostini, who still had to come in for his final pit stop. Despite this Gary pressed harder, determined to pass the 13-time World champ straight up. He pressed just a fraction too hard and on lap 37, dumped his Suzuki up the corner to the banking. A stunned partisan crowd watched Nixon sprint to his bike, but it was too badly damaged to continue. A terribly frustrated Gary Nixon was done, missing his best chance to recapture a Daytona win. Agostini didn't put a wheel wrong in the closing laps and crossed the stripe with Kenny Roberts surviving the day a distant 2nd. The often overlooked Hurley Wilvert, a brilliant rider/tuner, deftly rode his Kawasaki to well deserved 3rd spot. Don Castro was an impressive 4th, rounding out a great pavement debut for Yamaha. Rounding out the top 10 were Lansivuori, steady Gene Romero in his first Yamaha pavement ride, Ken Araoka aboard his Suzuki was the first non-Yamaha, Steve McLaughlin, Paul Smart and Akiyasu Motohashi. Yamahas dominated the race; they took 17 of the top 20 places. Scott Brelsford was the first four-stroke home in 33rd position.

Results

Race: 200 Mile Road Race National
Race Time: 1:4:39.50, (105.010 MPH, New Record)

Rank	Rider	Number	Make
1.	Giacomo Agostini, Bergamo, Italy	10	Yam
2.	Kenny Roberts, Woodside, Ca	1	Yam
3.	Hurley Wilvert, Westminster, Ca	39	Kaw
4.	Don Castro, Gilroy, Ca	11	Yam
5.	Teuvo Lansivuori, Isalmi, Finland	8	Yam
6.	Gene Romero, San Luis Obispo, Ca	3	Yam
7.	Ken Aroka, Tokyo, Japan	41	Suz
8.	Steve McLaughlin, Duarte, Ca	83	Yam
9.	Paul Smart, Santa Ana, Ca	33	Suz
10.	Akiyasu Motohashi, Japan	31	Yam

Rank	Rider	Number	Make
11.	Cliff Carr, Arlington, Mass	26	Kaw
12.	Dick Mann, Richmond, Ca	2	Yam
13.	Gary Fisher, Parkesburg, Pa	21	Yam
14.	Christian Bourgeois, Paris, France	55	Yam
15.	Jean Paul Boinet, Montlhery, France	44	Yam
16.	Dennis Varnes, Christiana, Pa	147	Yam
17.	Mike Clarke, Downey, Ca	143	Yam
18.	Marty Lunde, Hermosa Beach, Ca	56	Yam
19.	Harry Cone, Sherman, Tx	82	Yam
20.	Phil McDonald, Tulsa, Ok	109	Yam

Grand National Points Standings after Round 3

Rank	Rider	Pts
1.	Kenny Roberts	336
2.	Dave Hansen	270
3.	Mike Gerald	150
4.	Hurley Wilvert	130
5.	Don Castro	104
6.	Mike Kidd	101
7.	Tom Horton	100
8.	Gary Scott	83
9.	Roger Crump	80
10.	Gene Romero	70

*Extra Extra**

- The Daytona crowd was down a little, still numbering around 57,000.
- 80 riders from 14 nations started the event.
- It was Giacomo Agostini's first ride for Yamaha after leaving his long time MV Agusta ride.
- Agostini garnered $14,960.00 in purse money for the win, Kenny Roberts got $7995.00 for runner-up and Hurley Wilvert $4,800.00 for 3rd.
- Immediately after the event, Frenchman Patrick Pons filed a claim on Agostini's bike. He plunked down the required $5000.00, as did Ago in a counter claim. Pons won the bike in the drawing. The AMA had just recently changed the claiming rule, making the winners bike the only one in the field that could be claimed.
- Yamaha took 16 of the first 20 spots.
- Agostini, conditioned to "push" Grand Prix starts, practiced the U.S. style clutch start repeatedly. He was obviously a quick-learner!
- Ago turned in a number of 2:05 laps during the race, nearly three seconds quicker than Smart's pole speed.
- Clearly showing the rising speeds, Ago's race speed of 105.005 was faster than Dick Mann's 1971 win on the 3.81 mile course *sans* the chicane.
- Trap speeds taken during practice showed the Yamaha of Hideo Kanaya blazing by at 191.88, followed by Yvon DuHamel's Kawasaki at 186.33 and Gene Romero (Yam) at 184.04.
- The Italian champion Agostini was very well received by the fans and was complimentary towards the U.S. riders.
- In a case of mistaken identity, the Italian crew member who pushed Agostini's winning ride into Victory Circle was besieged by the press and fans till the real article arrived.
- Hurley Wilvert had his best ever Daytona finish in 3rd. Wilvert had worked for Kawasaki as both a tuner, (for Paul Smart), as well as a team rider. This year he had the luxury of mechanical help from tuner George Vukmonovich.

- It was Paul Smart's third pole position in four years. He finished 9th in the race despite gearbox trouble. It was the speedsters best and last 200 finish.
- Gene Romero managed to finish 6th despite seriously cracked pipes on his TZ700. A fate that befell many with new Yamaha.
- Tuner extraordinaire Kevin Cameron foresaw the problems with Yamahas flat sided chambers. He welded up a trick two-into one system for rider Jim Evans. Unfortunately chain trouble would strike Evans, thwarting his ride.
- It was two-time winner, (1970 and '71), Dick Mann's last 200. He came home 12th on a Don Vesco TZ700 after suffering several mechanical issues.
- Team Harley-Davidson had a pretty miserable day; Mark Brelsford, Gary Scott and Roger Reiman were listed in 55th, 61st and 65th respectively. Like Mann it was the last Daytona race for 1964 winner Reiman. For Brelsford, his DNF was still an improvement on 1973's race!
- There were a bunch of other high level DNF's, including; Barry Sheene, Yvon DuHamel, Steve Baker, Walter Villa, Gary Fisher, Pat Evans and Norton riders Peter Williams and Dave Aldana.
- Mike Clarke (Yam) was the biggest mover on the day, finishing 17th after starting in 54th spot.
- Hurley Wilvert and Cliff Carr's Kawasaki's were the only air cooled bikes in the top 20.
- Long-time Kawasaki tuner for Yvon DuHamel, Steve Whitelock, joined Erv Kanemoto in the Suzuki camp.
- Pat Hennen gave Yamaha it's first big TZ700 win in the Junior race, backed by retired racer Ron Grant.
- In the Lightweight race, Don Castro won his first ever road race victory. Castro capped a great weekend by finishing 4th in the 200.
- Dave Smith rode Junior rider Jack Burke's Yamaha to 5th place in the Lightweight race. He then qualified the too small to be legal machine for the 200. By the time officials decided to check the bike it was a legal 350cc. He finished 28th in his last Daytona start.
- Cliff Carr's Suzuki lost it's rear brake early in the event. He tried to compensate some by catching air with unzipped leathers!
- Topping all other period displays of streaking, a young woman rode a Honda across the front straight during pre-race festivities wearing nothing but a smile for the big crowd.

1974 San Jose Mile
Roberts Wins First Mile!

GNC Round #4 of 23 **Date:** May 19, 1974 **Type:** Mile **Venue:** Santa Clara Fairgrounds **Location:** San Jose, Ca	**Purse:** $15,000.00 **Surface:** Dirt **Course Length:** 1 Mile **Laps:** 25 **Distance:** 25 Miles

Grand National Champion Kenny Roberts outfoxed and outgunned rival Gary Scott on the last lap at the San Jose Mile. It was Roberts first ever Mile win and just the 5th National of his career. "Real" fans and racers considered this first outdoor oval of the season to be the first "real" race. Many had worked long and hard through the winter, extracting more horsepower from their machines. In the end there seemed near parity between the two big brands: Harley-Davidson and Yamaha. Roberts and 2nd place Gary Scott were glued together for many laps; power was near equal, the win was due to strategy. Closing up at the end was Team Yamaha member Gene Romero, who rounded out the podium. Besides Gary Scott, the most disappointed Harley-Davidson rider was 6th place Mert Lawwill. Lawwill and crew had worked very hard through the off season to put together the fastest XR at the track. It was, but a bad start and tire issues negated the extra power. Speaking of extra power, some neat multi-cylinder machines made their debut at San Jose. Erv Kanemoto put together a 750 Kawasaki triple for Gary Nixon and Rocky Cycle had assembled a Honda CB750-based machine for rookie Rick Hocking. The machines were well turned out and featured Champion frames. Both showed speed, particularly Nixon's, but suffered new bike teething.

Kenny Roberts' win added to his growing GNC points lead, his total now at 501. Dave Hansen's Houston points still had him in second, well back with 270. Hansen didn't make the National. Gary Scott's runner-up finish propelled him from way back, to third in points.

Time Trials

Near perfect weather conditions, great Harold Murrell track prep and increased horsepower led to a very fast times. Mert Lawwill shattered the old track record of 39.46 with an amazing 38.43. Around a half second back was new teammate Gary Scott at 38.96. Following were fellow Harley riders Charlie Seale (39.01) on a John Apple sponsored ride, and Scott Brelsford (39.07) on another factory bike. First non-Harley was rookie Roger Crump, running a 39.20 on Bill Kennedy's Triumph, rounded out the top 5. In all, 13 riders would break the old track record.

Heats

Mert Lawwill jetted away from the pack in Heat 1, leaving it to Gene Romero, Roger Crump and Jimmy Odom to put on the race. Making a rare National appearance, Odom looked good. He was safely in the top 4 who would go to the Main, but he pressed Romero and Crump. At the end it was Crump in 2nd on a very fast Triumph, just beating out Romero and Odom.

If one Scott wasn't enough, Kenny Roberts faced two, Gary and brother Hank, in Heat 2. Roberts was not easily intimidated though, controlling the early laps. Hank briefly scooted by for the lead on lap 4, with Roberts quickly reassuming the point, with Gary joining him in 2nd. In the fastest heat of the day, it was Roberts squeaking out the win by inches over Gary, with Hank in 3rd. Former GNC champion Mark Brelsford was shaking out the cobwebs, but was a solid 4th.

Frank Gillespie (Yam) shot out to the early lead in Heat 3, but was run down by Harley teamster Rex Beauchamp. Pressuring Beauchamp were more XR750's ridden by JR Rawls and Charlie Seale. After some drafting and swapping, the order at the finish read Beauchamp, Seale, Rawls and Yamaha mounted Pat McCaul.

Heat 4 saw Scott Brelsford make it three out of four wins for Team Harley. He headed the rapid AAR Yamaha of Chuck Palmgren, Tom Rockwood (HD) and Pat Marinacci (Tri).

Semis

Rookie Expert Bob Sanders (Yam) put on some wild moves to top Mike Collins (Yam) in Semi 1. Ascot stars Rob Morrison and Terry Dorsch battled through several other National wannabes to nail down the last available starting spots in Semi 2. Both were Yamaha mounted.

Trophy Race

All three big brands were at the front of the Trophy race with Tom Horton (Yam) taking the win over Tom White (HD) and Ron Moore (Tri).

National

Gary Scott rocketed off the line of the National, immediately pulling away with only Scott Brelsford close. Two of the expected favorites struggled to get going. Mert Lawwill had hit a slick spot right off the line and was near the back of the pack when he finally got traction. Kenny Roberts also hit a tricky spot, but it was in the 2nd turn and nearly spit him off. By the time he got rolling, Scott had a big lead. Roberts turned on the afterburners, reeling the front runners in, picking off Brelsford on the 4th lap and catching Scott two laps later. On lap 7, he went in front for the first time. Behind, last year's winner Gene Romero, and Rex Beauchamp were coming through the field, knocking Scott Brelsford back to 5th spot. Romero began checking out and gained distance on the leading duo. Lawwill had charged from way back in the field, managing to catch Brelsford, but his rear Goodyear was gone. The fastest bike at San Jose would advance no further. Back to the front, Scott and Roberts began the mile strategy game; both getting a feel of where they were fastest, Roberts frequently leading at the flag. Scott followed Roberts for several laps, going by with 5 to go. With two to go, Roberts tested his drive out of turn 4, moving up beside Scott. On the last lap, Roberts was running down low, setting up for the classic slingshot, with Scott up a little higher, thinking the Harley had enough to make it to the flag first. Out of turn 4, Scott slipped just a little, while Roberts hooked up, taking the win by less than a foot. Behind, Romero had gotten closer, with a big gap back to Beauchamp, Brelsford, Lawwill, Rockwood, McCaul, Sanders (great ride in first National), and Rob Morrison.

Results

Race: 25 Lap Mile National
Race Time: 16:41.47

Rank	Rider	Number	Make
1.	Kenny Roberts, San Carlos, Ca	1	Yam
2.	Gary Scott, Baldwin Park, Ca	64	HD
3.	Gene Romero, San Luis Obispo, Ca	3	Yam
4.	Rex Beauchamp, Milford, Mi	31	HD
5.	Scott Brelsford, Foster City, Ca	19	HD
6.	Mert Lawwill, San Francisco, Ca	7	HD
7.	Tom Rockwood, Gardena, Ca	88	HD
8.	Pat McCaul, San Jose, Ca	48Y	Yam
9.	Bob Sanders, Whittier, Ca	5R	Yam
10.	Rob Morrison, Granada Hills, Ca	10E	Yam
11.	Chuck Palmgren , Freehold, NJ	38	Yam
12.	Pat Marinacci, Seattle, Wa	67	Tri
13.	Jimmy Odom, Fremont, Ca	18	Yam
14.	Terry Dorsch, Granada Hills, Ca	22	Yam
15.	Mike Collins, Albuquerque, NM	84	HD
16.	Mark Brelsford, Daly City, Ca	6	HD
17.	Jim Rawls, Grand Prairie, Tx	93	HD
18.	Hank Scott, Hixson, Ca	20R	HD
19.	Charlie Seale, Imperial, Mo	47	HD
20.	Roger Crump, Resaca, Ga	4C	Tri

Race: 12 Lap Trophy Race
Race Time: 8:11.56

Rank	Rider	Number	Make
1.	Tom Horton, Lancaster, Ca	55	Yam
2.	Tom White, Huntington Beach, Ca	80	HD
3.	Ron Moore, San Bernardino, Ca	37	Tri
4.	John Gennai, Los Gatos, Ca	16Y	HD
5.	Dave Smith, Lakewood, Ca	20	Nor
6.	John Hateley, Van Nuys, Ca	98	Yam
7.	Michael Bailey, Eugene, Or	9Q	Yam
8.	Delbert Armour, Denver, Co	65	HD
9.	Sonny Burres, Portland, Ore	69	Yam
10.	Mark Williams, Springfield, Ore	70	Tri
11.	DeWayne Keeter, Ojai, Ca	44	HD
12.	Dave Hansen, Hayward, Ca	23	Yam

Grand National Points Standings after Round 4

Rank	Rider	Pts
1.	Kenny Roberts	501
2.	Dave Hansen	270
3.	Gary Scott	215
4.	Gene Romero	180
5.	Mike Gerald	150
6.	Hurley Wilvert	130
7.	Don Castro	104
8.	Mike Kidd	101
9.	Tom Horton	100
10.	Rex Beauchamp	88

Extra Extra

- A rocking crowd of 9,000 turned out for the day's racing.
- Kenny Roberts take from the purse was $2290.00, Gary Scott received $1430.00 and Gene Romero $1145.00.
- Roberts tuning crew of Shell Theutt, Bud Meyers and Bud Askland got bragging rights over Scott and Bill Werner (this time).
- Tom Horton took home $285.00 for his Trophy Race win.
- The exotic multis of Gary Nixon and Rick Hocking both had trouble. Nixon's Kawasaki suffered a broken chain and Hockings Honda a burnt piston.
- Mert Lawwill enlisted the talented help of cam grinder Sig Erson, Jim Belland, Mike Collins and Dud Perkins to build the fastest miler in the business. He spent the winter traveling to C.R. Axtell's shop in Los Angeles, honing his XR's engine to a fine edge. The 84 horsepower extracted showed as the Harley clearly had speed on all present. The Cycle World radar gun caught him at 121 mph, Nixon's Kawasaki was closest at 118.
- Dick Mann failed to qualify on the Champion Frames 750 Yamaha.
- There were several new Harley converts including Triumph stalwart Tom Rockwood, who made an impressive charge through the pack to 7th.
- Despite some fast British machines such as Roger Crump's Triumph, their numbers were dropping, with a corresponding rise in the Harley-Davidson and Yamaha ranks.
- Dave Aldana attempted to make the program but was hampered by a broken wrist, suffered at Ascot, May 3rd and mechanical problems.

- Almost 100 Experts signed in.
- A great Junior Invitational race saw Tom Berry top Bruce Hanlon and Alex Jorgensen.
- Mike Gerald and Honda failed to reach an agreement and Gerald would ride his own short track equipment the rest of the season.

Bonus!
Top 15 San Jose Mile Qualifying Times and Speeds

1.	Mert Lawwill	HD	38.43s, 93.67 MPH
2.	Gary Scott	HD	38.96 92.40
3.	Charlie Seale	HD	39.01 92.30
4.	Scott Brelsford	HD	39.07 92.16
5.	Roger Crump	Tri	39.20 91.84
6.	Mark Brelsford	HD	39.21 91.81
7.	Frank Gillespie	HD	39.22 91.78
8.	Tom Rockwood	HD	39.24 91.76
9.	Kenny Roberts	Yam	39.31 91.60
10.	Gene Romero	Yam	39.31 91.60
11.	Mike Kidd	Tri	39.33 91.54
12.	Jimmy Odom	Yam	39.39 91.53
13.	Jim Rice	HD	39.54 91.04
14.	Mark Williams	Tri	39.57 90.97
15.	Ron Moore	Tri	39.59 90.93

1974 Colorado Half-Mile
Lawwill Survives Denver Grind

GNC Round #5 of 23 **Date:** May 26, 1974 **Type:** Half-Mile **Venue:** Adams County Fairgrounds **Location:** Henderson, Co	**Purse:** $13,000.00 **Surface:** Dirt **Course Length:** 1/2 Mile **Laps:** 20 **Distance:** 10 Miles

Mert Lawwill used all of his savvy and experience to capture his 15th and final Grand National win. The victory was somewhat of a consolation prize after his disappointment at the San Jose Mile. As much as beating his fellow competitors, Lawwill beat the bombing range surface of the Adams County Fairgrounds track. The track was very rough, causing numerous accidents. The sandy, rocky track quickly came apart despite efforts to keep it patched up. Lawwill picked the fastest line(s) through the holes and pulled to a big lead over teammate Gary Scott, who had an equally large lead over Triumph's Mike Kidd. An enthusiastic crowd of around 11,000 waited patiently through repeated trips by the drag and water trucks between most every event. To preserve the track, the distances of the semis and Trophy Race were reduced. The National was also cut to 15 laps.

GNC points leader Kenny Roberts was challenging Gary Scott during the National, but was spit off. He still maintained a big point's advantage over Gary Scott, 511 to 355. Denver no show Dave Hansen was third with 270. Mert Lawwill's win moved him to fourth with 207. Mike Kidd was fifth with 201.

Time Trials

With the track still in decent shape, Mert Lawwill set fast time of 31.55 around the big, wide horse track on the Jim Belland/self-tuned Harley. Gary Scott was 2nd with a 31.95 on the Bill Werner-tuned XR750. Roger Crump ran an impressive 31.99 on the Kennedy Triumph for the last sub-32 lap. Rounding out the top 5 were Dave Aldana (Nor) 32.10 and Danny Hockie (Yam) 32.12.

Heats

Fast timer Mert Lawwill took an immediate lead in Heat 1 and led wire to wire. Rookie Danny Hockie on the Dirt Bike Magazine Yamaha, secured down 2nd after holding off challenges from GNC champ Kenny Roberts. John Hateley, aboard Mike Kidd's spare Triumph (Hateley's bikes were in Terry Dorsch's van which was in an accident, see *Extras*) pressured Roberts late in the race, followed by Triumph mounted Dick Mann.

It was all Harley-Davidson up front in Heat 2, led by Gary Scott, who motored away from everybody. Rookie John Gennai was a solid 2nd, with Florida's Charlie Seale taking the last transfer spot. Yamaha mounted Gene Romero was closing at the end, but was headed to the semis.

Heat 3 began on a nasty note before it started when Georgia's Roger Crump high-sided on the sighting lap. It looked bad initially, but Crump was not seriously injured. The race itself turned into one of the best of the day as Frank Gillespie (Yam), Jim Rice (HD), Chuck Palmgren (Yam), Jimmy Odom (Yam) and Eddie Wirth (Tri) waged a war up front. Palmgren and Odom moved past Rice and Gillespie to take the front spots. With three to go, Rice made a move in second turn, zapping both Odom and Palmgren for the lead. Rice pulled away to the win as further dicing saw Odom zap Palmgren for 2nd and Wirth came up to do the same to Gillespie for 4th.

Breaking up the Harley-Davidson sweep of the heats were Team British riders Dave Aldana (Nor) and Mike Kidd (Tri) and privateer Mark Williams (Tri). Aldana and Kidd pulled away cleanly for the top two spots. Harley-mounted Hank Scott was the early 3rd place runner, but faded back with Williams taking over. Teddy Poovey (HD) was 4th and 1972 GNC champ Mark Brelsford was 5th.

Semis

Former National champions Dick Mann and Gene Romero put on a nifty battle in Semi 1. Romero officially controlled the race, but Mann snuck by several times through the race. Mann attempted a last corner move, but slipped high and Romero was headed to the National, Mann to the Trophy Race.

Spectacular John Hateley blasted to a convincing win aboard his Triumph loaner. Sonny Burres topped a scuffle over Frank Gillespie, Teddy Poovey and Rex Beauchamp for second.

Trophy Race

Dick Mann now had the rough track figured and motored past early leader Pat McCaul (Yam). Mann put on a clinic on the cobby surface, stretching to a big win. McCaul held a safe 2nd to the finish. Frank Gillespie and Sonny Burres fought over 3rd with Burres taking the spot just past halfway.

National

Mert Lawwill spent a lot of time studying the other races and after conferring with Trophy Race victor Dick Mann, had picked out fast lines through the holes and bumps. Lawwill jumped out to an immediate lead in the National, his preferred lines working perfectly. Gary Scott running a distant 2nd, found the low line he used in his heat unworkable. By the time he made adjustments, Lawwill was long gone. From the back row, Kenny Roberts got a great start and by lap 3 was behind Scott. By half distance Roberts was challenging Scott, but hooked a rut and was tossed off the bike. He was unhurt, but out. Dave Aldana survived a similar, but more spectacular accident. Jim Rice was also a victim of the rough track. Lawwill was simply gone with Scott holding a big lead over a 3rd place battle between John Gennai and Mike Kidd. Gene Romero ran 5th till ignition failure late in the race. At the finish only nine bikes were running. Lawwill took the win, Scott 2nd, Kidd over Gennai late in the race followed by Chuck Palmgren, Charlie Seale, Mark Williams, Jimmy Odom and Danny Hockie.

Results

Race: 20 Lap Half-Mile National

Rank	Rider	Number	Make
1.	Mert Lawwill, San Francisco, Ca	7	HD
2.	Gary Scott, Baldwin Park, Ca	64	HD
3.	Mike Kidd, Euless, Tx	72	Tri
4.	John Gennai, Los Gatos, Ca	16Y	HD
5.	Chuck Palmgren, Freehold, NJ	38	Yam
6.	Charlie Seale, Imperial, Mo	47	HD
7.	Mark Williams, Springfield, Ore	70	Tri
8.	Jimmy Odom, Fremont, Ca	18	Yam
9.	Danny Hockie, Harbor City, Ca	45E	Yam
10.	Gene Romero, San Luis Obispo, Ca	3	Yam
11.	Kenny Roberts, San Carlos, Ca	1	Yam
12.	Dave Aldana, Santa Ana, Ca	13	Nor
13.	John Hateley, Van Nuys, Ca	98	Tri
14.	Jim Rice, Portola Valley, Ca	24	HD

Race: Trophy Race

Rank	Rider	Number	Make
1.	Dick Mann, Richmond, Ca	2	Tri
2.	Pat McCaul, San Jose, Ca	48Y	Yam
3.	Sonny Burres, Portland, Ore	69	Yam
4.	Frank Gillespie, Hayward, Ca	76	Yam
5.	Eddie Wirth, Dana Point, Ca	77	Yam
6.	Richard Wascher, Seattle, Wa	85W	Tri
7.	Tom White, Huntington Beach, Ca	80	Yam
8.	Jim Rawls, Grand Prairie, Tx	93	HD
9.	Teddy Poovey, Garland, Tx	94	HD
10.	Bruce Townsend, Oklahoma City, Ok	37G	Tri

Grand National Points Standings after Round 5

Rank	Rider	Pts
1.	Kenny Roberts	511
2.	Gary Scott	335
3.	Dave Hansen	270
4.	Mert Lawwill	207
5.	Mike Kidd	201
6.	Gene Romero	195
7.	Mike Gerald	150
8.	Hurley Wilvert	130
9.	Chuck Palmgren	121
10.	Don Castro	104

Extra Extra

- Mert Lawwill is one of the most iconic figures in AMA Grand National history. Lawwill could do it all; he was one of the best racers, tuners and chassis builders in the business. He won the 1969 Grand National Championship and captured 15 GNC victories. He won every type of dirt track event; short track, TT half-mile and mile. While this may portray him as a dirt-only specialist, he was a great road racer as well with high placings including a 2nd at Daytona as well as two other top 5's. He was a pavement victory short of a GNC "Grand Slam". He was one of the few 1960's stars able to race successful with the very different riders and machines of the 1970's. Lawwill's role in the legendary motorcycle movie, On Any Sunday will forever immortalize him as one of the premier stars of the sport. The movies positive impact on the sport is immeasurable. Lawwill's role in particular showed GNC racing to be a serious professional sport filled with talented, dedicated athletes. Though this race at Denver was his last National win, Lawwill continued racing successfully up to the 1977 season. His efforts in later years were hampered by inner ear problems that affected his balance. After retiring, Lawwill had success as an owner/tuner with champions such as Mike Kidd, Garth Brow, Steve Morehead, Wayne Rainey and Chris Carr, among others. He built and sold dirt track frames and components. He went on to develop revolutionary designs for bicycles and also prosthetic devices. He continues to build and sell Mert Lawwill Harley-Davidson Street trackers.
- Dave Aldana made the National despite his recent wrist injury.
- The Adams County Fairgrounds has a long history, which included racing from an early date. In the late 1880's, the first fairground site at Brighton was known as "Driving Park" due to the horse races that took place there. The first county fair held in 1904 hosted a wide variety of events including motorcycle, horse and foot races. The site at Brighton was used until 1956 when it moved to a huge site in Henderson. The fairgrounds have remained healthy and vibrant to present day and would continue to host occasional motorcycle racing.

- On the way to the Denver National, Terry Dorsch's van was involved in a serious traffic accident near Grand Junction, Co. Dorsch's longtime mechanic and supporter, Ron Bonner was killed in the accident. Dorsch was not badly injured, but returned home to California.

Bonus!
Top 10 Denver Qualifying Times

1.	Mert Lawwill	HD	31.55 seconds
2.	Gary Scott	HD	31.95
3.	Roger Crump	Tri	31.99
4.	Dave Aldana	Nor	32.10
5.	Danny Hockie	Yam	32.12
6.	Charlie Seale	HD	32.21
7.	Chuck Palmgren	Yam	32.48
8.	Mike Kidd	Tri	32.50
9.	Kenny Roberts	Yam	32.51
10.	John Gennai	HD	32.55

1974 Road Atlanta
Roberts Wins First Road Race!

GNC Round #6 of 23 **Date:** June 2, 1974 **Type:** Road Race **Venue:** Road Atlanta **Location:** Flowery Branch, Ga	**Purse:** $25,000.00 **Surface:** Pavement **Course Length:** 2.52 Miles **Laps:** 30 **Distance:** 75 Miles

Kenny Roberts' pavement skills were so strong at Road Atlanta, it was easy to forget that he had never won a National road race. He appeared supremely at ease scoring the double GNC and Lightweight races, both runaways. The big bike victory was National win number six for Roberts. His Yamaha was tuned by Shell Theutt, Bud Aksland and Bud Meyers. Finishing half-a-minute plus back from Roberts was teammate Gene Romero. Romero had to battle with a persistent Gary Nixon through much of the event, with the position undecided till the last lap. The weekend at Flowery Branch, GA was hampered by varying temperatures, rain, red clay, oily corners and a slow program. Though the races were sponsored by Kawasaki, on the track the former Kawasaki lions were much quieter than last year. Privateers on the new Yamahas were also very strong, while the remaining four stroke teams were practically nonexistent.

Kenny Roberts' win, combined with Gary Scott failing to score any points, gave him a towering lead in the GNC points battle, 676 points to Scott's 335 total. Gene Romero's runner-up placing moved him from sixth in points to third. Dave Hansen, Mert Lawwill and Mike Kidd all slid pack one spot. Mike Gerald, Hurley Wilvert and Chuck Palmgren maintained their positions. Gary Nixon's podium finish moved him into the top ten at Don Castro's expense.

Heats

Kenny Roberts (Yam) gave a taste of what was to come by totally dominating the first 8-lap heat. Gary Fisher (Yam) was in 2nd spot early on till Gene Romero (Yam) worked by. Cliff Carr (Suz) also quickly moved Fisher back a spot. Art Baumann (Kaw) was coming through the pack despite some setbacks. In practice he had seriously wrinkled his bike after hitting some oil dumped by Mark Brelsford's Harley. He muffed the start, but by mid-race he was by Fisher and as the laps wound down he passed Carr for third. At the finish, it was Roberts with a big lead, although Romero had closed a little, followed by Baumann, Carr and Fisher. Team Harley's Gary Scott was running towards the front, but pulled off on lap 5.

Ron Pierce (Yam) led Heat 2 all the way despite constant pressure from Steve McLaughlin (Yam). Next was Dave Aldana, aboard a new Winter Wonderland sponsored Yamaha. Norton had finally given in to the inevitable and thrown in the towel in road racing. Although Aldana had won at Talladega in 1970, he was still not yet thought of as a road racer. The three privateers topped heavy hitter Suzuki's riders Gary Nixon, Paul Smart and Kawasaki's Yvon DuHamel.

Due to the late running show, the Semi event was scrapped.

National

Ron Pierce gave it a good try, leading the first lap till around turn 5 when Kenny Roberts blitzed by with Gene Romero following. The early lead pack behind included; Dave Aldana, Steve McLaughlin, Art Baumann and Gary Fisher. Gary Nixon had a lousy start, but was working into the front after a few laps. Baumann and Nixon advanced into the lead pack with Nixon clear up to 4th by lap 6 and Baumann just behind. The pair broke from the pack, Nixon catching Romero by lap 12. The two former GNC champs battled hard, swapping paint and positions all over the circuit, with Baumann a safe 4th. Behind, Steve McLaughlin and Cliff Carr staged a similar battle. While Carr on the works Suzuki could control some of the twisty sections, McLaughlin's private Yamaha would blast by on the straights. As the laps waned, Roberts had a huge lead as he crossed the stripe but the battle(s) still raged behind. Nixon tried a few last second WFO moves, which Romero successful deflected, leading by less than a bike length. Baumann was a solid 4th, with McLaughlin topping Carr for 5th . Dave Aldana had a great first ride on the Yamaha, passing John Long and Paul Smart for 7th in the late going.

Results

Race: 75 Mile Road Race National
Race Time: 46:21, (97.848 MPH)

Rank	Rider	Number	Make
1.	Kenny Roberts, San Carlos, Ca	1	Yam
2.	Gene Romero, San Luis Obispo, Ca	3	Yam
3.	Gary Nixon, Cockeysville, Md	9	Suz
4.	Art Baumann, Brisbane, Ca	30	Kaw
5.	Steve McLaughlin, Duarte, Ca	83	Yam
6.	Cliff Carr, Arlington, Mass	26	Suz
7.	Dave Aldana, Santa Ana, Ca	13	Yam
8.	Paul Smart, Santa Ana, Ca	33	Suz
9.	John Long, Miami Beach, Fl	104	Yam
10.	Ron Pierce, Bakersfield, Ca	97	Yam
11.	Gary Fisher, Parkesburg, Pa	21	Yam
12.	Yvon DuHamel, LaSalle, Que., Can	17	Kaw
13.	Steve Baker, Bellingham, Wa	32	Yam
14.	Jim Evans, San Bernardino, Ca	27	Yam
15.	Phil McDonald, Tulsa, OK	109	Yam
16.	Mike Clarke, Downey, Ca	143	Yam
17.	Conrad Urbanowski, Miramar, Fl	28	Yam
18.	Hurley Wilvert, Westminster, Ca	39	Kaw
19.	Doug Libby, Milford, Mi	40	Yam
20.	Billy Labrie, St. Petersburg, Fl	139	Yam

Grand National Points Standings after Round 6

Rank	Rider	Pts
1.	Kenny Roberts	676
2.	Gary Scott	335
3.	Gene Romero	327
4.	Dave Hansen	270
5.	Mert Lawwill	207
6.	Mike Kidd	201
7.	Mike Gerald	150
8.	Hurley Wilvert	133
9.	Chuck Palmgren	121
10.	Gary Nixon	110

Extra Extra

- The factory Yamahas featured new expansion chambers to replace the troublesome flat sided units. Three pipes ran under the engine, with one pipe snaking through the frame and exiting by the upper right shock. Ron Pierce's bike featured a trick setup built by Mack Kambayashi. The pipes were completely tucked up under the bike, offering great ground clearance. They seemed to work well, but one pipe suffered a fracture during the race.

- Team Suzuki showed up with all new bikes. Redesigned frames and suspension had increased rake and trail. The engines featured new low end tuning and the bikes wore GP-style blue and white paint. The new bikes tested well in a private session before the weekend. Gary Nixon and Erv Kanemoto opted for their C&J framed machine, but had to switch to the new bike when Nixon hit oil and bent his favorite in pre-National practice.

- Most of the Kawasaki's were running new cylinders from Japan and while reliability seemed up, they struggled to keep up with the fastest bikes. Hurley Wilvert stuck with his own cylinder porting.
- Kevin Cameron and the Boston Cycles crew fixed a broken cylinder stud on Jim Evans Yamaha after his heat. The complete fix, including pulling the top end and helicoilng the offending stud, was finished in less than 30 minutes!

1974 Louisville Half-Mile
Keener Wins First at Louisville!

GNC Round #7 of 23	**Purse:** $13,000.00
Date: June 8, 1974	**Surface:** Limestone
Type: Half-Mile	**Course Length:** ½ Mile
Venue: Louisville Downs	**Laps:** 20
Location: Louisville, Ky	**Distance:** 10 Miles

Michigan cushion master Corky Keener earned his first-ever National win at the spectacular Louisville Downs race. Keener decimated the program, setting fast time, winning the fastest heat and the National going away. He was aboard three-time Louisville winner Bart Markel's Harley-Davidson, continuing the brands-domination since the inaugural race in 1967. Gary Scott battled through the lead pack to take the runner-up spot late in the race. Triumph's young star, Mike Kidd, took the remaining podium spot, spoiling an otherwise all-Harley top 10. It was 11 Harleys in the main, only broken up by Kidd's and Billy Eves' Triumphs and Kenny Roberts Yamaha.

There wasn't much change in the top order of the GNC points. Gary Scott's 2nd place run combined with Kenny Roberts 11th place finish helped narrow the gap between the leaders to 110 points. Corky Keener's win jumped him into the top 10 for the first time.

Time Trials

In the Harley-Davidson dominated qualifying session, Corky Keener was dialed in from the start, turning in a 26.004. Another Michigan rider, Dave Atherton, was a surprise second fastest with a 26.068. Gary and Hank Scott were next, turning in times of 26.088 and 26.236 respectively. Mert Lawwill, was 5th fastest at 26.423, Scott Brelsford 6th at 26.578, Rex Beauchamp 7th, and finally the first non-Harley, Dick Mann on a Champion Yamaha at 26.619.

Heats

Mike Kidd was sent to the penalty line on the first try to start Heat 1. Corky Keener took control on the restart and led to the win, although Mert Lawwill made a race of it in 2nd. Kidd put in a great ride, coming from the back, zapping John Hateley (Yam) on the last lap for the final transfer.

Georgia veteran Jimmy Maness on a factory/Dick Crenshaw Harley-Davidson sponsored XR750, pulled the holeshot in Heat 2, but a bobble in turn 2 helped Charlie Seale (HD) to take over the lead. Scott Brelsford also bumped Maness back a spot, a lap later. Gene Romero (Yam) and Scott Drake (BSA) also latched onto Maness, but they were in for a fight. The three swapped spots all over the place, but the tenacious Maness prevailed with the National spot. Seale took a comfortable win over Brelsford.

Rex Beauchamp, on the Babe DeMay-tuned factory Harley, was determined to continue the Harley sweep in Heat 3, but had to contend with a determined Billy Eves. Eves aboard the always-rapid Larry Mohan-tuned Triumph, worked the cushion hard and tracked Beauchamp down late in the race. The underdog Triumph drove by with two to go for the win. Behind, Gary Scott topped a spirited battle with Chuck Palmgren (Yam).

The Harley freight train continued in the last heat, with rookie Hank Scott motoring to a convincing win. Dick Mann tried to bring some diversity aboard his Yamaha, battling with Jim Rice (HD) and three time winner Dave Sehl (HD). Mann's bike developed trouble and quit late in the race. Scott was gone and Rice took the runner-up spot over Sehl.

Semis

A star-studded field lined up for Semi 1, including Mark Brelsford and most of Team Yamaha, Kenny Roberts and Gene Romero. Doug Sehl (HD) was not intimidated and stretched out to big lead. Things looked set till Sehl's bike quit late in the race, handing second place Roberts the win.

The best race of the night came in Semi 2. Chuck Palmgren (Yam) appeared to have things in hand till Rodney Bailey (HD) fell hard on lap 4. Upon the restart, Palmgren led again, but now faced heavy pressure from Steve Baker (Yam). Baker, known primarily as a great road racer, possessed great dirt track skills as well and he raced Palmgren side-by-side for several laps. Unnoticed by the leaders, Teddy Newton, aboard a Roy's Harley Davidson sponsored, Tex Peel tuned XR750, was on the charge and shot by both on the last lap, taking the final transfer spot of the night.

National

Due to threatening weather, the National was run before the Trophy Race. Corky Keener wasted no time and rocketed away from the pack, establishing a big lead in short order. Jimmy Maness was running a strong race, holding down 2nd place. A pressing Dave Sehl passed Maness four laps into the race. Gary Scott was closing from behind. Billy Eves and Rex Beauchamp battled in the lead pack till Eves overcooked it and fell. Beauchamp soon went out with mechanical trouble. On lap 9 Scott moved past Maness for 3rd. Mike Kidd had his Triumph wound up and was working through the pack. He and Mert Lawwill locked into a battle for 5th for several laps with Kidd moving forward. With five laps to go, Scott was by Sehl for 2nd. A rapidly closing-Kidd, knocked Sehl out of the final podium spot on the last lap. Nobody was close to Keener, who crossed the line for his first big win.

Trophy Race

Chuck Palmgren was determined to win the Trophy Race after missing his National shot in his semi. He was up and gone from flag-to-flag. Second quick qualifier Dave Atherton salvaged his night in 2nd and Scott Drake was 3rd aboard Delbert Bushes' BSA.

Results

Race: 20 Lap Half-Mile National

Rank	Rider	Number	Make
1.	Corky Keener, Flint, Mi	62	HD
2.	Gary Scott, Baldwin Park, Ca	64	HD
3.	Mike Kidd, Euless, Tx	72	Tri
4.	Dave Sehl, Waterdown, Ont., Can	16	HD
5.	Jimmy Maness, Augusta, Ga	71	HD
6.	Hank Scott, Hixson, Tn	20R	HD
7.	Mert Lawwill, San Francisco, Ca	7	HD
8.	Jim Rice, Portola Valley, Ca	24	HD
9.	Teddy Newton, Milford, Mi	40X	HD
10.	Charlie Seale, Imperial, Mo	47	HD
11.	Kenny Roberts, San Carlos, Ca	1	Yam
12.	Scott Brelsford, Foster City, Ca	19	HD
13.	Rex Beauchamp, Milford, Mi	31	HD
14.	Billy Eves, Phoenixville, Md	41	Tri

Race: Trophy Race

Rank	Rider	Number	Make
1.	Chuck Palmgren, Freehold, NJ	38	Yam
2.	Dave Atherton, White Pigeon, Mi	15E	HD
3.	Scott Drake, Xenia, Oh	7F	Tri
4.	Keith Ulicki, Kenosha, Wi	86	HD
5.	Steve Baker, Bellingham, Wa	32	Yam
6.	Mike Johnson, Flint, Mi	85	HD
7.	Frank Gillespie, Hayward, Ca	76	Yam
8.	Darryl Furst, Sanford, Mi	48X	HD
9.	Denny Palmgren, Freehold, NJ	49	HD
10.	Gene Romero, San Luis Obispo, Ca	3	Yam

Grand National Points Standings after Round 7

Rank	Rider	Pts
1.	Kenny Roberts	686
2.	Gary Scott	455
3.	Gene Romero	327
4.	Dave Hansen	270
5.	Mert Lawwill	247
6.	Mike Kidd	201
7.	Mike Gerald	150
8.	Corky Keener	150
9.	Hurley Wilvert	133
10.	Chuck Palmgren	127

Extra Extra

- A great 15,000-strong crowd turned out for the spectacular Louisville show.
- Corky Keener had earned his Expert card in the mid-1960's, but didn't race much till the early 1970's after some time in the military. A natural talent on the cushion, Keener had an easy-going, fun loving nature that made him very popular with fans and fellow racers. During the mid-70's, Keener was nearly unbeatable on the Regional Ohio and Michigan half-miles and always a threat at any National-level dirt oval.
- Keener further deepened his pockets on Sunday, capturing the $3000.00 Regional race. He topped Jimmy Maness and Billy Eves.
- Mike Kidd's factory Triumph in 3rd place broke up a top 10 Harley-Davidson sweep.
- Future super tuner Tex Peel had his first bike make a main event, with veteran Teddy Newton winning a semi and coming home 9th on Peel's Harley-Davidson in the National.
- Veteran Jimmy Maness was back in the top 5 for the first time since his 4th place run at the 1970 Atlanta Half-Mile.

1974 Loudon Road Race
Nixon Wins Weird, Wet Loudon

GNC Round #8 of 23 **Date:** June 16 &17, 1974 **Type:** Road Race **Venue:** Bryar Motorsports Complex **Location:** Loudon, NH	**Purse:** $25,000.00 **Surface:** Pavement **Course Length:** 1.6 Miles **Laps:** 47 **Distance:** 75 Miles

Gary Nixon won what had to be one of the strangest GNC races ever run. Due to a crash and then rain, the partially- completed race on Sunday ended up being finished on a Monday after a considerable amount of chaos and controversy. In the end, the day and the AMA's reputation was saved by a bit of good weather. For two-time Grand National Champion Gary Nixon, it was his 19th and final National victory. Although Nixon would have accepted the results either way, Gary was a fighter and that's the way he won his last AMA National. Repeating his second- place finish of Road Atlanta was Gene Romero. Romero fought his way forward on "day two" past Dave Aldana and Kenny Roberts. Aldana ended up third, well acclimated to his new Yamaha, with his best pavement finish since winning Talladega in 1970. Roberts ran with Nixon up front till his leathers began to shrink, causing muscle cramps. The champ still managed to finish 4th. Roberts' main GNC rival, Gary Scott was probably the second happiest Gary at Loudon. He won the Lightweight race aboard the new 250 Harley racer and managed a very credible 7th place finish in the National aboard the aging XRTT750. Probably the closest thing to a Harley-Davidson "double" possible in this era.

Heats

Although Saturday's preliminary races were nice and clear, the weather Sunday was damp and threatening. Heat race distances were halved. Gary Nixon (Suz) dominated the first heat after chasing down Yamaha factory riders Kenny Roberts, (USA) and Steve Baker (Canada). Hurley Wilvert (Kaw) took the Heat 2 win after early leader Cliff Carr crashed heavily when his helmet lense fogged up. His works Suzuki was broken into several pieces. Carr was shaken up, but okay.

National
Sunday June 16th

Rain caused the first start to be red flagged. After a short delay the race began, (without Heat 2 victor Hurley Wilvert whose Kawasaki failed to start), with Steve Baker getting the initial jump on the field. All over the Canadian were Kenny Roberts, Gary Nixon, Gene Romero and Dave Aldana. Baker staved off Roberts' attack till lap 3. when the GNC champ moved by. Baker fell on lap 4, but managed to remount and keep going. Romero was on the charge, moving clear to the front two laps later. Romero and Nixon battled as Yvon DuHamel (Kaw) made his way past Roberts. The order now read, Gary Nixon, Gene Romero, Kenny Roberts and Dave Aldana. Soon after, Art Baumann slid in oil in the last corner, falling hard as he came onto the straight. The red flag was out. Though scary at first, Baumann was not seriously injured. Soon after, the rain fell.

Confusion soon reigned, (sorry!); the AMA generally did not like to run races in the rain. Very few Nationals had been run in the rain. Most American riders had no experience in the wet, and generally the AMA shied away. But, the fans and promoters wanted to see a race and the under-pressure AMA decided to continue. This left the smaller teams unprepared. Many had no spares, let alone mounted and prepped "rains". This all became a moot point when the skies drowned out any possibility of continuing. This raised a new quandary; the riders would not get paid because they had not completed the 60% of the race as spelled out in the rules. Not knowing what else to do, everyone went home till Monday when a decision would be rendered.

Monday June 17th

When order(?) reconvened on Monday, indecision still ruled as more water had inundated the track. To get the laps in so the riders would be paid, it was decided to run the necessary amount of laps to get to 60% complete as "parade laps" with no passing to be allowed. Despite not being universally popular, it was at least a decision and bikes began to line up. No one was quite sure about what to do, or what was legal and a gamut of backup bikes appeared as well as several 250's! Lo and behold, as they got ready to go, the sky cleared and the track began drying. Eyeballing the heavens, officials reversed the decision and now the event would be run full distance under "normal racing conditions". Much gnashing of teeth and more general confusion later, a "proper" group of bikes lined up per Sunday's finishing order.

Gary Nixon immediately jumped out front on the Erv Kanemoto tuned Suzuki, stretching his lead clear to the finish. Gene Romero and Dave Aldana worked past Kenny Roberts whose aching muscles caused him to fade back to 4th spot. Yvon DuHamel retained 5th spot. Steve McLaughlin had a solid ride in 6th, Gary Scott pleased all the four stroke fans in 7th. Rounding out the top 10 were Steve Baker, Ron Pierce and John Long.

Results

Race: 75 Mile Road Race National

Rank	Rider	Number	Make
1.	Gary Nixon, Cockeysville, Md	9	Suz
2.	Gene Romero, San Luis Obispo, Ca	3	Yam
3.	Dave Aldana, Santa Ana, Ca	13	Yam
4.	Kenny Roberts, San Carlos, Ca	1	Yam
5.	Yvon DuHamel, LaSalle, Que., Can	17	Kaw
6.	Steve McLaughlin, Duarte, Ca	83	Yam
7.	Gary Scott, Baldwin Park, Ca	64	HD
8.	Steve Baker, Bellingham, Wa	32	Yam
9.	Ron Pierce, Bakersfield, Ca	97	Yam
10.	John Long, Miami, Fl	104	Yam
11.	Mike Clarke, Downey, Ca	143	Yam
12.	Gary Fisher, Parkesburg, Pa	21	Yam
13.	Billy Labrie, St. Petersburg, Fl	139	Yam
14.	Paul Smart, Santa Ana, Ca	33	Suz
15.	Dale Wylie, Christ Church, New Zealand	24	Yam
16.	Phil McDonald, Tulsa, Ok	109	Yam
17.	Mark Brelsford, Woodside, Ca	6	HD
18.	Bob Endicott, Balboa, Ca	110	Kaw
19.	Dennis Varnes, Christiana, Pa	147	Yam
20.	Dennis Purdie, Wayne, Mi	166	Yam

Grand National Points Standings after Round 8

Rank	Rider	Pts
1.	Kenny Roberts	774
2.	Gary Scott	499
3.	Gene Romero	459
4.	Mike Kidd	301
5.	Gary Nixon	275
6.	Dave Hansen	270
7.	Mert Lawwill	247
8.	Dave Aldana	172
9.	Steve McLaughlin	160
10.	Corky Keener	154

- This was Gary Nixon's 4th win at Loudon. He had won the race in two different decades on three different brands of motorcycles; 1968 on a 500cc Triumph T100/R, 1970 on a Triumph Trident, 1973 on a Kawasaki H2R and 1974 on the Suzuki TR750.
- Nixon's 4th win made him the all-time winner at the "new" Loudon. Brad Andres won 4 events at the old Laconia circuit.
- Gary Nixon continued to race with success in the U.S. and internationally through the 1970's . The Oklahoma native had an amazing career. He was a true journeyman Expert, on the circuit for several years, perfecting his skills, before his first National win at the Windber Road Race in 1963. He would become Grand National Champion in 1967 and 1968, and appeared headed to a third title in 1969 before his devastating leg injury at Santa Rosa. Though the injury limited his dirt track skills, he came back strong as ever in the road course events. While considered a pavement specialist, Nixon was one of the most versatile racers ever. He, along with Bobby Hill and Ralph White are the only riders to win both the Daytona 200 and the Springfield Mile. Nixon was only a TT win short of a GNC Grand Slam, coming up just short at the 1967 Peoria TT when Dick Mann passed him on the last lap. His 19 GNC wins tied him with Carroll Resweber and at the time of his Loudon victory, were only topped by Bart Markel, Joe Leonard and Dick Mann. Nixon crossed through two eras, riding for Triumph, Kawasaki and Suzuki factories and is one of the few riders to win on 40 HP, 1960's racers, as well as the 100HP two-stroke screamers of the 1970's. He was a tough dude, hurt badly and written off several times, then coming back to show the know-it-alls he could still win. His inner toughness and will to win were amazing, attributes that made him a true American hero.

1974 Columbus Half-Mile
A Final Triumph/A First for Kidd!

GNC Round #9 of 23	**Purse:** $15,000.00
Date: June 23, 1974	**Surface:** Dirt-Limestone
Type: Half-Mile	**Course Length:** ½ Mile
Venue: Ohio State Fairgrounds	**Laps:** 20
Location: Columbus, Oh	**Distance:** 10 Miles

Fast Texas youngster Mike Kidd nailed down his first National win after two years of trying. It was a big deal to win any GNC, but the Charity Newsies Half-Mile was a bigger than most: big payoff, big crowd and prestige. It was the first Triumph win at the Newsies since Gary Nixon win in 1968. It was also a historic last; the last GNC oval won by a Triumph. Brent Thompson had the tuning honors. For most of the National, it looked like a runaway win for GNC champ Kenny Roberts and a solid second place for two-time winner Mert Lawwill. Kidd came alive at the halfway point, catching Lawwill, then passing Roberts with two to go.

It was an unusual weather day at Columbus. Heavy rain fell right up to event time and the morning was cool and foggy. The event was a little behind, but skies cleared and the extra moisture made for a very racy track. It was a good day for most, but career ending fate awaited a former Grand National Champion.

Kenny Roberts gained more ground in the GNC points, doing well at a type of track he and his Yamaha usually struggled at, while rival Gary Scott had an off day at Columbus, finishing 7th. Gene Romero and Mike Kidd also added to their points totals, but stayed in third and fourth positions. Mert Lawwill's 3rd place run propelled him up to fifth in points. Gary Nixon slipped back to sixth. Dave Hansen continued hanging in there in the top order of points, now seventh in points. Chuck Palmgren moved up to eighth in points via a solid 5th place in the National. Dave Aldana was back to ninth, with Corky Keener held onto tenth.

Time Trials

Mert Lawwill was always strong at Columbus and the favorable track conditions allowed him to break his 1973 track record of 25.93 with a blazing 25.685. Scott Brelsford (HD) and John Hateley (Yam) rounded out the top 3.

Heats

Mert Lawwill took control of Heat 1 as the pack rocked out of turn 2 on the opening lap. Michigan rider Mike Johnson initially held 2nd spot, but slid down the next lap in the first turn. Mike Kidd assumed the runner-up position with Lawwill opening up a comfortable lead in the fastest heat of the day. Charlie Chapple (Yam) had the last transfer spot sewed up only to have his bike break on the last lap. This handed 3rd spot to Yamaha factory rider Gene Romero.

Heat 2 was an all-Milwaukee show up front as Harley-mounted Michigan cushion specialists Teddy Newton and Corky Keener tried to run away with the show. Newton led till halfway, when Keener on the Bart Markel Harley took control. The Brelsford brothers took the next two spots; Scott was headed to the National, Mark to the semi.

Yamahas provided most of the entertainment in Heat 3. Kenny Roberts pulled the holeshot at the start with relatively new Yamaha convert John Hateley blitzing by on lap 2. Roberts moved back by the next lap and led to the finish. Gary Scott (HD) motored to the third and final transfer spot.

Heat 4 saw Chuck Palmgren put another Yamaha in main, making it look easy in a wire-to-wire run. Behind there was a ferocious battle over the two remaining transfer positions. It included Rex Beauchamp (HD), Frank Gillespie (Yam), Larry Darr (HD), Dave Sehl (HD) and Rick Hocking (Yam). Gillespie held 2nd spot early, put was passed by Sehl and faded from the front. Dave Aldana (Nor) and TT ace Eddie Wirth (Tri) argued over 3rd, with Aldana taking the spot on the last lap. Beauchamp and Hocking headed to the semis.

Semis

Last year's winner at Columbus, Jim Rice, was the early leader in Semi 1, but Charlie Seale on the John Apple sponsored Harley came blasting by to lead lap 1. Seale really had a fire lit and ran away with the win. He had nearly a straightaway lead, taking the only National ticket over Rice and Rex Beauchamp.

Semi 2 saw an accident involving Mark Brelsford, Dick Mann and Dave Atherton. Brelsford received a badly fractured leg and other injuries. Complications from the injuries would eventually lead the 1972 Grand National champ Brelsford to retire. Upon the restart, rookie Hank Scott put his Harley ahead of Larry Darr's to take the final spot to the National.

Trophy Race

Last year's winner, Jim Rice looked a sure bet to take the "runner-ups" race, but East Coast teammate Rex Beauchamp had other ideas. Rice held the point early, with Beauchamp working by around halfway. The front two were locked in, but a good battle was on behind. Larry Darr was trying to salvage 3rd place, but first Frank Gillespie moved by followed by young Ohioan Steve Morehead. The top 5 were Beauchamp, Rice, Gillespie Morehead and Darr.

National

The National took a couple of attempts to get underway. Accused of being too quick on the first try were Hank Scott, Charlie Seale and Scott Brelsford; all went to the penalty line. The second try caught Dave Aldana and Brelsford again. Brelsford was moved back to a line of his own. On the next try, Kenny Roberts led the field away with Mert Lawwill, John Hateley and rest of the pack on his heels. Just behind, some strong runners had trouble. Harley mounted Corky Keener was soon out with valve train trouble. Chuck Palmgren had his Dan Gurney Yamaha stumble and he faded from the front. Mike Kidd was trying to shake out of his midpack start. Up front, Lawwill tried to close the gap, but Roberts opened up a several bike length lead. All the while, Kidd had found some fast lines and moved forward, moving past Hateley. Kidd latched onto Lawwill and moved into 2nd at halfway. He began to slowly reel in Roberts. Behind, Lawwill and Hateley were motoring safely in 3rd and 4th spots. Charlie Seale was 5th. Coming from nearly last spot to challenge Seale was Chuck Palmgren, whose Yamaha had cleared itself out, allowing a late race charge. Back up front, Kidd had caught Roberts with 3 to go. Kidd and Roberts ran wheel to wheel, but Kidd was soon by the champ and pulling away. It was a popular underdog win. Palmgren had worked by Seale, setting the top as; Kidd, Roberts, Lawwill, Hateley and Palmgren.

Results

Race: 20 Lap Half-Mile National

Rank	Rider	Number	Make
1.	Mike Kidd, Euless, Tx	72	Tri
2.	Kenny Roberts, San Carlos, Ca	1	Yam
3.	Mert Lawwill, San Francisco, Ca	7	HD
4.	John Hateley, Van Nuys, Ca	98	Yam
5.	Chuck Palmgren, Freehold, NJ	38	Yam
6.	Charlie Seale, Imperial, Mo	47	HD
7.	Gary Scott, Baldwin Park, Ca	64	HD
8.	Hank Scott, Hixson, Tn	20R	HD
9.	Scott Brelsford, Foster City, Ca	19	HD
10.	Dave Aldana, Santa Ana, Ca	13	Nor
11.	Dave Sehl, Waterdown, Ont., Can	16	HD
12.	Gene Romero, San Luis Obispo, Ca	3	Yam
13.	Teddy Newton, Milford, Mi	40X	HD
14.	Corky Keener, Flint, Mi	62	HD

Race: Trophy Race

Rank	Rider	Number	Make
1.	Rex Beauchamp, Milford, Mi	31	HD
2.	Jim Rice, Portola Valley, Ca	24	HD
3.	Frank Gillespie, Hayward, Ca	76	Yam
4.	Steve Morehead, Findlay, Oh	44F	Tri
5.	Larry Darr, Mansfield, Oh	20F	HD
6.	Randy Scott, Philomath, Ore	50	Yam
7.	Steve Droste, Waterloo, Ia	92	Yam
8.	Randy Cleek, Shawnee, Ok	11G	Yam
9.	John Gennai, Hayward, Ca	16Y	HD
10.	Eddie Wirth, Dana Point, Ca	77	Tri

Grand National Points Standings after Round 9

Rank	Rider	Pts
1.	Kenny Roberts	906
2.	Gary Scott	543
3.	Gene Romero	469
4.	Mike Kidd	466
5.	Mert Lawwill	466
6.	Gary Nixon	275
7.	Dave Hansen	270
8.	Chuck Palmgren	193
9.	Dave Aldana	189
10.	Corky Keener	162

Extra Extra

- An overflow crowd of 20,000 turned out for the 31st Annual Charity Newsies event.
- Mark Brelsford suffered complications from his severely fractured leg. He was placed in intensive care after an embolism occurred from the injury which lodged in a lung, causing serious respiratory trouble and Mark was placed on a ventilator. The hard luck 1972 Grand National Champion faced another long recovery. He would eventually decide to retire from the sport. The versatile racer should have been in his prime if not for his Daytona and Columbus injuries. Popular with both the fans and other riders, Brelsford's career was over way too early. He competed in the fewest amounts of races after becoming Number One than any other rider.
- Gary Nixon suffered serious injuries on June 21st while testing a Suzuki in Japan, for the Dutch GP. The bike seized, throwing Nixon off, breaking both arms, an ankle and severely bruising his back.
- Tom Rockwood had a big toe amputated after a crash at the Dayton, Oh Half-Mile on June 15th.
- Mike Kidd's come from behind win at Columbus, marked the Triumph marquees 56th modern era Grand National win; 23 TT 's, 10 miles, 10 half-miles, 9 road races and 4 short tracks. The majority of the races were won with the Meridian factories parallel twins, first appearing in the 1930's. The designs success and longevity were amazing, often competing with newer, purpose built racers for over forty years. While this was Triumphs last oval track win, they would still be a force to reckon with on the GNC TT tracks for years to come.

GNC Round #10 of 23 **Date:** July 7, 1974 **Type:** Mile **Venue:** Santa Clara Fairgrounds **Location:** San Jose, Ca	**Purse:** $15,000.00 **Surface:** Dirt **Course Length**: 1 Mile **Laps:** 25 **Distance:** 25 Miles

Gary Scott won his first race for Harley-Davidson at the "summer" San Jose Mile. It was Scott's first mile victory and his first National win in almost two years. It was GNC win number three for Gary. He controlled the majority of the Main event, but had to deal with pressure from his former Triumph ride as well as his younger brother. Columbus winner Mike Kidd showed there was still fire in the belly of the aging factory Triumph, which gave up little on this day, running a strong runner-up. Hank Scott was in the lead pack all day, scoring his best National finish in 3rd spot, making it a rare brother combination in victory circle. For Gary Scott and tuner Bill Werner it was sweet revenge over Kenny Roberts and the Yamaha team after a narrow loss at the spring running of the San Jose Mile. Roberts was in the lead pack, but wound up in 4th place.

Track conditions were much dryer and slicker than in spring. This may have contributed to the rash of accidents that occurred during the day. The slower track meant lap times were off compared to May. The only rider in practice below the 39 second mark was Mert Lawwill, still aboard the fastest XR in the land.

Gary Scott made up 77 points on Kenny Roberts, their points totals now at 994 and 708 points respectively. Roberts lessened the damage with his 4th place run. Mike Kidd's runner-up finish in the National moved him from fifth in points to third. Gene Romero was now back to fourth spot. Mert Lawwill, Gary Nixon and Dave Hansen remained in the next three spots. Hank Scott's podium run propelled him to eighth in points. Chuck Palmgren and Dave Aldana rounded out the top 10.

Time Trials

Mert Lawwill seemed a sure bet for the fastest time, but unbelievably, he hit an unassuming hole in turn 3 which launched him into a nasty high side, ending up against a post railing. His Harley was bent, but fortunately Mert was only bruised and battered. He returned to the pits and later would time in at 9th quickest on his spare. Chuck Palmgren's fast AAR Yamaha ended up with the best run of the day, a 39.20 lap, way off Lawwill's 38.43 record.

Heats

Heat 1 was an all-Yamaha show early, with Chuck Palmgren and Kenny Roberts battling. Interestingly, Palmgren's private entry appeared to have motor on the champ's factory bike, Roberts made up his time in the corners. Mert Lawwill was slowly reeling the leaders in, making the duo a trio late in the race. Timing the draft perfectly, Lawwill just took the win at the stripe, with Roberts 2nd and Palmgren 3rd. No doubt Lawwill was tough and so was his backup XR!

Starting a trend, a skirmish caused a Red flag and a restart in Heat 2. Jimmy Odom (Yam) took the early lead before rookie Hank Scott (HD) Gene Romero (Yam) and Corky Keener (HD) blasted by. Keener drafted to the front and stretched to a big lead. At the finish it was Keener, Scott, Romero, with Ron Moore (Tri) knocking Odom out of a transfer spot.

Heat 3 marked Don Castro's return from a serious knee injury suffered at a Cal Rayborn benefit race. Unfortunately, the race was plagued by crashes and restarts. On the second restart, Larry Gino catapulted nearly 100 feet from the track, over the 3rd turn wall, sustaining a compound leg fracture. Once the race got going, Gary Scott and Mike Kidd engaged in a classic mile battle, swapping positions several times a lap. Scott won by inches at the flag. Castro looked strong in his return and despite several run ins with aggressive Rob Morrison, took 3rd spot. Dave Aldana, on the factory Norton took the final transfer, sending Morrison to the semis.

Heat 4 had to be restarted because of (you guessed it!) a spill involving Dick Mann and JR Rawls. Mann suffered a tweaked ankle. It was one of those days! Upon the restart there was a three-way Yamaha struggle up front. Frank

Gillespie was the early leader on the Bike Jazz ride, with Rick Hocking on the Rocky Cycle Yamaha and Jardine Headers sponsored Terry Dorsch (Yam) giving chase. The 1972 winner Jim Rice on his self-tuned factory Harley came from midpack to score the win on the final circuit.

Semis

Early Semi 1 action saw Frank Gillespie and Jim Odom battle over the top spot. Rob Morrison, on the Ron Wood Norton altered their plan as he stormed to the win with Gillespie in 2ⁿᵈ spot. Both advanced to the National.

The second Semi was a bit of a replay of the first. John Hateley, on the Hateley Enterprises Yamaha battled with rookie Expert John Gennai on a factory-supported Harley-Davidson. The battle was disrupted by Bob Sanders (Yam). Sanders took over around lap 5. Soon after, an accident ended the race. It had run past halfway so Sanders and Hateley took the last two National spots.

Trophy Race

The Trophy Race was another "hide the number plates" affair with an all-out battle between DeWayne Keeter (HD), John Gennai, Dannie Hockie (Yam) and Jim Odom. Keeter had engine trouble up front and joined heavy hitters Mark Williams and Eddie Mulder on the sidelines. The situation was in doubt right to the end with Gennai taking the win over Hockie and Odom.

National

Gary Scott pulled the initial holeshot with Kenny Roberts and company giving chase. All was well the first lap, but a big crash ensued on Lap 2. By most accounts, a Rob Morrison maneuver had caused Jim Rice to go down, right in the path of hapless Mert Lawwill. Body and bike blew through the outside hay bales at near 100 mph. The bike went over the wall. Amazingly, Lawwill wasn't seriously hurt, but he was mercifully done for the day, as was Rice. Upon the restart, Scott and Kidd checked out with Roberts trying to keep up. Roberts soon fell into the clutches of Scott Brelsford, Corky Keener, Hank Scott and Don Castro. Scott showed some muscle, moving by the others and wrestling 3ʳᵈ from Roberts. The real fireworks were going on just behind. Rob Morrison joined a big fight over 5ᵗʰ spot with Brelsford, Castro, Keener and Chuck Palmgren. Morrison was giving his more experienced competitors fits by repeatedly steaming past on the Ron Wood Norton and throwing the bike dramatically sideways. The other riders were frequently taking evasive action. They could get back around in the corners but Morrison was much faster on the straights. Palmgren and Keener both dropped with piston failures late in the race. As the laps closed, Scott had a relatively safe lead over Kidd, with a big gap back to Hank Scott and Kenny Roberts. Roberts made a last lap bid on Scott but came up short. Morrison hung onto 5ᵗʰ spot despite a last lap run by Brelsford.

Results

Race: 25 Lap Mile National
Race Time: 16:39.42, (90.052 MPH)

Rank	Rider	Number	Make
1.	Gary Scott, Baldwin Park, Ca	64	HD
2.	Mike Kidd, Euless, Tx	72	Tri
3.	Hank Scott, Hixson, Tn	20R	HD
4.	Kenny Roberts, San Carlos, Ca	1	Yam
5.	Rob Morrison, Granada Hills, Ca	10E	Nor
6.	Scott Brelsford, Foster City, Ca	19	HD
7.	Don Castro, Gilroy, Ca	11	Yam
8.	Gene Romero, San Luis Obispo, Ca	3	Yam
9.	Frank Gillespie, Hayward, Ca	76	Yam
10.	Pat Marinacci, Seattle, Wa	67	Tri
11.	Terry Dorsch, Granada Hills, Ca	22	Yam
12.	John Hateley, Van Nuys, Ca	98	Yam
13.	Rick Hocking, Fremont, Ca	31Z	Yam
14.	Chuck Palmgren, Freehold, NJ	38	Yam
15.	Bob Sanders, Whittier, Ca	5R	Yam

Rank	Rider	Number	Make
16.	Dave Aldana, Santa Ana, Ca	13	Nor
17.	Corky Keener, Flint, Mi	62	HD
18.	Ron Moore, San Bernardino, Ca	37	Tri
19.	Jim Rice, Portola Valley, Ca	24	HD
20.	Mert Lawwill, San Francisco, Ca	7	HD

Race: 12 Lap Trophy Race
Race Time: 8:08.33, (88.465 MPH)

Rank	Rider	Number	Make
1.	John Gennai, Los Gatos, Ca	16Y	HD
2.	Dannie Hockie, Harbor City, Ca	45E	Yam
3.	Jimmy Odom, Fremont, Ca	18	Yam
4.	Tom White, Huntington Beach, Ca	80	HD
5.	Tom Horton, Lancaster, Ca	55	Yam
6.	Eddie Wirth, Dana Point, Ca	77	HD
7.	Devon Sowell, Manhattan Beach, Ca	59R	Tri
8.	Mike Bailey, Eugene, Ore	9Q	Yam
9.	Ike Reed, Salem, Ore	90	Tri
10.	DeWayne Keeter, Oak View, Ca	44	HD
11.	Mark Williams, Springfield, Ore	70	Tri
12.	Eddie Mulder, Northridge, Ca	12	Tri

Grand National Points Standings after Round 10

Rank	Rider	Pts
1.	Kenny Roberts	994
2.	Gary Scott	708
3.	Mike Kidd	598
4.	Gene Romero	502
5.	Mert Lawwill	358
6.	Gary Nixon	275
7.	Dave Hansen	270
8.	Hank Scott	216
9.	Chuck Palmgren	201
10.	Dave Aldana	194

Extra Extra

- Ron Morrison faced a bunch of angry riders after the race. For his part, the rookie was surprised at his reception, believing it had been a good race and that he had done nothing wrong. Jim Rice, Chuck Palmgren and the entire Yamaha team signed a protest over Morrison's rough riding. Morrison was not formally punished by the AMA and the matter was apparently dropped.
- A Junior Invitational was included in the program. Skip Aksland (Yam) topped Walt Foster (Tri) and Earl Meyer (Yam) in the 10 Lap Final.
- Rick Hocking rode a more traditional Yamaha twin instead of the Champion-framed Honda CB 750-based dirt tracker he tried out at the spring San Jose Mile.
- Charlie Seale was out of action due to a broken leg suffered at a regular Ascot Half-Mile event June 28th.

Top 10 San Jose Qualifying Times

1.		Chuck Palmgren	Yam	39.20 sec, 91.86 MPH
2.		Hank Scott	HD	39.38
3.		Mike Kidd	Tri	39.41
4.		Rick Hocking	Yam	39.54
5.		Kenny Roberts	Yam	39.59
6.		Gene Romero	Yam	39.59
7.		Gary Scott	HD	39.63
8.		Frank Gillespie	Yam	39.84
9.		Mert Lawwill	HD	39.85
10.		Corky Keener	HD	39.92

1974 Castle Rock TT
Gary Scott Wins 2nd in a Row at Castle Rock!

GNC Round #11 of 23 **Date:** July 13, 1974 **Type:** TT **Venue:** Mt. St. Helens Motorcycle Club Grounds	**Purse:** $15,000.00 **Location:** Castle Rock, Wa **Surface:** Dirt **Course Length:** ½ Mile **Laps:** 25

Gary Scott showed he could get his factory Harley-Davidson around a TT track as well as his former Triumph ride, scoring his second National win in a row at the Castle Rock. Redeeming his spill while leading the 1973 race here, Scott had to dice heavily in the closing laps with last year's winner Chuck Joyner, narrowly coming out on top. Joyner came up just short of a repeating his win. Pat Marinacci put in a great ride for 3rd place to round out the podium for his best-ever National finish.

Scott's win gave him momentum in the GNC points battle, helped even further when Kenny Roberts suffered a DNF while running up front in the National. At the midpoint of the season, Scott had narrowed down Roberts big points lead to a 143 point gap.

Time Trials

Mark Williams set the fast time of 23.81, almost exactly one second off his own track record. Local rider Charlie Brown gave the crowd a thrill by turning in second quick time. Northwest riders Randy Skiver and Chuck Joyner rounded out the top of the grid. The top four were all Triumph mounted.

As per the norm at Castle Rock, most of the fast guys were aboard Triumphs, so bike brands will only be mentioned if they are a non-Meriden based ride.

Heats

Houston TT winner Dave Hansen took a brief lead in Heat 1 before Mark Williams blew by. Hansen faded back and Randy Skiver and Chuck Joyner moved up. Joyner applied heavy pressure to Skiver, going past and setting out after Williams. Though Williams had a good lead, Joyner slowly reeled him in. With three laps to go, Joyner passed for the lead. Williams tried to fight back, but had to settle for the runner-up slot. Skiver maintained 3rd, fending off Eddie Wirth. Joyner set the fastest heat time of the night.

Heat 2 had to be restarted after Scott Brelsford (HD) and Steve Baker (Yam) got tangled up. Both made the restart, but in turn 1, Brelsford got tangled up again, this time in a nasty-looking wreck with John Hateley. Both riders and their machines went flying spectacularly. Brelsford suffered a hand injury with Hateley reportedly suffering some broken ribs. The race was a crowd-pleaser once it finally got underway. Local favorite Charlie Brown jumped out front and led to the checkers. John Gennai broke out of pack containing Randy Skiver, Steve Baker (Yam), Terry Dorsch and an on the charge Kenny Roberts (Yam). Roberts' charge brought him into transfer contention and he grabbed 3rd place from Skiver. At the flag it was Brown, Gennai and Roberts taking the transfers to the National.

Rex Beauchamp (HD) pulled a short-lived holeshot in Heat 3 before being swallowed up by the Triumphs of Dave Aldana, Mike Kidd and Pat Marinacci. Aldana bent his bike in practice and was on a Mike Kidd spare. Aldana was a quick study and scooted to the win in front of Kidd and Marinacci.

TT specialist Walter Mundt (Yam) was away first in Heat 4 with Paul Bostrom, Sonny Burres and Gary Scott in hot pursuit. Scott went to work, moving by Burres for 3rd in a couple laps. Bostrom took the lead from Mundt, followed by Scott. Scott took the lead in the infield, taking the win with Bostrom and Mundt following him to the National.

Semis

Dave Hansen pulled the holeshot in the first semi, but got tangled up with Eddie Wirth in Turn 1. They were joined by Randy Scott and Ike Reed. Terry Dorsch led the restart away and looked like a runaway winner till Randy Scott began to track him down. With two laps to go, Scott took the point, but both were going to the big race.

441

Sonny Burres led the second semi away, but a crash by Al Brackenbury caused a restart. It was Frank Gillespie out front this time, followed by rookie Rob Morrison and Burres. Gillespie won the race, followed by Morrison, with Gene Romero (Yam) bumping Burres out of 3rd.

Trophy Race

Sonny Burres got his Woodland Winter Track-sponsored Triumph dialed in take a comfortable win the Trophy event. Gene Romero was 2nd and Ike Reed 3rd.

National

After a requisite red flag on the first try to start the National, Gary Scott emerged with a very narrow lead over Chuck Joyner and Mark Williams. Kenny Roberts tried a banzai move around the pack in Turn 1, but there was no opening and the champ found himself at the rear of the pack. Scott eased out a little distance over Joyner as Williams faced pressure from John Gennai, Pat Marinacci and Randy Skiver. Kenny Roberts and Mike Kidd were charging through field and soon joined the lead pack. Gennai slipped down in the infield on lap 6. Roberts was working his Yamaha hard, up to around 7th place, passing competitors on any line available. He finally overcooked at mid-point of the race in the dog leg and was done for the night. Back up front, Scott was being tracked by Joyner, and Marinacci had won his battle with Skiver for a solid 3rd. As the laps closed, Joyner made his move, applying heavy pressure to the leader. He took the lead on lap 22. Scott was not ready to give up and stayed on Joyner's rear wheel. Scott got his chance with two laps to go. As the pair entered the half-mile section, Joyner got a little out of shape with Scott shooting by him on the outside, leading to the flag. Marinacci and Skiver held the next two spots. Behind, there was still some late lap dicing, with Kidd zapping several riders to take 5th . Rounding out the top ten were Williams, Paul Bostrom, Randy Scott, Frank Gillespie and Dave Aldana.

Results

Race: 25 Lap TT National
Race Time: 10:34.47

Rank	Rider	Number	Make
1.	Gary Scott, Baldwin Park,Ca	64	HD
2.	Chuck Joyner, Oregon City, Ore	60	Tri
3.	Pat Marinacci, Seattle, Wa	67	Tri
4.	Randy Skiver, Everett, Wa	35	Tri
5.	Mike Kidd, Euless, Tx	72	Tri
6.	Mark Williams, Springfield, Ore	70	Tri
7.	Paul Bostrom, San Roman, Ca	46	Tri
8.	Randy Scott, Philomath, Ore	50	Yam
9.	Frank Gillespie, Hayward, Ca	76	Tri
10.	Dave Aldana, Santa Ana, Ca	13	Tri
11.	Terry Dorsch, Granada Hills, Ca	22	Tri
12.	Walt Mundt, Parkdale, Ore	8Q	Yam
13.	John Gennai, Los Gatos, Ca	16Y	Tri
14.	Kenny Roberts, San Carlos, Ca	1	Yam

Race: 12 Lap Trophy Race
Race Time: 5:09.03

Rank	Rider	Number	Make
1.	Sonny Burres, Portland, Ore	69	Tri
2.	Gene Romero, San Luis Obispo, Ca	3	Yam
3.	Ike Reed, Salem, Ore	90	Tri
4.	Dave Hansen, Hayward, Ca	23	Yam
5.	Mike Branam, Rogue River, Ore	62Q	Yam
6.	Rick Hocking, Fremont, Ca	31Z	Yam
7.	Tom White, Huntington Beach, Ca	80	HD
8.	Richard Wascher, Seattle, Wa	85W	Tri
9.	Jim Herschbach, Salem, Ore	11Q	Tri
10.	Rex Beauchamp, Milford, Mi	31	HD
11.	Steve Baker, Bellingham, Wa	32	Yam
12.	Jim Jones, Kirkland, Wa	5W	Tri

Grand National Points Standings after Round 11

Rank	Rider	Pts
1.	Kenny Roberts	1001
2.	Gary Scott	858
3.	Mike Kidd	658
4.	Gene Romero	507
5.	Mert Lawwill	358
6.	Gary Nixon	275
7.	Dave Hansen	271
8.	Hank Scott	216
9.	Dave Aldana	209
10.	Chuck Palmgren	201

Extra Extra

- It was another SRO, race-crazed Castle Rock crowd.
- 68 Experts signed in.
- Harley-Davidson was fortunate that Gary Scott had a great run. His was the only full on factory bike in the National. John Gennai's semi-factory ride was 11th.
- It was Scott's 4th GNC win.
- Triumphs dominated the top ten, finishing 2nd through 8th.

GNC Round #12 of 23 **Date:** July 20, 1974 **Type:** TT **Venue:** Ascot Park **Location:** Gardena, Ca	**Purse:** $12,000.00 **Surface:** Dirt **Course Length**: ½ Mile, (approx.) **Laps:** 25

Making history and closing in on arch-rival Kenny Roberts in the championship, Gary Scott scored his third straight National win of 1974. He became the first rider to win three-in-a-row since Dick Mann in 1964. His chances of tying Carroll Resweber's four in a row mark from 1961 looked slim as the next National was on the pavement at Laguna Seca. Scott's win pulled him within 99 points of GNC champ Kenny Roberts' points lead. Roberts lessened the blow by finishing in 2nd after withstanding a near race-long assault from last year's winner Dave Aldana, who fell late in the race. Roberts was still in control of the GNC chase and was heavily favored at the upcoming Laguna Seca race. Yamaha teammate Gene Romero put in a late race charge to finish 3rd. Eddie Wirth posted his best finish in recent memory, taking 4th place late in the race.

Time Trials

Dave Aldana (Nor), hoping for a repeat win, blazed to the fast time of 46.00. He was way quicker than the rest of the field, with Gary Scott (HD) running a distant 46.78. Yamaha factory riders Kenny Roberts and Gene Romero were next at 47.02 and 47.11. Privateer Ron Powell (Tri) rounded out the top 5 at 47.37.

Heats

Dave Aldana ripped off the starting line in Heat 1 with only Eddie Wirth (Tri) keeping pace after turn 1. Wirth slowed because of a possible missed shift, allowing Rob Morrison and Paul Bostrom to blow by. Aldana flew out to a big lead, while Wirth remounted a charge and managed to take back the runner-up spot. Aldana led all four into the National.

Rex Beauchamp (HD) was impressive in Heat 2, grabbing the holeshot and leading the early going. The race was red flagged on lap 2 when Jimmy Odom and Rick Newby got together. Both riders walked away, but Odom's Yamaha went end-over-end, breaking off the forks. Beauchamp led the restart away and began facing heavy pressure from teammate Gary Scott. The Michigan oval specialist held tough, but Scott worked by with four laps to go. At the finish it was Scott, Beauchamp and Ascot veterans Dewayne Keeter (HD) and Dusty Coppage (Tri).

Triumph's Mike Kidd headed up the start of Heat 3 with Kenny Roberts breathing down his neck. The Champ carried on a "parry and thrust" routine against Kidd all around the course to no avail; Kidd held tough. Roberts settled into 2nd as his engine began to misfire, later attributed to a low battery charge. Mark Williams and Danny Hockie, both on Triumphs followed Kidd and Roberts to the big show.

1970 GNC champ Gene Romero narrowly led the way in the final heat with John Gennai (HD), Randy Skiver (Tri), 1966 Ascot TT winner Eddie Mulder (Tri) and Rick Hocking (Yam) close behind. Gennai really worked on the former champ, finally going by around halfway. Hocking had moved through the lead group, taking 2nd from Romero. Jim Rice (HD) joined the battle with Mulder and Skiver over the final transfer spot. Mulder took the spot with Rice overcooking it, going down unhurt. Transferring from the last heat was Gennai, Hocking, Romero and Mulder.

Semis

Chuck Joyner and Tom White (HD) took control early in Semi 1 and earned the two spots available to the National. Ron Powell and hard charging Frank Gillespie (Yam) pressed all the way, but were headed to the Trophy Race.

In Semi 2, Randy Skiver looked to have a runaway win till a sick engine put him out. Terry Dorsch (Tri) inherited the lead with Randy Scott joining him as the last riders to make the final. Mike Branan (Yam) and Don Dudek (Tri) were 3rd and 4th.

Trophy Race

Walt Mundt (Yam) looked good in the "consi", but a front wheel landing off the jump sent rider and machine into a violent tumble. Mundt reportedly suffered a ruptured spleen. Mike Branan took over after the restart and led Ron Powell and a closing Frank Gillespie to the finish.

National

Gary Scott led the 20 rider field away, but a big crash involving Rick Hocking, Randy Scott, Gene Romero, Eddie Wirth and Eddie Mulder brought the red flag out. Everyone made the restart, with Gary Scott again the quickest away. He was trailed by Mike Kidd, John Gennai, Dave Aldana and Kenny Roberts. Scott pulled away to a fairly comfortable lead, as first Aldana and then Roberts passed rookie Gennai. Roberts passed Aldana over the jump on the 9th lap, but Aldana quickly took the spot back. On lap 11, Roberts got by for good, but could not shake Aldana. Gennai fell into a very racy pack containing Rex Beauchamp, Mark Williams, Gene Romero, Eddie Wirth, Rick Hocking and others. Beauchamp had trouble with a fogged face shield and slipped back. Romero, Williams and Wirth began a march to the front. On lap 16 Kidd's engine began to slow and Roberts and Aldana went past. Kidd made a couple more laps and pulled off. Scott was out front and gone. Roberts was putting on a show tossing the big Yamaha twin all over the place. Aldana was working hard, staying right on Roberts. On lap 23, it appeared the two got together, with Aldana high siding out of the race. He was unhurt, but out. Scott sped to the finish with a big lead over Roberts. Romero's charge carried him to 3rd behind Roberts. Wirth managed to knock Williams out of 4th at the close of the race. Hocking was 6th; Beauchamp survived pretty well in 7th, Paul Bostrom was 8th, Chuck Joyner 9th and Gennai, who slipped back to 10th.

Results

Race: 25 Lap TT National
Race Time: 19:36.75

Rank	Rider	Number	Make
1.	Gary Scott, Baldwin Park, Ca	64	HD
2.	Kenny Roberts, San Carlos, Ca	1	Yam
3.	Gene Romero, San Luis Obispo, Ca	3	Yam
4.	Eddie Wirth, Dana Point, Ca	77	Tri
5.	Mark Williams, Springfield, Ore	70	Tri
6.	Rick Hocking, Fremont, Ca	31Z	Yam
7.	Rex Beauchamp, Milford, Mi	31	HD
8.	Paul Bostrom, San Roman, Ca	46	HD
9.	Chuck Joyner, Oregon City, Ore	60	Tri
10.	John Gennai, Los Gatos, Ca	16Y	HD
11.	Tom White, Huntington Beach, Ca	80	HD
12.	DeWayne Keeter, Oak View, Ca	44	HD
13.	Eddie Mulder, Northridge, Ca	12	Tri
14.	Danny Hockie, Harbor City, Ca	45E	Tri
15.	Dusty Coppage, Beaverton, Ore	32Q	Tri
16.	Dave Aldana, Santa Ana, Ca	13	Nor
17.	Mike Kidd, Euless, Tx	72	Tri
18.	Rob Morrison, Granada Hills, Ca	10E	Tri
19.	Randy Scott, Corvallis, Ore	50	Yam
20.	Terry Dorsch, Granada Hills, Ca	22	Tri

Race: Trophy Race

Rank	Rider	Number	Make
1.	Mike Branam, Rogue River, Ore	62Q	Yam
2.	Ron Powell, Quartz Hill, Ca	31E	Tri
3.	Frank Gillespie, Hayward, Ca	76	Yam
4.	John Sperry, Long Beach, Ca	28R	Tri
5.	Charlie Brown, Castle Rock, Wa	33W	Tri
6.	Bob Sanders, Whittier, Ca	5R	Yam
7.	Tom Clark, Seal Beach, Ca	66E	Tri
8.	Tom Horton, Lancaster, Ca	55	Yam
9.	Ricky Graves, White Salmon, Wa	15W	Tri

Grand National Points Standings after Round 12

Rank	Rider	Pts
1.	Kenny Roberts	1122
2.	Gary Scott	1023
3.	Mike Kidd	668
4.	Gene Romero	605
5.	Mert Lawwill	359
6.	Gary Nixon	275
7.	Dave Hansen	271
8.	Dave Aldana	217
9.	Hank Scott	216
10.	Mark Williams	205

Extra Extra

- Gary Scott joined Mert Lawwill as only the second rider to win both Ascot TT and Half-Mile Nationals.
- As compared to the Castle Rock TT, there was a lot of brand parity at Ascot. Triumph remained the dominant choice with 10 bikes. Harley-Davidson, lucky to have any bikes at Castle Rock, had 5 at Ascot. There were also 4 Yamahas and the lone Norton of Dave Aldana.
- The always hard-charging Frank Gillespie had a particularly wild night at Ascot; falling off and remounting on three different occasions! First in his heat, but managing to still grab a semi transfer. In his semi, he again came off, still getting a Trophy Race berth. In the Trophy Race, he slid off in the first corner, but charged back to 3rd! Though not making the National, he was definitely a crowd favorite!
- Mark Brelsford underwent surgery at the Ohio State University Hospital in Columbus, Oh, to have a pin placed in his broken left femur.

1974 Laguna Seca Road Race
Roberts Rocks in Monterey!

GNC Round #13 of 23	**Purse:** $25,0000.00
Date: July 28, 1974	**Surface:** Pavement
Type: Road Race	**Course Length**: 1.8 Miles
Venue: Laguna Seca Raceway	**Laps:** 40
Location: Monterey, Ca	**Distance:** 75 Miles

While Kenny Roberts was surely concerned about Gary Scott's three race win streak, he knew his turn was coming, and completely dominated the Laguna Seca National Road Race. Robert's reputation as a road racer had gone from mild praise the season before to comparisons in the press to legendary Mike Hailwood in 1974. Such lauditudes may have been a little premature as this was only Roberts's second GNC pavement win, but his raw talent was being honed and he easily defeated all players in the both Lightweight and National. It was his 7th National win. Historically significant for the sport, this was the first race in the new three race Camel Pro Series.

Riding with an injured hand and an underpowered mount, Kawasaki's Yvon DuHamel did all he could with a solid second spot. Turning in yet another pavement podium was Roberts's teammate, Gene Romero. He had constant pressure from Paul Smart through the event. Besides Roberts's domination, the ride of the weekend had to be Gary Scott on the aging Harley-Davidson V-twin. Scott rode the wheels of the aging warhorse, coming from way back in the field to snag 8th spot and valuable National points. Scott was forcing the machine to compete beyond it's intended era; a very impressive ride. Scott also finished runner-up to Roberts in the Lightweight race. Conspicuous by his absence was Gary Nixon. Right after the Loudon National, Nixon had flown to Japan to test a Suzuki 500 GP bike. A terrible crash had left Nixon with two broken arms which made his season in doubt. He was back at home, recuperating in Maryland. Also out with injury were three other former GNC champs, Mert Lawwill, Dick Mann and Mark Brelsford.

Heats

Yvon DuHamel tried to give Team Green some hope by sprinting out front early in Heat 1 in front of Kenny Roberts. DuHamel was using a specially made brake lever to ease pain in his hand caused by a practice crash. Those trying to keep pace included, Steve McLaughlin (Yam), Art Baumann (Kaw), a back to form Don Castro (Yam) and Paul Smart (Suz). Baumann fell a few laps into the event and was out for the day. DuHamel was doing all he could up front, but it was in vain as Roberts powered by on Lap 4. Smart moved up to 3rd spot and McLaughlin ended up 4th.

It was "Team Mexican" up front in Heat 2. Gene Romero (Yam) and Dave Aldana (Yam) battled fiercely for most of the race. After much paint trading, Romero pulled away for the win. In 3rd was rookie Pat Evans (Yam), contesting his first National race and looking good. John Boote from New Zealand (Yam) was 4th.

National

Kenny Roberts simply disappeared after the start of the 40-lap National. Other than a lap 5, miscue when he had an off-track excursion, Roberts was nearly perfect all day. Yvon DuHamel passed early runner-up Gene Romero and he was the last to see the vanishing Roberts. Romero was very solid in 3rd, but he had to work the rest of the day, fending off persistent Paul Smart. Smart had a lousy start, working through the pack, catching Romero around lap 10. He could just hang onto the 1970 GNC champ, but could not get past the Kel Carruthers-prepared TZ. Pat Evans was impressive in his debut, running smoothly in 5th. He was challenged heavily around the halfway mark by Team Kawasaki riders Hurley Wilvert and Gregg Hansford. They both blew by the young Evans, who was on cruise control. Not to be outdone, Evans cranked it up and left them behind. This set the top 5 for the rest of the race. Wilvert soon dropped out when his countershaft sprocket came loose. Dave Aldana moved past Hansford for 6th place. Gary Scott was riding his tail off close behind. Scott, who was as far back as 15th spot on Lap 1, was now challenging Hansford for 7th. He rolled by, but his rear Goodyear had had enough and Hansford slipped back by with just a few to go. Roberts took the win by a huge margin, with the rest of the top ten: DuHamel, Romero, Smart,

Evans, Aldana, Hansford, Scott, Warren Willing, and Phil McDonald. The next several events at played into Roberts favor and he was ready.

Results

Race: 75 Mile Road Race National
Race Time: 49:15.48, (92.68 MPH)

Rank	Rider	Number	Make
1.	Kenny Roberts, San Carlos, Ca	1	Yam
2.	Yvon DuHamel, LaSalle, Que., Can	17	Kaw
3.	Gene Romero, San Luis Obispo, Ca	3	Yam
4.	Paul Smart, Santa Ana, Ca	33	Suz
5.	Pat Evans, El Cajon, Ca	114	Yam
6.	Dave Aldana, Santa Ana, Ca	13	Yam
7.	Greg Hansford, Queensland, Australia	02	Kaw
8.	Gary Scott, Baldwin Park, Ca	64	HD
9.	Warren Willing, Dundas, N.S.W., Aus	62	Yam
10.	Phil McDonald, Tulsa, Ok	109	Yam
11.	Mike Clarke, Downey, Ca	143	Yam
12.	Cliff Carr, Arlington, Mass	26	Suz
13.	Reg Pridmore, Goleta, Ca	63	BMW
14.	Harry Cone, Sherman, Tx	82	Yam
15.	Eugene Brown, Portland, Ore	160	Yam
16.	Dennis Purdie, Wayne, Mi	166	Yam
17.	John Green, Sacramento, Ca	71	Kaw
18.	George Miller, Oakland, Ca	684	Yam
19.	Doug Libby, Milford, Mi	40	Yam
20.	Mike Devlin, La Mesa, Ca	127	Yam

Grand National Points Standings after Round 13

Rank	Rider	Pts
1.	Kenny Roberts	1287
2.	Gary Scott	1056
3.	Gene Romero	715
4.	Mike Kidd	668
5.	Mert Lawwill	358
6.	Gary Nixon	275
7.	Dave Aldana	272
8.	Dave Hansen	271
9.	Hank Scott	216
10.	Yvon DuHamel	208

1974 Sante Fe Short Track
Roberts Wins Again/Clinches Camel Crown

GNC Round #14 of 23 **Date:** August 9, 1974 **Type:** Short Track **Venue:** Sante Fe Speedway **Location:** Hinsdale, Ill	**Purse:** $14,000.00 **Surface:** Dirt **Course Length:** ¼ Mile **Laps:** 25

GNC Champ Kenny Roberts won his second National in a row at the Sante Fe speed plant. While a completely different event than Laguna Seca, the end result was the same: Roberts was in control. His win also clinched the "mini" Camel Pro Series with one event, Terre Haute, left to go. It was Roberts' 3rd win of the year as his overall win total climbed to 8. Roberts had to work hard on the small, tricky oval, duking it out with short track specialist Mike Gerald and Texan Mike Kidd. Gerald was back on a Yamaha after he and Honda had parted ways after winning Houston. The winner of the last two races at Sante Fe fought hard through night, pulling holeshots, leading, falling off, but Roberts was just too strong. John Hateley took the last podium spot from Gary Scott late in the race. Though hoping for four dirt victories in a row, Scott once again squeezed all he could from an aging Harley racer, this time a Sprint instead of an XRTT, finishing 4th.

The 1974 season continued to be darkened by a string of crashes and injuries to some of the best in the business, including two that threatened to end the seasons for Mert Lawwill and Mike Kidd.

Kenny Roberts win continued to pad his points lead over Gary Scott, (now at 301 points), nearing the numbers he had before Scott went on his three race streak. There was little other change in the top ten except for Mike Gerald and Chuck Palmgren just sliding into the last two spots.

Like last year's Sante Fe; Yamaha machinery dominated, and brands will only be noted when they are non-Yamaha.

Time Trials

Kenny Roberts set the short track specialists a worrin' as he reeled off the fastest lap of the night. Darryl Hurst was a distant 2nd and John Hateley was 3rd quickest. The track at Sante Fe this night was fast with a second groove coming in up high as the night wore on.

Heats

Setting the tone for the night, Heat 1 required three restarts to get going. One of the spills involved a back to action Mert Lawwill, who had his handlebars taken from him, crashed hard, further damaging a an already sore shoulder. On the final try, Gerald jumped out front with Roberts hot on his rear wheel. Gerald controlled till halfway when Roberts rolled by and on to the win. Steve Morehead who had went down in Lawwill's accident, grabbed 3rd. The top 3 were all on Yamahas.

Once again Gary Scott knew he was behind the "8 Ball", but made the most of it, taking the still rapid Sprint to an impressive wire-to wire in Heat 2. Rookie Randy Cleek ran a strong 2nd on the K&N ride, with 1971 Sante Fe winner Robert E. Lee 3rd.

Heat 3 had Charlie Chapple holding off a determined run from a strengthening Don Castro. Despite a strong bid for the lead, Castro had to settle for runner-up. George Wills was trying hard to make it into his first National, but Paul Pressgrove went by with 3 to go.

Breaking up the Yamaha monopoly in Heat 4 was Team Bultaco's Mike Kidd. Kidd worked ahead of Robert E. Lee's younger brother Jimmy, and Dan Gurney's rider Chuck Palmgren.

Semis

With each Semi only taking one rider each, some great racing was assured. JR Rawls (Bul) topped Corky Keener (HD) and fellow Texan Teddy Poovey in Semi 1. Billy Schaeffer (Bul) had Semi 2 under control till the halfway point, when Lil' John Hatelely sped past, taking the last National spot.

Trophy Race

Billy Schaefer dominated the Trophy Race, staying out of battle between Phil McDonald, Gene Romero, Corky Keener and others for the other podium spots. Rookie McDonald ended up in the runner-up slot, with Keener in 3rd spot.

National

Mike Gerald's boasting of his "the fastest starts in short track" was backed up again, but unfortunately the Ragin' Cajun promptly fell down in Turn 1. The restart saw a three-way stack up of Steve Morehead, Jimmy Lee and JR Rawls. Rawls was out, along with Don Castro, whose Yamaha stuck a piston. On the third start, Mike Kidd topped all with his holeshot, chased by Gerald and Roberts. Kidd found a fast line up near the cushion, with Roberts running a similar line, knocking Gerald back to 3rd. He went to school on the diminutive Texan, slipping by around Lap 6. Behind was Gary Scott, soon accompanied by John Hateley who had worked through the pack. As Kidd was challenging Roberts for the lead, his Bultaco seized. He got it going again, but had slipped way back in the field. Trying to regain positions, Kidd missed a shift, crashed into the turn 3 wall, breaking his left femur, (what else!). The lengthy delay before the final restart gave many riders a chance to make changes to their machines for the final laps. Gerald performed a gearing swap and Roberts' crew put in a new plug, hoping to cure some obvious detonation. Gerald made the most of the restart, zapping Roberts into turn 1. Roberts followed for a couple of laps before making the completing the last lead swap of the night. Gerald couldn't retaliate and motored home in 2nd. Hateley pressured Scott hard for 3rd, slipping past on the last lap. Chuck Palmgren held onto a solid 5th place ride. Rookies Randy Cleek, Steve Morehead and Jimmy Lee impressed, coming home in positions 6-8. Charlie Chapple and Robert E. Lee rounded out the top 10. Kenny Roberts. versatility and skill were growing, whether on a TZ700 at Laguna Seca or a 360 short tracker at Sante Fe, he was well on his way to becoming "King Kenny".

Results

Race: 25 Lap Short Track National

Rank	Rider	Number	Make
1.	Kenny Roberts, San Carlos, Ca	1	Yam
2.	Mike Gerald, Baton Rouge, La	15	Yam
3.	John Hateley, Van Nuys, Ca	98	Yam
4.	Gary Scott, Baldwin Park, Ca	64	HD
5.	Chuck Palmgren, Freehold, NJ	38	Yam
6.	Randy Cleek, Shawnee, Ok	11G	Yam
7.	Steve Morehead, Findlay, Oh	44F	Yam
8.	Jimmy Lee, Bedford, Tx	19N	Yam
9.	Charlie Chapple, Flint, Mi	36	Yam
10.	Robert E. Lee, Fort Worth, Tx	54	Yam
11.	Paul Pressgrove, Tecumseh, Kan	74	Bul
12.	Mike Kidd, Euless, Tx	72	Bul
13.	Don Castro, Gilroy, Ca	11	Yam
14.	Jim Rawls, Grand Prairie, Tx	93	Bul

Race: Trophy Race

Rank	Rider	Number	Make
1.	Billy Schaffer, Pinegrove, Pa	96	Bul
2.	Phil McDonald, Tulsa, Ok	9G	Yam
3.	Corky Keener, Flint, Mi	62	Yam
4.	Gene Romero, San Luis Obispo, Ca	3	Yam
5.	Tom Cummings, Flint, Mi	33X	Yam
6.	Ed Salley, Roswell, Ga	62C	Kaw
7.	George Wills, Riverdale, Ill	10P	Yam
8.	Pat McCaul, San Jose, Ca	48Y	Yam
9.	Tim Buckles, Houston, Tx	23N	Bul
10.	Keith Ulicki, Kenosha, Wi	86	Yam

Grand National Points Standings after Round 14

Rank	Rider	Pts
1.	Kenny Roberts	1437
2.	Gary Scott	1136
3.	Gene Romero	718
4.	Mike Kidd	677
5.	Mert Lawwill	358
6.	Gary Nixon	275
7.	Dave Aldana	272
8.	Dave Hansen	271
9.	Mike Gerald	270
10.	Chuck Palmgren	261

Camel Pro Series Points Standings after Round 2

Rank	Rider	Pts
1.	Kenny Roberts	315
2.	Yvon DuHamel	132
3.	Mike Gerald	120
4.	Gene Romero	113
5.	Gary Scott	113
6.	John Hateley	100
7.	Paul Smart	88
8.	Jim Evans	66
9.	Dave Aldana	55
10.	Randy Cleek	50

- A full house of 7,500 fans watched the race.
- Kenny Roberts garnered around $3500.00 for his win.
- Adding to the "walking wounded" atmosphere, Dave Aldana, troubled by muscle swelling, pushed wheelchair bound Gary Nixon around the facility.
- Mark Brelsford was finally able to leave the hospital in Columbus, Oh and headed for some rest and recreation.
- John Hateley's podium run was his best finish of the season.
- Sante Fe favorite Charlie Chapple was running in the top 5 early in the National till slowed with brake trouble. He wound up in 9th spot.
- Many strong competitors missed the main, including ace short trackers Darryl Hurst, Neil Keen, John Gennai and Rick Hocking.

GNC Round #15 of 23 **Date:** August 18, 1974 **Type:** TT **Venue:** Peoria Motorcycle Club Grounds **Location:** Peoria, Ill	**Purse:** $14,000.00 **Surface:** Dirt **Course Length:** ½ Mile **Laps:** 25

"King Kenny" Roberts could not have had a much better weekend than he did on a hot August day at Peoria. His third straight GNC win gave him a TT to add to his win column, giving him a "Grand Slam" of all five disciplines in Grand National racing; short track, half-mile, mile, TT and road race. He joined Dick Mann as the only riders yet to accomplish the feat. Mann accumulated his wins over 14 years; Roberts did it in three. Roberts also equaled Gary Scott's earlier three race streak. He thoroughly decimated the Peoria competition: he broke his own track record in qualifying, had the fastest heat and set a new 25 lap mark. He also added to his GNC point lead over Gary Scott. Scott worked hard against the Roberts momentum, moving through the pack for a strong second place in the National. Local Illinois favorite Mike Caves had a great run to third spot on a ride sponsored by former GNC champ Roger Reiman.

Time Trials

Heavy early morning showers may have given a little extra bite, as Kenny Roberts (Yam) ran a 29.00 lap, shattering his 29.22 record from last year. Mark Williams (Tri) equaled last year's top time. Chuck Palmgren (Yam) was third quickest at 29.60.

Heats

Kenny Roberts quickly took control of Heat 1, stretching to the days fastest 10 laps, ahead of Harley mounted riders Gary Scott and an impressive Mike Caves. Ironically the three finished in the same order as the National.

Heat 2 saw a battle of Northwestern TT stars. Sonny Burres controlled the race till just shy of halfway, when Mark Williams went by for the lead and held on for the win. Both were Triumph mounted. K-R Racings Pat McCaul (Yam) nailed down 3rd.

Chuck Palmgren tried his best to runaway with Heat 3, but Chuck Joyner (Tri) had other ideas, taking the victory. Rookie John Gennai took the final transfer aboard a factory supported Harley.

Rookie Expert Randy Cleek (Yam) had people trying to figure out who #11G was, as he smoked to the final heat win. He topped veteran Yamaha mounted TT riders Randy Scott and Terry Dorsch.

Semis

John Hateley topped the first semi, with Rick Hocking grabbing 2nd spot to move to the National. Both California riders were aboard Yamahas.

Ike Reed and Eddie Wirth (Tri) raced with crowd pleaser Dave Aldana at the beginning of Semi 2. Aldana pulled out to the win. Reed and Wirth battled hard for the remaining spot, with the result being a crash that took them both out. A surprised Scott Drake (Tri), who had been motoring along in 4th, found himself going to his first National.

Trophy Race

Rick Roberts (Tri) took the early lead in the Trophy event and held a small lead over the field. Veteran Buddy Powell (Yam) slowly reeled in Roberts and took the top spot around halfway. Frank Gillespie (Yam) worked his way to 3rd by the flag.

National

Chuck Palmgren blasted out front early in the National, with Kenny Roberts and crew close behind. Roberts applied heavy pressure to the leader, with Chuck Joyner, Mike Caves, Mark Williams and Gary Scott trailing. On lap

3, Roberts went by Palmgren for the lead. Joyner also went by Palmgren, with Chuck now 3rd. Gary Scott moved forward into the 4th spot. Around lap 10, Scott passed Palmgren for the number three spot. Soon after, Joyner had his drive chain come apart and he was out. Scott was now solidly in the runner-up spot. Up front, Roberts was on cruise control, stretching his lead. Action still continued in lead pack; Caves moved into the podium spot, with Palmgren finally settling into a secure 4th. Dave Aldana passed more riders than anybody else in the main. David had been last on lap 1, but worked himself clear up to the 5th spot in the late laps. Randy Cleek was close behind for his second 6th place finish in a row. Mark Williams ended up in 7th. At the finish, Roberts had a huge lead and set a new record time for the National. Following at a distance, the rest of the top ten were Gary Scott, Caves, Palmgren, Aldana, Cleek, Williams, Rick Hocking, Terry Dorsch and Randy Scott.

Results

Race: 25 Lap TT National

Rank	Rider	Number	Make
1.	Kenny Roberts, San Carlos, Ca	1	Yam
2.	Gary Scott, Baldwin Park, Ca	64	HD
3.	Mike Caves, Galesburg, Ill	2P	HD
4.	Chuck Palmgren, Freehold, NJ	38	Yam
5.	Dave Aldana, Santa Ana, Ca	13	Nor
6.	Randy Cleek, Shawnee, Ok	11G	Yam
7.	Mark Williams, Springfield, Ore	70	Tri
8.	Rick Hocking, Fremont, Ca	31Z	Yam
9.	Terry Dorsch, Granada Hills, Ca	22	Yam
10.	Randy Scott, Corvallis, Ore	50	Yam
11.	John Hateley, Van Nuys, Ca	98	Yam
12.	Pat McCaul, San Jose, Ca	48Y	Yam
13.	Scott Drake, Xenia, Oh	7F	Tri
14.	John Gennai, Los Gatos, Ca	16Y	HD
15.	Sonny Burres, Portland, Ore	69	Yam
16.	Chuck Joyner, Oregon City, Ore	60	Tri

Race: Trophy Race

Rank	Rider	Number	Make
1.	Buddy Powell, Noblesville, Ind	18H	Yam
2.	Rick Roberts, Heyworth, Ill	26P	Tri
3.	Frank Gillespie, Hayward, Ca	76	Yam
4.	Charlie Brown, Castle Rock, Wa	33W	Tri
5.	Punk Wells, Portage, Mi	8X	HD
6.	Mike Gerald, Baton Rouge, La	15	Yam
7.	John Skinner, Auburn, Al	66	Tri
8.	Doug Sehl, Waterdown, Ont., Can	45	HD
9.	Max Horton, South Bend, In	19H	Tri
10.	Pat Marinacci, Seattle, Wa	67	Tri
11.	Tom White, Huntington Beach, Ca	80	HD
12.	Jerry Powell, Noblesville, Ind	23H	Yam

Grand National Points Standings after Round 15

Rank	Rider	Pts
1.	Kenny Roberts	1589
2.	Gary Scott	1268
3.	Gene Romero	718
4.	Mike Kidd	677
5.	Mert Lawwill	358
6.	Dave Aldana	338
7.	Gary Nixon	275
8.	Dave Hansen	271
9.	Mike Gerald	271
10.	Chuck Palmgren	261

Extra Extra

- It was Kenny Roberts 5th win of the season.
- The win was the first for a Japanese motorcycle at Peoria.
- 12,000 fans witnessed Roberts's runaway win.
- All of the season's attrition took toll on the entry list; just 44 Experts signed in.
- The factory teams presence was very thin. Gary Scott was the only full-on Harley rider in the National. Last year's winner Mert Lawwill, Rex Beauchamp and Mark Brelsford were all out with injuries. While Kenny Roberts decimated the field, his teammates had trouble. Gene Romero had mechanical trouble in his heat. Don Castro was still on the mend and just couldn't take Peoria's pounding. Dave Aldana was able to overcome his muscle swelling issues for a fine ride on the factory Norton. Privateers filled out most of the National grid.
- Peoria's oppressive heat and humidity gave rise to some creative cooling solutions. Rick Hocking taped a water bottle with straw, to his leathers. Kenny Roberts crammed his leathers into the refrigerator of his RV before the National. The first cool suit?

Bonus!
Top 10 Peoria Qualifying Times

1.	Kenny Roberts	Yam	29.00 Sec, 60.80 MPH
2.	Mark Williams	Tri	29.22
3.	Chuck Palmgren	Yam	29.60
4.	Dave Aldana	Nor	29.63
5.	Mike Caves	HD	29.63
6.	Frank Gillespie	Yam	29.78
7.	Chuck Joyner	Tri	29.79
8.	Scott Drake	Tri	29.80
9.	Gary Scott	HD	29.85
10.	Jim Jones	Tri	29.88

1974 Indianapolis Mile
Romero Romps at Indy!

GNC Round #16 of 23 **Date:** August 24, 1974 **Type:** Mile **Venue:** Indianapolis State Fairgrounds **Location:** Indianapolis, In	**Purse:** $15,000.00 **Surface:** Dirt **Course Length**: 1 Mile **Laps:** 25 **Distance:** 25 miles

Gene Romero won a thrilling edition of the Indy Mile in one of the best mile contests of the era. The annual event held during the Indiana State Fair was charged with excitement and the 11,000-plus who turned out saw great races throughout the event. Romero worked up through the field on a very fast Shell Theutt factory Yamaha, joining the lead pack in the late laps. He edged out a heartbroken Doug Sehl who controlled most of the late goings on an equally rapid Poole's Cycle Harley-Davidson.. Corky Keener finished 3rd, after being in contention for the win most of the race. It was Romero's milestone 10th GNC win and his first as a Yamaha team member.

Gary Scott finished in 4th spot, gaining ground on Kenny Roberts whose Yamaha had engine trouble and finished last in the National. The gap between the two now stood at 245 points. While Roberts had lost some cushion, the upcoming Talladega Road Race clearly favored him.

Time Trials

A big surprise in qualifying was relatively unknown Jimmy Zeigler turning in fast time of 39.60. "Ziggy" was an Ohio cushion specialist whose Harley-Davidson was tuned by legendary Edgar Fuhr. Zeigler was the first rider out, indicating a slowing track for the rest of the field. Chuck Palmgren was 2nd quickest and the fastest Yamaha rider at 39.66. The rest of the top 5 was Doug Sehl (HD), and the Yamahas of John Hateley and Don Castro.

Heats

It was most of Team Yamaha out front in Heat 1, with Don Castro and Gene Romero sprinting out front. The two exchanged the lead a couple of times before Castro took the advantage, possibly helped when Romero's seat base came loose. Eddie Wirth sprinted through the pack and latched onto Romero with four laps to go. Castro scooted away to a comfortable win. Romero and Wirth diced with a last lap charge by Wirth coming up just short. Fast timer Jimmy Zeigler was 4th and headed to his first National.

Chuck Palmgren tried his best to run away with Heat 2. He was mostly successful, as his powerful AAR Yamaha jetted away from 2nd place Gary Scott. Scott managed to close up in the corners, but Palmgren pulled away from the factory Harley on the straights and took the win. Behind the two leaders, there was a nifty battle for the remaining transfer spots between Harley riders John Gennai and Mert Lawwill and Billy Eves fast Triumph. The order shifted back and forth with rookie Gennai taking 3rd, Lawwill 4th and Eves semi-bound in 5th.

Rex Beauchamp and Corky Keener were quickly out front on their Harley-Davidsons in Heat 3. They ran as a duo for much of the race, until Beauchamp pulled away to the fastest heat win of the night. Keener tried to shake off a determined Hank Scott who arrived late in the race. Scott took the runner-up spot with two to go. Dave and Doug Sehl argued over the last transfer spot with Doug muscling ahead in the late laps.

John Hateley pulled the holeshot in Heat 4 and controlled much of the race. Most of the crowd's attention though was focused on Kenny Roberts (Yam). The GNC champ had gotten mired in the back at the start and was knifing spectacularly through the pack. He caught Hateley as the laps ran out, passing for the lead on the white flag lap. Hateley got a better drive as they came out of turn 4, just nipping Roberts at the line. Both experienced trouble that would come back to haunt them in the National. Hateley had his axle adjusters back off and Roberts' engine was going flat. The final regular transfer spots went to Terry Dorsch (Yam) and Mike Caves (HD) who emerged from a battle with Triumph riders Steve Morehead and Rob Morrison.

Semis

Ohio veteran Larry Darr (HD) blasted away to a big win in Semi 1. Georgia veteran Jimmy Maness (HD) topped a battle with Yamaha riders Danny Hockie and Ricky Campbell to take the other transfer spot.

Semi 2 saw the only red flag of the night when Dave Aldana fell and was collected by Steve Morehead. Aldana suffered a fractured pelvis; a rare injury for the rider nicknamed "Rubberball" for escaping injury from many hair raising spills over the years. Morehead walked away from the high speed get off. Dave Sehl took control as the green waved again and took the win. Behind, another hard fought battle developed over the final transfer spot of the night between, (mostly) Rick Hocking (Yam), Mark Williams (Tri) and Tom White (HD). Hocking dropped out late in the race when his Yamaha burnt a piston. Williams took the spot by a narrow margin in front of the pack, putting the only Triumph in the National.

Trophy Race

The Trophy Race was another thriller, with half the starting field engaged in the lead battle. Yamaha mounted Ohio rookie Ricky Campbell won the race by inches over Georgia rookie Roger Crump aboard the Kennedy Triumph. Very close behind were Danny Hockie (Yam) and Steve Dalgarno (Tri).

National

Terry Dorsch, John Gennai, Eddie Wirth and Mark Williams, were accused of being too quick on the first attempt to start the National, and were sent to the penalty stripe. When the green flagged waved it was Gary Scott out front, shadowed by Rex Beauchamp, Corky Keener, Chuck Palmgren, Mert Lawwill, Doug Sehl and a host of others including Kenny Roberts and Gene Romero. Beauchamp drafted into the lead on lap with Scott having trouble finding grip. Beauchamp controlled the next 5-6 laps which also saw Keener bumping Scott back another spot. Kenny Roberts had worked up as high as 6th place, but suffered engine problems and dropped out of the race. Fast-timer Jimmy Zeigler had dropped out earlier with mechanical trouble. John Hateley slipped back as his rear axle worked loose again. By lap 10 Beauchamp's grip on the lead loosened as Keener and Palmgren both took turns at the front. Just behind ran Sehl, Scott and a pressing Gene Romero. With 10 laps to go, Sehl turned up the wick and drafted into the lead, bringing Romero and Scott along. Sehl stayed in front for the next 10 laps or so, with positions in lead pack constantly in flux. Beauchamp had slipped back due to a slight misfire in his Harleys engine, dropping back to 6th. Terry Dorsch ran behind, all alone in 7th, having made great progress from his 4th row, penalty stripe start. With two laps to go, Romero, with Keener glued to him, drafted past Sehl. On the last lap the trio ran down the back straight side by side. Coming out of the last turn, Romero got just a little better drive than Sehl and led him across the line by about two bike lengths. Keener was back about three lengths. Scott just managed to top Palmgren at the stripe for 4th. It had been a classic "Hold your breath" race for 25 miles for everyone present, with the front runners absolutely exhausted. It was jubilation for Romero and crushing disappointment for Sehl, who just missed his best chance for a National win.

Results

Race: 25 Lap Mile National
Race Time: 16:45.90, (89.472 MPH)

Rank	Rider	Number	Make
1.	Gene Romero, San Luis Obispo, Ca	3	Yam
2.	Doug Sehl, Waterdown, Ont., Can	45	HD
3.	Corky Keener, Flint, Mi	62	HD
4.	Gary Scott, Baldwin Park, Ca	64	HD
5.	Chuck Palmgren, Freehold, NJ	38	Yam
6.	Rex Beauchamp, Milford, Mi	31	HD
7.	Mert Lawwill, San Francisco, Ca	7	HD
8.	Terry Dorsch, Granada Hills, Ca	22	Yam
9.	Dave Sehl, Waterdown, Ont., Can	16	HD
10.	Don Castro, Gilroy, Ca	11	Yam

Rank	Rider	Number	Make
11.	John Gennai, Los Gatos, Ca	16Y	HD
12.	Larry Darr, Mansfield, Oh	20F	HD
13.	Mike Caves, Galesburg, Ill	2P	HD
14.	Jimmy Maness, Augusta, Ga	71	HD
15.	John Hateley, Van Nuys, Ca	98	Yam
16.	Mark Williams, Springfield, Ore	70	Tri
17.	Hank Scott, Hixson, Tn	20R	HD
18.	Eddie Wirth, Dana Point, Ca	77	HD
19.	Kenny Roberts, San Carlos, Ca	1	Yam
20.	Jimmy Zeigler, Bellville, Oh	89	HD

Race: Trophy Race

Rank	Rider	Number	Make
1.	Ricky Campbell, Milford, Oh	21F	Yam
2.	Roger Crump, Resaca, Ga	4C	Tri
3.	Danny Hockie, Harbor City, Ca	45E	Yam
4.	Steve Dalgarno, Baltimore, Md	99	Yam
5.	Darryl Hurst, Houston, Tx	34	Yam
6.	Dave Atherton, White Pigeon, Mi	15X	HD
7.	Moe Frazier, Hamilton, Ont., Can	10T	Tri
8.	Tom White, Huntington Beach, Ca	80	HD
9.	Steve Droste, Waterloo, Ia	92	HD
10.	Mike Johnson, Flint, Mi	85	HD
11.	Rob Morrison, Granada Hills, Ca	10E	Nor

Grand National Points Standings after Round 16

Rank	Rider	Pts
1.	Kenny Roberts	1589
2.	Gary Scott	1344
3.	Gene Romero	883
4.	Mike Kidd	677
5.	Chuck Palmgren	407
6.	Mert Lawwill	402
7.	Dave Aldana	332
8.	Corky Keener	280
9.	Gary Nixon	275
10.	Dave Hansen	271

GNC Round #17 of 23 **Date:** September 1, 1974 **Type:** Road Race **Venue:** Alabama International Motor Speedway	**Purse:** $25,500.00 **Location:** Talladega, Al **Surface:** Pavement **Course Length**: 1.8 Miles **Laps**: 41 **Distance:** 75 Miles

Kenny Roberts once again topped all pavement scratchers to take his third road race national of the year. It was Roberts' 6th win of the year and milestone 10th of his career. His Lightweight win gave him his third "Double" of the year. Roberts along with all of Team Yamaha struggled with handling problems right up to race time. Reworking all of the bikes front forks seemed to cure the ills. Testifying to this was Don Castro's factory Yamaha running a solid, if distant runner-up. Putting in a rare privateer podium was Jim Evans, on the Kevin Cameron-tuned Boston Cycle Yamaha in 3rd. British GP star Barry Sheene put in a surprise appearance and was the first non-Yamaha in 4th.

The Suzuki and Kawasaki Teams continued to struggle against the Yamaha domination, with varying results. Limits imposed by their street bike heritage plagued both teams, particularly Team Green. They were way down on speed, a deficit not easily made up on the very fast Talladega circuit. The Suzuki's were the strongest of any of the machines in practice. They were good handling, but by race time lacked the lap times of the fastest Yamahas. Gary Nixon was in attendance, but still on the mend from his Japanese crash. Paul Smart would ride Gary's Erv Kanemoto-prepared machine this day.

The Talladega race had been shortened from the previous year's 200 mile distance to just 75 miles. This meant a 41 lap scramble with no fuel stops. Many worried if their machines would make it on one tank of fuel.

Gary Scott suffered a broken collarbone when his lightweight Harley seized in practice, potentially ending his championship hopes. Roberts' win really seemed to assure repeating his championship. Scott would miss some races and Roberts had around double the quantity over third place in points, teammate Gene Romero.

Heat Races

After a brief tussle with a lead pack that included Yvon DuHamel (Kaw), Don Castro, Ron Pierce (Yam) and Gary Fisher (Yam), Kenny Roberts jetted away to an easy win in the first and fastest heat. Paul Smart went out early with a fried clutch.

Heat 2 was a little more dramatic. Steve Baker was out front early, but fell. Hurley Wilvert (Kaw) took over and was pursued by Gene Romero (Yam) and Cliff Carr (Suz). Romero was out quickly with clutch problems. Carr reeled in his former teammate, passing for the lead on lap 3. Though he went on for the win, Carr had to deal with a persistent Wilvert till the checkers on lap 5. Carr's fastest lap was nearly two seconds off of Roberts' best time.

National

A back-in-form Don Castro led the pack away from the line, but teammate Roberts was by early in the twisties. Yvon DuHamel was close behind, but stepped off hard as he entered the banking. Others also having early trouble were Paul Smart with a suspect front tire, Gary Fisher with engine woes and Mike Clarke who crashed. Gene Romero had to start at the rear of the field, but had joined the lead pack in just a couple laps. It was all Team Yellow up front by the end of lap 2: Roberts, Castro and an amazing Romero. Cliff Carr was the first non-yellow bike in 4th. As he and Romero argued over 3rd, Romero tossed it away, losing a decent chunk of leathers and skin, but no serious injuries. Hurley Wilvert was now 4th, followed by Steve McLaughlin (Yam). A charging Jim Evans soon made his presence known, dispatching Wilvert and pressuring Carr for third. Up front, Roberts was pulling a huge lead, gaining over a second of a lap over Castro. Castro had a similar lead over his pursuers. Speaking of which, Evans moved to 3rd with 5 laps to go. As the laps waned, Barry Sheene made his appearance in the top 5. Sheene had gotten a poor start and had been steadily marching his way forward. He pressured Carr as the laps ticked off. With two laps remaining, Carr's Suzuki began missing as fuel ran low. Sheene quickly shot ahead of his teammate. This set the top finishing order: At the flag, it was Roberts, Castro, Evans, Sheene, (who too ran short of fuel, coasting in), and Carr.

Results

Race: 75 Mile Road Race National
Race Time: 40:43.80, (111.957 MPH)

Rank	Rider	Number	Make
1.	Kenny Roberts, San Carlos, Ca	1	Yam
2.	Don Castro, Gilroy, Ca	11	Yam
3.	Jim Evans, San Bernardino, Ca	27	Yam
4.	Barry Sheene, Surrey, Eng	7	Suz
5.	Cliff Carr, Arlington, Mass	26	Suz
6.	Hurley Wilvert, Westminster, Ca	39	Kaw
7.	Steve McLaughlin, Duarte, Ca	83	Yam
8.	Ted Henter, St. Petersburg, Fl	12	Yam
9.	Jean Lysight, Tracy, Que., Can	59	Yam
10.	Billy Labrie, St. Petersburg, Fl	139	Yam
11.	Len Fitch, Woodslee, Ont., Can	62	Yam
12.	Dennis Purdie, Wayne, Mi	66	Yam
13.	Mike Ninci, Kansas City, Mo	95	Yam
14.	Bart Myers, New Brunswick, NJ	53	Yam
15.	Gary Fisher, Parkesburg, Pa	21	Yam
16.	Robert Wakefield, Indianapolis, Ind	78	Yam
17.	Dave Smith, Lakewood, Ca	20	Yam
18.	Art Baumann, Brisbane, Ca	30	Kaw
19.	Peter Chancey, Pte. Claire, Que., Can	55	Yam
20.	Doug Libby, Milford, Mi	40	Yam

Grand National Points Standings after Round 17

Rank	Rider	Pts
1.	Kenny Roberts	1754
2.	Gary Scott	1344
3.	Gene Romero	883
4.	Mike Kidd	677
5.	Chuck Palmgren	407
6.	Mert Lawwill	402
7.	Dave Aldana	350
8.	Don Castro	332
9.	Corky Keener	280
10.	Gary Nixon	275

Extra Extra

- Kenny Roberts' win was worth $3685.00 from the purse.
- In what may have been a first, there were only Japanese two-strokes on the grid for a GNC road race. There were no other brands, (read 4-strokes), present. Gary Scott and Harley pulled up stakes and left after his crash. The very fast Talladega course made it an exercise in futility to show up without competitive horsepower. Relying on good handling would not cut it.
- Reflecting this, only 32 riders made up the field.
- Not surprisingly, this was the last National to be held at Talladega. Oppressive weather, low rider counts and most importantly, fan disinterest, let the event die.

1974 Syracuse Mile
Hank Scott Wins First at Syracuse National!

GNC Round #18 of 23 **Date:** September 8, 1974 **Type:** Mile **Venue:** New York State Fairgrounds **Location:** Syracuse, NY	**Purse:** $15,000.00 **Surface:** Dirt **Course Length**: 1 Mile **Laps:** 25 **Distance:** 25 Miles

Rookie Hank Scott swept to his first National victory at the first championship race held at the Syracuse Mile since 1953. A great crowd of around 10,000 fans turned out for the return to the "Mile". Hank upheld the family honor as brother Gary was forced to sit out the event due to a broken collarbone from the Talladega National. Hank was himself had just recovered from back injuries suffered at Kenton, Ohio in July. Although now wearing Nasco Oil leathers instead of Team Harley duds, Scott was still receiving some factory help on the XR750 out of Drew Pate's shop. Finishing a distant second to Scott was Rex Beauchamp on the works Harley. Canadian Doug Sehl made it two mile podiums in a row aboard the Pooles Cycle Harley. A down-on-power Kenny Roberts finished in fourth. Hank Scott didn't hurt his chances by winning a Regional event at Syracuse the week before the National.

With Roberts earning solid points in fourth, his points lead over injured Gary Scott ballooned to 498 points. If Roberts had a decent showing at the upcoming Terre Haute National, he would clinch the GNC title again. Gene Romero was beginning to threaten Scott's second place standing. There was no change in Mike Kidd, Chuck Palmgren and Mert Lawwill's positions. Hank Scott's win shot up to seventh via his win. Don Castro hung onto eighth place. Dave Aldana was 9th and Rex Beauchamps's runner-up finish moved him to tenth in points.

Time Trials

The fastest bikes this day were all Harley-Davidsons. Rex Beauchamp's factory Babe DeMay-tuned ride was by far the fastest, running a 38.36 at 93.85 mph. Indy fast qualifier Jimmy Zeigler was a ways back at 39.05. Doug Sehl ran a 39.18, Dave Sehl a 39.21 and Hank Scott a 39.32.

Heats

Fast qualifier Rex Beauchamp ran down Hank Scott on the last lap to take the win in Heat 1. A classic "hide the number plates" battle developed further behind between Denny Palmgren's always fast XR750, Triumph mounted Billy Eves and the Harley-Davidsons of Corky Keener and John Gennai. All took a turn in third position, with Palmgren taking the spot. Keener took the last transfer.

Talladega road rash victim Gene Romero (Yam) had lost no speed, battling early in Heat 2 with Ohio's Jimmy Zeigler (HD) and Mark Williams (Tri). All had a go up front, but Romero powered the Yamaha Company ride away for the win. Zeigler outdueled Williams for the runner-up spot. Dave Atherton's Harley developed an oil leak, but he managed to hold unto 4th spot.

Heat 3 saw Mert Lawwill's awful 1974 luck continue as he was caught up in a spill with Mike Johnson and Dennis Varnes. Lawwill tweaked his ankle, with Varnes receiving suspected rib and back injuries; Johnson was not injured. Once underway, a great mile battle ensued between Kenny Roberts (Yam) and Doug Sehl. The lead was swapped all over the place, with Roberts nearly always leading at the stripe, except for the last circuit, when Sehl out-powered the champ. Roberts' teammate Castro followed along with Ron Moore (Tri).

Dave Sehl quickly saw an early lead in the last heat disappear as a trio of fast Yamahas, ridden by Chuck Palmgren, Terry Dorsch and Billy Schaffer, steamed past. Palmgren had a little edge and slowly inched ahead of Dorsch and Schaeffer, who battled through the event. The matter wasn't decided till the last lap when Schaeffer found some extra speed, passing Dorsch and nearly catching Palmgren at the stripe. Sehl maintained 4th for the final transfer.

Semis

Rookie John Gennai outran former car jumper Steve Droste and a fast-closing Keith Ulicki in Semi 1. All were Harley mounted. The second semi was a barn burner between Ohio riders Rod Bailey and Steve Morehead versus Californian Frank Gillespie. They put on a great show for the crowd, with the issue settled in a near photo finish with Bailey taking the nod over Gillespie and Morehead. Brand wise it was Harley, Yamaha and Triumph.

National

With threatening weather moving in during the semis, it was decided to run the National before the Trophy Race. Kenny Roberts was the first away at the start of the National with Hank Scott right behind. On the backstretch, Rex Beauchamp drafted by for the lead with Doug Sehl moving by Scott and Roberts before the first lap was complete. Scott followed for a couple of laps, slipping by Roberts and latching unto Sehl's rear wheel. Just behind, in 5th spot, Denny Palmgren faced his first batch of challengers which included Corky Keener and Gene Romero. Up front, Beauchamp still led, with Scott drafting by Sehl into second. Scott soon began harassing Beauchamp and on the 11th go around, took the top spot. The top three had pulled away from the pack, with Roberts a solid 4th. Denny Palmgren survived early advances by Keener and Romero when both eventually dropped out with mechanical ills, a common trend at Syracuse this day. They were soon replaced by a cast including brother Chuck, Don Castro and Ron Moore. The 5th spot was heavily contested, with Chuck Palmgren taking the spot, but Roberts was too far away to catch. Denny Palmgren slipped back in the order eventually nailing down 7th, behind Castro. As the laps wound down, Sehl closed up on Beauchamp and the two traded 2nd spot several times, with Beauchamp taking over for good with 4 laps left. Scott built healthy lead by the finish over Beauchamp, Sehl, and a distant Roberts. The rest of the field strung out over the big oval. Many riders dropped out with various mechanical trouble, leaving only 12 bikes running at the finish.

Trophy Race

John Hateley (Tri) led most of the Trophy Race with Steve Morehead giving chase. Morehead took the lead for two circuits late in race, with Hateley retaking the position and the win. Keith Ulicki kept them honest in 3rd spot.

Results

Race: 25 Lap Mile National
Race Time: 16:12.32, (92.56 MPH)

Rank	Rider	Number	Make
1.	Hank Scott, Hixson, Tn	20R	HD
2.	Rex Beauchamp, Milford, Mi	31	HD
3.	Doug Sehl, Waterdown, Ont., Can	45	HD
4.	Kenny Roberts, San Carlos, Ca	1	Yam
5.	Chuck Palmgren, Freehold, NJ	38	Yam
6.	Don Castro, Gilroy, Ca	11	Yam
7.	Denny Palmgren, Lutherville, Md	4S	HD
8.	Ron Moore, San Bernardino, Ca	37	Tri
9.	John Gennai, Los Gatos, Ca	16Y	HD
10.	Frank Gillespie, Hayward, Ca	76	Yam
11.	Dave Atherton, White Pigeon, Mi	15X	HD
12.	Jimmy Zeigler, Bellville, Oh	89	HD
13.	Mark Williams, Springfield, Ore	70	Tri
14.	Rodney Bailey, Warren, Oh	52F	HD
15.	Gene Romero, San Luis Obispo, Ca	3	Yam
16.	Billy Schaffer, Pinegrove, Pa	96	Yam
17.	Dave Sehl, Waterdown, Ont., Can	16	HD
18.	Corky Keener, Flint, Mi	62	HD
19.	Steve Droste, Waterloo, Ia	92	HD
20.	Terry Dorsch, Granada Hills, Ca	22	Yam

Race: Trophy Race

Rank	Rider	Number	Make
1.	John Hateley, Van Nuys, Ca	98	Yam
2.	Steve Morehead, Findlay, Oh	44F	Tri
3.	Keith Ulicki, Kenosha, Wi	86	HD
4.	Charlie Chapple, Flint, Mi	36	HD
5.	Tom Cummings, Flint, Mi	33X	HD
6.	Roger Crump, Resaca, Ga	4C	Tri
7.	George Richtmeyer, Schenectady, NY	10B	BSA
8.	George Longabaugh, Leola, Pa	9A	HD
9.	Ricky Campbell, Milford, Oh	21F	Yam
10.	Lou Moniz Jr., Lincoln, RI	21U	BSA
11.	John Leale, Hackettstown, NJ	14U	HD
12.	Steve Dalgarno, Baltimore, Md	99	Yam

Grand National Points Standings after Round 18

Rank	Rider	Pts
1.	Kenny Roberts	1842
2.	Gary Scott	1344
3.	Gene Romero	890
4.	Mike Kidd	677
5.	Chuck Palmgren	473
6.	Mert Lawwill	402
7.	Hank Scott	385
8.	Don Castro	360
9.	Dave Aldana	332
10.	Rex Beauchamp	330

Extra Extra

The New York State Fairgrounds, also known as the Empire Expo Center, is home to the Syracuse Mile race track. Syracuse was the location of the state's first fair in 1841. From 1842-1889 the fair rotated its home to 11 different cities. In 1889, the Syracuse Land Company donated land that would make Syracuse the permanent home of the fair. The fair grew over the years, becoming a area huge happening. The event takes place over 12 days and attendance topped 1 million for the first time in 2001. Racing began at the fairgrounds on a half-mile track in 1890. The mile began hosting events in 1903. Horses, cars and motorcycles have all competed at Syracuse. The AAA/USAC raced Indy cars there till 1962. Other USAC divisions have frequented the track. NASCAR made some appearances in the 1950's. Motorcycles raced in Class "A" and "C" championships before WWII. AMA National racing returned in 1952 and 1953, with Bobby Hill winning both events. Promoter Don Brymer brought the circuit back in 1974. The return of motorcycles at Syracuse was successful and the race became a regular stop on the tour. The main form of motorsports at the track today is the areas Modified stock cars. DIRT Motorsports hosts the popular Super Dirt Week races there every year.

1974 Toledo Half-Mile
Beauchamp Rebounds to Take Toledo
Harley Sweeps First Five

GNC Round #19 of 23	**Purse:** $13,000.00
Date: September 21, 1974	**Surface:** Limestone
Type: Half-Mile	**Course Length:** ½ Mile
Venue: Toledo Raceway Park	**Laps:** 20
Location: Toledo, Oh	**Distance:** 10 Miles

Rex Beauchamp won his 2nd GNC race at the first ever Toledo Half-Mile. The big 5/8 mile cushion track developed a narrow groove by National time, forcing mostly follow the leader action. Beauchamp jumped out front early on the Babe DeMay tuned factory Harley-Davidson and was gone. Second in the National was Louisville winner Corky Keener. Finishing 3rd and just keeping his GNC crown hopes afloat was Gary Scott. Title rival Kenny Roberts salvaged a 7th on a decidedly Harley-Davidson track. Steve Droste scored his best National finish yet in 4th place. The night was a testament to the toughness and dedication of the National competitors. The year had seen a dizzying amount of injuries plague the circuit. On this night Beauchamp led a comeback of several riders hurt during the season. Beauchamp had ruptured his spleen just a month earlier. Gary Scott was riding with a brace on a healing collarbone from his Talladega accident. It was also the return of Dave Aldana, Scott Brelsford and Charlie Seale. In this league it was one thing to be a fast rider; it was much harder thing to come back after an injury.

Despite Gary Scott's valiant effort, Kenny Roberts was very close to clinching his second crown. He had a 438 point advantage and Scott was rapidly running out of season. Roberts just had to pretty much show up at the upcoming Terre Haute National to seal the title.

Time Trials

Gary Scott, injured collarbone and all, set the fastest time on the Bill Werner-prepared factory Harley at 29.748. Very close behind was the Bart Markel Harley with Corky Keener aboard, running a 29.750. Michigan cushion specialist Tom Cummings (HD) raised a few eyeballs with his third quick time of 29.893. Fourth was Hank Scott (HD) and rounding the top 5 was Steve Morehead on the Bill Kennedy Triumph.

Heats

It was all Gary Scott in Heat 1. He took control off the line and led to the checkers by a comfortable margin. Steve Morehead was a solid 2nd. Harley riders John Gennai and Teddy Newton argued over 3rd, till Newton's bike gave up with three laps to go. Chuck Palmgren was 4th and headed to the semis, along with Charlie Seale and Frank Gillespie.

Corky Keener was first off the stripe in Heat 2, with Jimmy Zeigler (HD), Rick Hocking (Yam) and Rex Beauchamp in hot pursuit. Beauchamp mounted a charge, disposing of Hocking and Zeigler by lap 4. He was soon on Keener's rear wheel, passing with two to go and leading to the checkers. He set the fast heat time along the way. Hocking managed to get by Zeigler for the final transfer spot.

Heat 3 was red flagged on lap 1 when Scott Drake fell hard coming out of Turn 2. Doug Sehl (HD) had no place to go, collecting the fallen machine, also taking a serious tumble. Drake was done for the night, but Sehl made the restart despite a tweaked ankle. Upon the restart, Terry Dorsch (Yam) blasted off the line first, but soon gave way to Doug Sehl and Steve Droste (HD). GNC champ Kenny Roberts worked up to 4th, struggling with the track and brake trouble.

Ohio native Jimmy Osborne fell in the opening lap of Heat 4, causing yet another restart. Dave Sehl ran away for the win, giving Harley-Davidson a clean sweep of the heats. Harley riders Denny Palmgren and Eddie Wirth took the last heat transfers to the National with Hank Scott (HD) going to the semis.

Semis

Frank Gillespie tried hard to take the only National spot available in Semi 1, but fellow Yamaha pilot took the lead on lap 3 and powered to the win. Nothing illustrated that this track was Harley territory better than the fact that the entire Yamaha team was in Semi 2! Kenny Roberts, Gene Romero and Don Castro had to battle with each other and rest of the field for the last remaining National ticket. Roberts blasted out front, pursued by his teammates and Hank Scott. Castro had mechanical trouble and fell back in the order. Scott made a race of it, but after slipping off the groove, Roberts was home free. Romero was 3rd.

Trophy Race

Frank Gillespie worked hard his Yamaha hard to score the "consi" win. Hank Scott hounded Gillespie through much of the race, particularly so in the closing laps. Scott challenged hard in the corners, but Gillespie managed to edge away on the straights. On the last lap, a final charge by Scott came up a half a length short at the stripe.

National

Steve Droste on a Tex Peel tuned Harley, pulled a brief holeshot in front the thundering 14 rider National field, but it was Rex Beauchamp who took command as the pack hit the back straight. Corky Keener was all over Droste and went by after two laps. Gary Scott was mounting a charge after getting tangled up at the start of the race. Scott also tracked Droste down and took 3rd place on lap 8. As the laps ticked off, Beauchamp pulled to comfortable lead with Keener just able to keep a close eye on his Michigan teammate. Scott was a safe second, not close enough to pressure Keener, but a good distance ahead of Droste and company. Droste managed to keep 4th, but only after fighting off Dave Sehl. Chuck Palmgren brought his Yamaha home 6th to be the first non-Milwaukee finish. Kenny Roberts managed to work up to 7th, Denny Palmgren was 8th with Rick Hocking and Terry Dorsch rounding out the top 10.

Results

Race: 20 Lap Half Mile National
Race Time: 9:43.048, (61.74 MPH)

Rank	Rider	Number	Make
1.	Rex Beauchamp, Milford, Mi	31	HD
2.	Corky Keener, Flint, Mi	62	HD
3.	Gary Scott, Baldwin Park, Ca	64	HD
4.	Steve Droste, Waterloo, Ia	92	HD
5.	Dave Sehl, Waterdown, Ont., Can	16	HD
6.	Chuck Palmgren, Freehold, NJ	38	Yam
7.	Kenny Roberts, San Carlos, Ca	1	Yam
8.	Denny Palmgren, Lutherville, Md	4S	HD
9.	Rick Hocking, Fremont, Ca	31Z	Yam
10.	Terry Dorsch, Granada Hills, Ca	22	Yam
11.	Steve Morehead, Findlay, Oh	44F	Tri
12.	Doug Sehl, Waterdown, Ont., Can	45	HD
13.	Eddie Wirth, Dana Point, Ca	77	HD
14.	John Gennai, Los Gatos, Ca	16Y	HD

Race: Trophy Race

Rank	Rider	Number	Make
1.	Frank Gillespie, Hayward, Ca	76	Yam
2.	Hank Scott, Hixson, Tn	20R	HD
3.	Tom Cummings, Flint, Mi	33X	HD
4.	Gene Romero, San Luis Obispo, Ca	3	Yam
5.	Mark Williams, Springfield, Ore	70	Tri
6.	Ricky Campbell, Milford, Oh	21F	Yam
7.	Charlie Chapple, Flint, Mi	36	Yam
8.	Billy Schaffer, Pinegrove, Pa	96	Yam
9.	John Hateley, Van Nuys, Ca	98	Yam
10.	Ron Moore, San Bernardino, Ca	37	Tri
11.	Larry Darr, Mansfield, Oh	94	HD
12.	Randy Scott, Corvallis, Ore	50	Tri

Grand National Points Standings after Round 19

Rank	Rider	Pts
1.	Kenny Roberts	1882
2.	Gary Scott	1444
3.	Gene Romero	890
4.	Mike Kidd	677
5.	Chuck Palmgren	523
6.	Rex Beauchamp	480
7.	Mert Lawwill	402
8.	Hank Scott	391
9.	Don Castro	360
10.	Dave Aldana	332

Extra Extra

- Toledo Raceway Park was built as an auto racing track in 1949 by the Jechura family. It was converted to a horse racing facility in 1959. In 1962 the ½ mile was converted to a 5/8 mile length. The track was a successful part of the Toledo-area culture for decades. The AMA Grand National circuit visited the facility from 1974-'76. A fire destroyed the grandstands in 1976. The AMA moved the race dates scheduled there in 1977, to Louisville Downs. Though the races were successful, they never returned to Toledo. The grandstands were rebuilt and horse racing continued. The Jechura family sold the facility to Penn National Gambling in 1988. In a strange situation, Penn National Gambling opened a casino in Toledo in 2012, threatening its own business at Raceway Park. As of this writing, Penn National is seeking state government permission to move the racetrack operation, en masse', to Dayton, Oh!

1974 Terre Haute Half-Mile
Keener Takes Win/Roberts Wins Two Titles!!!

GNC Round #20 of 23	**Purse:** $12,000.00
Date: September 22, 1974	**Location:** Terre Haute, In
Type: Half-Mile	**Surface:** Dirt
Venue: Terre Haute Speedway	**Course Length**: ½ Mile
	Laps: 20
Location: Terre Haute, In	**Distance:** 10 Miles

Corky Keener won his second race of the year at Terre Haute, which was the rescheduled final round of the three race Camel Pro Series. Keener led home the troops, most still weary from the previous nights Toledo National. A slim 40 rider field signed in. Keener blitzed out front early, stretching to a huge lead at the end of the race. Keener's bike was very strong, despite tuner Bart Markel having to replace a burnt valve after practice. Kenny Roberts notched a strong second place, locking up the Grand National Championship for the second time in a row. He also sewed up the inaugural Camel Pro title and the bulk of it's $15,000 top prize. Dave Aldana put on the ride of the day, coming from back in the pack on injured Mike Kidd's Triumph. The 1970 winner of this event was spectacular, despite nursing a cracked pelvis from the Indy Mile. Keener and Aldana also fared well in the Camel Pro monies, with Aldana's charge netting him second, bumping Keener back to third.

The day at Terre Haute was unseasonably cool and windy. This didn't help the tired riders and crews, but did lead to a fast surface with many racing lines. GNC title contender Gary Scott had to give up his bid for the title. He really needed for Roberts to have an off day. It didn't happen and Scott's 10th place finish just wasn't enough.

Time Trials

John Hateley found the setup on his Yamaha, stopping the clocks at 24.903, shattering Dave Aldana's track record time of 25.63. Hateley was the only rider below the 25 second mark. Toledo winner Rex Beauchamp (HD) was next with a 25.020. In all, 7 riders all broke Aldana's 1972 record.

Heats

Steve Droste (HD) solidly controlled Heat 1 despite race-long pressure from fast timer John Hateley. Giving a preview of the coming National, Dave Aldana moved through the pack to nail down the last transfer.

Team Harley riders Gary Scott and Rex Beauchamp controlled the start of Heat 2, only to have Yamaha's main man Kenny Roberts rocket past. Roberts charged to the quickest heat time, giving him the pole for the National. Beauchamp got by a beat-up and tiring Scott for the runner-up slot.

It was Corky Keener all the way in the third heat. TT ace Mark Williams (Tri) gave chase, followed by Yamaha's Gene Romero. Chuck Palmgren mounted a charge from the back, knocking both Williams and Romero back a spot. Williams suffered a DNF with three to go.

It took a couple of tries to get the last heat going, with 1971 winner Dave Sehl (HD) in early control. Close behind were rookies Steve Morehead (Tri) and John Gennai (HD). Blasting from the rear of the pack was Billy Schaeffer (Yam); He had found a line that really worked and just past midway he moved by Gennai. He quickly did the same to 2nd place Morehead. He then ran down a surprised Sehl in the closing laps.

Semis

Don Castro (Yam) appeared National bound, in Semi 1, but a persistent Hank Scott (HD) moved by mid-race to take the last National ticket. John Gennai topped fellow Californian Rick Hocking in the second, hard-fought semi. Hocking was nursing a dislocated thumb suffered at Toledo.

Trophy Race

Stylish rookie Rick Hocking, hurt thumb and all, sped to the Trophy Race win with Harley pilots Tom Cummings and Mike Caves giving chase.

National

With track conditions helping to give parity to all brands present, most riders had an equal chance. Corky Keener was first away from the line, with Chuck Palmgren latching on, with Dave Sehl, Steve Droste, and Kenny Roberts a little further back. Roberts began charging, dropping Droste and Sehl back. He soon caught up to Palmgren and after a several lap duel, Roberts was in 2nd spot. During this time Keener had flat checked out, already with a big lead. Rex Beauchamp was also on the move, locking horns with Palmgren for third. After several laps, Beauchamp pulled a little breathing room, leaving Palmgren to face a flying Dave Aldana. Aldana had a slow start but was tearing through the pack, 'ala Bart Markel by mid-race. With 3 laps to go, Aldana buzzed by Palmgren's Yamaha. With time running out, Aldana caught Beauchamp on the last lap, got a great drive out of turn 4, beating Beauchamp by a bike length at the flag. Turned out to be a great move for David, as the pass moved him from 3rd in the Camel Pro standings to 2nd, adding $1000.00 to his awards. The top spots at the finish were; Keener, Roberts, Aldana, Beauchamp, Palmgren and Droste.

Results

Race: 20Lap Half-Mile National
Race Time: 8:56.922, (67.05 MPH) New Record,
Old Record set in 1973 by Rex Beauchamp

Rank	Rider	Number	Make
1.	Corky Keener, Flint, Mi	62	HD
2.	Kenny Roberts, San Carlos, Ca	1	Yam
3.	Dave Aldana, Santa Ana, Ca	13	Tri
4.	Rex Beauchamp, Milford, Mi	31	HD
5.	Chuck Palmgren, Freehold, NJ	38	Yam
6.	Steve Droste, Waterloo, Ia	92	HD
7.	Gene Romero, San Luis Obispo, Ca	3	Yam
8.	Hank Scott, Hixson, Tn	20R	HD
9.	Dave Sehl, Waterdown, Ont., Can	16	HD
10.	Gary Scott, Baldwin Park, Ca	64	HD
11.	Steve Morehead, Findlay, Oh	44F	Tri
12.	John Gennai, Los Gatos, Ca	16Y	HD
13.	Billy Schaffer, Pinegrove, Pa	96	Yam
14.	John Hateley, Van Nuys, Ca	98	Yam

Race: 12 Lap Trophy Race
Race Time: 5:29.303

Rank	Rider	Number	Make
1.	Rick Hocking, Fremont, Ca	31Z	Yam
2.	Tom Cummings, Flint, Mi	33X	HD
3.	Mike Caves, Galesburg, Ill	2P	HD
4.	Randy Scott, Corvallis, Ore	50	Tri
5.	Don Castro, Gilroy, Ca	11	Yam
6.	Doug Sehl, Waterdown, Ont., Can	45	HD

Grand National Points Standings after Round 20

Rank	Rider	Pts
1.	Kenny Roberts	2002
2.	Gary Scott	1459
3.	Gene Romero	933
4.	Mike Kidd	677
5.	Chuck Palmgren	583
6.	Rex Beauchamp	560
7.	Corky Keener	553
8.	Dave Aldana	432
9.	Hank Scott	420
10.	Mert Lawwill	402

Final Camel Pro Series Points and Payout

Rank	Rider	Pts	Payout
1.	Kenny Roberts	435	$5,000.00
2.	Dave Aldana	155	3,000.00
3.	Corky Keener	154	2,000.00
4.	Gene Romero	153	1,000.00
5.	Yvon DuHamel	132	900.00
6.	Gary Scott	128	800.00
7.	Mike Gerald	120	625.00
8.	Chuck Palmgren	120	625.00
9.	John Hateley	107	550.00
10.	Paul Smart	88	500.00

GNC Round #21 of 23 **Date:** September 29, 1974 **Type:** Mile **Venue:** Golden Gate Field **Location:** Albany, Ca	**Purse:** 15,000.00 **Surface:** Dirt **Course Length:** 1 Mile **Laps:** 25 **Distance:** 25 miles

Rookie Rick Hocking scored his first Grand National win at the rough and tumble Golden Gate Mile. The cushion surface on the big track quickly came apart, turning bumpy and rough despite constant attention. Hocking was a tough, strong, natural born throttle twister and wore out the closest completion. Rex Beauchamp made a late race effort from back in the pack, but there was no catching Hocking. GNC champ Kenny Roberts finished out the podium in 3rd. Due to the deteriorating track conditions, the National was shortened from 25 to 16 laps. The repeated track maintenance included a lot of watering, which combined with the thick cushion, produced a concrete-like rooster tail that was like getting hit by a fire hose. It made riders slow immediately when hit with the spray, blinding many. Gary Scott ran into an outside pole, suffering a painful blow to his foot.

Noise concerns raised by local residents forced promoter Mike Goodwin to require all the competitors to run mufflers. Most used a product from Discojet who were was on hand to install their product. Team Harley came up with their own "boom box". The mufflers didn't seem to hurt horsepower production, in fact several thought it helped low end power. The mufflers had to be intact at the end of any race or the rider would be disqualified.

Scott Brelsford had left his factory Harley-Davidson ride for the opportunity to ride Erv Kanemoto's radical Kawasaki 750 H2R dirt tracker. Brelsford was convinced the bike could be a winner and was eyeballing the huge Kawasaki contingency monies.

Time Trials

Despite running the requisite mufflers, several riders broke Jim Rice's record of 40.56, set at a non-National the previous year. They were led by Rex Beauchamp (HD) with a 40.07 time. Kenny Roberts (Yam) was second fastest at 41.26. Tying for third fastest were Harley mounted Hank Scott and Corky Keener at 41.14. Local hero Mert Lawwill was next at 41.59. Dave Aldana, on Mike Kidd's Triumph, ran a 41.63. Scott Brelsford turned a 41.66 on the screaming Erv Kanemoto Kawasaki. Finishing out the top ten were Gary Scott (HD), a 41.68. Don Castro (Yam) a 42.02 and John Hateley at 42.07.

Heats

Rob Morrison was a little too quick at the start of Heat 1 and was sent to the penalty line. Rex Beauchamp was up and gone when the race started. Mert Lawwill was runner-up early, chased by the Yamahas of Frank Gillespie and Dewayne Keeter. They soon caught Lawwill whose was troubled by a still-tender ankle. Doug Sehl (HD) was on a charge, as was Rob Morrison from the penalty line. Sehl railed past everybody but Beauchamp, who had disappeared to set yet another National fast heat time. Gillespie was 3rd and Lawwill managed to hang onto the final transfer spot in 4th.

It was a Yamaha shootout in Heat 2. Chuck Palmgren and Kenny Roberts were quickly out front. Palmgren ran down at the rail, with Roberts hitting the high line. The two diced hard, with Dave Aldana (Tri) in the mix early on. Roberts took control early, with Palmgren blasting by to lead through mid-race. Roberts gassed it back up, retaking the lead with four laps to go. Palmgren briefly surged back into the lead, but slowed with a fractured exhaust. Roberts went on for the win with Palmgren hanging onto 2nd. Aldana was caught first by local rider Terry Sage, then Randy Scott and Gene Romero. Sage dropped back with an issue and Scott managed to nail down 3rd. Romero took the last transfer with Aldana ending up 5th. Dick Mann returned to action in this heat for the first time since early in the season, but had to retire with engine trouble.

Heat 3 saw one of the best battles of the day between John Hateley (Yam) and Hank Scott (HD). The two exchanged spots all race long with Hateley taking a narrow win. Eddie Wirth controlled 3rd most of the race till his

Harley's engine went off-song late in the race, helping Jim Rice to take over on the final lap. Scott Brelsford struggled with the Kawasaki triple, but a late race rip through the field garnered him a 5th and a semi berth.

Harley-Davidson's win leaders Gary Scott and Keener had a ding-dong battle in the final heat. Keener held the advantage in the opening laps, with Scott buzzing by on lap 3. Keener was able to retaliate soon after. They continued to stage a close dice when Keener slowed dramatically, running on one cylinder. Scott surged ahead with Keener being passed by Yamaha riders Rick Hocking and Danny Hockie. With Dave Hansen (Tri) closing, an alert Keener spotted a plug wire that had came off. He got the wire back on and the Bart Markel Harley was back to full song. He was able to nail down 4th and a National berth.

Semis

Dave Aldana and Rob Morrison (Nor) were the class of Semi 1, and shot way in front of the field. Aldana led but Morrison briefly took over. Aldana was back in the lead as Morrison appeared to slow, and was nearly caught by Dewayne Keeter, who was riding a Shell Yamaha. Morrison managed to wick it back up and followed Aldana into the National. Keeter got blasted by Morrison's rooster tail and gave up 3rd to Tom Cummings (HD).

Scott Brelsford, on the radical Kawasaki took any early lead after shaking off Bob Sanders (Yam) and Dave Hansen. He put on a spectacular show trying to control the 100 HP two-stroke. John Gennai (HD) soon tracked Brelsford down, stealing some thunder, (shrieking?) with his traditional XR750. Gennai took the win with Brelsford putting the first two-stroke in a dirt track National since Yvon DuHamel did it with a Yamaha in 1968.

Trophy Race

The red flag came out on lap 2 of the Trophy Race when Tom Cummings went down in Turn 3. A close following Ron Davies ran over Cummings bike and went down hard; Bob Sanders was also involved. Davies went to the hospital, Cummings was done for the day and Sanders made the restart. Tom White (HD) took control on the restart and withstood pressure from Dewayne Keeter to take the win. Rookie "Big" Mike Renslow (HD) was 3rd.

National

More endless dragging and packing of the sandy surface didn't help matters much and the decision was made to cut the National distance. Mert Lawwill scratched from the National due to his weak ankle. He was joined by Hank Scott, whose Harley sprung an oil leak on the line and was pulled from the grid. John Hateley pulled the holeshot and looked strong up front till his Yamaha had an ignition failure on lap 2. He was soon joined by Scott Brelsford, who had made it up 8th place after a lousy start before a seizure ended his day. Rick Hocking took over the lead with Kenny Roberts and Corky Keener in hot pursuit. Roberts moved into the top spot on lap 3, with Keener pushing Hocking. Keener mounted a charge, zapping Hocking and taking the lead from Roberts on lap 5. It didn't last long, as Hocking took the lead back. He and Keener continued to dice, with Hocking taking over for good by lap 8. Gary Scott and Chuck Palmgren had been running behind the leaders and were joined by Rex Beauchamp and John Gennai. Beauchamp put on a late race charge flying past by Palmgren, Scott, Roberts and Keener. Scott dropped out after brushing the outside fencing and breaking six bones in his foot and ankle. Beauchamp worked by Roberts whose Yamaha was a little off song and a fading Keener. By the time he broke free Hocking was long gone for a popular home state win.

Results

Race: 25 Lap Mile National
Race Time: 11:30.44, (83.42 MPH)

Rank	Rider	Number	Make
1.	Rick Hocking, Fremont, Ca	31Z	Yam
2.	Rex Beauchamp, Milford, Mi	31	HD
3.	Kenny Roberts, San Carlos, Ca	1	Yam
4.	Corky Keener, Flint, Mi	62	HD
5.	Chuck Palmgren, Freehold, NJ	38	Yam
6.	John Gennai, Los Gatos, Ca	16Y	HD
7.	Rob Morrison, Granada Hill, Ca	10E	Nor
8.	Danny Hockie, Harbor City, Ca	45E	Yam
9.	Doug Sehl, Waterdown, Ont., Can	45	HD
10.	Jim Rice, Portola Valley, Ca	24	HD
11.	Gene Romero, San Luis Obispo, Ca	3	Yam
12.	Dave Aldana, Santa Ana, Ca	13	Tri
13.	Randy Scott, Corvallis, Ore	50	Yam
14.	Gary Scott, Baldwin Park, Ca	64	HD
15.	Frank Gillespie, Hayward, Ca	76	Yam
16.	Eddie Wirth, Dana Point, Ca	77	HD
17.	Scott Brelsford, Foster City, Ca	19	HD
18.	John Hateley, Van Nuys, Ca	98	Yam
19.	Hank Scott, Hixson, Tn	20R	HD
20.	Mert Lawwill, San Francisco, Ca	7	HD

Race: 10 Lap Trophy Race
Race Time: 7:20.31, (81.391 MPH)

Rank	Rider	Number	Make
1.	Tom White, Huntington Beach, Ca	80	HD
2.	DeWayne Keeter, Oak View, Ca	44	Yam
3.	Mike Renslow, Fremont, Ca	45Y	HD
4.	Terry Sage, Stockton, Ca	20Z	Tri
5.	Bob Sanders, Whittier, Ca	5R	Yam
6.	John Ogilvie, Los Gatos, Ca	5Y	HD
7.	Ike Reed, Salem, Ore	90	Tri
8.	Charles Thielke, Torrance, Ca	56E	Tri
9.	Paul Bostrom, San Ramon, Ca	46	HD
10.	Ron Moore, San Bernardino, Ca	37	Tri

Grand National Points Standings after Round 21

Rank	Rider	Pts
1.	Kenny Roberts	2112
2.	Gary Scott	1467
3.	Gene Romero	944
4.	Rex Beauchamp	692
5.	Mike Kidd	677
6.	Chuck Palmgren	649
7.	Corky Keener	641
8.	Dave Aldana	442
9.	Hank Scott	422
10.	Mert Lawwill	403

Extra Extra

- Despite the issues with the track, a great crowd of over 7000 turned out for the "L&M Golden Gate Super Mile".
- Although the race was an apparent success financially, all the hassles involved with noise issues and track preparation probably helped make the Golden Gate Mile a one-time event.
- Rick Hocking joined Hank Scott as the only rookies to win a National in 1974.
- Hocking was aboard a Yamaha loaned by A&A Racing after his regular Rocky Cycle/Champion Frame sponsored ride developed transmission trouble.
- Michael Goodwin and the Media Max promotion team worked with the Albany City Council and local residents and agreed that the motorcycles would meet a 92 dba level. They were also required to put up a $3000.00 bond from which fines would extracted for any noise violations.
- The commonly used Discojet muffler system, better known today as Supertrapp mufflers, used varying quantities of stacked metal discs to quiet exhaust systems. The company not only helped with installation, they gave refunds to those who didn't make the program and posted contingency money to the purse.
- Most riders had good luck with the Discojet system, but there were a few exceptions. Don Castro's bike spit out it's discs as he waited for his semi. Castro pulled out of the lineup as he faced disqualification if he competed.
- The bumpy fast track saw Mert Lawwill and Rex Beauchamp break out old school 21" front wheels and tires to smooth out the ride. Always the innovator, Lawwill fitted a front fender to his XR750 to deal with the wet cushion spray.
- The spray was so strong that Bart Markel was sure it was the cause for the spark plug wire coming off during Corky Keener's heat race.
- Dick Mann appeared for the first time since the spring San Jose Mile since suffering an early season MX leg injury. He was doing business in his heat race till mechanical trouble struck.
- Jim Rice made the decision during the Golden Gate National to retire. The 12 time-National winner, one of the best riders never to win the Grand National Championship, was ready to pursue other interests in his life. He would return to have some fun when invited to compete in some of the first "Superbikers" competitions.

1974 Ontario Road Race
Romero Wins First on Pavement!

GNC Round #22 of 23 **Date:** October 6, 1974 **Type:** Road Race **Venue:** Ontario Motor Speedway **Location:** Ontario, Ca	**Purse:** $50,000.00 **Surface:** Pavement **Course Length:** 2.9 Miles **Laps:** 43 Per Segment **Distance:** 250 Miles, 2 X 125 Mile Segments

Gene Romero defeated all the pavement stars, foreign and domestic at the final road race of the year at Ontario. Romero's stock as a road racer had risen considerably of late and winning this event confirmed the talent that insiders always knew. For Romero, it was his first National pavement win and his 11th overall GNC victory. He knocked off GNC champ Kenny Roberts, Barry Sheene, along with the GNC foreigner "regulars". Even 14-time World Champion Giacomo Agostini made an appearance, albeit a brief one, crashing on lap 1 of the first leg. Romero won the first leg outright and finished 2nd in the second leg. This just topped teammate Roberts, who was slowed in leg one with the wrong rear tire; he came back to win the second segment. Boston Cycle's Jim Evans once again struck a blow for privateers with fantastic 2-3 finishes. The Ontario race always carried controversy and the 1974 event was no different. On the plus side was the marquee attraction of Agostini taking on Roberts, Sheene, etc. The crowd was way up over previous years, maybe as a result. In addition, spectator viewing areas were much improved. This was partially the result of the promoters reconfiguring the track layout. The course was longer and was run in reverse direction than normal. Although helping the spectators with a better view, some racers were not happy as it created some dangerous situations on the track, (see *Extras*).

Heats Races

The two 5-lap, 15-mile qualifying races were held on Saturday, with the National(s) on Sunday. Yamaha teammates Kenny Roberts and Don Castro squabbled some over the top spot in the first heat, with Castro taking the win. More Yamahas followed, with Jim Evans and Warren Willing from Australia.

Barry Sheene controlled Heat 2 aboard the works Suzuki, but not without heavy pressure from American privateer Steve McLaughlin on the Mel Dineson Yamaha. Gene Romero held 3rd spot till the last circuit when Agostini snuck by.

National
Segment 1

Don Castro led the talented pack off the line with Kenny Roberts and rookie Phil McDonald in tow. Fireworks ensued behind in Turn 6 when Agostini made contact with both Jim Evans and Steve McLaughlin, went down hard and was done for the day. Evans received no damage, but McLaughlin's bike ingested some dirt and slowed. The amazing young McDonald managed to zap both Roberts and Castro in Turn 6 to grab the lead. McDonald headed the pack for a couple more laps, until Castro worked back by. In third, Roberts was struggling with his tire choice (hard) and was fending off the following group of Jim Evans, Yvon DuHamel (Kaw), Barry Sheene and Gene Romero. Evans led Romero and Sheene towards the front, up to leader Castro. Romero surged ahead on lap 8 to take the lead. Gas stops did not change the lead order. Up front, Castro, nearly as hungry as Romero for a pavement win, followed the 1970 GNC champ through traffic. With 3 laps to go, Castro attempted to lap Teppi Lansivouri, ran out of room, brushed the wall and slid off. At the end, Romero was way ahead, Evans retained 2nd, Roberts worked back to 3rd, McDonald was an impressive 4th and Sheene 5th.

Segment 2

Kenny Roberts got his tire selection figured out (soft) took the lead from Phil McDonald and smoked away from the field, setting the days fastest laps in the process. Phil McDonald and Gene Romero were arguing over 2nd spot when McDonald hit a corner marker and had his day end in a big get-off. The early order was Roberts, Romero, Hansford, Teppi Lansivouri, Jim Evans and Barry Sheene. Sheene also benefited from a change in tire compound and charged through the lead pack into 3rd position. He began to harass Romero for the runner-up spot. Romero knew he had to keep the spot if he was going to take the overall win. Sheene was just determined to get past. Sheene's Suzuki lacked the 6-speed gearbox that Romero's TZ700's had, slowing him in comparison through the infield. Although he had an edge on the fast sections, Romero always managed to get back by. The gas stops were the turning point of the race for Romero. His stop was flawless; Sheene's was slower and he ended up behind Jim Evans, giving Romero the cushion he needed. Romero even closed slightly on Roberts as the laps wound down. No worry though, it was Gene's day. Roberts win gave him 2nd overall, Evans in 3rd gave him another podium, Sheene ended up 4th and steady Teppi Lansivouri was 5th overall.

Results

Race: 250 Mile Road Race National
Race Time: 1:05, (93.33 MPH)

Rank	Rider	Number	Make
1.	Gene Romero, San Luis Obispo, Ca	3	Yam
2.	Kenny Roberts, San Carlos, Ca	1	Yam
3.	Jim Evans, San Bernardino, Ca	27	Yam
4.	Barry Sheene, Surrey, England	7	Suz
5.	Teuvo Lansivuori, Isalmi, Finland	8	Yam
6.	Warren Willing, Dundas, N.S.W., Aus	62	Yam
7.	Mick Grant, England	25	Kaw
8.	Jim Dunn, Everett, Wa	75	Yam
9.	Hurley Wilvert, Westminster, Ca	39	Kaw
10.	Mike Clarke, Downey, Ca	143	Yam
11.	Dale Wylie, Christ Church, New Zealand	24	Yam
12.	Doug Libby, Milford, Mi	40	Yam
13.	Yvon DuHamel, LaSalle, Ont., Can	17	Kaw
14.	Phil McDonald, Tulsa, Ok	69	Yam
15.	Doug Sehl, Waterdown, Ont., Can	45	HD
16.	Dennis Purdie, Wayne, Mi	66	Yam
17.	John Boote, Christchurch, NZ	80	Yam
18.	Greg Hansford, Queensland, Australia	61	Yam
19.	Mike Devlin, La Mesa, Ca	127	Yam
20.	George Miller, Oakland, Ca	84	Yam

Extra Extra

- Gene Romero became the first American to win the Ontario National.
- Romero won $8000.00 from the purse, $1000.00 from Champion Sparkplugs, another $1000.00 from L&M Cigarettes for being voted the "Outstanding Racer" by the present journalists, as well as other contingency awards.
- The new track layout did appear to offer better spectator visibility, but many riders thought safety was compromised. The entrance and exit onto the main straight were tight and narrow. Pit lane was located in a fast portion of the track, making it dangerous to navigate. Despite rider protests, no changes were made.
- Whether it was the track layout change or aggressive marketing, something helped to breathe some new life into the event with a good crowd of 20,000 turning out.
- Gary Nixon had hoped to have healed by Ontario, but it just didn't happen. Dave Aldana rode the Erv Kanemoto prepped machine, but had trouble, finishing outside the top 20.

1974 Ascot Half-Mile
Hocking Rocks Ascot for 2nd Win!

GNC Final Round # 23	**Purse:** $14,000.00
Date: October 12, 1974	**Surface:** Dirt
Type: Half-Mile	**Course Length:** ½ Mile
Venue: Ascot Park	**Laps:** 20
Location: Gardena, Ca	**Distance:** 10 Miles

Rick Hocking became the winningest rookie of 1974 by capturing his second National win at the Ascot season finale. He had also won at the previous dirt track National at Albany, Ca a few weeks before. He had to dice hard with Rex Beauchamp for most of the race before pulling out the win. Beauchamp was another of the late season's hottest riders. He had caught fire at the end of the season, winning at Toledo, finishing runner-up at Albany and setting fast time and winning the fastest heat at several Nationals. In 3rd, was the nation's other hottest rookie Hank Scott. He made a late charge to capture the last podium spot. Hocking and Hank Scott were the only rookie winners of the season. Scott, who won the Syracuse Mile, was higher in the GNC points standings due to a more consistent season. While Michigan riders Beauchamp and Corky Keener loomed as potential non-California threats to win Ascot, in the end, just Beauchamp and Oregon's Mark Williams (who finished a very strong 4th), were the only Ascot outsiders to make the National.

Heats

Two-time Ascot winner Mert Lawwill took the lead in Heat 1, despite still riding with an injured foot. He led till four laps to go when fast qualifier Rex Beauchamp took the spot and in what was becoming a habit late in the year, set the fastest heat time. Lawwill held onto 2nd, with Gene Romero (Yam) a solid 3rd.

Heat 2 was dominated by the fast Yamahas of Rick Hocking, Dewayne Keeter and John Hateley. They were challenged early on by Harley-Davidson's Corky Keener. Keener had dominated a regular Friday night Ascot race earlier and like Beauchamp, looked like an Easterner who would threaten for the win. He ran with leader Hocking early on, but just couldn't get hooked up. Hocking led every lap, with Keener being picked off by Keeter at midway, then with three to go by Hateley. All three Yamaha pilots had cut their teeth at Ascot, with Hocking winning three main events leading up to the National aboard the Rocky Cycle ride that was tuned by Champion Frames Doug Schwerma.

The third heat was a great race with John Gennai (HD) pulling the holeshot with a mob giving chase. Gennai led the first three laps, till TT ace Mark Williams managed to slip by for the lead. Kenny Roberts (Yam) was on the charge behind and zapped Williams for the win with three to go.

Heat 4 was a swap fest like the previous race. John Sperry (HD) surprised everybody present, by commanding the first four laps of the race. Dave Aldana (Tri) took the lead for a couple of laps till the nations other hottest rookie, Syracuse winner, Hank Scott, ripped by late in the race for the win. Frank Gillespie, on a borrowed Vista-Sheen Harley, edged out Sperry for the final transfer spot.

Semis

Paul Bostrom (HD) out-distanced a cast of talented riders to take the first semi win. Corky Keener was in the hunt until lap 2 when he laid his bike down in front of most of the pack. He was very fortunate to miss being collected. Behind Bostrom at the finish was local rookie Mike Renslow (Yam) and Canadian Doug Sehl (HD).

Semi 2 was a great battle between Ascot aces Terry Dorsch (aboard injured Tom Rockwood's Triumph) and Ron Moore, also Triumph mounted. The two ran wheel-to-wheel for much of the race with Moore out front for most of the race. Dorsch managed to eke out a lead late, but Moore would not be denied and powered ahead for the win.

Trophy Race

It was all Terry Dorsch in the Trophy Race. The stylish Californian had his new ride figured out and blitzed away from the pack, taking the win by a big margin. Pat McCaul (Yam) was a distant 2nd, followed by Steve Droste (HD), Mike Renslow and Tom White (HD).

National

It was Michigan invader Rex Beauchamp out front at the start of the 20-lap National. Rick Hocking was right on his rear wheel, with a gap back to Mert Lawwill, Mark Williams, Dave Aldana and crew. Williams quickly moved past Lawwill for 3rd. Hocking took the point briefly on lap 6, with Beauchamp quickly grabbing the lead back. Hank Scott had missed some shifts off the line, but was rocketing through the field. He was into the lead pack and by the halfway point was into 4th. Lawwill was beginning to fade back, his foot injury not helping. He wound up in 9th place at the finish. Up front, the lead battle was still raging, with Beauchamp and Hocking still just inches apart. Entering turn 1 on the 12th lap, Hocking dove in deep and took the lead for good. Hocking opened up a little a small lead over Beauchamp, flying to a new Ascot 20- lap record. On the last lap, Hank Scott took the last podium spot from Williams. In 5th from back of the pack, was John Hateley. Rounding out the top 10 were Dewayne Keeter, Danny Hockie, Kenny Roberts, Mert Lawwill and Ron Moore.

Results

Race: 20 Lap Half-Mile National
Race Time: 7:39.05, (68.627 MPH)

Rank	Rider	Number	Make
1.	Rick Hocking, Fremont, Ca	31Z	Yam
2.	Rex Beauchamp, Milford, Mi	31	HD
3.	Hank Scott, Hixson, Tn	20R	HD
4.	Mark Williams, Springfield, Ore	70	Tri
5.	John Hateley, Van Nuys, Ca	98	Yam
6.	DeWayne Keeter, Oak View, Ca	44	Yam
7.	Danny Hockie, Harbor City, Ca	45E	Yam
8.	Kenny Roberts, San Carlos, Ca	1	Yam
9.	Mert Lawwill, San Francisco, Ca	7	HD
10.	Ron Moore, San Bernardino, Ca	37	Tri
11.	Dave Aldana, Santa Ana, Ca	13	Tri
12.	Frank Gillespie, Hayward, Ca	76	HD
13.	Gene Romero, San Luis Obispo, Ca	3	Yam
14.	Paul Bostrom, San Ramon, Ca	46	HD

Race: Trophy Race

Rank	Rider	Number	Make
1.	Terry Dorsch, Granada Hills, Ca	22	Tri
2.	Pat McCaul, San Jose, Ca	48Y	Yam
3.	Steve Droste, Waterloo, Ia	92	HD
4.	Mike Renslow, Fremont, Ca	45Y	Yam
5.	Tom White, Huntington Beach, Ca	80	HD
6.	Doug Sehl, Waterdown, Ont., Can	45	HD
7.	Ron Powell, San Bernardino, Ca	37	Tri
8.	Jimmy Odom, Fremont, Ca	18	Tri
9.	Eddie Wirth, Daly City, Ca	77	HD
10.	John Gennai, Los Gatos, Ca	16Y	HD

Final Grand National Points Standings

Rank	Rider	Pts
1.	Kenny Roberts	2286
2.	Gary Scott	1467
3.	Gene Romero	1132
4.	Rex Beauchamp	812
5.	Mike Kidd	677
6.	Chuck Palmgren	649
7.	Corky Keener	641
8.	Hank Scott	522
9.	Rick Hocking	490
10.	Dave Aldana	452

. *Extra Extra*

- The Ascot National offered a rich purse. Besides the $14,000.00 purse, there was an additional $4000.00 in contingency dollars and lap money of $100.00 per circuit available.
- Rick Hocking became the third rookie to win the Ascot National. Dan Haaby did it in 1967 and Gary Scott in 1972.
- Yamaha was the brand of choice in the National with 6 bikes. Harley-Davidson had 5 and Triumph 3.
- Repeat GNC champ Kenny Roberts had an off night, struggling at the back of the pack, working hard to finish 8th.
- Norton rider Dave Aldana finished out the year on Mike Kidd's Triumph, finishing 11th.
- Rex Beauchamp joined Carroll Resweber and Bart Markel as the only non-Californians to set fast time at an Ascot National.
- While Michigan riders Beauchamp and Corky Keener loomed as potential non-California threats to win Ascot, in the end just Beauchamp and Oregon's Mark Williams, (who finished a very strong 4th), were the only Ascot outsiders to make the National.

1974 Season Review

1. Kenny Roberts
2286 Points

The 1974 Grand National Championship season was the year that established "King Kenny" Roberts. He utterly dominated the year on his way to his second consecutive title, scoring six wins, and his points advantage over rival Gary Scott was a whopping 800 points plus. Roberts point total of 2286 was the highest attained in the history of the series. His wins came at the spring San Jose Mile, Road Atlanta, a three-in-row run at Laguna Seca, Sante Fe and Peoria, scoring his last win at Talladega. His three run streak answered a similar run by Gary Scott and helped him win the inaugural Camel Pro "mini-series". The season saw his first pavement wins, taking half of the six races on the schedule. His win at Peoria gave him the TT victory he needed to accomplish a GNC "Grand Slam"; a win in every competition discipline. During the 1974 season he scored wins in all the different types of events except for a half-mile, which he had won at the season ending Ascot in 1973. He became just the second rider to accomplish the 'Slam. Many had come close, including Carroll Resweber, Bart Markel, and Gary Nixon, but Dick Mann was the first. His victories took place between 1959 and 1972, a 14 year time span. Roberts accomplished it in just 3, from 1972-'74. His versatility was comparable to three-time GNC champ Joe Leonard who was also a threat to win any event, regardless of the type. Leonard never won a National short track, an event introduced to the circuit near the end of his career. Another amazing 1974 statistic was Roberts consistency; he made the every National on the 23 event schedule. No other rider was even close. This was testimonial to his versatility and excellent machine preparation and reliability. He was the first GNC champ since Carroll Resweber to make every National scheduled. Another stat that should quiet anyone that credits road racing alone for repeating his title: Counting dirt track points only, Roberts would have still beat Gary Scott by 14 points!

Besides Roberts's six wins, his podium runs were also impressive. He was 2nd at, the Houston TT, Daytona, Columbus, Ascot TT, Terre Haute and Ontario. He was 3rd at the Golden Gate Mile. Runs in the top 5 were scored at the Houston Short Track, Loudon and the summer San Jose Mile. Finishes in the top 10 included the Toledo and Ascot Half-Miles. Roberts finished outside the top 10 just four times, at Denver, Louisville, Castle Rock TT and the Indy Mile.

2. Gary Scott
1467 Points

For Gary Scott it was another "best of times/worst of times" or "good news/bad news" year. It was his first year riding for Team Harley-Davidson. As expected, he ran well at the big bore dirt track events and salvaged points at the shorter road races. He trailed Roberts as the season entered the midway point. He then ran off an amazing three race streak at the summer San Jose Mile, Castle Rock and Ascot TT's. After going winless in 1973, it was a very satisfying time for Scott. In the points battles, the victories allowed him to reel in Roberts and he looked to have a real shot at the title. Unfortunately for Gary, arch-rival Roberts unbelievably reeled off three wins-in-row himself, reassuming command of the championship battle. Scott tried his best to retaliate, but a broken collarbone on his lightweight ride at Talladega derailed his chances. He missed the following Syracuse National, bravely returning at Toledo where he finished third. It wasn't enough as Roberts clinched the title at the next race at Terre Haute. Scott suffered an injured foot at the Golden Gate race, missing the last two races of the year as Roberts piled on the points. In addition to his wins, Scott was 2nd at the spring San Jose Mile, Denver, Louisville and Peoria. He was in the top 5 at the Houston TT, Sante Fe and Indy Mile. He was in the top 10 at the Columbus and Terre Haute Half-Miles and impressive on the outdated XRTT at Loudon and Laguna Seca. He scored points in 16 of the 23 Nationals.

Scott was a fierce competitor who was deadly serious in his efforts. While salvaging some pride in his three victories and a runner-up finish in the championship for Harley-Davidson, Scott would not be satisfied till he became Grand National Champion. He had the ability, he just needed some luck.

3. Gene Romero
1132 Points

1970 Grand National Champion Gene Romero showed he still had the goods as he adapted well to his new Yamaha machinery in 1974. The longtime Triumph factory rider had an off-year in 1973 and knew it was time to move on. Romero got on well with the new TZ700 as well as the dirt track machinery. Early season success included a 6th at Daytona and a 3rd at the Spring San Jose Mile. Showing rapid progress on TZ; he was runner-up at both Road Atlanta and Loudon. At mid-season he had back-to-back 3rd places finishes at very different tracks; at the Ascot TT and Laguna Seca Road Race. Showing dirt track savvy and Yamaha factory horsepower, he won a thrilling race at the Indy Mile. Romero rounded out the year, finally scoring a road race win, a big one, at the Ontario National. Romero had been close for years, including consecutive runner-ups at Daytona. The elusive victory was made all the sweeter by the huge payday against the worlds best pavement racers. He became the first American rider to win the event. Romero's career had definitely hit it's second wind.

4. Rex Beauchamp
812 Points

Michigan dirt tracker Rex Beauchamp had his best ever GNC season. He scored a win at the Toledo Half-Mile. He finished 2nd three times; at the Syracuse and Golden Gate Miles and was runner-up at the Ascot Half-Mile, one of the few outsiders to run so well on it's unique surface. He was in the top 5 at the spring San Jose Mile and at Terre Haute. He was 6th at the Indy Mile and an impressive 7th at the Ascot TT. He scored points in 9 of the 23 Nationals, all on dirt.

5. Mike Kidd
677 Points

The last official Team Triumph rider, Mike Kidd, was a legitimate title contender till a broken leg at Sante Fe took him out for the year. Despite scoring points in just 7 of 23 races, Kidd was still 5th in points. He was in the top 5 of all the races he finished, except at Sante Fe. Riding the still potent Triumph dirt trackers, wrenched by Brent Thompson, Kidd won the long Harley dominated Columbus National for Triumphs last ever oval track National win. Showing surprising Triumph horsepower and Kidd's growing skills, the combination came home 2nd at the summer San Jose Mile. Kidd was also 3rd at the Denver and Louisville Half-Miles and 5th at the Castle Rock TT. If Kidd had remained healthy he may not have been able to catch Roberts, but he would have surely been a contender for the top three spots in points.

6. Chuck Palmgren
649 Points

Veteran Chuck Palmgren returned to the GNC Top Ten after an off-year in 1973. Palmgren didn't score a win or even a podium finish during the year. His best finish was a strong 4th at Peoria. His high placing in the championship was mainly due to an amazing run of seven 5th place finishes. He was scored in that spot at Denver, Columbus, Sante Fe, Indy, Syracuse, Terre Haute and the Golden Gate Mile. Palmgren ran well on all the dirt surfaces and the AAR Yamahas were still putting out potent power. He made 11 of the 23 Nationals.

7. Corky Keener
641 Points

Corky Keener had held an Expert card since the middle 1960's, but the Michigan dirt tracker had his career take off when he teamed up with Bart Markel. Aboard Markel's XR750, Keener won his first National at the deep cushion Louisville Half-Mile. Keener won again at the late season Terre Haute National. Other top finishes for the year included a 2nd at Toledo and a 4th at the Golden Gate Mile. Keener made 8 of 23 Nationals, but fought mechanical trouble at many races. Given more reliable machinery, Keener was destined for more winning days. Like teammate Beauchamp, Keener was a natural throttle twister, ala' Bart Markel and was always a threat to win on dirt.

8. Hank Scott
522 Points

Gary Scott's younger brother Hank was the top rookie of 1974, narrowly topping fellow Californian Rick Hocking. Dirt tracker Scott benefited from back-door Harley support and scored a win at the Syracuse Mile. He was also on the podium at the summer San Jose Mile and the Ascot Half-mile. Scott scored top tens at the Houston Short Track, at Louisville, Columbus and Terre Haute. He made 10 of the 23 races. Hank and Gary became the first brothers in the top ten in points since Chuck and Larry Palmgren in 1969.

9. Rick Hocking
490 Points

Rick Hocking was another great all around dirt tracker who was having a solid, if not spectacular rookie season. Showing his TT skills, he was 5th at the season opening Houston TT, 6th at the Ascot TT and 8th at Peoria. There was also a 9th at the Toledo Half-Mile. Even though suffering a dislocated thumb at Terre Haute, Hocking caught fire late in the year, reeling off home state wins at the Golden Gate Mile and season ending Ascot Half-Mile. Despite his two wins, he didn't have as consistent season as rookie rival Scott, making 7 of 23 races, thus coming in just behind him in the standings.

10. Dave Aldana
452 Points

While scoring points in 13 of the 23 Nationals, veteran Dave Aldana struggled with injury and machinery through the year. He fought muscle soreness and swelling much of the year and suffered a rare serious injury, a cracked pelvis at the Indy Mile. Aboard his Norton dirt trackers, he did managed to score a 5th at the Peoria TT. Late in the year Aldana began riding injured Mike Kidd's Triumph with a best finish a 3rd at Terre Haute. One of the other bright spots for Aldana was on pavement aboard a new Yamaha TZ700. He was 3rd at Loudon, 6th at Laguna Seca and 7th at Road Atlanta.

There were 13 different winners in the 23 event schedule. The amount of different winners was down from 1973's record number, mostly due to Kenny Roberts 6 wins. Riders scoring Grand National points reached 110, one of the highest years on record.

Yamaha was the dominant brand and took the Manufacturer Championship with 11 wins, again mostly attributable to Roberts's domination. Harley-Davidson scored 8 wins, Triumph 2, Honda and Suzuki 1 each. For the first time since 1970, Kawasaki went winless, way off their 1973 mark of 5 wins.

The 1974 season was marked by Kenny Roberts, the new Camel Pro "mini-series" and widespread injuries among many of series top riders. Roberts' season was his most successful ever in the series. He absolutely dominated the show and luck seemed to go his way. Camel, the AMA and the riders all seemed pleased with the three-race mini-series and negotiations were underway for a full season in 1975. On the darker side, the rider injury rate seemed to be at a series high. Gary Nixon and Mert Lawwill both scored the final GNC wins of their careers in 1974, but were knocked out of most of the year and the top ten in points. Dick Mann ran his last year on the circuit, suffering a leg injury at the summer San Jose Mile, missing most of the season. For Lawwill, it was the first time he finished out of the top 10 since 1964! Mark Brelsford's comeback was derailed at Columbus and the talented 1972 champ retired all too early. Gary Scott suffered a broken collarbone at a pivotal part of the championship, and returned, only to injure his foot at the Golden Gate Mile. Fellow title contender Mike Kidd suffered a badly broken leg at the Sante Fe Short Track ruining his year. Don Castro had suffered a bad leg injury at a Cal Rayborn benefit race and struggled through the year, out of the Top 10 for the first time since ever since turning Expert in 1970. Seemingly unbreakable "Rubberball" Dave Aldana suffered a cracked pelvis at the Indy Mile but returned. John Hateley suffered mid-season rib injuries but was able to return. Jim Rice, a fixture at the top of the standings since 1970 suffered enough spills and frustrating mechanical failures to cause his retirement. Though mercifully there were no fatalities, the injuries were troubling. They may have played a part in former Grand National Champions, Gary Nixon, Dick Mann and Mark Brelsford retiring or semi-retiring from the series. They also changed the complexion of the championship. There was a changing of the guard as the series moved into the middle of the decade.

The Junior class of 1974 would produce the most talented riders since the bumper crop of 1972 that produced Kenny Roberts, Gary Scott and Mike Kidd. The top Junior riders of the year included Jay and Ken Springsteen from Michigan, Greg Sassaman and Jay Ridgeway from Georgia, Guy McClure and Bubba Rush from Texas, Steve Freeman from South Carolina, Scott Rader and Chuck Jordan from Ohio, Alex Jorgensen, Tom Berry and Kenny Roberts' protégé from California, Skip Aksland. The coming 1975 Camel Pro Series would promise to be an exciting year!

1974 GNC Winners

Event	Location	Winner	Machine
TT	Houston, Tx	Dave Hansen, Hayward, Ca	Tri
Short Track	Houston, Tx	Mike Gerald, Baton Rouge, La	Hon
Road Race	Daytona, Fl	Giacomo Agostini, Italy	Yam
Mile	San Jose, Ca	Kenny Roberts, Modesto, Ca	Yam
Half-Mile	Denver, Co	Mert Lawwill, San Francisco, Ca	HD
Road Race	Braselton, Ga	Kenny Roberts, Modesto, Ca	Yam
Half-Mile	Louisville, Ky	Corky Keener, Flint, Mi	HD
Road Race	Loudon, NH	Gary Nixon, Cockeysville, MD	Suz
Half-Mile	Columbus, Oh	Mike Kidd, Euless, Tx	Tri
Mile	San Jose, Ca	Gary Scott, Baldwin Park, Ca	HD
TT	Castle Rock, Wa	Gary Scott, Baldwin Park, Ca	HD
TT	Gardena, Ca	Gary Scott, Baldwin Park, Ca	HD
Road Race	Monterey, Ca	Kenny Roberts, Modesto, Ca	Yam
Short Track	Hinsdale, Ill	Kenny Roberts, Modesto, Ca	Yam
TT	Peoria, Ill	Kenny Roberts, Modesto, Ca	Yam
Mile	Indianapolis, Ind	Gene Romero, San Luis Obispo, Ca	Yam
Road Race	Talladega, Al	Kenny Roberts, Modesto, Ca	Yam
Mile	Syracuse, NY	Hank Scott, Hixson, Tn	HD
Half-Mile	Toledo, Oh	Rex Beauchamp, Drayton Plains, Mi	HD
Half-Mile	Terre Haute, Ind	Corky Keener, Flint, Mi	HD
Mile	Albany, Ca	Rick Hocking, Fremont, Ca	Yam
Road Race	Ontario, Ca	Gene Romero, San Luis Obispo, Ca	Yam
Half-Mile	Gardena, Ca	Rick Hocking, Fremont, Ca	Yam

Bonus!
1974 Year End Point Fund Awards

1.	Kenny Roberts	2286 Points	$7,876.83
2.	Gary Scott	1467	3,177.05
3.	Gene Romero	1132	2,451.55
4.	Rex Beauchamp	812	1,758.53
5.	Mike Kidd	677	1,466.17
6.	Chuck Palmgren	649	1,405.53
7.	Corky Keener	641	1,388.20
8.	Hank Scott	522	1,130.49
9.	Rick Hocking	490	1,061.18
10.	Dave Aldana	452	978.89
11.	Mert Lawwill	423	916.08
12.	Don Castro	362	783.98
13.	Mark Williams	342	740.66
14.	John Hateley	338	732.00
15.	Doug Sehl	282	610.72
16.	Gary Nixon	275	595.56
17.	Dave Hansen	271	586.90
18.	Mike Gerald	270	584.74
19.	Jim Evans	238	515.43
20.	John Gennai	231	500.28
		Total Point Fund	$29,260.77

1975 GNC Season Preview

The biggest news for the 1975 AMA Grand National season was the official announcement that Camel cigarettes would become the series sponsor. For what would now be called the Camel Pro Series, the company would post $75,000.00 in points money. There would be a $14,000.00 payout at midseason and another at the end of the year for Top 10 riders. An additional $47,000.00 would be paid out to the overall series riders according to their point totals. Total combined purse money reached over $750,000.00. The successful 1974 three race "mini-series" that paid out $15,000.00, paved the way for the full season in 1975. It was the first time the AMA had a series sponsor, setting a precedent for the future. It was ground-breaking moment to have a non-motorcycle company play such a large role in the sport.

Although not perceived as a big deal at the time, the tweaked 1975 Camel Pro Schedule had big ramifications for all teams and riders. After reaching a series high of 9 road races in 1973, the AMA had reduced the number to 6 in 1974; still a sizable number. In a move mostly attributed to the Japanese factories cutting back support, as well as low attendance at some events, the pavement races were reduced to a paltry 3 for the 1975 season. Road races at Talladega and Loudon were off the schedule, with Road Atlanta being cancelled, (while low attendance was possible with the other two events, Loudon's strong crowds meant there was probably a disagreement between the promoters and the AMA). Also off the schedule were the Denver Half-Mile and the Golden Gate Mile, both one-off dirt tracks. New on the schedule was an indoor short track at Dallas, Tx and a fairgrounds cushion half-mile at Harrington, Del. The number of overall races dropped from 23 to just 20. The loss of so many pavement races was a blow to all the Japanese teams. Gone were the huge teams of the past. The three race schedule did not warrant a huge racing budget. While the factories would field large international efforts at Daytona, the domestic teams were much abbreviated.

For Yamaha and Kenny Roberts, the schedule change was not a fatal blow to defending his title, but the big points paying pavement races were a place he could gain a cushion over Team Harley. Roberts was still a formidable dirt tracker, particularly on the TT's and short tracks. The Yamahas were not as successful on the big ovals. To try and gain some ground back, Roberts made a major change in tuners. Shell Theutt was gone, off to start a new team with Hank Scott. Tim Witham of the S&W motorcycle suspension company was brought in. Bud Aksland stayed on with the team. It was hoped the new combination could coax significantly more power out of the dirt track engine. If his luck held, Roberts still had a great chance of taking his third title. His lone, official teammate for 1975 was Gene Romero. Romero had a great debut season in 1974, his road race prowess growing by the event. Don Castro, on the team since 1973, was released. Castro had a difficult year in 1974, struggling with a wounded leg through the season. Roberts was the only rider with full-up support at all events. Romero's road race efforts had full support, but he had to run his own dirt track efforts. He enlisted the aid of C.R. Axtell for engine help and had C&J build the chassis. There was some updates for factory machinery. The formidable TZ700 was enlarged to a full 750. The standard racer still retained the previous twin shock configuration. The top rider at each international distributer received a new model with monoshock rear suspension. In the U.S., only Roberts received one. The XS based 750 dirt tracker received better breathing cylinder heads. There was a radical Yamaha dirt track machine under development, though not directly involving the U.S. team. Steve Baker and his Canadian Yamaha sponsor Bob Work, thought the new TZ700/750 might make a workable miler. Champion Frames wizard Doug Schwerma loved the idea and began work on a design, with 6 bikes slated to be produced. Ken Clark, the Yamaha U.S. team boss was contacted, but wanted no part of it; at least yet. There will be more to this story!

The revised schedule seemingly played right into Harley-Davidson hands and Gary Scott's title aspirations. The pavement races had been his weak spot and their number had been halved. On big dirt ovals the Harley's were dominant, and in 1975 there were 6 half-miles and 4 miles on the schedule. Scott was a great TT rider and there 4 on the calendar. Short tracks were the only weak link in the team's dirt assault. Scott and crew would still field the old Sprints, despite rumors the engine from the RR250 lightweight road racer would be tried. Joining Scott for the official 1975 team was 1970 champ Mert Lawwill, Rex Beauchamp and now full-fledged team member Corky Keener. The newest member of the team was rookie Greg Sassaman. He was an unknown quantity to many, coming out of Georgia, a state not usually known for flat tracking. He had been a top Junior in 1974 riding for long time Harley faithful Powell Hassell. Mark Brelsford had retired and brother Scott was off the team. Dave and Doug Sehl and several other riders also received support. Though not a factory effort, much was expected of Michigan rookies, brothers Jay and Ken Springsteen. They were two of the best Junior racers of 1974. The two rode for Vista Sheen, a t-shirt business run by racing enthusiast Rich Gawthrop.

There was a run of 100 new XR750's, the engine receiving refinement in many areas including the cylinder heads and oiling system. The frames received some minor changes as well, all from lessons learned from racing the 1972

XR. Already the best dirt tracker available, the continued improvements were rapidly obsoleting the competition. The same could not be said for the XRTT road racer. For the first time ever the Harley-Davidson team would not field machines at Daytona. It was a hard pill for Dick O'Brien and crew to swallow. Gary Scott was a very capable road racer and would race the bike where it made sense. There was some hope that the 500cc big brother of the lightweight racer would provide an answer, only time would tell.

The individual Triumph and Norton race teams were no more, but were reorganized like their respective companies as the Norton-Villers-Triumph (NVT) team. Norton dirt trackers would be their main weapon, with Triumphs occasionally used. Riders were Rob Morrison, veteran Mark Williams and former factory Triumph rider Mike Kidd. While seemingly a long shot, the bikes were still making competitive power and there was no shortage of rider talent.

Despite the abbreviated pavement schedule, Kawasaki and Suzuki still fielded capable, if smaller teams. Team Green was now down to just veteran Yvon DuHamel and Jim Evans. Suzuki fielded the talented trio of Gary Nixon, Dave Aldana and rookie Pat Hennen. Various GP stars were imported by all the Japanese teams for the big events.

A new player in the motorcycle world, PowerDyne Vehicles, (PDV), planned to enter into the Camel Pro Series. Based in Rhode Island, they manufactured small displacement motorcycles (mostly dirt bikes) and planned to enter all important short track races. Their machines were a combination of copies of Yamaha engines and designs of Doug Schwerma's Champion Frames products (which would later get them into a serious lawsuit.) As the bikes used familiar designs, they were competitive with other short trackers. A talented group of riders was assembled. JR Rawls, Teddy Poovey, Larry Cooper, George Richtmeyer and Louis Moniz made up the team. They were known as "Team Gringo", a moniker the company used for their bikes as well.

1975 National Numbers

1. Kenny Roberts, Villa Park, Ca
2. Dick Mann, Richmond, Ca
3. Gene Romero, San Luis Obispo, Ca
4. Bart Markel, Flint, Mi
5. Roger Reiman, Kewanee, Ill
6. Mark Brelsford, Anchorage, Ak
7. Mert Lawwill, Tiburon, Ca
8. Unassigned
9. Gary Nixon, Cockeysville, Md
10. Dave Aldana, Santa Ana, Ca
11. Don Castro, Gilroy, Ca
12. Eddie Mulder, Northtridge, Ca
13. Rick Hocking, Fremont, Ca
14. Hank Scott, Hixson, Tn
15. Mike Gerald, Baton Rouge, La
16. Dave Sehl, Waterdown, Ont., Can
17. Yvon DuHamel, LaSalle, Quebec, Can
18. Jimmy Odom, Fremont, Ca
19. Scott Brelsford, Foster City, Ca
20. John Gennai, Los Gatos, Ca
21. Gary Fisher, Parkesburg, Pa
22. Terry Dorsch, Granada Hills, Ca
23. Dave Hansen, Hayward, Ca
24. Jim Rice, Portola Valley, Ca
25. Rob Morrison, Perris, Ca
26. Cliff Carr, Irvine, Ca
27. Jim Evans, Bonners Ferry, Id
28. Mike Caves, Galesburg, Ill
29. Randy Cleek, Shawnee, Ok
30. Art Baumann, Brisbane, Ca
31. Rex Beauchamp, Milford, Mi
32. Steve Baker, Bellingham, Wa
33. Paul Smart, Santa Ana, Ca
34. Darryl Hurst, Houston, Tx
35. Randy Skiver, Everett, Wa
36. Charlie Chapple, Flint, Mi
37. Ron Moore, San Bernardino, Ca
38. Chuck Palmgren, Santa Ana, Ca
39. Hurley Wilvert, Westminster, Ca
40. Doug Libby, Milford, Mi
41. Billy Eves, Phoenixville, Pa
42. Steve Morehead, Findlay, Oh
43. Roger Crump, Resaca, Ga
44. DeWayne Keeter, Oak View, Ca
45. Doug Sehl, Waterdown, Ontario, Can
46. Paul Bostrom, San Ramon, Ca
47. Charlie Seale, Santa Ana, Ca
48. Pat McCaul, San Jose, Ca
49. Denny Palmgren, Lutherville, Md
50. Randy Scott, Corvallis, Ore
51. Pat Evans, El Cajon, Ca
52. Mike Clarke, Downey, Ca
53. Ted Henter, St. Petersburg, Fl
54. Robert E. Lee, Hurst, Tx
55. Tom Horton, Lancaster, Ca
56. John Long, Miami Beach, Fl
57. James Lee, Bedford, Tx
58. Phil McDonald, Sapulpa, Ok
59. Jean Lysight, Tracy, Que., Can
60. Chuck Joyner, Oregon City, Ore
61. Teddy Newton, Pontiac, Mi
62. Corky Keener, Flint, Mi
63. Robert Sanders, Whittier, Ca
64. Gary Scott, Baldwin Park, Ca
65. Billy Labrie, St. Petersburg, Fl
66. Robert Ewell, Dallas, Tx
67. Pat Marinacci, Seattle, Wa
68. Dennis Purdie, Wayne, Mi
69. Sonny Burres, Portland, Ore
70. Mark Williams, Springfield, Ore
71. Jimmy Maness, Augusta, Ga
72. Mike Kidd, Fort Worth, Tx
73. Terry Pletch, Frankfort, Ind
74. Paul Pressgrove, Chillicothe, Ill
75. Jim Dunn, Everett, Wa
76. Frank Gillespie, Hayward, Ca
77. Eddie Wirth, Dana Point, Ca
78. Charles Brown, Longview, Wa
79. Tom Cummings, Flint, Mi
80. Tom White, Huntington Beach, Ca
81. Gordon Duesenbery, Witchita, Ks
82. Rickey Campbell, Milford, Oh
83. Steve McLaughlin, Duarte, Ca
84. Dan Hockie, Harbor City, Ca
85. Mike Johnson, Flint, Mi
86. Bill Wascher, Seattle, Wa
87. Tim Buckles, Houston, Tx
88. Tom Rockwood, Gardena, Ca
89. Jimmy Zeigler, Bellville, Oh
90. Ike Reed, Salem, Ore
91. Scott Drake, Xenia, Oh
92. Steve Droste, Waterloo, Ia
93. Jim Rawls, Grand Prairie, Tx
94. Ted Poovey, Garland, Tx
95. Ricky Graves, White Salmon, Wa
96. Bill Schaeffer, Pine Grove, Pa
97. Ron Pierce, Bakersfield, Ca
98. John Hateley, Van Nuys, Ca
99. Dale Wylie, Atlanta, Ga

1975
Grand National Championship
Schedule

	Race	Location	Date
1	Houston TT	Houston, Tx	January 31, 1975
2	Houston Short Track	Houston, Tx	February 1, 1975
3	Daytona 200 Mile Road Race	Daytona Beach, Fl	March 9, 1975
4	Dallas Short Track	Dallas, Tx	April 12, 1975
5	San Jose Mile	San Jose, Ca	May 18, 1975
6	Louisville Half-Mile	Louisville, Ky	June 7, 1975
7	Harrington Half-Mile	Harrington, Del	June 14, 1975
8	Columbus Half-Mile	Columbus, Oh	June 22, 1975
9	Castle Rock TT	Castle Rock, Wa	July 12, 1975
10	Ascot TT	Gardena, Ca	July 26, 1975
11	Laguna Seca 75 Mile Road Race	Monterey, Ca	August 3, 1975
12	Peoria TT	Peoria, Ill	August 10, 1975
13	Sante Fe Short Track	Hinsdale, Ill	August 15, 1975
14	Terre Haute Half-Mile	Terre Haute, Ind	August 17, 1975
15	Indy Mile	Indianapolis, Ind	August 23, 1975
16	Syracuse Mile	Syracuse, NY	September 7, 1975
17	Toledo Half-Mile	Toledo, Oh	September 13, 1975
18	San Jose Mile	San Jose, Ca	September 21, 1975
19	Ascot Half-Mile	Gardena, Ca	September 27, 1975
20	Ontario 200 Mile Road Race	Ontario, Ca	October 5, 1975

1975 Houston Astrodome TT and Short Track
Kenny Roberts Finally Takes Houston TT!
Local Darryl Hurst Wins Short Track!

GNC Round #1 & 2 of 20 **Date:** January 31 & February 1 , 1975 **Type:** TT and Short Track **Venue:** Houston Astrodome **Location:** Houston, Tx	**Purse:** $32,000.00 **Surface:** Dirt **Course Length:** ¼ mile **Laps:** 25 TT, 20 Short Track

Grand National Champion Kenny Roberts, the most dominant, (and winless!), rider at the Houston TT since 1972 finally got the monkey off his back in 1975. In 1972 and 1973 he stalled his Yamaha's engine with races he had completely in his control. In 1974, a bad start saw him come up just short to Dave Hansen. Over the winter months of the off-season, Roberts, Bud Aksland and new tuner Tim Witham, burned the midnight oil to come up with the perfect Houston TT frame, which Champion Frame's Doug Schwerma built. It featured motocross-inspired long-travel suspension. In reality, all Roberts really needed was a bit of good luck, which he finally got. As expected, Roberts dominated the race and became the first rider to win both the TT and short track at Houston, (he won the short track events in 1972 and '73). He was also in position to become the first rider to win both events in one weekend. Unfortunately, all the effort spent on the TT bike may have been at the expense of his short track program. For the first time since turning Expert, Roberts failed to make the short track event. Instead, Darryl Hurst, a local racer who owned a nearby Yamaha shop, became the first home-state winner at Houston, thrilling the partisan crowd. It was a perfect main event for Hurst, running away with the 20 lap National.

Time Trials

To no-one's surprise, Roberts's and his new Champion-framed Yamaha were the night's fastest qualifier at 27.35. Former GNC champ Mert Lawwill on a Harley XR750, was second quickest with a 27.48. Oregon rider Diane Cox, the first female Expert rated rider, was attempting to make her first National. An experienced TT rider, she just missed the cut and would return for the next nights short track

Heats

Kenny Roberts was on the pole for Heat 1, and was favored to take all of his events. Minor engine troubles made this harder than expected. Roberts' traditional rival, second year Harley-Davidson team member Gary Scott, pulled the holeshot and would lead from wire-to-wire. Behind him, Roberts ran in 2nd, but an engine stutter allowed Oregon TT star Mark Williams (Nor) and last year's winner Dave Hansen (Tri) to slip by. Roberts' engine cleared up and he charged back by Hansen and Williams. Hansen didn't give up easily and briefly passed Roberts back. Roberts surged back into 2nd, but Gary Scott was now long gone. Williams moved past Hansen to take the third and last transfer to the National.

The second heat was a crash-filled event requiring four restarts. The first attempt was called back after Frank Gillespie (HD) was involved in a crash. The restart saw Dannie Hockie (Yam) fall off and was unavoidably T-boned by Sonny Burres (Tri). Hockie was not seriously injured, but sat out the restart. The third try saw several riders jump the start and were called back. Mercifully, the fourth try was the charm and Mert Lawwill jumped out front chased by Texas rookie Guy McClure (Yam), 1972 Winner John Hateley (Nor) and Rick Hocking (Yam). Smooth-riding Lawwill stayed out front and led unchallenged to the finish. McClure lost a battle with Hateley and Hocking; both going by for 2nd and 3rd places.

Dan Gurney-sponsored Chuck Palmgren was extremely upset when his B50 BSA quit before the start of Heat 3. He and the only 4-stroke single in the program, were out for the night. Randy Skiver (Tri) led the race from flag-to-flag. In exciting action behind Skiver, 1971 winner Jimmy Odom and John Gennai were 2nd and 3rd aboard Harley XR750's. Rookie Skip Aksland (Yam) charged to the front. He moved by Gennai and began hounding Odom. On the last lap, Aksland moved inside Odom. Not to be outdone, close-following Gennai put in a great move, passing both for 2nd place. Odom managed to beat Aksland to the line for 3rd.

Dave Aldana (HD), resplendent in his "Bones" skeleton leathers, caused delays in starting Heat 4. First he was under the two minute clock to clear up some mechanical issues and once the race started, laid his bike down in Turn 1. On the restart, Eddie Mulder (Tri) showed his reflexes were still in great shape, getting another holeshot. Ron Powell (Tri) was right on Mulder and when "Steady Eddie" slipped wide coming onto the straightaway, Powell took the lead. Mulder continued to backslide, with future super star Jay Springsteen (HD) and Dave Aldana both moving past him for 2nd and 3rd.

Semis

After a restart, caused by Bruce Hanlon (HD) crashing off the jump, Dave Hansen led the pack with rookies Alex Jorgensen (Tri) and Dennis Briggs in pursuit. Briggs was riding the strong ex-Gary Scott, ex-Dave Aldana 350 Kawasaki. He got a great drive in the infield and banged into Jorgensen, who in turn took out leader Hansen. Defending race champion Hansen was done for the night. Briggs managed to keep his bike upright and with the other front runners by the wayside, took the win.

The second semi had to be restarted after a spectacular opening lap accident involving Steve Dalgarno (Yam), Ohio rookie Chuck Jordan (Yam) and Tom White (HD). On the restart, Team K&N's Randy Cleek (Yam) took control, followed by a battle between JR Rawls (HD) and Ascot veteran Paul Bostrom (Tri). The two duked it out with Bostrom taking the spot.

Trophy Race

Paul Bostrom and Tom White diced through much of the Trophy Race with Bostrom coming up with the victory.

National

Friday night's big crowd of around 29,000 watched Gary Scott repeat his opening holeshot of 1974. He led the first lap till Kenny Roberts took over. He immediately began stretching his lead. Once in front, the only guy that could beat Kenny Roberts was himself. He now just had to concentrate and avoid making the mistakes that had cost him the victories in the previous years. He had it all together this night, putting on a great show for the fans, tossing the 750 Yamaha around like a lightweight. John Hateley caught Scott in the early laps and took over 2nd after Scott made some miscues. It was short lived however, as Hateley dropped back with mechanical problems. Scott reassumed the runner-up spot for another good TT showing. Hateley's teammate, Mark Williams, moved into 3rd place. Dennis Briggs was very impressive in 4th. The rookie came from the back row with his unconventional Kawasaki, the only two-stroke in the field. Fellow rookie John Gennai was in 5th. Rounding out the top ten were Ron Powell, Mert Lawwill, Jimmy Odom, Rick Hocking and Dave Aldana.

Short Track National

A huge crowd of around 40,000 watched an equally large field of 136 riders shoot for 48 spots. Last year's second place finisher, Dave Hansen, again Honda mounted, was the fastest qualifier at 15.14. Hometown hero Darryl Hurst on his Jon Easton/self-tuned Yamaha was just behind with a 15.17. The 1971 winner Jimmy Odom (Hon) was 3rd. Gary Scott, now more accustomed to the Harley Sprint was 4th. Kenny Roberts (Yam) waved off his first attempt and qualified 21st on the second try. Mike Gerald, minus the factory Honda, riding with an injured shoulder, aboard a Bultaco Astro, qualified a dismal 28th. Diane Cox made history by becoming the first woman to qualify for an AMA Grand National Championship race. She took the 48th and final spot in the program with a respectable 15.69. How respectable? There were nearly 90 riders behind her.

Heats

After Rick Hocking (Yam) was placed on the penalty line on the initial start of Heat 1, Chuck Palmgren (Yam) turned in an impressive flag-to-flag win. Palmgren was still recovering from recent back surgery. Dave Hansen thumped along behind on the XL350-based machine. Hocking put on an impressive ride from the penalty stripe. He charged past John Hateley (Tri) and then zapped Kenny Roberts for 3rd. Roberts and Hateley were semi bound.

Factory Bultaco rider Guy McClure and Georgia rookie Jay Ridgeway (Kaw) jumped the start of Heat 2 and were sent to the penalty line. On the second attempt, local resident Darryl Hurst (Yam) jumped out ahead of the Shell Yamaha of Hank Scott and the Texas crowd went nuts. Denny Palmgren (Yam) looked good in the third and final transfer. That is until McClure and Ridgeway stormed by on the last lap from their penalty line start.

In Heat 3, Dave Aldana (Yam) appeared to leverage Jimmy Odom out of his way on lap 2, with Odom unceremoniously dumped to the dirt. Aldana received a rough riding penalty on the spot, which was surprising revoked after a challenge by Aldana. On the restart, Aldana jumped out front chased by Mark Williams on a very trick B50 "Triumph". New Harley Team member Corky Keener, on a Sprint, managed to just edge Charlie Chapple (Yam) out of the last transfer spot.

Diane Cox (Yam) made her GNC debut in Heat 4. In a royal Houston initiation, Cox was involved in a big crash at the start of the race with Randy Skiver, Randy Scott and Allen Mundt. Cox, along with the others, gamely made the restart. Skiver (Yam) recovered nicely and led the race wire-to-wire. Randy Cleek (Yam) ran 2nd with Texan Jimmy Lee (Yam) taking the last direct transfer of the night. Behind, Alex Jorgenson topped crowd favorite, (at least the large Louisiana throng), Mike Gerald. Gary Scott could manage no better than 7th on his Sprint. Diane Cox was 10th, the last rider running.

Semis

Kenny Roberts battled with heat race rivals Guy McClure and Jay Ridgeway during the early laps of Semi 1. McClure surged ahead as Roberts rode the wheels off his bike to stay ahead of Ridgeway and his Woody Kyle Kawasaki. McClure took the clear victory, but crashed after the finish, injuring his arm. Roberts' 2nd place wasn't good enough and for the first time in his Expert career, failed to start a Houston National race.

Houston youngster David "Bubba" Rush (Bul) surprised the regulars by winning Semi 2. Fellow Texan JR Rawls ran 2nd on his factory PDV for most of the race. Randy Scott moved by Rawls with 2 laps to go along with a disappointed Mike Gerald.

Trophy Race

Kenny Roberts took out his frustrations on not making the National, by obliterating the Trophy Race field. Roberts led wire-to-wire in a spectacular one-man show.

National

With Kenny Roberts out of the picture, the huge crowd's favorites were hometown heroes Darryl Hurst and Bubba Rush. Chuck Palmgren and Dave Hansen led the first starts, but were called back. Hansen was warned not to jump again. It was all Darryl Hurst on the third attempt. Hansen did his best to catch Hurst, but relived the 1974 race: He could close up, but could not get around. It was Hurst's night, as he rode a near perfect race for the 20-lap distance. He thrilled the Texas crowd with a neat victory wheelie. Hansen hung tight for 2nd. Randy Cleek was a solid 3rd for his best finish at the 'Dome. Mark Williams was impressive on his B50 hybrid. His short track finish, combined with his 3rd at the TT put him in the early Camel Pro series point lead. After the race, an ecstatic Darryl Hurst celebrated with his family, crew and thousands of new friends.

Results

Race: 25 Lap TT National
Race Time: 12:13.10

Rank	Rider	Number	Make
1.	Kenny Roberts, Villa Park, Ca	1	Yam
2.	Gary Scott, Springfield, Oh	64	HD
3.	Mark Williams, Springfield, Ore	70	Nor
4.	Dennis Briggs, Tustin, Ca	26R	Kaw
5.	John Gennai, Los Gatos, Ca	20	HD
6.	Ron Powell, Quartz Hill, Ca	31E	Tri
7.	Mert Lawwill, San Francisco, Ca	7	HD
8.	Jimmy Odom, Fremont, Ca	18	Tri
9.	Rick Hocking, Fremont, Ca	13	Yam
10.	Dave Aldana, Santa Ana, Ca	10	HD
11.	Randy Skiver, Everett, Wa	35	Tri
12.	Randy Cleek, Shawnee, Ok	29	Yam
13.	John Hateley, Van Nuys, Ca	98	Nor
14.	Jay Springsteen, Flint, Mi	65X	HD

Race: 12 Lap Trophy Race
Race Time: 5:57.07

Rank	Rider	Number	Make
1.	Paul Bostrom, San Roman, Ca	46	Tri
2.	Tom White, Huntington Beach, Ca	80	HD
3.	Eddie Wirth, Dana Point, Ca	77	HD
4.	Robert E. Lee, Fort Worth, Tx	54	Bul
5.	Greg Sassaman, Macon, Ga	80C	HD
6.	DeWayne Keeter, Ojai, Ca	44	Yam
7.	Chuck Jordan, Powell, Oh	99F	Yam
8.	Jim Rawls, Grand Prairie, Tx	93	HD
9.	Terry Dorsch, Granada Hills, Ca	22	Tri

Race: 20 Lap Short Track National
Race Time: 5:14.72

Rank	Rider	Number	Make
1.	Darryl Hurst, Houston, Tx	34	Yam
2.	Dave Hansen, Hayward, Ca	23	Hon
3.	Randy Cleek, Shawnee, Ok	29	Yam
4.	Mark Williams, Springfield, Ore	70	Tri
5.	Dave Aldana, Santa Ana, Ca	10	Kaw
6.	Rick Hocking, Fremont, Ca	13	Yam
7.	Randy Skiver, Everett, Wa	35	Hon
8.	Hank Scott, Springfield, Oh	14	Yam
9.	Jimmy Lee, Bedford, Tx	57	Yam
10.	Corky Keener, Flint, Mi	62	HD
11.	Chuck Palmgren, Santa Ana, Ca	38	Yam
12.	Bubba Rush, Houston, Tx	41N	Bul
13.	Billy Schaffer, Pine Grove, Pa	96	Yam
14.	Guy McClure, Fort Worth, Tx	50N	Bul

Race: 12 Lap Trophy Race
Race Time: 3:06.85

Rank	Rider	Number	Make
1.	Kenny Roberts, Villa Park, Ca	1	Yam
2.	Alex Jorgensen, Stockton, Ca	62Z	Suz
3.	Jim Rawls, Grand Prairie, Tx	93	PDV
4.	Mike Gerald, Baton Rouge, La	15	Bul
5.	Charlie Brown, Longview, Wa	78	Kaw
6.	Roger Sterling, Mont Belvieu, Tx	30N	Bul
7.	Randy Scott, Philomath, Ore	50	Yam
8.	Jay Ridgeway, Atlanta, Ga	9C	Bul
9.	Frank Gillespie, Hayward, Ca	76	Yam
10.	Gene Romero, San Luis Obispo, Ca	3	Yam

Grand National Points Standings after Rounds 1 & 2

Rank	Rider	Pts
1.	Mark Williams	198
2.	Kenny Roberts	172
3.	Darryl Hurst	165
4.	Gary Scott	132
5.	Dave Hansen	132
6.	Randy Cleek	120
7.	Dennis Briggs	88
8.	Dave Aldana	83
9.	Rick Hocking	77
10.	John Gennai	66

Extra Extra

- Mike Kidd missed the whole weekend because of a broken leg sustained at the Ross Downs (Texas) TT track. John Hateley was riding his machines.
- The Norton/Triumph team's short tracker was a very tweaked BSA B50 based machine. The destroked 350 machines featured numerous one-off bits. Although faced with new bike gremlins, the bikes ran very strong with Mark Williams scoring a 4th in the National.
- For the first time since 1972, a Harley Sprint was back in the short track National. In a one-off ride, Corky Keener finished 10th on a trick lightweight machine out of Powell Hassel's shop.
- Dennis Briggs 4th place finish on his Kawasaki was the best finish in the TT event for a two-stroke.
- Rookie Jay Springsteen made his GNC debut at the TT race taking 3rd in his heat. He had mechanical issues in the main, finishing 14th.
- Guy McClure was given the pay and points for last spot in the short track National though he couldn't start the race. No doubt Kenny Roberts would have volunteered to act as his alternate!
- Yamaha gave Kenny Roberts and crew some early practice time by renting the 'Domes tracks on Thursday before the races.
- Mark Williams, Randy Cleek, Dave Aldana and Rick Hocking made the Nationals both nights.
- Chuck Palmgren was rarin' to go at the 'Dome races after successful back surgery over the winter months relieved some long present pain.
- A Junior invitational termed the Gulf Coast Championship had it's main run on Saturday. Larry Beale Jr. survived a late race run in with fellow Texan Terry Poovey to win a whale of a race.
- Continuing the Astrodome tradition of exhibition races was a speedway match race between USA and European riders. Stars on the US team including Steve Bast, Sammy Nutter and Rick Woods put up a good struggle, but the European stars led by Barry Briggs, Ivan Mauger and Peter Collins came out on top, final score 67 to 45.

Top 10 Houston TT Qualifying Times

1.	Kenny Roberts	Yam	27.35 seconds
2.	Mert Lawwill	HD	27.48
3.	Chuck Palmgren	BSA	27.52
4.	Ron Powell	Tri	27.54
5.	Gary Scott	HD	27.56
6.	John Hateley	Nor	27.58
7.	Skip Aksland	Yam	27.62
8.	Dave Aldana	HD	27.66
9.	Alex Jorgenson	Tri	27.70
10.	Guy McClure	Yam	27.72

Top 10 Houston Short Track Qualifying Times

1.	Dave Hansen	Hon	15.14 seconds
2.	Darryl Hurst	Yam	15.17
3.	Jimmy Odom	Hon	15.21
4.	Gary Scott	HD	15.26
5.	Chuck Palmgren	Yam	15.35
6.	Jay Springsteen	Bul	15.35
7.	Dave Aldana	Kaw	15.35
8.	Randy Cleek	Yam	15.37
9.	Gene Romero	Yam	15.37
10.	Hank Scott	Yam	15.37

GNC Round #3 of 20 **Date:** March 9, 1975 **Type:** Road Race **Venue:** Daytona International Speedway **Location:** Daytona, Florida	**Purse:** $67,000.00 **Surface:** Pavement **Course Length:** 3.84 miles **Laps:** 52 **Distance:** 200 Miles

The 1975 running of the Daytona 200 promised a continuation of Yamaha's domination via an even more powerful version of it's big bore road racer. The new production TZ750 featured increased displacement and power. The newest factory version featured monoshock suspension and was doled out to Yamahas International distributers with Kenny Roberts, Giacomo Agostini, Hirdyuki Kawasaki, and Steve Baker each receiving a machine. Regular U.S. team members Gene Romero and Don Castro received the more conventional machines. If one of the factory bikes failed to finish, any number of private entries including Steve McLaughlin, Ron Pierce, Warren Willing and Jim Dunn among others, were capable of winning.

Suzuki was the only other team with a clear chance of winning. Further development of their engine showed near equal speed to the fastest Yamahas. New for 1975 was a 6-speed transmission and long travel suspension. Team riders were slated to be Barry Sheene, Gary Nixon, Teuvo Lansivuori, and new members Dave Aldana, Hurley Wilvert and Pat Hennen. The one ingredient Suzuki always seemed to lack for victory at Daytona was some good luck. Things were to go no better this year. Barry Sheene was out the week before after a terrifying testing crash. While running nearly flat out on the banking, Sheene had his rear Dunlop tire suddenly blow apart. Sheene was thrown from the bike at over 160 mph. He received numerous broken bones and was lucky to be alive. Holland's Klassen suffered the same fate on the banking and Dunlop pulled its tire from the event, making Goodyear the main tire supplier. Suzuki's other main star Gary Nixon, was still on the mend from serious injuries suffered in a testing session while in Japan the previous year. Fresh out of an arm cast, Nixon struggled, but showed competitive speed in practice. Despite the worries over the teams stars, Wilvert, Lansivuori, Aldana and rookie Hennen each could win the event.

Kawasaki still fielded a talented team. Mainstay Yvon DuHamel was back, joined by Jim Evans, Mick Grant and Takao Abe. The team bikes were now water-cooled, Kawasaki benefiting from the AMA reducing the required number of bikes or engines from 200 to 25 examples. The new engines failed to develop the hoped for power boost. It wasn't for a lack of trying; DuHamel's tuner Steve Johnson burned the midnight oil. DuHamel and Evans tried so hard they both took trips to the infield hospital after practice crashes. DuHamel would continue; Evans was out with a broken collarbone.

While passing without much fanfare, this marked the first time in GNC history there was not a major factory four-stroke effort. While Harley-Davidson would continue to occasionally field it's XRTT in the future, it was at shorter courses like Loudon and Laguna Seca. Honda continued to sit on the sidelines. There were no British teams present. It was hard to think of the 165 mph Beezumphs as slow. Butler & Smith did turn out again with their trick BMWs with Reg Pridmore and Kurt Liebmann aboard. Their noble effort put the only two four-strokes in the field.

Time Trials

Grand National Champion Kenny Roberts was clearly the fastest rider in practice and set a NTR of 111.08 mph in qualifying. Flying the Suzuki flag high was Teuvo Lansivuori turning in second quick time of 109.77, but was way off Roberts' speed. The big surprise was John Cecotto in 3rd at 109.09 on a standard TZ700. Unknown in the U.S., the 19-year old Venezuelan was a star in South America. Gene Romero ran a 108.71, Steve Baker on the Yamaha of Canada monoshocker a 108.30. Ron Pierce (Yam) was the first privateer at 107.80. Steve McLaughlin had picked up a Larry Worrell-prepped TZ700 just before the 200. Pat Hennen, the top pavement Junior in 1974, ran a 107.40. Last year's winner, Giacomo Agostini, ran a "slow" 107.30. Rounding out the top 10 was Kawasaki pilot Takao Abe.

Gary Nixon was just coming up to speed when the stress of riding caused the plates holding his arm together separated. The gritty champion decided to qualify anyway, coming in 28th fastest. In a tough decision, Nixon had to face the fact that he was in no condition to last 200 miles. The fast Erv Kanemoto tuned-Suzuki would sit the rest of the week.

National

Teuvo Lansivuori, fighting for his own and Suzuki's battered honor, blasted to an immediate lead in front of 67,000 plus spectators. Crowd favorite Kenny Roberts gave chase, followed by, Giacomo Agostini, Gene Romero, Steve McLaughlin, Steve Baker and Yvon Duhamel. Johnny Cecotto was left sitting in last spot as his crew hastily repaired a fluid leak. He left the line in 73rd position in hot pursuit of the pack. Amazingly, in just 3 laps, he is up to 26th place! DuHamel is quickly out when the shift shaft breaks on his Kawasaki. Roberts sets a punishing pace and by the 4th lap catches and passes Lansivuori. By lap 10, Cecotto is in 10th place; Two laps later, he is in 7th. Roberts sets a torrid pace once in front and leads by a huge margin in just a handful of laps. Behind him Agostini fades back in the pack with Romero, McLaughlin and Baker swapping positions. Disaster strikes for Roberts, who pits way too early on lap 15. He is the victim of a broken clutch hub and is done for the day. Romero pits for his fuel and is away with no trouble. Romero's day nearly ends shortly after as well. While negotiating a fast infield turn, his Yamaha begins to tie up. Romero alertly pulls in the clutch; sure he's done, when almost as an afterthought, he pops the clutch. The engine refires, never missing a beat the rest of the day. At this point Lansivuori heads to the pits, needing fuel and with a very loose chain. The crew misses the chain and the Finnish rider pits again, all the while dropping positions. When he returned to the race he pressed very hard to make up distance. The talented Finn finally pushed a little too much and dropped his bike in one of the infield corners and was done for the day. Dark horse privateer McLaughlin has a great stop and is now leading the event. Romero is on the charge, working past Agostini and the Baker into 2nd. Moving past the halfway mark and Romero begins seriously reeling in young front runner. McLaughlin knows Romero is coming and makes his only slip of the day exiting the infield onto the banking. He drops his bike in nearly the same spot as Gary Nixon had the year before. McLaughlin scrambles to the bike and gets going, but not before falling to 7th spot. Romero has big lead over Baker, even after his last pit stop. With just a few laps to go, Cecotto passes Agostini to secure the podium spot. Romero who was never given his due as a world-class racer, despite two runner-up Daytona finishes in 1970 and '71, crossed the stripe with a comfortable margin to take a well deserved win. He set a new race record of 106.451 mph.

Results

Race: 200 Road Race National
Race Time: 1:52:32.88, (106.451 MPH) New Record

Rank	Rider	Number	Make
1.	Gene Romero, San Luis Obispo, Ca	3	Yam
2.	Steve Baker, Bellingham, Wa	32	Yam
3.	Johnny Cecotto, Caracas, Venezuela,	96	Yam
4.	Giacomo Agostini, Bergamo, Italy	4	Yam
5.	Warren Willing, Dundas, Australia	85	Yam
6.	Steve McLaughlin, Duarte, Ca	83	Yam
7.	Hirdyuki Kawasaki, Nagoya, Japan	61	Yam
8.	Ron Pierce, Bakersfield, Ca	97	Yam
9.	Don Castro, Gilroy, Ca	11	Yam
10.	Harry Cone, Sherman, Tx	82	Yam
11.	Tommy Byars, Beaumont, Tx	13	Yam
12.	James Allen, Racine, Que., Can	16	Yam
13.	Larry Bleil, DelRay Beach, Fl	71	Yam
14.	Cliff Carr, Irvine, Ca	26	Yam
15.	Len Fitch, Woodslee, Ont., Can	62	Yam
16.	Roger Marshall, Halifax, England	91	Yam
17.	Jim Dunn, Everett, Wa	75	HD
18.	Phil Gurner, Dinnington, Eng	46	Yam
19.	Billy Labrie, St. Petersburg, Fl	65	Yam
20.	Marcel Ankone, Oldenzaal, Holland	28	Suz

Grand National Points Standings after Round 3

Rank	Rider	Pts
1.	Mark Williams	198
2.	Gene Romero	195
3.	Kenny Roberts	172
4.	Darryl Hurst	165
5.	Steve Baker	156
6.	Gary Scott	132
7.	Dave Hansen	132
8.	Steve McLaughlin	130
9.	Randy Cleek	120
10.	Ron Pierce	104

Extra Extra

- Gene Romero had a great day, taking home $17,485.00 from the Camel Pro purse.
- Romero had complained bitterly about not receiving one of the latest monoshock machines. Turns out he didn't need it anyway!
- Kel Carruthers tuned both Kenny Roberts and Gene Romero's winning machine.
- Yamaha dominated the event, taking 19 of the first 20 spots.
- Some of the day's happenings were very reminiscent of past Daytona events. John Cecotto's amazing run from 73rd to the podium was very reminiscent of Dick Mann's 1973 run from 62nd to 4th. Gene Romero's mid-race seizure also happened to 1972 winner Don Emde. Teuvo Lansivuori's early race sprint was similar to Giacomo Agostini's of last year. Unfortunately for Yvon DuHamel, he had transmission trouble too similar to 1974.
- Speaking of Dick Mann, it was strange not to see the two-time winner present. Same for Paul Smart and Mark Brelsford.
- The clutch trouble Kenny Roberts suffered seemed a common problem for Team Yamaha. Trouble was detected during race day practice and all bikes received clutch attention. Giacomo Agostini's bike was reportedly slowing through the race with clutch issues, as was Romero's at race end.
- Running lap times at least equal to his qualifying laps, Roberts began lapping the field in 6 laps.
- Roberts did capture the Lightweight event with Gary Scott scoring a runner-up on Harley-Davidson's new RR250 racer.
- Don Castro had visor problems, making it difficult for him to see well during much of the race. He still managed to finish in 9th place.
- Steve Baker's Yamaha of Canada had several broken cylinder studs that were repaired just in time for the 200 miler.
- Steve McLaughlin rode for the "Hole in the Wall" team from Mississippi.
- The crack-prone Yamaha flat pipes from the previous year had been largely replaced by a Kel Carruthers design that routed 3 pipes underneath the motor and one high in the frame.
- Japanese racer Hirdyuki Kawasaki rode a factory Yamaha to 7th place, tuned by a gentleman named Suzuki. Whew!
- Suzuki's change to long travel suspension seemed to work well handling-wise. Unfortunately it caused problems keeping proper drive chain tension. This would surely played a part in Teuvo Lansivuori's problems.
- Adding to Suzuki's horrible week, Pat Hennen dropped out with chain woes and Hurley Wilvert had his engine tie up. The only team rider to finish, Dave Aldana, had a scoring snafu. According to most accounts, Aldana was running in the top ten at the finish. Aldana turned off the track as soon as he passed the stripe. He had been doused with gasoline on a pit stop and sought quick relief. This may have led to scorer's confusion. By the time the team realized there was a problem, it was too late to protest. He was credited with 27th place. Marcel Ankone was ranked the first Suzuki home in 20th.

- Aldana wowed everyone present with his Open Production (pre-Superbike) win. He tossed a heavyweight Kawasaki around like a TT bike.
- Gary Nixon's idle Suzuki was the cause for much pit gossip. Everyone from Gary Fisher to Gary Scott was rumored to take over the controls. The bike stayed put in the pits.
- Takae Abe was the only Kawasaki in the top 10 in qualifying. Yvon DuHamel was 17th, Mick Grant, 26th. Things only got worse in the race; no team bikes finished. The highest Green Machine home was Barry Ditchburn in 41st.
- Reg Pridmore soldiered home 31st on his BMW. There were a lot of two-strokes behind him!
- The much-publicized claiming of Giacomo Agostini's Yamaha after last year's event caused much consternation by the big teams. Yamaha's exotic monoshock TZ's carried a high price tag. Not surprisingly, the claiming rule was conveniently dropped before the race and was not renewed.
- Dirt tracker Mark Williams managed to stay atop the GNC points by a narrow 3 points over Daytona winner Romero, who scored no points at Houston.

Bonus!
Top 20 Daytona 200 Qualifying Speeds

1.		Kenny Roberts	Yam	111.08 MPH
2.		Teuvo Lansivuori	Suz	109.77
3.		John Cecotto	Yam	109.09
4.		Gene Romero	Yam	108.71
5.		Steve Baker	Yam	108.30
6.		Ron Pierce	Yam	107.80
7.		Steve McLaughlin	Yam	107.80
8.		Pat Hennen	Suz	107.40
9.		Giacomo Agostini	Yam	107.30
10.		Takao Abe	Kaw	106.80
11.		Don Castro	Yam	106.70
12.		Warren Willing	Yam	106.50
13.		Randy Cleek	Yam	106.40
14.		Hirdyuki Kawasaki	Yam	106.30
15.		Hurley Wilvert	Suz	106.20
16.		Dave Aldana	Suz	106.20
17.		Yvon DuHamel	Kaw	106.10
18.		Wes Cooley Jr.	Yam	105.80
19.		Patrick Pons	Yam	105.80
20.		Tommy Byars	Yam	105.10

1975 Dallas Short Track
Roberts Jets Back for Dallas Win
Takes Points Lead

GNC Round #4 of 20 **Date:** April 12, 1975 **Type:** Short Track **Venue:** Texas Stadium **Location:** Irving, Tx	**Purse:** $14,000.00 **Surface:** Dirt **Course Length:** ¼ Mile **Laps:** 20

GNC champ Kenny Roberts overcame jet lag and rough track conditions to win the inaugural Dallas Short Track event. Roberts, suffering from overseas blahs and an injured thumb from the Imola road race, led the rough and tumble short track wire to wire. It was Roberts' 2nd win of the year and 12th of his career. The win put Roberts in charge of the Camel Pro points standings. Mild-mannered in appearance only, Randy Cleek hammered through the pack to grab second spot in the National. Hank Scott lost 2nd to Cleek before midway, hanging onto third for the rest of the event.

Pace Management thought that if one Texas stadium race was good, two might be better. One of the big differences though was the venue; differing from the Astrodome, the Dallas Unidome didn't have a full dome. This allowed the rain preceding the event to wreak havoc with Harold Murrell's track prep. While he managed to dry up the rain with truckloads of material, the result was a rough, lumpy mess. Fast times were only had by hanging on and trying to pick a way through the bumps.

Kenny Roberts' win put him atop the Camel Pro points for the first time with a 322 total. Runner-up in the race, Randy Cleek moved into second with 240 points. Despite a credible 9th in the National, early points leader Mark Williams dropped back to third at 218 points. Daytona winner Gene Romero slipped back to fourth. Dave Hansen finished 6th in the National, moving to fifth in points.

Time Trials

Dave Hansen set fast time on the Champion XL350 Honda at 13.696. Hot rookie Jay Springsteen (Bul) was 2nd at 13.766 and Phil McDonald (Yam) in 3rd with a 13.799. Kenny Roberts (Yam) made the show but was way back in 30th spot.

Heats

Heat 1 had Dave Hansen thump his way to the win in the fastest heat of the night. Hank Scott on the Shell Yamaha, had a classic high/low race long battle with NVT factory rider Mark Williams over 2nd spot. Scott stayed down on the pole to take the position.

Randy Cleek, on the K&N Yamaha controlled most of Heat 2, pursued early on by Vista Sheen's Jay Springsteen and Team Bultaco's Guy McClure. Kenny Roberts was coming from the back row, blasting though the front runners to grab 2nd place. Roberts nipped Cleek at the flag in a last lap charge.

Gary Scott's ancient Team Harley Sprint proved it was still relevant, topping all the trick, modern machines in Heat 3. Home state rider JR Rawls tickled the crowd by taking 2nd aboard a PDV factory machine. John Gennai (Bul) fought his way out of a battling pack of riders for the final transfer.

Tough Rick Hocking on the Rocky Cycle Yamaha, took control of the final heat. Hocking appeared to have the race wired till a determined Mike Caves (Bul), ran him down. He took the lead late in the goings. John Hateley was 3rd on another factory Triumph.

Semis

With just one rider making the National from each semi, competition on the tight oval was fierce. Guy McClure led every lap of Semi 1, but had to fend off Floridian Billy Labrie's Alco Motors Yamaha the whole race.

Danny Hockie (Kaw) led the early stages of the second semi, before Randy Skiver worked by on his Honda. A crash involving front runners Jimmy Lee and Pat McCaul caused a red flag and the race was called complete.

Trophy Race

Billy Labrie would not be denied in the Trophy Race, taking control early and leading Rob Morrison (Tri) and Danny Cartwright (Bul) home.

National

Kenny Roberts pulled the holeshot into turn 1. Those up front early included Randy Cleek, Gary and Hank Scott, and Dave Hansen. Lines run around the small oval were as numerous as the brands competing. Much position swapping and wheel-to-wheel racing ensued. Hank Scott took over 2nd spot with brother Gary was sliding backwards through the pack. Guy McClure was headed the other direction; from back row start into the lead pack in just a handful of laps. Rick Hocking made a similar charge. The top order around laps 6-7 now read, Roberts, Hank Scott, Cleek, and Hocking, with McClure closing. Cleek soon put a move on Scott for 2nd with the two rubbing elbows and Cleek forcing his way ahead. On lap 12, Hocking was out with engine trouble. This moved McClure moved into 4th, followed by John Hateley and Dave Hansen. Jay Springsteen was applying pressure to this group when he low sided in the middle of the first corners. He was up and away, but lost a lot of positions. Roberts was way ahead up front and with 5 laps to go the top spots were nailed down as Roberts, Cleek, Scott, McClure, Hateley, and Hansen. Roberts bobbled some, allowing Cleek to close up a little, but he still had a good margin at the flag.

Results

Race: 20 Lap Short Track National
Race Time: 4:46.06

Rank	Rider	Number	Make
1.	Kenny Roberts, Villa Park, Ca	1	Yam
2.	Randy Cleek, Shawnee, Ok	29	Yam
3.	Hank Scott, Springfield, Oh	14	Yam
4.	Guy McClure, Fort Worth, Tx	50N	Bul
5.	John Hateley, Van Nuys, Ca	98	Tri
6.	Dave Hansen, Hayward, Ca	23	Hon
7.	Jim Rawls, Grand Prairie, Tx	93	PDV
8.	John Gennai, Los Gatos, Ca	20	Bul
9.	Mark Williams, Springfield, Ore	70	Tri
10.	Randy Skiver, Everett, Wa	35	Hon
11.	Mike Caves, Galesburg, Ill	28	Bul
12.	Jay Springsteen, Flint, Mi	65X	Bul
13.	Gary Scott, Springfield, Oh	64	HD
14.	Rick Hocking, Fremont, Ca	13	Yam

Race: Trophy Race

Rank	Rider	Number	Make
1.	Billy Labrie, St. Petersburg, Fl	65	Yam
2.	Rob Morrison, Mission Hills, Ca	25	Tri
3.	Danny Cartwright, Tulsa, Ok	64G	Bul
4.	Chuck Palmgren, Santa Ana, Ca	38	Yam
5.	Teddy Poovey, Garland, Tx	94	PDV
6.	Gene Romero, San Luis Obispo, Ca	3	Yam
7.	Phil McDonald, Tulsa, Ok	58	Yam
8.	Mike Eades, Petersburg, Va	6S	Yam
9.	Danny Hockie, Harbor City, Ca	84	Kaw
10.	Ken Springsteen, Flint, Mi	76X	Bul

Grand National Points Standings after Round 4

Rank	Rider	Pts
1.	Kenny Roberts	322
2.	Randy Cleek	240
3.	Mark Williams	218
4.	Gene Romero	196
5.	Dave Hansen	182
6.	Darryl Hurst	165
7.	Steve Baker	156
8.	Gary Scott	140
9.	Hank Scott	133
10.	Steve McLaughlin	130

Extra Extra

- Three-time GNC short track winner Mike Gerald, riding with an injured shoulder, failed to qualify for the National.
- Randy Cleek and Phil McDonald, like Kenny Roberts, had also competed at Imola. McDonald qualified well and placed 7th in the Trophy Race.
- JR Rawl's 7th place on his factory PDV was the highest GNC finish for the fledgling company.
- Ted Boody won a Junior program that was run Friday before the National. Boody's Montesa featured lay down rear shocks that may have helped him cope with atrocious track conditions.
- Mike Kidd was released from the NVT Team due to his pre-Houston leg injuries. John Hateley would stay with the team in his place.
- Texas Stadium was built in 1971 to replace the Cotton Bowl as the home for the Dallas Cowboys. It was actually built in the city of Irving, Texas. The stadium was originally going to have a retracting roof, but the design was changed to have a stationary roof to cover most seats, but the playing field was left open to the elements. The facility originally had seating for 65,000. In addition to being home to the Cowboys, the stadium was also a frequent site for college and high schools football games, soccer games, wrestling tournaments and numerous concerts. The AMA GNC raced at the facility in 1975 and '76, not drawing the hoped for crowds. Though successful through the years, the aging stadium was replaced as the home for the Cowboys in 2009 by the new Cowboys Stadium. Texas Stadium was destroyed in 2010 by a planned implosion. It is currently used as a storage site by the Texas Department of Transportation.

GNC Round #5 of 20
Date: May 18, 1975
Type: Mile
Venue: Santa Clara Fairgrounds
Location: San Jose, Ca

Purse: $16,000.00
Surface: Dirt
Course Length: 1 Mile
Laps: 25
Distance: 25 Miles

The first big-bike race of the season always had its share of surprises. New teams, machines, riders and long winters prying more horsepower to beat the other guy all figured into the equation. At the spring San Jose Mile, the surprise was bigger than usual. To say that rookie Greg Sassaman was an unknown talent, especially in California, would be an understatement. The young Georgia rider had a successful Novice and Junior career, but had the crowd, and a lot of pit road, digging through their programs. The fact that he was aboard a Nick Deligianis/Carroll Resweber-tuned factory Harley-Davidson didn't hurt his chances, but Sassaman turned in a great ride, topping the Harley teams best hope for the title, Gary Scott. Scott controlled the early stages of the event, swapping the lead with Sassaman till being forced to settle for the runner-up slot late in the race. Rex Beauchamp took the final podium spot after a race long duel with perennial San Jose favorite Mert Lawwill. After a couple of seasons with a horsepower edge on the miles, the rest of Team Harley had at least pulled even with dynamometer guru Lawwill. GNC champ Kenny Roberts ran hard all day, ending up in 4th. Despite a new engine from legendary Tim Withman, Roberts was obviously underpowered. The other big surprise at San Jose was the strong run of Scott Brelsford aboard the Erv Kanemoto Kawasaki triple two-stroke. The former Harley team rider took delight in the excess horsepower. The bike was handling well and only minor trouble in the National prevented a top placing.

Kenny Roberts' run in 5th boosted his Camel Pro points lead. Gary Scott's runner-up finish shot him from barely in the top 10 to second in points. Mark Williams finished 8th on the day and maintained third in the standings. Gene Romero ran 7th in the National to hold onto fourth. Randy Cleek did not make the main and fell from second in points to fifth. Dave Hansen slipped back a spot to sixth. Greg Sassaman's big win moved him from nowhere to seventh. Darryl Hurst and Steve Baker were eighth and ninth. Mert Lawwill's 4th in the race moved him into the top ten.

Time Trials

The Team Harley quest for horsepower dominated the top spots at San Jose. Rex Beauchamp, aboard the Babe DeMay tuned XR750, was fastest at 39.19. Mert Lawwill was very close with a 39.23. Greg Sassaman raised the first few eyeballs with a 39.24. A pleasant surprise in the next slot was Triumph mounted rookie Walt Foster on the Tony Denius owned machine.

Heats

Rex Beauchamp thoroughly outgunned the competition in Heat 1. His only competition was Hank Scott, but the fast Shell Motors Yamaha dropped out with mechanical trouble. With Scott's departure, Beauchamp won in a runaway. Behind, Frank Gillespie won the battle over 2nd place over Dave Aldana and Tom White. That's how they finished and all were Harley mounted. Long-time parallel twins faithful Gillespie (Triumph and Yamaha) and Aldana (anything British), had finally given into the Harley-Davidson tide. The former was on a Dud Perkins supported ride, the latter on his own, with a little help from Nick Deligianis and friends.

John Sperry took the early lead in Heat 2, but stepped off on lap 2. Mert Lawwill took the point position and proceeded to pull away from the field. Scott Brelsford's screaming Kawasaki got everybody's attention as he blasted through the field to nail down 2nd. Veteran Yamaha riders Terry Dorsch and Jimmy Odom followed Lawwill and Brelsford into the National.

Kenny Roberts pulled the holeshot in Heat 3 and tried his best to pull away. Greg Sassaman's Harley was a rocket and within 3 circuits had caught and passed the champ. Behind, Harley mounted John Gennai and JR Rawls battled fiercely with Gennai just taking third at the flag.

Gary Scott completed Team Harley's domination of the heats, winning the last race comfortably. Rookie Jay Springsteen ran just behind Scott early before low sliding in Turn 4. Finishing in 2nd spot was Walt Foster, making believers out of those who thought the clocks might have been quick on his Triumph's qualifying run. Mark Williams, on a factory Norton took 3rd place, with teammate John Hateley barely edging out Team Harleys Corky Keener at the flag for 4th.

Semis

Classic mile racing was seen throughout both hard fought semi races, which advanced only the top two riders. Rick Hocking, on the A&A Racing Yamaha, took the first semi just edging a swapfest that included Pat McCaul on a backup Ron Wood Norton, and Harley riders Eddie Wirth and Bruce Hanlon.

One of the best races of the day was Semi 2. Daryl Hurst (Yam) was the early leader, but was soon swallowed up by a snarling pack that included rookies Skip Aksland (Yam) and Ken Springsteen (HD), Corky Keener, JR Rawls and Don Castro on the other Kanemoto Kawasaki. The group thrilled the crowd with passing all over the big oval. The wildest ride was from Rawls, who would run deep and high through turns, only to be swallowed up by the fastest bikes of Aksland and Keener coming out of the turns. In the end, Kenny Roberts' protégé Aksland took the win with Keener in 2nd.

Trophy Race

Semi survivors had one more shot at glory in the Trophy Race. Great racing continued as JR Rawls led early, but was quickly caught by a big pack, headed sometimes by Ken Springsteen, Bruce Hanlon and Eddie Wirth. Position swapping was the norm rather than exception, with the crowd on its feet and the outcome in doubt. On lap 3, Daryl Hurst blasted through the pack to grab the lead. He and Hanlon developed as the front runners and swapped the lead constantly as did the mob behind them. Hanlon topped Houston winner Hurst on the last round in a thriller.

National

Gary Scott pulled the holeshot over the three-row, 20 rider field. Kenny Roberts, Mert Lawwill, Rex Beauchamp, Greg Sassaman and Scott Brelsford gave the closest chase. Over the first couple of laps, the pack rearranged itself with Sassaman moving up to 3rd, with Beauchamp with Brelsford right behind. Roberts was the loser in all this and slid back to 6th. Walt Foster had a huge getoff on lap 3 in the last corner, suffering possible hand/arm/shoulder injuries. His bike was destroyed. Up front, Sassaman reeled Scott in as Brelsford trailed a short distance behind. Beauchamp was also on the move, passing Lawwill and challenging Brelsford for 3rd spot. Suddenly, Brelsford's Kawasaki was out; a loose air cleaner had allowed one cylinder to suck in dirt and the triple was out. Sassaman made his move on lap 8, taking the lead for the first time. Sassaman had an edge in power and controlled the straights. Veteran Scott dove hard into the corners to make up time and pressure the rookie. Though repeated lap after lap, Sassaman was up to the challenge and began to edge ahead around lap 18. The leaders pulled a huge lead on the rest of the pack. Next back was Beauchamp who was dealing with a persistent Lawwill, who had caught back up after Beresford's departure. Further back, a battle raged between Kenny Roberts, Frank Gillespie, Gene Romero, Dave Aldana, Corky Keener, Skip Aksland and Mark Williams. This was the best racing in the National. Positions were swapped constantly in a great "hide the number plates" dicing. Roberts managed to clear the pack to take 5th position. As the laps ticked down, Sassaman's stretched to a big lead over Scott, with Beauchamp closing. Lawwill was lucky to salvage 4th as his XR went on one cylinder on the last lap. The rest of the top ten was Roberts, Gillespie, Romero, Williams, Aksland, and Keener.

Race: 25 Lap Mile National
Race Time: 16:33.37

Rank	Rider	Number	Make
1.	Greg Sassaman, Macon, Ga	80C	HD
2.	Gary Scott, Springfield, Oh	64	HD
3.	Rex Beauchamp, Drayton Plains, Mi	31	HD
4.	Mert Lawwill, San Francisco, Ca	7	HD
5.	Kenny Roberts, Villa Park, Ca	1	Yam
6.	Frank Gillespie, Hayward, Ca	76	HD
7.	Gene Romero, San Luis Obispo, Ca	3	Yam
8.	Mark Williams, Springfield, Ore	70	Nor
9.	Skip Aksland, Manteca, Ca	72Y	Yam
10.	Corky Keener, Flint, Mi	62	HD
11.	Dave Aldana, Santa Ana, Ca	10	HD
12.	Rick Hocking, Fremont, Ca	13	Yam
13.	Pat McCaul, San Jose, Ca	48	Tri
14.	Tom White, Huntington Beach, Ca	80	HD
15.	Terry Dorsch, Granada Hills, Ca	22	Yam
16.	John Hateley, Van Nuys, Ca	98	Nor
17.	John Gennai, Los Gatos, Ca	20	HD
18.	Scott Brelsford, Foster City, Ca	19	Kaw
19.	Walt Foster, Colton, Ca	57R	Tri
20.	Jimmy Odom, Fremont, Ca	18	Yam

Race: Trophy Race

Rank	Rider	Number	Make
1.	Bruce Hanlon, Redwood City, Ca	78Z	HD
2.	Darryl Hurst, Houston, Tx	34	Yam
3.	Ken Springsteen, Flint, Mi	76X	HD
4.	Eddie Wirth, Dana Point, Ca	77	HD
5.	Randy Cleek, Shawnee, Ok	29	Yam
6.	Jim Rawls, Grand Prairie, Tx	93	HD
7.	Mike Myers, Crestline, Ca	84R	HD
8.	Rob Morrison, Perris, Ca	25	Nor
9.	Diane Cox, Salem, Ore	66Q	Tri
10.	Dick Wascher, Seattle, Wa	86	Tri
11.	Charlie Brown, Longview, Wa	78	Yam
12.	Bob Sanders, Whittier, Ca	5R	Tri

Grand National Points Standings after Round 5

Rank	Rider	Pts
1.	Kenny Roberts	388
2.	Gary Scott	272
3.	Mark Williams	251
4.	Gene Romero	240
5.	Randy Cleek	240
6.	Dave Hansen	182
7.	Greg Sassaman	167
8.	Darryl Hurst	165
9.	Steve Baker	156
10.	Mert Lawwill	132

Extra Extra

- A big 9000+ crowd proved it was probably a safe bet to have a second San Jose Mile later in the year.
- Greg Sassaman became the first Georgia rider to win a GNC.
- Sassaman took home around $5000.00.
- Nick Deligianis and Carroll Resweber were reportedly getting 88 horsepower out of Sassaman's Harley.
- The top four were all on factory Harleys.
- Jim Odom was left sitting on the sidelines when his Yamaha failed to fire for the National.
- Rick Hocking rode to 12th place in the National despite a seriously twisted ankle sustained at a previous Ascot half-mile incident.
- Diane Cox made her mile racing debut. She qualified 42nd, advanced through the program, ending up 9th in the Trophy Race.
- The dangerous inside fencing at San Jose had been torn down, helping to improve safety. In 1972, Jim Rice had banged off the railing, breaking his shoulder on his way to winning the National.
- Chuck Palmgren tried a monstrous looking 5:10 X 16 Pirelli Universal on the back of the Gurney Yamaha. He was fast in practice, but results were inconclusive when bike problems struck.
- 1972 Grand National Champion Mark Brelsford, Malcolm Smith and Bruce Brown were interested spectators at San Jose.
- Mechanical attrition is often a problem on the mile, particularly so on this day. Some of the many who experienced trouble before racing even started included the aforementioned Palmgren, Hank Scott, Alex Jorgensen, Charlie Seale, Randy Scott, Eddie Mulder, Corky Keener and Pat McCaul. Keener switched to a spare Bart Markel ride with McCaul, as mentioned, on the Ron Wood Norton.
- Corky Keener and Bart Markel parted ways after San Jose, with Keener in line for more factory Harley help.
- Popular California rider DeWayne Keeter was fatally injured at Ascot Park on May 1, 1975. In the accident, another rider fell, and with nowhere to go, Keeter hit his bike. Keeter won numerous main events at Ascot, on a wide variety of motorcycles. He was a top ten GNC competitor, always a threat when the circuit came to his home state of California. His best National finish was a runner-up at the 1968 Ascot Half-Mile National. The soft-spoken Keeter was 29-years old.

1975 Louisville Half-Mile
Rookie Jay Springsteen Scores at Louisville!

GNC Round #6 of 20 **Date:** June 7, 1975 **Type:** Half-Mile **Venue:** Louisville Downs **Location:** Louisville, Ky	**Purse:** $16,000.00 **Surface:** Limestone **Course Length:** ½ Mile **Laps:** 20 **Distance:** 10 Miles

Rookie sensation Jay Springsteen wowed the crowd at the packed Louisville Downs facility. He was unstoppable in the National and became the youngest racer ever racer to win an AMA Grand National race; he was just barely past his 18th birthday. Though Springsteen held great promise, the early season Nationals didn't give a chance for him to showcase his talent. He was further overshadowed by fellow rookie Greg Sassaman, who won the San Jose Mile, while Jay fell off in a sure transfer spot. Springsteen grew up on east coast cushion half-miles and this race showcased his blazing speed. If ever there was a pure natural dirt track talent, Jay was it. He was sponsored by Vista Sheen, a T-shirt printing company, riding a fast Jimmy Clarke-tuned Harley-Davidson. Last year's winner, Corky Keener, ran a distant second, just keeping the fast teenage Springsteen in sight. Gary Scott came in third and had to put in overtime to do it; He came from the back of the National after transferring via the semi. Bad starts hampered Scott all night.

Kenny Roberts did not have a good night, making the National but eventually suffering a DNF. This allowed Gary Scott to really tighten up the Camel Pro points race, just 15 points behind: 397 to Roberts 382. Mark Williams scored just a single point on the night, but hung onto third in the standings. Randy Cleek won the Trophy Race, giving him enough points to move past Gene Romero for fourth. Greg Sassaman had a good run in the National, moving up a spot to sixth. Making his first appearance in the top 10 was Hank Scott in seventh via a 5th place run in the race. Dave Hansen did not figure in the results and dropped back to eighth. New to the top 10 were National winner Jay Springsteen and Michigan buddy Corky Keener.

Time Trials
Gary Scott, aboard the Bill Werner-tuned factory Harley, stopped the lights the quickest at 26.096. Jay Springsteen and Rex Beauchamp rounded out the top 3.

Heats
Hank Scott (Yam) and veteran Jimmy Maness (HD) led the pack at the beginning of Heat 1. Corky Keener had a mediocre start, but came ripping through the field "high wide and handsome" to knock Scott out of the top position. Gary Scott had gotten an even worse start after getting snookered by the starter, and the fast qualifier was really struggling. Three-time Louisville winner Dave Sehl (HD) knocked Hank Scott back another spot. At the finish, rooster-tailing Keener was way out front, followed by Sehl, Hank Scott and 4th place and semi-bound Gary Scott.

Foreshadowing later action, Jay Springsteen flat checked-out in Heat 2, scorching to the fastest heat of the night. He left veterans, Jimmy Zeigler on the Edgar Fuhr-tuned Harley to battle with Chuck Palmgren's Gurney AAR Yamaha and the fast Larry Mohan-wrenched Triumph of Billy Eves. Zeigler found a fast line to a solid 2nd, as Eves and Palmgren dueled. Eves ran low with Palmgren up wailing on the cushion. Eves managed to just edge by at the flag for the transfer.

Heat 3 was another Harley runaway, this time with Rex Beauchamp up on his Babe DeMay-prepped ride. Greg Sassaman got a terrible start, then wowed the crowd using all of the factory power his XR750 had by blitzing through the field. Literally riding the wheels off of his bike, Sassaman came from last to 2nd at the flag. Paul Pressgrove (HD) was 3rd, headed to his first National, just nosing out veteran Eddie Wirth (HD).

GNC champ Kenny Roberts had his Yamaha up front in Heat 4, trying his best to run away from the field. Yet another fast rookie, this time Texan Bubba Rush (HD) had other ideas and moved past Roberts at midway. Taking the last "regular" transfer was Steve Droste (HD).

Semis

Chuck Palmgren survived some serious challenges to earn the first semi ticket to the National. Steve Morehead ran down leader Palmgren after the first few laps, but spun out the Bill Kennedy Triumph shortly after taking the lead. Palmgren next faced Ken Springsteen, Jay's older brother. Palmgren was about to be outpowered again, but the savvy veteran managed to shunt the rookie's charge on the last lap.

Leaving no doubt of his intentions, Gary Scott put the hammer down in Semi 2 and motored away for the win. Business-like Scott was not interested in a show for the fans, just a National ticket. The entertainment was behind Gary, as Randy Cleek, aboard Bart Markel's Harley-Davidson, argued with several riders, including cushion specialist Teddy Newton (HD). The two moved ahead of the pack, with Newton just managing to edge Cleek.

Trophy Race

Teddy Newton was up front early, doing his best to grab some glory in the Trophy Race. Randy Cleek, who was getting the hang of his first XR750 ride, had other ideas. He caught Newton late in the race and led to the finish. Keith Ulicki (HD) was 3rd.

National

Jay Springsteen shot from his outside pole position to lead the pack into Turn 1. His small advantage became a big one as he rocketed away from the field on the back straight. Everybody else struggled to keep him in sight. Dave Sehl was 2nd with Corky Keener hot on his heels. Rex Beauchamp was with the lead pack till his bike dropped a cylinder. Bubba Rush's XR developed a problem and he was out. Gary Scott had again been stymied at the start and was momentarily stuck mid-pack. Greg Sassaman repeated his last man on the line start like his heat race. Keener soon passed Sehl for the runner-up position, with Gary Scott rapidly closing. As the race neared midway, Springsteen was way out in front with Keener trying to close. Scott moved by Sehl for 3rd spot. Further back, Kenny Roberts was still working the cushion, trying to advance past a group that contained Steve Droste, Billy Eves and a closing Sassaman. Roberts was out when his bike broke its rear axle. As the laps wound down, Keener's bid to catch Springsteen came up short, as did Scott's run on Keener. Sehl was a solid 4th, with Hank Scott moving past Steve Droste. A fired up Sassaman also dropped Droste a spot, ending his run in 6th from 14th spot. A big celebration, led by Team Vista Sheen's owner Rich Gawthrop surely began as Springsteen crossed the line at 20 laps followed by Keener, Gary Scott, Sehl, Hank Scott, (first non-Harley rider), Sassaman, Droste, Eves, Beauchamp and Chuck Palmgren.

Results

Race: 20 Lap Half-Mile National
Race Time: 8:40.588

Rank	Rider	Number	Make
1.	Jay Springsteen, Flint, Mi	65X	HD
2.	Corky Keener, Flint, Mi	62	HD
3.	Gary Scott, Springfield, Oh	64	HD
4.	Dave Sehl, Waterdown, Ont., Can	16	HD
5.	Hank Scott, Springfield, Oh	14	Yam
6.	Greg Sassaman, Macon, Ga	80C	HD
7.	Steve Droste, Flint, Mi	92	HD
8.	Billy Eves, Birchrunville, Pa	41	Tri
9.	Rex Beauchamp, Drayton Plains, Mi	31	HD
10.	Chuck Palmgren, Santa Ana, Ca	38	Yam
11.	Jimmy Zeigler, Bellville, Oh	89	HD
12.	Paul Pressgrove, Tecumseh, Ks	74	HD
13.	Kenny Roberts, Villa Park, Ca	1	Yam
14.	Bubba Rush, Houston, Tx	41N	HD

Race: 12 Lap Trophy Race
Race Time: 5:10.114

Rank	Rider	Number	Make
1.	Randy Cleek, Shawnee, Ok	29	HD
2.	Teddy Newton, Pontiac, Mi	61	HD
3.	Keith Ulicki, Kenosha, Wi	8K	HD
4.	Mike Caves, Galesburg, Ill	28	HD
5.	Mike Johnson, Flint, Mi	85	HD
6.	Mark Williams, Springfield, Ore	70	Nor
7.	Ken Springsteen, Flint, Mi	76X	HD
8.	Scott Drake, Xenia, Oh	91	HD
9.	Ricky Campbell, Milford, Oh	82	Yam
10.	Steve Freeman, Simpsonville, SC	68C	HD

Grand National Points Standings after Round 6

Rank	Rider	Pts
1.	Kenny Roberts	397
2.	Gary Scott	382
3.	Mark Williams	252
4.	Randy Cleek	247
5.	Gene Romero	240
6.	Greg Sassaman	222
7.	Hank Scott	199
8.	Dave Hansen	182
9.	Jay Springsteen	182
10.	Corky Keener	166

Extra Extra

- A whopping 108 Experts signed in for the race.
- Jay Springsteen's heat race time set tongues wagging in the pits. It was 4 seconds quicker than teammate and last year's winner Corky Keener's time.
- Keener was running a new chassis fitted with a motor previously run by 1972 National Champion Mark Brelsford.
- Harley-Davidson's domination at Louisville continued. The field was composed of 10 XR750's, 3 Yamahas and 1 Triumph.
- After missing much of 1974 due to injury, Roger Crump made an appearance at Louisville, looking good and qualifying for the program. Engine trouble forced him to scratch from the program.
- National Number 50, Randy Scott, was put out of action around the time of the Louisville National after breaking his ankle while riding his motocross bike.
- Mike Gerald broke his collarbone trail riding and his recovery was slowed because of a pin placed after the injury kept coming loose.
- Rookie Expert Chuck Jordan was killed at a Pro race at Greenville, Oh on May 25, 1975. His handlebars touched the fencing and he was unavoidably struck by another rider. Jordan was one of the top Junior racers of 1974 and had a promising career. His first GNC outing had netted a 7th place in the Houston TT Trophy Race. He was still on the mend from injuries suffered earlier in the year. To keep honor his memory, the Chuck Jordan Memorial Race was soon established and became a fixture for years at various tracks in Ohio.

1975 Harrington Half-Mile
Springsteen Makes it Two in a Row!
Gary Scott Takes Over Camel Points!

GNC Round #7 of 20	**Purse:** $14,000.00
Date: June 14, 1975	**Surface:** Limestone
Type: Half-Mile	**Course Length:** ½ Mile
Venue: Harrington Raceway	**Laps:** 20
Location: Harrington, De	**Distance:** 10 Miles

Proving that his Louisville Downs win was no fluke, 18 year-old Jay Springsteen dominated the first National race ever held in Delaware. Springsteen set fast time, won the fastest heat and for the second week in a row, ran away with the National. Fellow Michigan rider Rex Beauchamp led the race early, before Springsteen flashed by. Harley teammate Gary Scott also held the point early, settling for the last podium spot. He just edged out GNC rival Kenny Roberts, who rode the cushion in spectacular fashion to shoot through the field in the late stages of the race.

The Harrington fairground course reminded many of Louisville, with narrower turns. The track developed into a slippery wide groove, with a few brave souls, (well at least "King Kenny"), riding the deep cushion. Thick dust plagued the event throughout the program.

Gary Scott's podium run just ahead of GNC rival Kenny Roberts gave him the number one spot in points by a slim 5 point margin, 482 to 477. Jay Springsteen's second win in a row catapulted him from ninth to third in points. Greg Sassaman had another solid ride in 7th and moved to fourth in the standings. Runner-up in the race, Rex Beauchamp, blasted clear up to fifth, making his first showing in the top ten. Mark Williams, Randy Cleek and Gene Romero all failed to make the race and each slid back three spots.

Time Trials

It was all Michigan riders on Harley's up front in qualifying. Jay Springsteen ran a 26.20 lap to decimate area Expert Denny Palmgren's 1971 Regional event mark of 27.11. Corky Keener was next at 26.67 and Rex Beauchamp a 26.90. Harley riders dominated the top 10, with Hank Scott sneaking into 9th on the Shell Yamaha.

Heats

Jay Springsteen ran off and hid in Heat 1, literally leaving the field in a cloud of dust. Canadian Doug Sehl (HD) squabbled over 2nd place with Eddie Wirth (HD). Sehl pulled away, leaving Wirth to deal with rookie Steve Freeman. Freeman took the final transfer spot away from veteran Wirth on the last lap. Springsteen's time was the fastest of the night.

Chuck Palmgren's AAR Yamaha looked very strong during the early stages of Heat 2. Corky Keener slowly reeled him in though, with Palmgren dropping out soon after with engine woes. Gary Scott worked through the field into 2nd place with 4 laps to go. He was threatened late in the go by Kenny Roberts, who had given up on the groove and was riding up near the hay bales. Roberts was closing as the laps ran out.

It was all Team Harley in the third heat, as Rex Beauchamp led the way home with Greg Sassaman following closely. John Hateley put his factory Norton in the Main after inheriting 3rd spot from Dave Aldana, who overcooked it early and Georgia rookie Jay Ridgeway, who had his bike break.

The early leader of Heat 4 was semi-retired Denny Palmgren on a Larry Schafer tuned Harley: he had previous success at this facility in Regional events. He was kept honest though by Steve Droste, aboard Tex Peels' Harley, who nipped by to lead a few laps. The patient veteran followed for a while before powering by to grab the lead for good. Cushion artist Dave Sehl (HD) also dropped Droste back a spot late in the race.

Semis

Hank Scott (Yam) and Billy Eves (Tri) gave the crowd some brand diversity along with some good racing in Semi 1. Scott led the early stages of the race with aggressive Eves all over him. Eves' job got a little easier when Scott's Yamaha went off song and slipped back. Eves went on to a popular win, with Scott just able to fend off Mert Lawwill.

California 'shoe Frank Gillespie, on the Dud Perkins Harley, was out front early, chased by veteran Jimmy Maness (HD). Rookie Brent Lowe, on the Richmond Harley-Davidson XR750, closed up on his more experienced competitors. He first displaced Georgian Maness, then latched onto Gillespie. On the last go around, Lowe put himself into his first National with a neat last corner pass.

Trophy Race

Michigan rider Mike Johnson, on a Nasco Oils-sponsored Harley, led some heavy hitters in the non-qualifiers final. Former National winners Hank Scott, Mert Lawwill and Rick Hocking were all in the Trophy event. Johnson led early, pressured heavily by Scott. After several laps, Scott was by, but almost immediately had his Yamaha fall flat again and he retired. Johnson's own machine then began slowing, just holding off an approaching Mert Lawwill.

National

A really messy start was let stand and Gary Scott led the field away. Rex Beauchamp took over as the field began the 2nd lap. Jay Springsteen and Corky Keener were flying up behind the lead duo. By lap 5, both passed Scott. Keener had a camshaft issue and was out. Soon after, Springsteen moved by Beauchamp and really set sail. Following the top 3 were Doug Sehl, an impressive Brent Lowe and Denny Palmgren. Greg Sassaman had a great run going, moving momentarily by Gary Scott before slipping way-off the groove to miss a downed rider. By midway, Kenny Roberts was barely in the top 10, skittering around with everybody else on the groove. With nothing to lose, Roberts began barnstorming the cushion again, wowing the crowd. It was not only spectacular, it worked and Roberts began picking off riders lap-after-lap. He worked clear up to 3rd place Scott and was applying pressure as the race ended. Springsteen had stretched to a huge lead at the end of the race, with Beauchamp a solid 2nd, Scott being hassled by Roberts, Sehl another good ride in 5th, Lowe with a great first National in 6th, Sassaman salvaging 7th; rounding out the top ten were Steve Droste, Dave Sehl and John Hateley.

Results

Race: 20 Lap Half-Mile National
Race Time: 9:21.09

Rank	Rider	Number	Make
1.	Jay Springsteen, Flint, Mi	65X	HD
2.	Rex Beauchamp, Drayton Plains, Mi	31	HD
3.	Gary Scott, Springfield, Oh	64	HD
4.	Kenny Roberts, Villa Park, Ca	1	Yam
5.	Doug Sehl, Waterdown, Ont., Can	45	HD
6.	Brent Lowe, Wakefield, Va	36S	HD
7.	Greg Sassaman, Macon, Ga	80C	HD
8.	Steve Droste, Flint, Mi	92	HD
9.	Dave Sehl, Waterdown, On., Can	16	HD
10.	John Hateley, Van Nuys, Ca	98	Nor
11.	Billy Eves, Birchrunville, Pa	41	Tri
12.	Denny Palmgren, Lutherville, MD	49	HD
13.	Corky Keener, Flint, Mi	62	HD
14.	Steve Freeman, Simpsonville, SC	68C	HD

Race: Trophy Race

Rank	Rider	Number	Make
1.	Mike Johnson, Flint, Mi	85	HD
2.	Mert Lawwill, San Francisco, Ca	7	HD
3.	Frank Gillespie, Hayward, Ca	76	HD
4.	Rick Hocking, Fremont, Ca	13	Yam
5.	Don Doutre, Atlas, Mi	6X	Yam
6.	George Richtmeyer, Schenectady, NY	10B	HD

Grand National Points Standings after Round 7

Rank	Rider	Pts
1.	Gary Scott	482
2.	Kenny Roberts	477
3.	Jay Springsteen	332
4.	Greg Sassaman	262
5.	Rex Beauchamp	252
6.	Mark Williams	252
7.	Randy Cleek	247
8.	Gene Romero	240
9.	Hank Scott	199
10.	Dave Hansen	182

Extra Extra

- Way off of Louisville's entries, only around 60 Experts signed up.
- Jay Springsteen made history as the first rookie to win dirt track Nationals back to back. Brad Andres was the first to win double victories, his occurring at the "road courses" of Daytona and Laconia.
- Possibly due to the slicker track conditions, it was a Harley-Davidson dominated show, even more than Louisville. The National was made up of 11 Harleys, and one each Yamaha, Norton and Triumph.
- Local favorite Denny Palmgren had a top ten run going in the National on his Larry Schafer prepared Harley when he went down with two laps to go after another rider got into him.
- It was a tough night for many riders, particularly for a bunch of the long haul California riders. Talent like Dave Aldana, Mert Lawwill, Gene Romero, Rick Hocking, Frank Gillespie, Paul Bostrom, veteran Shorty Seabourne and Terry Dorsch, (who won the 1973 Race of Champions at Harrington), all missed the show.
- The recent success of Michigan riders Jay Springsteen, Rex Beauchamp and Corky Keener led to them being dubbed the "Michigan Mafia".
- Harrington Raceway opened in 1946 and is located at the Delaware State Fairgrounds. The track is one of the most prominent half-mile horse racing tracks in the country. The live betting horse track coexists with a large casino. Motorcycle racing has been a feature through the years at Harrington, including AMA Pro Regional and National events. In 2002-'03, the track was reconfigured with wider turns, making a faster surface.

1975 Columbus Half-Mile
Gary Scott Claims 4th Straight Harley Win

GNC Round #8 of 20	**Purse:** $16,000.00
Date: June 22, 1975	**Surface:** Dirt-Limestone
Type: Half-Mile	**Course Length:** ½ Mile
Venue: Ohio State	**Laps:** 20
Fairgrounds	**Distance:** 10 Miles
Location: Columbus, Oh	

Gary Scott scored his first Grand National win of the year at the 32nd Annual Charity Newsies Half-Mile. The win helped boost his points lead over arch rival Kenny Roberts. The GNC champ had an ignition failure in his heat and was out for the day. Finishing in the next three positions were "Michigan Mafia" members Corky Keener, Jay Springsteen and Rex Beauchamp. The track developed a typical daytime Charity Newsies narrow groove, leading to a rather uneventful main event. Harley-Davidson again dominated, sweeping the first seven spots. It was the fourth Harley National victory in a row.

The recent string of dirt tracks, were playing into Harley-Davidson's hand, and its riders were beginning to dominate the top of the points order. Gary Scott's win boosted him to a huge 170 point advantage over Kenny Roberts. Jay Springsteen's podium run solidified his third spot in points and was now closing up on Roberts. Yet another strong ride by Rex Beauchamp moved him to fourth, just ahead of teammates Greg Sassaman and Corky Keener, who moved way up in the standings via his runner-up performance.

Time Trials

The nation's hottest dirt tracker, Jay Springsteen nailed down the fastest time on his Vista-Sheen Harley, turning in a 25.852. Kenny Roberts ran his Yamaha wide open to nail down 2nd spot at 25.953. Rex Beauchamp was 3rd fastest on his factory Harley at 26.031.

Heats

Dave Sehl (HD) was first off the line first in Heat 1, but Jay Springsteen was by as they entered the back stretch on lap 1. He quickly pulled to a good size lead and the win. Dave and Doug Sehl (HD) ran in 2nd and 3rd. Gene Romero was determined to make the National and began to apply heavy pressure to Doug Sehl. Romero ran a little too hard and slipped into the marbles. Sehl pulled away and Romero had his hands full with Frank Gillespie. On the last lap, Doug Sehl's bike quit and Romero just edged out Gillespie for the transfer behind Springsteen and Dave Sehl.

Kenny Roberts put on a great show for half of Heat 2. He pulled the holeshot but was soon trailing the Harleys of Corky Keener, Keith Ulicki and Mike Caves going down the back straight. Showing why he was known as "King Kenny", Roberts just ran it in deep in Turns 3 & 4 up near the hay bales and blew by all of them. He proceeded to run it spectacularly around the top of the track till a condenser wire broke. Keener went on to an easy win. Chuck Palmgren, (aboard brother Denny's Harley after his AAR Yamaha broke), topped challenges from Keith Ulicki (HD) and Mark Williams (Nor). Rick Hocking had the Champion Frames-sponsored Yamaha wound up late in the race, buzzing by Ulicki and Williams for 3rd spot over the last two laps.

Ohio's best hopes for a home state win, Jimmy Zeigler (HD) and Steve Morehead (Tri) squared off in Heat 3. Quick starting Zeigler was out in front till midway, when Morehead steamed by. Morehead went on for the win with Rex Beauchamp dropping Zeigler to 3rd on lap 6.

It was a factory Harley duel in the final heat. Two-time event winner, (1969 & '72), Mert Lawwill led the first two laps till Gary Scott rolled by on Lap 3 and headed straight to the checkers. Lawwill hung onto 2nd ahead of rookie teammate Greg Sassaman. Billy Eves (Tri) was 4th, with rookie Jay Ridgeway (HD), from Georgia like Sassaman, beating Alabama rookie Steve Freeman (HD) for 5th.

Semis

Only the winner from each semi would transfer to the National and in the first race, John Hateley was up and gone on his factory Norton, leading every lap. Teammate Mark Williams and Keith Ulicki were involved in a crash in Turn 3 of lap 1. The two hit the hay bales with Williams being drug along the tops of the bales before letting go. Neither rider was injured. Mike Johnson (HD) ran 2nd till close to halfway when Dave Aldana took the spot. Both were Harley mounted.

In Semi 2, Jay Ridgeway controlled the early laps, but a hard charging Billy Eves took the lead on Lap 2. Hank Scott was coming through the field on the Shell Yamaha and bumped Ridgeway out of 2nd with 4 laps to go. Scott was flying, but Eves was too far out front to catch and earned the last National ticket.

Trophy Race

It was all Hank Scott and the Shell Racing Yamaha in the Trophy Race. He led every lap, but did face a late-race challenge from Paul Bostrom. Bostrom had to wrestle 2nd place from Mike Johnson before he set out after the leader. He caught Scott and managed to show him a wheel or two, but Scott hung onto the win. Scott's Yamaha led a nine Harley sweep home.

National

Pole sitter Gary Scott hooked up on the rubbered-up outside groove and led the National away. Jay Springsteen, Rex Beauchamp and Corky Keener gave chase. Scott pulled away on lap 2 as Springsteen got out of shape and Keener, who had earlier slipped by Beauchamp, took the 2nd spot. Scott was headed to the win, with Keener and Springsteen formed up with a gap back to the Harleys of Beauchamp, Chuck Palmgren and Greg Sassaman. Jimmy Zeigler and Steve Morehead were ahead of scuffle between Gene Romero and Billy Eves. With the narrow groove allowing little passing, the race was mostly follow-the-leader. In the end Scott took a comfortable win ahead of Keener, Springsteen and Beauchamp. Sassaman managed a final lap pass around Palmgren. Zeigler took 7th ahead of Romero. Morehead had used up his tire and slipped back; Eves' Triumph gave up on lap 15.

Results

Race: 20 Lap Half-Mile National
Race Time: 8:50.543

Rank	Rider	Number	Make
1.	Gary Scott, Springfield, Oh	64	HD
2.	Corky Keener, Flint, Mi	62	HD
3.	Jay Springsteen, Flint, Mi	65X	HD
4.	Rex Beauchamp, Drayton Plain, Mi	31	HD
5.	Greg Sassaman, Macon, Ga	80C	HD
6.	Chuck Palmgren, Santa Ana, Ca	38	Yam
7.	Jimmy Zeigler, Bellville, Oh	89	HD
8.	Gene Romero, San Luis Obispo, Ca	3	Yam
9.	Dave Sehl, Waterdown, Ont., Can	16	HD
10.	Rick Hocking, Fremont, Ca	13	Yam
11.	Steve Morehead, Findlay, Oh	42	Tri
12.	John Hateley, Van Nuys, Ca	98	Nor
13.	Mert Lawwill, San Francisco, Ca	7	HD
14.	Billy Eves, Birchrunville, Pa	41	Tri

Race: Trophy Race

Rank	Rider	Number	Make
1.	Hank Scott, Springfield, Oh	14	Yam
2.	Paul Bostrom, San Roman, Ca	46	HD
3.	Mike Johnson, Flint, Mi	85	HD
4.	Don Doutre, Atlas, Mi	6X	HD
5.	Randy Cleek, Shawnee, Ok	29	HD
6.	Steve Droste, Flint, Mi	92	HD
7.	Teddy Poovey, Garland, Tx	94	HD
8.	Keith Ulicki, Kenosha, Wi	8K	HD
9.	Dave Aldana, Santa Ana, Ca	10	HD
10.	Jay Ridgeway, Atlanta, Ga	9C	HD

Grand National Points Standings after Round 8

Rank	Rider	Pts
1.	Gary Scott	647
2.	Kenny Roberts	477
3.	Jay Springsteen	442
4.	Rex Beauchamp	340
5.	Greg Sassaman	328
6.	Corky Keener	305
7.	Gene Romero	273
8.	Mark William	252
9.	Randy Cleek	249
10.	Hank Scott	206

GNC Round #9 of 20 **Date:** July 12, 1975 **Type:** TT **Venue:** Mt. St. Helens Motorcycle Club Grounds **Location:** Castle Rock, Wa	**Purse:** $15,000.00 **Location:** Castle Rock, Wa **Surface:** Dirt **Course Length:** ½ Mile **Laps:** 25

The loyal Castle Rock crowd, with liberal numbers of the lunatic fringe, went nuts as area Northwestern riders swept the podium spots over the National stars. 1973 winner Chuck Joyner made his move to the front about halfway, passing then leader Charlie Brown and won over a closing Sonny Burres. Burres came from way back in the field to capture the runner-up spot. The veteran had momentum, but ran out of time to catch leader Joyner. Charlie Brown put in the ride of his life. He pulled the holeshot and led till halfway when Joyner and then Burres went by. Two-time Castle Rock winner Mert Lawwill, (1967 and 1969), was the first "outsider", regular touring pro in 4th place. Always a tough place for outsiders, the Castle Rock this night was smooth, but seemed extra slick. The crowds at the Mt. St. Helens M/C facility normally bordered on out of control, but this 9000-strong group went above and beyond the call. Besides the serious race fans, there were numerous rowdies who merrily engaged in lots of drinking, fighting, streaking and other forms of public nudity and illicit behavior. They were loud, obnoxious and fiercely loyal to "their" Pacific Northwest favorites. This included Diane Cox, who put in several strong rides, but came up short at the end of the night. Grand National Champ Kenny Roberts met up with some local attitude when he ran across tough Randy Skiver's front wheel in the National. Roberts was knocked out and carted off the track, but was not seriously injured.

With the TT specialists taking many of the top spots, the Camel Pro points remained relatively stable for the first time in 1975. Gary Scott put in a solid 5th in the race, his advantage over Kenny Roberts, (scored 16th), was now a whopping 230 points. Jay Springsteen put in a great first ride at Castle Rock, finishing 9th. Other than Mert Lawwill's reappearance in the top ten after his strong 4th in the National, there were no other changes in the top order.

Time Trials

The locals took advantage of the tricky track conditions and dominated qualifying. Sonny Burres set fast time of 24.62, followed by Ed Hermann (24.72), Darrell Hendrickson (24.79), Charlie Brown (24.80), Mark Williams on a Norton with a 24.84, Bruce Hanlon (24.85), Randy Skiver (24.85), John Gennai (24.88), Jim Jones (24.89) and Rex Beauchamp (HD) a 24.93. Unless otherwise noted, the brand of choice was a Triumph. Only three of the top 10, Williams, Gennai and Beauchamp, could be considered Camel Pro regulars. Where were the normal GNC TT fast guys? Mert Lawwill (HD) was 13th, Kenny Roberts (Yam), despite wowing the crowd on his attempt was 25th and last year's winner Gary Scott (HD) barely made the program in 47th, despite the fact his time of 25.76 was only about a second off the pole.

Heats

Mert Lawwill pulled the holeshot in Heat 1, with Team Norton's Mark Williams and John Hateley giving close support. Kenny Roberts shot from his second row start, first knocking off Jim Jones (Tri) and latching onto the Norton duo. He was quickly by Hateley and soon heavily pressuring Williams. It took Roberts two laps but he was by Williams and heading for the leader. Roberts passed Lawwill in the infield with two laps to go, on his way to setting fast time of the night. Roberts was clearly figuring the track out and would be the biggest threat to a local victory. Even the partisan crowd had begrudging respect for Roberts' talent. No one laid a bike on it's cases like KR.

Last year's Junior winner, Bruce Hanlon, headed Ed Hermann early in Heat 2 till his bike went belly up. Hermann took over the lead chased by Chuck Joyner and Harley mounted Steve Droste. California rider Ron Powell was 4th. The crowd was really into it as next came Diane Cox on the Torco Oils/Suzuki Sport Center Triumph, chased by former GNC champ Gene Romero! Cox was moving up on Powell, whose chain parted, sending him hard into the first turn hay bales. The red flag came out on lap 6 and the race was called complete with the order Hermann, Joyner, and Droste, with Cox one spot out of the National and semi-bound!

Randy Skiver jumped out front quickly in Heat 2 and set a torrid pace. Darrell Hendrickson was running a distant 2nd. Michigan rookie Jay Springsteen was known as a half-miler, but he wheeled the Vista-Sheen Harley around well enough to send 4th place, defending race champ Gary Scott, to the semis.

John Gennai, done with his factory Harley support and back on his familiar Triumph, took the holeshot in Heat 4. Veteran Terry Dorsch (Tri) was quickly by, with another Michigan half-miler, Corky Keener (HD) running 3rd. Charlie Brown was on the charge and soon ripped through the front runners for the lead. Gennai was under heavy pressure from Keener. It was a neat battle; Gennai had finesse, Keener the horsepower. Keener squeaked by, but a mistake gave Gennai the spot back. Both moved Dorsch back to 4th. Brown motored to a big win followed by Gennai and Keener.

Semis

Jim Jones looked strong and led the first semi flag-to-flag. The night's pole-sitter, Sonny Burres had to run the semi after failing to get going in Heat 1. He was getting on track and took the second and last spot into the National over Mark Williams and Gene Romero. Diane Cox didn't get a transfer to the Trophy Race after being caught up in an accident.

Gary Scott eventually ran away with Semi 2, with Frank Gillespie (HD) keeping it close till halfway. A riding wounded Randy Scott (Tri), Pat McCaul (Tri) and Rick Hocking followed.

Trophy Race

Norton's Rob Morrison shot out in front of the Trophy Race with teammate and crowd favorite Mark Williams and Gene Romero on the CR Axtell tuned, Alex's Tamale Wagon sponsored Yamaha, in pursuit. Morrison was dominating the event, but was slowed by engine blahs, letting Williams by for the win followed by Romero. Morrison hung on for 3rd.

National

Kenny Roberts pulled out front at the start of the National, but Charlie Brown and Randy Skiver quickly shuffled by. Roberts was followed by Mert Lawwill, Chuck Joyner and Jay Springsteen. GNC champ Roberts was applying heavy pressure to Skiver and after several laps tried a move on the outside going into the last turn. Roberts bobbled and cut across Skiver's front wheel, both went down, Roberts hard enough to temporarily knock himself out. A very unhappy Skiver stood over the prone Roberts and unleashed his opinion about the move. Roberts may or may not have heard and was soon carted off the track. Roberts seriously tweaked his shoulder and was very beat-up. Skiver and crew rushed to repair his Triumph. The restart saw Brown reassume the lead, on his Bob's Body Shop Triumph, with Chuck Joyner passing Lawwill for 2nd. Gary Scott got a great restart and moved into 4th. Sonny Burres emerged from a scrap with John Gennai and John Hateley. Burres soon caught Scott and took away the spot. Behind, several strong runners had problems: John Hateley's charge was slowed by an off-song engine, Jay Springsteen had slipped backwards, Corky Keener and Ed Hermann tangled. With the halfway mark approaching, Burres passed Scott for 4th and his target was now Lawwill. Soon afterword Joyner and Brown diced heavily for the lead. After a couple of back and forths, Joyner took over for good. Burres pushed Lawwill hard and went past for 3rd. He soon caught Brown and with the laps waning went by in pursuit of Joyner. He was gaining at the finish, but it was Joyner's night. The top-10 at the stripe were Joyner, Burres, Brown, Lawwill, Scott, Hateley, Skiver in a strong ride from the back, Gennai, Springsteen and Jim Jones.

Results

Race: 25 Lap TT National

Rank	Rider	Number	Make
1.	Chuck Joyner, Oregon City, Ore	60	Tri
2.	Sonny Burres, Portland, Ore	69	Tri
3.	Charlie Brown, Longview, Wa	78	Tri
4.	Mert Lawwill, San Francisco, Ca	7	HD
5.	Gary Scott, Springfield, Oh	64	HD
6.	John Hateley, Van Nuys, Ca	98	Nor
7.	Randy Skiver, Everett, Wa	35	Tri
8.	John Gennai, Los Gatos, Ca	20	Tri
9.	Jay Springsteen, Flint, Mi	65X	HD
10.	Jim Jones, Kirkland, Wa	5W	Tri
11.	Darrell Hendrickson, Seattle, Wa	86W	Tri
12.	Frank Gillespie, Hayward, Ca	76	HD
13.	Steve Droste, Flint, Mi	92	HD
14.	Ed Hermann, Portland, Ore	12Q	Tri
15.	Corky Keener, Flint, Mi	62	HD
16.	Kenny Roberts, Villa Park, Ca	1	Yam

Race: Trophy Race
Race Time: 5:07.95

Rank	Rider	Number	Make
1.	Mark Williams, Springfield, Ore	70	Nor
2.	Gene Romero, San Luis Obispo, Ca	3	Yam
3.	Rob Morrison, Mission Hills, Ca	25	Nor
4.	Don Dodge, Portland, Ore	57Q	Tri
5.	Pat McCaul, San Jose, Ca	48	Tri
6.	Ike Reed, Salem, Ore	90	Tri
7.	Rex Beauchamp, Drayton Plains, Mi	31	HD
8.	Hank Scott, Springfield, Oh	14	Yam
9.	Brad Tibbitts, Spanaway, Wa	14W	Tri
10.	Rick Hocking, Fremont, Ca	13	Yam
11.	John Hartman, Federal Way, Wa	52W	Tri
12.	Randy Scott, Albany, Ore	50	Tri

Grand National Points Standings after Round 9

Rank	Rider	Pts
1.	Gary Scott	713
2.	Kenny Roberts	483
3.	Jay Springsteen	464
4.	Rex Beauchamp	340
5.	Greg Sassaman	328
6.	Corky Keener	313
7.	Gene Romero	276
8.	Mark William	256
9.	Randy Cleek	249
10.	Mert Lawwill	239

- Scott Brelsford, aboard the Erv Kanemoto Kawasaki 750, made history by winning the first big race for a two-stroke. He captured the $8000.00 Pacific Regional Championship event in Stockton, Ca, on July 6th.

Bonus!
Top 20 Castle Rock TT Qualifying Times

1.	Sonny Burres	Tri	24.62 seconds
2.	Ed Hermann	Tri	24.72
3.	Darrell Hendrickson	Tri	24.79
4.	Charlie Brown	Tri	24.80
5.	Mark Williams	Nor	24.84
6.	Bruce Hanlon	HD	24.85
7.	Randy Skiver	Tri	24.85
8.	John Gennai	Tri	24.88
9.	Jim Jones	Tri	24.89
10.	Rex Beauchamp	HD	24.93
11.	Tom White	HD	24.99
12.	Frank Gillespie	HD	25.03
13.	Mert Lawwill	HD	25.08
14.	Diane Cox	Tri	25.09
15.	Eddie Wirth	HD	25.12
16.	Corky Keener	HD	25.13
17.	John Hateley	Nor	25.15
18.	Ron Powell	Tri	25.16
19.	Jay Springsteen	HD	26.17
20.	Ike Reed	Tri	25.21

1975 Ascot TT
Gary Scott Flys at Ascot TT!
Roberts Grounded

GNC Round #10 of 20 **Date:** July 26, 1975 **Type:** TT **Venue:** Ascot Park **Location:** Gardena, Ca	**Purse:** $14,000.00 **Surface:** Dirt **Course Length:** ½ Mile, (approx.) **Laps:** 25

Gary Scott earned his second National of the season win at Ascot, and benefitted mightily when his GNC points rival Kenny Roberts suffered a thrown chain while leading the National. Roberts' DNF ended what would have been storybook finish to his night. Roberts was doubtful even to ride at Ascot after seriously banging up his shoulder at Castle Rock. He made it into a semi-event as a distant alternate and had started at the rear of the National, knifing through to the front. It was a strange night that saw a run of sprocket/chain failures that hit Roberts in both his heat, and the National, as well as several other riders, including John Hateley, Steve Droste and Jay Springsteen. The likely cause for the failures, were likely a tacky Ascot surface, lightweight drivetrain components and ever increasing horsepower. Finishing in second place was John Gennai. He had recently traded his Harley-Davidson ride for a Triumph, a brand that had brought him a lot of success at Ascot. It appeared the right choice as he led much of National before settling for the runner-up spot. Rick Hocking put in a late race charge for the last podium spot. He was challenging Gennai when the race ended.

Gary Scott's back-to-back win gave him another huge boost in his quest for the GNC crown. He received the lion's share of the Camel Pro mid-season point's payoff, pocketing $5000.00. (See *Extras* for the rest of the Camel Pro monies.) Scott's lead over Kenny Roberts was 377 points. Roberts' troubles in the two National TT's couldn't have come at a worst time. With Harley's growing domination of the ovals, the TT races were a chance to level the playing surface and score some points. With the upcoming Nationals at Laguna Seca, Peoria and Sante Fe, Roberts still had a good chance to strike back.

Time Trials
Dave Aldana (HD) the 1973 TT winner and 1974 fast qualifier, was quickest again with a 46.13 lap. John Hateley on a factory Norton turned a 46.24 and Kenny Roberts (Yam) rounded out the top 3 with a 46.28 time.

Heats
Starting out a weird night right in Heat 1, Phil McDonald and Ron Powell locked bars at the start and went tumbling down; Dave Aldana also fell in Turn 1. Dave Hansen (Yam) led the restart, but Mark Williams (Nor) soon took over. Rex Beauchamp (HD) gave chase behind, slipping by Hansen around Lap 5. On the charge was Dave Aldana, who also bumped Hansen back a spot. He was all over Beauchamp, only to have his engine quit on the last lap. Going to the National were Williams, Beauchamp, Hansen and Charlie Brown (Tri).

Terry Dorsch (Tri) was away first in Heat 2, heavily challenged by John Hateley whose Norton soon tossed its chain. Hateley got going again, but was way back. Hard-charging Frank Gillespie crashed hard after the jump and was out. Dorsch ran away for a sizable win with John Allison (Yam), Paul Bostrom (HD) and Danny Hockie (Tri) capturing the other transfers.

In Heat 3, Rick Hocking (Yam) and John Gennai led the field away, but Kenny Roberts blasted by both for the lead. Perennial Ascot rivals Hocking and Gennai battled hard, with Gennai taking a narrow advantage. Roberts was long gone, but on Lap 8 his rear sprocket failed and the champ was out. Gennai went on for the win, followed by Hocking, Hank Scott (Yam) and Tom White (HD).

Heat 4 saw a restart after Eddie Wirth (HD) jumped the first try. Gary Scott (HD) pulled ahead to lead the early laps. Mert Lawwill bailed off in order to miss Randy Skiver in first lap traffic. Scott ran strong till he began having trouble with his shifter. He slowed slightly, allowing a charging Wirth and Randy Skiver to close up. Both went by Scott. Scott retaliated, taking back 2nd from Skiver. A surprising Jay Springsteen (HD) closed up on Skiver, pressuring the TT ace all around the course. He pushed a little too hard, tangling handlebars with Skiver and going

517

down. Wirth put in a great ride from the penalty stripe and headed to the National along with Scott, Skiver and 1966 winner Eddie Mulder (Tri). Lawwill chased down the pack to earn a semi-berth.

Semis

In a real long shot, fourth alternate Kenny Roberts got into the first semi when the riders in front of him either scratched or didn't show up in time. Steve Droste (HD) pulled the holeshot as John Hateley and Bruce Hanlon soon pulled in behind him. Roberts was up to mid-pack before the first lap was out. Hanlon passed Hateley for 2nd and soon zapped Droste for the lead. Roberts had moved up and followed Hanlon's charge forward. Hateley's bike had tossed it's chain again and he pulled off. Roberts' task up front was made a little easier when Hanlon's bike quit and he raced to the checkers. Droste was facing a challenge from 1970 GNC champ Gene Romero for the last transfer spot. Romero was in the National with his teammate when unbelievably, Droste's rear sprocket failed in the same way Roberts had earlier.

It was rookie Expert Tom Berry (HD) out front in Semi 2 with Rob Morrison (Nor), rookie Skip Aksland and 1970 TT winner Mert Lawwill (HD) giving chase. Morrison slipped back as Aksland and Lawwill both passed Berry. Veteran Lawwill and rookie Aksland battled right up to the checkers, with a last second move by Aksland giving him the win.

Trophy Race

Walt Foster (Tri) zapped early front runners Rob Morrison, Randy Cleek (Yam) and Rick Kraft (Yam) in a daring pass and went on to win. The others diced hard till Morrison pulled off with mechanical trouble. Cleek topped Kraft and they were followed in by Phil McDonald and Corky (Where's the next oval") Keener.

National

A packed grandstand of over 9,200 was on hand to watch the 25-Lap National. Terry Dorsch was a little too quick on the first try to start the race and he was sent way back to the penalty line. The lone factory rider on the front row, Norton's Mark Williams, pulled a nice holeshot. It was brief, as the Norton soon went off-song and Williams was swallowed up by the pack. John Gennai took over the top spot; chasing behind were Gary Scott, Hank Scott and Paul Bostrom. By lap 2, Roberts had cut through the pack and was clear up to 8th spot. Just in front of him, Eddie Wirth and John Allison got tangled up with both falling down. Both were able to continue, but not before several riders, including Roberts, now in 6th, went by. As the laps ticked by, Roberts was into 3rd, having passed Hank Scott and Bostrom. Around lap 10, Roberts was by Gary Scott and set out after Gennai. With the King right on his tail, Gennai didn't give in easily and when Roberts surged by after the jump, the youngster went back by. Roberts managed to get back by, with Gennai and Scott close. Roberts pulled a small lead and looked set for the win, but with 5 laps to go, the chain popped off his Yamaha and he was done. Scott passed Gennai for the lead and went on for the win. Rick Hocking had been working his way through the pack and now pressured Gennai in the closing laps. Scott and Bostrom were 4th and 5th, Wirth mounted another impressive come from behind charge to grab 6th, Dorsch came from the penalty line and was 7th. Mert Lawwill and Gene Romero were 8th and 9th and John Allison regrouped from his fall for 10th. It was Gary Scott's second win of the season and his second win in a row at the Ascot TT.

Results

Race: 25 Lap TT National
Race Time: 19:49.90

Rank	Rider	Number	Make
1.	Gary Scott, Springfield, Oh	64	HD
2.	John Gennai, Los Gatos, Ca	20	Tri
3.	Rick Hocking, Fremont, Ca	13	Yam
4.	Hank Scott, Springfield, Oh	14	Yam
5.	Paul Bostrom, San Roman, Ca	46	HD
6.	Eddie Wirth, Dana Point, Ca	77	HD
7.	Terry Dorsch, Granada Hills, Ca	22	Tri
8.	Mert Lawwill, San Francisco, Ca	7	HD
9.	Gene Romero, San Luis Obispo, Ca	3	Yam
10.	John Allison, Poway, Ca	83R	Yam
11.	Eddie Mulder, Northridge, Ca	12	Tri
12.	Rex Beauchamp, Drayton Plains, Mi	31	HD
13.	Danny Hockie, Harbor City, Ca	84	Tri
14.	Skip Aksland, Manteca, Ca	72Y	Yam
15.	Charlie Brown, Longview, Ca	78	Tri
16.	Mark Williams, Springfield, Ore	70	Nor
17.	Tom White, Huntington Beach, Ca	80	HD
18.	Kenny Roberts, Villa Park, Ca	1	Yam
19.	Dave Hansen, Hayward, Ca	23	Yam
20.	Randy Skiver, Everett, Wa	35	Tri

Race: 12 Lap Trophy Race
Race Time: 9:38.70

Rank	Rider	Number	Make
1.	Walt Foster, Colton, Ca	57R	Tri
2.	Randy Cleek, Shawnee, Ok	29	Yam
3.	Rick Kraft, Phoenix, Az	69G	Yam
4.	Phil McDonald, Tulsa, Ok	58	HD
5.	Corky Keener, Flint, Mi	62	HD

Grand National Points Standings after Round 10

Rank	Rider	Pts
1.	Gary Scott	863
2.	Kenny Roberts	486
3.	Jay Springsteen	464
4.	Rex Beauchamp	349
5.	Greg Sassaman	328
6.	Corky Keener	313
7.	Gene Romero	296
8.	Hank Scott	286
9.	Mert Lawwill	264
10.	Mark Williams	261

Camel Pro Mid-Season Points Payout

Rank	Rider	Payout
1.	Gary Scott	$5000.00
2.	Kenny Roberts	3000.00
3.	Jay Springsteen	1300.00
4.	Rex Beauchamp	900.00
5.	Greg Sassaman	800.00
6.	Corky Keener	700.00
7.	Gene Romero	650.00
8.	Hank Scott	600.00
9.	Mert Lawwill	550.00
10.	Mark Williams	500.00

Extra Extra

- Hospital stops hit a couple of top East Coast riders. Dave Atherton received a badly broken leg on July 18th at a short track race in Webster, Ind. A hospital stay of 4 weeks or more was expected. Charlie Seale received a broken arm in a multi-rider crash at Adrian, Mi on July 25th.

1975 Laguna Seca Road Race
Roberts Rocks in Monterey!
NVT Team Disbands

GNC Round #11 of 20
Date: August 3, 1975
Type: Road Race
Venue: Laguna Seca
Raceway
Location: Monterey, Ca

Purse: $27,0000.00
Surface: Pavement
Course Length: 1.8 Miles
Laps: 40
Distance: 75 Miles

A top finish at Laguna Seca was imperative for GNC champ Kenny Roberts. A string of bad luck and mechanical troubles left him trailing Gary Scott in the points battle by 221 points. With only three road races on the schedule, Roberts had to capitalize at each. Roberts had a heated battle with Yvon DuHamel for the top spot, but overheated tires gave him reason to seemingly concede the win to the Kawasaki rider. Duhamel however, pitched way his bike late in the race, a victim of his own oil leak. Roberts cruised home to victory. It was his 3rd win of the year, the 13th of his career. Unknown in the US, New Zealand rider John Boote stunned everyone present by coming from dead last in the field, (39th position!), to take the runner-up slot. Boote had bad luck and struggled all weekend, getting very little practice and not starting his heat race. The last victim of Boote's charge was Steve Baker. Like Roberts, Baker's tires had gone away during the event, and was unable to hold off Boote's late race charge.

The Yamaha team appeared organized, fast and well prepared at Laguna Seca. Head tuner Kel Carruthers, Roberts and Daytona winner Gene Romero were backed up by hordes of fast privateers. The other teams were still struggling to keep pace. Yvon DuHamel was the only full Kawasaki works rider. His water-cooled 750 was still underpowered, but was handling well, turning competitive times out of the box. The team even brought along a bike featuring experimental parallelogram rear suspension. The designed sought better stability while braking and accelerating. DuHamel professed to like the setup, but rode his faster, conventional setup. Dave Aldana' factory Suzuki appeared to be the fastest non-Yamaha with Suzuki-mate Pat Hennen also a solid contender. Gary Scott would debut the new Harley-Davidson RR-500, the bigger brother of the two-stroke RR-250. The bike showed promise, but was no threat for the win on this day. Scott hoped only to score a few points to offset expected Roberts success.

Heats

Dave Aldana served notice that his Suzuki had the ponies to compete with the Yamahas in Heat 1. He topped Gene Romero (Yam) and Pat Evans (Suz) as proof. Gary Scott and the new Harley had a less than auspicious start when a carb induction boot came adrift before the race. Scott started the race two laps down, finishing last.

Heat 2 had more fireworks as Kenny Roberts (Yam) and Yvon DuHamel (Kaw) faced off. After a spirited discussion, Roberts took the win. Steve Baker was 3rd on the Canadian factory Yamaha.

National

Yvon DuHamel pulled a 3-4 bike length holeshot to lead the pack away from the grid. Tucked close behind were Kenny Roberts, Dave Aldana, Gene Romero and Steve Baker. Roberts closed the gap on the leader but had a big moment on lap 2, at the tight corner before the straight. When he tried to force his Yamaha inside of DuHamel, it responded with a nasty tankslapper that Roberts somehow rode out of. He settled back to a more sedate rhythm. Aldana appeared at ease in 3rd position, but his bike began misfiring and he was out on lap 5. Roberts remounted his drive, and on lap 6 passed DuHamel for the lead. He immediately began to pull away. DuHamel maintained a solid 2nd, with Romero heading Baker. Just behind, a dicing pack of riders including Ron Pierce, Steve McLaughlin and Pat Hennen were joined by John Boote. The New Zealand rider had a miraculous charge through the field. Starting dead last, Boote was up to 12th position at the end of lap 1! Boote's ascension would continue through this pack, which all the while was reeling in Steve Baker. Back up front, Roberts' times began to fall off as his new compound Goodyears were losing grip. DuHamel steadily gained ground, retaking the top spot on lap 17. Roberts did not press the issue, happy with a top finish and the valuable points which went with it. On lap 25, Romero's day ended when his TZ suffered the first seizure for Team Yamaha since the bike was introduced. Just four laps later, Yvon

DuHamel's bike pitched him off in the corkscrew. His machine had developed an oil leak which coated the rear tire. Suddenly, Roberts was back in charge. He cruised to the finish with a huge lead on the pack. As the laps wound down, Boote had moved to 3rd and was closing on Baker. Baker was running the same compound tires as Roberts and was fighting his machine. Boote caught Baker on the last lap at the corkscrew, shooting by for the runner-up slot. The remainder of the top ten were; Pierce, Hennen, McLaughlin, Hurley Wilvert, Randy Cleek, Pat Evans and Don Castro. Gary Scott soldiered home 13th with broken motor mounts.

Results

Race: 75 Mile Road Race National
Race Time: 49:06.567, (92.822 MPH)

Rank	Rider	Number	Make
1.	Kenny Roberts, Villa Park, Ca	1	Yam
2.	John Boote, Christchurch, NZ	22	Yam
3.	Steve Baker, Bellingham, Wa	32	Yam
4.	Ron Pierce, Bakersfield, Ca	97	Yam
5.	Pat Hennen, San Mateo, Ca	80	Yam
6.	Steve McLaughlin, Duarte, Ca	83	Yam
7.	Hurley Wilvert, Westminster, Ca	39	Kaw
8.	Randy Cleek, Shawnee, Ok	29	Yam
9.	Pat Evans, El Cajon, Ca	51	Yam
10.	Don Castro, Gilroy, Ca	11	Yam
11.	Mike Devlin, Anaheim, Ca	77	Yam
12.	Phil McDonald, Tulsa, Ok	58	Yam
13.	Gary Scott, Springfield, Oh	64	HD
14.	Len Fitch, Woodslee, Ont., Can	62	Yam
15.	Doug Libby, Milford, Mi	40	Yam
16.	Bart Myers, New Brunswick, NJ	87	Yam
17.	Reg Pridmore, Goleta, Ca	62	BMW
18.	George Miller, Oakland, Ca	66	Yam
19.	Bob Wakefield, Indianapolis, Ind	78	Yam
20.	John Clark, Litchfield, Ct	42	Yam

Grand National Points Standings after Round 11

Rank	Rider	Pts
1.	Gary Scott	872
2.	Kenny Roberts	651
3.	Jay Springsteen	464
4.	Rex Beauchamp	349
5.	Greg Sassaman	328
6.	Corky Keener	313
7.	Gene Romero	296
8.	Hank Scott	286
9.	Randy Cleek	282
10.	Steve Baker	266

- An impressive crowd of 39,250 watched the National.
- It was Kenny Roberts' second win in a row at Laguna Seca.
- Only Roberts and Steve Baker rode monoshock TZ750's machines.
- Roberts scored another double by also taking the Combined Lightweight win.
- Novice Steve Souter from North Vancouver, BC was killed in his Novice heat race. Souter had fallen and was struck by another rider.
- Expert dirt tracker Jay Springsteen finished 3rd in the Novice main.
- John Boote arrived from New Zealand with the makings of a TZ750 in his suitcases. Upon assembly, Boote had nothing but trouble getting ready for the National. Due to a seizure, a broken chain and running out of gas, he got next to no practice. The bike then broke a radiator hose in his heat. Fortunately, Boote had some knowledge of the track, competing here in 1974. His ride from the rear of the grid to runner-up was nothing short of amazing.
- In major dirt track news, just before Laguna Seca, Norton-Triumph announced it was suspending the official Norton/NVT team. Though allowed to keep their machines if they wished, Mark Williams, John Hateley and Rob Morrison would no longer receive official factory support.

GNC Round #12 of 20 **Date:** August 20, 1975 **Type:** TT **Venue:** Peoria Motorcycle Club Grounds **Location:** Peoria, Ill	**Purse:** $15,000.00 **Surface:** Dirt **Course Length:** ½ Mile **Laps:** 25

Sonny Burres scored the second and final GNC win of his career at the tough Peoria TT. The 39 year-old Oregon rider put in an impressive flag-to-flag run on a very rough racetrack. Dave Aldana, always a Peoria favorite, didn't let the extra bulk of his Harley-Davidson slow down his high-flying antics on his way to second place. Mert Lawwill, the 1973 Peoria winner, took 3rd on the last lap from Chuck Joyner. Last year's winner, Kenny Roberts, was having a good day, battling with Dave Aldana, until he was one again sidelined with chain problems. His championship rival and points leader Gary Scott soldiered in with a 7th place finish.

While Gary Scott didn't have the day he wanted, he added 34 points to his GNC total. Kenny Roberts' horrible dirt track luck hit again, relegating him to a 12th place finish. The points at the top were Scott 916, Roberts 661. Jay Springsteen thumped in on one cylinder, the last bike running. Mert Lawwill had another great TT ride, his 3rd place finish moving him from outside the top 10 to fourth. Rex Beauchamp crashed while running up front in the race and he slipped to fifth in points. Greg Sassaman was now sixth, Gene Romero added some points, but was still seventh with Corky Keener sliding to eighth. Sonny Burres win moved him up to ninth with Hank Scott rounding out the top 10.

Time Trials

Kenny Roberts (Yam) ran a 28.37 in qualifying to shatter his own track record of 29.00. Dave Aldana (HD) was 2nd quickest at 28.46 and Rex Beauchamp (HD) a 28.79. These were the first laps under 29 seconds at the famed course.

Heats

Kenny Roberts was up and gone in Heat 1, leading every lap. John Gennai (Tri) ran 2nd with Mark Williams (Tri) and Mert Lawwill (HD) reeling him in. Both passed a fading Gennai. Lawwill managed to sneak by Williams for the runner-up spot. Paul Bostrom (HD) was 4th.

Dave Aldana and Sonny Burres (Tri), provided fireworks in Heat 2. The two diced the whole distance, with Burres taking a narrow win. Early 3rd place runner Eddie Wirth (HD) had transmission trouble and dropped out. Randy Skiver (Tri) took 3rd and was on his way to another TT National.

Oval specialist Corky Keener (HD) pulled the holeshot in Heat 3, but quickly went backwards in the field. Hank Scott (Yam) took over the lead with Michigan Harley riders Rex Beauchamp and Jay Springsteen in hot pursuit. Beauchamp passed Scott for the win with three laps to go. Scott remained in 2nd, and Springsteen held off veteran Chuck Palmgren (Yam) for the last transfer.

Mike Caves (HD) didn't let a first lap crash deter him from rebounding to win Heat 4 after the restart. He tracked down leader Gary Scott (HD), who was slowed by a rear sprocket that was coming loose. Scott drifted back a little and was also passed by Chuck Joyner. He was very fortunate to keep 3rd place to transfer directly to the National.

Semis

1970 GNC champ Gene Romero (Yam) led the whole distance in the first semi, despite race long pressure from Paul Bostrom. Both were headed to the National.

Jim Jones (Tri) was out front in Semi 2 with Chuck Palmgren all over him. Palmgren was quickly by, holding on for the win. Jones survived heavy pressure from John Hateley (Tri) to get the final ticket to the main.

Trophy Race

  Steve Droste (HD) led the opening laps of the "Consolation race" before a sticking throttle allowed Randy Cleek (Yam) and John Hateley past. Cleek was gone for the win, with Droste remounting a charge to take 2nd back from Hateley.

National

  Sonny Burres beat everyone, including pole-sitter Kenny Roberts, into the first turns and over the jump. Dave Aldana Rex Beauchamp and Kenny Roberts tried to stay with the veteran, who was on a mission to win at Peoria. Burres began pulling away each lap, amassing a big lead. Other than a bobble on lap 10, he turned in a near perfect ride. Aldana held a solid 2nd over a closing Roberts. Beauchamp ran alone in 4th. Behind the leaders, Chuck Joyner and Mike Caves fought over 5th. Mert Lawwill was closing in behind. He had come from way back in the field after having his XR750 being knocked out of gear in an opening lap skirmish. Lawwill passed Caves and started working on Joyner. Beauchamp missed a gear and crashed on lap 16. On the next lap, Roberts passed Aldana for 2nd only to have his chain break. Burres sailed to the win a comfortable gap over Aldana. Lawwill zapped Joyner coming out of the last corner to take 3rd. Caves was 5th. Chuck Palmgren topped a battle with Gary Scott and Mark Williams. Gene Romero and Jim Jones rounded out the top 10.

Results

Race: 25 Lap TT National

Rank	Rider	Number	Make
1.	Sonny Burres, Portland, Ore	69	Tri
2.	Dave Aldana, Santa Ana, Ca	10	HD
3.	Mert Lawwill, San Francisco, Ca	7	HD
4.	Chuck Joyner, Oregon City, Ore	60	Tri
5.	Mike Caves, Galesburg, Ill	28	HD
6.	Chuck Palmgren, Santa Ana, Ca	38	Yam
7.	Gary Scott, Springfield, Oh	64	HD
8.	Mark Williams, Springfield, Ore	70	Tri
9.	Gene Romero, San Luis Obispo, Ca	3	Yam
10.	Jim Jones, Kirkland, Wa	5W	Tri
11.	Jay Springsteen, Flint, Mi	65X	HD
12.	Kenny Roberts, Villa Park, Ca	1	Yam
13.	Rex Beauchamp, Drayton Plains, Mi	31	HD
14.	Randy Skiver, Everett, Wa	35	Tri
15.	Paul Bostrom, San Roman, Ca	46	HD
16.	Hank Scott, Enon, Oh	14	Yam

Race: Trophy Race

Rank	Rider	Number	Make
1.	Randy Cleek, Shawnee, Ok	29	Yam
2.	Steve Droste, Flint, Mi	92	HD
3.	John Hateley, Van Nuys, Ca	98	Tri
4.	Ike Reed, Salem, Ore	90	Tri
5.	Buddy Powell, Noblesville, Ind	18H	Yam
6.	Phil McDonald, Tulsa, Ok	58	Yam
7.	Bruce Hanlon, Redwood City, Ca	78Z	HD
8.	Terry Sage, Stockton, Ca	20Z	Tri
9.	Mike Gerald, Baton Rouge, La	15	Yam
10.	Joe Peterson, Kenney, Ill	70P	HD
11.	Jay Ridgeway, Atlanta, Ga	9C	HD
12.	John Gennai, Los Gatos, Ca	20	Tri

Grand National Points Standings after Round 12

Rank	Rider	Pts
1.	Gary Scott	916
2.	Kenny Roberts	661
3.	Jay Springsteen	475
4.	Mert Lawwill	374
5.	Rex Beauchamp	358
6.	Greg Sassaman	328
7.	Gene Romero	318
8.	Corky Keener	313
9.	Sonny Burres	297
10.	Hank Scott	292

1975 Sante Fe Short Track
Hank Scott Tops Rookies at Sante Fe

GNC Round #13 of 20 **Date:** August 15, 1975 **Type:** Short Track **Venue:** Sante Fe Speedway **Location:** Hinsdale, Ill	**Purse:** $14,000.00 **Surface:** Dirt **Course Length:** ¼ Mile **Laps:** 25

Hank Scott topped a varied field of rookies, short track specialists and GNC regulars to score his second National win. Scott took the lead early in the event and scooted to a comfortable victory. Scott attributed the win to his recent visit to Sante Fe's tough Wednesday-night regular program. He won the event, figuring out a good setup for the upcoming National. Scott was followed by two rookie short track specialists. Steve Freeman led the initial laps of the race and held on for a solid runner-up spot. Freeman's family ran a short track in their native South Carolina. Though a rookie, he probably had as many laps on the short courses as anyone. Third-place finisher was Bubba Rush from Texas. The Lone Star state was noted for turning out great short trackers. Rookie Rush had honed his ability even further by rarely missing a Sante Fe Wednesday race during the 1975 season. Rush had to battle hard for the podium, including going toe-to-toe with GNC champ Kenny Roberts. He secured the spot late in the race. Neither contenders for the National Championship, Gary Scott and Kenny Roberts had a great night at Sante Fe. Scott ended up 12th, with Roberts faring better, actually finishing a dirt track event, winding up in 5th. Mike Kidd made his first return to GNC racing since breaking his leg during the National here a year ago and again before Houston. Kidd made the National, via a Semi win, ending up in 13th spot.

Kenny Roberts had a good dirt track finish for a change, his top 5 run narrowing the points gap by 51 points. Gary Scott was still firmly in command though with the totals 925 and 721 respectively. Jay Springsteen turned in a good 4th place run, still solidly in third in points with 555. Hank Scott's win made him the big mover of the week moving from tenth in points to fourth. None of the rest of the top 10 made the National.

Time Trials

The top three time trialers would also top the National, albeit in a slightly different order. Hank Scott aboard the Shell Theutt Yamaha nailed down the fastest lap at 15.895. The only other rider below the 16 second mark was Bubba Rush on the Baytown Bultaco ride at 15.984. Steve Freeman on the Surefire Distributing Yamaha was third with a 16.116.

Heats

Randy Cleek, another Sante Fe regular, put his K&N/Bel-Ray Yamaha out front at the start of Heat 1. Vista Sheen's Jay Springsteen (Bul) and Hank Scott were close behind. It took a little while for Scott to get moving, but he moved by Springsteen and set out after Cleek. With two laps to go, Scott passed for the lead and the heat win.

Dave Aldana, on an ex-Mike Gerald Yamaha, looked strong in Heat 2, but at the midway point was joined by Jimmy Lee (Yam), Bubba Rush and Steve Morehead (Yam). Aldana began running wide as a brake pad slipped out of the caliper. Lee moved past, as did Rush a short while later. Aldana salvaged 3rd and headed to the pits to make repairs.

After a restart of Heat 3 was necessitated by a minor spill, Rocky Cycle rider Rick Hocking (Yam) led the field away. A flying Steve Freeman soon took over, blitzing to the win in the fastest heat of the night. Hocking hung unto 2nd place. Gary Scott rode his Harley Sprint aggressively to hold off Danny Cartwright (Bul) and a returning to action Mike Kidd (Yam). Scott's Sprint looked a little more modern with Bill Werner's addition of a front Lester mag wheel. Pretty cool!

Southern short tracker Brent Lowe (Bul) led wire-to-wire in the final heat. He managed to outrun Team Bultaco rider Guy McClure. McClure in turn held off a persistent Kenny Roberts (Yam).

Semis

Corky Keener tried his best to keep his factory Sprint out front in Semi 1, but Steve Morehead had other ideas. Morehead, on the KK Supply/Nasco Oils sponsored Yamaha, took over early and led to the finish. Keener faded as rookie Skip Aksland (Yam), two-time Sante Fe winner Mike Gerald (Yam) and John Gennai (Bul), tried to catch the leader. It was to no avail, as Morehead took the only ticket to the National.

The second semi was a Texas shootout between Mike Kidd, on the Kruger Racing Yamaha and big JR Rawl's factory Powerdyne machine. After swapping the top position several times, Kidd took over around halfway. Rawls stayed close, but was out of luck. Rookie Jay Ridgeway was 3rd on the Woodie Kyle tuned-Champion Kawasaki Big Horn.

Trophy Race

John Gennai, on a factory Bultaco Astro, controlled the Trophy event. Fellow California rider Skip Aksland pressured him for most of the distance, settling for 2nd. Jim Rawls was 3rd, ahead of Mike Gerald and Jay Ridgeway.

National

A very revved up Steve Freeman nailed the holeshot with Hank Scott right on his heels. Close behind, Bubba Rush headed a screaming pack which included Jimmy Lee, Guy McClure, Kenny Roberts and Rick Hocking. Scott closed up on Freeman and hustled by on lap 3. Scott and Freeman kept a good gap between themselves and moved ahead of the rest of the pack. Rush tried his best to hang unto 3rd ahead of an aggressive Kenny Roberts. Close behind, Lee faced the same pressure from Jay Springsteen. Back in the pack, Steve Morehead had found a good line and was mounting a mid-race charge. Many early front runners had missed the setup on the tricky oval and slipped rearward. Randy Cleek, Guy McClure, Rick Hocking and Brent Lowe all suffered from a lack of traction. Gary Scott tried to hang on in the middle of the pack, but steadily drifted back. With six laps to go, Rush finally moved ahead of Roberts. Lee slipped the groove, allowing Springsteen by, and was soon caught by Morehead. As the laps wound down, Scott and Freeman had a big lead on the pack, with Rush a solid 3rd. On lap 21, Springsteen moved by Roberts into 4th spot, with Morehead challenging the champ right to the flag. The final order was; Scott, Freeman, Rush, Springsteen, Roberts, Morehead, Lee, McClure, Lowe, Hocking, Aldana, Gary Scott, Kidd and Cleek.

Results

Race: 25 Lap Short Track
Race Time: 6:46.52

Rank	Rider	Number	Make
1.	Hank Scott, Enon, Oh	14	Yam
2.	Steve Freeman, Simpsonville, SC	68C	Yam
3.	Bubba Rush, Houston, Tx	41N	Bul
4.	Jay Springsteen, Flint, Mi	65X	Bul
5.	Kenny Roberts, Villa Park, Ca	1	Yam
6.	Steve Morehead, Findlay, Oh	42	Yam
7.	Jimmy Lee, Bedford, Tx	57	Yam
8.	Guy McClure, Fort Worth, Tx	50N	Bul
9.	Brent Lowe, Wakefield, Va	36S	Bul
10.	Rick Hocking, Fremont, Ca	13	Yam
11.	Dave Aldana, Santa Ana, Ca	10	Yam
12.	Gary Scott, Springfield, Oh	64	HD
13.	Mike Kidd, Fort Worth, Tx	72	Yam
14.	Randy Cleek, Shawnee, Ok	29	Yam

Race: Trophy Race
Race Time: 3:16.17

Rank	Rider	Number	Make
1.	John Gennai, Los Gatos, Ca	20	Bul
2.	Skip Aksland, Manteca, Ca	72Y	Yam
3.	Jim Rawls, Grand Prairie, Tx	93	PDV
4.	Mike Gerald, Baton Rouge, La	15	Yam
5.	Jay Ridgeway, Atlanta, Ga	9C	Kaw
6.	Corky Keener, Flint, Mi	62	HD
7.	Ken Springsteen, Flint, Mi	76X	Bul
8.	Darryl Hurst, Houston, Tx	34	Yam
9.	Robert E. Lee, Hurst Tx	54	Yam
10.	John Evers, Morenci, Mi	67X	Bul

Grand National Points Standings after Round 13

Rank	Rider	Pts
1.	Gary Scott	925
2.	Kenny Roberts	721
3.	Jay Springsteen	555
4.	Hank Scott	442
5.	Mert Lawwill	374
6.	Rex Beauchamp	358
7.	Greg Sassaman	328
8.	Gene Romero	318
9.	Corky Keener	314
10.	Sonny Burres	297

Extra Extra

- Gary Scott put the last ever Harley-Davidson Sprint into a Grand National event, finishing 13th. The Sprint had been Mark Brelsford's ride in the past.

1975 Terre Haute Half-Mile
Kidd Returns for All Harley Benefit

GNC Round #14 of 20 **Date:** August 17, 1975 **Type:** Half-Mile **Venue:** Terre Haute Speedway **Location:** Terre Haute, Ind	**Purse:** $14,000.00 **Surface:** Dirt **Course Length:** ½ Mile **Laps:** 20 **Distance:** 10 Miles

Diminutive, but tough Texan, Mike Kidd returned to the winner's circle in only his second National race since breaking his leg twice in one year. Kidd was injured at Sante Fe in 1974, then rebroke the leg just before Houston. He overcame some other big odds; he had been let go by the now defunct NVT team. Switching from his familiar British twins to a Harley-Davidson XR750 was definitely not a guarantee for success. On a slick one-groove track where the start is everything, Kidd got through turns one and two first, leading the entire race. It was his second National win. Rex Beauchamp led off the start, but was forced to play catch up afterwards from the second spot. The follow-the-leader track helped thwart a charge on Kidd, but Beauchamp made it close at the end. Gary Scott put in the ride of the day, starting last without a clutch, passing most of the field on his way to the podium. Scott's drive through the field was impressive on the freight train groove. He perhaps had motivation to pile on as many points as possible, as GNC rival Kenny Roberts failed to make the main. Roberts struggled from the onset as his primary machine lunched it's gearbox in practice. Thrashing on the spare ensued, but it was down on power and handling. Roberts was not alone though. The tricky track conditions uniquely favored the Milwaukee 45-degree V-twin. For the first time in history, Harley-Davidson was the lone brand at an AMA Grand National Championship dirt track event. Those with foresight could see this day coming. The Harley's were just hitting their stride in development while the other brands were struggling. The Yamaha teams made good horsepower, but could only hook up when track conditions were favorable. With a few exceptions, (Billy Eves, Steve Morehead), the Triumphs were down on power and had reached their peak. The Terre Haute track conditions were the perfect non-Harley storm.

Harley's main title contender, Gary Scott, surged ahead adding almost another 100 points on Kenny Roberts, his total breaking the 1000 point margin. The point contest at the top now stood at 1025 to 724. It was going to be an uphill battle for Roberts to retain his title. Jay Springsteen's 4th place finish added to his total, but Scott's growing total made it unlikely the rookie could catch him. Rex Beauchamp's runner up effort moved him back into fourth place.

As has been customary in the past with one brand domination, brands may only be mentioned when they are non-Harley-Davidsons.

Time Trials
Corky Keener was atop the field in qualifying. His Nick Deligianis-tuned factory Harley stopped the clocks at 25.704. Dave Aldana on his self-sponsored Harley (also helped by the busy Deligianis on the side), was next at 25.881. John Hateley on his self-supported Triumph was third at 25.955. The tracks conditions caused the times to be way off Hateley's 1973 record of 24.903.

Heats
Fast-timer Corky Keener pulled the holeshot in Heat 1, but it was teammate Greg Sassaman that led lap 1. Rookie Brent Lowe got off hard during the first lap and headed to the hospital with cuts and suspected back injuries. Back to the action, Billy Eves, Gary Scott and crew trailed the leaders. Coming from midpack was Frank Gillespie on the Dud Perkins XR750. Gillespie got a handle on the track, rapidly picking off other riders, including leader Sassaman. Sassaman stayed in 2nd, Keener was 3rd with teammate Scott behind and headed to the semis.

Dave Sehl, 1971 Terre Haute winner, jumped out in front of Heat 2, never to be seen by the pack again. Jimmy Zeigler ran behind early, chased by Guy McClure and Jimmy Osborne. McClure took over 2nd when Zeigler dropped out. At the finish it was Sehl, McClure and Osborne headed to the main. Behind, and looking for another chance was Dave Aldana and JR Rawls.

Gene Romero gave Yamaha fans something to cheer about, albeit briefly, in Heat 3. Romero was out front early, soon overwhelmed by the Harley power of Rex Beauchamp and Mike Kidd. Beauchamp controlled lap 1, with Kidd steaming by for the win; a preview of the coming National. Moving into 3rd was Jay Springsteen for the lat transfer. Late in the race, Romero was dropped to 5th by Triumph mounted John Gennai.

Heat 4 was won by Paul Bostrom, chased by Scott Drake, both were Harley mounted. Behind the two front-runners, GNC champ Kenny Roberts running several positions out of a transfer spot, went into desperation mode. He couldn't do business on the slick groove, so he moved up to what cushion there was at Terre Haute. He rode amazingly, up near the guardrail, very sideways, but to no avail. This was not the damp night cushion of Louisville or Harrington, where such pyrotechnic tactics worked. There was just dry dust at Terre Haute and the champ just slipped backwards by the finish.

Semis

JR Rawls led the first couple of circuits of Semi 1, as Gary Scott worked up from mid pack. It was do-or-die for Scott and he passed for the lead on lap 2. Also on the move were Billy Eves and Dave Aldana. They also knocked Rawls back in the standings. Eves began pulling up on Scott as the British fans cheered at the last chance for a Meridian twin to make the show. Eves nearly did it, getting a great drive coming out of the last corner, but Scott narrowly took the National ticket.

Kenny Roberts had one more chance in the last semi. His chances coming from Row 2 grew a little as the riders right in front of him were accused of jumping the start, giving Roberts a clean view. It wasn't enough though, as Kenny struggled from the start. Up front there was still hope for a non-Harley as former GNC Champ Gene Romero held the point again. He looked good and was riding hard, but fellow GNC Champ Mert Lawwill was reeling him in. Lawwill slowly moved up and took the lead for good at the midpoint of the race. Romero was soon caught by a Roberts/Eddie Wirth duel. Roberts would dive bomb past the two riders deep into the corners, but lost any advantage as he slid up high. At the end it was Lawwill, Romero, Wirth and Roberts.

Trophy Race

In a crowd pleasing win, Billy Eves, on the Larry Mohan-tuned Triumph, salvaged a little pride and glory as he led the event wire-to-wire. Eddie Wirth and Dave Aldana gave chase behind, as Roberts frustratingly chased his tail in 4th for a few meager points.

National

Rex Beauchamp pulled a small holeshot off the line with Dave Sehl, Mike Kidd and the rest of the field following. The two frontrunners drifted just a little high, but it was all Kidd needed as he got the Kruger Racing XR750 turned and went to the lead. For all intents and purposes, the race was Kidd's. Gary Scott's start from the third row only momentarily slowed Team Harleys brightest star. Within just a handful of laps he joined the pack of Beauchamp, Sehl, Greg Sassaman, Jay Springsteen, Corky Keener and Frank Gillespie. All were either partial or full Harley factory riders. Beauchamp managed to pull a little distance towards Kidd and away from Sehl. Scott used all of the Bill Werner supplied power and some savvy riding to move up to 4th spot. Sassaman began applying heavy pressure on Sehl. Soon after halfway, Sassaman got in a little hot in turn 1 on lap 13, got into Sehl and high sided. The young Georgian rider's year was probably done with a badly broken arm. The top order now read, Kidd, Beauchamp, Sehl, Scott and Springsteen. Up front, a tiring Kidd allowed Beauchamp to close, but he maintained a safe distance. As the laps wound down, Scott closed up and motored by Sehl. Springsteen did likewise a couple of laps later. The top finishers crossed the line as; Kidd, Beauchamp, Scott, Springsteen, Sehl, Keener, Scott Drake, (in his best GNC finish so far), Mert Lawwill, Frank Gillespie and Paul Bostrom.

Results

Race: 20 Lap Half-Mile National

Rank	Rider	Number	Make
1.	Mike Kidd, Fort Worth, Tx	72	HD
2.	Rex Beauchamp, Drayton Plains, Tx	31	HD
3.	Gary Scott, Springfield, Oh	64	HD
4.	Jay Springsteen, Flint, Mi	65X	HD
5.	Dave Sehl, Waterdown, Ont., Can	16	HD
6.	Corky Keener, Flint, Mi	62	HD
7.	Scott Drake, Xenia, Oh	91	HD
8.	Mert Lawwill, San Francisco, Ca	7	HD
9.	Frank Gillespie, Hayward, Ca	76	HD
10.	Paul Bostrom, San Roman, Ca	46	HD
11.	Guy McClure, Fort Worth, Tx	50N	HD
12.	Jimmy Osborne, Toledo, Oh	36F	HD
13.	Bubba Rush, Houston, Tx	41N	HD
14.	Greg Sassaman, Macon, Ga	80C	HD

Race: Trophy Race
Race Time: 5:29.97

Rank	Rider	Number	Make
1.	Billy Eves, Birchrunville, Pa	41	Tri
2.	Eddie Wirth, Dana Point, Ca	77	HD
3.	Dave Aldana, Santa Ana, Ca	10	HD
4.	Kenny Roberts, Villa Park, Ca	1	Yam
5.	Rick Hocking, Fremont, Ca	13	Yam
6.	Steve Droste, Flint, Mi	92	HD
7.	Gene Romero, San Luis Obispo, Ca	3	Yam
8.	Billy Schaeffer, Pine Grove, Pa	96	Yam
9.	Jim Rawls, Grand Prairie, Tx	93	HD
10.	Sonny Burres, Portland, Ore	69	Yam

Grand National Points Standings after Round 14

Rank	Rider	Pts
1.	Gary Scott	1025
2.	Kenny Roberts	724
3.	Jay Springsteen	635
4.	Rex Beauchamp	478
5.	Hank Scott	442
6.	Mert Lawwill	404
7.	Corky Keener	364
8.	Greg Sassaman	335
9.	Gene Romero	318
10.	Sonny Burres	297

Extra Extra

- The all-Harley finale had to be sweet revenge for Dick O'Brien and Team Harley. The Milwaukee faithful had suffered through the long iron XR years. This race was a reversal of races like San Jose in 1970 where there were no Harleys in the National.

Bonus!
Top 10 Terre Haute Qualifying Times

1.		Corky Keener	HD	25.704 seconds
2.		Dave Aldana	HD	25.881
3.		John Hateley	Tri	25.955
4.		Mert Lawwill	HD	26.013
5.		Hank Scott	Yam	26.014
6.		Jay Ridgeway	HD	26.017
7.		Mike Kidd	HD	26.048
8.		Paul Bostrom	HD	26.110
9.		Billy Eves	Tri	26.184
10.		Guy McClure	HD	26.185

1975 Indianapolis Mile
King Kenny Stuns with TZ at Indy!

GNC Round #15 of 20	**Purse:** $16,000.00
Date: August 23, 1975	**Surface:** Dirt
Type: Mile	**Course Length**: 1 Mile
Venue: Indianapolis State Fairgrounds	**Laps:** 25
Location: Indianapolis, In	**Distance:** 25 miles

Leaving no doubt of why he earned the title "King Kenny" Roberts, the GNC Champ set the racing world on its ear by storming to victory aboard a Yamaha TZ750-powered dirt tracker. Although he claimed it "rode" him, Roberts manhandled the radical machine to a storybook, come from behind victory. He nipped surprised Harley riders Corky Keener and Jay Springsteen right at the line. The Champion-framed machine had in the neighborhood of 120 horsepower, compared to the 75 or so of Roberts' "regular" XS750 machine. Astoundingly, Roberts had not even seen the machine till the Indy race. There were five total TZ750-powered machines; Steve Baker, Rick Hocking, Randy Cleek and Skip Aksland were all similarly equipped. In addition, there were three Kawasaki triples. Scott Brelsford was the only two-stroke multi pilot with success; He had won a non-national at Stockton, Ca and has a strong run at the spring San Jose Mile. He and Don Castro would ride identical Erv Kanemoto prepared machines; Danny Hockie was also aboard a similar machine. Though Roberts' machine was successful, even he questioned it's safety and whether the AMA should ban the machines. The multis had so much straightaway speed that closing rates on other bikes was downright scary. Much debate ensued and time would soon tell if the machines had a future in dirt track.

While Roberts' win was spectacular, it only made a dent in Gary Scott's huge lead. Unfortunately for Roberts, Scott soldiered in with a solid 4th place run, blunting Roberts' charge. He only gained 77 points on Scott, still with a 224 point lead, (1113 to 889). Jay Springsteen's chance at the title was slim, but he was closing up on Roberts with 745 points. Hank Scott's strong Yamaha ride in 6th moved him back to fourth, followed by 2nd place finisher Corky Keener. Both knocked Rex Beauchamp back to sixth and Mert Lawwill to seventh. Gene Romero moved up a couple of spots to eighth. Injured Greg Sassaman held onto ninth and Sonny Burres' Peoria win still had him in tenth.

Time Trials

Rex Beauchamp, aboard the Babe DeMay-tuned factory Harley-Davidson, turned a fast 37.253 to break Mert Lawwill's two-year old record of 37.52. Lawwill turned in the 2nd fastest time, followed by Chuck Palmgren's rapid Dan Gurney sponsored Yamaha twin. Roberts timed in the 6th fastest time, even though he wasn't even sure if wanted to ride the four-cylinder monster after practice. Brelsford was 9th quickest on the Kawasaki, sticking a piston in the process.

Heats

Rex Beauchamp absolutely scorched to victory in the first heat. The Michigan rider left no doubt who had the fastest bike, (well, Harley), in the field. Scott Brelsford's Kawasaki was running strong, showing little evidence of the earlier seizure. Brelsford had a big advantage over 3rd place Dave Aldana (HD). Tom Berry (HD) emerged from a battle with the likes of Mark Williams (Nor), Frank Gillespie (HD) and Steve Droste (HD), to take 4th and the last transfer spot.

In Heat 2, anticipation rose as Kenny Roberts joined the grid. Mert Lawwill was not concerned, nearly copying his teammate Beauchamp's performance from the first event. Mert checked out, leaving the racing to those behind. Doug Sehl on the Poole's Cycle Harley, ran in the runner-up spot for the first part of the race. He then fell under attack from Paul Bostrom (HD) and later Hank Scott on the Shell Motors Yamaha. Both passed Sehl, but he hung unto 4th spot. Roberts was getting the TZ figured out and worked up to 5th, but was semi-bound.

Corky Keener hoped for a runaway in the third heat, like his teammates had enjoyed. Keener did indeed take the win, but he had to work for it. Ohio rider Ricky Campbell on a fast XR750 closed up and pressured Keener hard. He was soon joined by Gene Romero and a draft-fest ensued. Keener usually led at the line and he managed a tight victory over his pursuers. Romero was 2nd, Campbell an impressive 3rd and Eddie Wirth (HD) 4th. Don Castro was close behind on the other Kanemoto Kawasaki.

Jay Springsteen headed the field at the start of the last heat. "Springer" was aboard injured Greg Sassaman's fast Carroll Resweber/Nick Deligianis-tuned XR750. Gary Scott was right with Springsteen and took over on lap 2. A great- lead swapping battle ensued, with Springsteen taking the win. Behind the leaders, Mike Kidd (HD) and Skip Aksland (Yam TZ750) diced, with Kidd taking the advantage.

Semis

Billy Schaeffer (HD) led the initial laps in the first semi. Kenny Roberts soon screamed by for the lead. Roberts had figured out the TZ was faster if downshifted going into the corner. Roberts pulled a small advantage as the pack diced behind him. Schaeffer fell into the clutches of Steve Droste and Jay Ridgeway, both also Harley mounted. Droste showed speed, drafting to the front of the battle, even gaining some on Roberts. Both Roberts and Droste were National bound.

The last semi offered up the two last National tickets. Robert Deiss (HD) was out front early, with the Dud Perkins Harley of Frank Gillespie and the rapid Bill Kennedy Triumph of Steve Morehead right with him. Close behind, Don Castro's triple screamer was hounded by Harley riders Billy Labrie and Jimmy Zeigler. Gillespie had an edge but as the lead trio came out of turn 4 on the last lap, he got into the front straight wall and suffered a hard crash. Gillespie reportedly received a broken bone in his hand, a fractured wrist and leg injuries. His bike was totally trashed. Morehead put the only British bike in the field along with Deiss.

Trophy Race

Don Castro was spectacular in the consolation race. His Kawasaki would scream ahead of all comers down the straights, only to lose the advantage by going high in the corners. It was similar to the old technique of diamonding off the corners, 'a la Bart Markel. Lap after lap, Castro tried to fend off pursuers like Scott Drake and Dave Sehl. The Harley riders would sneak past in the corners and then watch Castro blast by. Sehl slipped off the groove and fell back. Pat Marinacci (HD) joined the battle up front. Sehl re-exerted himself and managed to keep just ahead of Castro at the flag. Marinacci took 3rd, Drake 4th and Jimmy Zeigler was 5th.

National

The motorcycle line up for the 25 Mile National was indeed unique: making up the field were 14 Harley XR750's, three multi-two-stroke machines-two Yamaha TZ750's and one Kawasaki triple- two Yamaha 750 twins and one 750 Triumph. Safe money was still on Team Harley, but Roberts on the TZ had to be the ultimate unknown quantity at a dirt track National!

Jay Springsteen pulled the holeshot to start the National, with Rex Beauchamp and Corky Keener giving chase. Springsteen held the point for the first two circuits, with Beauchamp taking over. Where was Roberts? Blasting from his third row starting position, Roberts had worked his way into the pack that was shadowing the leaders, headed by Gary Scott and Mert Lawwill. Roberts knew that to have a chance at the end he had to save his rear tire. He seemed content to motor around at this point with the lead group. Early retirees included the other two-strokes in the field; both Scott Brelsford and Skip Aksland were gone. Dave Aldana also dropped out. As the race neared completion of the first 10 laps, Keener and Springsteen began applying friendly pressure to Beauchamp. Roberts began to turn up the wick. He had moved up higher and higher on the track, literally brushing the hay bales. He got a tremendous drive out of turn 2, passing Lawwill and Scott in a single zigzag swoop. Up front, Springsteen drafted back in front to lead laps 14-17. Beauchamp was game and drove back by. On lap 18, Beauchamp was out with ignition failure. By this point Springsteen and Keener had pulled away and didn't spot the yellow and black screamer closing on them. The Michigan buddies began trading the lead back and forth, having fun. Keener led a couple with Springsteen returning the favor. Meanwhile Roberts and the TZ were gobbling up the straight-aways. With one to go, Keener took the point as they crossed the line, Springsteen going by on the back straight with Keener diving in a little deeper into turn 3. Now Roberts really closed up. As the duo became a trio, Roberts went very high in the last corners searching for moisture, getting a great drive and rocketing towards the stripe. Springsteen sensed/heard/saw the coming buzz saw. It was too late, as Robert ripped by Springer and an unsuspecting Keener, scoring the win by two feet. Bedlam ensued as no one including Roberts, expected the dramatic win. The Keener/Springsteen duel was classic, Roberts arrival at the finish was legendary. Although oft quoted, nothing can top Roberts' statement that "They don't pay me enough to ride that thing!"

Results

Race: 25 Lap Mile National
Race Time: 16:15.56, New Record

Rank	Rider	Number	Make
1.	Kenny Roberts, Villa Park, Ca	1	Yam
2.	Corky Keener, Flint, Mi	62	HD
3.	Jay Springsteen, Flint, Mi	65X	HD
4.	Gary Scott, Springfield, Oh	64	HD
5.	Mert Lawwill, San Francisco, Ca	7	HD
6.	Hank Scott, Enon, Oh	14	Yam
7.	Ricky Campbell, Milford, Oh	82	HD
8.	Paul Bostrom, San Ramon, Ca	46	HD
9.	Gene Romero, San Luis Obispo, Ca	3	Yam
10.	Eddie Wirth, Dana Point, Ca	77	HD
11.	Mike Kidd, Fort Worth, Tx	72	HD
12.	Tom Berry, Huntington Beach, Ca	11E	HD
13.	Steve Droste, Flint, Mi	92	HD
14.	Bob Deiss, Pekin, Ill	27P	HD
15.	Doug Sehl, Waterdown, Ont., Can	45	HD
16.	Steve Morehead, Findlay, Oh	42	Tri
17.	Rex Beauchamp, Drayton Plains, Mi	31	HD
18.	Skip Aksland, Manteca, Ca	72Y	Yam
19.	Scott Brelsford, Foster City, Ca	19	Kaw
20.	Dave Aldana, Santa Ana, Ca	10	HD

Race: 12 Lap Trophy Race
Race Time: 7:56.23

Rank	Rider	Number	Make
1.	Dave Sehl, Waterdown, Ont., Can	16	HD
2.	Don Castro, Gilroy, Ca	11	Kaw
3.	Pat Marinacci, Seattle, Wa	67	HD
4.	Scott Drake, Xenia, Oh	91	HD
5.	Jimmy Zeigler, Bellville, Oh	89	HD
6.	Denny Palmgren, Lutherville, MD	49	HD
7.	Billy Schaeffer, Pine Grove, Pa	96	HD
8.	Darryl Hurst, Houston, Tx	34	Yam
9.	Jay Ridgeway, Atlanta, Ga	9C	HD
10.	Ken Springsteen, Flint, Mi	76X	HD

Grand National Points Standings after Round 15

Rank	Rider	Pts
1.	Gary Scott	1113
2.	Kenny Roberts	889
3.	Jay Springsteen	745
4.	Hank Scott	497
5.	Corky Keener	496
6.	Rex Beauchamp	482
7.	Mert Lawwill	470
8.	Gene Romero	340
9.	Greg Sassaman	335
10.	Sonny Burres	297

Extra Extra

- Kenny Roberts Indy Mile win gave him 4 out 5 types of GNC competition in 1975. He only lacked only a half-mile win to complete a single season "Grand Slam".
- Norton-Triumph closed corporate facilities in Baltimore, Md and Atlanta, Ga. The office in Duarte, Ca remained open with a reduced workforce.

1975 Syracuse Mile
Keener Leads a Michigan Sweep!

GNC Round #16 of 20 **Date:** September 7, 1975 **Type:** Mile **Venue:** New York State Fairgrounds **Location:** Syracuse, NY	**Purse:** $16,000.00 **Surface:** Dirt **Course Length**: 1 Mile **Laps:** 25 **Distance:** 25 Miles

Corky Keener topped fellow "Michigan Mafia" members Rex Beauchamp and Jay Springsteen in a Harley-Davidson slug-fest at the Syracuse Mile. The top-three were all on factory Harleys, albeit with rookie Springsteen aboard injured Greg Sassaman's ride. Beauchamp tried some last lap heroics, but came up short of Keener at the flag. It was Keener's third National win and his first and only Mile victory. The Michigan riders led a 15 rider Harley sweep. It was not a good day for Kenny Roberts. He, along with a handful of other riders tried out their multi-cylinder two-stroke machines, but they just plain didn't work at Syracuse. Roberts switched back to his traditional 4-stroke twin, but a heat race crash put him out for the day, costing him valuable championship points. GNC rival Gary Scott had a decent day, finishing 7th, with minor mechanical troubles preventing a higher finish.

Like Roberts, most of the other big bore two-stroke riders like Rick Hocking, Skip Aksland and Randy Cleek, hopped aboard more traditional dirt trackers. Yamaha's Steve Baker, and Kawasaki riders Danny Hockie, Scott Brelsford and Don Castro had no backups and stuck with their radical shriekers. All barely made the program, with Baker's 8th in the Trophy Race the highest placing.

Gary Scott's finish padded his points lead, picking up another 44 points, giving him a 1157 total to Roberts' 889. Kenny Robert rarely let the pressure get to him, but his heat race fall came at a critical time in the championship. In reality, he would have needed a lot of luck for his outgunned Yamaha to have cut Scott's advantage if he had made the main. Roberts was now being pressured by Jay Springsteen, whose total stood at 855. Fourth place in the points had been a revolving door of late, with a different rider each week. This week, it was race winner Corky Keener with 661 points. He was trailed by two Harley teammates, runner-up Rex Beauchamp at 614 and 4th place finisher Mert Lawwill with 558. Hank Scott had engine trouble in the main and he dropped from fourth in the standings to seventh. Gene Romero, Greg Sassaman stayed eighth and ninth, with 5th place finisher Dave Aldana joining the top ten for the first time in 1975.

Time Trials

With top Harley rider and tuner bragging rights at stake, Rex Beauchamp shattered his own lap record of 38.36 with a 37.88 lap on the rocket ship XR750 prepared by Babe DeMay. Corky Keener's XR750, prepared by tuning wizard Nick Deligianis, was close with a 37.98 time. The Carroll Resweber tuned Harley of rookie Jay Springsteen was next at 38.12. Getting some bragging rights of their own was the All-American Racing crew with Chuck Palmgren ripping a very fast Yamaha through the clocks at 38.18. Gary Scott was 5th fastest on the Bill Werner tuned-XR750 at 38.24. Bill Schaeffer took some notes from the past, fitting a 21" front Dunlop on his XR750 to turn a 38.32. All six of these riders broke Beauchamp's previous record.

Heats

After some first corner dicing, Gary Scott emerged as the leader of Heat 1. Locked in behind him were teammate Rex Beauchamp and the Harleys of Dave Aldana and Doug Sehl, (second here last year). Scott held the lead till halfway, when Beauchamp steamed by. Beauchamp powered to a new heat race record.

Californian Tom Berry showed his privateer XR had some ponies, leading Heat 2 till lap 3, when Corky Keener drafted by on his factory machine. Billy Schaeffer gave chase in 3rd, followed by the "Xenia Zephyr", Ohio's Scott Drake, on another XR. Kenny Roberts was struggling to keep up and on lap 6, he laid his bike down to avoid another rider. The race was called complete and Kenny was done for the day.

Heat 3 produced the first classic mile racing of the day. Mark Williams aboard Bart Markel's Harley, jumped out to an early lead, pursued by a mob led by Jay Springsteen, Dave Sehl (HD) and Steve Morehead (Tri). By lap 3,

Springsteen took the lead and powered away from the pack. Williams continued to battle with Sehl and Morehead till he slowed a little and drifted back. Sehl managed to pull a little edge on Morehead and both pulled away from the pack. Williams fell back and barely held the last transfer over Paul Bostrom (HD), Randy Cleek (Yam) and Billy Eves (HD).

Chuck Palmgren rode the fastest Yamaha present into the lead of Heat 4 ahead of Mert Lawwill and last year's winner Hank Scott, this year on a Shell Yamaha rather than a Harley. It took Lawwill most of the race to run Palmgren down, going by for the lead with two laps to go. Behind was a serious mile battle for the last transfer spot. A pack of Harleys ridden by Ken Springsteen, Ricky Campbell, Terry Dorsch, Eddie Wirth, Denny Palmgren and Steve Droste all wanted the spot. Terry Dorsch took 4th by inches at the line.

Semis

The first semi was a barn burner between Rocky Cycles Rick Hocking (Yam), K&N's Phil McDonald and Mike Kidd aboard Jay Springsteen's vacated Vista-Sheen Harley (after Kidd wadded his bike up in practice). The three swapped places all through the race, with Hocking and McDonald heading to the National. Kidd headed to the Trophy race, followed by Steve Baker and his TZ750.

Semi 2 turned into a two-man race after Billy Eves and Eddie Wirth ran off from the field. They traded the lead repeatedly over the 10 laps with Wirth finally taking the win. Both went to the National.

Trophy Race

Steve Droste pulled the holeshot in the Trophy Race. He was trailed by Ricky Campbell, Mike Kidd, Jay Ridgeway , Randy Cleek and Ken Springsteen. Campbell took over on the third circuit with Kidd and Cleek pressuring. Droste was fading back. On lap 7, Kidd took over, with Campbell hot on his heels. Kidd held on for the win, followed by Campbell, Cleek and Ridgeway.

National

Dave Sehl emerged as the leader as the big pack roared down Syracuse's back straight. Rex Beauchamp held 2nd till Chuck Palmgren included him in a daring multi-rider draft pass. Behind the lead trio was Corky Keener, Jay Springsteen, Steve Morehead and Gary Scott. On lap 4, Palmgren's tightly wound Yamaha exploded right in front of Beauchamp and Keener on the back stretch. All were fortunate to avoid a big wreck. Keener continued to gas it and soon took the lead from Sehl. Springsteen, Beauchamp and Steve Morehead moved forward as Sehl's Harley began slipping rearward. By lap 14, Beauchamp had taken over 2nd, and was mounting a charge on Keener. Springsteen and Morehead continued to fight over 3rd, with Morehead's Kennedy Triumph appearing to have near Harley speed. Mert Lawwill was drawing close though, followed by Dave Aldana, Phil McDonald (from the 3rd row) and Gary Scott's slightly slowing XR750. As the laps ran down, Beauchamp was closing on Keener; Morehead had a flat tire and dropped out with less than three to go. Beauchamp was really coming now, but Keener still took the win by 60 feet. Rounding out the top 10 were; Springsteen, Lawwill, Aldana, McDonald with a great run, Gary Scott, Tom Berry, Scott Drake and Eddie Wirth. Dave Sehl slipped back to 12th.

Results

Race: Mile National
Race Time: 15:47.17, New Record

Rank	Rider	Number	Make
1.	Corky Keener, Flint, Mi	62	HD
2.	Rex Beauchamp, Drayton Plains, Mi	31	HD
3.	Jay Springsteen, Flint, Mi	65X	HD
4.	Mert Lawwill, San Francisco, Ca	7	HD
5.	Dave Aldana, Santa Ana, Ca	10	HD
6.	Phil McDonald, Tulsa, Ok	58	HD
7.	Gary Scott, Springfield, Oh	64	HD
8.	Tom Berry, Huntington Beach, Ca	11E	HD
9.	Scott Drake, Xenia, Oh	91	HD
10.	Eddie Wirth, Dana Point, Ca	77	HD
11.	Dave Sehl, Waterdown, Ont., Can	16	HD
12.	Terry Dorsch, Granada Hills, Ca	22	HD
13.	Billy Eves, Birchrunville, Pa	41	HD
14.	Doug Sehl, Waterdown, Ont., Can	45	HD
15.	Billy Schaeffer, Pine Grove, Pa	96	HD
16.	Steve Morehead, Findlay, Oh	42	Tri
17.	Rick Hocking, Fremont, Ca	13	Yam
18.	Mark Williams, Springfield, Ore	70	HD
19.	Chuck Palmgren, Santa Ana, Ca	38	Yam
20.	Hank Scott, Enon, Oh	14	Yam

Race: 12 Lap Trophy Race

Rank	Rider	Number	Make
1.	Mike Kidd, Fort Worth, Tx	72	HD
2.	Ricky Campbell, Milford, Oh	82	HD
3.	Randy Cleek, Shawnee, Ok	29	HD
4.	Jay Ridgeway, Atlanta, Ga	9C	HD
5.	Ken Springsteen, Flint, Mi	76X	HD
6.	Keith Ulicki, Kenosha, Wi	8K	HD
7.	Mike Caves, Galesburg, Ill	28	HD
8.	Steve Baker, Bellingham, Wa	32	Yam
9.	Steve Droste, Flint, Mi	92	HD
10.	Skip Aksland, Manteca, Ca	72Y	Yam
11.	Paul Bostrom, San Ramon, Ca	46	HD
12.	Jim Osborne, Toledo, Oh	36F	HD

Grand National Points Standings after Round 16

Rank	Rider	Pts
1.	Gary Scott	1157
2.	Kenny Roberts	889
3.	Jay Springsteen	855
4.	Corky Keener	661
5.	Rex Beauchamp	614
6.	Mert Lawwill	558
7.	Hank Scott	498
8.	Gene Romero	340
9.	Greg Sassaman	335
10.	Dave Aldana	307

Extra Extra

- After Kenny Roberts Indy Mile win, Team Harley went into overdrive to coax more power from the XR750. Corky Keener's tuner, Nick Deligianis, related that a lot of midnight oil was burned at the factory dynos, right up to the Syracuse event.
- It was Rex Beauchamp's second Mile fast time in a row.
- Last year's winner, Hank Scott, had the ignition on his Shell Yamaha give out early in the National.
- Steve Morehead's Ohio-based Bill Kennedy Triumph impressed all with its ability to run with some of the fastest Harleys at Syracuse. A flat tire spoiled a high placing.
- Road race specialist Steve Baker earned a lot of dirt track respect aboard his TZ750. Baker was one of the driving forces in the Champion TZ development. He was the only guy to turn competitive speed on a big two-stroke.
- There were 16 Harleys, 3 Yamahas and 1 Triumph in the National. Harleys swept the first 15 positions. There continued to be converts like Billy Schaeffer and Billy Eves who were trying an XR750 out on the mile.

Bonus!
Top 20 Syracuse Mile Qualifying Times

1.	Rex Beauchamp	HD	37.88 seconds
2.	Corky Keener	HD	37.98
3.	Jay Springsteen	HD	38.12
4.	Chuck Palmgren	Yam	38.18
5.	Gary Scott	HD	38.24
6.	Billy Schaeffer	HD	38.32
7.	Dave Sehl	HD	38.38
8.	Hank Scott	Yam	38.44
9.	Dave Aldana	HD	38.44
10.	Tom Berry	HD	38.60
11.	Mark Williams	HD	38.67
12.	Mert Lawwill	HD	38.69
13.	Doug Sehl	HD	38.73
14.	Kenny Roberts	Yam	39.00
15.	Jimmy Zeigler	HD	39.05
16.	Ken Springsteen	HD	39.07
17.	Jimmy Osborne	HD	39.08
18.	Rick Hocking	Yam	39.11
19.	Steve Morehead	Tri	39.11
20.	Terry Dorsch	HD	39.11

GNC Round #17 of 20	**Purse:** $14,000.00
Date: September 13, 1975	**Surface:** Limestone
Type: Half-Mile	**Course Length:** ½ Mile
Venue: Toledo Raceway	**Laps:** 20
Location: Toledo, Oh	**Distance:** 10 Miles

Gaining late season momentum, Corky Keener and tuner Nick Deligianis notched their second GNC win in a row at the Toledo, Oh Half-Mile. Fresh off his Syracuse Mile victory, Keener passed leader Jimmy Zeigler early in the National, then ran off to a big win on the grooved-up limestone racetrack. GNC points leader Gary Scott was solid all night, nailing down the runner-up spot, further adding to his points lead. A surprise third place was Triumph-mounted Billy Eves. Eves had worked his way through the pack from a last row semi berth. He was given a real gift when Jimmy Zeigler's bike broke on the last lap while holding down the final podium spot.

Gary Scott's runner-up finish all but iced the cake for his first championship. As long as he had a decent day at the upcoming San Jose National, the crown was his. His points total stood at 1277, well ahead of rival Kenny Roberts, who had a 939 total. Roberts and the peaky Yamaha struggled on the slippery track, but salvaged a 6th place finish on the night. Jay Springsteen's machine had a rare mechanical problem, with the rookie scoring no points. Teammate Corky Keener's win closed him up close to his young Michigan buddy. The preponderance of half-mile specialists cut the amount of top 10 GNC riders down to just four in the main. There were no changes in the top order in points

Time Trials

The fastest time of the night went to Jay Springsteen (HD), who was the last rider to make an attempt. It wasn't by choice, as tuner Jimmy Clarke replaced a lunched valve and just got the bike buttoned back up. Springsteen broke Gary Scott's year old record of 29.74, running a 29.70. Dave Sehl (HD) was second quickest at 29.75, with Mert Lawwill running a 29.76 for third. Steve Morehead, on the Kennedy Triumph broke up the Harley-Davidson domination up front by clocking in 10th fastest.

Heats

One of the several very fast Ohio racers this night was Scott Rader, who despite turning to his backup Harley-Davidson after problems with his primary machine, blitzed to the first heat win. Fast timer Jay Springsteen's night ended quickly with magneto problems. Following Rader early in the race were Scott Drake (HD), Steve Freeman (HD) and Kenny Roberts (Yam). Freeman and Roberts engaged in a battle that moved them past Drake. Roberts worked the cushion in spectacular fashion and managed to displace the pole riding Freeman, but only for a couple laps. Drake found himself being challenged by Randy Cleek (HD). As the race closed, Rader had a sizeable lead, Freeman just held off a charging Roberts and Drake topped Cleek.

Canadian cushion master Dave Sehl blasted out front for a dominant win in Heat 2. Trying to keep pace, Steve Morehead and Mike Kidd (HD) battled over the runner-up slot. Morehead appeared in control till loose battery cables slowed him, handing the spot to Kidd. David "Bubba" Rush (HD) was on a charge from the pack and on the last lap, just nosed Morehead and his ailing ride out of the last transfer.

The third heat contained most of the Harley-Davidson team, including Gary Scott, Corky Keener, Mert Lawwill and last year's winner, Rex Beauchamp. Billy Schaffer pulled the holeshot and was leading early till Keener zipped past, headed for the win. Schaffer managed to hold off Scott for two laps before giving in. Beauchamp also dropped the belabored Schaffer back another spot, taking the last transfer. Billy Eves took the 5th spot.

Chuck Palmgren put his high horsepower Yamaha out front of Heat 4, quickly facing pressure from some Ohio area hot shoes. Jimmy Zeigler (HD) scooted by on lap 1 and went on for the win. Palmgren next faced pressure from Toledo's own Jimmy Osborne. Osborne took 2nd with two laps to go. Doug Sehl fell early in the event, sustaining an injured ankle.

Semis

The two semis were crowd pleasers as Triumph riders Steve Morehead and Billy Eves struck a blow against the night's Milwaukee brand domination, winning both races. Morehead topped the first race over rookie Jay Ridgeway aboard a John Apple/Nasco Oils sponsored Harley and privateer Scott Drake. In Semi 2, Eves passed early leader Steve Droste (HD) just before halfway. Eves was headed for the National, Bill Schaeffer worked past Droste for 2nd.

Trophy Race

Steve Droste was out front in the Trophy Race with a determined Billy Schaffer giving chase. Schaeffer passed Droste with three laps to go and crossed the line with a thin advantage. Jay Ridgeway topped a battle with Rick Hocking (Yam), and Keith Ulicki (HD) for 3rd.

National

By National time, the track had turned to a narrow groove, but there was some traction up high in the cushion for those brave enough to try it. At the start of the race, Ohio's own Jimmy "Ziggy" Zeigler got the holeshot of his career and emerged with the lead down the backstretch. Corky Keener was in hot pursuit, trailed by Gary Scott, Jimmy Osborne and Mike Kidd. "Ziggy" did his best to runaway with the race, but the red hot Keener went past without incident on the second lap. Scott soon latched onto Zeigler and a battle for 2nd position ensued. Bubba Rush had mechanical troubles and was out very early. GNC champ Kenny Roberts was blinded by limestone spray at the start and was mounting a charge from last spot. As in his heat race, he was wowing the crowd, making up time, up high in the thick cushion.

At the point, Keener was pulling a big lead on the pack. Scott had caught Zeigler on lap 5 and the two scuffled for several laps before Scott moved by. Keener was long gone, with Scott a distant 2nd. Zeigler had a secure lead over Osborne, Chuck Palmgren and Mike Kidd.

From the back of the field, several riders mounted a mid-race charge, making their presence known, including, Steve Morehead, Billy Eves, Rex Beauchamp and the aforementioned Roberts. Morehead took over 4th from Osborne on lap 11, only to have another battery cable fail five laps later and he was out. The midpack order changed rapidly as Chuck Palmgren and Mike Kidd both suffered mechanical troubles. Eves worked past Osborne with one lap to go, with Beauchamp and Roberts behind. It seemed the front order was set as first Keener and then Scott crossed the line a final time. Close behind with his best ever finish in hand, Zeigler's bike sputtered to a stop within yards of the flag. All of this was unbeknownst to Billy Eves, who crossed the line in 3rd for his best ever National finish. It was the same story for rookie Jimmy Osborne, finishing 4th in front of his hometown crowd.

Results

Race: 20 Lap Half-Mile National

Rank	Rider	Number	Make
1.	Corky Keener, Flint, Mi	62	HD
2.	Gary Scott, Springfield, Oh	64	HD
3.	Billy Eves, Birchrunville, Pa	41	Tri
4.	Jim Osborne, Toledo, Oh	36F	HD
5.	Rex Beauchamp, Drayton Plains, Mi	31	HD
6.	Dave Sehl, Waterdown, Ont., Can	16	HD
7.	Kenny Roberts, Villa Park, Ca	1	Yam
8.	Scott Rader, Lebanon, Oh	89F	HD
9.	Steve Freeman, Simpsonville, SC	68C	HD
10.	Chuck Palmgren, Santa, Ana, Ca	38	Yam
11.	Mike Kidd, Fort Worth, Tx	72	HD
12.	Jimmy Zeigler, Bellville, Oh	89	HD
13.	Steve Morehead, Findlay, Oh	42	Tri
14.	Bubba Rush, Houston, Tx	41N	HD

Race: Trophy Race

Rank	Rider	Number	Make
1.	Billy Schaeffer, Pine Grove, Pa	96	HD
2.	Steve Droste, Flint, Mi	92	HD
3.	Jay Ridgeway, Atlanta, Ga	9C	HD
4.	Rick Hocking, Fremont, Ca	13	Yam
5.	Keith Ulicki, Kenosha, Wi	8K	HD
6.	Hank Scott, Enon, Oh	14	Yam

Grand National Points Standings after Round 17

Rank	Rider	Pts
1.	Gary Scott	1277
2.	Kenny Roberts	939
3.	Jay Springsteen	855
4.	Corky Keener	811
5.	Rex Beauchamp	674
6.	Mert Lawwill	558
7.	Hank Scott	499
8.	Gene Romero	340
9.	Greg Sassaman	335
10.	Dave Aldana	307

Extra Extra

- A Junior Invitational race sponsored by Nasco Oils and run as the Chuck Jordan Memorial, had a surprise ending. Vista-Sheen's Ted Boody had a big lead aboard Bart Markel's Harley-Davidson on the last lap, only to run out of gas. Fellow Michigan rider Terry Brow (HD) breezed in for a big win. Canada's Norm Carr (HD) was 2nd, with Billy Kennedy Jr. aboard one of his father's Triumphs-rounding out the podium.

Bonus!
Top 10 Toledo Qualifying Times

1.	Jay Springsteen	HD	29.70 seconds
2.	Dave Sehl	HD	29.75
3.	Mert Lawwill	HD	29.76
4.	Jim Osborne	HD	29.82
5.	Scott Drake	HD	29.87
6.	Ricky Campbell	HD	29.90
7.	Corky Keener	HD	29.96
8.	Jimmy Zeigler	HD	29.97
9.	Scott Rader	HD	29.97
10.	Steve Morehead	Tri	29.98

GNC Round #18 of 20 **Date:** September 21, 1975 **Type:** Mile **Venue:** Santa Clara Fairgrounds **Location:** San Jose, Ca	**Purse:** $16,000.00 **Surface:** Dirt **Course Length**: 1 Mile **Laps:** 25 **Distance:** 25 Miles

It was a day of great racing and high drama at the second San Jose Mile of the season. Rex Beauchamp won his first mile race in a slugfest up front that saw nearly 50 unofficial lead changes. Despite wrenching his knee during the National, Beauchamp won by a narrow margin, over Jay Springsteen, Corky Keener and Hank Scott. Riding out the day in 5th was the new Grand National Champion, Gary Scott. Scott was deep in the lead battle early, but faded with an exhaust leak. Fifth place was more than Scott had to have; the title was his. Jay Springsteen's runner-up finish put him in a narrow advantage over GNC champ Kenny Roberts in the Camel Pro points standings. Roberts' day was a microcosm of the season. His hard riding could not overcome deficiencies in machinery. He had success early in the day, winning his heat, but during the main, a tire selection gamble did not work and Roberts slipped from the front and eventually retired from the race. Track conditions were once again the deciding factor and the one thing Roberts could not control. The track was tacky and fast early in the day, but by main event time was hard and slick. Roberts had tried his traditional 750 twin as well as the TZ750 machine in practice. The radical TZ had been reworked since Syracuse, with motor placement altered and it was fitted with 18" wheels. The Goodyear tires fitted to the bike were actually wet weather Grand Prix items. Despite weird handling and brushing the wall during practice and tearing off the brake lever, Roberts opted for the 4-cylinder machine. Roberts felt he had no choice. Less Steve Baker, all of the multi-cylinder machines and riders that appeared at Indy were here. While failing to place high in the standings, it was a watershed event for the two-stroke multis. Six of the radical stokers made the main, with Scott Brelsford's 9th place finishing the highest. It was the last appearance of multi-cylinder bikes in AMA dirt track competition.

The day was marred by a couple of scary crashes that produced serious injuries. Mark Williams was injured in a practice crash, suffering spinal injuries that would eventually paralyze the great veteran racer from Oregon from the waist down. Frank Gillespie was involved in a grinding crash in his semi. Serious injuries included a head injury and several broken bones. He was semi-conscious for over a week after the accident and had multiple operations to plate and pin broken bones.

Time Trials

Despite a rapidly drying track, Rex Beauchamp still managed to set a new one lap mark of 38.21 on the Babe DeMay-tuned Harley flyer. Harleys took the next three spots, with Corky Keener at 38.56, Jay Springsteen at 38.64 and Mert Lawwill still turning out the power with a 38.68 lap. Giving hope to the multi-fans, Scott Brelsford (Kaw) and Kenny Roberts were 5th and 6th fastest.

Heats

Hank Scott showed there was still life yet in those Yamaha twins, by taking the lead in Heat 1 aboard the Shell Motors ride. Pat Marinacci was trying to do the same on a Triumph as he and Mike Kidd (HD) began drafting with Scott. Marinacci soon had engine trouble and was gone. He was quickly replaced by Scott Brelsford and Rex Beauchamp. Much drafting and passing ensued. Kidd slipped a little into the clutches of John Hateley and Rick Hocking (Yam TZ750). At the finish, Brelsford managed a great drive to edge Beauchamp and Scott with Hocking slipping through to take the last transfer spot.

Steve Morehead blitzed ahead in Heat 2, riding an XR750 instead of his usual Kennedy Triumph. Kenny Roberts and Corky Keener were in hot pursuit. Roberts soon drafted into the lead followed by Keener. Another slipstream party ensued. As expected, Roberts ruled the straights, but got into the corners very hot, allowing Keener to challenge. Roberts finally edged ahead and Keener was beat at the flag by savvy Morehead, who stayed with the leaders the entire go. It was the first time Morehead would put a Harley-Davidson into a National. K&N/Bel-Ray

sponsored Randy Cleek was fourth, putting another multi in the field. Roberts looked strong in the heat, but he and team were shocked to see the Goodyear rain tire completely destroyed by the short heat race. There was no way it would last in the main. They took a gamble and would set the bike up with a hand-grooved slick.

Jay Springsteen blasted by the field in Heat 3 for the fastest time of the day. It took Springer a little while to get warmed up, as he first had to run down Paul Bostrom and Tom Berry, both Harley mounted. Don Castro was getting used to Erv Kanemoto's Kawasaki triple as he closed up to harass Berry. At the finish, it was Springsteen by a wide margin, then Bostrom and Berry, who outlasted Castro's screamer. Make it five multi's in the main!

Former GNC champ Mert Lawwill showed he could still compete with the best by going wheel-to-wheel with Gary Scott in the last heat. Lawwill controlled most of the distance with Scott keeping him honest. Gene Romero put his traditional CR Axtell-tuned Yamaha into 3rd place, just ahead of John Gennai's fast Triumph.

Semis

Skip Aksland (Yam TZ750) and Mike Kidd on the Kruger Racing Harley squirted away from the field in Semi 1. Aksland took the top spot with a neat last lap move, but both headed to the National. John Hateley (Yam) was third. The multi count was now at 6.

Dave Aldana was out front early in Semi 2, determined to put his Harley in the National. Behind, Chuck Palmgren (Yam), Rob Morrison (Yam), Steve Droste (HD) and Frank Gillespie fought over the last remaining slot for the National. Droste drafted through to the runner-up spot at halfway. Soon after, Chuck Palmgren got out of shape and was hit by Morrison, Gillespie had nowhere to go, striking Morrison's bike. Gillespie hit the fence, adding concussion, broken arm and leg to his Indy injuries. Palmgren made the restart; Morrison was shaken up and out. On the restart, Droste managed to pass Aldana, but it was short-lived as "Mr. Bones" led to the flag. Palmgren regrouped and challenged Droste hard the rest of the race, but it was Aldana and Droste headed to the main.

Trophy Race

The "consolation" event turned into a 12-lap battle. John Hateley and Jimmy Odom headed the huge multi-wheeled spectacle at the start. Bubba Rush (HD), Bruce Hanlon, Chuck Palmgren, Terry Dorsch and Chuck Joyner (Tri) played "hide the number plates" with Hateley and Odom. Odom dropped out with mechanicals with Hateley taking the win, followed by Hanlon and Joyner.

National

Gary Scott nailed the holeshot to start the 25–Mile National with Mert Lawwill on his tail section. Right behind were Jay Springsteen, Rex Beauchamp, Corky Keener and Hank Scott, with Kenny Roberts already slipping back. Lawwill quickly took the lead as Springsteen moved by Scott for 2nd. Lawwill had a spark plug issue and slipped back to 6th. Springsteen and Gary Scott diced in front Beauchamp, Keener and Hank Scott. The Harley mob passed and repassed, each up front at some point. Hank Scott tried his best, but the underpowered Yamaha could not quite top the pack. Roberts' rear tire was clearly not working and the champ went rapidly rearwards. He would retire after the midway point. Up front Gary Scott fell a little off the pace with a cracked exhaust clamp. As the laps waned, Springsteen, Beauchamp and Keener began trading the lead furiously with Hank Scott close, and brother Gary watching. With one to go, Springsteen led at the stripe. Beauchamp put on a big move down the back straight, nabbing the lead for good. Hank Scott managed to duck under Keener as they headed for the flag. Beauchamp held off Springsteen by a small margin at the finish, with Scott and Keener close behind. Scott trailed further back. It didn't matter though, after following in Kenny Roberts shadow throughout his professional career, Scott had finally taken the title.

Results

Race: 25 Lap Mile National

Rank	Rider	Number	Make
1.	Rex Beauchamp, Drayton Plains, Mi	31	HD
2.	Jay Springsteen, Flint, Mi	65X	HD
3.	Hank Scott, Enon, Oh	14	Yam
4.	Corky Keener, Flint, Mi	62	HD
5.	Gary Scott, Springfield, Oh	64	HD
6.	Mert Lawwill, San Francisco, Ca	7	HD
7.	Tom Berry, Huntington Beach, Ca	11E	HD
8.	Dave Aldana, Santa Ana, Ca	10	HD
9.	Scott Brelsford, Foster City, Ca	19	Kaw
10.	Gene Romero, San Luis Obispo, Ca	3	Yam
11.	Rick Hocking, Fremont, Ca	13	Yam
12.	Randy Cleek, Shawnee, Ok	29	Yam
13.	Skip Aksland, Manteca, Ca	72Y	Yam
14.	Mike Kidd, Fort Worth, Tx	72	HD
15.	Don Castro, Gilroy, Ca	11	Kaw
16.	Steve Droste, Flint, Mi	92	HD
17.	Steve Morehead, Findlay, Oh	42	HD
18.	John Gennai, Los Gatos, Ca	20	Tri
19.	Paul Bostrom, San Roman, Ca	46	HD
20.	Kenny Roberts, Villa Park, Ca	1	Yam

Race: Trophy Race

Rank	Rider	Number	Make
1.	John Hateley, Van Nuys, Ca	98	Yam
2.	Bruce Hanlon, Redwood City, Ca	78Z	HD
3.	Chuck Joyner, Oregon City, Ore	60	Tri
4.	Chuck Palmgren, Santa Ana, Ca	38	Yam
5.	Terry Dorsch, Granada Hills, Ca	22	HD
6.	Dennis Briggs, Tustin, Ca	26R	Yam
7.	Bubba Rush, Houston, Tx	41N	HD
8.	Pat McCaul, San Jose, Ca	48	HD
9.	Darryl Hurst, Houston, Tx	34	Yam

Grand National Points Standings after Round 18

Rank	Rider	Pts
1.	Gary Scott	1343
2.	Jay Springsteen	987
3.	Kenny Roberts	930
4.	Corky Keener	899
5.	Rex Beauchamp	839
6.	Mert Lawwill	613
7.	Hank Scott	609
8.	Gene Romero	357
9.	Dave Aldana	340
10.	Greg Sassaman	335

Bonus!
Top 20 San Jose Mile Qualifying Times

1.	Rex Beauchamp	HD	38.21 seconds
2.	Corky Keener	HD	38.56
3.	Jay Springsteen	HD	38.64
4.	Mert Lawwill	HD	38.68
5.	Scott Brelsford	Kaw	38.86
6.	Kenny Roberts	Yam	39.13
7.	Paul Bostrom	HD	39.21
8.	Dave Aldana	HD	39.22
9.	Hank Scott	Yam	39.25
10.	Steve Morehead	HD	39.26
11.	Tom Berry	HD	39.31
12.	Gene Romero	Yam	39.44
13.	John Hateley	Yam	39.57
14.	Randy Cleek	Yam	39.60
15.	Don Castro	Kaw	39.61
16.	John Gennai	Tri	39.65
17.	Rick Hocking	Yam	39.71
18.	Terry Dorsch	HD	39.73
19.	Pat McCaul	HD	39.80
20.	Steve Droste	HD	39.83

1975 Ascot Half-Mile
Roberts Grand Slams 'Em at Ascot!

GNC Round #19 of 20	**Purse:** $14,000.00
Date: September 27, 1975	**Surface:** Dirt
Type: Half-Mile	**Course Length**: ½ Mile
Venue: Ascot Park	**Laps:** 20
Location: Gardena, Ca	**Distance:** 10 Miles

Kenny Roberts may have lost the National title, but his win at Ascot confirmed him as preeminent rider of his era and perhaps the greatest ever. The Ascot win on a "riders" track was impressive in itself; more importantly, the victory completed a single season AMA Grand National "Grand Slam". Roberts had won each of the championship's five disciplines in one season; TT, (Houston), Short Track, (Dallas), Road Race, (Laguna Seca), Mile, (Indy) and now the Ascot Half-Mile. He and Dick Mann were the only riders at this point to accomplish a "Grand Slam". It had taken Mann 13 years to do it once. Showing Roberts' extreme versatility, 1975 marked the second time Roberts had done it since becoming an Expert in 1972! The first time it took three seasons. To this day, Roberts remain the only rider in history to do it in one season, as well as repeating the feat. There can be little doubt that the title "King Kenny" Roberts is well deserved. It was Roberts' 15th National win. The victory moved him back to second in GNC points ahead of Jay Springsteen.

Perhaps it helped Roberts some that the pressure of the title chase with Gary Scott was gone. He could just concentrate on racing. While Roberts, tuners Tim Withman, Bud Aksland, and all other non-Harley teams would once again face the Harley powerhouse that had won every half-mile and mile event save the Indy Mile, the Ascot track itself was a great equalizer. It rewarded home track knowledge like no other facility. National stars who had not "grown up" there often struggled to keep up with local stars, unknown outside of the area. The track had a unique tackiness that allowed a wide variety of machinery to run up front there if they had the power. Weird stuff like Royal-Enfields, Velocettes and more recently Nortons, machines that didn't do well anywhere else, commonly won at Ascot. The track this night at Ascot was even more of a machinery equalizer than usual. Extra watering, whether intentional or not, made the track very tacky and fast. This evening would be no typical Harley half-mile benefit, 'a la Terre Haute. Turning the tables, at least momentarily, on the dominant Harley-Davidsons, Yamahas swept the first four places. Robert's protégé, rookie Skip Aksland was an impressive 2nd place on his DART Yamaha. Hank Scott steered the Shell Yamaha to 3rd. Rick Hocking brought his Rocky Cycle Machine 4th. Hot Ascot rookie Alex Jorgensen was 5th on the fast Ron Wood Norton.

Time Trials

Confirming that this indeed would be a different night; local rookie Alex Jorgenson on the Ron Wood Norton, set a blazing 22.18. It was all-Yamahas for the next three spots; Rick Hocking, 22.26, Kenny Roberts, 22.27 and Hank Scott at 22.29. Next was Dave Aldana on the first Harley at 22.31. The first five had all spent considerable time at Ascot during their careers. Where were the dominant Harleys? Unbelievably Gary Scott, Rex Beauchamp and Jay Springsteen had tied for the 10th fastest time. Scott, although a 'local", had a misfiring engine on his lap.

Heats

Alex Jorgenson was rockin' & rolling in Heat 1, setting fast heat time in an unchallenged win. He had been dominant of late in Ascot's weekly shows. Dave Aldana ran 2nd, but could not match Jorgensen's pace. Mert Lawwill (HD) was an early 3rd, chased by Skip Aksland (Yam). Aksland challenged Aldana hard in the closing laps, but could not get by. On the last lap, Aldana's bike quit, with Aksland and Lawwill following"Jorgy" into the National. Aldana beat on his machine in frustration.

Hoping to restore some order, Team Harley's Rex Beauchamp took command of Heat 2. He and last year's winner, Rick Hocking (Yam), quickly shot away from the field. Suddenly, Beauchamp pulled off the track, having wrenched his still tender San Jose knee and was unable to continue. Hocking sped to an uncontested win over John Hateley (Yam) and Steve Morehead, this week on a borrowed Yamaha.

Heat 3 provided a shocker. All eyes were on heavy hitters Gary Scott and Kenny Roberts. Steve Droste (HD) impressed, pulling the holeshot and leading the new and old GNC champs early, the trio trailed by local Tom Berry (HD). Droste and Scott got loose in the first corner, Roberts made adjustments and Berry swooped by all three for the lead! Berry scooted on to the win, chased by Scott. Roberts managed to pass Droste's Tex Peel-tuned Harley to take the final National ticket. Berry's win surprised everyone, even himself, although he had turned in some other great runs earlier this year. It was one of those nights!

Hank Scott powered the Shell Yamaha out front early in Heat 4, checking out to an easy win. Michigan Mafia members Jay Springsteen and Corky Keener diced all around the oval. Keener was a little quicker in the turns and finally slid in front of Springsteen to nail down 2nd.

Semis

Mike Kidd (HD) ducked out front early in Semi 1, taking a runaway win and one ticket available to the National. The race was marred by a violent accident involving Rob Morrison and Danny Hockie. The two got together, sending riders and machines cart-wheeling. Both were shaken up, but no serious injuries were reported.

Paul Bostrom (HD) was trying his best to runaway with the last semi. Eddie Wirth (HD) was charging from a back row start after he jumped the initial start. He passed Bostrom late in the race for the final National slot.

Trophy Race

Pat McCaul pulled the holeshot in the consolation race aboard the second Ron Wood Norton. Behind, Mike Meyers (HD), John Gennai (Tri) and Paul Bostrom, gave heated chase. Pressure on McCaul was intense, as the riders behind swapped spots. Meyers was suddenly the leader just past midway as McCaul's bike developed problems. Bostrom continually ran it in deep down into the last corners, with Meyer and Gennai faster everywhere else. Meyers took the win, with Gennai handing 2nd to Bostrom when his Triumph dropped a cylinder. John Allison (Yam) rounded out the top three.

National

Rick Hocking and Hank Scott led the field away at the start of the National, with Gary Scott and Alex Jorgensen close behind. Gary Scott almost immediately began sliding back due to a sticky caliper. Kenny Roberts and Skip Aksland were on the move, by Scott, Tom Berry, John Hateley and Mert Lawwill into the lead pack. Lawwill was soon out with bike trouble. Hank Scott took over the top spot after a serious bobble by Hocking. Roberts was on the move, taking 3rd from Jorgensen. With Jorgy in tow, Roberts made Hocking his next victim. Roberts was soon by into 2nd, with Jorgy and Hocking battling hard. Losing the handle a little bit, Hocking lost the spot and soon lost another to rim-riding Aksland. Roberts closed on Scott at the halfway point with barnstorming Aksland moving by Jorgensen for third. A rear shock change for Scott just before the National wasn't working and he soon lost two places to the Roberts/Aksland show. Behind the lead pack, Tom Berry was the fastest Harley, ahead of Jay Springsteen and Corky Keener. The two Michigan riders never found the right setup and were slithering all over the place, dreaming of crushed limestone. John Hateley was next, with Gary Scott hanging on behind. Setting a new 20-lap record, Roberts and Aksland flew across the line followed by Hank Scott, Hocking, Jorgensen, Berry, Springsteen, Keener, Hateley and Gary Scott.

Results

Race: 20 Lap Half-Mile National
Race Time: 7:37.71

Rank	Rider	Number	Make
1.	Kenny Roberts, Villa Park, Ca	1	Yam
2.	Skip Aksland, Manteca, Ca	72Y	Yam
3.	Hank Scott, Enon, Oh	14	Yam
4.	Rick Hocking, Fremont, Ca	13	Yam
5.	Alex Jorgensen, Stockton, Ca	62Z	Nor
6.	Tom Berry, Huntington Beach, ca	11E	HD
7.	Jay Springsteen, Flint, Mi	65X	HD
8.	Corky Keener, Flint, Mi	62	HD
9.	John Hateley, Van Nuys, Ca	98	Yam
10.	Gary Scott, Springfield, Oh	64	HD
11.	Eddie Wirth, Dana Point, Ca	77	HD
12.	Mike Kidd, Fort Worth, Tx	72	HD
13.	Steve Morehead, Findlay, Oh	42	Yam
14.	Mert Lawwill, San Francisco, Ca	7	HD

Race: Trophy Race

Rank	Rider	Number	Make
1.	Mike Meyers, Crestline, Ca	84R	HD
2.	Paul Bostrom. San Ramon, Ca	46	HD
3.	John Allison, Poway, Ca	83R	Yam
4.	Jimmy Odom, Fremont, Ca	18	Yam
5.	Randy Skiver, Everett, Wa	35	HD
6.	Steve Droste, Flint, Mi	92	HD
7.	John Sperry, Long Beach, Ca	28R	Yam
8.	John Gennai, Los Gatos, Ca	20	Tri
9.	Pat McCaul, San Jose, Ca	48	Tri
10.	Gene Romero, San Luis Obispo, Ca	3	Yam

Grand National Points Standings after Round 19

Rank	Rider	Pts
1.	Gary Scott	1353
2.	Kenny Roberts	1080
3.	Jay Springsteen	1027
4.	Corky Keener	929
5.	Rex Beauchamp	839
6.	Hank Scott	709
7.	Mert Lawwill	620
8.	Gene Romero	357
9.	Dave Aldana	340
10.	Greg Sassaman	335

1975 Ontario Road Race
Roberts Goes Out in Style!

GNC Final Round #20	**Purse:** $40,000.00
Date: October 5, 1975	**Surface:** Pavement
Type: Road Race	**Course Length:** 2.9 Miles
Venue: Ontario Motor Speedway	**Laps:** 2 X 69 Lap Segments
Location: Ontario, Ca	**Distance:** 200 Miles, 2 X 100 Mile Segments

He may have had to give up the #1 plate, but Kenny Roberts' take-no-prisoners attitude won his second National in a row at the last race of the year at Ontario. He dominated both of the Olympic-scored 100-mile legs, winning each by huge margins. It gave Roberts two of the three pavement races of the year. Roberts' win tally for the year was 6 races, raising his career tally to 16. Roberts helped the Yamaha Motor Company salvage a little pride as he and the bevy of TZ750 riders present helped Yamaha to take the Manufacturers Cup away from Harley-Davidson.

A surprise in the runner-up spot in the race, (at least to U.S. fans), was Japanese star Takazumi Katayama. The factory Yamaha rider was impressive in runs of 4th and 3rd to take the runner-up spot. Whatever he lacked in the English language department, he made up with an easy going personality and blazing speed. Ranked in third, (7th and 2nd), Yvon DuHamel was very pleased with the performance of his parallelogram-suspended Kawasaki. His finish in the first segment would surely have been higher if not for an oil leak which oiled down his tire. Gary Nixon was finally able to return to competition, showing no loss of speed or bravery. A crash in practice cracked a shoulder blade, but Nixon showed little effects in the National. He sped to a fantastic runner-up to Roberts in leg one, but was sabotaged by clutch trouble in the remaining race. He still finished 8th overall. Gary Scott gave his factory XRTT one last try to gain a few Harley manufacturers points. The aging ride was completely outgunned and he withdrew with mechanical trouble. This was to be the last race run at the troubled Ontario Motor Speedway. It was amazing that the event hung on as long as it did. Plagued by rider dislike of the course, (but not the money!), low attendance, and a featureless landscape, the "Champion Spark Plug Classic" managed to hang around much longer than expected by the naysayers. A credit to the promoters and sponsors.

Tires were a major story at Ontario. Team Yamaha ran Goodyear slicks of varying compounds. Kawasaki riders mostly ran Dunlops. In the Suzuki camp, it came down to rider preference, with most using the aforementioned brands, with a few on Michelins.

Heats

Kenny Roberts surprised no one in the first heat, romping to an easy win on the Kel Carruthers tuned TZ750. Steve Baker, on the Yamaha of Canada ride, was 2nd with Gary Nixon mounting a late race charge to pass teammate Tepi Lansivuori for 3rd place.

Pat Hennen, on a factory Suzuki, did surprise in Heat 2. Not because of his dominant win: His heat time was faster than Roberts, giving him the pole for the National.

National
Segment 1

A pumped Pat Hennen led the way off the start, heading Kenny Roberts, Steve Baker, Pat Evans, Gary Nixon and Takazumi Katayama. First lap shakeups saw Evans jump to 2nd and Baker to 3rd, with Roberts playing it cool and keeping pace. As the tires and engines heated up, so did the action up front. Baker moved around Evans and began to pressure Hennen, as Roberts followed. Baker took the point on lap 3. Roberts was feeling out Hennen and soon drafted by. He closed up on Baker and by lap 6 was ahead and moving on. Hennen latched onto Baker with a drafting battle ensuing. This lasted till Baker overcooked it in the infield and went down. Nixon had been close the whole time and he closed up on Hennen. The two raced hard, with Nixon taking spot the on lap 15. Hennen retook the spot briefly before Nixon surged ahead for good. Pit stops briefly shuffled the order, but as the laps wound down, Roberts took the win by a huge margin over Nixon and Hennen. Katayama headed a long battle with Steve McLaughlin, Pat

Evans, Mick Grant and Yvon DuHamel for 4th spot. DuHamel slipped back with the oily tire and Grant lost an engine.

Segment 2

Kenny Roberts stopped fooling around and just checked out from the very start of the final segment. Behind, Gary Nixon, Pat Hennen, Yvon DuHamel, Steve McLaughlin and Takazumi Katayama fought over the remaining podium spots. For awhile it was like the "old-days" as Nixon and DuHamel waged a spirited battle early in the race. Nixon's comeback ride was short-changed when his clutch began acting up and he dropped from the front. Katayama had an off-track excursion that dropped him back in the order. Warren Willing, Pat Evans and others took advantage of his misfortune. Mick Grant's crew had installed another engine during the long intermission. He was in the hunt until his bike blew a rear tire on the banking, leading to a scary get off. Grant was fortunately uninjured. Pits stops provided little excitement, except for Steve McLaughlin overshooting his pit. He rammed his pit board, knocked down a crew member and smashing his windscreen in the process. The damage didn't seem to slow him much though. Way out front, Roberts continued to stretch his lead, with Duhamel a comfortable second. Katayama worked his way back to 3rd past Willing. McLaughlin was up and down in the order through the race, but matched his 5th of segment 1. (McLaughlin was the only rider to finish in the top ten in each of the seasons road races). Roberts ended the day with a nearly 30-second lead. Although Kenny Roberts didn't have the season he wished, he finished out the year strongly with back-to-back wins. Despite equaling the 6 wins of his previous championship year, it wasn't enough. Uncharacteristic bad luck and mechanical trouble really hurt his chances. Also, while having a nearly unbeatable package for road racing and being strong at short tracks and TT's, the predominance of the schedule was on half-miles and miles. With the growing dominance of Harleys XR750 at these tracks, the odds were becoming more difficult for even King Kenny to overcome.

Results

Race: 200 Mile Road Race National

Rank	Rider	Number	Make
1.	Kenny Roberts, Villa Park, Ca	1	Yam
2.	Takazumi Katayama, Japan	34	Yam
3.	Yvon DuHamel, LaSalle, Que., Can	17	Kaw
4.	Steve McLaughlin, Duarte, Ca	83	Yam
5.	Pat Evans, El Cajon, Ca	51	Yam
6.	Murray Sayle, Brisbane, Australia	44	Kaw
7.	Dave Aldana, Santa Ana, Ca	10	Suz
8.	Gary Nixon, Cockeysville, Md	9	Suz
9.	Gene Romero, San Luis Obispo, Ca	3	Yam
10.	Randy Cleek, Shawnee, Ok	29	Yam
11.	Ted Henter, St. Petersburg, Fl	53	Yam
12.	Pat Hennen, San Mateo, Ca	80	Yam
13.	Phil McDonald, Tulsa, Ok	58	Yam
14.	John Long, Miami, Fl	56	Yam
15.	Mike Clarke, Downey, Ca	52	Yam
16.	Gary Fisher, Parkesburg, Pa	21	BMW
17.	Pee Wee Gleason, Chattanooga, Tn	55	Kaw
18.	Greg Hansford, Brisbane, Australia	74	Kaw
19.	Cliff Carr, Irvine, Ca	26	Yam
20.	Robert Wakefield, Indianapolis, Ind	78	Yam

Final Grand National Points Standings

Rank	Rider	Pts
1.	Gary Scott	1358
2.	Kenny Roberts	1260
3.	Jay Springsteen	1027
4.	Corky Keener	929
5.	Rex Beauchamp	839
6.	Hank Scott	709
7.	Mert Lawwill	620
8.	Dave Aldana	388
9.	Gene Romero	381
10.	Greg Sassaman	335

1975 Season Review

1. Gary Scott
1358 Points

Long-suffering Gary Scott, runner-up in the GNC series since 1972, finally achieved his goal, finally winning the #1 plate in the inaugural Camel Pro Series/AMA Grand National Championship. Scott never gave up, after finishing behind Mark Brelsford in his rookie year of 1972, and then following perennial rival Roberts in the chase the subsequent two years. The luck and schedule that had seemed to favor Roberts finally swung Scott's way in 1975. He rode well in all events and the reliable and fast Bill Werner prepared machinery allowed him to post top finishes in 17 of 20 events. The schedule was heavy with dirt tracks, with a series low of three road races. Scott's move to Harley-Davidson in 1974 seemed to have finally paid off. Despite solid performances, Scott trailed early in the year; first behind veteran Mark Williams and then Roberts. He moved steadily up the standings, taking the points lead at Round #6 in Harrington, and a win a week later at Columbus which put him way out in front. He hit his stride at the Ascot TT, scoring win number two, while Robert began struggling with crashes and the DNF's. By mid-season, Scott had a 400 point lead. Though Roberts reeled off numerous National wins, Scott's steady finishes kept him firmly in control of the championship. He wrapped up the title at the fall San Jose Mile, with two races remaining. In addition to his two wins, Scott finished 2nd at the Houston TT, the spring San Jose Mile and at Toledo. He was 3rd at the Harrington, Louisville and Terre Haute Half-Miles. Top 5's were scored at the Castle Rock TT, Indy Mile and the summer San Jose Mile. Finishes in the top 10 included the Peoria TT, Syracuse Mile and Ascot Half-Mile. He put the last Harley Sprint in a National at Sante Fe and was a credible 13th on his XRTT at Laguna Seca. Scott's championship year was a testament to his skill, perseverance, excellent machine preparation and the most difficult to control intangible, good luck, which finally swung his way in 1975.

2. Kenny Roberts
1260 Points

Kenny Roberts had strange season of remarkable high and low points. He equaled his 1974 season win total of 6 Nationals, scoring an amazing single season "Grand Slam" along the way. He ticked off each discipline as the season rolled on, winning the season opening Houston TT, Dallas Short Track, Laguna Seca Road Race, Indy Mile, Ascot Half-Mile (wrapping up the "Grand Slam") and adding on a win at the Ontario Road Race for good measure. It was Roberts second 'Slam, achieving the first from 1972-'74. Despite this historic accomplishment, he lost the title in a big way to Gary Scott, who scored just 2 wins. What happened? In a year reminiscent of Jim Rice in 1970, if Roberts didn't win, he struggled. Despite new tuner Tim Witham's efforts, the Yamaha dirt trackers were rapidly losing touch with the Harley-Davidsons, causing Roberts use of the TZ750 at Indy. He also struggled with plain-old bad luck. He failed to score any points at the Houston TT or at Daytona, both events he was a clear favorite. Weird DNF's caused by sprocket/chain issues knocked him out at the Ascot and Peoria TT's. Crashes at the Castle Rock TT and Syracuse Mile cost him dearly as well. For the first time the champ was off his game. In some amazing statistics, he scored no podiums, just two top 5's (spring San Jose Mile and Sante Fe) and only one top ten, at Toledo. While the lack of road races clearly hurt Roberts in defending his title, his loss to Scott more due to not being able to notch consistent finishes across the board; something he had always managed previously. Roberts' last two wins were at the end of the year and did not figure in the championship. Despite a disappointing year in some ways, Roberts clearly showed he was the most skilled and versatile rider on the circuit. Even his considerable skills could not make up for obsolescing equipment and changes in fortune.

3. Jay Springsteen
1027 Points

Flint, Michigan rookie sensation Jay Springsteen started the year out well, if unspectacularly, making his first National at the Houston TT, winding up 14th. He followed this up with a 12th at the Dallas Short Track. At the spring San Jose Mile, he overcooked it in his heat race while in a sure transfer spot. A win at San Jose by fellow rookie Greg Sassaman assured he received little press coverage. This would all change when the circuit returned to Springsteen's Midwest stomping grounds. At the Louisville Half-Mile, "Springer" showed blazing speed and dominated the event. His wide-open style reminded many of fellow Flint native, Bart Markel. A win at the following weeks Harrington Half-Mile showed that Louisville was no fluke. Soon after he was on the podium again at Columbus, finishing 3rd. Springsteen continued to run strong through the rest of the year, making every dirt oval National except for Toledo, where he suffered mechanical trouble after setting fast time. He was 4th at both the Sante

Fe Short Track and Terre Haute Half-Mile. Aboard injured Greg Sassaman's factory Harley-Davidson, he was 3rd at both the Indy and Syracuse Miles. He was 7th at his first trip to the famed Ascot Half-Mile. Showing that he was a capable TT rider as well, he made 3 of the 4 races on the schedule; a 9th at Castle Rock his best finish. Still ranked as a Novice road racer, Springsteen scored all his points on the dirt. He made 13 of 20 races on the schedule. His rides aboard Sassaman's Harley would help to pave the way for a factory connection. In GNC points, he led home fellow the Michigan Mafia members Corky Keener and Rex Beauchamp. There was much to come from the teenager from Michigan!

4. Corky Keener
929 Points

Corky Keener had a year reminiscent of fellow Flint resident Jay Springsteen. Keener's year just took longer to get cooking. The first half of the year was relatively lackluster, save for his runner-up finish at Columbus, a pair of 10th place finishes at the Houston Short Track and San Jose Mile. Keener hit a slump at mid-season, missing four Nationals in a row. Things picked back up with a 6th at Terre Haute and then a close 2nd to Kenny Roberts at the Indy Mile. At the next National, Keener put in a convincing ride at Syracuse to claim his lone Mile win. At the next weeks Toledo Half-Mile, Keener made it two-in-a-row. In his element on the cushion, Keener took an early lead and dominated the event. He rounded out his season with a 4th at the fall San Jose Mile. Keener made 11 of the 20 Nationals on his way to his best finish in the championship.

5. Rex Beauchamp
839 Points

Rex Beauchamp rounded out the Michigan trio in the GNC points. He had a frustrating early season, scoring no points till the spring San Jose Mile where he was 3rd. Through the season, Beauchamp came agonizingly close to victory, finishing 2nd at Harrington, Terre Haute and Syracuse. He was also 4th at Columbus and 5th at Toledo. The very competitive veteran finally got satisfaction by winning his Mile win at the fall San Jose Mile. Like teammate Keener, Beauchamp competed in 11 of the 20 National.

6. Hank Scott
709 Points

Hank Scott had a pretty successful sophomore year, riding Shell Theutt's Yamaha's full-time. He had great success on the short tracks, claiming a win at Sante Fe and was 3rd at Dallas. On the big ovals his best runs were 3rd place runs at the fall San Jose Mile and the Ascot Half-Mile. Other top finishes were a 4th at the Ascot TT, a 5th at Louisville, a 6th at the Indy Mile and an 8th at the Houston Short Track.

7. Mert Lawwill
620 Points

1969 National Champion Mert Lawwill may not have had the season he wanted, not scoring a win, but he was healthy and competitive through the year. It was a huge improvement over his injury plagued 1974 season. His best finish was a 3rd at the Peoria TT. Other top performances were 4th places at the spring San Jose Mile, the Castle Rock TT and the Syracuse Mile. He was 5th at the Indy Mile. He also was in the top 10 at the Houston and Ascot TT's, the Terre Haute Half-Mile and fall San Jose Mile. Lawwill made the main events in 11 of 20 Nationals. This year marked the final year that he finished in the top ten of GNC points.

8. Dave Aldana
388 Points

For the 1975 season, veteran Dave Aldana competed on a Nick Deligianis prepped-Harley-Davidson on the big dirt tracks and a factory Suzuki for pavement events. His best dirt track finishes were a 2nd at the Peoria TT and 5th place runs at the Houston TT and Syracuse Mile. He was in the top 10 at the Houston TT and the fall San Jose Mile. He didn't have great luck on his new Suzuki pavement ride, but did manage a fine 7th at the season ending Ontario event.

9. Gene Romero
381 Points

The year started off rough as usual at Houston for 1970 GNC champ Gene Romero, scoring no points. He rebounded for one of the biggest wins of his career, finally bagging the Daytona 200, where he had been runner-up twice previously. The lack of pavement races hurt his chances for finishing higher in the standings. He had his bike seize at Laguna Seca, and managed a 9th at Ontario. Romero struggled on his semi-factory Yamaha dirt tracker. His best finish was a 7th at the spring San Jose Mile. He was in the top 10 four other times, at Columbus, Peoria, Indy and the fall San Jose Mile. While Romero scored in points in just 7 events, he was in the top 10 at each.

10. Greg Sassaman
335 Points

Georgia rookie Greg Sassaman fulfilled the faith Harley-Davidson had in him by notching a neat win at the spring San Jose Mile. Sassaman was a dirt oval specialist and his Nick Deligianis/Carroll Resweber-tuned rides were fast. All was well through mid-season as Sassaman ran strong, scoring a come-from-behind 6th at Louisville, a 7th at Harrington and a 5th at Columbus. Mid-season TT's, road races and short tracks were not Sassaman's forte' and he missed the next several races. He was running strong at the Terre Haute Half-Mile, when he fell and suffered a badly broken leg. Despite missing the remaining 6 events, his early season performances allowed him to squeak into the top ten in Camel Pro points for the only time in his career.

There were 12 different winners in the 20 championship rounds. A total of 110 riders scored National points during the season. Yamaha and Harley-Davidson machines each won 9 races, with Yamaha taking the Manufacturer Championship. Triumphs won the remaining 2 races.

The story of the 1975 season was the change to a more dirt track oriented schedule. This played right into Team Harley-Davidson's hands. Riders on Harley dirt track machinery took 7 of the top 10 positions in the title chase. While the schedule change in itself didn't hand Gary Scott the title, it definitely changed the momentum of the championship. Kenny Roberts was under tremendous pressure to perform and did not have the "luxury" of extra road race events that would make up for any dirt track deficiency. Adding to his troubles was fact that the Yamaha dirt trackers were near the end of their development just as the XR750 was hitting its stride. Roberts was not as competitive on the big ovals in the past, thus forcing the desperation of running the radical TZ750 dirt tracker. Compounding his troubles was a turn in luck. Roberts suffered uncharacteristic mechanical failures and spills. He could not match his performance of 1974 where he finished well in every National. Despite the amazing single season "Grand Slam" and 6 wins Roberts did not finish well when he did not win. Gary Scott was finally in the right place in the right time. His Harley-Davidson machinery was perfectly prepared, and he finished well across the board at the seasons rich number quantity of dirt track events. He had luck go his way, managing to avoid the falls and injuries that had cost him so dearly in the past. The best illustration of the dirt track heavy schedule changing things was the "Michigan Mafia" of Jay Springsteen, Corky Keener and Rex Beauchamp finishing 3-5 in the championship. These riders excelled at the traditional Midwest half-miles that made up most of the season. Others who normally benefited from a more diverse schedule were great all-arounders like Team Mexican's Dave Aldana and Gene Romero, both who struggled through the year. There were not enough pavement races to offset any deficiencies in their dirt track programs. Pure road racers played no part in this year's point's race.

In the fall of 1975, the AMA banned all multi-cylinder machines from dirt track competition. The machines were difficult to ride, and their closing speeds on more traditional machines, was a major concern. With even Team Yamaha having mixed feelings about TZ750, the ruling was not a surprise.

In a move that effectively put the PowerDyne Company out of business, a California court ordered the company to pay $465,000.00 in damages to Doug Schwerma of Champion Frames. The bikes frames were exact copies of Schwerma's own and an actual Champion Frame was used in PowerDyne advertisements!

The first Camel Pro Series was a huge success for all involved. The series drew a total of 369,400 fans during 1975, a 10% increase over 1974. Camels total payout was $75,000, with $47,000.00 paid out in end of the year points monies. The extra point money allowed the riders to earn some serious money, many for the first time in their careers. New GNC champ Gary Scott was awarded $15,000.00. The sponsorship was a real feather in the cap for the AMA and the Grand National Series. The importance of a non-industry related series sponsor was groundbreaking in motorcycle racing and it's impact cannot be understated. It gave extra advertising, prestige and presence to the sport. Nicely dovetailing with Winston's sponsoring of NASCAR, the Camel Pro Series was a fixture on the circuit for years to come.

1975 GNC Winners

Event	Location	Winner	Machine
TT	Houston, Tx	Kenny Roberts, Villa Park, Ca	Yam
Short Track	Houston, Tx	Darryl Hurst, Houston, Tx	Yam
Road Race	Daytona Beach, Fl	Gene Romero, San Luis Obispo, Ca	Yam
Short Track	Dallas, Tx	Kenny Roberts, Villa Park, Ca	Yam
Mile	San Jose, Ca	Greg Sassaman, Macon, Ga	HD
Half-Mile	Louisville, Ky	Jay Springsteen, Flint, Mi	HD
Half-Mile	Harrington, Del	Jay Springsteen, Flint, Mi	HD
Half-Mile	Columbus, Oh	Gary Scott, Springfield, Oh	HD
TT	Castle Rock, Wa	Chuck Joyner, Oregon City, Ore	Tri
TT	Gardena, Ca	Gary Scott, Springfield, Oh	HD
Road Race	Monterey, Ca	Kenny Roberts, Villa Park, Ca	Yam
TT	Peoria, Ill	Sonny Burres, Portland, Ore	Tri
Short Track	Hinsdale, Ill	Hank Scott, Findlay, Oh	Yam
Half-Mile	Terre Haute, Ind	Mike Kidd, Ft. Worth, Tx	HD
Mile	Indianapolis, Ind	Kenny Roberts, Villa Park, Ca	Yam
Mile	Syracuse, NY	Corky Keener, Burton, Mi	HD
Half-Mile	Toledo, Oh	Corky Keener, Burton, Mi	HD
Mile	San Jose, Ca	Rex Beauchamp, Drayton Plains, Mi	HD
Half-Mile	Gardena, Ca	Kenny Roberts, Villa Park, Ca	Yam
Road Race	Ontario, Ca	Kenny Roberts, Villa Park, Ca	Yam

Epilogue

The AMA GNC saw unprecedented growth through the mid-1970's. Factory involvement rose to an all-time high, especially in 1972-'73. Teams from Harley-Davidson, Yamaha, Triumph, BSA, Norton, Kawasaki, Suzuki, Ossa and Bultaco, all posted Grand National wins. Top ten finishers in dirt track and road races often contained five different brands. The explosion of popularity of motorcycling in the United States coincided with the release of Bruce Brown's movie, On Any Sunday. If you were going to be a professional motorcycle racer, you aimed at the Grand National Championship Series, with winning the #1 plate was your ultimate goal. Factory contracts and purse money was finally lucrative and things only got better when the Camel Pro Series pumped serious cash into the sport. Motocross racing was just taking off and the best motorcycle racers competed in flat track and road races. Illustrating the extreme competitiveness of the period was 1973, when an amazing 18 different riders won each of the 24 Nationals. To win the GNC, you needed to be the best across the board in all events. Grand National Champions from 1970-1975; Gene Romero, Dick Mann, Mark Brelsford, Kenny Roberts and Gary Scott were all models of the skill and versatility that it took to be Number 1 in the era. Kenny Roberts' consecutive championships coincided with the peak of the sport. Roberts was arguably the greatest rider in the history of the sport, dominating when the competition level of other riders and machines were at their highest. Gary Scott was among the last to compete for the Grand National Championship in the traditional sense; by competing in all types of events. His switch to Harley-Davidson in 1974 gave him the best chance to do well across the board. Though the team's road racers were the weak link, Scott still ran most pavement events, scoring in front of much more sophisticated machinery. His championship year of 1975 saw a reduction in the amount of road racing, lessing the disciplines importance in the series and increasing his chances of taking the title. This trend would continue and the racers on the trail took notice. This coincided with ascension of Harley-Davidson's XR750 on the dirt and Yamaha's TZ750 on pavement. The British factories pulled out of racing, with Triumph and Norton fighting for their existence. Kawasaki and Suzuki struggled to keep up with their production based machines on pavement. Yamaha was losing ground on the dirt, it's twin reaching it's peak and the TZ750 outlawed on the ovals. The series began to be a victim of it's own success; racing did improve the breed. The XR750 and TZ750 were so good that were running everything else off the track. To race successfully you needed one of each, a daunting price tag for privateer teams to afford. Flat trackers realized that if they scored well on dirt through the season, they stood a good chance of winning the title. Road racers could not do the same. There just were not enough events. Gary Nixon was the last racer to take a run at the title mostly on pavement points in the road race rich season of 1973. The series would never see such a schedule again. Though not necessarily by design, the GNC was becoming a separate series. Changes in machinery, schedule and attitudes were moving the series away from it's original concept. The attendance and popularity of the sport would continue into the next decade. The changes in the series would take nothing away from the quality of racing and levels of competition. In fact, there would still be battles between the all-arounders and pure dirt trackers for the crown. Fantastic races and fierce championship battles between series veterans and newcomers waited.

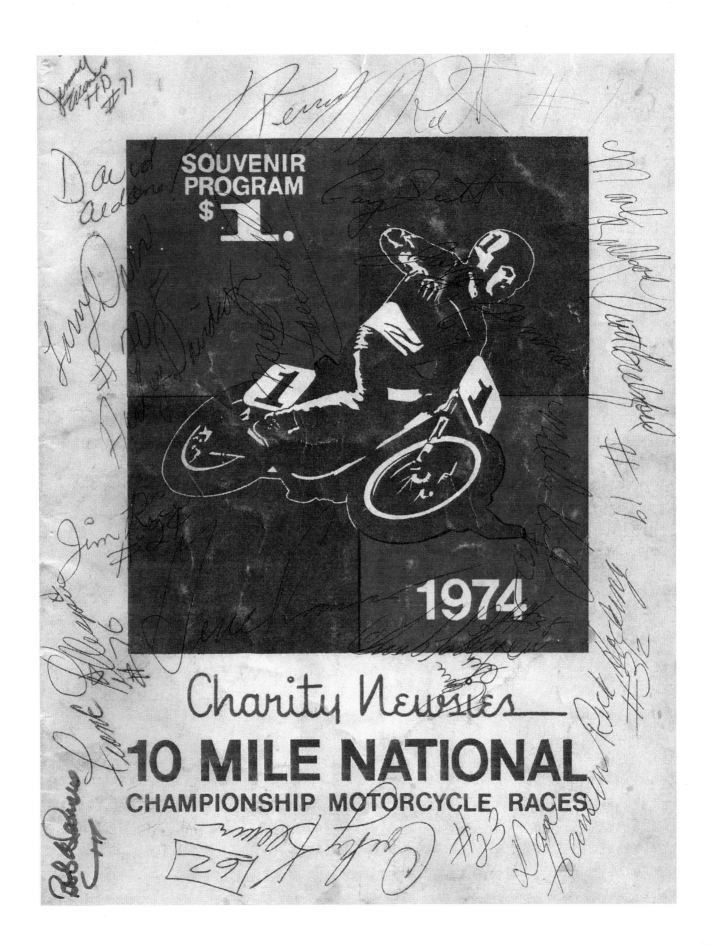

SOUVENIR PROGRAM $1.

1974.

Charity Newsies
10 MILE NATIONAL
CHAMPIONSHIP MOTORCYCLE RACES

Whew!.....man, am I glad this thing is done!!!!
Craig Stocks Photo